COOK'S

ILLUSTRATED

2001

$29.95

Copyright 2001 © by *Cook's Illustrated*
All rights reserved including the right of reproduction in
whole or in part in any form

Published by
Boston Common Press Limited Partnership
17 Station Street
Brookline, MA 02445

ISBN: 0-936184-56-6
ISSN: 1068-2821

To get home delivery of *Cook's Illustrated*, call 800-526-8442 inside the U.S., or 515-247-7571 if calling from outside the U.S., or subscribe online at http://www.cooksillustrated.com.

In addition to the Annual Hardbound Editions, *Cook's Illustrated* offers the following publications:

The *How To Cook* series features 25 single-topic cookbooks.

Topics include pies, cakes, stir-fry, ice cream, pizza, holiday desserts, pasta sauces, salad, grilling, simple fruit desserts, cookie jar favorites, holiday roasts and birds, stew, shrimp and other shellfish, barbecue and roasting on the grill, garden vegetables, pot pies and casseroles, soup, potatoes, quick appetizers, sauces and gravies, sauté, Chinese favorites, muffins, biscuits, and scones, and chicken breasts. Boxed sets are available in attractive, protective slipcases and make great gifts.

The Best Recipe Series

The Best Recipe This 560-page best-selling cookbook contains the 700 best recipes from seven years of *Cook's Illustrated* plus cookware reviews, quick tips, food-tasting results, and explanations of the hows and whys of cooking. This unique 560-page volume was called "the perfectionist's *Joy of Cooking*" by *The Amherst Bulletin*.

The Best Recipe: Grilling & Barbecue More than 400 recipes, with both charcoal and gas grill variations, cover just about everything that has ever been grilled, from steaks and chops to ribs and pulled pork. Three hundred illustrations present preparation techniques in clear, step-by-step detail, and the equipment tests and ingredient tastings tell you which products are best and why.

The Best Recipe: Soups & Stews This 368-page cookbook covers soup and stew favorites, from Manhattan Clam Chowder, Cream of Tomato Soup, and Lobster Bisque, to Irish Stew, Gumbo, and Cassoulet. Includes more than 200 recipes and 200 illustrations, plus equipment testings and food-tasting results.

The America's Test Kitchen Cookbook

This beautifully photographed, hardcover book takes you inside our new hit television series, *America's Test Kitchen*. Includes more than 200 recipes and outtakes from the most popular segments of the show, including Science Desk, Equipment Corner, and Tasting Lab.

1993–2001 Master Index

Quickly find every article and recipe *Cook's Illustrated* has published from the Charter Issue in 1992 through the most recent year-end issue. Recipe names, authors, article titles, subject matter, equipment testings, food tastings, cookbook reviews, wine tastings, and ingredients are all now instantly at your fingertips.

The Cook's Bible, The Yellow Farmhouse Cookbook, and *The Dessert Bible*

Written by Christopher Kimball and published by Little, Brown and Company.

To order any of the books listed above, call 800-611-0759 inside the U.S., or 515-246-6911 if calling from outside the U.S.

You can order subscriptions, gift subscriptions, and any of our books by visiting our online store at
http://www.cooksillustrated.com

BC=Back Cover

COOK'S ILLUSTRATED INDEX 2001

A

Adzuki beans, field guide ....Jan/Feb 01   BC
Aebleskive pans, Danish ....Mar/Apr 01   3
Agglomeration process ....May/Jun 01   2
Air-drying brined poultry ....Nov/Dec 01   17
Aji chiles, field guide ....May/Jun 01   BC
Alford, Jeffrey (*Hot Sour Salty Sweet*) ....Jul/Aug 01   31;
                                              ..Nov/Dec 01   31

Almond(s)
   Green Beans with Buttered Bread Crumbs and ....Nov/Dec 01   18
   paste, hardened, reconstituting ....May/Jun 01   4
   Warm-Spiced Pan Sauce with Currants and ....Mar/Apr 01   13
Amatista chiles, field guide ....May/Jun 01   BC
American Home Cooking (C. A. Jamison and B. Jamison) ...Nov/Dec 01   31
Amines ....May/Jun 01   3
Anchovies, Madeira Pan Sauce with Mustard and ....May/Jun 01   9
Anise and anise seeds ....Nov/Dec 01   3
Appaloosa beans, field guide ....Jan/Feb 01   BC
Apple(s)
   cake ....Sep/Oct 01   22–23
      distributing batter for ....Sep/Oct 01   23
      Master Recipe for ....Sep/Oct 01   23
   Cameo ....Sep/Oct 01   30
   Cider and Brown Sugar Glaze ....Mar/Apr 01   10
   cider vinegar, film on surface of ....Jan/Feb 01   2
   coring ....Sep/Oct 01   5
   Curried Tuna Salad with Currants and ....May/Jun 01   13
   pie, Dutch, errata ....Mar/Apr 01   3
   turnovers ....Jan/Feb 01   22–23
      with commercial puff pastry ....Mar/Apr 01   30
      Flaky ....Jan/Feb 01   23
      fraisage technique for ....Jan/Feb 01   22
      Quickest Puff Pastry for ....Jan/Feb 01   23
      shaping ....Jan/Feb 01   23
Appliances
   cleaning nooks, crannies, and crevices on .....May/Jun 01   4
   coffee grinders
      inexpensive, rating of ....Nov/Dec 01   28–29
      sources for ....Nov/Dec 01   32
   dishwashers, unloading silverware from ....Mar/Apr 01   5
   electric knives, scoring skin of fresh ham with ..May/Jun 01   30
   food processors
      grater attachments of, keeping dried mushrooms
         submerged while rehydrating with ....Jan/Feb 01   4
      juicing fruits for jam in ....Sep/Oct 01   5
   freezers, storing flour in ....Jul/Aug 01   5
   microwave ovens
      cleaning inside ....Jan/Feb 01   4
      cleaning nooks, crannies, and crevices on ..May/Jun 01   4
      storing flour in ....Jul/Aug 01   5
   refrigerators ....Mar/Apr 01   16–17
      crisper in ....Mar/Apr 01   17
      vase for herbs in ....Jul/Aug 01   5
      where to store what in ....Mar/Apr 01   17
   rice cookers
      rating of ....Mar/Apr 01   30
      sources for ....Mar/Apr 01   32
   washing machine, chilling beverages in ....Nov/Dec 01   5
Argentinian-Style Fresh Parsley and
   Garlic Sauce (Chimichurri) ....May/Jun 01   9
Aromatic Stir-Fried Shrimp ....Jan/Feb 01   19
Arugula
   and Grilled Potato Salad with Dijon Mustard Vinaigrette ...Jul/Aug 01   11
   and Ricotta Pesto ....Jan/Feb 01   11
Asian (cuisines). *See also* Chinese (cuisine)
   cookbooks
      The Hali'imaile General Store Cookbook (Gannon) ....Jul/Aug 01   31
      Hot Sour Salty Sweet (Alford and Duguid) ....Jul/Aug 01   31;
                                              ..Nov/Dec 01   31
   ingredients
      fish sauce, sources for ....Mar/Apr 01   32
      noodles, dried, sources for ....May/Jun 01   32
      noodles, types of ....May/Jun 01   7
      oyster sauce ....Jan/Feb 01   2–3
      sesame oil ....May/Jun 01   30
   Kanom krok pans ....Mar/Apr 01   3
   shrimp, stir-fried ....Jan/Feb 01   18–19

Asian (cuisines) *(cont.)*
   Aromatic ....Jan/Feb 01   19
   Cantonese-Style ....Jan/Feb 01   19
   Simplest Shrimp Broth for ....Jan/Feb 01   19
   Singapore Chili ....Jan/Feb 01   19
   Thai-Style Curried Chicken Fried Rice ....Mar/Apr 01   19
Asparagus
   Broiled, Simple ....Mar/Apr 01   11
   snapping off tough ends of ....Mar/Apr 01   11
   vinaigrettes for
      Bacon, Red Onion, and Balsamic ....Mar/Apr 01   11
      Lemon-Shallot ....Mar/Apr 01   11
      Soy-Ginger ....Mar/Apr 01   11
      Tomato-Basil ....Mar/Apr 01   11
Avocados, mashing with pastry blender ....Jan/Feb 01   17

B

Baba ghanoush ....Jul/Aug 01   18–19
   Charcoal-Grill Method ....Jul/Aug 01   19
   Gas-Grill Method ....Jul/Aug 01   19
   Israeli-Style ....Jul/Aug 01   19
   Oven Method ....Jul/Aug 01   19
   preparing eggplant for ....Jul/Aug 01   19
   with Sautéed Onions ....Jul/Aug 01   19
Baby bok choy ....May/Jun 01   20
   Braised with Shiitake Mushrooms ....May/Jun 01   20
Bacon
   Onion, and Scallion Filling (for cheese omelet) ...May/Jun 01   19
   Red Onion, and Balsamic Vinaigrette, Asparagus with ...Mar/Apr 01   11
   spaghetti alla carbonara ....Sep/Oct 01   6–7
      Master Recipe for ....Sep/Oct 01   7
   -Wrapped Filet Mignon ....May/Jun 01   9
Baked-on goo, removing ....Jan/Feb 01   5
Baker's peels, sources for ....Jan/Feb 01   32
Bakeware and baking supplies
   adhering parchment paper to ....Nov/Dec 01   4
   baker's peels, sources for ....Jan/Feb 01   32
   baking sheets
      half-sheet pans, sources for ....Sep/Oct 01   32
      rotating in oven ....Nov/Dec 01   5
   baking stones
      benefits of ....Mar/Apr 01   3
      sources for ....Jan/Feb 01   32;
                                              ..Mar/Apr 01   32
   bread blankets
      canvas as ....Jan/Feb 01   30
      sources for ....Jan/Feb 01   32
   bundt pans, sources for ....Sep/Oct 01   32
   cake pans
      combining greasing and flouring of ....Nov/Dec 01   5
      flipping with dish towel ....Jan/Feb 01   17
      rotating with tongs ....Jan/Feb 01   16
   cooling racks, improvised ....Jul/Aug 01   4
   half-sheet pans, sources for ....Sep/Oct 01   32
   muffin pans
      cooking stuffed peppers in ....Sep/Oct 01   5
      liberating stuck muffins from ....Mar/Apr 01   5
      portioning dough into ....Sep/Oct 01   21
   parchment paper
      adhering to pan ....Nov/Dec 01   4
      commercial ....Jan/Feb 01   30
      making bread sling with ....May/Jun 01   5
      sources for ....Jan/Feb 01   32
   pie weights
      baking time with ....Jul/Aug 01   30
      ovenproof cooking bags for ....Mar/Apr 01   4
      pennies as ....May/Jun 01   5
      sources for ....Jul/Aug 01   32
   pizza stones
      benefits of ....Mar/Apr 01   3
      sources for ....Jan/Feb 01   32;
                                              ..Mar/Apr 01   32
   ramekins
      removing with tongs ....Jan/Feb 01   16
      securing in hot-water bath ....Jan/Feb 01   17
      sources for ....Nov/Dec 01   32
   removing baked-on goo from ....Jan/Feb 01   5

Bakeware and baking supplies *(cont.)*
  tart pans
    sources for . . . . .Jul/Aug 01   32
    testing of different finishes on .Jul/Aug 01   23
    tube-pan inserts, as makeshift vertical roasters . . . . .Jan/Feb 01   5
    tube pans, cooking stuffed peppers in . . . . .Sep/Oct 01   5
Baking sheets
  half-sheet pans, sources for . . . . .Sep/Oct 01   32
  rotating in oven . . . . .Nov/Dec 01   5
Baking stones
  benefits of . . . . .Mar/Apr 01   33
  sources for . . . . .Jan/Feb 01   32;
  . . . . .Mar/Apr 01   32
Balsamic vinegar
  Bacon, and Red Onion Vinaigrette, Asparagus with . . . .Mar/Apr 01   11
  and Mustard Vinaigrette . . . . .Sep/Oct 01   12
  and Red Wine Reduction, Strawberries and Grapes with . . . . .Jul/Aug 01   20
  sources for . . . . .Jul/Aug 01   32
  tasting of . . . . .Jul/Aug 01   26–27
  Tuna Salad with Grapes and . . . . .May/Jun 01   13
Bamboo skewers
  sources for . . . . .Jul/Aug 01   32
  as story sticks for reductions . . . . .Jan/Feb 01   5
Bar cookies, cutting with dough scraper . . . . .Jan/Feb 01   16
Bartlett pears, field guide . . . . .Nov/Dec 01   BC
Basil
  field guide . . . . .Jul/Aug 01   BC
  leftover, using up in sandwiches . . . . .Mar/Apr 01   4
  Stuffed Bell Peppers with Chicken, Smoked Mozzarella and . . . . . . .Mar/Apr 01   7
  Tomato Vinaigrette, Asparagus with . . . . .Mar/Apr 01   11
Basting brushes, impromptu . . . . .Jul/Aug 01   5
Basting oils for vegetables
  Garlic . . . . .May/Jun 01   17
  Lemon-Rosemary . . . . .May/Jun 01   17
Bay leaves
  sources for . . . . .Mar/Apr 01   32
  Turkish vs. California . . . . .Sep/Oct 01   30
Bayless, Rick *(Mexico One Plate at a Time)* . . . . .May/Jun 01   31;
  . . . . .Nov/Dec 01   31
Bean(s). *See also* Green beans
  dried
    field guide . . . . .Jan/Feb 01   BC
    fresh, sources for . . . . .Jan/Feb 01   32
    freshness of . . . . .Jan/Feb 01   21
    white, soup, Tuscan . . . . .Jan/Feb 01   20–21
      leftover, making ribollita with . . . . .Jan/Feb 01   21
      Master Recipe for . . . . .Jan/Feb 01   21
      Quick . . . . .Jan/Feb 01   21
      with Winter Vegetables . . . . .Jan/Feb 01   21
Bean Sprouts, Fried Rice with Peas and . . . . .Mar/Apr 01   19
Beef
  bright color and freshness of . . . . .Mar/Apr 01   17
  Burgundy . . . . .Jan/Feb 01   12–14
    advance preparation of . . . . .Jan/Feb 01   14
    making vegetable and herb bouquet for . . . . .Jan/Feb 01   14
    Master Recipe for . . . . .Jan/Feb 01   13
    trimming meat for . . . . .Jan/Feb 01   14
    wine for . . . . .Jan/Feb 01   14
  filet mignon . . . . .May/Jun 01   8–9
    Argentinian-Style Fresh Parsley and
      Garlic Sauce for (Chimichurri) . . . . .May/Jun 01   9
    Bacon-Wrapped . . . . .May/Jun 01   9
    butchering quality of . . . . .May/Jun 01   9
    Madeira Pan Sauce with Mustard and Anchovies for . . .May/Jun 01   9
    Pan-Seared . . . . .May/Jun 01   9
  roast, protecting brown crust of . . . . .Mar/Apr 01   5
  steak au poivre . . . . .Sep/Oct 01   8–9
    adhering pepper to . . . . .Sep/Oct 01   9
    with Brandied Cream Sauce . . . . .Sep/Oct 01   9
    crushing peppercorns for . . . . .Sep/Oct 01   8
    right grind of peppercorns for . . . . .Sep/Oct 01   8
  storing in refrigerator . . . . .Mar/Apr 01   16
  Stuffed Bell Peppers, Classic . . . . .Mar/Apr 01   7
  tenderloin . . . . .Nov/Dec 01   19
    Dry-Aged, for Beef Wellington . . . . .Nov/Dec 01   10
  Wellington . . . . .Nov/Dec 01   19–21
    assembling . . . . .Nov/Dec 01   20
    Dry-Aged Beef Tenderloin for . . . . .Nov/Dec 01   20

Beef *(cont.)*
    Duxelles for . . . . .Nov/Dec 01   20
    Master Recipe for . . . . .Nov/Dec 01   21
    Red Wine Sauce for . . . . .Nov/Dec 01   21
    timeline for . . . . .Nov/Dec 01   21
Beets, preventing stains on cutting board from . . . . .Jan/Feb 01   4
Bench scrapers, checking evenness of cookie dough with . . . . .Nov/Dec 01   5
Beranbaum, Rose Levy *(The Pie and Pastry Bible)* . . . . .Nov/Dec 01   31
Berry(ies). *See also* specific berries
  Mixed, Tart . . . . .Jul/Aug 01   22
Beurré Bosc pears, field guide . . . . .Nov/Dec 01   BC
Beurré d'Anjou pears, field guide . . . . .Nov/Dec 01   BC
Beverages
  anise-flavored liqueurs . . . . .Nov/Dec 01   3
  chilling for party . . . . .Nov/Dec 01   5
Biscuit Topping, for Sour Cherry Cobbler . . . . .Jul/Aug 01   25
Black-eyed peas, field guide . . . . .Jan/Feb 01   BC
Blanching
  iceless ice baths for . . . . .Nov/Dec 01   4
  potatoes before grilling . . . . .Jul/Aug 01   11
Blenders, cleaning nooks, crannies, and crevices on . . . . .May/Jun 01   4
Blind tastings. *See* Tastings
Blueberry(ies)
  Honeydew, and Mango with Lime-Ginger Reduction . . . .Jul/Aug 01   20
  Kiwi, and Raspberry Tart . . . . .Jul/Aug 01   22
  muffins . . . . .Sep/Oct 01   20–21
    Best . . . . .Sep/Oct 01   21
    Cinnamon-Sugar-Dipped . . . . .Sep/Oct 01   21
    filling tins for . . . . .Sep/Oct 01   21
    Ginger-Glazed or Lemon-Glazed . . . . .Sep/Oct 01   21
    problems with . . . . .Sep/Oct 01   21
  Nectarines, and Raspberries with
    Champagne-Cardamom Reduction . . . . .Jul/Aug 01   20
  Rhubarb Fool with Fresh Ginger . . . . .May/Jun 01   22
Boiling, simmering vs. . . . . .Sep/Oct 01   30
Bok choy . . . . .May/Jun 01   20–21
  baby . . . . .May/Jun 01   20
    Sesame-Soy-Glazed . . . . .May/Jun 01   21
  braised
    with Garlic . . . . .May/Jun 01   21
    with Shiitake Mushrooms . . . . .May/Jun 01   21
  preparing . . . . .May/Jun 01   21
  stir-fried
    with Oyster Sauce and Garlic . . . . .May/Jun 01   21
    with Soy Sauce and Ginger . . . . .May/Jun 01   21
  varieties of . . . . .May/Jun 01   20
Bok choy sum . . . . .May/Jun 01   20
Boning knives, sources for . . . . .Jan/Feb 01   32
Book of Jewish Food, The (Roden) .Mar/Apr 01   31
Book reviews. *See also* Cookbooks
  The Book of Jewish Food (Roden) . . . . .Mar/Apr 01   31
  Charlie Palmer's Casual Cooking (Palmer) . . . . .Jan/Feb 01   31;
  . . . . .Mar/Apr 01   31
  The Hali'imaile General Store Cookbook (Gannon) . . . . .Jul/Aug 01   31
  Hot Sour Salty Sweet (Alford and Duguid) . . . . .Jul/Aug 01   31
  Mexico One Plate at a Time (Bayless) . . . . .May/Jun 01   31
  The Naked Chef (Oliver) . . . . .May/Jun 01   31
  1,000 Jewish Recipes (Levy) . . . . .Mar/Apr 01   31
  Second Helpings from Union Square Cafe
    (Meyer and Romano) . . . . .Sep/Oct 01   31
  Staffmeals (Waltuck and Phillips) . . . . .Jan/Feb 01   31
  Tom Douglas' Seattle Kitchen (Tom Douglas) . . . . .Sep/Oct 01   31
Bouillabaisse . . . . .Sep/Oct 01   13–15
  choosing seafood for . . . . .Sep/Oct 01   15
  Fish Stock for . . . . .Sep/Oct 01   15
  Garlic-Rubbed Croutons for . . . . .Sep/Oct 01   15
  licorice-flavored ingredients in . . . . .Nov/Dec 01   3
  Rouille for . . . . .Sep/Oct 01   15
  -Style Fish Stew . . . . .Sep/Oct 01   15
Bouquet
  garni, improvised . . . . .Jul/Aug 01   4
  vegetable and herb . . . . .Jan/Feb 01   14
Bowls, warming . . . . .May/Jun 01   5
Brandy(ied)
  Cinnamon Reduction, Red Plums and Figs with . . . . . . .Jul/Aug 01   20
  Cream Sauce . . . . .Sep/Oct 01   9
Brassica family, field guide . . . . .Mar/Apr 01   BC
  errata . . . . .May/Jun 01   3

Bread(s). *See also* Muffins
  breakfast strata ....Nov/Dec 01   14–15
    assembling ....Nov/Dec 01   15
    with Potatoes, Rosemary, and Fontina ....Nov/Dec 01   15
    with Sausage, Mushrooms, and Monterey Jack ....Nov/Dec 01   15
    with Spinach, Shallots, and Gruyère ....Nov/Dec 01   15
  crescent rolls ....Nov/Dec 01   12–13
    Master Recipe for ....Nov/Dec 01   13
    shaping ....Nov/Dec 01   13
    tasting of supermarket brands ....Nov/Dec 01   13
  croutons
    Buttered Cinnamon-Sugar ....Nov/Dec 01   8
    Garlic ....Jul/Aug 01   9
    Garlic-Rubbed ....Sep/Oct 01   15
  Crumbs, Buttered, Green Beans with Almonds and ....Nov/Dec 01   18
  dough, canvas as work surface for ....Jan/Feb 01   30
  proofing stage in rising of dough for ....Mar/Apr 01   2
  quick, sling for ....May/Jun 01   5
  ribollita ....Jan/Feb 01   21
  slashing top of, prior to baking ....Jul/Aug 01   5
  yeast for ....Jan/Feb 01   25–27
    expired, performance of ....Jan/Feb 01   27
    instant ....Jan/Feb 01   25–26
    proofing ....Mar/Apr 01   2
    superior flavor development during long fermentations of .....Jan/Feb 01   27
    tasting of ....Jan/Feb 01   27
    types of ....Jan/Feb 01   25–26
Bread bags, closing tight ....May/Jun 01   5
Bread blankets
  canvas as ....Jan/Feb 01   30
  sources for ....Jan/Feb 01   32
Breading, coating chicken cutlets with ....Sep/Oct 01   11
Bread knives, sources for ....Mar/Apr 01   32
Breakfast and brunch fare. *See* Muffins; Omelets
Breakfast strata ....Nov/Dec 01   14–15
  assembling ....Nov/Dec 01   15
  with Potatoes, Rosemary, and Fontina ....Nov/Dec 01   15
  with Sausage, Mushrooms, and Monterey Jack ....Nov/Dec 01   15
  with Spinach, Shallots, and Gruyère ....Nov/Dec 01   15
Brining ....Nov/Dec 01   16–17
  air-drying after ....Nov/Dec 01   17
  best candidates for ....Nov/Dec 01   16
  with Coke ....Mar/Apr 01   10
  curing vs. ....Nov/Dec 01   30
  equipment for ....Nov/Dec 01   17
    sources for ....Nov/Dec 01   32
  explanation of process for ....Nov/Dec 01   16
  koshering and ....Jan/Feb 01   3
  two types of salt for ....Nov/Dec 01   16
  universal formula for ....Nov/Dec 01   17
Broccoli, field guide ....Mar/Apr 01   BC
Broccoli rabe, field guide ....Mar/Apr 01   BC
Broiler pans, sources for ....Nov/Dec 01   32
Broth. *See also* Stocks
  Shrimp, Simplest ....Jan/Feb 01   19
  Vegetable ....May/Jun 01   15
Brownies, cutting with dough scraper ....Jan/Feb 01   16
Brown sugar. *See* Sugar—brown
Bruschetta, oiling surface of ....May/Jun 01   4
Brushes
  basting, impromptu ....Jul/Aug 01   5
  pastry
    for glazing fruit tarts ....Jul/Aug 01   30
    sources for ....May/Jun 01   32;
    ....Jul/Aug 01   32;
    ....Nov/Dec 01   32
Brussels sprouts, field guide ....Mar/Apr 01   BC
Bucatini ....Jan/Feb 01   2
Bundt Cake, Apple ....Sep/Oct 01   23
Bundt pans, sources for ....Sep/Oct 01   32
Burgundy. *See* Beef—Burgundy
Butcher's twine, binding roast with ....Mar/Apr 01   30
Butter(ed)
  Brown, Green Beans with Toasted Hazelnuts and ....Nov/Dec 01   18
  Cinnamon-Sugar Croutons ....Nov/Dec 01   8
  cutting with dough scraper ....Jan/Feb 01   16
  dotting baked goods with ....Sep/Oct 01   4
  measuring ....Sep/Oct 01   17

Butter(ed) *(cont.)*
  Shortbread, Buttery ....Nov/Dec 01   25
Buttercream
  Coconut ....Mar/Apr 01   25
  curdled or broken, rescuing ....Mar/Apr 01   30
Butter dishes, covered, storing goat cheese in ....May/Jun 01   5
Buttermilk ....Jul/Aug 01   3
  Sweet Curry Marinade with ....Jul/Aug 01   15
Butternut squash soup ....Nov/Dec 01   8
  Buttered Cinnamon-Sugar Croutons for ....Nov/Dec 01   8
  Curried, with Cilantro Yogurt ....Nov/Dec 01   8
  Silky ....Nov/Dec 01   8

C

Cabbage. *See also* Bok choy
  field guide ....Mar/Apr 01   BC
Cake flour ....May/Jun 01   2
  storing and measuring ....May/Jun 01   4
  testing necessity of ....Sep/Oct 01   23
Cake pans
  combining greasing and flouring of ....Nov/Dec 01   5
  flipping with dish towel ....Jan/Feb 01   17
  rotating with tongs ....Jan/Feb 01   16
Cakes
  apple ....Sep/Oct 01   22–23
    distributing batter for ....Sep/Oct 01   23
    Master Recipe for ....Sep/Oct 01   23
  chocolate sheet, all-purpose ....Jan/Feb 01   24
    Creamy Milk Chocolate Frosting for ....Jan/Feb 01   24
    Simple ....Jan/Feb 01   24
  coconut layer ....Mar/Apr 01   24–25
    assembling ....Mar/Apr 01   25
    coconut extract for ....Mar/Apr 01   24
    Master Recipe for ....Mar/Apr 01   25
Cambro buckets
  for brining ....Nov/Dec 01   17
  sources for ....Nov/Dec 01   32
Candlestands, impromptu ....May/Jun 01   4
Cannellini beans
  dried
    fresh, sources for ....Jan/Feb 01   32
    freshness of ....Jan/Feb 01   21
  field guide ....Jan/Feb 01   BC
  Tuscan white bean soup ....Jan/Feb 01   20–21
    leftover, making ribollita with ....Jan/Feb 01   21
    Master Recipe for ....Jan/Feb 01   21
    Quick ....Jan/Feb 01   21
    with Winter Vegetables ....Jan/Feb 01   21
Canisters, keeping measuring cups in ....Sep/Oct 01   4
Cantonese-Style Stir-Fried Shrimp ....Jan/Feb 01   19
Canvas, working bread dough on ....Jan/Feb 01   30
Capers ....Jan/Feb 01   7
Caramel sauce, rewarming ....Jul/Aug 01   30
Carbonara. *See* Spaghetti—alla carbonara
Cardamom-Champagne Reduction, Nectarines,
  Blueberries, and Raspberries with ....Jul/Aug 01   20
Carrots
  baby ....Jan/Feb 01   15
  mirepoix ....Mar/Apr 01   3
  roasted ....Jan/Feb 01   15
    with Ginger-Orange Glaze ....Jan/Feb 01   15
    Maple, with Browned Butter ....Jan/Feb 01   15
    Simple ....Jan/Feb 01   15
  shaving with vegetable peeler ....Jan/Feb 01   16
  White Bean Soup with Winter Vegetables ....Jan/Feb 01   21
Carving
  ham roasts ....Mar/Apr 01   10
  steadying roast or large bird during ....Jan/Feb 01   16
  turkey, butterflied ....Nov/Dec 01   11
Castellane, field guide ....Sep/Oct 01   BC
Cast-iron cookware
  Danish aebleskive pans ....Mar/Apr 01   3
  for frying chicken ....May/Jun 01   11
  Thai Kanom krok pans ....Mar/Apr 01   3
Cauliflower
  field guide ....Mar/Apr 01   BC
  Tuna Salad with Jalapeño, Cilantro and ....May/Jun 01   13

Cavatappi, field guide . . . Sep/Oct 01 BC
Celery
  mirepoix . . . Mar/Apr 01 3
  White Bean Soup with Winter Vegetables . . . Jan/Feb 01 21
Chalazae, removing from egg yolks . . . May/Jun 01 25;
  . . . Jul/Aug 01 23
Champagne-Cardamom Reduction, Nectarines,
  Blueberries, and Raspberries with . . . Jul/Aug 01 20
Chanterelle mushrooms . . . Mar/Apr 01 21;
  . . . May/Jun 01 3
Charcoal, dividing into bags for individual fires . . . Jul/Aug 01 5
Charcoal grills
  emptying cool ashes from . . . Jul/Aug 01 4
  measuring temperature of . . . Jul/Aug 01 3
  restarting fire in . . . Jul/Aug 01 5
Charlie Palmer's Casual Cooking (Palmer) . . . Jan/Feb 01 31;
  . . . Mar/Apr 01 31
Cheddar cheese, slicing with vegetable peeler . . . Jan/Feb 01 16
Cheese
  breakfast strata . . . Nov/Dec 01 14–15
    assembling . . . Nov/Dec 01 15
    with Potatoes, Rosemary, and Fontina . . . Nov/Dec 01 15
    with Sausage, Mushrooms, and Monterey Jack . . . Nov/Dec 01 15
    with Spinach, Shallots, and Gruyère . . . Nov/Dec 01 15
  Feta, Stuffed Bell Peppers with Spiced Lamb, Currants and . . . Mar/Apr 01 7
  goat, storing in covered butter dish . . . May/Jun 01 5
  grating with microplane grater . . . Jan/Feb 01 17
  microplane grater/zester for . . . May/Jun 01 32
  Mozzarella, Smoked, Stuffed Bell Peppers with
    Chicken, Basil and . . . Mar/Apr 01 7
  omelets . . . May/Jun 01 18–19
    with Bacon, Onion, and Scallion Filling . . . May/Jun 01 19
    Perfect . . . May/Jun 01 19
    with Sautéed Mushroom Filling with Thyme . . . May/Jun 01 19
    with Sauteed Red Bell Pepper Filling with
      Mushroom and Onion . . . May/Jun 01 19
  Parmesan, Breaded Chicken Cutlets with (Chicken Milanese) . . . Sep/Oct 01 11
  Pecorino Romano . . . Nov/Dec 01 2
  Ricotta and Arugula Pesto . . . Jan/Feb 01 11
  Romano . . . Nov/Dec 01 2
  slicing or shaving with vegetable peeler . . . Jan/Feb 01 16
  spaghetti alla carbonara . . . Sep/Oct 01 6–7
    Master Recipe for . . . Sep/Oct 01 7
  storing in refrigerator . . . Mar/Apr 01 16
Chef's knives . . . Mar/Apr 01 15
Cherry(ies)
  Balaton . . . Jul/Aug 01 25
  cobbler . . . Jul/Aug 01 24–25
    Sour . . . Jul/Aug 01 25
    Sour, Fresh . . . Jul/Aug 01 25
    tasting of "processed" cherries for . . . Jul/Aug 01 25
  sources for . . . Jul/Aug 01 32
Cherry pepper chiles, field guide . . . May/Jun 01 BC
Chez Panisse Vegetables (Waters) . . . Nov/Dec 01 31
Chicken
  brining . . . Nov/Dec 01 16–17
    air-drying after . . . Nov/Dec 01 17
    containers for . . . Nov/Dec 01 17, 32
  contamination vigilance with . . . Jul/Aug 01 30
  cutlets
    getting to even thickness . . . Jul/Aug 01 7;
      . . . Sep/Oct 01 11
    slicing . . . Jan/Feb 01 6
  cutlets, breaded . . . Sep/Oct 01 10–11
    breading technique for . . . Sep/Oct 01 11
    Crisp . . . Sep/Oct 01 11
    Deviled . . . Sep/Oct 01 11
    with Garlic and Oregano . . . Sep/Oct 01 11
    with Parmesan (Chicken Milanese) . . . Sep/Oct 01 11
  cutlets, grilled . . . Jul/Aug 01 6–7
    Charcoal- . . . Jul/Aug 01 7
    Cucumber and Mango Relish with Yogurt for . . . Jul/Aug 01 7
    diamond-pattern grill marks on . . . Jul/Aug 01 7
    Gas- . . . Jul/Aug 01 7
    Salad with Sesame-Miso Dressing . . . Jul/Aug 01 7
    Spicy Tomatillo and Pineapple Salsa for . . . Jul/Aug 01 7
  fat, reusing . . . May/Jun 01 30
  fried . . . May/Jun 01 10–12
Chicken *(cont.)*
    breadings for . . . May/Jun 01 11
    cookware for . . . May/Jun 01 32;
      . . . Jul/Aug 01 3
    cutting chicken into parts for . . . May/Jun 01 12
    Ultimate Crispy . . . May/Jun 01 12
  Fried Rice, Thai-Style Curried . . . Mar/Apr 01 19
  koshering . . . Jan/Feb 01 3
  makeshift vertical roasters for . . . Jan/Feb 01 5
  oven-fried, shortcut for . . . Jan/Feb 01 5
  piccata . . . Jan/Feb 01 6–7
    with Black Olives . . . Jan/Feb 01 7
    Master Recipe for . . . Jan/Feb 01 7
    Peppery . . . Jan/Feb 01 7
    with Prosciutto . . . Jan/Feb 01 7
  raw, getting firm grip on . . . Sep/Oct 01 5
  Stuffed Bell Peppers with Smoked Mozzarella, Basil and . . . Mar/Apr 01 7
Chickpeas (garbanzo beans), field guide . . . Jan/Feb 01 BC
Chiffon pie, chocolate . . . May/Jun 01 30
Chilean sea bass . . . Jul/Aug 01 12–13
  fillets, grilled
    Black Olive and Citrus Relish for . . . Jul/Aug 01 13
    Charcoal- . . . Jul/Aug 01 13
    Gas- . . . Jul/Aug 01 13
    Orange and Soy Marinade for . . . Jul/Aug 01 13
    Spicy Fresh Tomato Relish for . . . Jul/Aug 01 13
  "real" sea bass vs. . . . Jul/Aug 01 12
  thickness of fillets . . . Jul/Aug 01 13
Chiles. *See also* Red pepper flakes
  chipotle . . . Sep/Oct 01 3
    en adobo . . . Sep/Oct 01 3
  fresh, field guide . . . May/Jun 01 BC
  Jalapeño, Tuna Salad with Cauliflower, Cilantro and . . . May/Jun 01 13
  Poblano, Spicy Grilled Potato Salad with Corn and . . . Jul/Aug 01 11
Chili Stir-Fried Shrimp, Singapore . . . Jan/Feb 01 19
Chilling beverages for party . . . Nov/Dec 01 5
Chimichurri (Argentinian-Style Fresh Parsley and Garlic Sauce) . . . May/Jun 01 9
Chimney starters, filling neatly with charcoal . . . Jul/Aug 01 5
Chinese (cuisine)
  bok choy . . . May/Jun 01 20–21
    See also Bok choy
  fried rice . . . Mar/Apr 01 18–19
    with Peas and Bean Sprouts . . . Mar/Apr 01 19
    with Shrimp, Pork, and Peas . . . Mar/Apr 01 19
  lop cheong sausages, sources for . . . Mar/Apr 01 32
  noodles . . . May/Jun 01 7
    sources for . . . May/Jun 01 32
  Sichuan (Szechuan) ingredients, sources for . . . May/Jun 01 32
  Sichuan noodles . . . May/Jun 01 6–7
    Spicy (Dan Dan Mian) . . . May/Jun 01 7
    Spicy, with Shiitake Mushrooms . . . May/Jun 01 7
Chipotle chiles . . . Sep/Oct 01 3
  en adobo . . . Sep/Oct 01 3
Chocolate
  bittersweet
    Sauce . . . Sep/Oct 01 24
    tasting of . . . Sep/Oct 01 24
    unsweetened chocolate vs. . . . May/Jun 01 24
  chiffon pie . . . May/Jun 01 30
  chip cookies . . . Mar/Apr 01 22–23
    morsels for . . . Mar/Apr 01 23
    Thin, Crispy . . . Mar/Apr 01 23
  Cookie Crumb Crust . . . May/Jun 01 25
  cream pie . . . May/Jun 01 23–25;
    . . . May/Jun 01 30
    Master Recipe for . . . May/Jun 01 25
  custard pie . . . May/Jun 01 30
  grating with microplane grater . . . Jan/Feb 01 17
  Milk, Frosting, Creamy . . . Jan/Feb 01 24
  mousse pie . . . May/Jun 01 30
  sheet cake, all-purpose . . . Jan/Feb 01 24
    Creamy Milk Chocolate Frosting for . . . Jan/Feb 01 24
    Simple . . . Jan/Feb 01 24
  tastings of
    bittersweet . . . Sep/Oct 01 24
    morsels . . . Mar/Apr 01 23
Chopping, with pastry blender . . . Jan/Feb 01 17
Chopsticks, as story sticks for reductions . . . Jan/Feb 01 5

Cider and Brown Sugar Glaze . . . Mar/Apr 01 10
Cider vinegar, film on surface of . . . Jan/Feb 01 2
Cilantro
  and Garlic Marinade with Garam Masala . . . Jul/Aug 01 15
  Tuna Salad with Cauliflower, Jalapeño and . . . May/Jun 01 13
  Yogurt, Curried Butternut Squash Soup with . . . Nov/Dec 01 8
Cinnamon
  Brandy Reduction, Red Plums and Figs with . . . Jul/Aug 01 20
  Orange, and Star Anise Glaze . . . Mar/Apr 01 10
  sugar
    Buttered Croutons . . . Nov/Dec 01 8
    -Dipped Blueberry Muffins . . . Sep/Oct 01 21
Citrus. *See also* specific citrus fruits
  and Black Olive Relish . . . Jul/Aug 01 13
  zest, collecting neatly . . . Mar/Apr 01 5
Cleaning
  baked-on goo . . . Jan/Feb 01 5
  charcoal grills, emptying cool ashes from . . . Jul/Aug 01 4
  cutting boards . . . May/Jun 01 28;
  . . . Jul/Aug 01 30
  grill racks without brush . . . Jul/Aug 01 5
  microwave ovens . . . Jan/Feb 01 4
  nooks, crannies, and crevices on appliances . . . May/Jun 01 4
  utensils during dinner preparation . . . Mar/Apr 01 4
  work surface with dough scraper . . . Jan/Feb 01 16
Cleavers, hatchets as substitutes for . . . Jul/Aug 01 5
Cloves . . . Mar/Apr 01 2
Cobbler, cherry . . . Jul/Aug 01 24–25
  Sour . . . Jul/Aug 01 25
  Sour, Fresh . . . Jul/Aug 01 25
  tasting of "processed" cherries for . . . Jul/Aug 01 25
Coca-Cola Ham . . . Mar/Apr 01 10
Coconut
  Buttercream . . . Mar/Apr 01 25
  extract
    sources for . . . Mar/Apr 01 32
    tasting of . . . Mar/Apr 01 24
  layer cake . . . Mar/Apr 01 24–25
    assembling . . . Mar/Apr 01 25
    coconut extract for . . . Mar/Apr 01 24
    Master Recipe for . . . Mar/Apr 01 25
  shaving with vegetable peeler . . . Jan/Feb 01 16
Coffee, in Espresso Crème Brûlée . . . Nov/Dec 01 23
Coffee filters, paper, improvising bouquet garni with . . . Jul/Aug 01 4
Coffee grinders
  inexpensive, rating of . . . Nov/Dec 01 28–29
  sources for . . . Nov/Dec 01 32
Colanders
  rating of . . . Sep/Oct 01 28–29
  sources for . . . Sep/Oct 01 32
  strainers vs. . . . Sep/Oct 01 29
Cookbooks. *See also* Book reviews
  top-10 list from last 5 years
    American Home Cooking (C. A. Jamison and B. Jamison) . . . Nov/Dec 01 31
    Chez Panisse Vegetables (Waters) . . . Nov/Dec 01 31
    Hot Sour Salty Sweet (Alford and Duguid) . . . Nov/Dec 01 31
    In Nonna's Kitchen (Field) . . . Nov/Dec 01 31
    The Italian Country Table (Kasper) . . . Nov/Dec 01 31
    Jacques Pépin's Table (Pépin) . . . Nov/Dec 01 31
    Mexico One Plate at a Time (Bayless) . . . May/Jun 01 31
    The Naked Chef (Oliver) . . . May/Jun 01 31
    The Pie and Pastry Bible (Beranbaum) . . . Nov/Dec 01 31
    Sweet Simplicity: Jacques Pépin's Fruit Desserts (Pépin) . . . Nov/Dec 01 31
Cookie(s)
  bar, cutting with dough scraper . . . Jan/Feb 01 16
  burnt, rescuing . . . Nov/Dec 01 5
  chocolate chip . . . Mar/Apr 01 22–23
    morsels for . . . Mar/Apr 01 23
    Thin, Crispy . . . Mar/Apr 01 23
  crumb crusts
    Chocolate . . . May/Jun 01 25
    forming . . . May/Jun 01 25
  dough, rolling out evenly . . . Nov/Dec 01 5
  frosted, drying . . . Nov/Dec 01 4
  keeping fresh and out of sight . . . Nov/Dec 01 4
  rotating baking sheets in oven . . . Nov/Dec 01 5
  shortbread . . . Nov/Dec 01 24–25
    Buttery . . . Nov/Dec 01 25
Cookie(s) *(cont.)*
  shaping . . . Nov/Dec 01 25
Cookie cutters, making ice cream slices with . . . Sep/Oct 01 4
Cookie droppers . . . May/Jun 01 3
Cookie jars, keeping cookies fresh in . . . Nov/Dec 01 4
Cookie sheets, removing baked-on goo from . . . Jan/Feb 01 5
Cooking spray . . . May/Jun 01 15
  adhering parchment paper to pan with . . . Nov/Dec 01 4
  for knife used to slash top of bread prior to baking . . . Jul/Aug 01 5
Cookware
  aebleskive pans, Danish . . . Mar/Apr 01 3
  broiler pans, sources for . . . Nov/Dec 01 32
  crêpe pans . . . May/Jun 01 30
  Dutch ovens
    All-Clad, clarification of terminology for . . . Jul/Aug 01 3
    for fried chicken . . . May/Jun 01 11;
    . . . Jul/Aug 01 3
    sources for . . . May/Jun 01 32
  for fried chicken . . . May/Jun 01 11;
  . . . Jul/Aug 01 3
  for fried rice . . . Mar/Apr 01 19
  fry pans, All-Clad, sources for . . . Mar/Apr 01 32
  hot, alerting others to danger of . . . Jan/Feb 01 17
  Kanom krok pans, Thai . . . Mar/Apr 01 3
  nonstick, protecting surfaces of . . . Sep/Oct 01 4
  pommes Anna pans . . . Jan/Feb 01 2
  removing baked-on goo from . . . Jan/Feb 01 5
  removing hot lids from . . . Jan/Feb 01 16
  roasting racks, sources for . . . Mar/Apr 01 32
  sauté pans
    copper, reconsideration of . . . Nov/Dec 01 30
    rating of . . . Jan/Feb 01 28–29
    sources for . . . Jan/Feb 01 32;
    . . . Mar/Apr 01 32
    T-Fal Thermospot . . . Mar/Apr 01 13, 32
  skillets, specialized . . . May/Jun 01 30
  stockpots, All-Clad, using as Dutch oven . . . Jul/Aug 01 3
Coolers, for brining . . . Nov/Dec 01 17
Cooling racks, improvised . . . Jul/Aug 01 4
Copper sauté pans, reconsideration of . . . Nov/Dec 01 30
Cork crumbs, fishing out of wine bottles . . . Nov/Dec 01 4
Corkscrews
  as handle for potatoes during peeling . . . Mar/Apr 01 4
  puncturing corn on the cob pieces with,
    for skewering . . . Jul/Aug 01 4
Corn
  on the cob
    grilling . . . May/Jun 01 17
    hot boiled, draining . . . Jul/Aug 01 4
    skewering pieces of, for grilling . . . Jul/Aug 01 4
  Spicy Grilled Potato Salad with Poblano Chiles and . . . Jul/Aug 01 11
Cornbread, in Sausage Dressing . . . Nov/Dec 01 10
Cornflakes, as breading for fried chicken . . . May/Jun 01 11
Cornish hens, brining . . . Nov/Dec 01 16–17
  containers for . . . Nov/Dec 01 17
Cream
  pasteurized vs. ultrapasteurized . . . May/Jun 01 2–3
  pies
    chocolate . . . May/Jun 01 23–25
    Chocolate, Master Recipe for . . . May/Jun 01 25
    chocolate, terminology for . . . May/Jun 01 30
    protecting from plastic wrap . . . Sep/Oct 01 5
  Sauce, Brandied . . . Sep/Oct 01 9
Crème brûlée . . . Nov/Dec 01 22–23
  Classic . . . Nov/Dec 01 23
  curdled vs. creamy . . . Nov/Dec 01 23
  Espresso . . . Nov/Dec 01 23
  ramekins for . . . Nov/Dec 01 32
  Tea-Infused . . . Nov/Dec 01 23
Cremini mushrooms . . . Mar/Apr 01 21
  grilling . . . May/Jun 01 17
Crêpe pans . . . May/Jun 01 30
Crêpes, nonspecialized skillets for . . . May/Jun 01 30
Crescent rolls . . . Nov/Dec 01 12–13
  Master Recipe for . . . Nov/Dec 01 13
  shaping . . . Nov/Dec 01 13
  tasting of supermarket brands . . . Nov/Dec 01 13
Crostini, oiling surface of . . . May/Jun 01 4

Croutons
Buttered Cinnamon-Sugar ...Nov/Dec 01 8
Garlic ...Jul/Aug 01 9
Garlic-Rubbed ...Sep/Oct 01 15
Crusts
Chocolate Cookie Crumb ...May/Jun 01 25
crumb, forming ...May/Jun 01 25
pie weights for
baking time with ...Jul/Aug 01 30
ovenproof cooking bags for ...Mar/Apr 01 4
pennies as ...May/Jun 01 5
sources for ...Jul/Aug 01 32
Cucumber(s)
gazpacho ...Jul/Aug 01 8–9
chopping vegetables for ...Jul/Aug 01 9
Garlic Croutons for ...Jul/Aug 01 9
getting texture "right" for ...Jul/Aug 01 9
Master Recipe for ...Jul/Aug 01 9
Quick Food Processor ...Jul/Aug 01 9
and Mango Relish with Yogurt ...Jul/Aug 01 7
shaving with vegetable peeler ...Jan/Feb 01 16
Curing, brining vs. ...Nov/Dec 01 30
Currants
Curried Tuna Salad with Apples and ...May/Jun 01 13
fresh vs. dried ...May/Jun 01 3
Stuffed Bell Peppers with Spiced Lamb, Feta Cheese and ...Mar/Apr 01 7
Warm-Spiced Pan Sauce with Almonds and ...Mar/Apr 01 13
Curry(ied)
Butternut Squash Soup with Cilantro Yogurt ...Nov/Dec 01 8
Chicken Fried Rice, Thai-Style ...Mar/Apr 01 19
Marinade with Buttermilk, Sweet ...Jul/Aug 01 15
Tuna Salad with Apples and Currants ...May/Jun 01 13
Custard
chocolate, pie ...May/Jun 01 30
crème brûlée ...Nov/Dec 01 22–23
Classic ...Nov/Dec 01 23
curdled vs. creamy ...Nov/Dec 01 23
Espresso ...Nov/Dec 01 23
ramekins for ...Nov/Dec 01 32
Tea-Infused ...Nov/Dec 01 23
Cutting, with dough scraper ...Jan/Feb 01 16
Cutting boards
cleaning ...May/Jun 01 28;
...Jul/Aug 01 30
preventive care for ...Jan/Feb 01 4
rating of ...May/Jun 01 28–29
safety concerns and ...May/Jun 01 28;
...Jul/Aug 01 30
separate, for different purposes ...May/Jun 01 28
sources for ...May/Jun 01 32
special features on ...May/Jun 01 28
warping of ...May/Jun 01 28–29
Cutting mats ...May/Jun 01 28

D

Dan Dan Mian (Spicy Sichuan Noodles) ...May/Jun 01 7
Danish aebleskive pans ...Mar/Apr 01 3
Defatting
pan drippings ...Nov/Dec 01 4
stocks and sauces ...Jan/Feb 01 5
Demerara sugar, sources for ...Nov/Dec 01 32
Desserts. *See also* Cakes; Cookie(s); Ice creams; Pie(s); Tart(s)
apple turnovers ...Jan/Feb 01 22–23
with commercial puff pastry ...Mar/Apr 01 30
Flaky ...Jan/Feb 01 23
fraisage technique for ...Jan/Feb 01 22
Quickest Puff Pastry for ...Jan/Feb 01 23
shaping ...Jan/Feb 01 23
Bittersweet Chocolate Sauce for ...Sep/Oct 01 24
cherry cobbler ...Jul/Aug 01 24–25
Sour ...Jul/Aug 01 25
Sour, Fresh ...Jul/Aug 01 25
tasting of "processed" cherries for ...Jul/Aug 01 25
crème brûlée ...Nov/Dec 01 22–23
Classic ...Nov/Dec 01 23
curdled vs. creamy ...Nov/Dec 01 23
Espresso ...Nov/Dec 01 23
Desserts *(cont.)*
ramekins for ...Nov/Dec 01 32
Tea-Infused ...Nov/Dec 01 23
fruit salads, summer ...Jul/Aug 01 20
Honeydew, Mango, and Blueberries with Lime-Ginger Reduction ...Jul/Aug 01 20
Nectarines, Blueberries, and Raspberries with
Champagne-Cardamom Reduction ...Jul/Aug 01 20
Red Plums and Figs with Brandy-Cinnamon Reduction ...Jul/Aug 01 20
Strawberries and Grapes with Balsamic and Red Wine Reduction ...Jul/Aug 01 20
The Pie and Pastry Bible (Beranbaum) ...Nov/Dec 01 31
rhubarb fool ...May/Jun 01 22
Blueberry, with Fresh Ginger ...May/Jun 01 22
Master Recipe for ...May/Jun 01 22
Strawberry ...May/Jun 01 22
Sweet Simplicity: Jacques Pépin's Fruit Desserts (Pépin) ...Nov/Dec 01 31
Deviled
Breaded Chicken Cutlets ...Sep/Oct 01 11
eggs, stabilizing for transporting ...Mar/Apr 01 5
Diamond steels ...Jul/Aug 01 16
sources for ...Jul/Aug 01 32
Dinosaur kale, field guide ...Mar/Apr 01 BC
Dips. *See* Baba ghanoush
Dish racks, draining hot boiled corn on the cob in ...Jul/Aug 01 4
Dish towels, uncommon uses for ...Jan/Feb 01 17
Dishwashers, unloading silverware from ...Mar/Apr 01 5
Dough scrapers, uncommon uses for ...Jan/Feb 01 16
Douglas, Tom *(Tom Douglas' Seattle Kitchen)* ...Sep/Oct 01 31
Doyenné du Comice pears, field guide ...Nov/Dec 01 BC
Dressing, Sausage ...Nov/Dec 01 10
Dressings, salad. *See also* Vinaigrettes
Sesame-Miso ...Jul/Aug 01 7
Drop cookie makers ...May/Jun 01 3
Duguid, Naomi *(Hot Sour Salty Sweet)* ...Jul/Aug 01 31;
...Nov/Dec 01 31
Dumplings, Danish aebleskive ...Mar/Apr 01 3
Dutch apple pie, errata ...Mar/Apr 01 3
Dutch ovens
All-Clad, clarification of terminology for ...Jul/Aug 01 3
for fried chicken ...May/Jun 01 11;
...Jul/Aug 01 3
sources for ...May/Jun 01 32
Duxelles ...Nov/Dec 01 20

E

Egg(s)
adding one at a time ...May/Jun 01 4
breakfast strata ...Nov/Dec 01 14–15
assembling ...Nov/Dec 01 15
with Potatoes, Rosemary, and Fontina ...Nov/Dec 01 15
with Sausage, Mushrooms, and Monterey Jack ...Nov/Dec 01 15
with Spinach, Shallots, and Gruyère ...Nov/Dec 01 15
chopping with pastry blender ...Jan/Feb 01 17
deviled, stabilizing for transporting ...Mar/Apr 01 5
hot, transferring to ice-water bath ...Mar/Apr 01 5
omelets. *See also* Omelets
cheese ...May/Jun 01 18–19
pasteurized ...Sep/Oct 01 2
separating, avoiding contamination during ...Mar/Apr 01 4
spaghetti alla carbonara ...Sep/Oct 01 6–7
Master Recipe for ...Sep/Oct 01 7
whites
Coconut Buttercream ...Mar/Apr 01 25
French, Swiss, and Italian meringues ...Jul/Aug 01 2
yolks, removing *chalazae* from ...May/Jun 01 25;
...Jul/Aug 01 23
Eggplant
baba ghanoush ...Jul/Aug 01 18–19
Charcoal-Grill Method ...Jul/Aug 01 19
Gas-Grill Method ...Jul/Aug 01 19
Israeli-Style ...Jul/Aug 01 19
Oven Method ...Jul/Aug 01 19
preparing eggplant for ...Jul/Aug 01 19
with Sautéed Onions ...Jul/Aug 01 19
ratatouille ...Sep/Oct 01 18–19
Master Recipe for ...Sep/Oct 01 19
salting and pressing ...Sep/Oct 01 18, 19
Ejector spoons ...May/Jun 01 3

Endive, grilling . . . May/Jun 01 16
Equipment. *See also* Appliances; Bakeware and baking supplies; Cookware; Cutting boards; Gadgets and utensils; Grilling equipment; Knives; Storing and storage equipment
  ratings of
    coffee grinders, inexpensive . . . Nov/Dec 01 28–29
    colanders . . . Sep/Oct 01 28–29
    cutting boards . . . May/Jun 01 28–29
    garlic presses . . . Mar/Apr 01 28–29
    ice cream scoops . . . Sep/Oct 01 26
    pepper mills . . . Jul/Aug 01 28–29
    rice cookers . . . Mar/Apr 01 30
    sauté pans . . . Jan/Feb 01 28–29
    steak knives . . . Sep/Oct 01 9
    tongs . . . Jul/Aug 01 15
    torches . . . Nov/Dec 01 23
Escarole, in White Bean Soup with Winter Vegetables . . . Jan/Feb 01 21
Espresso Crème Brûlée . . . Nov/Dec 01 23

F

Farfalle, field guide . . . Sep/Oct 01 BC
Fat
  chicken, reusing . . . May/Jun 01 30
  defatting
    pan drippings . . . Nov/Dec 01 4
    stocks and sauces . . . Jan/Feb 01 5
Fatback, salt pork vs. . . . Jan/Feb 01 30
Fennel . . . Nov/Dec 01 3
  grilling . . . May/Jun 01 17
Fennel seeds . . . Nov/Dec 01 3
  field guide . . . Jul/Aug 01 BC
Feta Cheese, Stuffed Bell Peppers with Spiced Lamb, Currants and . . Mar/Apr 01 7
Field, Carol *(In Nonna's Kitchen)* . . . Nov/Dec 01 31
Field guides
  beans, dried . . . Jan/Feb 01 BC
  Brassica family . . . Mar/Apr 01 BC
    errata . . . May/Jun 01 3
  chiles, fresh . . . May/Jun 01 BC
  herbes de Provence . . . Jul/Aug 01 BC
  pasta, dried . . . Sep/Oct 01 BC
  pears . . . Nov/Dec 01 BC
Figs and Red Plums with Brandy-Cinnamon Reduction . . . Jul/Aug 01 20
Filet mignon . . . May/Jun 01 8–9
  Argentinian-Style Fresh Parsley and Garlic Sauce for (Chimichurri) . . . May/Jun 01 9
  Bacon-Wrapped . . . May/Jun 01 9
  butchering quality of . . . May/Jun 01 9
  Madeira Pan Sauce with Mustard and Anchovies for . . . May/Jun 01 9
  Pan-Seared . . . May/Jun 01 9
Fines Herbes, Mustard Vinaigrette with Lemon and . . . Sep/Oct 01 12
Fish. *See also* Seafood; Shrimp
  Bouillabaisse . . . Sep/Oct 01 13–15
    See also Bouillabaisse
  Chilean sea bass . . . Jul/Aug 01 12–13
    See also Chilean sea bass
  Monkfish Fra Diavolo with Linguine . . . Nov/Dec 01 7
  stock . . . Sep/Oct 01 14
    for Bouillabaisse-Style Fish Stew . . . Sep/Oct 01 14
  storing in refrigerator . . . Mar/Apr 01 16
  striped bass . . . Jul/Aug 01 12
  tuna salad . . . May/Jun 01 13
    with Balsamic Vinegar and Grapes . . . May/Jun 01 13
    with Cauliflower, Jalapeño, and Cilantro . . . May/Jun 01 13
    Classic . . . May/Jun 01 13
    Curried, with Apples and Currants . . . May/Jun 01 13
    with Lime and Horseradish . . . May/Jun 01 13
Flageolets, field guide . . . Jan/Feb 01 BC
Flour(s)
  all-purpose . . . Jan/Feb 01 30
    testing in cakes . . . Sep/Oct 01 23
  cake . . . May/Jun 01 2
    storing and measuring . . . May/Jun 01 4
    testing necessity of . . . Sep/Oct 01 23
  measuring . . . Sep/Oct 01 17
    sifting and . . . Sep/Oct 01 17
  for pizza dough . . . Jan/Feb 01 9
Flour(s) *(cont.)*
  proper ratio of yeast to . . . Jan/Feb 01 25
  rice, sources for . . . Nov/Dec 01 32
  sifting . . . Sep/Oct 01 17
  storing in summer . . . Jul/Aug 01 5
  tapioca . . . Nov/Dec 01 2
  weighing in brown paper bag . . . May/Jun 01 5
  Wondra . . . May/Jun 01 2
Flour canisters
  keeping measuring cups in . . . Sep/Oct 01 4
  lids of, as sifter coasters . . . Mar/Apr 01 5
Flouring cake pans, combining greasing with . . . Nov/Dec 01 5
Flour sifters, coasters for . . . Mar/Apr 01 5
Fluid ounce . . . Sep/Oct 01 30
Fontina, Breakfast Strata with Potatoes, Rosemary and . . . Nov/Dec 01 15
Food processors
  grater attachments of, keeping dried mushrooms submerged while rehydrating with . . . Jan/Feb 01 4
  juicing fruits for jam in . . . Sep/Oct 01 5
Fool, rhubarb . . . May/Jun 01 22
  Blueberry, with Fresh Ginger . . . May/Jun 01 22
  Master Recipe for . . . May/Jun 01 22
  Strawberry . . . May/Jun 01 22
Forelle pears, field guide . . . Nov/Dec 01 BC
Four-Vegetable Soup . . . May/Jun 01 15
Fra diavolo
  Monkfish, with Linguine . . . Nov/Dec 01 7
  Scallops, with Linguine . . . Nov/Dec 01 7
  shrimp . . . Nov/Dec 01 6–7
    with Linguine . . . Nov/Dec 01 7
Fraisage technique . . . Jan/Feb 01 22
Freezers, storing flour in . . . Jul/Aug 01 5
Freezing
  ice cream, preserving freshness of . . . Jan/Feb 01 4
  pizza dough . . . Jan/Feb 01 10
  single servings of soup . . . Jan/Feb 01 4
French (cuisine)
  beef Burgundy . . . Jan/Feb 01 12–14
    advance preparation of . . . Jan/Feb 01 14
    making vegetable and herb bouquet for . . . Jan/Feb 01 14
    Master Recipe for . . . Jan/Feb 01 13
    trimming meat for . . . Jan/Feb 01 14
    wine for . . . Jan/Feb 01 14
  Bouillabaisse . . . Sep/Oct 01 13–15
    See also Bouillabaisse
  cookbooks
    Jacques Pépin's Table (Pépin) . . . Nov/Dec 01 31
    Sweet Simplicity: Jacques Pépin's Fruit Desserts (Pépin) . . . Nov/Dec 01 31
  crème brûlée . . . Nov/Dec 01 22–23
    Classic . . . Nov/Dec 01 23
    curdled vs. creamy . . . Nov/Dec 01 23
    Espresso . . . Nov/Dec 01 23
    ramekins for . . . Nov/Dec 01 32
    Tea-Infused . . . Nov/Dec 01 23
  persillade . . . May/Jun 01 3
  pommes Anna, pans for . . . Jan/Feb 01 2
Fried chicken. *See* Chicken—fried
Fried rice. *See* Rice—fried
Frostings
  buttercream
    Coconut . . . Mar/Apr 01 25
    curdled or broken, rescuing . . . Mar/Apr 01 30
  icings vs. . . . Sep/Oct 01 3
  Milk Chocolate, Creamy . . . Jan/Feb 01 24
Fruit(s). *See also* specific fruits
  fresh, tarts . . . Jul/Aug 01 21–23
    Classic . . . Jul/Aug 01 23
    glazing . . . Jul/Aug 01 30
    Kiwi, Raspberry, and Blueberry . . . Jul/Aug 01 22
    Mixed Berry . . . Jul/Aug 01 22
    Strawberry . . . Jul/Aug 01 22
  juicing for jam . . . Sep/Oct 01 5
  salads, summer . . . Jul/Aug 01 20
    Honeydew, Mango, and Blueberries with Lime-Ginger Reduction . . . Jul/Aug 01 20
    Nectarines, Blueberries, and Raspberries with Champagne-Cardamom Reduction . . . Jul/Aug 01 20
    Red Plums and Figs with Brandy-Cinnamon Reduction . . . Jul/Aug 01 20
    Strawberries and Grapes with Balsamic and Red Wine Reduction . . Jul/Aug 01 20

Fruit(s) *(cont.)*
storing in refrigerator . . . Mar/Apr 01 16
Sweet Simplicity: Jacques Pépin's Fruit Desserts (Pépin) . . . Nov/Dec 01 31
Fry pans, All-Clad, sources for . . . Mar/Apr 01 32

G

Gadgets and utensils. *See also* Cutting boards; Knives; Measuring cups and spoons
basting brushes, impromptu . . . Jul/Aug 01 5
butcher's twine, binding roast with . . . Mar/Apr 01 30
candlestands, impromptu . . . May/Jun 01 4
colanders
rating of . . . Sep/Oct 01 28–29
sources for . . . Sep/Oct 01 32
strainers vs. . . . Sep/Oct 01 29
cookie cutters, making ice cream slices with . . . Sep/Oct 01 4
cookie droppers . . . May/Jun 01 3
corkscrews
as handle for potatoes during peeling . . . Mar/Apr 01 4
puncturing corn on the cob pieces with, for skewering . . . Jul/Aug 01 4
cutting mats . . . May/Jun 01 28
dish racks, draining hot boiled corn on the cob in . . . Jul/Aug 01 4
dish towels, uncommon uses for . . . Jan/Feb 01 17
garlic peelers
loading pepper grinders with . . . Jan/Feb 01 5
sources for . . . Mar/Apr 01 32
garlic presses . . . Mar/Apr 01 15
rating of . . . Mar/Apr 01 28–29
sources for . . . Mar/Apr 01 32
ice cream scoops
rating of . . . Sep/Oct 01 26
sources for . . . Mar/Apr 01 32;
. . . Sep/Oct 01 32
stainless steel . . . Mar/Apr 01 32
ice cream spades . . . Sep/Oct 01 26
sources for . . . Sep/Oct 01 32
ice packs, for brining . . . Nov/Dec 01 17
keeping clean and on hand . . . Mar/Apr 01 4
marrow spoons . . . Jan/Feb 01 3
microplane grater/zester
collecting zest neatly with . . . Mar/Apr 01 5
rescuing burnt cookies with . . . Nov/Dec 01 5
sources for . . . May/Jun 01 32;
. . . Sep/Oct 01 32
uncommon uses for . . . Jan/Feb 01 17
mortars and pestles . . . Mar/Apr 01 15
sources for . . . Mar/Apr 01 32
orange peelers . . . Jul/Aug 01 3
osso buco spoons . . . Jan/Feb 01 3
pasta rakes, wooden, sources for . . . Mar/Apr 01 32
pasta servers, transferring hot eggs to ice-water bath with . . . Mar/Apr 01 5
pastry bags, stands for . . . Sep/Oct 01 4
pastry blenders, uncommon uses for . . . Jan/Feb 01 17
pastry brushes
for glazing fruit tarts . . . Jul/Aug 01 30
sources for . . . May/Jun 01 32;
. . . Jul/Aug 01 32;
. . . Nov/Dec 01 32
peach pitters . . . Sep/Oct 01 3
pepper mills
loading . . . Jan/Feb 01 5;
. . . Jul/Aug 01 4
motorizing . . . May/Jun 01 5
rating of . . . Jul/Aug 01 28–29
sources for . . . Jul/Aug 01 32
pizza wheels, sources for . . . Nov/Dec 01 32
pop-up timers, in poultry . . . Mar/Apr 01 2–3
rolling pins
sources for . . . Jan/Feb 01 32;
. . . Nov/Dec 01 32
tapered French-style . . . Jan/Feb 01 32
scissors, uncommon uses for . . . Jan/Feb 01 17
scrapers
bench, checking evenness of cookie dough with . . . Nov/Dec 01 5
dough, uncommon uses for . . . Jan/Feb 01 16
flexible, sources for . . . Nov/Dec 01 32
shrimp deveiners . . . Jan/Feb 01 19

Gadgets and utensils *(cont.)*
sifter coasters . . . Mar/Apr 01 5
skewers
bamboo, as story sticks for reductions . . . Jan/Feb 01 5
bamboo, sources for . . . Jul/Aug 01 32
metal, sources for . . . May/Jun 01 32;
. . . Jul/Aug 01 32
spatulas
heatproof, sources for . . . Mar/Apr 01 32
flexible, sources for . . . May/Jun 01 32
story sticks
chopsticks or bamboo skewers as . . . Jan/Feb 01 5
metal rulers as . . . Sep/Oct 01 4
thermometers
in ham roasts . . . Mar/Apr 01 10
Thermapen, sources for . . . May/Jun 01 32;
. . . Nov/Dec 01 32
tongs
caddy for . . . Mar/Apr 01 5
rating of . . . Jul/Aug 01 15
sources for . . . May/Jun 01 32;
. . . Jul/Aug 01 32
uncommon uses for . . . Jan/Feb 01 16
torches
rating of . . . Nov/Dec 01 23
sources for . . . Nov/Dec 01 32
vegetable peelers
dotting baked goods with butter with . . . Sep/Oct 01 4
uncommon uses for . . . Jan/Feb 01 16
vertical roasters, makeshift . . . Jan/Feb 01 5
whipped cream siphons, sources for . . . May/Jun 01 32
whisks, making gnocchi ridges with . . . Sep/Oct 01 5
Gannon, Beverly (*The Hali'imaile General Store Cookbook*) . . . Jul/Aug 01 31
Garam Masala, Garlic and Cilantro Marinade with . . . Jul/Aug 01 15
Garbanzo beans (chickpeas), field guide . . . Jan/Feb 01 BC
Garlic
Basting Oil . . . May/Jun 01 17
Bok Choy Braised with . . . May/Jun 01 21
Breaded Chicken Cutlets with Oregano and . . . Sep/Oct 01 11
and Cilantro Marinade with Garam Masala . . . Jul/Aug 01 15
Croutons . . . Jul/Aug 01 9
dehydrated minced . . . Jul/Aug 01 2–3
finely mincing with microplane grater . . . Jan/Feb 01 17
fra diavolo
Monkfish, with Linguine . . . Nov/Dec 01 7
Scallops, with Linguine . . . Nov/Dec 01 7
shrimp . . . Nov/Dec 01 6–7
Shrimp, with Linguine . . . Nov/Dec 01 7
and Fresh Parsley Sauce, Argentinian-Style (Chimichurri) . . . May/Jun 01 9
mail-order sources for . . . Mar/Apr 01 32
pasta with oil and . . . Mar/Apr 01 14–15
Master Recipe for (Pasta Aglio e Olio) . . . Mar/Apr 01 15
persillade . . . May/Jun 01 3
preventing cutting board from picking up odor of . . . Jan/Feb 01 4
rendering little bits of . . . Mar/Apr 01 15
Roasted, and Mustard Vinaigrette . . . Sep/Oct 01 12
Rosemary-Mint Marinade with Lemon and . . . Jul/Aug 01 15
-Rubbed Croutons . . . Sep/Oct 01 15
softneck and hardneck varieties of . . . Mar/Apr 01 14–15
Stir-Fried Bok Choy with Oyster Sauce and . . . May/Jun 01 21
Garlic peelers
loading pepper grinders with . . . Jan/Feb 01 5
sources for . . . Mar/Apr 01 32
Garlic powder . . . Jul/Aug 01 2–3
Garlic presses . . . Mar/Apr 01 15
rating of . . . Mar/Apr 01 28–29
sources for . . . Mar/Apr 01 32
Gastrique technique . . . Jul/Aug 01 20
Gazpacho . . . Jul/Aug 01 8–9
chopping vegetables for . . . Jul/Aug 01 9
Garlic Croutons for . . . Jul/Aug 01 9
getting texture "right" for . . . Jul/Aug 01 9
Master Recipe for . . . Jul/Aug 01 9
Quick Food Processor . . . Jul/Aug 01 9
Gemelli, field guide . . . Sep/Oct 01 BC
German-Style Grilled Potato Salad . . . Jul/Aug 01 11
Gigli, field guide . . . Sep/Oct 01 BC

Ginger
Fresh, Blueberry-Rhubarb Fool with . . . May/Jun 01 22
-Glazed Blueberry Muffins . . . Sep/Oct 01 21
grating with microplane grater . . . Jan/Feb 01 17
Lime Reduction, Honeydew, Mango, and Blueberries with . . . Jul/Aug 01 20
Orange Glaze, Roasted Carrots with . . . Jan/Feb 01 15
Pineapple Glaze, Spicy . . . Mar/Apr 01 10
Soy Vinaigrette, Asparagus with . . . Mar/Apr 01 11
Stir-Fried Bok Choy with Soy Sauce and . . . May/Jun 01 21
Warm-Spiced Parsley Marinade with . . . Jul/Aug 01 15
Glazes
for fruit tarts
Classic Fresh Fruit Tart . . . Jul/Aug 01 23
tips for . . . Jul/Aug 01 30
for ham
Apple Cider and Brown Sugar . . . Mar/Apr 01 10
Orange, Cinnamon, and Star Anise . . . Mar/Apr 01 10
Spicy Pineapple-Ginger . . . Mar/Apr 01 10
mess-free application of . . . Sep/Oct 01 5
Gnocchi, making ridges in . . . Sep/Oct 01 5
Goat cheese, storing in covered butter dish . . . May/Jun 01 5
Gomitoni, field guide . . . Sep/Oct 01 BC
Gouda, smoked, in Cheese Omelet with Bacon, Onion, and Scallion Filling . . . May/Jun 01 19
Grapefruit, in Black Olive and Citrus Relish . . . Jul/Aug 01 13
Grapes
and Strawberries with Balsamic and Red Wine Reduction . . . Jul/Aug 01 20
Tuna Salad with Balsamic Vinegar and . . . May/Jun 01 13
Grater attachments, keeping dried mushrooms submerged while rehydrating with . . . Jan/Feb 01 4
Graters. *See* Microplane grater/zester
Gravy
defatting pan drippings for . . . Nov/Dec 01 4
Kitchen Bouquet for . . . Nov/Dec 01 2
Turkey . . . Nov/Dec 01 10
Green beans . . . Nov/Dec 01 18
Blanched . . . Nov/Dec 01 18
with Buttered Bread Crumbs and Almonds . . . Nov/Dec 01 18
with Sautéed Shallots and Vermouth . . . Nov/Dec 01 18
with Toasted Hazelnuts and Brown Butter . . . Nov/Dec 01 18
Greens, storing in refrigerator . . . Mar/Apr 01 16
Grilled (foods)
baba ghanoush . . . Jul/Aug 01 18–19
Charcoal-Grill Method . . . Jul/Aug 01 19
Gas-Grill Method . . . Jul/Aug 01 19
Israeli-Style . . . Jul/Aug 01 19
with Sautéed Onions . . . Jul/Aug 01 19
chicken cutlets . . . Jul/Aug 01 6–7
Charcoal- . . . Jul/Aug 01 7
Cucumber and Mango Relish with Yogurt for . . . Jul/Aug 01 7
diamond-pattern grill marks on . . . Jul/Aug 01 7
Gas- . . . Jul/Aug 01 7
Salad with Sesame-Miso Dressing . . . Jul/Aug 01 7
Spicy Tomatillo and Pineapple Salsa for . . . Jul/Aug 01 7
Chilean sea bass fillets . . . Jul/Aug 01 12–13
Black Olive and Citrus Relish for . . . Jul/Aug 01 13
Charcoal- . . . Jul/Aug 01 13
Gas- . . . Jul/Aug 01 13
Orange and Soy Marinade for . . . Jul/Aug 01 13
Spicy Fresh Tomato Salsa for . . . Jul/Aug 01 13
corn on the cob . . . May/Jun 01 17
skewering pieces of . . . Jul/Aug 01 4
diamond-pattern grill marks on . . . Jul/Aug 01 7
doneness tests for . . . May/Jun 01 30
potato(es)
and Arugula Salad with Dijon Mustard Vinaigrette . . . Jul/Aug 01 11
blanching step for . . . Jul/Aug 01 11
Gas-Grill Variation . . . Jul/Aug 01 11
salad . . . Jul/Aug 01 10–11
Salad, German-Style . . . Jul/Aug 01 11
for Salad, Master Recipe for . . . Jul/Aug 01 10
Salad with Corn and Poblano Chiles, Spicy . . . Jul/Aug 01 11
shish kebab . . . Jul/Aug 01 14–15
Charcoal-Grilled . . . Jul/Aug 01 14
Garlic and Cilantro Marinade with Garam Masala for . . . Jul/Aug 01 15
Gas-Grilled . . . Jul/Aug 01 15
prepping onions for . . . Jul/Aug 01 15
Rosemary-Mint Marinade with Garlic and Lemon for . . . Jul/Aug 01 15
Sweet Curry Marinade with Buttermilk for . . . Jul/Aug 01 15
Grilled (foods) *(cont.)*
Warm-Spiced Parsley Marinade with Ginger for . . . Jul/Aug 01 15
vegetables . . . May/Jun 01 16–17
basting oils for . . . May/Jun 01 17
equipment sources for . . . May/Jun 01 32
essential equipment for . . . May/Jun 01 17
general guidelines for . . . May/Jun 01 16
preparing for . . . May/Jun 01 16
Grill grates, sources for . . . May/Jun 01 32
Grilling equipment
basting brushes, impromptu . . . Jul/Aug 01 5
charcoal, dividing into bags for individual fires . . . Jul/Aug 01 5
charcoal grills
emptying cool ashes from . . . Jul/Aug 01 4
measuring temperature of . . . Jul/Aug 01 3
restarting fire in . . . Jul/Aug 01 5
chimney starters, filling neatly with charcoal . . . Jul/Aug 01 5
gas grills, measuring temperature of . . . Jul/Aug 01 3
grill grates, sources for . . . May/Jun 01 32
grill racks, cleaning without brush . . . Jul/Aug 01 5
skewers, sources for . . . May/Jun 01 32;
. . . Jul/Aug 01 32
tongs
rating of . . . Jul/Aug 01 15
sources for . . . Jul/Aug 01 32
for vegetables . . . May/Jun 01 17
sources for . . . May/Jun 01 32
Grill racks, cleaning without brush . . . Jul/Aug 01 5
Grill temperature, measuring . . . Jul/Aug 01 3
Gruyère
Breakfast Strata with Spinach, Shallots and . . . Nov/Dec 01 15
Cheese Omelet with Sautéed Mushroom Filling with Thyme . . . May/Jun 01 19
Guacamole, mashing with pastry blender . . . Jan/Feb 01 17

H

Habanero chiles, field guide . . . May/Jun 01 BC
Hair dryers, restarting grill fire with . . . Jul/Aug 01 5
Half-sheet pans, sources for . . . Sep/Oct 01 32
Hali'imaile General Store Cookbook, The (Gannon) . . . Jul/Aug 01 31
Ham roast, fresh . . . Mar/Apr 01 8–10
carving . . . Mar/Apr 01 10
Coca-Cola . . . Mar/Apr 01 10
glazes for
Apple Cider and Brown Sugar . . . Mar/Apr 01 10
Orange, Cinnamon, and Star Anise . . . Mar/Apr 01 10
Spicy Pineapple-Ginger . . . Mar/Apr 01 10
Master Recipe for . . . Mar/Apr 01 9
scoring skin of . . . Mar/Apr 01 9
with electric knife . . . May/Jun 01 30
thermometer placement in . . . Mar/Apr 01 10
two sections of . . . Mar/Apr 01 9
Hatchets, as cleaver substitutes . . . Jul/Aug 01 5
Hawaiian (cuisine), in *The Hali'imaile General Store Cookbook* (Gannon) . . . Jul/Aug 01 31
Hazelnuts, Toasted, Green Beans with Brown Butter and . . . Nov/Dec 01 18
Headaches after drinking wine . . . May/Jun 01 3
Herb(s). *See also* specific herbs
Fines Herbes, Mustard Vinaigrette with Lemon and . . . Sep/Oct 01 12
Herbes de Provence, field guide . . . Jul/Aug 01 BC
leftover, using up in sandwiches . . . Mar/Apr 01 4
plastic milk jug as vase for . . . Jul/Aug 01 5
sachets, improvising with in paper coffee filters . . . Jul/Aug 01 4
and vegetable bouquet . . . Jan/Feb 01 14
Herbes de Provence, field guide . . . Jul/Aug 01 BC
Histamines . . . May/Jun 01 3
Honey
measuring . . . Sep/Oct 01 17
Mustard Pan Sauce with Tarragon (for turkey cutlets) . . . Mar/Apr 01 13
Honeydew, Mango, and Blueberries with Lime-Ginger Reduction . . . Jul/Aug 01 20
Horseradish, Tuna Salad with Lime and . . . May/Jun 01 13
Hosui pears, field guide . . . Nov/Dec 01 BC
Hotcakes, Thai Kanom krok . . . Mar/Apr 01 3
Hot Sour Salty Sweet (Alford and Duguid) . . . Jul/Aug 01 31;
. . . Nov/Dec 01 31
Hot-water baths
removing ramekins from . . . Jan/Feb 01 16
securing ramekins in . . . Jan/Feb 01 17

Hydrogenation . . . . .May/Jun 01   24
   of peanut butters . . . . .May/Jun 01   26

I

Ice baths, iceless . . . . .Nov/Dec 01   4
Ice creams
   keeping fresh . . . . .Jan/Feb 01   4
   melting speed of . . . . .Sep/Oct 01   25
   rock-hard, serving . . . . .Sep/Oct 01   4
   vanilla
      sources for . . . . .Sep/Oct 01   32
      tasting of . . . . .Sep/Oct 01   25–27
Ice cream scoops
   rating of . . . . .Sep/Oct 01   26
   sources for . . . . .Mar/Apr 01   32;
   . . . . .Sep/Oct 01   32
   stainless steel . . . . .Mar/Apr 01   32
Ice cream spades . . . . .Sep/Oct 01   26
   sources for . . . . .Sep/Oct 01   32
Ice packs, for brining . . . . .Nov/Dec 01   17
Icings, frostings vs. . . . . .Sep/Oct 01   3
Ingredients, ratings of. *See* Tastings
In Nonna's Kitchen (Field) . . . . .Nov/Dec 01   31
Israeli-Style Baba Ghanoush . . . . .Jul/Aug 01   19
Italian (cuisine). *See also* Pasta; Pizza
   Breaded Chicken Cutlets with Parmesan
      (Chicken Milanese) . . . . .Sep/Oct 01   11
   chicken piccata . . . . .Jan/Feb 01   6–7
      with Black Olives . . . . .Jan/Feb 01   7
      Master Recipe for . . . . .Jan/Feb 01   7
      Peppery . . . . .Jan/Feb 01   7
      with Prosciutto . . . . .Jan/Feb 01   7
   cookbooks
      In Nonna's Kitchen (Field) .Nov/Dec 01   31
      The Italian Country Table (Kasper) . . . . .Nov/Dec 01   31
      Second Helpings from Union Square Cafe
         (Meyer and Romano) . . . . .Sep/Oct 01   31
   fra diavolo
      Monkfish, with Linguine . . . . .Nov/Dec 01   7
      Scallops, with Linguine . . . . .Nov/Dec 01   7
      shrimp . . . . .Nov/Dec 01   6–7
      Shrimp, with Linguine . . . . .Nov/Dec 01   7
   piccata, use of term . . . . .Mar/Apr 01   2
   ribollita . . . . .Jan/Feb 01   21
   Tuscan white bean soup . . . . .Jan/Feb 01   20–21
      leftover, making ribollita with . . . . .Jan/Feb 01   21
      Master Recipe for . . . . .Jan/Feb 01   21
      Quick . . . . .Jan/Feb 01   21
      with Winter Vegetables . . . . .Jan/Feb 01   21
   Italian Country Table, The (Kasper) . . . . .Nov/Dec 01   31

J

Jacob's cattle beans, field guide . . . . .Jan/Feb 01   BC
Jacques Pépin's Table (Pépin) . . . . .Nov/Dec 01   31
Jalapeño chiles
   field guide . . . . .May/Jun 01   BC
   Tuna Salad with Cauliflower, Cilantro and . . . . .May/Jun 01   13
Jamaican hot chiles, field guide . . . . .May/Jun 01   BC
Jamison, Bill (*American Home Cooking*) . . . . .Nov/Dec 01   31
Jamison, Cheryl Alters (*American Home Cooking*) . . . . .Nov/Dec 01   31
Jams
   juicing fruits for . . . . .Sep/Oct 01   5
   use of term . . . . .Jul/Aug 01   2
Jar lids
   sticky, preventing . . . . .Sep/Oct 01   5
   stubborn, opening . . . . .Mar/Apr 01   5
Jellies, use of term . . . . .Jul/Aug 01   2
Jewish cooking
   The Book of Jewish Food (Roden) . . . . .Mar/Apr 01   31
   1,000 Jewish Recipes (Levy) . . . . .Mar/Apr 01   31

K

Kale
   field guide . . . . .Mar/Apr 01   BC
   White Bean Soup with Winter Vegetables . . . . .Jan/Feb 01   21

Kanom krok pans, Thai . . . . .Mar/Apr 01   3
Kasper, Lynne Rossetto (*The Italian Country Table*) . . . . .Nov/Dec 01   31
Kidney beans, field guide . . . . .Jan/Feb 01   BC
Kitchen Bouquet . . . . .Nov/Dec 01   2
Kiwi
   peeling . . . . .Jul/Aug 01   22
   Raspberry, and Blueberry Tart . . . . .Jul/Aug 01   22
Knives
   boning, sources for . . . . .Jan/Feb 01   32
   bread, sources for . . . . .Mar/Apr 01   32
   chef's . . . . .Mar/Apr 01   15
   cleavers, hatchets as substitute for .Jul/Aug 01   5
   cooling rack improvised with . . . . .Jul/Aug 01   4
   detecting burrs on . . . . .Jul/Aug 01   17
   electric, scoring skin of fresh ham with . . . . .May/Jun 01   30
   sharpening. *See also* Sharpening steels; Sharpening stones
      by hand . . . . .Jul/Aug 01   16–17
      professional, sources for . . . . .Jul/Aug 01   32
   sharpness tests for . . . . .Jul/Aug 01   16
   steak
      rating of . . . . .Sep/Oct 01   9
      sources for . . . . .Sep/Oct 01   32
   transporting safely . . . . .Jul/Aug 01   4
Kohlrabi, field guide . . . . .Mar/Apr 01   BC
Koshering . . . . .Jan/Feb 01   3

L

Lamb
   shish kebab . . . . .Jul/Aug 01   14–15
      Charcoal-Grilled . . . . .Jul/Aug 01   14
      Garlic and Cilantro Marinade with Garam Masala for . . . . .Jul/Aug 01   15
      Gas-Grilled . . . . .Jul/Aug 01   15
      prepping onions for . . . . .Jul/Aug 01   15
      Rosemary-Mint Marinade with Garlic and Lemon for . . . . .Jul/Aug 01   15
      Sweet Curry Marinade with Buttermilk for . . . . .Jul/Aug 01   15
      Warm-Spiced Parsley Marinade with Ginger for . . . . .Jul/Aug 01   15
   Spiced, Stuffed Bell Peppers with Currants, Feta Cheese and . . . . .Mar/Apr 01   7
Lavender, field guide . . . . .Jul/Aug 01   BC
Leeks
   Four-Vegetable Soup . . . . .May/Jun 01   15
   White Bean Soup with Winter Vegetables . . . . .Jan/Feb 01   21
Lemon
   -Glazed Blueberry Muffins . . . . .Sep/Oct 01   21
   Mustard Vinaigrette with Fines Herbes and . . . . .Sep/Oct 01   12
   Rosemary Basting Oil . . . . .May/Jun 01   17
   Rosemary-Mint Marinade with Garlic and . . . . .Jul/Aug 01   15
   Shallot Vinaigrette, Asparagus with . . . . .Mar/Apr 01   11
Lettuce leaf, as impromptu basting brush . . . . .Jul/Aug 01   5
Levy, Faye (*1,000 Jewish Recipes*) . . . . .Mar/Apr 01   31
Lids
   hot, removing from cookware . . . . .Jan/Feb 01   16
   jar
      sticky, preventing . . . . .Sep/Oct 01   5
      stubborn, opening . . . . .Mar/Apr 01   5
Lime
   Ginger Reduction, Honeydew, Mango, and Blueberries with . . . . .Jul/Aug 01   20
   Tuna Salad with Horseradish and . . . . .May/Jun 01   13
Linguine
   Monkfish Fra Diavolo with . . . . .Nov/Dec 01   7
   Scallops Fra Diavolo with . . . . .Nov/Dec 01   7
   Shrimp Fra Diavolo with . . . . .Nov/Dec 01   7
Liqueurs, anise-flavored . . . . .Nov/Dec 01   3
Lop cheong sausages, sources for . . . . .Mar/Apr 01   32
Lunchmeats, storing in refrigerator . . . . .Mar/Apr 01   16

M

Macho green chiles, field guide . . . . .May/Jun 01   BC
Macho red chiles, field guide . . . . .May/Jun 01   BC
Madeira Pan Sauce with Mustard and Anchovies . . . . .May/Jun 01   9
Main dishes
   beef
      Burgundy . . . . .Jan/Feb 01   13
      Filet Mignon, Bacon-Wrapped . . . . .May/Jun 01   9
      Filet Mignon, Pan-Seared . . . . .May/Jun 01   9
      Steak au Poivre with Brandied Cream Sauce . . . . .Sep/Oct 01   9
      Wellington . . . . .Nov/Dec 01   21

Main dishes (cont.)

Bouillabaisse-Style Fish Stew ....Sep/Oct 01   15

chicken

Cutlets, Breaded, Crisp ....Sep/Oct 01   11
Cutlets, Breaded, Deviled ....Sep/Oct 01   11
Cutlets, Breaded, with Garlic and Oregano ....Sep/Oct 01   11
Cutlets, Breaded, with Parmesan (Chicken Milanese) ....Sep/Oct 01   11
Cutlets, Charcoal-Grilled ....Jul/Aug 01   7
Cutlets, Gas-Grilled ....Jul/Aug 01   7
Fried, Ultimate Crispy ....May/Jun 01   12
Grilled, Salad with Sesame-Miso Dressing ....Jul/Aug 01   7
Piccata ....Jan/Feb 01   7
Piccata, Peppery ....Jan/Feb 01   7
Piccata with Black Olives ....Jan/Feb 01   7
Piccata with Prosciutto ....Jan/Feb 01   7

Chilean sea bass

Fillets, Charcoal-Grilled ....Jul/Aug 01   13
Fillets, Gas-Grilled ....Jul/Aug 01   13

fried rice

with Peas and Bean Sprouts ....Mar/Apr 01   19
with Shrimp, Pork, and Peas ....Mar/Apr 01   19
Thai-Style Curried Chicken ....Mar/Apr 01   19

ham

Coca-Cola ....Mar/Apr 01   10
Roast Fresh ....Mar/Apr 01   9

Monkfish Fra Diavolo with Linguine ....Nov/Dec 01   7

noodles, Sichuan

Spicy (Dan Dan Mian) ....May/Jun 01   7
Spicy, with Shiitake Mushrooms ....May/Jun 01   7

omelets, cheese

with Bacon, Onion, and Scallion Filling ....May/Jun 01   19
Perfect ....May/Jun 01   19
with Sautéed Mushroom Filling with Thyme ....May/Jun 01   19
with Sautéed Red Bell Pepper Filling with Mushroom and Onion ....May/Jun 01   19

pasta

with Garlic and Oil (Pasta Aglio e Olio) ....Mar/Apr 01   15
Monkfish Fra Diavolo with Linguine ....Nov/Dec 01   7
Scallops Fra Diavolo with Linguine ....Nov/Dec 01   7
Shrimp Fra Diavolo with Linguine ....Nov/Dec 01   7
Spaghetti alla Carbonara ....Sep/Oct 01   7

peppers, stuffed bell

with Chicken, Smoked Mozzarella, and Basil ....Mar/Apr 01   7
Classic ....Mar/Apr 01   7
with Spiced Lamb, Currants, and Feta Cheese ....Mar/Apr 01   7

Pizza, Crisp Thin-Crust ....Jan/Feb 01   9
Scallops Fra Diavolo with Linguine ....Nov/Dec 01   7

shish kebab

Charcoal-Grilled ....Jul/Aug 01   14
Gas-Grilled ....Jul/Aug 01   15

shrimp

Fra Diavolo with Linguine ....Nov/Dec 01   7
Stir-Fried, Aromatic ....Jan/Feb 01   19
Stir-Fried, Cantonese-Style ....Jan/Feb 01   19
Stir-Fried, Singapore Chili ....Jan/Feb 01   19

turkey

Crisp-Skin High-Roast Butterflied, with Sausage Dressing .....Nov/Dec 01   10
Cutlets, Sautéed ....Mar/Apr 01   13

Mango

and Cucumber Relish with Yogurt ....Jul/Aug 01   7
Honeydew, and Blueberries with Lime-Ginger Reduction ....Jul/Aug 01   20

Maple Carrots with Browned Butter, Roasted ....Jan/Feb 01   15

Marinades

Fish and Shellfish ....Sep/Oct 01   15
Orange and Soy, for Grilled Chilean Sea Bass Fillets ....Jul/Aug 01   13

for shish kebab

Garlic and Cilantro, with Garam Masala ....Jul/Aug 01   15
Rosemary-Mint, with Garlic and Lemon ....Jul/Aug 01   15
Sweet Curry, with Buttermilk ....Jul/Aug 01   15
Warm-Spiced Parsley, with Ginger ....Jul/Aug 01   15

Marjoram, field guide ....Jul/Aug 01   BC
Marrow spoons ....Jan/Feb 01   3
Mashing, with pastry blender ....Jan/Feb 01   17
Matzo, as breading for fried chicken ....May/Jun 01   11
Measuring ....Sep/Oct 01   16–17
brown sugar, packing and ....Sep/Oct 01   17
butter ....Sep/Oct 01   17
dry ....Sep/Oct 01   16, 30
dip and sweep technique for ....Sep/Oct 01   16

Measuring (cont.)

flour ....Sep/Oct 01   17
sifting and ....Sep/Oct 01   17
fluid ounce ....Sep/Oct 01   30
liquid ....Sep/Oct 01   16, 30
peanut butter ....Sep/Oct 01   17
shortening ....Sep/Oct 01   17
sticky ingredients ....Sep/Oct 01   17
water ....May/Jun 01   5

Measuring cups and spoons

for dry ingredients ....Sep/Oct 01   16, 30
problematic handle styles of ....Sep/Oct 01   16
improvised, yogurt cups as ....Jul/Aug 01   4
keeping in canisters with dry ingredients ....Sep/Oct 01   4
for liquid ingredients ....Sep/Oct 01   16, 30
metal teaspoons, coring apples with ....Sep/Oct 01   5
sources for ....Sep/Oct 01   32

Meats. See also specific meats

bright color and freshness of ....Mar/Apr 01   17
storing in refrigerator ....Mar/Apr 01   16

Melba toast crumbs, coating chicken with ....Jan/Feb 01   5
Meringues, French, Swiss, and Italian ....Jul/Aug 01   2
Mexico One Plate at a Time (Bayless) ....May/Jun 01   31;
....Nov/Dec 01   31
Meyer, Danny (*Second Helpings from Union Square Cafe*) ......Sep/Oct 01   31

Microplane grater/zester

collecting zest neatly with ....Mar/Apr 01   5
rescuing burnt cookies with ....Nov/Dec 01   5
sources for ....May/Jun 01   32;
....Sep/Oct 01   32
uncommon uses for ....Jan/Feb 01   17

Microwave ovens

cleaning

inside ....Jan/Feb 01   4
nooks, crannies, and crevices ....May/Jun 01   4
storing flour in ....Jul/Aug 01   5

Middle Eastern (cuisine). See Baba ghanoush

Milk jugs, plastic

fashioning grill scoop from ....Jul/Aug 01   4
making vase for herbs from ....Jul/Aug 01   5

Mint-Rosemary Marinade with Garlic and Lemon ....Jul/Aug 01   15
Mirepoix ....Mar/Apr 01   3
Miso-Sesame Dressing, Grilled Chicken Salad with ....Jul/Aug 01   7
Molasses, measuring ....Sep/Oct 01   17
Monkfish Fra Diavolo with Linguine ....Nov/Dec 01   7

Monterey Jack

Breakfast Strata with Sausage, Mushrooms and ....Nov/Dec 01   15
Cheese Omelet with Sautéed Red Bell Pepper Filling
with Mushroom and Onion ....May/Jun 01   19

Mortars and pestles ....Mar/Apr 01   15
sources for ....Mar/Apr 01   32
Mostaccioli, field guide ....Sep/Oct 01   BC
Mothers (films on surface of vinegar) ....Jan/Feb 01   2
Mousse pie, chocolate ....May/Jun 01   30
Mozzarella, Smoked, Stuffed Bell Peppers with Chicken, Basil and .....Mar/Apr 01   7

Muffin pans

cooking stuffed peppers in ....Sep/Oct 01   5
liberating stuck muffins from ....Mar/Apr 01   5
portioning dough into ....Sep/Oct 01   21

Muffins

blueberry ....Sep/Oct 01   20–21
Best ....Sep/Oct 01   21
Cinnamon-Sugar-Dipped ....Sep/Oct 01   21
filling tins for ....Sep/Oct 01   21
Ginger-Glazed or Lemon-Glazed ....Sep/Oct 01   21
problems with ....Sep/Oct 01   21
trapped, liberating ....Mar/Apr 01   5

Mushroom(s)

Breakfast Strata with Sausage, Monterey Jack and ....Nov/Dec 01   15
button ....Mar/Apr 01   21
cleaning with dish towel ....Jan/Feb 01   17
dried, keeping submerged while rehydrating ....Jan/Feb 01   4
Duxelles ....Nov/Dec 01   20
grilling ....May/Jun 01   17
Pesto with Parsley and Thyme ....Jan/Feb 01   11
Sautéed, Filling with Thyme (for cheese omelet) ....May/Jun 01   19
Sautéed Red Bell Pepper Filling with Onion and (for cheese omelet) ..May/Jun 01   19
shiitake ....Mar/Apr 01   21

Mushroom(s) *(cont.)*
Bok Choy Braised with . . . May/Jun 01 21
Spicy Sichuan Noodles with . . . May/Jun 01 7
trimming with scissors . . . Jan/Feb 01 17
soup . . . Mar/Apr 01 20–21
Creamy . . . Mar/Apr 01 21
Sautéed Wild Mushroom Garnish for . . . Mar/Apr 01 21
storing . . . Nov/Dec 01 30
wild
Sautéed, Garnish . . . Mar/Apr 01 21
varieties of . . . Mar/Apr 01 21;
. . . May/Jun 01 3
Mustard
Honey Pan Sauce with Tarragon (for turkey cutlets) . . . Mar/Apr 01 13
Madeira Pan Sauce with Anchovies and . . . May/Jun 01 9
vinaigrette . . . Sep/Oct 01 12
Balsamic and . . . Sep/Oct 01 12
Dijon, Grilled Potato and Arugula Salad with . . . Jul/Aug 01 11
with Lemon and Fines Herbes . . . Sep/Oct 01 12
Roasted Garlic and . . . Sep/Oct 01 12
Mustard greens, field guide . . . Mar/Apr 01 BC

N
Naked Chef, The (Oliver) . . . May/Jun 01 31;
. . . Nov/Dec 01 31
Nectarines, Blueberries, and Raspberries with
Champagne-Cardamom Reduction . . . Jul/Aug 01 20
Nonpareils . . . Jan/Feb 01 7
Nonstick surfaces, protecting . . . Sep/Oct 01 4
Noodles. *See also* Pasta
Asian, dried, sources for . . . May/Jun 01 32
Chinese, fresh and dried varieties of . . . May/Jun 01 7
Sichuan . . . May/Jun 01 6–7
Spicy (Dan Dan Mian) . . . May/Jun 01 7
Spicy, with Shiitake Mushrooms . . . May/Jun 01 7
Nut(s). *See also* specific nuts
Toasted, and Parsley Pesto . . . Jan/Feb 01 11
Nutmeg, grating with microplane grater . . . Jan/Feb 01 17

O
Oil(s)
basting, for vegetables
Garlic . . . May/Jun 01 17
Lemon-Rosemary . . . May/Jun 01 17
pasta with garlic and . . . Mar/Apr 01 14–15
Master Recipe for (Pasta Aglio e Olio) . . . Mar/Apr 01 15
sesame
cold-pressed . . . May/Jun 01 30
roasted, dark, or Asian . . . May/Jun 01 30
Olive(s), black
Chicken Piccata with . . . Jan/Feb 01 7
and Citrus Relish . . . Jul/Aug 01 13
Olive oil
applying to surface of crostini and bruschetta . . . May/Jun 01 4
extra-virgin
tasting of . . . Mar/Apr 01 26–27
as term . . . Mar/Apr 01 26
Oliver, Jamie *(The Naked Chef)* . . . May/Jun 01 31;
. . . Nov/Dec 01 31
Omelets
cheese . . . May/Jun 01 18–19
with Bacon, Onion, and Scallion Filling . . . May/Jun 01 19
Perfect . . . May/Jun 01 19
with Sautéed Mushroom Filling with Thyme . . . May/Jun 01 19
with Sautéed Red Bell Pepper Filling with Mushroom and Onion . . . May/Jun 01 19
overcooking . . . May/Jun 01 19
pans for . . . May/Jun 01 30
preparing . . . May/Jun 01 19
1,000 Jewish Recipes (Levy) . . . Mar/Apr 01 31
Onion(s)
Bacon, and Scallion Filling (for cheese omelet) . . . May/Jun 01 19
grilling . . . May/Jun 01 16
mirepoix . . . Mar/Apr 01 3
older, keeping track of . . . Nov/Dec 01 5
prepping for shish kebab . . . Jul/Aug 01 15
ratatouille . . . Sep/Oct 01 18–19
Onion(s) *(cont.)*
Master Recipe for . . . Sep/Oct 01 19
Red, Bacon, and Balsamic Vinaigrette, Asparagus with . . . Mar/Apr 01 11
Sautéed, Baba Ghanoush with . . . Jul/Aug 01 19
Sautéed Red Bell Pepper Filling with Mushroom and (for cheese omelet) . . . May/Jun 01 19
slippery skin on . . . Jan/Feb 01 3
Opening stubborn jar lids . . . Mar/Apr 01 5
Orange(s)
Black Olive and Citrus Relish . . . Jul/Aug 01 13
Cinnamon, and Star Anise Glaze . . . Mar/Apr 01 10
Ginger Glaze, Roasted Carrots with . . . Jan/Feb 01 15
and Soy Marinade for Grilled Chilean Sea Bass Fillets . . . Jul/Aug 01 13
Orange peelers . . . Jul/Aug 01 3
Orecchiette, field guide . . . Sep/Oct 01 BC
Oregano, Breaded Chicken Cutlets with Garlic and . . . Sep/Oct 01 11
Oreos . . . May/Jun 01 24
Chocolate Cookie Crumb Crust . . . May/Jun 01 25
Osso buco spoons . . . Jan/Feb 01 3
Ounce, as liquid vs. weight measure . . . Sep/Oct 01 30
Ouzo . . . Nov/Dec 01 3
Oven mitts, protecting from dirt and grease . . . Nov/Dec 01 5
Oyster mushrooms . . . Mar/Apr 01 21;
. . . May/Jun 01 3
Oyster sauce . . . Jan/Feb 01 2–3
Stir-Fried Bok Choy with Garlic and . . . May/Jun 01 21

P
Pacific Rim (cuisines)
The Hali'imaile General Store Cookbook (Gannon) . . . Jul/Aug 01 31
Hot Sour Salty Sweet (Alford and Duguid) . . . Jul/Aug 01 31;
. . . Nov/Dec 01 31
Packham pears, field guide . . . Nov/Dec 01 BC
Palmer, Charlie *(Charlie Palmer's Casual Cooking)* . . . Jan/Feb 01 31;
. . . Mar/Apr 01 31
Pan drippings, defatting . . . Nov/Dec 01 4
Panko, as breading for fried chicken . . . May/Jun 01 11
Pans. *See* Cookware
Paper towel rolls, transporting knives safely in . . . Jul/Aug 01 4
Parchment paper
adhering to pan . . . Nov/Dec 01 4
commercial . . . Jan/Feb 01 30
making bread sling with . . . May/Jun 01 5
sources for . . . Jan/Feb 01 32
Parmesan
Breaded Chicken Cutlets with (Chicken Milanese) . . . Sep/Oct 01 11
shaving with vegetable peeler . . . Jan/Feb 01 16
Parsley
Arugula and Ricotta Pesto . . . Jan/Feb 01 11
curly vs. flat-leaf . . . Jul/Aug 01 30
Fresh, and Garlic Sauce, Argentinian-Style (Chimichurri) . . . May/Jun 01 9
leftover, using up in sandwiches . . . Mar/Apr 01 4
Marinade with Ginger, Warm-Spiced . . . Jul/Aug 01 15
Mushroom Pesto with Thyme and . . . Jan/Feb 01 11
persillade . . . May/Jun 01 3
and Toasted Nut Pesto . . . Jan/Feb 01 11
Pasta. *See also* Noodles
all'Amatriciana, pasta shape for . . . Jan/Feb 01 2
cooking water, saving and thinning sauce with . . . Sep/Oct 01 5, 7
dried, field guide . . . Sep/Oct 01 BC
fra diavolo
Monkfish, with Linguine . . . Nov/Dec 01 7
Scallops, with Linguine . . . Nov/Dec 01 7
shrimp . . . Nov/Dec 01 6–7
Shrimp, with Linguine . . . Nov/Dec 01 7
with garlic and oil . . . Mar/Apr 01 14–15
Master Recipe for (Pasta Aglio e Olio) . . . Mar/Apr 01 15
gnocchi, making ridges in . . . Sep/Oct 01 5
shape and sauce matchups . . . Jan/Feb 01 2
spaghetti
alla carbonara . . . Sep/Oct 01 6–7
Alla Carbonara (recipe) . . . Sep/Oct 01 7
tasting of . . . Sep/Oct 01 7
Pasta rakes, wooden, sources for . . . Mar/Apr 01 32
Pasta sauces
pasta shape matchups and . . . Jan/Feb 01 2
pestos, winter . . . Jan/Feb 01 11
Arugula and Ricotta . . . Jan/Feb 01 11

Pasta sauces *(cont.)*
    Mushroom, with Parsley and Thyme ....Jan/Feb 01   11
    Roasted Red Pepper ....Jan/Feb 01   11
    Toasted Nut and Parsley ....Jan/Feb 01   11
  thinning with pasta water ....Sep/Oct 01   5, 7
Pasta servers, transferring hot eggs to ice-water bath with ....Mar/Apr 01   5
Pasteurization ....May/Jun 01   2–3
  of eggs ....Sep/Oct 01   2
Pastry(ies). *See also* Pie(s); Puff pastry; Tart(s)
  apple turnovers ....Jan/Feb 01   22–23
    with commercial puff pastry ....Mar/Apr 01   30
    Flaky ....Jan/Feb 01   23
    fraisage technique for ....Jan/Feb 01   22
    Quickest Puff Pastry for ....Jan/Feb 01   23
    shaping ....Jan/Feb 01   23
  The Pie and Pastry Bible (Beranbaum) ....Nov/Dec 01   31
Pastry bags, stands for ....Sep/Oct 01   4
Pastry blenders, uncommon uses for ....Jan/Feb 01   17
Pastry brushes
  for glazing fruit tarts ....Jul/Aug 01   30
  sources for ....May/Jun 01   32;
  ....Jul/Aug 01   32;
  ....Nov/Dec 01   32
Pastry cream
  for chocolate cream pie ....May/Jun 01   23
    Chocolate Pastry Cream Filling ....May/Jun 01   25
  for Classic Fresh Fruit Tart ....Jul/Aug 01   23
  making ....May/Jun 01   25
  removing *chalazae* from egg yolks for ....May/Jun 01   25;
  ....Jul/Aug 01   23
  right consistency for ....Nov/Dec 01   3
Pâté, sources for ....Nov/Dec 01   32
Pâte Sucrée (Tart Pastry) ....Jul/Aug 01   23
Peach pitters ....Sep/Oct 01   3
Peanut butters
  hydrogenated ....May/Jun 01   26
  measuring ....Sep/Oct 01   17
  Spicy Sichuan Noodles (Dan Dan Mian) ....May/Jun 01   7
    with Shiitake Mushrooms ....May/Jun 01   7
  tasting of ....May/Jun 01   26–27
Pears, field guide ....Nov/Dec 01   BC
Peas
  Four-Vegetable Soup ....May/Jun 01   15
  Fried Rice with Bean Sprouts and ....Mar/Apr 01   19
  Fried Rice with Shrimp, Pork and ....Mar/Apr 01   19
  frozen
    fresh peas vs. ....May/Jun 01   15
    tasting of ....May/Jun 01   15
Pecorino Romano cheese ....Nov/Dec 01   2
Pectin ....Jul/Aug 01   2
Penne ....Jan/Feb 01   2
Pennies, for pie weights ....May/Jun 01   5
Pennoni, field guide ....Sep/Oct 01   BC
Pépin, Jacques
  Jacques Pépin's Table ....Nov/Dec 01   31
  Sweet Simplicity: Jacques Pépin's Fruit Desserts ....Nov/Dec 01   31
Pepper(s) (bell)
  charring indoors ....Sep/Oct 01   30
  color and taste differences in ....Mar/Apr 01   7
  gazpacho ....Jul/Aug 01   8–9
    chopping vegetables for ....Jul/Aug 01   9
    Garlic Croutons for ....Jul/Aug 01   9
    getting texture "right" for ....Jul/Aug 01   9
    Master Recipe for ....Jul/Aug 01   9
    Quick Food Processor ....Jul/Aug 01   9
  grilling ....May/Jun 01   17
  red
    Roasted, Pesto ....Jan/Feb 01   11
    Rouille ....Sep/Oct 01   15
    Sautéed, Filling with Mushroom and Onion (for cheese omelet) ...May/Jun 01   19
  stuffed ....Mar/Apr 01   6–7
    with Chicken, Smoked Mozzarella, and Basil ....Mar/Apr 01   7
    Classic ....Mar/Apr 01   7
    filling technique for ....Mar/Apr 01   7
    keeping upright during cooking ....Sep/Oct 01   5
    with Spiced Lamb, Currants, and Feta Cheese ....Mar/Apr 01   7
Peppercorns
  crushing ....Sep/Oct 01   8

Peppercorns *(cont.)*
  Peppery Chicken Piccata ....Jan/Feb 01   7
  Sichuan ....May/Jun 01   32
  sources for ....May/Jun 01   32;
  ....Sep/Oct 01   32
  steak au poivre ....Sep/Oct 01   8–9
    adhering pepper to ....Sep/Oct 01   9
    with Brandied Cream Sauce ....Sep/Oct 01   9
    crushing peppercorns for ....Sep/Oct 01   8
    right grind of peppercorns for ....Sep/Oct 01   8
Pepper mills
  loading ....Jan/Feb 01   5;
  ....Jul/Aug 01   4
  motorizing ....May/Jun 01   5
  rating of ....Jul/Aug 01   28–29
  sources for ....Jul/Aug 01   32
Peppers (chile). *See* Chiles
Pernod ....Nov/Dec 01   3
Persillade ....May/Jun 01   3
Pestos, winter ....Jan/Feb 01   11
  Arugula and Ricotta ....Jan/Feb 01   11
  Mushroom, with Parsley and Thyme ....Jan/Feb 01   11
  Roasted Red Pepper ....Jan/Feb 01   11
  Toasted Nut and Parsley ....Jan/Feb 01   11
Phillips, Melicia *(Staffmeals)* ....Jan/Feb 01   31
Phyllo dough, cutting with scissors ....Jan/Feb 01   17
Piccata
  chicken ....Jan/Feb 01   6–7
    with Black Olives ....Jan/Feb 01   7
    Master Recipe for ....Jan/Feb 01   7
    Peppery ....Jan/Feb 01   7
    with Prosciutto ....Jan/Feb 01   7
  use of term ....Mar/Apr 01   2
Pie(s)
  apple, Dutch, errata ....Mar/Apr 01   3
  chocolate chiffon ....May/Jun 01   30
  chocolate cream ....May/Jun 01   23–25;
  ....May/Jun 01   30
    Master Recipe for ....May/Jun 01   25
  chocolate custard ....May/Jun 01   30
  chocolate mousse ....May/Jun 01   30
  cream, protecting from plastic wrap ....Sep/Oct 01   5
  dough, cutting and venting with scissors ....Jan/Feb 01   17
  improvised cooling rack for ....Jul/Aug 01   4
  The Pie and Pastry Bible (Beranbaum) ....Nov/Dec 01   31
Pie and Pastry Bible, The (Beranbaum) ....Nov/Dec 01   31
Pie weights
  baking time with ....Jul/Aug 01   30
  ovenproof cooking bags for ....Mar/Apr 01   4
  pennies as ....May/Jun 01   5
  sources for ....Jul/Aug 01   32
Pimento chiles, field guide ....May/Jun 01   BC
Pineapple
  Ginger Glaze, Spicy ....Mar/Apr 01   10
  and Tomatillo Salsa, Spicy ....Jul/Aug 01   7
Pine nuts ....Sep/Oct 01   3
Pinto beans, field guide ....Jan/Feb 01   BC
Pizza
  cutting with scissors ....Jan/Feb 01   17
  dough
    achieving proper consistency for ....Jan/Feb 01   9
    flour for ....Jan/Feb 01   9
    freezing ....Jan/Feb 01   10
  paraphernalia for, sources for ....Jan/Feb 01   32
  thin-crust ....Jan/Feb 01   8–10
    Crisp ....Jan/Feb 01   9
    perfect, six steps to ....Jan/Feb 01   10
    topping options for ....Jan/Feb 01   9
    virtues of pizza stones for ....Mar/Apr 01   3
    Tomato Sauce for, Quick ....Jan/Feb 01   10
Pizza stones
  benefits of ....Mar/Apr 01   3
  sources for ....Jan/Feb 01   32;
  ....Mar/Apr 01   32
Pizza wheels, sources for ....Nov/Dec 01   32
Plastic wrap
  extrawide, sources for ....Jan/Feb 01   32
  keeping ice cream fresh with ....Jan/Feb 01   4

Plastic wrap *(cont.)*
protecting cream pies from . . . . . Sep/Oct 01 5
in space-saving vegetable prep . . . . . Jan/Feb 01 4
Plastic zipper-lock bags
for brining . . . . . Nov/Dec 01 17
coating chicken pieces in . . . . . Jan/Feb 01 5
crushing garlic in . . . . . Jan/Feb 01 4
crushing peppercorns in . . . . . Sep/Oct 01 8
defatting stocks and sauces with . . . . . Jan/Feb 01 5
glazing with, mess-free . . . . . Sep/Oct 01 5
storing and measuring brown sugar in . . . . . Mar/Apr 01 4
storing and measuring flour in . . . . . May/Jun 01 4
storing in cookie jars with . . . . . Nov/Dec 01 4
Plums, Red, and Figs with Brandy-Cinnamon Reduction . . . . . Jul/Aug 01 20
Poblano chiles
field guide . . . . . May/Jun 01 BC
Spicy Grilled Potato Salad with Corn and . . . . . Jul/Aug 01 11
Pommes Anna pans . . . . . Jan/Feb 01 2
Pop-up timers, in poultry . . . . . Mar/Apr 01 2–3
Pork. *See also* Bacon; Ham roast, fresh
brining . . . . . Nov/Dec 01 16–17
containers for . . . . . Nov/Dec 01 17, 32
Fried Rice with Shrimp, Peas and . . . . . Mar/Apr 01 19
roasts, binding with butcher's twine . . . . . Mar/Apr 01 30
salt
fatback vs. . . . . . Jan/Feb 01 30
trimming . . . . . Jan/Feb 01 13
sausage(s)
Breakfast Strata with Mushrooms, Monterey Jack and . . . . . Nov/Dec 01 15
Dressing . . . . . Nov/Dec 01 10
lop cheong, sources for . . . . . Mar/Apr 01 32
Spicy Sichuan Noodles (Dan Dan Mian) . . . . . May/Jun 01 7
with Shiitake Mushrooms . . . . . May/Jun 01 7
storing in refrigerator . . . . . Mar/Apr 01 16
Potato(es)
Breakfast Strata with Rosemary, Fontina and . . . . . Nov/Dec 01 15
Four-Vegetable Soup . . . . . May/Jun 01 15
grilled, salad . . . . . Jul/Aug 01 10–11
with Arugula and Dijon Mustard Vinaigrette . . . . . Jul/Aug 01 11
blanching step for . . . . . Jul/Aug 01 11
German-Style . . . . . Jul/Aug 01 11
Grilled Potatoes for, Gas-Grill Variation . . . . . Jul/Aug 01 11
Grilled Potatoes for, Master Recipe . . . . . Jul/Aug 01 10
Spicy, with Corn and Poblano Chiles . . . . . Jul/Aug 01 11
mashed, warming bowl for . . . . . May/Jun 01 5
peeling . . . . . Mar/Apr 01 4
pommes Anna, pans for . . . . . Jan/Feb 01 2
White Bean Soup with Winter Vegetables . . . . . Jan/Feb 01 21
Potholders, dish towels as . . . . . Jan/Feb 01 17
Pots. *See* Cookware
Poultry. *See also* Chicken; Turkey
brining . . . . . Nov/Dec 01 16–17
air-drying after . . . . . Nov/Dec 01 17
pop-up timers in . . . . . Mar/Apr 01 2–3
storing in refrigerator . . . . . Mar/Apr 01 16
Preserves, use of term . . . . . Jul/Aug 01 2
Pringles cans, as pastry bag stands . . . . . Sep/Oct 01 4
Proofing, use of term . . . . . Mar/Apr 01 2
Prosciutto, Chicken Piccata with . . . . . Jan/Feb 01 7
Provençal (cuisine)
Bouillabaisse . . . . . Sep/Oct 01 13–15
See also Bouillabaisse
ratatouille . . . . . Sep/Oct 01 18–19
Master Recipe for . . . . . Sep/Oct 01 19
salting and pressing eggplant for . . . . . Sep/Oct 01 18, 19
Puff pastry
for apple turnovers . . . . . Jan/Feb 01 22–23
for Beef Wellington . . . . . Nov/Dec 01 21
commercial . . . . . Mar/Apr 01 30
fraisage technique for . . . . . Jan/Feb 01 22
Quickest . . . . . Jan/Feb 01 23
sources for . . . . . Nov/Dec 01 32
Purple kohlrabi, field guide . . . . . Mar/Apr 01 BC

R

Racks, roasting, sources for . . . . . Mar/Apr 01 32
Radiatore, field guide . . . . . Sep/Oct 01 BC
Radicchio, grilling . . . . . May/Jun 01 16
Ramekins
removing with tongs . . . . . Jan/Feb 01 16
securing in hot-water bath . . . . . Jan/Feb 01 17
sources for . . . . . Nov/Dec 01 32
Raspberry(ies)
Kiwi, and Blueberry Tart . . . . . Jul/Aug 01 22
Nectarines, and Blueberries with
Champagne-Cardamom Reduction . . . . . Jul/Aug 01 20
Ratatouille . . . . . Sep/Oct 01 18–19
Master Recipe for . . . . . Sep/Oct 01 19
salting and pressing eggplant for . . . . . Sep/Oct 01 18, 19
Ratings. *See* Equipment—ratings of; Tastings
Red Bartlett pears, field guide . . . . . Nov/Dec 01 BC
Red pepper flakes
fra diavolo
Monkfish, with Linguine . . . . . Nov/Dec 01 7
Scallops, with Linguine . . . . . Nov/Dec 01 7
shrimp . . . . . Nov/Dec 01 6–7
Shrimp, with Linguine . . . . . Nov/Dec 01 7
tasting of . . . . . Nov/Dec 01 7
Reductions, story sticks for . . . . . Jan/Feb 01 5;
. . . . . Sep/Oct 01 4
Refrigerators . . . . . Mar/Apr 01 16–17
crisper in . . . . . Mar/Apr 01 17
storing flour in freezer of . . . . . Jul/Aug 01 5
vase for herbs in . . . . . Jul/Aug 01 5
where to store what in . . . . . Mar/Apr 01 17
Rehydrating dried mushrooms . . . . . Jan/Feb 01 4
Relishes
Black Olive and Citrus . . . . . Jul/Aug 01 13
Cucumber and Mango, with Yogurt . . . . . Jul/Aug 01 7
Rhubarb
buyer's guide for . . . . . May/Jun 01 30
fool . . . . . May/Jun 01 22
Blueberry, with Fresh Ginger . . . . . May/Jun 01 22
Master Recipe for . . . . . May/Jun 01 22
Strawberry . . . . . May/Jun 01 22
peeling . . . . . May/Jun 01 30
Ribollita . . . . . Jan/Feb 01 21
Rice
absorbing steam from . . . . . Jan/Feb 01 17
fried . . . . . Mar/Apr 01 18–19
with Peas and Bean Sprouts . . . . . Mar/Apr 01 19
with Shrimp, Pork, and Peas . . . . . Mar/Apr 01 19
Thai-Style Curried Chicken . . . . . Mar/Apr 01 19
wok vs. skillet for . . . . . Mar/Apr 01 19
length of grain and stickiness of . . . . . Mar/Apr 01 3
stuffed bell peppers
with Chicken, Smoked Mozzarella, and Basil . . . . . Mar/Apr 01 7
Classic . . . . . Mar/Apr 01 7
with Spiced Lamb, Currants, and Feta Cheese . . . . . Mar/Apr 01 7
Rice beans, field guide . . . . . Jan/Feb 01 BC
Rice cookers
rating of . . . . . Mar/Apr 01 30
sources for . . . . . Mar/Apr 01 32
Rice flour, sources for . . . . . Nov/Dec 01 32
Ricotta and Arugula Pesto . . . . . Jan/Feb 01 11
Roasts
binding with butcher's twine . . . . . Mar/Apr 01 30
defatting pan drippings from . . . . . Nov/Dec 01 4
mirepoix for . . . . . Mar/Apr 01 3
protecting brown crust of . . . . . Mar/Apr 01 5
steadying during carving . . . . . Jan/Feb 01 16
Roden, Claudia *(The Book of Jewish Food)* . . . . . Mar/Apr 01 31
Rolling pins
sources for . . . . . Jan/Feb 01 32;
. . . . . Nov/Dec 01 32
tapered French-style . . . . . Jan/Feb 01 32
Rolls, crescent . . . . . Nov/Dec 01 12–13
Master Recipe for . . . . . Nov/Dec 01 13
shaping . . . . . Nov/Dec 01 13
tasting of supermarket brands . . . . . Nov/Dec 01 13
Romano, Michael *(Second Helpings from Union Square Cafe)* . . . . . Sep/Oct 01 31
Romano cheese . . . . . Nov/Dec 01 2
Rosemary
Breakfast Strata with Potatoes, Fontina and . . . . . Nov/Dec 01 15
field guide . . . . . Jul/Aug 01 BC

Rosemary (cont.)
Lemon Basting Oil . . . . .May/Jun 01   17
Mint Marinade with Garlic and Lemon . . . . .Jul/Aug 01   15
Rotelle, field guide . . . . .Sep/Oct 01   BC
Rouille . . . . .Sep/Oct 01   15
Rulers, metal, as story sticks . . . . .Sep/Oct 01   4
Rutabaga, field guide . . . . .Mar/Apr 01   BC
errata . . . . .Mar/Apr 01   BC

S

Safety concerns
with cutting boards . . . . .May/Jun 01   28;
. . . . .Jul/Aug 01   30
pasteurized eggs and . . . . .Sep/Oct 01   2
Saffron
sources for . . . . .Sep/Oct 01   32
tasting of . . . . .Nov/Dec 01   30
Sage, field guide . . . . .Jul/Aug 01   BC
Salad dressings. *See also* Vinaigrettes
Salads
Chicken, Grilled, with Sesame-Miso Dressing . . . . .Jul/Aug 01   7
fruit, summer . . . . .Jul/Aug 01   20
Honeydew, Mango, and Blueberries with Lime-Ginger Reduction . . .Jul/Aug 01   20
Nectarines, Blueberries, and Raspberries
with Champagne-Cardamom Reduction . . . . .Jul/Aug 01   20
Red Plums and Figs with Brandy-Cinnamon Reduction . . . . .Jul/Aug 01   20
Strawberries and Grapes with Balsamic and
Red Wine Reduction . . . . .Jul/Aug 01   20
potato, grilled . . . . .Jul/Aug 01   10–11
See also Potato(es)—grilled, salad
tuna . . . . .May/Jun 01   13
with Balsamic Vinegar and Grapes . . . . .May/Jun 01   13
with Cauliflower, Jalapeño, and Cilantro . . . . .May/Jun 01   13
Classic . . . . .May/Jun 01   13
Curried, with Apples and Currants . . . . .May/Jun 01   13
with Lime and Horseradish . . . . .May/Jun 01   13
Salmonella, pasteurized eggs and . . . . .Sep/Oct 01   2
Salsas
Tomatillo and Pineapple, Spicy .Jul/Aug 01   7
Tomato, Spicy Fresh . . . . .Jul/Aug 01   13
Salt
for brining . . . . .Nov/Dec 01   16
kosher . . . . .Nov/Dec 01   16
sea, sources for . . . . .Mar/Apr 01   32
Salt pork
fatback vs. . . . . .Jan/Feb 01   30
trimming . . . . .Jan/Feb 01   13
Sandwiches
leftover fresh herbs in . . . . .Mar/Apr 01   4
overstuffed, stabilizing in bulky rolls . . . . .Mar/Apr 01   4
tuna salad . . . . .May/Jun 01   13
See also Tuna salad
Sauces
Brandied Cream . . . . .Sep/Oct 01   9
caramel, rewarming . . . . .Jul/Aug 01   30
Chocolate, Bittersweet . . . . .Sep/Oct 01   24
defatting . . . . .Jan/Feb 01   5
for filet mignon
Argentinian-Style Fresh Parsley and Garlic (Chimichurri) . . . . . . .May/Jun 01   9
Madeira Pan, with Mustard and Anchovies . . . . .May/Jun 01   9
mirepoix for . . . . .Mar/Apr 01   3
pasta
shapes and sauce matchup . . . . .Jan/Feb 01   2
thinning with pasta water . . . . .Sep/Oct 01   5, 7
pestos, winter . . . . .Jan/Feb 01   11
Arugula and Ricotta . . . . .Jan/Feb 01   11
Mushroom, with Parsley and Thyme . . . . .Jan/Feb 01   11
Roasted Red Pepper . . . . .Jan/Feb 01   11
Toasted Nut and Parsley . . . . .Jan/Feb 01   11
Red Wine, for Beef Wellington .Nov/Dec 01   21
Red Wine Reduction for . . . . .Nov/Dec 01   26–27
Rouille . . . . .Sep/Oct 01   15
Tomato, for Pizza, Quick . . . . .Jan/Feb 01   10
for turkey cutlets (pan)
Honey-Mustard, with Tarragon . . . . .Mar/Apr 01   13
Warm-Spiced, with Currants and Almonds . . . . .Mar/Apr 01   13

Sausage(s)
Breakfast Strata with Mushrooms, Monterey Jack and . . . . .Nov/Dec 01   15
Dressing . . . . .Nov/Dec 01   10
lop cheong, sources for . . . . .Mar/Apr 01   32
Sauté pans
copper, reconsideration of . . . . .Nov/Dec 01   30
rating of . . . . .Jan/Feb 01   28–29
sources for . . . . .Jan/Feb 01   32;
. . . . .Mar/Apr 01   32
T-Fal Thermospot . . . . .Mar/Apr 01   13, 32
Savory, summer, field guide . . . . .Jul/Aug 01   BC
Scallion(s)
Bacon, and Onion Filling (for cheese omelet) . . . . .May/Jun 01   19
slicing with scissors . . . . .Jan/Feb 01   17
Scallops
faux . . . . .Sep/Oct 01   2–3
Fra Diavolo with Linguine . . . . .Nov/Dec 01   7
processed . . . . .Sep/Oct 01   3
Scarlet runner beans, field guide .Jan/Feb 01   BC
Science of cooking
brining . . . . .Nov/Dec 01   16
with Coke . . . . .Mar/Apr 01   10
curing vs. . . . . .Nov/Dec 01   30
chocolate, bittersweet vs. unsweetened . . . . .May/Jun 01   24
flours
cake . . . . .Sep/Oct 01   23
Wondra vs. regular . . . . .May/Jun 01   2
meat, bright color and freshness of . . . . .Mar/Apr 01   17
pasteurization . . . . .May/Jun 01   2–3
peanut butters, hydrogenated . . . . .May/Jun 01   26
rhubarb, acidity and red color of . . . . .May/Jun 01   22
rice, length of grain and stickiness of . . . . .Mar/Apr 01   3
yeast, fermentation of . . . . .Jan/Feb 01   26
Scissors, uncommon uses for . . . . .Jan/Feb 01   17
Scrapers
bench, checking evenness of cookie dough with . . . . .Nov/Dec 01   5
dough, uncommon uses for . . . . .Jan/Feb 01   16
flexible, sources for . . . . .Nov/Dec 01   32
Sea bass
Chilean . . . . .Jul/Aug 01   12–13
See also Chilean sea bass
"real" . . . . .Jul/Aug 01   12
Seafood. *See also* Chilean sea bass; Fish; Shrimp
Bouillabaisse . . . . .Sep/Oct 01   13–15
See also Bouillabaisse
brining . . . . .Nov/Dec 01   16–17
scallops
faux . . . . .Sep/Oct 01   2–3
Fra Diavolo with Linguine . . . . .Nov/Dec 01   7
processed . . . . .Sep/Oct 01   3
storing in refrigerator . . . . .Mar/Apr 01   16
Seckel pears, field guide . . . . .Nov/Dec 01   BC
Second Helpings from Union Square Cafe
(Meyer and Romano) . . . . .Sep/Oct 01   31
Serrano chiles, field guide . . . . .May/Jun 01   BC
Sesame
Miso Dressing, Grilled Chicken Salad with . . . . .Jul/Aug 01   7
oil
cold-pressed . . . . .May/Jun 01   30
roasted, dark, or Asian . . . . .May/Jun 01   30
paste, sources for . . . . .May/Jun 01   32
Soy-Glazed Baby Bok Choy . . . . .May/Jun 01   21
Shallot(s)
Breakfast Strata with Spinach, Gruyère and . . . . .Nov/Dec 01   15
finely mincing with microplane grater . . . . .Jan/Feb 01   17
Lemon Vinaigrette, Asparagus with . . . . .Mar/Apr 01   11
Sautéed, Green Beans with Vermouth and . . . . .Nov/Dec 01   18
using raw . . . . .Jul/Aug 01   30
Shanghai bok choy . . . . .May/Jun 01   20
Sharpening knives
by hand . . . . .Jul/Aug 01   16–17
professionally, sources for . . . . .Jul/Aug 01   32
Sharpening steels . . . . .Jul/Aug 01   16
diamond . . . . .Jul/Aug 01   16, 32
sources for . . . . .Jul/Aug 01   32
using . . . . .Jul/Aug 01   17
Sharpening stones . . . . .Jul/Aug 01   16
lubricating . . . . .Jul/Aug 01   16

Sharpening stones (cont.)
sources for ....Jul/Aug 01   32
using ....Jul/Aug 01   17
Shellfish. See Seafood; Shrimp
Shiitake mushrooms ....Mar/Apr 01   21
Bok Choy Braised with ....May/Jun 01   21
Spicy Sichuan Noodles with ....May/Jun 01   7
trimming with scissors ....Jan/Feb 01   17
Shish kebab ....Jul/Aug 01   14–15
Charcoal-Grilled ....Jul/Aug 01   14
Gas-Grilled ....Jul/Aug 01   15
marinades for
Garlic and Cilantro, with Garam Masala ....Jul/Aug 01   15
Rosemary-Mint, with Garlic and Lemon ....Jul/Aug 01   15
Sweet Curry, with Buttermilk ....Jul/Aug 01   15
Warm-Spiced Parsley, with Ginger ....Jul/Aug 01   15
prepping onions for ....Jul/Aug 01   15
Shortbread ....Nov/Dec 01   24–25
Buttery ....Nov/Dec 01   25
shaping ....Nov/Dec 01   25
Shortening, measuring ....Sep/Oct 01   17
Shrimp
brining ....Nov/Dec 01   16
containers for ....Nov/Dec 01   17
Broth, Simplest ....Jan/Feb 01   19
codes on packages of ....Jan/Feb 01   30
deveining ....Jan/Feb 01   19
fra diavolo ....Nov/Dec 01   6–7
with Linguine ....Nov/Dec 01   7
Fried Rice with Pork, Peas and ....Mar/Apr 01   19
peeling ....Nov/Dec 01   5
stir-fried ....Jan/Feb 01   18–19
Aromatic ....Jan/Feb 01   19
Cantonese-Style ....Jan/Feb 01   19
Simplest Shrimp Broth for ....Jan/Feb 01   19
Singapore Chili ....Jan/Feb 01   19
Shrimp deveiners ....Jan/Feb 01   19
Sichuan (Szechuan) (cuisine)
ingredients, sources for ....May/Jun 01   32
noodles ....May/Jun 01   6–7
Spicy (Dan Dan Mian) ....May/Jun 01   7
Spicy, with Shiitake Mushrooms ....May/Jun 01   7
peppercorns ....May/Jun 01   32
Side dishes
asparagus
with Bacon, Red Onion, and Balsamic Vinaigrette ....Mar/Apr 01   11
Broiled, Simple ....Mar/Apr 01   11
with Lemon-Shallot Vinaigrette ....Mar/Apr 01   11
with Soy-Ginger Vinaigrette ....Mar/Apr 01   11
with Tomato-Basil Vinaigrette ....Mar/Apr 01   11
baba ghanoush
Charcoal-Grill Method ....Jul/Aug 01   19
Gas-Grill Method ....Jul/Aug 01   19
Israeli-Style ....Jul/Aug 01   19
Oven Method ....Jul/Aug 01   19
with Sautéed Onions ....Jul/Aug 01   19
bok choy
Baby, Sesame-Soy-Glazed ....May/Jun 01   21
Braised with Garlic ....May/Jun 01   21
Braised with Shiitake Mushrooms ....May/Jun 01   21
Stir-Fried, with Oyster Sauce and Garlic ....May/Jun 01   21
Stir-Fried, with Soy Sauce and Ginger ....May/Jun 01   21
carrots
Roasted, Simple ....Jan/Feb 01   15
Roasted, with Ginger-Orange Glaze ....Jan/Feb 01   15
Roasted Maple, with Browned Butter ....Jan/Feb 01   15
fruit salads, summer
Honeydew, Mango, and Blueberries with Lime-Ginger Reduction .....Jul/Aug 01   20
Nectarines, Blueberries, and Raspberries
with Champagne-Cardamom Reduction ....Jul/Aug 01   20
Red Plums and Figs with Brandy-Cinnamon Reduction ....Jul/Aug 01   20
Strawberries and Grapes with Balsamic and Red Wine Reduction ..Jul/Aug 01   20
green beans
Blanched ....Nov/Dec 01   18
with Buttered Bread Crumbs and Almonds ....Nov/Dec 01   18
with Sautéed Shallots and Vermouth ....Nov/Dec 01   18
with Toasted Hazelnuts and Brown Butter ....Nov/Dec 01   18
peppers, bell
Stuffed, Classic ....Mar/Apr 01   7

Side dishes (cont.)
Stuffed, with Chicken, Smoked Mozzarella, and Basil ......Mar/Apr 01   7
Stuffed, with Spiced Lamb, Currants, and Feta Cheese .....Mar/Apr 01   7
potato(es)
Grilled, and Arugula Salad with Dijon Mustard Vinaigrette ....Jul/Aug 01   11
Grilled, for Salad ....Jul/Aug 01   10
Grilled, Salad, German-Style ....Jul/Aug 01   11
Grilled, Salad with Corn and Poblano Chiles, Spicy ....Jul/Aug 01   11
Ratatouille ....Sep/Oct 01   19
Sausage Dressing ....Nov/Dec 01   10
Sifters, coasters for ....Mar/Apr 01   5
Simmering, boiling vs. ....Sep/Oct 01   30
Singapore Chili Stir-Fried Shrimp ....Jan/Feb 01   19
Skewers
bamboo
sources for ....Jul/Aug 01   32
as story sticks for reductions ....Jan/Feb 01   5
metal, sources for ....May/Jun 01   32;
....Jul/Aug 01   32
Skillets
cast-iron, for fried chicken ....May/Jun 01   11
for fried rice ....Mar/Apr 01   19
specialized ....May/Jun 01   30
Snow peas, neatly opening pods for stuffing ....May/Jun 01   4
Soups
butternut squash ....Nov/Dec 01   8
Buttered Cinnamon-Sugar Croutons for ....Nov/Dec 01   8
Curried, with Cilantro Yogurt ....Nov/Dec 01   8
Silky ....Nov/Dec 01   8
freezing single servings of ....Jan/Feb 01   4
gazpacho ....Jul/Aug 01   8–9
chopping vegetables for ....Jul/Aug 01   9
Garlic Croutons for ....Jul/Aug 01   9
getting texture "right" for ....Jul/Aug 01   9
Master Recipe for ....Jul/Aug 01   9
Quick Food Processor ....Jul/Aug 01   9
mirepoix for ....Mar/Apr 01   3
mushroom ....Mar/Apr 01   20–21
Creamy ....Mar/Apr 01   21
Sautéed Wild Mushroom Garnish for ....Mar/Apr 01   21
vegetable ....May/Jun 01   14–15
Four-Vegetable ....May/Jun 01   15
white bean, Tuscan ....Jan/Feb 01   20–21
leftover, making ribollita with ....Jan/Feb 01   21
Master Recipe for ....Jan/Feb 01   21
Quick ....Jan/Feb 01   21
with Winter Vegetables ....Jan/Feb 01   21
Southeast Asian (cuisines). See also Thai (cuisine)
Hot Sour Salty Sweet (Alford and Duguid) ....Jul/Aug 01   31;
....Nov/Dec 01   31
Soy (sauce)
Ginger Vinaigrette, Asparagus with ....Mar/Apr 01   11
and Orange Marinade for Grilled Chilean Sea Bass Fillets ..Jul/Aug 01   13
Sesame-Glazed Baby Bok Choy ....May/Jun 01   21
Stir-Fried Bok Choy with Ginger and ....May/Jun 01   21
Spaghetti
alla carbonara ....Sep/Oct 01   6–7
Master Recipe for ....Sep/Oct 01   7
tasting of ....Sep/Oct 01   7
Spanish (cuisine). See Gazpacho
Spatulas
heatproof, sources for ....Mar/Apr 01   32
flexible, sources for ....May/Jun 01   32
Spinach
Breakfast Strata with Shallots, Gruyère and ....Nov/Dec 01   15
Four-Vegetable Soup ....May/Jun 01   15
Squash. See also Zucchini
butternut, soup ....Nov/Dec 01   8
Buttered Cinnamon-Sugar Croutons for ....Nov/Dec 01   8
Curried, with Cilantro Yogurt ....Nov/Dec 01   8
Silky ....Nov/Dec 01   8
summer, grilling ....May/Jun 01   16
Staffmeals (Waltuck and Phillips) ....Jan/Feb 01   31
Star Anise, Orange, and Cinnamon Glaze ....Mar/Apr 01   10
Steak au poivre ....Sep/Oct 01   8–9
adhering pepper to ....Sep/Oct 01   9
with Brandied Cream Sauce ....Sep/Oct 01   9
crushing peppercorns for ....Sep/Oct 01   8
right grind of peppercorns for ....Sep/Oct 01   8

Steak knives			
rating of	Sep/Oct 01	9	
sources for	Sep/Oct 01	32	
Steuben yellow eye beans, field guide	Jan/Feb 01	BC	
Stews			
beef Burgundy	Jan/Feb 01	12–14	
advance preparation of	Jan/Feb 01	14	
making vegetable and herb bouquet for	Jan/Feb 01	14	
Master Recipe for	Jan/Feb 01	13	
trimming meat for	Jan/Feb 01	14	
wine for	Jan/Feb 01	14	
Bouillabaisse	Sep/Oct 01	13–15	
See also Bouillabaisse			
ratatouille	Sep/Oct 01	18–19	
Master Recipe for	Sep/Oct 01	19	
salting and pressing eggplant for	Sep/Oct 01	18, 19	
Sticky ingredients, measuring	Sep/Oct 01	17	
Sticky jar lids, preventing	Sep/Oct 01	5	
Stir-fried			
bok choy			
with Oyster Sauce and Garlic	May/Jun 01	21	
with Soy Sauce and Ginger	May/Jun 01	21	
shrimp	Jan/Feb 01	18–19	
Aromatic	Jan/Feb 01	19	
Cantonese-Style	Jan/Feb 01	19	
Simplest Shrimp Broth for	Jan/Feb 01	19	
Singapore Chili	Jan/Feb 01	19	
Stockpots, All-Clad, using as Dutch oven	Jul/Aug 01	3	
Stocks. *See also* Broth			
defatting	Jan/Feb 01	5	
fish			
for Bouillabaisse-Style Fish Stew	Sep/Oct 01	15	
simmering vs. sweating bones and vegetables for	Sep/Oct 01	14	
mirepoix for	Mar/Apr 01	3	
Storing and storage equipment. *See also* Plastic wrap;			
Plastic zipper-lock bags			
brown sugar, in premeasured portions	Mar/Apr 01	4	
in cookie jars, airtight	Nov/Dec 01	4	
flour			
cake	May/Jun 01	4	
in summer	Jul/Aug 01	5	
goat cheese, in covered butter dish	May/Jun 01	5	
herbs, vase for	Jul/Aug 01	5	
ice cream, preserving freshness of	Jan/Feb 01	4	
mushrooms	Nov/Dec 01	30	
in refrigerator	Mar/Apr 01	16–17	
Story sticks			
chopsticks or bamboo skewers as	Jan/Feb 01	5	
metal rulers as	Sep/Oct 01	4	
Strainers, colanders vs.	Sep/Oct 01	29	
Strata. *See* Breakfast strata			
Strawberry(ies)			
cleaning with dish towel	Jan/Feb 01	17	
and Grapes with Balsamic and Red Wine Reduction	Jul/Aug 01	20	
Rhubarb Fool	May/Jun 01	22	
Tart	Jul/Aug 01	22	
Striped bass	Jul/Aug 01	12	
Sugar			
brown			
and Apple Cider Glaze	Mar/Apr 01	10	
measuring	Sep/Oct 01	17	
storing and measuring	Mar/Apr 01	4	
cinnamon			
Buttered Croutons	Nov/Dec 01	8	
-Dipped Blueberry Muffins	Sep/Oct 01	21	
Demerara, sources for	Nov/Dec 01	32	
superfine, sources for	Nov/Dec 01	32	
Sulfites	May/Jun 01	3	
Summer rental kitchens, improvising in	Jul/Aug 01	4–5	
Summer savory, field guide	Jul/Aug 01	BC	
Sweet Simplicity: Jacques Pépin's Fruit Desserts (Pépin)	Nov/Dec 01	31	

T

Tapioca	Nov/Dec 01	2–3	
flour	Nov/Dec 01	2	
instant, Minute, or quick	Nov/Dec 01	2	
pearl	Nov/Dec 01	2	
Tarragon, Honey-Mustard Pan Sauce with (for turkey cutlets)	Mar/Apr 01	13	

Tart(s)			
fruit, fresh	Jul/Aug 01	21–23	
Classic	Jul/Aug 01	23	
glazing	Jul/Aug 01	30	
Kiwi, Raspberry, and Blueberry	Jul/Aug 01	22	
Mixed Berry	Jul/Aug 01	22	
Strawberry	Jul/Aug 01	22	
Pastry (Pâte Sucrée)	Jul/Aug 01	23	
Tart pans			
sources for	Jul/Aug 01	32	
testing of different finishes on	Jul/Aug 01	23	
Tastings			
balsamic vinegar	Jul/Aug 01	26-27	
bay leaves, Turkish vs. California	Sep/Oct 01	30	
bell peppers in different colors	Mar/Apr 01	7	
capers	Jan/Feb 01	7	
cherries, "processed"	Jul/Aug 01	25	
chocolate			
bittersweet, for sauces	Sep/Oct 01	24	
morsels	Mar/Apr 01	23	
coconut extract	Mar/Apr 01	24	
cream, pasteurized vs. ultrapasteurized	May/Jun 01	2-3	
eggs, pasteurized vs. ordinary	Sep/Oct 01	2	
olive oil, extra-virgin	Mar/Apr 01	26-27	
oyster sauce	Jan/Feb 01	3	
peanut butters	May/Jun 01	26-27	
peas, frozen	May/Jun 01	15	
red pepper flakes	Nov/Dec 01	7	
red wines for cooking	Nov/Dec 01	26-27	
rolls, supermarket bake 'n serve	Nov/Dec 01	13	
saffron	Nov/Dec 01	30	
spaghetti	Sep/Oct 01	7	
tomato juice	Jul/Aug 01	8	
vanilla ice creams	Sep/Oct 01	25-27	
yeast	Jan/Feb 01	27	
Taylor's Gold pears, field guide	Nov/Dec 01	BC	
Tea-Infused Crème Brûlée	Nov/Dec 01	23	
T-Fal Thermospot sauté pan	Mar/Apr 01	13	
Thai (cuisine)			
Curried Chicken Fried Rice	Mar/Apr 01	19	
fish sauce, sources for	Mar/Apr 01	32	
Kanom krok pans	Mar/Apr 01	3	
Thermometers			
in ham roasts	Mar/Apr 01	10	
Thermapen, sources for	May/Jun 01	32;	
	Nov/Dec 01	32	
Thyme			
field guide	Jul/Aug 01	BC	
Mushroom Pesto with Parsley and	Jan/Feb 01	11	
Sautéed Mushroom Filling with (for cheese omelet)	May/Jun 01	19	
Timers, pop-up, in poultry	Mar/Apr 01	2-3	
Tomatillo and Pineapple Salsa, Spicy	Jul/Aug 01	7	
Tomato(es)			
Basil Vinaigrette, Asparagus with	Mar/Apr 01	11	
chopping with pastry blender	Jan/Feb 01	17	
gazpacho	Jul/Aug 01	8-9	
chopping vegetables for	Jul/Aug 01	9	
Garlic Croutons for	Jul/Aug 01	9	
getting texture "right" for	Jul/Aug 01	9	
Master Recipe for	Jul/Aug 01	9	
Quick Food Processor	Jul/Aug 01	9	
juice, tasting of	Jul/Aug 01	8	
ratatouille	Sep/Oct 01	18-19	
Master Recipe for	Sep/Oct 01	19	
Salsa, Spicy Fresh	Jul/Aug 01	13	
Sauce for Pizza, Quick	Jan/Feb 01	10	
Tom Douglas' Seattle Kitchen (Tom Douglas)	Sep/Oct 01	31	
Tongs			
caddy for	Mar/Apr 01	5	
rating of	Jul/Aug 01	15	
sources for	May/Jun 01	32;	
	Jul/Aug 01	32	
uncommon uses for	Jan/Feb 01	16	
Torches			
rating of	Nov/Dec 01	23	
sources for	Nov/Dec 01	32	
Tube-pan inserts, as makeshift vertical roasters	Jan/Feb 01	5	
Tube pans, cooking stuffed peppers in	Sep/Oct 01	5	
Tuna salad	May/Jun 01	13	

Tuna salad (cont.)
    with Balsamic Vinegar and Grapes . . . . .May/Jun 01   13
    with Cauliflower, Jalapeño, and Cilantro . . . . .May/Jun 01   13
    Classic . . . . .May/Jun 01   13
    Curried, with Apples and Currants . . . . .May/Jun 01   13
    with Lime and Horseradish . . . . .May/Jun 01   13
Tupperware containers, for brining . . . . .Nov/Dec 01   17
Turkey
    brining . . . . .Nov/Dec 01   16-17
        containers for . . . . .Nov/Dec 01   17, 32
    butterflied, carving . . . . .Nov/Dec 01   11
    butterflying . . . . .Nov/Dec 01   11
    cutlets
        butchering quality of . . . . .Mar/Apr 01   12-13
        Honey-Mustard Pan Sauce with Tarragon for . . . . .Mar/Apr 01   13
        Sautéed, Master Recipe for . . . . .Mar/Apr 01   13
        sautéing . . . . .Mar/Apr 01   12-13
        T-Fal Thermospot sauté pan for .Mar/Apr 01   13
        Warm-Spiced Pan Sauce with Currants and Almonds for . . . . . .Mar/Apr 01   13
    Gravy . . . . .Nov/Dec 01   11
    high-roast . . . . .Nov/Dec 01   9-11
        Crisp-Skin Butterflied, with Sausage Dressing . . . . .Nov/Dec 01   10
        timeline for . . . . .Nov/Dec 01   10
    koshering . . . . .Jan/Feb 01   3
    pop-up timers in . . . . .Mar/Apr 01   2-3
    steadying during carving . . . . .Jan/Feb 01   16
    turning during cooking . . . . .Nov/Dec 01   5
Turnips, field guide . . . . .Mar/Apr 01   BC
    errata . . . . .May/Jun 01   3
Turnovers
    apple . . . . .Jan/Feb 01   22-23
        with commercial puff pastry . . . . .Mar/Apr 01   30
        Flaky . . . . .Jan/Feb 01   23
        fraisage technique for . . . . .Jan/Feb 01   22
        Quickest Puff Pastry for . . . . .Jan/Feb 01   23
        shaping . . . . .Jan/Feb 01   23
    as term . . . . .Jan/Feb 01   30
Tuscan white bean soup . . . . .Jan/Feb 01   20-21
    leftover, making ribollita with . . . . .Jan/Feb 01   21
    Master Recipe for . . . . .Jan/Feb 01   21
    Quick . . . . .Jan/Feb 01   21
    with Winter Vegetables . . . . .Jan/Feb 01   21
Tyramines . . . . .May/Jun 01   3

U
Ultrapasteurization . . . . .May/Jun 01   2-3

V
Vanilla ice creams
    sources for . . . . .Sep/Oct 01   32
    tasting of . . . . .Sep/Oct 01   25-27
Vase for herbs, plastic milk jug as . . . . .Jul/Aug 01   5
Vegetable(s)
    basting oils for
        Garlic . . . . .May/Jun 01   17
        Lemon-Rosemary . . . . .May/Jun 01   17
    blanching, iceless ice baths for . . . . .Nov/Dec 01   4
    Chez Panisse Vegetables (Waters) . . . . .Nov/Dec 01   31
    chopped, lifting with dough scraper .Jan/Feb 01   16
    grilling . . . . .May/Jun 01   16-17
        basting oils for . . . . .May/Jun 01   17
        equipment sources for . . . . .May/Jun 01   32
        essential equipment for . . . . .May/Jun 01   17
        general guidelines for . . . . .May/Jun 01   16
        preparing vegetables for . . . . .May/Jun 01   16
    and herb bouquet . . . . .Jan/Feb 01   14
    soup . . . . .May/Jun 01   14-15
        Four-Vegetable . . . . .May/Jun 01   15
    space-saving preparation of . . . . .Jan/Feb 01   4
    storing in refrigerator . . . . .Mar/Apr 01   16, 17
Vegetable peelers
    dotting butter over baked goods with . . . . .Sep/Oct 01   4
    uncommon uses for . . . . .Jan/Feb 01   16
Vermouth, Green Beans with Sautéed Shallots and . . . . .Nov/Dec 01   18
Vertical roasters, makeshift . . . . .Jan/Feb 01   5

Vinaigrettes
    for asparagus
        Bacon, Red Onion, and Balsamic . . . . .Mar/Apr 01   11
        Lemon-Shallot . . . . .Mar/Apr 01   11
        Soy-Ginger . . . . .Mar/Apr 01   11
        Tomato-Basil . . . . .Mar/Apr 01   11
    mustard . . . . .Sep/Oct 01   12
        Balsamic and . . . . .Sep/Oct 01   12
        Dijon, Grilled Potato and Arugula Salad with . . . . .Jul/Aug 01   11
        with Lemon and Fines Herbes . . . . .Sep/Oct 01   12
        Roasted Garlic and . . . . .Sep/Oct 01   12
Vinegar. *See also* Balsamic vinegar
    cider, film on surface of . . . . .Jan/Feb 01   2

W
Waltuck, David (*Staffmeals*) . . . . .Jan/Feb 01   31
Washing machine, chilling beverages in .Nov/Dec 01   5
Washtubs, for brining . . . . .Nov/Dec 01   17
Water, measuring accurately . . . . .May/Jun 01   5
Waters, Alice (*Chez Panisse Vegetables*) . . . . .Nov/Dec 01   31
Weighing flour in brown paper bag . . . . .May/Jun 01   5
Wellington. *See* Beef—Wellington
Whipped cream
    pasteurized vs. ultrapasteurized cream for . . . . .May/Jun 01   2-3
    rhubarb fool . . . . .May/Jun 01   22
        Blueberry, with Fresh Ginger . . . . .May/Jun 01   22
        Master Recipe for . . . . .May/Jun 01   22
        Strawberry . . . . .May/Jun 01   22
    Topping . . . . .May/Jun 01   25
Whipped cream siphons, sources for . . . . .May/Jun 01   32
Whisks, making gnocchi ridges with . . . . .Sep/Oct 01   5
White beans. *See* Cannellini beans
White kohlrabi, field guide . . . . .Mar/Apr 01   BC
Wine
    Champagne-Cardamom Reduction, Nectarines,
        Blueberries, and Raspberries with . . . . .Jul/Aug 01   20
    headaches after drinking . . . . .May/Jun 01   3
    red
        and Balsamic Reduction, Strawberries and Grapes with . . . . . . .Jul/Aug 01   20
        beef Burgundy . . . . .Jan/Feb 01   12-14
            See also Beef—Burgundy
        for cooking, tasting of . . . . .Nov/Dec 01   26-27
        Reduction for Sauces . . . . .Nov/Dec 01   26
        Sauce for Beef Wellington . . . . .Nov/Dec 01   21
Wine bottles, fishing cork crumbs out of . . . . .Nov/Dec 01   4
Winter Vegetables, White Bean Soup with . . . . .Jan/Feb 01   21
Woks, for fried rice . . . . .Mar/Apr 01   19
Wondra flour . . . . .May/Jun 01   2
Work surfaces, cleaning with dough scraper . . . . .Jan/Feb 01   16

Y
Yeast . . . . .Jan/Feb 01   25-27
    expired, performance of . . . . .Jan/Feb 01   27
    instant . . . . .Jan/Feb 01   25-26
    proofing, use of term . . . . .Mar/Apr 01   2
    proper ratio of flour to . . . . .Jan/Feb 01   25
    sources for . . . . .Jan/Feb 01   32
    superior flavor development during long fermentations of . . . . . .Jan/Feb 01   26
    tasting of . . . . .Jan/Feb 01   27
    types of . . . . .Jan/Feb 01   25-26
Yogurt
    Cilantro, Curried Butternut Squash Soup with . . . . .Nov/Dec 01   8
    Cucumber and Mango Relish with . . . . .Jul/Aug 01   7
Yogurt cups, as improvised measuring cups . . . . .Jul/Aug 01   4

Z
Zante grapes . . . . .May/Jun 01   3
Zest, collecting neatly . . . . .Mar/Apr 01   5
Zipper-lock bags. *See* Plastic zipper-lock bags
Zucchini
    grilling . . . . .May/Jun 01   16
    ratatouille . . . . .Sep/Oct 01   18-19
        Master Recipe for . . . . .Sep/Oct 01   19

NUMBER FORTY-EIGHT

JANUARY & FEBRUARY 2001

COOK'S
ILLUSTRATED

Double Chocolate Sheet Cake
Easy Cake, Deep Chocolate Taste

Beef Burgundy
Ideal Pairing of Beef and Red Wine

Crisp and Tender Thin-Crust Pizza

Is a $200 Sauté Pan Worth the Money?
We Test 8 Pans to Find Out

Chicken Piccata
Simple, Quick, and Fresh

The Truth about Yeast
Does Brand Matter?

How to Stir-Fry Shrimp
Winter Pestos
No-Fuss Roasted Carrots
New Uses for Kitchen Tools
Tuscan White Bean Soup
Superflaky Apple Turnovers

$4.95 U.S./$6.95 CANADA

CONTENTS

January & February 2001

2 **Notes from Readers**
Readers ask questions and suggest solutions.

4 **Quick Tips**
Quick and easy ways to perform everyday kitchen tasks.

6 **Chicken Piccata Done Right**
For brightly flavored, fresh-tasting chicken piccata, use a whopping quarter cup of lemon juice and don't use flour to thicken the sauce. BY JACK BISHOP

8 **Crisp and Tender Thin-Crust Pizza**
Giving the dough a long refrigerator rise and baking the crust directly on parchment paper produce a no-stick, crackling crisp pizza with big flavor. BY KAY RENTSCHLER

11 **Winter Pestos**
When fresh basil is out of season, use arugula, nuts, mushrooms, or even roasted peppers to make quick, full-flavored pestos. BY JULIA COLLIN

12 **The Best Beef Burgundy**
The essence of this hearty French beef stew is flavor, and lots of it. The secrets? Use the right cut of meat, salt pork, and a brown roux; forget canned beef stock; and buy the best bottle of wine you can afford. BY DAWN YANAGIHARA

15 **No-Fuss Roasted Carrots**
With a broiler pan and a hot oven, you can produce perfectly cooked, caramelized roasted carrots in just 30 minutes. BY RAQUEL PELZEL

16 **Uncommon Uses for Common Kitchen Tools**
Learn some new and uncommon uses for six ordinary kitchen tools. BY RAQUEL PELZEL

18 **How to Stir-Fry Shrimp**
A simple shrimp broth boosts flavor, while a dash of cornstarch gives the sauce just the right body. BY ADAM RIED

20 **The Secrets of Tuscan White Bean Soup**
For perfectly cooked, richly flavored beans, go against tradition: Forget about presoaking, and don't spare the salt. BY BRIDGET LANCASTER

22 **Superflaky Apple Turnovers**
The combination of fast food-processor puff pastry and grated apples makes a turnover vastly superior to those made with store-bought pastry or precooked apples. BY RAQUEL PELZEL

24 **All-Purpose Chocolate Sheet Cake**
For an easy, foolproof, last-minute cake that packs in great chocolate flavor, just whisk together a few ingredients and bake. BY CHRISTOPHER KIMBALL

25 **Understanding and Using Yeasts**
Months of kitchen tests determined that there is almost no difference in baking results when using different types and brands of yeast. It's how you use them that matters. BY KAY RENTSCHLER AND JULIA COLLIN

27 **How to Buy a Premium Sauté Pan**
Among pricey sauté pans, good performance is a safe bet, but subtle design features separate the winners from the losers. BY ADAM RIED

30 **Kitchen Notes**
Test results, buying tips, and advice related to stories past and present, directly from our test kitchen. BY KAY RENTSCHLER

31 **Restaurant Chefs and Home Cooks**
Chef-written cookbooks routinely claim to contain "recipes for the home cook." We chose two examples and went into the test kitchen to check them out. BY CHRISTOPHER KIMBALL

32 **Resources**
Products from this issue, plus a curved boning knife, fresh dried beans, heavy-duty parchment paper, and a French-style rolling pin.

COOK'S
ILLUSTRATED

www.cooksillustrated.com

PUBLISHER AND EDITOR
Christopher Kimball

SENIOR EDITOR
John Willoughby

SENIOR WRITER
Jack Bishop

CORPORATE MANAGING EDITOR
Barbara Bourassa

TEST KITCHEN DIRECTOR
Kay Rentschler

ASSOCIATE EDITORS
Adam Ried
Dawn Yanagihara
Raquel Pelzel

RECIPE TESTING AND DEVELOPMENT
Bridget Lancaster
Julia Collin

ASSISTANT EDITOR
Shannon Blaisdell

CONSULTING FOOD EDITOR
Jasper White

CONTRIBUTING EDITOR
Elizabeth Germain

ART DIRECTOR
Amy Klee

COPY EDITOR
India Koopman

EDITORIAL INTERNS
Tammy Inman
Matthew Card

SPECIAL PROJECTS
Barry Estabrook

ASSOCIATE EDITOR,
ONLINE EDUCATION
Becky Hays

ASSISTANT EDITOR, WEB SITE
Shona Simkin

MARKETING MANAGER
Pamela Caporino

SALES REPRESENTATIVE
Jason Geller

MARKETING ASSISTANT
Connie Forbes

CIRCULATION DIRECTOR
David Mack

CIRCULATION MANAGER
Larisa Greiner

PRODUCTS MANAGER
Steven Browall

CIRCULATION ASSISTANT
Jennifer McCreary

INBOUND MARKETING REPRESENTATIVES
Adam Dardeck
Jacqui Valerio

VICE PRESIDENT OPERATIONS
AND TECHNOLOGY
James McCormack

ASSISTANT PRODUCTION MANAGER
Jessica Lindheimer

PRODUCTION ARTIST
Daniel Frey

PRODUCTION COORDINATOR
Mary Connelly

PRODUCTION INTERN
Christine Rizzo

SYSTEMS ADMINISTRATOR
Richard Cassidy

WEB MASTER
Nicole Morris

CONTROLLER
Mandy Shito

OFFICE MANAGER
Juliet Nusbaum

PUBLICITY
Deborah Broide

For list rental information, contact The SpecialLISTS, 1200 Harbor Blvd. 9th Floor, Weehawken, NJ 07087; (201) 865-5800; fax (201) 867-2450. Editorial office: 17 Station Street, Brookline, MA 02445; (617) 232-1000; fax (617) 232-1572. Editorial contributions should be sent to: Editor, *Cook's Illustrated*. We cannot assume responsibility for manuscripts submitted to us. Submissions will be returned only if accompanied by a large self-addressed envelope. Postmaster: Send all new orders, subscription inquiries, and change of address notices to: *Cook's Illustrated*, P.O. Box 7446, Red Oak, IA 51591-0446. PRINTED IN CHINA.

DRIED BEANS

DRIED BEANS Beans are part of every known cuisine. Although they are also used fresh, they are much more common in dried form. By far the largest bean family is the haricot, which encompasses most of the beans native to the Americas. These include the familiar kidney bean; flageolet, which are immature white kidney beans; pintos and their ancestors, the appaloosa; cannellini, white beans associated with Tuscan food; and rice beans, the cannellini's dwarf cousin. Other beans indigenous to the Americas include scarlet runner beans, esteemed for their ornamental flowers and crisp, lightly fruity flavor; Jacob's cattle, nutty tasting tepary beans well adapted to desert climates; and Steuben yellow eyes, excellent for bean salads and stews. Old World beans include smoky African black-eyed peas; Japanese adzuki beans, made into sweetened red bean paste for Asian confections; and garbanzo beans, native to Asia but popular throughout the world, particularly in the Middle East.

COVER (*Swiss Chard*): ELIZABETH BRANDON, BACK COVER (*Dried Beans*): JOHN BURGOYNE

THE ANTIQUE

I n a nod to my childhood in this small mountain town, I still cook many of the family meals on a wood cookstove, a Richmond model made by Olds & Whipple of Hartford, Conn. This black behemoth is bedecked with fancy nickel plating featuring two naked cherubs holding bunches of grapes and plenty of Victorian-era scrollwork. The four dampers are used to control the fire and regulate the extent to which the heat either goes under the cooktop and up the flue or takes a circuitous route around the oven for the purpose of baking. It also has a copper-plated reservoir on the right side that heats up about three gallons of water. The trick to starting the stove is to use very fine kindling and not too much of it. A small, hot fire gets a draft going, which then sucks out the smoke that otherwise would leak out into the kitchen and cause the fire alarm to sound, a not uncommon occurrence in our household.

Using a wood cookstove takes some practice. Birch is good for a quick, hot fire. Seasoned, split oak or butternut is better for a longer, slower burn. Maintaining a moderate oven temperature is pretty easy, but getting the oven hot enough for, say, biscuits is another matter. On a cold morning, the stove can refuse to start a draft or it can start to cool suddenly right in the middle of bread baking. But over time, one gains a sixth sense about such things, and the cookstove becomes a part of the family. Like a good friend, my antique offers unexpected pleasures. The warming shelf is great for holding dinner plates and letting doughs rise. It keeps a kettle of water at a simmer all day, handy for a quick cup of tea.

On a cold winter's morning, the kitchen fills with the faint smell of wood smoke and maple syrup as the kids tumble out of bed in nightshirts to a pancake breakfast.

My neighbor John purchased a new pickup a few years back, a bright red Dodge Ram with a snowplow on the front. It cost him nearly $30,000, so he sold me his 1981 Ford F-150 to help offset the expense. The Ford had more than 150,000 miles on it, the truck bed was badly rusted, the tires were almost bald, and the front bench seat was starting to lose its covering. I had some bodywork done, had it painted red, bought new tires, had the tie rods and muffler replaced, had the clutch adjusted, and put on a new rear bumper.

John and I met on the road one day, each of us in our pickups, his new and mine old. He didn't say much at first, just looked at his old friend in its new coat of paint, and then asked about the corn crop. A few months later, I noticed that he kept his new truck parked up by the cabin and drove around town in an old brown Rabbit that started only about half the time. He often talked about getting the Rabbit fixed, but never did—he had to give it a push down his driveway to get it going most mornings. Two years after he sold me the F-150, the Ram was gone, sold to a farmer over in New York State. He never said a word about selling it, but he admitted over a glass of stout that he sure did like the way that old Ford rode.

Christopher Kimball

Today, John is getting on in years, but he still works every day up in the woods, clearing land, pulling down "widow-makers" (trees that have been blown over and get hung up in the branches of neighboring trees), and, I think, enjoying himself out-of-doors while making himself useful. One knee made it difficult to walk a year ago, but a simple operation put things right, and he's back to going full steam. He's making sausages, raising pigs, and doing a little Polish cooking on the side.

Back at the stove one morning, I had biscuits in the oven and eggs scrambling in a cast-iron skillet on top. The tea kettle was steaming and the fire was good and steady, just right for warming the feet of my four kids, who had come down for breakfast. I glanced over at the new gas range nearby and thought that, yes, sometimes the old is better than the new. I had rescued this old cookstove from a decorator's kitchen, where it would have served out the rest of its days as an "antique," a place to display family photos, knickknacks, or baskets full of potpourri. Antiques are things that no longer serve a useful purpose, yet deep in the soul of every old car or old man is a yearning to carry a load. The day will come when our paint will be peeling, our truck beds rusted, and our engines run a bit rough, but we're ready, willing, and able to do our part. We just need to be given a jump-start and a chance.

ABOUT COOK'S ILLUSTRATED

Visit our expanded Web site The *Cook's* Web site features original editorial content not found in the magazine as well as searchable databases for recipes, equipment tests, food tastings, buying advice, step-by-step technique illustrations, and quick tips. The site also features our online bookstore, cooking courses, a question and answer message board, and a sign-up form for *e-Notes*, our free newsletter on cooking. Join us online today at www.cooksillustrated.com.

The Magazine *Cook's Illustrated* (ISSN 1068-2821) is published bimonthly (6 issues per year) by Boston Common Press Limited Partnership, 17 Station Street, Brookline, MA 02445. Copyright 2001 Boston Common Press Limited Partnership. Periodical postage paid at Boston, Mass., and additional mailing offices, USPS #012487. A one-year subscription is $29.70, two years is $55, and three years is $75. Add $6 postage per year for Canadian subscriptions and $12 per year for all other foreign countries. To order subscriptions in the U.S. call 800-526-8442; from outside the U.S. call 515-247-7571. Gift subscriptions are available for $24.95 each. Postmaster: Send all new orders, subscription inquiries, and change of address notices to *Cook's Illustrated*, P.O. Box 7446, Red Oak, IA 51591-0446.

Cookbooks and other products *Cook's Illustrated* offers cookbooks and magazine-related items for sale through its online bookstore. Products offered include annual hardbound editions of the magazine, an eight-year (1993–2000) reference index for the magazine, single-subject cookbooks from

our How to Cook Master Series, as well as copies of *The Best Recipe, The Complete Book of Pasta and Noodles, The Complete Book of Poultry, The Cook's Bible,* and *The Yellow Farmhouse Cookbook*. Prices and ordering information are available by calling 800-611-0759 inside the U.S. or 515-246-6911 from outside the U.S. or visiting our bookstore at www.cooksillustrated.com. Back issues of *Cook's Illustrated* are available for sale by calling 800-611-0759 inside the U.S. or 515-246-6911 from outside the U.S.

Questions about your book order? Visit our customer care page at www.cooksillustrated.com, or call 800-611-0759 inside the U.S. or 515-246-6911 from outside the U.S.

Reader submissions *Cook's* accepts reader submissions for Quick Tips. We will provide a one-year complimentary subscription for each tip that we print. Send your tip, name, address, and daytime telephone number to Quick Tips, *Cook's Illustrated*, P.O. Box 470589, Brookline, MA 02447. Questions, suggestions, or submissions for Notes from Readers should be sent to the same address.

Questions about your subscription? Visit our customer care page at cooksillustrated.com where you can manage your subscription, including changing your address, renewing your subscription, paying your bill, or viewing answers to frequently asked questions. You can also direct questions about your subscription to *Cook's Illustrated*, P.O. Box 7446, Red Oak, IA 51591-0446, or call 800-526-8442.

Why No Pommes Anna Pan?

I made your pommes Anna (see "Pommes Anna for Home Cooks," November/December 2000) in a nonstick, ovenproof skillet and had wonderful results, but I was wondering why, if there is a pan made specifically for a dish, you didn't use the pommes Anna pan instead?

MARY HOFFMAN
SHORT HILLS, N.J.

➤ While most of us have a large nonstick skillet in our kitchens, very few of us have a $200 pommes Anna pan. Almost as beautiful as the potato cake itself, this elegant receptacle is a heavy, tin-lined, 3-inch-deep copper pan with straight sides, a cuffing lid, and small handles on either side of both the pan and the lid. Apart from its expense and rarity, the primary reason we didn't use it for our recipe is simple: it just didn't work well enough to justify it.

In their book *The Well-Tooled Kitchen* (Hearst, 1991), Fred Bridge and Jean F. Tibbetts explain that the copper surrounding the layered potato slices retains and distributes the high heat necessary to brown the top, bottom, and sides of the cake. We weren't so lucky. We tested the pan entirely in the oven as well as with a start on the stovetop, and in neither case did our potatoes brown deeply or evenly. In fact, they didn't brown enough on the bottom or sides to allow for the clean release that makes the presentation of the dish so unique. Weighing in at seven pounds, this pan is also a bit cumbersome. Although the pommes Anna pan is a classic, we were relieved to discover that we didn't need one after all to make our recipe.

Pasta and Sauce Matchups

I recently made the pasta all'Amatriciana (see "The Best Pasta Amatriciana," November/December 2000) but did not serve it with the recommended pasta, bucatini. I used the penne I had in my pantry. A friend told me that pastas and sauces have specific marriages. Is this true?

JULIE KRAMER
BAR HARBOR, MAINE

➤ Italians have created dozens of shapes of dried pasta. No matter what the shape of the pasta or type of sauce, we adamantly believe that the pasta, not the sauce, should be the focal point. Our senior writer, Jack Bishop, author of *Pasta e Vedura* (HarperCollins, 1996), notes that Italians eat pasta with sauce, not sauce "stretched" with some pasta, as is the case in many American restaurants. But whether any one dish demands a particular type

of pasta is a different question entirely. In our recently published *Complete Book of Pasta and Noodles* (Clarkson Potter, 2000), we state our position on this issue. In Italy, matching pasta shapes with certain sauces is a fine art. In fact, some Italians would rather forgo a dish than make it with something other than the traditional pasta shape. At *Cook's* we are considerably more relaxed in our matching of pasta shapes and sauces, following just one general rule: You should be able to eat some pasta and sauce easily with each bite. This means that the texture and consistency of the sauce should work with the pasta shape.

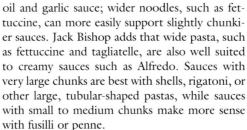

Bucatini

Penne

In general, long strands are best with smooth sauces or sauces with very small chunks, such as a traditional oil and garlic sauce; wider noodles, such as fettuccine, can more easily support slightly chunkier sauces. Jack Bishop adds that wide pasta, such as fettuccine and tagliatelle, are also well suited to creamy sauces such as Alfredo. Sauces with very large chunks are best with shells, rigatoni, or other large, tubular-shaped pastas, while sauces with small to medium chunks make more sense with fusilli or penne.

Pasta all'Amatriciana is traditionally made with bucatini, a long tubular pasta that works best with pesto and sauces containing pancetta, vegetables, and cheeses. With help from the Pecorino, the small chunks of pancetta, onion, and tomato in the Amatriciana bind to the pasta, while the sauce works its way into the hollow tubes. With every bite you experience the full effect of the dish. If using penne, the body of the sauce is likely to slip away from the short, tubular pasta and collect on the bottom of the bowl.

Dealing with Mother

Soon after I purchased a gallon of cider vinegar, a white film formed on the surface. Can you tell me what it is and if it is safe to use the vinegar?

JULIA ANASOULIS
PEABODY, MASS.

➤ The white film on the surface of your cider vinegar is called a mother, a gelatinous mat of cellulose (the molecular form of fiber found in vegetables and grains) and acetic bacteria that grow across the top of fermenting vinegar. Mothers can be thick or thin, and though they are usually suspended on

top of the vinegar, they can, if disturbed, settle to the bottom of the bottle. Most have a chalky white hue, but they vary from vinegar to vinegar and may be clear, light brown, or even black.

Mothers are essential to the production of all kinds of vinegar (hence the name). Apple cider vinegar, for example, begins as apple juice, rich in sugars and carbohydrates, and is converted to alcohol (think hard cider) by means of yeast. Next, a vinegar culture of acetic bacteria from another batch of vinegar is added to the mix to turn the alcohol into acetic acid, or vinegar.

Mothers develop on the surface of bottled vinegar if it is exposed to atmospheric bacteria and oxygen. The moment a bottle of vinegar is opened, it is susceptible to both, and if the conditions are right for bacterial breeding, a mother will form. Many consumers mistakenly assume the film is an indicator of spoiled or turned vinegar, but this is not the case. The film is completely harmless. However, it is advisable to remove it soon after it appears because if it sinks to the bottom of the bottle and is left alone it will die. Deprived of oxygen, the thin mat of bacteria and cellulose will begin to decay and unpleasantly influence the taste and smell of the vinegar. For this reason, Lawrence Driggs of the International Vinegar Museum in Roslyn, S.D., recommends filtering the vinegar through cheesecloth into a small bottle (or bottles) at first sign of a mother. Store the new bottle in the refrigerator. At 45 degrees Fahrenheit, bacteria goes dormant, and further growth is supressed. One way to avoid having to filter your vinegar, said Driggs, is to buy cider vinegar in small bottles as opposed to gallon-sized jugs. Small bottles limit the vinegar's exposure to oxygen and so discourage mother growth.

The Two Oyster Sauces

I am delighted to find so many ethnic ingredients in mainstream grocery stores these days but have trouble deciding what to buy. I am very interested in Asian ingredients, as my family loves stir-fries, and wonder if you can tell me what oyster sauce is, how to use it, and which brand is the best?

KERRY COOPER
BETHESDA, MD.

➤ Oyster sauce can be divided into two categories. The first is bottled oyster sauce, which is actually called oyster-flavored sauce. The second is a prepared sauce that contains bottled sauce, such as the "Broccoli with Oyster Sauce" you might order from the menu in a Chinese restaurant.

Bottled oyster-flavored sauce is a rich, concentrated mixture of oyster extracts, soy sauce, brine, and assorted seasonings. This brown sauce is thick, salty, and strong. It is used sparingly to enhance the flavor of many dishes that typically include a number of other aromatic ingredients (one example being the recipe for stir-fried shrimp on page 19 of this issue).

Cooked oyster sauce, on the other hand, is a mixture of various ingredients, such as chicken broth, soy sauce, sake, rice wine, sherry, sesame oil, and sugar, in addition to prepared oyster-flavored sauce. It is often thickened with cornstarch and tossed with a wide array of vegetable, beef, chicken, and seafood stir-fries.

A trip to our local grocery store and Asian market turned up five different brands of bottled oyster sauce. Lee Kum Kee dominated the shelves with three varieties: Choy Sun, Panda Brand, and Premium. Coin Tree and Sa Cheng rounded out the list. Although bottled oyster-flavored sauce is too strong to be used as a condiment, we thought it important to take note of the raw, unadulterated flavor of each bottle before using it to make a cooked oyster sauce. Each brand of the potent sauce received the same standard comments: "salty," "biting," and "fishy." However, when we mixed the bottled oyster-flavored sauces with other ingredients—sherry, soy sauce, sesame oil, sugar, and freshly ground pepper—and then made simple stir-fries, the tasters were able to detect a wider range of flavors.

The most authentic cooked oyster sauce of the group was undoubtedly that which contained Lee Kum Kee's Premium Oyster Flavored Sauce. Admittedly intense and somewhat fishy, it was the only sauce with true depth of flavor; its saltiness was balanced by sweet caramel undertones, and the oyster flavor was strong. This sauce is not for the faint of heart; one taster proclaimed, "My American taste buds can't take it." According to Jason Wong, president of AsiaFoods.com, Lee Kum Kee's Premium sauce is the favorite among Boston's Asian population and the "only one" used in restaurants nationwide. All of this notwithstanding, the other favorite among our tasters was the cooked oyster sauce made with Sa Cheng Oyster Flavored Sauce, preferred because it was mild and "gravylike." The other three bottled sauces we tried didn't seem to add much to the cooked sauces. As one taster put it, they "may just as well have been soy sauce."

What's That Slippery Skin

Do you know what the slippery skin on an onion is? I often remove it but don't really know if I should or shouldn't.

GREG ROGERS
AUSTIN, TEXAS

➤ According to Dr. Irwin Goldman, associate professor of horticulture at the University of Wisconsin, the slippery membrane found between each scale, or layer, of the flesh of an onion bulb is the epidermis, a layer of cells that covers the leaves and (in this case) young parts of a plant.

The fact that an onion's epidermal layers peel away so readily sets it apart from other plants. The ease of separation, Goldman explained, has to do with the release of tension in the bulb when an onion is cut. The pressure exerted by the knife relieves stress between the epidermal layers and the scales, and they fall away from one another. When they do, cells are disrupted, and the dissolved substances within, consisting largely of sugars, leach out and lubricate the membrane, thus making it slick.

Though it may be slippery to work around in the kitchen, in the scientific world, the onion's epidermis is considered an ideal specimen. A single sheet of cells that can be removed with ease in its entirety, it is used by instructors to teach students about cell makeup as well as in research.

The outermost layer of epidermis has been known to send a few knives off course, but can easily be removed. If it gets in the way of chopping or slicing, peel it away. Otherwise, let it be. It is edible and flavorful.

Understanding Koshering

In your recipe for high-roast chicken (see "High-Roast Chicken Perfected," March/April 2000), you suggest using a kosher chicken, which is salted, when not planning to brine the chicken, as recommended. Can you tell me why a kosher chicken is salted, and how this is similar to brining?

ANNE NASH
NEW YORK, N.Y.

➤ In accordance with the dietary laws that govern the selection and preparation of foods eaten by observant Jews, chicken is processed in a prescribed manner to make it kosher, or fit to eat. The process of koshering a chicken involves soaking, salting, and washing the chicken, as does brining.

The primary function of koshering chicken (as well as other meats) is to remove blood, the consumption of which is prohibited by the dietary laws. After slaughter, inspection, and butchering, kosher chickens are soaked in cool, constantly replenished water for one-half hour and then set out to dry before being covered entirely—inside and out—with coarse kosher salt. The chicken is left to sit and drain for an hour, at which point it is rinsed three times to remove the salt. According to Dr. Joe Regenstein, professor of food science at Cornell University, when salt is applied to the surface of the chicken, the free-flowing liquid within the proteins is drawn out. The salt, in turn, is absorbed back into the proteins. The salt denatures, or unwinds, the coiled strands of proteins, thereby priming them for the absorption of more liquid when the salt is rinsed off. The water and salt molecules, tangled in the web of protein strands, are what makes the koshered chicken moist and flavorful.

Essentially, *Cook's* technique of brining combines all of these steps into one. Immersed in a large container of salt, sugar, and water, the chicken (or turkey) goes through much the same process as a koshered chicken. Liquid rushes out of the proteins to dilute the solution of salt (and, in the case of our chicken brine, sugar), which is then absorbed back into the meat, causing the protein strands to unravel and eventually absorb and trap additional moisture.

WHAT IS IT?

While at a Houston steak house, I noticed that my place was set with the usual assortment of forks, knives, and spoons as well as a utensil like this one. Having never seen one before, I was a little embarrassed to ask what it was, so I ate the whole meal without touching it. Can you fill me in?

JOSEPH P. MANZELLA
NAPLES, FLA.

Making the occasional appearance in ultratraditional steak houses, what you came across was a marrow spoon. Designed to extract marrow—the tissue that fills bone cavities—from the bones of meat, a marrow spoon is long and thin and has a scoop on each end of a flat grip area: one narrow scoop for hard-to-reach spaces and the other a little bit broader. According to the *Glutton's Glossary* by John Ayto (Routledge, 1990), marrow spoons were popular in Europe from the 17th to the 19th centuries, when marrow had a widespread reputation as a culinary delicacy. Today, a marrow spoon is apt to accompany the Italian veal shank stew osso buco, but it is otherwise a tool known and used by only a few. A handful of antique dealers told us that the spoons were customarily made from silver and that while they can still be found in antique shops, they are rare and quite expensive. The proprietors of Bridge Kitchenware (214 East 52nd Street, New York, NY 10022; 800-247-3435; www.bridgekitchenware.com) had been searching for a marrow spoon to carry in their store for some time before they came across an Italian osso buco spoon. Carved from natural horn and highly polished, these unique spoons were created specifically for the dish. They sell for $35 (item BSSO).

Quick Tips

Space-Saving Vegetable Prep

Recipes for soups and stews often call for adding different vegetables and other ingredients at different points during the cooking time. Instead of placing each prepared ingredient in its own smaller bowl or into piles crowded onto a cutting board, David Theobald of Montclair, N.J., saves both space and dirty dishes by layering the ingredients in a single large bowl and separating the layers with sheets of wax paper or plastic wrap. (Make sure that the ingredients are in the right order, with the one you'll need first on top.)

Keeping Dried Mushrooms Submerged While Rehydrating

It's often the case when rehydrating dried mushrooms or tomatoes that the pieces float to the surface of the hot water, where they plump up slowly and unevenly. Hunter Harwood of Ocean, N.J., solves this problem by putting the mushroom or tomato pieces in a small bowl, covering them with boiling water, then placing the grater attachment from his food processor in the bowl. The holes in the grater allow water to pass through, and the grater sinks and keeps the food submerged.

Preventive Care for Cutting Boards

Some cooks have multiple cutting boards designated for different purposes, but cooks with more limited storage space often make do with one. Readers suggested two tips that keep their cutting boards from picking up stains and odors.

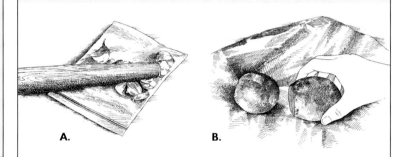

A.　　　　　　　　　**B.**

A. When Gary and Barb Listermann of Cincinnati, Ohio, crush garlic cloves to flavor a brine or the like, they put the cloves in a plastic sandwich bag, mash them with a pan or rolling pin right in the bag, and dump them directly from the bag into the pot. This way, no odor pervades their board because no garlic ever touches it.
B. Diane Gottfred-Clouthier of Denver, Colo., likes roasted beets but hates the way they stain her cutting board when she peels and slices them after roasting. She has solved this problem by lining the roasting pan with a square of foil that is large enough to act as a board liner when it comes time to peel and slice the roasted beets.

Easy Microwave Cleaning

In busy households where the microwave sees a lot of use, people sometimes forget to cover a dish when reheating food. This results in splatters inside the oven. Since scrubbing is tedious and has the potential to damage the interior surfaces, Sondra Jackson de Cadirola of Chevy Chase, Md., devised a simple cleaning method. She places a microwave-safe bowl full of water in the oven and heats it on high for 10 minutes; the steam loosens dried food particles so they can be wiped off with ease.

Quick Single Soup Servings

Homemade soup is a winter treat that's easy to freeze. But most people freeze it in large multiserving portions that make for a lot of unnecessary defrosting when the need for just one or two servings arises. Linda Michael of Middletown, Conn., has an easy system for freezing convenient single servings.

1. Set out a number of 10- or 12-ounce paper cups for hot beverages and fill each with a portion of cooled soup (but not all the way to the top). Label, wrap, and freeze each cup.
2. Whenever you want a quick cup of soup, remove as many servings as necessary from the freezer and microwave them until they're hot and ready to serve.

Keeping Ice Cream Fresh

If ice cream isn't eaten right away, it can lose its fresh taste and form ice crystals on the surface as it sits in the freezer. Lydia Golub of Upper Montclair, N.J., suggests a way to keep the crystals at bay. Before replacing the ice cream in the freezer, cover the portion remaining in the carton with heavy-duty plastic wrap, pressing the wrap right down onto the surface of the ice cream.

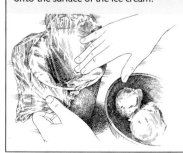

Send Us Your Tip We will provide a complimentary one-year subscription for each tip we print. See page 1 for information.

Oven-Fried Chicken Shortcut

The illustrations in the *Cook's* May/June 1999 article "Oven-Fried Chicken" demonstrate Melba toasts being crushed in a heavy-duty plastic freezer bag and then transferred to a pie plate before they are used to coat the chicken. Bonner Kyle of Austin, Texas, recommends a way to shortcut this step, saving both time and mess. First, use a large bag and simply leave the crumbs in it, then add the vegetable oil, seal the bag, and toss to coat the crumbs. One by one, carefully add all of the egg-coated chicken and press the crumbs onto the pieces (through the sides of the bag, so that your hands stay clean) until evenly and thoroughly coated.

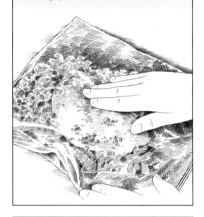

Easier Pepper Grinder Loading

The filler opening of many pepper grinders is so small that the only way to fill them is by using a funnel. But even that trick has its problems, as peppercorns can easily catch in the neck of the funnel and block it. Fed up with this process, Darcie O'Grady of Columbus, Ohio, turned to another gadget: her rubber garlic peeler. It's both wide and malleable, so it's perfect for the job.

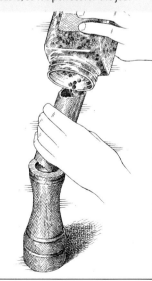

Story Sticks for Accurate Reductions

In woodworking, a story stick is marked and used to transfer measurements from one object to another, avoiding the possible inaccuracies introduced with a ruler. While some cooks are comfortable eyeballing the level to which liquid has reduced in a sauce, jam, or jelly, others would like more precision. For those in the latter group, Lorraine Skibo of Saratoga Springs, N.Y., has adapted the story stick for culinary use.

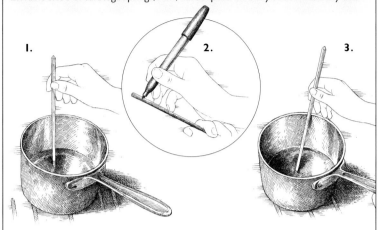

1. Say you are supposed to reduce the liquid to one-half cup. Measure one-half cup water into the pan you're using for the reduction and stand a wooden chopstick or bamboo skewer in the center for several seconds, long enough for the water to mark the wood.
2. Pull the chopstick or skewer out of the pan and mark the water level with a non-toxic marker.
3. As you are reducing the sauce, check the liquid level periodically with the story stick. When the level reaches the mark on the stick, you can be confident of an accurate reduction.

Removing Baked-On Goo

Some folks argue that the baked-on coating of burnt cheese and sauce left at the bottom of a fondue dish or macaroni-and-cheese pan is the tastiest part of the dish. But for those who find it unpalatable, this residue presents a formidable cleaning task. Here's how two readers handle the challenge.

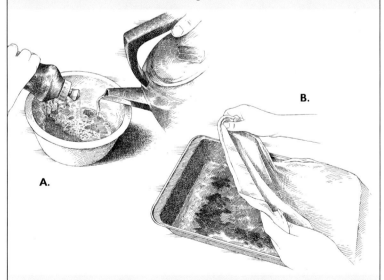

A. Gail Emley of Cleves, Ohio, covers the burned-on mess with dishwashing soap and a small amount of boiling water and allows it to rest overnight. The next morning, the mess washes away with ease.
B. Billie Ducharme of Hooksett, N.H., doesn't let her small sink deter her from soaking large cookie sheets and baking pans. To get around the size problem, she soaks a dishrag thoroughly in warm water and places it directly on the surface of the dirty pan. In as little as a few minutes, the mess washes right off, just as if the pan had been soaked in a sink.

Makeshift Vertical Roaster

Though using a vertical roaster to roast chicken is not *Cooks'* preferred method, many cooks do it anyway because it's quick and it eliminates the need to turn the bird. One night, when Cheryl Vieira of Germantown, Tenn., found herself in need of a second vertical roaster, she improvised by using a tube-pan insert sprayed with nonstick cooking spray and placed in a shallow dish.

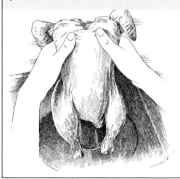

Another Way to Defat Stocks and Sauces

Although overnight refrigeration is the best way to defat a stock or sauce, several methods can be used to accomplish this while the liquid is hot. Jason Valdes Greenwood of Somerville, Mass., uses the following method.

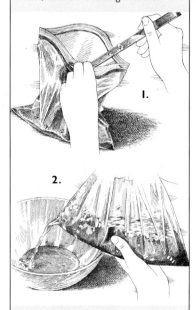

1. Allow the liquid to cool just slightly and then place it in a large, heavy-duty zipper-lock bag. Seal the bag and allow time enough for the fat to rise to the surface of the liquid.
2. Hold the bag by one of the top corners and cut off the point of one of the bottom corners to act as a spout. As soon as the liquid is drained, pinch the spout to capture the fat in the bag.

Chicken Piccata Done Right

For brightly flavored, fresh-tasting chicken piccata, use a whopping quarter cup of lemon juice, and don't use flour to thicken the sauce.

≥ BY JACK BISHOP ≤

When I was a kid, my mother told me to order grilled cheese in any diner or eatery that looked suspicious. She figured it was hard to mess up something so simple. When I eat out in Italian restaurants, chicken or veal piccata is my grilled cheese. Piccata is one of those appealing Italian recipes that tastes complex but is actually easy to prepare. Even mediocre chefs can usually turn out a credible version.

I imagined that piccata would be easy to perfect—and it was, after I realized that most recipes are missing the point. To begin with, many cookbook authors add extraneous ingredients and thereby ruin the pure simplicity of the dish. The other major problem is blandness. Many recipes contain just a tablespoon of lemon juice and a teaspoon of capers, neither of which provides much flavor. My goals were simple: to cook the chicken properly and make a streamlined sauce that really tastes of lemons and capers.

Thin lemon slices soften in the reducing sauce and add a wonderful bright lemon flavor to the finished dish.

Chicken First

Over the years, *Cook's* has run several recipes for sautéed boneless, skinless chicken breasts. Other than using plenty of heat, the technique is simple. But regular six- to eight-ounce breasts—the kind we had always called for—didn't feel right in this dish. Piccata began as something you made with veal, so I decided that thin chicken cutlets were a must.

I bought thinly sliced chicken cutlets at my supermarket but found that some packages contained ragged bits of meat that were less than ¼ inch thick. These cutlets were so thin that they looked like chicken carpaccio. On other occasions I had better luck, and the thinly sliced cutlets were just fine. My conclusion: Shop carefully if you want to use this convenience product.

My supermarket sells several brands of premium chicken breasts, including kosher cutlets, that I think taste better than mass-market brands. The cutlets are the standard thickness—¾ to 1 inch—and I found they could easily be readied for

piccata. Simply remove the tenderloin (which will prevent the underside of the cutlet from cooking evenly) and then slice the main part of the cutlet in half horizontally (see illustrations, below).

Many piccata recipes suggest pounding the cutlets, even thin ones. I found this step to be unnecessary; cutlets less than ½ inch thick will cook quickly enough. Pounding not only makes the cutlets thinner but increases their surface area, making it harder to fit the cutlets in the pan. Then you're forced to cook them in three batches to make enough for four people, dramatically increasing your chances of burning the pan drippings. Without pounding, you can cook 1½ pounds of thin cutlets in a 12-inch skillet in two batches.

Many piccata recipes call for flouring or breading the cutlets. As in past tests conducted at the magazine, I found that floured cutlets browned better and were less likely to stick to the pan. Tasters did not like breaded cutlets—what's the point of developing a crisp crust only to douse

it with sauce? I also tried dipping the cutlets in milk as well as beaten eggs before flouring them. Although the crust was a bit thicker when cooked, tasters felt that there was little advantage to this extra step.

Sleuthing the Sauce

With my chicken tests completed, I turned my attention to the sauce. I wanted a strong lemon flavor that wasn't harsh or overly acidic. I also wanted a sauce that was thick enough to nap the sautéed cutlets. I knew I would want to deglaze the empty skillet used to cook the chicken with some liquid to loosen the flavorful browned bits and would then reduce the liquid and thicken it.

Most of the recipes I uncovered in my research called for 1 or 2 tablespoons of lemon juice. All of my tasters agreed that these sauces weren't lemony enough. I found that ¼ cup delivered a nice lemon punch. Recipes that instructed the cook to deglaze the hot pan with lemon juice and then simmer the sauce for several minutes tasted flat. Adding the lemon juice toward the end of the cooking time helped keep the lemon juice tasting fresh.

My caper testing led me to a similar conclusion. You need to use a lot of capers—2 tablespoons is just right—and they should be added when the sauce is nearly done so the capers retain their structural integrity.

I next focused on the liquid I would use to deglaze the pan. Chicken stock and white wine were the most obvious candidates. The wine seemed like a good idea, but it contributed more acid to the sauce, something it did not need. Stock proved to be a more neutral base for the lemon juice and capers.

TECHNIQUE | SLICING THE CUTLETS

After removing the tenderloin, place each cutlet smooth-side up on a cutting board. Holding one hand on top of the cutlet, carefully slice the cutlet in half horizontally to yield two pieces, each between ⅜ and ½ inch thick.

Before deglazing the pan, I sautéed some aromatics in the pan drippings. I tested shallots, onions, scallions, and garlic separately. All were fine, although tasters preferred the shallots and garlic. Just make sure to watch the pan carefully so that the aromatics don't burn. Add the broth to the pan as soon as the garlic or shallots start to color.

At this point, my sauce was quite good, but I wondered if there was another way to add lemon flavor. In my research, I uncovered several recipes that called for lemon slices. I halved a lemon and then cut it into very thin half circles. I tried adding the lemon slices with the lemon juice, but the slices were too crunchy and numerous. For my next test, I used just half a lemon and added the slices with the broth. They simmered for five minutes and softened considerably. The longer simmering time also allowed oils from the peel to flavor the sauce. I tried replacing the sliced lemons with grated zest but found the sliced lemons more appealing and less work.

The last remaining issue for testing was thickening the sauce. Some recipes called for a roux (stirring flour into fat before adding the liquid) while others added either softened butter or softened butter mixed with flour once the sauce was cooked. A roux made the sauce too thick. Several times I ended up with a sauce as thick as Spackle. Thickening the sauce at the end seemed more practical. The butter-flour paste gave the sauce a floury taste that dulled the flavors of lemon and capers. Plain butter proved best. Some parsley added with the butter gave the sauce some color.

The key is to keep the flavors simple and allow the lemon and capers to take center stage. You can add your own embellishments, but remember my mother's advice about the grilled cheese: Keep it simple.

CHICKEN PICCATA
SERVES 4

If you like, use thinly sliced cutlets available at many supermarkets. These cutlets don't have any tenderloins and can be used as is.

- 2   large lemons
- 4   boneless, skinless chicken breasts (about 1½ pounds), preferably kosher or Bell and Evans, rinsed, dried thoroughly, trimmed of excess fat, and prepared according to illustrations on page 6
-     Salt and ground black pepper
- ½   cup all-purpose flour
- 4   tablespoons vegetable oil
- 1   small shallot, minced (about 2 tablespoons) or 1 small garlic clove, minced (about 1 teaspoon)
- 1   cup chicken stock or canned low-sodium chicken broth
- 2   tablespoons drained small capers
- 3   tablespoons unsalted butter, softened
- 2   tablespoons minced fresh parsley leaves

What Are Capers?

Many people associate capers with anchovies and assume that they come from the sea. Others assume that they must be related to peas or beans because of their shape. Capers are actually pickles made from the unopened flower buds of the caper shrub, which grows in the Mediterranean region. These briny morsels are used in countless Italian, Spanish, and Greek recipes.

Capers can be preserved in one of two ways. Most often, the flower buds are soaked in a saltwater brine and then packed in brine or a mixture of brine and vinegar. This is how capers are sold in most supermarkets. The

 Caperberries    Gruesas   Nonpareils    Salt-cured

other option is to cure them with salt. This kind of caper costs more and is available only in specialty markets.

In addition to differences in preservation, capers vary in size. The smallest capers—no larger than small peas—are called nonpareils. There are several more grades, the largest being the size of small olives and called *gruesas*. If you drink martinis, you may also have seen something called *caperberries*. These oval berries form if the flower buds are allowed to open and set fruit. Caperberries are pickled in brine, just like capers.

To make some sense of these variables, I purchased six brands of capers and held a small tasting. We tasted small and large capers packed in brine and vinegar as well as

one brand of salted capers. For cooking, tasters agreed that small capers are best because they can be used as is; larger capers are too potent to eat whole and should be chopped. Besides adding an extra step, chopped capers disintegrate when added to sauces.

The taste differences in the various brands were subtle, although most tasters felt that the brand packed in wine vinegar was the least harsh and therefore the most flavorful. (Labels on the other bottles just said "vinegar.")

Capers packed in salt were unbearably salty straight from the bottle. Rinsing didn't do much to lessen their sting. Soaking in cool water for at least 20 minutes (and preferably an hour) washed out enough of the salt to reveal the flavor of the capers. Without the salt (because there's no vinegar), I picked up hints of herbs (especially oregano) and mustard that I never tasted in the brined capers. These salted capers were delicious, but once I used them in piccata their subtle traits faded behind other ingredients.

Many sources suggest rinsing brined capers, too. I think you can skip this step. Drain the capers well and taste one. If they seem very salty or vinegary, you can rinse them. In most cases, this step won't be necessary. —J.B.

---

1. Adjust oven rack to lower-middle position, set large heatproof plate on rack, and heat oven to 200 degrees.

2. Halve one lemon pole to pole. Trim ends from one half and cut crosswise into slices ⅛ to ¼ inch thick; set aside. Juice remaining half and whole lemon to obtain ¼ cup juice; reserve.

3. Sprinkle both sides of cutlets generously with salt and pepper. Measure flour into pie tin or shallow baking dish. Working one cutlet at a time, coat with flour, and shake to remove excess.

4. Heat heavy-bottomed 12-inch skillet over medium-high heat until hot, about 2 minutes; add 2 tablespoons oil and swirl pan to coat. Lay half of chicken pieces in skillet. Sauté cutlets, without moving them, until lightly browned on first side, 2 to 2½ minutes. Turn cutlets and cook until second side is lightly browned, 2 to 2½ minutes longer. Remove pan from heat and transfer cutlets to plate in oven. Add remaining 2 tablespoons oil to now-empty skillet and heat until shimmering. Add remaining chicken pieces and repeat.

5. Add shallot or garlic to now-empty skillet and return skillet to medium heat. Sauté until fragrant, about 30 seconds for shallot or 10 seconds for garlic. Add stock and lemon slices, increase heat to high, and scrape skillet bottom with wooden

spoon or spatula to loosen browned bits. Simmer until liquid reduces to about ⅓ cup, about 4 minutes. Add lemon juice and capers and simmer until sauce reduces again to ⅓ cup, about 1 minute. Remove pan from heat and swirl in butter until butter melts and thickens sauce; swirl in parsley. Spoon sauce over chicken and serve immediately.

PEPPERY CHICKEN PICCATA

Follow recipe for Chicken Piccata, adding ½ teaspoon coarsely ground black peppercorns along with lemon juice and capers.

CHICKEN PICCATA WITH PROSCIUTTO

Follow recipe for Chicken Piccata, adding 2 ounces thinly sliced prosciutto, cut into pieces 1 inch long and ¼ inch wide, along with shallot or garlic and sauté just until prosciutto is lightly crisped, about 45 seconds.

CHICKEN PICCATA WITH BLACK OLIVES

Follow recipe for Chicken Piccata, adding ¼ cup pitted and chopped black olives along with lemon juice and capers.

Crisp and Tender Thin-Crust Pizza

Giving the dough a long refrigerator rise and baking the crust directly on parchment paper produce a no-stick, crackling crisp pizza with big flavor.

⇒ BY KAY RENTSCHLER ⇐

I n my opinion, a good pizza can be defined largely by what it is not. A good pizza is not puffy white bread under a sea of tomato sauce or tough cardboard stamped into a circle. It is not a mountainous antipasto glued to blistering cheese. A good pizza is not damp, molten, saucy, messy, or bready.

What it is, however, is something both simpler and more complicated than any of the above, something well worth spending some time in the kitchen to achieve. What remains after everything else drops away is a slice of postmodern minimalism: a shatteringly crisp, wafer-thin crust with a deeply caramelized flavor that bears no trace of raw yeast or flour and toppings that are sleek, light, and off the charts in flavor.

Ease, Heat, and Rest

One thing I knew was that this dough must not only taste remarkably good, it must be easy to produce and cooperative as well. Pizza is casual fare and should shape up easily. My first inclination, therefore, was to advance to the food processor and give it a whirl against the standing mixer and hand methods. It buried the competition for ease and speed, producing gorgeous, supple doughs in about 30 seconds, or faster than you could say "large pepperoni."

I was keen to make a big, free-form pizza, and I knew that a thin crust would need every bit of conventional oven heat it could get in the 10 minutes or so it would take to bake. That meant 500 degrees and a giant pizza stone with an hour's head start to preheat. (Though I tested a slightly lower oven heat as well, the extra minutes the pizza needed to brown left the finished crust more tough than crisp.) Wanting the crackerlike simplicity of a rich burnished crust to prevail, I dressed the pizzas with sauce and mozzarella only.

A handful of the pizza recipes I reviewed offered ideas that contributed significantly to the success of my future recipe. Overnight fermentation (the dough's first long rise) in the refrigerator was a key first precept. The finished dough is put to bed in chilly quarters—where it rises at its leisure—and is then stretched and baked the following day. Granted, this approach removes home pizza making from the world of whimsy and impulse, but the fact that the dough was so easy to handle and the baked pizza so flavorful and crisp more than made up for the delay.

To our great surprise, we found that a dough about the size of an apple could be stretched to a crackling 14-inch disk.

By letting the dough rest overnight, I was able to use less yeast and gain more flavor from fermentation. The chilled, rested dough also handled easily, having become pliant and less sticky in the intervening hours. Even better, I could toss the dough into the fridge and forget about it altogether until the next day—I didn't need to wait around to punch it down after a two- or three-hour rise at room temperature. By using warm water to process the dough, the yeast got enough of a jump to take off in the cold climate of the refrigerator; the refrigerated dough holds for up to two days without depleting the energy of just one-half teaspoon of yeast.

The second precept was that a soft, supple, and frankly moist dough produces a light, crisp crust.

This proved true time after time. Surprisingly, and to my everlasting relief, moist doughs were also easier to work with than drier ones.

Stick with Me, Baby

Having long been a fan of the neo-Neapolitan-style pizza, which is just a couple of hairs thinner than the original thin-crust pizza of Naples, I knew the only instrument equal to the task of achieving a crust as thin as a credit card was a rolling pin. Armed with my overnight-rested, food-processor dough and a tapered French rolling pin, I dusted a large sheet of parchment paper lightly with flour and commenced rolling as one would with a pie.

The dough was fully compliant under the pin until I made an effort to turn it like a regular pie dough. At that point, the dough gripped the parchment for dear life. Though thinner and wider it rolled, I could not shake it loose. A potentially maddening situation morphed into a saving grace when I realized the parchment could accompany the dough to the oven. As the pizza baked, it loosened from the paper automatically, and the stone remained clean. Best yet, the tackiness of the dough against the parchment prevented the dough from springing and shrinking back, eliminating the need for excess flouring when rolling out. Eventually, I refined this technique by positioning an 18-inch piece of plastic wrap directly onto the top surface of the dough during rolling. Thus insulated, the dough could be rolled effortlessly and flipped about like a sandwich. It did not dry out. Once the dough was rolled, the plastic wrap peeled off like a post-vacation sunburn; the thin round could be dressed and hurried into the oven without further ado.

Weights and Measures

While Americans have a propensity for using high-protein flour in breads, my research indicated that Italians use fairly soft flour. Here at the magazine, King Arthur all-purpose is generally the test kitchen's flour of choice. A fairly strong all-purpose flour with no chemical additives, King Arthur all-purpose has the light yellow color associated with unbleached, untampered-with flour. Its flavor is outstanding. I had been using it throughout testing, occasionally in combination with softer flours such as cake or rye to lighten the dough (these flour combinations produced unexceptional pizzas). But doughs made exclusively with King Arthur were occasionally less than cracker-crisp, especially during damp weather. At the suggestion of Maggie Glezer, a baker certified by the American Institute of Baking and a wizard with yeast, I switched from King Arthur all-purpose flour at 11.7 percent protein to Gold Medal unbleached all-purpose

Topping Options

A thin crust cannot bear the weight and water of raw vegetables or a stifling canopy of cheese. During their stay in the oven, crust and topping must become one, sustaining temperatures that drive off moisture as they toast the crust mahogany, bake the sauce to a lacquer, and graft cheese to the top. What this means is that moisture is the natural enemy of a thin-crust pizza, and it is best to avoid watery or uncooked vegetables in toppings. Instead, try putting one, two, or three of these options on your pizza:

BEFORE BAKING: Caramelized onions; roasted mushrooms; roasted bell pepper strips.
AFTER BAKING: Goat cheese medallions; thin layer of pesto; tapenade. —K.R.

flour at 10.5 percent protein. Flours with a higher protein content require more vigorous kneading to create structure in the dough and more water to achieve proper hydration. The lower-protein Gold Medal flour yielded uniformly light doughs that were as full-flavored as those made with King Arthur.

Working initially with measures of volume—2 cups flour to ¾ cup water—the results became unpredictable enough to convince me to switch to weights. I discovered stunning discrepancies between liquid measuring cups at that volume (up to a tablespoon), and with my meager dough ball, a few drops of water more or less made quite an impact.

A final note or two. Force of habit persuaded me to transfer the hot, sliced pizza to a cooling rack. Though the pizza seldom survived long enough to underscore the merits of this method, on the occasions that it did, the air circulating under the crust kept it crisp. In fact, the crusts generally became more crisp a few minutes after being removed from the oven—like a cookie might. And although a 14-inch pizza may sound

extra *lahge*, as they say in Boston, one of these will satisfy only two restrained, polite adults. So serve them as snacks, as appetizers, make two, make a salad.

CRISP THIN-CRUST PIZZA
MAKES TWO 14-INCH PIZZAS

All-purpose unbleached flour with a protein percentage no higher than 10.5 makes the lightest, crispiest pizzas. We recommend weighing the flour and water, but because many factors affect the flour's capacity to absorb water, heed visual and tactile clues to achieve a dough with the proper consistency. For rolling out the dough, we prefer commercial-sized parchment paper sheets (see Resources, page 32, for mail-order sources), though parchment sold in rolls 14 inches wide also works. Keep in mind that it is more important for the rolled dough to be of even thinness than to be a perfect circle. For topping the pizzas, we recommend buying a chunk of whole milk mozzarella and shredding it by hand; do not use fresh or prepackaged shredded mozzarella, and resist the temptation to sprinkle on more cheese than is recommended. Between baking pizzas, allow the baking stone to reheat for 15 minutes.

10	ounces (about 2 cups) unbleached all-purpose flour, preferably Gold Medal, protein content no higher than 10.5 percent
½	teaspoon instant yeast
½	teaspoon honey
½	teaspoon salt
6.2	ounces (about ¾ cup plus 1½ teaspoons) water, preferably filtered or spring, 100 to 105 degrees
¼	cup olive oil
1	cup Quick Tomato Sauce for Pizza (see page 10)
10	ounces whole milk mozzarella, shredded (about 2 cups)

TESTING | HOW TO ACHIEVE THE PROPER DOUGH CONSISTENCY

A freshly processed dough with adequate water will look shaggy and stick to the counter. A few "throws" against the counter will help the dough become supple and fine-textured.

On the other hand, a freshly processed dough that is too dry will form a clean ball, feel more oily than moist, and look slightly curdy on the surface.

To moisten a processed dough that is too dry, add 1 teaspoon water and throw the dough against the counter 10 times. The dough may take up to 2 teaspoons additional water.

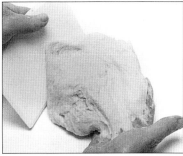

A properly kneaded dough with enough water will be supple and fine-textured. Though moist and sticky, the dough should have structure and not feel "batter-like."

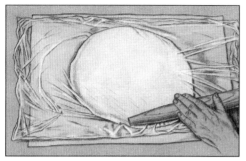

1. Once the dough is about 8 inches in diameter, use the rolling pin as illustrated to stretch and feather the dough.

2. If the parchment wrinkles, flip the dough sandwich over and smooth the wrinkles with a metal dough scraper.

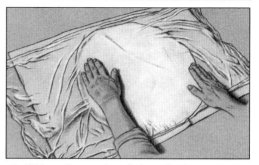

3. Glide a palm over the rolled-out dough to get a sense of its evenness.

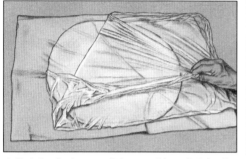

4. Peel the plastic wrap off the top of the rolled dough.

5. Use a soup spoon to smooth ½ cup sauce to the edges of the dough.

6. Slide the pizza, parchment and all, onto the pizza stone.

Day 1

1. Combine flour, yeast, honey, and salt in workbowl of food processor fitted with steel blade. With machine running, add all but 2 tablespoons water through feed tube. With machine still running, add olive oil through feed tube and process until dough forms a ball, about 30 seconds. Turn dough out onto work surface. See "How to Achieve the Proper Consistency," page 9, to see if dough needs more water and to finish kneading.

2. Place dough in gallon-sized, heavy-duty zipper-lock plastic bag and seal. Refrigerate overnight or up to 48 hours.

Day 2

1. Adjust oven rack to lowest position, set baking stone on rack, and heat oven to 500 degrees. Heat baking stone 1 hour before proceeding.

2. Remove dough from plastic bag and divide in half with pastry scraper. Set each half in center of lightly floured large sheet parchment paper. Cover each with two 18-inch lengths plastic wrap overlapping in center (alternatively, use one 18-inch length of extrawide plastic wrap); let doughs rest 10 minutes.

3. Setting one dough aside, follow illustrations 1 through 3 to roll one dough into 14-inch round with even thinness of 1/32 inch, using tackiness of dough against parchment to help roll.

4. Following illustrations 4 and 5, peel off plastic wrap, sauce dough, then sprinkle with about 1 cup cheese. With scissors, trim excess parchment so that it is just larger than dough.

5. Slip dough with parchment onto pizza peel, inverted rimmed baking sheet, or rimless cookie sheet, then, following illustration 6, slide onto hot baking stone. Bake until deep golden brown, about 10 minutes. Remove from oven with pizza peel or pull parchment with pizza onto baking sheet. Transfer pizza to cutting board, slide parchment out from under pizza; cut pizza into wedges and slide onto wire rack. Let cool 2 minutes until crisp; serve.

6. While first pizza is baking, repeat steps 1 through 5 to roll and sauce second pizza; allow baking stone to reheat 15 minutes after baking first pizza, then repeat step 6 to bake second pizza.

Thin-Crust Pizza on Hold

Our recipe makes two rail-thin 14-inch pizzas. If you're hungry for just one pizza, make the full recipe anyway. Roll out both doughs, but roll one of them to 15 inches. Dress the dough rolled to the standard 14 inches with sauce and topping and bake it; poke the larger dough everywhere with a fork, but leave it undressed. Bake the undressed dough on the stone for 2 minutes, then remove it from the parchment and cool it on a rack. (The dough will look like a large flour tortilla and will have shrunk to 14 inches.) Wrap well and freeze on a baking sheet (yes, it is pretty big, but the sheet can be balanced on top of other frozen goods). When you're in the mood for pizza, heat up the stone for an hour, defrost and dress the frozen dough, slide it onto parchment, and bake it for nine minutes. The pizzas done this way were so good our tasters could not distinguish them from the fresh. A frozen disk will keep nicely for up to three weeks in the freezer—but can you wait that long to have another? —K.R.

QUICK TOMATO SAUCE FOR PIZZA
MAKES ABOUT 1½ CUPS

We adapted this pizza sauce from a recipe in the May/June 1995 issue of *Cook's* simply by processing the tomatoes to create a smoother sauce. Note that this recipe makes a bit more sauce than needed to sauce two thin-crust pizzas.

- 1 can (14.5 ounces) crushed tomatoes
- 1 large garlic clove, minced or pressed through garlic press
- 1 tablespoon olive oil
  Salt and ground black pepper

1. Process tomatoes in workbowl of food processor fitted with steel blade until smooth, about five 1-second pulses.

2. Heat garlic and oil in medium saucepan over medium heat until garlic is sizzling, about 40 seconds. Stir in tomatoes; bring to simmer and cook, uncovered, until sauce thickens enough to coat wooden spoon, about 15 minutes. Season to taste with salt and pepper.

Winter Pestos

When fresh basil is out of season, use arugula, nuts, mushrooms, or even roasted peppers to make a quick, full-flavored pesto.

⇒ BY JULIA COLLIN ⇐

I have been known to be impatient, which is why I like pesto. A quick whiz around the food processor with a bunch of herbs, a little garlic, and some olive oil, and you have a fragrant sauce that can transform plain pasta, chicken, or toasted bread into something fresh and flavorful. Over the years, the traditional pesto, a hand-pounded basil and garlic sauce from the Italian province of Liguria, has succumbed to modern appliances and a broader range of ingredients. The term *pesto* now refers not only to basil but to a multitude of pureed, oil-based sauces. Many of them—including all of the sauces here—have the advantage of using ingredients available in the dead of winter, when fresh basil can be scarce.

In a previous article ("Pesto at Its Best," July/August 1996), we found the food processor to be the fastest way to produce a consistently good basil pesto. Three keys to a flavorful sauce included bruising the basil prior to pureeing, using extra-virgin olive oil, and finely grating a high-quality Parmesan. My fellow tasters and I found all three of these rules to hold true with these winter pestos, and we added one of our own: Use toasted garlic rather than raw. Its mellowed and slightly sweetened flavor pairs better with the heartier flavors of toasted nuts and roasted vegetables.

Note that when adding any pesto to cooked pasta it is important to include three or four tablespoons of the cooked pasta water for proper consistency and even distribution. These pestos can be kept in the refrigerator for up to three days if they are covered with a sheet of plastic wrap or a thin film of oil. All recipes make about 1½ cups, enough to sauce one pound of cooked and drained pasta.

ARUGULA AND RICOTTA PESTO

- 3   medium unpeeled garlic cloves
- ¼   cup pine nuts, walnuts, or almonds
- 1   cup packed fresh arugula leaves, washed and dried thoroughly
- 1   cup packed fresh parsley leaves, washed and dried thoroughly
- 7   tablespoons extra-virgin olive oil
- ⅓   cup ricotta cheese
- 2   tablespoons finely grated Parmesan
      Salt and ground black pepper

1. Toast garlic in small dry skillet over medium heat, shaking pan occasionally, until softened and spotty brown, about 8 minutes; when cool, remove and discard skins. While garlic cools, toast nuts in skillet over medium heat, stirring frequently, until golden and fragrant, 4 to 5 minutes.

2. Place arugula and parsley in heavy-duty, quart-sized, zipper-lock plastic bag; bruise all leaves with meat pounder.

3. In workbowl of food processor fitted with steel blade, process garlic, nuts, arugula, parsley, and oil until smooth, stopping as necessary to scrape down sides of bowl. Transfer mixture to small bowl and stir in cheeses; season to taste with salt and pepper.

MUSHROOM PESTO WITH PARSLEY AND THYME

- 10   ounces white mushrooms, sliced ¼-inch thick
- 9   tablespoons extra-virgin olive oil
      Salt and ground black pepper
- 3   medium unpeeled garlic cloves
- ½   ounce dried porcini mushrooms, rehydrated in ½ cup boiling water until softened, about 5 minutes, hydrating liquid strained through damp paper towel–lined sieve and reserved
- 1   small shallot, chopped coarse
- 1   tablespoon fresh thyme leaves
- ¼   cup packed parsley leaves, washed and dried thoroughly
- ¼   cup finely grated Parmesan

1. Adjust oven rack to lowest position and heat oven to 450 degrees; line rimmed baking sheet with heavy-duty foil. Toss sliced mushrooms with 2 tablespoons oil and salt and pepper in medium bowl; spread evenly on prepared baking sheet. Roast, stirring occasionally, until browned and crisp, about 25 minutes.

2. Meanwhile, toast garlic in small dry skillet over medium heat, shaking pan occasionally, until softened and spotty brown, about 8 minutes; when cool, remove and discard skins.

3. In workbowl of food processor fitted with steel blade, process roasted mushrooms, garlic, porcini and liquid, shallot, thyme, parsley and remaining 7 tablespoons oil until smooth, stopping as necessary to scrape down sides of bowl. Transfer mixture to small bowl and stir in cheese; season to taste with salt and pepper.

TOASTED NUT AND PARSLEY PESTO

- 3   medium unpeeled garlic cloves
- 1   cup pecans, walnuts, whole blanched almonds, skinned hazelnuts, unsalted pistachios, or pine nuts, or any combination thereof
- ¼   cup packed fresh parsley leaves, washed and dried thoroughly
- 7   tablespoons extra-virgin olive oil
- ¼   cup finely grated Parmesan
      Salt and ground black pepper

1. Toast garlic in small dry skillet over medium heat, shaking pan occasionally, until softened and spotty brown, about 8 minutes; when cool, remove and discard skins.

2. Toast nuts in medium dry skillet over medium heat, stirring frequently, until golden and fragrant, 4 to 5 minutes.

3. In workbowl of food processor fitted with steel blade, process garlic, nuts, parsley, and oil until smooth, stopping as necessary to scrape down sides of bowl. Transfer mixture to small bowl and stir in cheese; season to taste with salt and pepper.

ROASTED RED PEPPER PESTO

- 2   medium red bell peppers, roasted, peeled, and cut into rough 2-inch pieces
- 3   medium unpeeled garlic cloves
- 1   small shallot, chopped coarse
- 1   tablespoon fresh thyme leaves
- ¼   cup packed parsley leaves, washed and dried thoroughly
- 7   tablespoons extra-virgin olive oil
- ¼   cup finely grated Parmesan
      Salt and ground black pepper

1. Toast garlic in small dry skillet over medium heat, shaking pan occasionally, until softened and spotty brown, about 8 minutes; when cool enough to handle, remove and discard skins.

2. In workbowl of food processor fitted with steel blade, process peppers, garlic, shallot, thyme, parsley, and oil until smooth, stopping as necessary to scrape down sides of bowl. Transfer mixture to small bowl and stir in cheese; season to taste with salt and pepper.

The Best Beef Burgundy

The essence of this hearty French beef stew is flavor, and lots of it. The secrets?
Use the right cut of meat, salt pork, and a brown roux; forget canned beef stock;
and buy the best bottle of wine you can afford.

⇒ BY DAWN YANAGIHARA ⇐

If the Louvre were just a museum, then *boeuf à la bourguignonne* might be just beef stew. Both are French and utterly extraordinary, but only one can be enjoyed at home. But boeuf à la bourguignonne is not, as it is sometimes claimed, highfalutin' French cuisine—it's comforting, comfortable regional French fare. Its relation to American beef stew lies in its common ingredients and similar preparation, and perhaps it is for this reason that it is often esteemed no higher and that it is frequently met with gastronomic ennui, at least in this country. But there are definite differences. Beef stew is served in a bowl and eaten with a spoon; boeuf à la bourguignonne (hereafter referred to as beef Burgundy) is served in a soup plate and eaten with a fork.

In fact, I liken beef Burgundy more to a fabulous prime steak napped with a rich, silken red wine reduction sauce than to a mundane beef stew. The beef in beef Burgundy is cut into satisfyingly large chunks that become utterly tender. Their braising liquid, brimming with voluptuous wine and infused with aromatic vegetables, garlic, and herbs, is finessed into a sauce of burgundy velvet studded with mushrooms and pearl onions. Beef Burgundy is earthy, big, robust, warm, and welcoming in a brooding sort of way.

At least that's what it is at its best. I have had versions that fell far short of this, with tough meat or a dull sauce with no flavor complexity. I wanted to find a way to bring this classic dish to its full potential in a home kitchen.

Charting the Course

Nearly every basic French cookbook or general cookbook in the French vein contains a recipe for beef Burgundy. They are much alike. Aromatic vegetables (onions and carrots), red wine, stock, herbs, mushrooms, and pearl onions are all requisite ingredients; their combinations and proportions and the variations in preparation and technique are where the recipes diverge.

Rich, dark, and deeply flavored, beef Burgundy may be the ultimate beef stew.

I started by completing four recipes, and from these four I deduced a couple of things. First, marinating the beef in the red wine and herbs that will later go into the braise—a common recommendation in recipes—does not improve the flavor of the cooked meat. Second, the braising liquid requires straining to rid it of bits of aromatic vegetables and herbs so that it may become a silky sauce. I found that bundling in cheesecloth all the goods that must eventually come out of the pot made their extraction possible in one easy step. When wrapped in cheesecloth, however, the aromatic vegetables cannot first be sautéed—a customary step, the omission of which I feared would adversely affect the flavors of the braise. Remarkably, it did not. But perhaps this is why it took such generous amounts of chopped onions, carrots, and garlic as well as parsley, thyme, peppercorns, and bay leaves to create a balanced mélange of flavors.

The cut of beef best suited to the long braise of beef Burgundy is a chuck roast. It's the cut that almost every recipe calls for and the one we at *Cook's* also preferred in a regular beef stew because of its rich, meaty flavor (see "Simple, Satisfying Beef

Stew," January/ February 1996). Because the beef in a beef Burgundy is cut into chunks larger than those in a beef stew—a good 1½ to 2 inches—I found it necessary to take extra care to trim off as much fat and silver skin as possible; larger pieces of beef also mean larger, more detectable bites of these undesirables. Spurred by a few comments that the beef chunks were too large, I cut them smaller, but these smaller pieces were not as satisfying and the dish lost its substance. The focus on beef and sauce became blurred, and the braise began to resemble a less interesting beef stew.

Pork, Stock, and Wine

Each and every beef Burgundy begins with either salt pork or bacon cut into lardons, or small strips, and fried to a crisp; the fat that results is used to brown the beef chunks. The crisped pork is added to the pot to simmer alongside the beef so that it may relinquish its flavors to the braise, providing a subtle, sweet underpinning and lending the sauce roundness and depth. I tried both bacon and salt pork and favored the cleaner, purer, more honest flavor of salt pork; the smoke and sugar in bacon—irresistible with eggs in the morning—were unwelcome. Moreover, the thicker, more toothsome strips of salt pork had better texture than the lifeless, thin pieces of bacon. Salt pork can be a challenge to find in grocery stores, so I reasoned that just as blanching salt pork removes excess salt that would otherwise crystallize on the surface during frying, blanching thick-cut bacon ought to calm the smoke and sugar and make it appropriate for beef Burgundy. This worked well. The thick-cut bacon had more textural appeal than regular bacon. Like my tasters in the test kitchen, I considered blanched thick-cut bacon a suitable substitute for salt pork.

As for the stock that goes into the braise, most recipes call for beef, preferably homemade. Just about no one has or makes homemade beef stock, and from our experience at *Cook's* I knew that canned beef broth would not make an acceptable

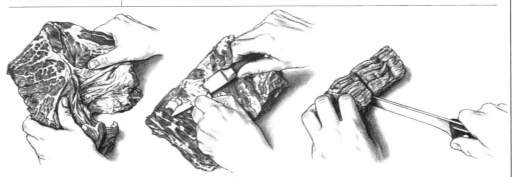

1. Pull apart the roast at its major seams (delineated by lines of fat and silver skin). Use a knife as necessary.

2. With a paring knife, trim off all visible fat and silver skin.

3. Cut the meat into large chunks measuring about 1 ½ to 2 inches.

substitute (see "Tasting Beef Broth," January/February 1998). Therefore, in all subsequent tests, I used what we have found to be the next best option—canned chicken broth—with excellent results. Still, beef Burgundy necessitates a good amount of liquid for braising, and too much chicken broth just tasted too chickeny. Water was a fine filler, especially since the braising liquid is later reduced to create the sauce. I then tried something a bit unorthodox to boost flavor. Just a small amount of dried porcini mushrooms wrapped into the cheesecloth package brought the meatiness and savory quality that homemade beef broth would conceivably have added. A modicum of tomato paste added color and sprightliness.

Wine was the next issue. Beef Burgundy does not exist without a healthy dose of it. I concluded after several batches that anything less than a whole bottle left the sauce lacking and unremarkable. After numerous experiments, I had determined that a Burgundy, or at least a decent Pinot Noir, is indeed the wine of choice (see "Does It Have to Be Burgundy?" page 14). Though most recipes indicate that all of the wine should be added at the outset, one recipe, as well as one wine expert, recommended saving just a bit of the wine to add at the very end, just before serving. This late embellishment of raw wine vastly improved the sauce, brightening its flavor, giving it resonance, and making it sing.

Midway through testing, I decided I needed an alternative to browning the meat in the Dutch oven, where it would eventually be braised. Browning in batches took too long, and the drippings, or *fond*, that are essential flavor providers frequently burned. Evidently, the small cooking surface of even a large Dutch oven was a liability. I took to browning the beef in two batches in a heavy, large 12-inch skillet. To keep the fond from going to waste, I deglazed the pan with a bit of water and poured it directly into the braising pot, where it would eventually marry with the broth and wine.

Next I went to work to find the best means of adding flour to thicken the braising liquid that

must blossom into a velvety sauce. Tossing the beef in flour before browning interfered with the color the beef could attain and ultimately affected its flavor. Tossing the flour into the browned beef and cooking until the flour took on some color was imprecise and messy, especially since browning was now taking place in a separate skillet. I found it preferable to make a roux right in the skillet and add broth and water to it, then have it join the beef, wine, and vegetable and herb bouquet in the braising pot. This afforded me the opportunity to cook the roux until it achieved a toasty brown color, which made a favorable impact on the flavor of the dish.

With everything assembled in the Dutch oven, into the oven it went, where the constant, all-encompassing heat produced an even simmer that required little attention. This was the time to prepare the mushrooms and pearl onions, both of which would later join the sauce. Peeling fresh pearl onions is a nuisance, but opening a bag isn't. I embraced already-peeled frozen pearl onions that, contrary to expectations, are not inferior in flavor or texture to fresh when browned, as they are when boiled. A brisk simmer in a skillet with some water, butter, and sugar, and then a quick sauté with the mushrooms created glazed beauties that were ready to grace the sauce. The final flourish was a swish of brandy that added richness and warmth to an already magnificent boeuf à la bourguignonne.

If you cannot find salt pork, thick-cut bacon can be substituted. Cut it crosswise into ¼-inch pieces and treat it just as you would salt pork, but note that you will have no rind to include in the vegetable and herb bouquet. To make this dish a day or two in advance, see "Advance Preparation of Beef Burgundy" (page 14). Boiled potatoes are the traditional accompaniment, but mashed potatoes or buttered noodles are nice as well.

Beef Braise

- 6 ounces salt pork, trimmed of rind (see below), rind reserved, and salt pork cut into ¼ inch by ¼ inch by 1-inch pieces
- 10 sprigs fresh parsley, torn into quarters
- 6 sprigs fresh thyme
- 2 medium onions, chopped coarse
- 2 medium carrots, chopped coarse
- 1 medium garlic head, cloves separated and crushed but unpeeled
- 2 bay leaves, crumbled
- ½ teaspoon black peppercorns
- ½ ounce dried porcini mushrooms, rinsed (optional)
- 4-4¼ pounds beef chuck roast, prepared according illustrations 1 to 3 (above)
  Salt and ground black pepper
- 4 tablespoons unsalted butter, cut into 4 pieces
- ⅓ cup all-purpose flour
- 1¾ cups canned low-sodium chicken broth
- 1 bottle (750 ml) wine, red Burgundy or Pinot Noir
- 1 teaspoon tomato paste

Onion and Mushroom Garnish

- 36 frozen pearl onions (about 7 ounces)
- 1 tablespoon unsalted butter
- 1 tablespoon sugar
- ½ teaspoon salt
- 10 ounces white mushrooms, whole if small, halved if medium, quartered if large

- 2 tablespoons brandy
- 3 tablespoons minced fresh parsley leaves

1. Bring salt pork, reserved salt pork rind, and 3 cups water to boil in medium saucepan over high heat. Boil 2 minutes, then drain well.

2. Cut two 22-inch lengths cheesecloth. Following illustrations 1 to 3 on page 14, wrap parsley, thyme, onions, carrots, garlic, bay leaves, peppercorns, porcini mushrooms, and blanched salt pork rind in cheesecloth and set in 8-quart nonreactive Dutch oven. Adjust oven rack to lower-middle position and heat oven to 300 degrees.

3. Set 12-inch skillet with salt pork over medium heat; sauté until lightly brown and crisp, about 12 minutes. Remove with slotted spoon to Dutch oven; pour off all but 2 teaspoons fat and

Steady the salt pork with one hand, and with the other slide the blade of a sharp chef's knife between the rind and the fat, using a wide sawing motion to cut away the rind in one piece.

reserve. Season beef with salt and pepper. Increase heat to high and brown half of beef in single layer, turning once or twice, until deep brown, about 7 minutes; transfer browned beef to Dutch oven. Pour ½ cup water into skillet and scrape pan with wooden spoon to loosen browned bits; when pan bottom is clean, pour liquid into Dutch oven.

4. Return skillet to high heat and add 2 teaspoons reserved pork fat; swirl to coat pan bottom. When fat begins to smoke, brown remaining beef in single layer, turning once or twice, until deep brown, about 7 minutes; transfer browned beef to Dutch oven. Pour ½ cup water into skillet and scrape pan with wooden spoon to loosen browned bits; when pan bottom is clean, pour liquid into Dutch oven.

5. Set now-empty skillet over medium heat; add butter. When foaming subsides, whisk in flour until evenly moistened and pasty. Cook, whisking constantly, until mixture has toasty aroma and resembles light-colored peanut butter, about 5 minutes. Gradually whisk in chicken broth and 1½ cups water; increase heat to medium-high and bring to simmer, stirring frequently, until thickened. Pour mixture into Dutch oven. Add 3 cups wine, tomato paste, and salt and pepper to taste to Dutch oven and stir to combine. Set Dutch oven over high heat and bring to boil. Cover and set pot in oven; cook until meat is tender, 2½ to 3 hours.

6. Remove Dutch oven from oven and, using tongs, transfer vegetable and herb bouquet to strainer set over pot. Press out liquid into pot and discard bouquet. With slotted spoon, remove beef to medium bowl; set aside. Allow braising liquid to settle about 15 minutes, then, with wide shallow spoon, skim fat off surface and discard.

7. Bring liquid in Dutch oven to boil over medium-high heat. Simmer briskly, stirring occasionally to ensure that bottom is not burning, until sauce is reduced to about 3 cups and thickened to the consistency of heavy cream, 15 to 25 minutes.

8. While sauce is reducing, bring pearl onions, butter, sugar, ¼ teaspoon salt, and ½ cup water

to boil in medium skillet over high heat; cover and reduce heat to medium-low and simmer, shaking pan occasionally, until onions are tender, about 5 minutes. Uncover, increase heat to high, and simmer until all liquid evaporates, about 3 minutes. Add mushrooms and ¼ teaspoon salt; cook, stirring occasionally, until liquid released by mushrooms evaporates and vegetables are browned and glazed, about 5 minutes. Transfer vegetables to large plate and set aside. Add ¼ cup water to skillet and stir with wooden spoon to loosen browned bits. When pan bottom and sides are clean, add liquid to reducing sauce.

9. When sauce has reduced to about 3 cups and thickened to the consistency of heavy cream, reduce heat to medium-low; stir in beef, mushrooms and onions (and any accumulated juices), remaining wine from bottle, and brandy into Dutch oven. Cover pot and cook until just heated through, 5 to 8 minutes. Adjust seasonings with salt and pepper and serve, sprinkling individual servings with minced parsley.

ADVANCE PREPARATION OF BEEF BURGUNDY

The braise can be made a day or two ahead, and the sauce, along with the onion and mushroom garnish, can be completed the day you intend to serve.

1. Follow recipe for beef Burgundy through step 5. Using tongs, transfer vegetable and herb bouquet to mesh strainer set over Dutch oven. Press out liquid back into pot and discard bouquet. Let beef cool to room temperature in braising liquid in Dutch oven, then cover and refrigerate 1 to 2 days.

2. With slotted spoon, skim congealed fat off top and discard. Set pot over medium-high heat and bring to simmer; with slotted spoon remove beef to medium bowl and set aside. Simmer sauce briskly, stirring occasionally to ensure that bottom is not burning, until reduced to about 3 cups and thickened to the consistency of heavy cream.

3. Continue with recipe from step 8.

Does It Have to Be Burgundy?

Beef burgundy is rightfully made with true Burgundy wine. This means a red wine made from the Pinot Noir grape grown in the French province of Burgundy. Characteristically, these wines are medium-bodied but also deep, rich, and complex, with earthy tones and a reticent fruitiness. They are also expensive. Throughout my testing, into each batch of beef Burgundy, I emptied a $12 bottle of Burgundy—the least expensive I could find. Quite frankly, it was making outstanding beef Burgundies. Nonetheless, I tried more costly, higher-quality Burgundies and found that they bettered the dish—a $30 bottle gave a stellar, rousing performance. I thought it worth exploring other wines, but, wanting to remain faithful to the spirit of the dish, I limited myself to Pinot Noirs made on the West Coast of the United States, which are

$30 French Burgundy $9 California Pinot Noir

slightly less expensive than Burgundies. I made beef Burgundies with domestic Pinot Noirs of three different price points, and even the least expensive wine—a $9 bottle—was perfectly acceptable, although its flavors were simpler and less intriguing than those of its Burgundian counterpart.

Both the Burgundies and Pinot Noirs exhibited the same pattern—that is, as the price of the wine increased, so did the depth, complexity, and roundness of the sauce. I can advise with some confidence to set your price, then seek out a wine—either Burgundy or Pinot Noir—that matches it. But if your allegiance is to a true Burgundy, be warned that they can be difficult to find because production is relatively limited. I also caution you to beware of several very inexpensive mass-produced wines from California of questionable constitutions that are sold as "Burgundy." They are usually made from a blend of grape varieties, and whether or not they actually contain so much as a drop of Pinot Noir is a mystery. I made a beef burgundy with one of these "Burgundy" wines as well, and it resulted in a fleeting, one-dimensional, fruity, sweet sauce that, though palatable, lacked the deep, lavish flavors I have come to expect in a beef Burgundy. —D.Y.

STEP-BY-STEP | MAKING THE VEGETABLE AND HERB BOUQUET

1. Cut two 22-inch lengths of cheesecloth and unfold each piece once lengthwise so that each forms a 2-ply, 22 by 8-inch piece.

2. Lay the cheesecloth in a medium bowl, stacking the sheets. Place the designated ingredients in the cheesecloth-lined bowl.

3. Gather the edges of the cheesecloth securely and fasten with kitchen twine. Trim excess cheesecloth with scissors if necessary.

No-Fuss Roasted Carrots

With a broiler pan and a hot oven, you can produce perfectly cooked, caramelized roasted carrots in just 30 minutes.

≥ BY RAQUEL PELZEL ≤

Roasted carrots' sublime nature lies in their rustic charm. Simple, sweet, and pure, their perfectly caramelized outer layer gently gives way to a smooth, tender interior—unless they are undercooked and have a crisp, bitter center or, on the opposite end of the spectrum, are subjected to such intense heat that they become wan, limp, and utterly unpalatable.

My ideal roasted carrot recipe, I decided, would be one that let me throw a couple of ingredients together, toss the carrots into the oven, and let them roast until they were done—a simple and painless side dish. But I wasn't willing to settle for just any roasted carrot; it had to be inviting and pleasurable from start to finish, which included not waging war on the pan when it came time to clean up.

I started with the basic question of what type of carrot to use. I tested bunch carrots (those with greens still attached), bagged carrots, and bagged baby carrots. The bagged whole carrots were too toothy, fibrous, and bitter. Baby and bunch carrots were the best—sweet and tender. While the flavor and presentation of bunch carrots edged out the bagged babies (bunch carrots were breathtaking when roasted whole with just a nub of green stem left attached), the baby carrots needed no peeling, trimming, or chopping. They were effortless and easy, just what I had in mind. (See "What Are Those Babies?" at right).

Still, without a little help from a fatty cohort, I knew that the glossy, bronzed carrots I envisioned would not be possible. So I tossed batches of carrots with vegetable oil, olive oil, extra-virgin olive oil, butter, and clarified butter and roasted them. I was surprised to discover that my favorite was plain olive oil; it neither masked the carrots' sweetness, as did extra-virgin olive and vegetable oils, nor changed their texture, as did the butter.

Initially, I had been using pepper as well as salt to season the carrots prior to roasting; with a little more testing, I discovered that eliminating the pepper brightened the carrots' flavor. Next I lined up several varieties of salt, including table, kosher, and sea. While the sea salt had the cleanest flavor, the grains didn't distribute themselves evenly among the carrots, so in one bite the carrots would taste bland and in the next, salty. Kosher salt presented the same problem. I concluded that plain old table salt was the most reliable flavor enhancer.

Never to be underestimated in their importance, roasting method, time, and temperature did not escape intense scrutiny. I tried covering the broiler pan with foil to help keep the carrots moist and hasten the roasting, but when I pulled these carrots out from their sealed bed, they had become reminiscent of cafeteria carrots: slightly bitter, pale, and soggy. Carrots covered for only part of the roasting time fared little better. The best batch was the most straightforward: 475 degrees for 20 minutes, until the carrots were brown and caramel colored.

I wasn't done with this recipe yet, though. I proceeded to roast carrots in different sorts of pans to see which would give me the best color and the easiest cleanup. After pitting broiler-pan bottoms against cookie sheets and roasting pans against Pyrex glass dishes and nonstick aluminum pans, I found the broiler-pan bottom to be the best for browning the carrots without burning them. It also made for stress-free cleanup long after the carrots had been devoured.

SIMPLE ROASTED CARROTS
SERVES 8 AS A SIDE DISH

Inspect your bag of baby carrots carefully for pockets of water. Carrots taken from the top of the supermarket's carrot pile are often waterlogged. This not only makes carrots mealy, it also dashes any hopes of caramelization in the oven.

- 2 pounds baby carrots (two 16-ounce bags)
- 2 tablespoons olive oil
- 1/2 teaspoon salt

Adjust oven rack to middle position and heat oven to 475 degrees. Toss carrots, oil, and salt in broiler-pan bottom. Spread into single layer and roast 12 minutes. Shake pan to toss carrots; continue roasting about 8 minutes longer, shaking pan twice more, until carrots are browned and tender.

ROASTED MAPLE CARROTS WITH BROWNED BUTTER
SERVES 8 AS A SIDE DISH

Follow recipe for Simple Roasted Carrots, decreasing oil to 1½ teaspoons. After carrots have roasted 10 minutes, heat 1 tablespoon butter in small saucepan over medium heat, swirling occasionally, and simmer until deep gold, about 1 minute. Off heat, stir in 1 tablespoon maple syrup and drizzle mixture over carrots after 12 minutes of roasting; shake pan to coat, and continue roasting according to recipe.

ROASTED CARROTS WITH GINGER–ORANGE GLAZE
SERVES 8 AS A SIDE DISH

Follow recipe for Simple Roasted Carrots. After carrots have roasted 10 minutes, bring 1 heaping tablespoon orange marmalade, 1 tablespoon water, and ½ teaspoon grated fresh ginger to simmer in small saucepan over medium-high heat. Drizzle mixture over carrots after 12 minutes of roasting; shake pan to coat, and continue roasting according to recipe.

What Are Those Babies?

During testing, I came to wonder just what a baby carrot was. Although potentially misleading when applied to bagged baby carrots, the term baby refers to the carrots' size, not their age. Bagged baby carrots are made by taking long, thin carrots (usually carrot varieties grown for their high sugar and beta carotene content, which makes them sweet and bright in color) and forcing them through a carrot-trimming machine that peels the carrots and cuts them down to their ubiquitous baby size. Real baby carrots, however, are varieties of carrots that are miniature in size when mature; contrary to popular belief, they are not carrots of the standard length that are picked early. Unfortunately, most baby carrots are available only through specialty produce purveyors that sell to restaurants and other professional kitchens. If you are lucky enough to spy true, greens-still-attached, tapered baby carrots in your grocery store or farmer's market, buy them in the cooler months. Baby carrots harvested in the warmer spring and summer months tend to be less sweet and have more of a metallic, turpentine-like flavor. —R.P.

Uncommon Uses for Common Kitchen Tools

Learn some new ways to use six ordinary kitchen tools. BY RAQUEL PELZEL

Walk into a restaurant kitchen, or even the test kitchen here at *Cook's*, and you're apt to see tools being used for purposes that their manufacturers never imagined. It's all about efficiency—reaching for the tool that's going to get the job done the easiest way in the least time, with minimal searching through kitchen cabinets and drawers. In the interest of efficiency, we've found that several kitchen staples—a dish towel, vegetable peeler, microplane rasp, pair of tongs, metal dough scraper, scissors, and pastry blender—offer a bounty of uses besides the ordinary. We hope the tips in this guide help you to cook better, faster, and easier in your home kitchen.

TONGS

Tongs can be used for more than just flipping a steak on the grill or chicken breasts in a pan. We often use tongs as a more durable extension of our arm, whether for removing ramekins from a hot water bath, reaching for an ingredient on the top shelf of the cupboard, or rotating a cake during baking—the tongs can grab onto the lip of the cake pan, whereas a hand clad in a bulky oven mitt risks marring the surface of the cake. We also use tongs to remove hot pan lids (for this purpose, a long pair of tongs works best) and to steady a roast or large bird during carving.

ROTATING A CAKE

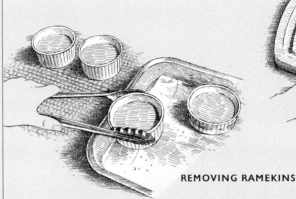

REMOVING RAMEKINS

STEADYING A ROAST

METAL DOUGH SCRAPER

You have probably seen these rectangular metal blades with plastic (or sometimes wood) handles in kitchen supply stores, but have you ever tried using one? Once you have, there's no turning back; it will become one of your most precious pieces of kitchen paraphernalia. We find a dough scraper incredibly handy for transferring chopped vegetables to a sauté pan, cutting butter quickly into small cubes, and cutting bar cookies or brownies. A scraper is also unmatched when it comes to cleaning up a sticky, doughy, work surface, the kind of mess that will ruin a sponge forever.

LIFTING CHOPPED VEGETABLES

CUTTING BUTTER

CLEANING A WORK SURFACE

VEGETABLE PEELER

A vegetable peeler can do more than peel potatoes. It's a handy tool for making thin slices of cheddar cheese for a grilled cheese sandwich, shaving coconut, and making thin ribbons of carrots, cucumbers, or Parmesan cheese, as shown here, to elegantly dress a salad.

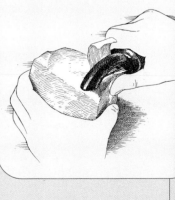

Illustration: John Burgoyne

DISH TOWEL

Dish towels, like T-shirts, seem to stack up in the closet until they reach skyscraper proportions. But don't throw your old ones away—they're good for a lot more than just drying dishes. For one, they can be used to line a pan that will be used as a hot-water bath for baking custards, a tactic that prevents the ramekins from sliding all over the place; another towel can be snaked around the ramekins so that they remain evenly separated and bake evenly. Double- or triple-folded dish towels can be used as potholders, and a dampened dish towel can be used to clean mushrooms or strawberries. A long, thin dish towel comes in handy when flipping a cake out of a still-warm pan, a task for which potholders sometimes seem too bulky. Any dish towel can be draped over a hot pan to alert others to its dangerous temperature, and a towel can also be used to absorb steam from rice just after it comes off the stove.

FLIPPING A CAKE

SECURING RAMEKINS

ABSORBING STEAM

MAKING GUACAMOLE

CHOPPING TOMATOES

PASTRY BLENDER

Since the introduction of the food processor, that old standby, the hand pastry blender, probably has not seen the light of day in your kitchen. But we find it useful for lots of kitchen duties, such as mashing avocados for guacamole, chopping eggs for salad, and chopping whole, canned tomatoes for a quick sauce.

SCISSORS

You might not consider them as such, but a pair of scissors can be a great kitchen tool. For pie dough, we use scissors to trim dough and cut vents in the top crust. We also use scissors to slice scallions quickly and thinly and to trim the woody stems from dried shiitake mushrooms. Scissors can also be used to cut phyllo dough for individual-sized appetizer portions, and to cut through hot pizza.

CUTTING PIZZA

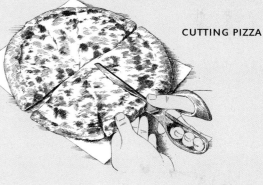

SNIPPING VENTS

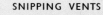

SLICING SCALLIONS

MICROPLANE RASP

In 1999 we tested the microplane-style rasp and found its ability to finely grate cheese unparalleled. We now find ourselves using it constantly for much more—from grating nutmeg and ginger to achieving a fine mince of shallot or garlic. We also like to use it to grate chocolate for a final decorative touch on a steaming cup of hot chocolate with whipped cream, as shown.

GRATING CHOCOLATE

How to Stir-Fry Shrimp

A simple shrimp broth boosts flavor, while a dash of cornstarch gives the sauce just the right body.

≥ BY ADAM RIED ≤

When it comes to shrimp, simpler is better. Streamlined classics such as shrimp cocktail, grilled shrimp, and stir-fried shrimp all come to mind. The benefits of stir-frying are compelling. Once the ingredients are ready, the actual cooking time is next to nothing. The method also makes the most of shrimp's sweet, delicate flavor, and it opens the door to many different sauce possibilities. But there are pitfalls, too, especially when it comes to the sauce. If it's too thin, the shrimp seem to slip right through it without picking up any flavor. On the other hand, overly thick sauces give a stir-fry a pasty, leaden quality. I favor a sauce thickened just enough to gently coat the shrimp, with a light mouthfeel and deep flavor. Of course, beyond the sauce, you also have to choose the best shrimp, prepare them properly, and cook them so as to optimize their flavor and texture.

Because the aromatics in this dish—garlic, ginger, and scallion—burn easily, we add them to the pan near the end of cooking.

Beyond the Peel

The recipes I researched recommended many different techniques for preparing the shrimp prior to cooking. I tried brining as well as successive salting and rinsing, but both methods made the shrimp too salty, especially with the soy sauce (which is salty, too) in the recipes. From there I moved on to—and eventually rejected—sprinkling the shrimp with salt and sugar, butterflying them fully (so that each shrimp was separated into halves connected only at the tail), and deveining while leaving the shells in place. Cooking the shrimp in their shells did seem to add flavor, but eating them this way required too much extra effort (and too many napkins).

In the end, I went with a partial butterfly, in which the peeled shrimp are cut along their backs just enough to remove their veins. Though we in the test kitchen are not a squeamish lot, we did not enjoy our occasional encounters with the large, gritty veins in these jumbo shrimp. With this method, the shrimp also flared open a tiny bit when they cooked, which made for an especially attractive, restaurant-style presentation.

Getting the Sauce Right

Most cooks know that stir-frying means cooking small bits of food very quickly over high heat in a skillet or wok, tossing or stirring them frequently to achieve even cooking. The key to successful stir-frying is intense heat that will evaporate the juices in the food quickly, promoting caramelization and concentration of flavors.

Fortunately, I had a head start from the kitchen testing done for previous *Cook's* articles on stir-frying. I knew, for instance, to choose a skillet over a wok because the flat surface of a skillet makes more efficient use of the heat generated by the flat burners on an American stove than does the rounded surface of a wok. I also knew to preheat the skillet long and hard before adding the food; to marinate the shrimp for the best flavor; and to add the aromatic seasonings—garlic, ginger, and scallion—at the very end of cooking to avoid burning them. Last, I knew that the shrimp shouldn't cook for more than about a minute before I began to build the sauce, lest they become overcooked and rubbery by the time the stir-fry was completed.

The wild card here was the composition of the sauce. Many recipes call for chicken stock as the base, while others favor water or even bottled clam juice. To that lineup, I added a very simple shrimp broth made by boiling the shells in water briefly, an idea inspired by the method for poaching shrimp in our July/August 1997 *Cook's* article "Building a Better Shrimp Cocktail." The tasters' favorite among these options was the sauce made with shrimp broth, which had the sweetest, fullest shrimp flavor. Their next favorite was the sauce made with water, which was the lightest and most aromatic, not to mention the easiest. Water was definitely the best substitute for shrimp broth.

Although we at *Cook's* generally don't use a thickener in stir-fries, I felt this dish called for one. But I was unsure about how much cornstarch to use and when to use it. With sauces based on ½ cup liquid, I tried as little as ½ teaspoon cornstarch right on up to 2 teaspoons, moving in increments of ¼ teaspoon. My tasters and I agreed that the sauce made with 1 teaspoon achieved just the light, silky consistency I was after.

When and how to add the cornstarch to the pan was another question. In some of the recipes I researched, the full amount was added to the marinade for the shrimp. Others split the amount between the shrimp marinade and the sauce ingredients, and some simply added all the cornstarch in a slurry to the sauce ingredients. Noted Chinese food expert, chef, and cookbook author Nina Simonds explained why the shrimp were sometimes marinated in some or all of the cornstarch. She said that cornstarch was meant to serve as a binder, in effect helping the marinade ingredients stick to the shrimp. Each time we tried this method, though, small bits of cornstarch that had failed to dissolve completely gelled on the shrimp and browned in the heat of the pan. Not only were these bits unattractive, their texture was gummy and unappealing. Adding more of the liquid marinade ingredients—soy sauce and sherry—was not the answer because their flavors then dominated, throwing the overall flavor of the stir-fry out of balance. In the end, the old standby method of adding the cornstarch last, along with the other liquid sauce ingredients, consistently provided quick, thorough, reliable, and easy thickening.

Shrimp Tales

With the basics of my sauce worked out, I turned to a quick study of the shrimp itself. As part of our shrimp cocktail article, we sampled all of the commonly available species of shrimp and declared Mexican Whites and Gulf Whites the best, followed by the ubiquitous Black Tigers. I repeated these tests and agreed with the conclusions. Almost 100 percent of the shrimp available to consumers is frozen right after being caught. In our earlier article, we recommended buying the shrimp still frozen, as do I. They needn't be used immediately, like thawed shrimp, and they defrost in just a couple of minutes under cold running water. With regard to shrimp size, the descriptors "small, medium, large, jumbo" and so forth are less precise than the numbers that tell you how many pieces of said shrimp it would take to make a pound. Shrimp labeled 21/25, indicating that 21 to 25 pieces equal one pound, were large, easy to peel, succulent to eat, and generous looking. Paired with a sauce that is deeply flavorful and softly thickened, these stir-fried shrimp are both easy and slightly decadent.

AROMATIC STIR–FRIED SHRIMP
SERVES 4

1	pound jumbo shrimp (21 to 25 count), peeled and deveined (see illustration below)
1	tablespoon dry sherry
2	teaspoons soy sauce
2–3	scallions, white and light green parts, minced (about 1 tablespoon), plus 2 tablespoons scallion greens, sliced thin and reserved
2	medium garlic cloves, minced (about 2 teaspoons)
1	piece fresh gingerroot (about ½ inch), peeled and minced (about 2 teaspoons)
½	cup Simplest Shrimp Broth (see recipe at right) or water
2	teaspoons Asian sesame oil
2	teaspoons oyster sauce
¼	teaspoon sugar
1	teaspoon cornstarch
2	tablespoons peanut or vegetable oil

1. Toss shrimp with sherry and soy sauce in medium bowl; set aside to marinate 10 minutes. Combine minced scallion, garlic, and ginger in small bowl; set aside. Stir together shrimp broth (or water), sesame oil, oyster sauce, sugar, and cornstarch in small bowl or measuring cup; set aside.

2. Heat 12-inch skillet over high heat until hot, 3 to 4 minutes. Add 1 tablespoon oil and swirl to coat bottom of pan. Add shrimp and cook, stirring every 10 seconds, until just opaque, about 1 minute. Push shrimp to sides of skillet, clearing a spot in center of pan. Add remaining 1 tablespoon oil and scallion mixture

Do Shrimp Deveiners Really Work?

Cookware stores sell an array of tools designed to devein, and even shell, shrimp quickly and effortlessly. We found three basic types to test. One design, shared by the the Good Cook Seafood Club Shrimp Tool and the Progressive International One-Step Shrimp Peeler, featured a perfectly smooth, slightly curved prong that in our tests mangled the shrimp without actually removing the vein. The Oxo Good Grips Shrimp Cleaner and the Quickso Shrimp Cleaner added serrations to their prongs and, while still rather ineffective, did slightly better because the veins would get snagged on the serrations, occasionally coming out when we removed the prong. These two tools also butterflied the shrimp. The Better Housewares Shrimp Sheller/Deveiner and the Williams-Sonoma Shrimp Deveiner were the best of the lot. Each had a metal prong sharpened at the front to cut through the shell and serrations along the bottom edge to catch the veins—which, in our tests, they did more often than the other tools but still not 100 hundred percent of the time. Even after working through several pounds of shrimp with each, we never got accustomed to the front-facing blades. We worked slowly to avoid cutting ourselves, and, consequently, not even the best of these tools saved us any time. After all was said and deveined, we wouldn't bother with any of the tools we tested. We found it faster and easier to shell the shrimp and then use a sharp paring knife to partially butterfly and devein them. —A.R.

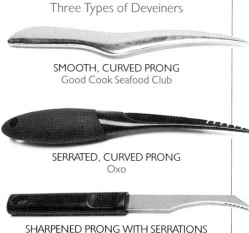

Three Types of Deveiners

SMOOTH, CURVED PRONG
Good Cook Seafood Club

SERRATED, CURVED PRONG
Oxo

SHARPENED PRONG WITH SERRATIONS
Williams-Sonoma

to clearing and mash with spoon; cook until fragrant, 10 to 15 seconds, then stir mixture into shrimp. Remix broth mixture and stir into skillet; cook until sauce has thickened, 30 to 45 seconds. Transfer to serving plate, sprinkle with reserved scallion greens, and serve.

SIMPLEST SHRIMP BROTH
MAKES ENOUGH FOR ONE STIR-FRY

	Shells from 1 pound jumbo shrimp (21 to 25 count)
¾	cup cold water

Bring shells and water to boil in small saucepan over medium-high heat. Cover pan and reduce heat to low; simmer until fragrant, 10 to 15 minutes. Strain; set ½ cup aside for use in one stir-fry recipe.

CANTONESE–STYLE STIR–FRIED SHRIMP

1. Follow recipe for Aromatic Stir-Fried Shrimp through step 1, increasing sugar to 1 teaspoon and adding ¼ teaspoon ground black or white pepper to shrimp broth.

2. Stir-fry shrimp as directed in step 2 until just opaque, about 1 minute; transfer shrimp to large plate and set aside. Return skillet to high heat, add ½ tablespoon oil and swirl to coat pan bottom. Add 3 ounces ground pork, broken into rough 1-inch pieces, and cook until pork turns opaque, about 1 minute, breaking down pieces as small as possible with wooden spoon or spatula. Push pork to sides of pan, clearing a spot in center. Add remaining ½ tablespoon oil and scallion mixture and mash with spoon; cook

until fragrant, 10 to 15 seconds, then stir mixture into pork. Return shrimp to pan and stir to combine. Remix broth mixture and stir into skillet; cook, stirring constantly, until sauce has thickened, 30 to 45 seconds. Off heat, stir 2 large eggs whites into skillet until opaque and gently set. Transfer to serving plate, sprinkle with scallion greens, and serve.

SINGAPORE CHILI STIR–FRIED SHRIMP

Adapted from a well-known dish in Singapore called chili crab, this very spicy dish is complemented nicely by lime wedges and mung bean sprouts, passed at the table.

1. Follow recipe for Aromatic Stir-Fried Shrimp through step 1, adding 2 medium jalapeño chiles, seeded and minced (about 2 tablespoons) to minced scallion mixture; substituting ¼ cup tomato juice for equal amount broth and 3 tablespoons Asian chili sauce (Sriracha) for sesame oil; and increasing sugar to ½ teaspoon.

2. Continue with recipe from step 2.

Deveining Hold the shelled shrimp between thumb and forefinger and cut down the length of its back, about ⅛ to ¼ inch deep, with a sharp paring knife. If the shrimp has a vein, it will be exposed and can be pulled out easily.

The Secrets of Tuscan White Bean Soup

For perfectly cooked, richly flavored beans, go against tradition:
Forget about presoaking, and don't spare the salt.

> BY BRIDGET LANCASTER

I would like to begin this story with the tale of the quaint Italian village where I first tasted my favorite white bean soup, but in reality that occasion was in a city more famous for beans of the baked persuasion—Boston. Before that, I had never given Tuscan white bean soup so much as a second glance. I thought of it as a choice between soup with mushy, exploded beans in an unmemorable broth and soup filled with beans reminiscent of pebbles.

But on the recommendation of a friend, I found myself ordering the *zuppa di giorno* at the local trattoria. One bite and I was converted. This soup, a testament to restraint, comprised only two components: tender, creamy beans, and a broth perfumed with the fragrance of garlic and rosemary. I surmised that soup so simple would be easy to duplicate. I had no idea.

Bean and Nothingness

Because I was writing about white bean soup, I based my initial research on Italian recipes that used navy, great Northern, or cannellini (white kidney) beans. After cooking a few batches, I found that I preferred the larger size and appearance of the cannellini beans, so I centered my testing on them. Many of these recipes came with tips and warnings on how to achieve a cooked bean with perfect texture. "Always soak the beans overnight to ensure even cooking" and "Never salt the beans while they are cooking or they will become tough or split open" were not uncommon counsel. Surely these "rules" were established for a reason. They couldn't be merely rural myths, could they?

I decided to find out and started with rule number one: Always soak the beans. I cooked up three batches of beans. Prior to cooking, I soaked one batch overnight and another according to the "quick-soak" method (water and beans simmer for two minutes, then are placed off heat, covered, and allowed to sit in the water for one hour). I didn't presoak the third batch at all. The results were altogether disappointing. Both batches of soaked beans split or exploded. The unsoaked beans looked better, but their texture was uneven; by the time half of the beans were tender, the other half had overcooked and disintegrated.

Drizzle each bowl of soup with extra-virgin olive oil before serving.

I wondered what would happen if I cooked unsoaked beans until just barely done, then let them sit off heat in their still-hot cooking liquid. Would the residual heat from the liquid finish cooking the beans without any splitting or bursting? The answer was yes. This batch produced perfectly cooked, creamy, yet not soggy beans that retained their texture.

Now I could take on rule number two: Never salt the beans during cooking. Recipes that warned against salting stated that it would cause the outer shell of the bean to toughen. I tested beans cooked in salted water against unsalted beans, and the salted beans were indeed slightly more toothsome on the outside. However, these beans were not any less cooked on the inside than the unsalted beans. In addition, the small amount of resistance that the salted beans had developed on the outside seemed to prevent them from bursting. The beans were now softly structured on the outside and tooth-tender on the inside.

This Little Pig

One other advantage of using salted water is flavor. The seasoned beans were simply much tastier than those cooked in unsalted water. I reasoned that by adding other ingredients to the cooking liquid, I could improve the flavor of the beans that much more. In my initial testing, tasters preferred the beans flavored with pork rather than chicken. But because meat is not called for in the finished soup (only the extracted flavor of the meat is used), I didn't want to use expensive cuts of pork, such as loin chops, in the broth only to throw out the meat later. I reasoned that a ham hock or bacon would do the job, but smoked meats, I found out, added an unwanted sugary-smoky flavor reminiscent of canned soup wrapped in a red label. I tried an unsmoked ham hock, but the flavor lacked the punch that I was looking for. Finally, I tried pancetta, a salt-cured, nonsmoked Italian bacon. The pancetta gave the beans a welcome sweet and sour flavor, and the rendered fat boosted the pork flavor of the broth. Cutting the pancetta into large cubes made it easy to remove once the beans were cooked. Onion, garlic, and a bay leaf were a traditional addition; their flavors permeated the beans.

So now I had perfectly cooked beans, full of flavor from the pork and aromatics. Surely the finished soup would take little more than some chopped rosemary and a light drizzling of olive oil to finish. Wrong. Although the beans were delicious enough to be eaten on their own, the broth was lacking that bright, full garlic flavor I remembered. It was clear that I would have to add a second batch of vegetables toward the end of the cooking process. I cooked another batch of beans with all of the accouterments, strained them from their cooking liquid, and allowed them to cool on the side while I proceeded. Sautéing was key to releasing the flavors from the aromatics quickly, and a short swim in the bean water helped to blend the flavors.

Now I needed to work in the flavor of rosemary, an herb traditional to white bean soup. I tried cooking the rosemary with the beans, but

Fresh Dried Beans?

While Bridget Lancaster stood over pots of beans during testing of her Tuscan bean soup, she began to wonder if there might be a way to tell if the beans were fresh. Noticing a pile of raw beans shriveling in a bowl of water, our colleague Jack Bishop observed that beans shrivel when they are old. Bridget herself became aware that some of the beans she cooked were old when, instead of being creamy, their interiors were gritty or mealy. Because bean bags contain no "sell by" date, however, we were uncertain as to how to determine if the beans we pulled off the supermarket shelves were fresh.

For more information, we contacted legume expert Dr. Barry Swanson at Washington State University. Yes, shriveling during soaking is generally a sign of age, he told us. That is because beans should absorb moisture only through their *hilum*, the part of the bean that attaches to the pod. But beans are not handled with much care, Swanson said: "People think of them as piles of rocks or gravel." Beans that have been knocked around a bit can develop holes in their seed coats. Even carefully handled beans develop these holes (called "checks") over time because of fluctuations in temperature, moisture, and fungi growth. These holes subsequently admit water, shriveling the bean. Dr. Swanson admits that apart from soaking, there is no way to tell if the beans you buy are fresh. His advice: "If you find some fresh beans, buy some more." —Kay Rentschler

Stale bean   "Fresh" bean

that produced a bitter, medicinal broth. Recalling a technique used in our article "Shrimp Bisque Simplified" (November/December 2000), I allowed the herb to steep off heat in the hot liquid for just a few minutes at the finish of my recipe. It worked—just the right amount of bright, fresh rosemary flavor was infused into the broth.

TUSCAN WHITE BEAN SOUP
MAKES ABOUT 2½ QUARTS, SERVING 6 TO 8

If possible, use fresh dried beans in this soup (see "Fresh Dried Beans?" above). For a more authentic soup, place a small slice of lightly toasted Italian bread in the bottom of each bowl and ladle the soup over. To make this a vegetarian soup, omit the pancetta and add a 4-ounce piece of Parmesan rind to the pot along with the halved onion and unpeeled garlic in step 1.

- 6   ounces pancetta, one 1-inch-thick slice, cut into 1-inch cubes
- 1   pound dried cannellini beans, rinsed and picked over
- 1   large onion, unpeeled and halved pole to pole, plus 1 small onion, diced medium
- 4   medium unpeeled garlic cloves, plus 3 medium garlic cloves, minced
- 1   bay leaf
  Salt and ground black pepper
- ¼   cup extra-virgin olive oil, plus extra for serving
- 1   sprig fresh rosemary
  Balsamic vinegar, for serving

1. In large, heavy-bottomed Dutch oven, cook pancetta over medium heat until just golden, 8 to 10 minutes. Add 12 cups water, beans, halved onion, unpeeled garlic, bay leaf, and 1 teaspoon salt; bring to boil over medium-high heat. Cover pot partially; reduce heat to low, and simmer, stirring occasionally, until beans are almost tender, 1 to 1¼ hours. Remove

beans from heat, cover, and let stand until beans are tender, about 30 minutes. Drain beans, reserving cooking liquid (you should have about 5 cups; if not, add more water); discard pancetta, onion, garlic, and bay leaf. Spread beans in even layer on baking sheet and cool.

2. While beans are cooling, heat oil in now-empty Dutch oven over medium heat until shimmering; add diced onion and cook, stirring occasionally, until softened, 5 to 6 minutes. Stir in minced garlic and cook until fragrant, about 30 seconds. Add cooled beans and cooking liquid; increase heat to medium-high and bring to simmer. Submerge rosemary sprig in liquid, cover and let stand off heat 15 to 20 minutes. Discard rosemary sprig and season to taste with salt and pepper. Ladle soup into individual bowls, drizzle each bowl with extra-virgin olive oil, and serve, passing balsamic vinegar separately.

WHITE BEAN SOUP WITH WINTER VEGETABLES
MAKES ABOUT 4 QUARTS, SERVING 10 TO 12

1. Follow recipe for Tuscan White Bean Soup through step 1, adding enough water to reserved bean cooking liquid to equal 9 cups. While beans are cooking, cut 2 small carrots and 2 celery ribs into medium dice; slice white and light green parts of 2 small leeks, washed thoroughly, crosswise into ½-inch pieces. Remove stems from 4 ounces kale and 4 ounces escarole and cut leaves into ½-inch strips (you should have about 3 cups each). Peel and cut 2 small boiling potatoes into medium dice.

2. In step 2, add carrot, celery, and leeks to Dutch oven along with diced onion and cook until vegetables are softened but not browned, about 7 minutes; stir in minced garlic and cook until fragrant, about 30 seconds. Add bean cooking liquid, kale, and escarole to pot. Increase heat to medium-high and bring to boil; cover, reduce heat to low, and simmer 30 minutes. Add potatoes and one

14½-ounce can diced tomatoes, drained; cover and cook until potatoes are tender, about 20 minutes. Add cooled beans; increase heat to medium-high and bring to simmer. Add rosemary; cover and let stand off heat 15 to 20 minutes. Discard rosemary, and season to taste with salt and pepper. Ladle soup into individual bowls, drizzle each bowl with extra-virgin olive oil, and serve.

QUICK TUSCAN WHITE BEAN SOUP
MAKES ABOUT 2 QUARTS, SERVING 6

This quick variation uses canned beans and can be on the table in just 40 minutes.

- 6   ounces pancetta, one 1-inch-thick slice, cut into 1-inch cubes
- 2   tablespoons extra-virgin olive oil, plus extra for serving
- 1   small onion, diced medium
- 3   medium garlic cloves, minced
  Salt and ground black pepper
- 4   cans (15½ ounces each) cannellini beans, drained and rinsed
- 1   sprig fresh rosemary
  Balsamic vinegar, for serving

In large heavy-bottomed Dutch oven, cook pancetta over medium heat until just golden, 8 to 10 minutes; discard pancetta and add oil to pot with pancetta fat. Add onion and cook, stirring occasionally, until softened, 5 to 6 minutes; stir in garlic and cook until fragrant, about 30 seconds. Add beans, ½ teaspoon salt, and 3½ cups water. Increase heat to medium-high and bring to simmer. Submerge rosemary in liquid; cover and let stand off heat 15 to 20 minutes. Discard rosemary and adjust seasonings with salt and pepper. Ladle soup into individual bowls, drizzle each bowl with extra-virgin olive oil, and serve, passing balsamic vinegar separately.

Leftovers Are Good

If you find yourself with a plethora of leftover bean soup, have no fear. In Tuscany, where nothing is wasted, leftover soup is not seen as a problem but rather is the last step in creating a delicious, homey dish called *ribollita*, Italian for "reboiled." The leftover soup is reheated over medium-low heat until warm. Slices of rustic day-old bread are submerged into the soup until completely softened, then the mixture is blended or mashed until very thick. True ribollita connoisseurs say that it must be thick enough to eat with a fork. Don't be put off by the strange appearance of this dish—what ribollita lacks in beauty it more than makes up for in flavor. But do be sure to use a good-quality artisan or rustic bread when making ribollita; a fluffy, market bread will result in a mushy, sloppy mess. —B.L.

Superflaky Apple Turnovers

Fast food-processor puff pastry and grated apples make a turnover vastly superior to those made with store-bought pastry or precooked apples.

> BY RAQUEL PELZEL ≤

Eating an apple turnover should be the kind of thing you do in private, or only with close friends. Because when you eat an apple turnover—and I mean a real apple turnover, not those mass-produced imitations—the flaky dough should shatter all over your plate and yourself, requiring a stand-up and shakedown to get your clothes presentable again. But if you eat a bad apple turnover, the experience couldn't be more disheartening—the filling is bland and mushy and the dough soggy, more like a bad prepackaged pie than "apples in slippers" or *chaussons aux pomme*, the French name for this tantalizing pastry.

The problem with making great apple turnovers is this: the dough typically used for turnovers, *pâte feuilletée* (known by Anglophiles as puff pastry, a superflaky dough with hundreds of buttery layers), is incredibly labor intensive. It involves wrapping the dough around a square of butter, rolling the dough, folding the dough over itself at least four and no more than six times, and chilling the dough for at least one hour in between folds. Before you know it, you've lost a day and all of your desire to make turnovers. No, I'm an impatient urbanite; I wanted to make the dough, assemble the turnovers, and eat them all in the same day—without losing the hundreds of flaky layers that make a turnover so much fun to eat.

Getting the Pastry Right

I started with some puff recipes. There was a traditional takes-all-day puff; a quick puff (in which the butter was cut in a fashion similar to that for a pie dough and then given four folds rather than six); a very flaky rugalach dough we had had luck with in the test kitchen on prior occasions; *Cook's* standard American pie dough; and an interesting food-processor puff pastry recipe developed for *Cook's* back in 1994 by Nick Malgieri, author of *How to Bake* (HarperCollins, 1995).

The only doughs that did any justice to the apple filling were the three puffs—they were

For extraflaky turnovers, it is essential that the dough be rolled very thinly—just under ⅛ inch thick.

strong enough to hold the filling in place (which the pie dough version wasn't) and delicate enough to flake upon impact (which the rugalach dough wasn't). But the traditional puff was too time consuming, and even the "quick"

puff wasn't quick enough for me. This left me with Malgieri's food processor version. This puff was buttery and tender, and I knew that with one extra fold it was potentially a very flaky turnover dough.

My hunch that I could boost the dough's flakiness by giving it an extra turn was no coincidence. I knew from practice that the more folds, or turns, you give a puff pastry, the flakier it will become. This happens for two reasons. First, the mere action of rolling and folding (also known as *turning*) the dough creates paper-thin sheaths of fat in between the layers of dough. Then, when the butter in the dough meets the heat of the oven, the water in the butter steams away, pushing up the hundreds of layers of dough. Initially, my dough got one business letter–style fold and was then rolled into a spiral shape from right to left. If I repeated this sequence, I suspected that I could double the flaky layers. While the new dough was flaky beyond what I had secretly wished for and was definitely worth the extra 45 minutes (most of which was chilling time in the refrigerator), it still lacked that melt-in-your-mouth tenderness I had experienced with the more labor-intensive varieties.

Up until now, I had been sticking with the *Cook's* prescribed method of incorporating water into a dry pastry mixture—gently pressing it together with a rubber spatula. But a colleague suggested that the classical *fraisage* method—placing the water-tossed dry ingredients on a flat surface and pushing one handful of dough at a time against the work surface so the butter is

TECHNIQUE | FRAISAGE MAKES FOR TENDER PASTRY

1. Turn the shaggy dough mass onto the work surface and press it together with both hands.

2. Use the heel of one hand braced against the work surface to drag a small portion of the dough forward in a short, brisk stroke. Repeat with the remaining dough portions.

3. Gather the dough together with a bench scraper and repeat the fraisage a second time. Press the dough into an 8 by 4-inch rectangle, wrap in plastic, and refrigerate at least 30 minutes.

forced into thin sheets (see illustrations on page 22)—might be the way to make the pastry more tender. My colleague was correct. The fraisage took just a few minutes to complete, and the results were right on: these turnovers were tender and incredibly flaky.

A Grate Discovery

Now that my dough had come full circle, it was time to pool my efforts and tackle the turnover filling. During my research, I had come across an interesting method recommended by Mark Bittman, author of *How to Cook Everything* (Macmillan, 1998). Instead of dicing, chopping, or precooking the apples, as proposed in other cookbooks, Bittman simply grated his apples on the large holes of a box grater. Contrary to the other failed filling methods, the turnovers with the shredded apples exuded fresh apple flavor, providing just the right contrast with the rich pastry. Since I felt that pairing a plain apple filling with the flaky, tender pastry didn't do the turnovers justice, I went ahead and tested a few ways to spike the flavor. After trying varying amounts of sugar, cinnamon, flour, lemon (zest and juice), and salt, the crowd pleasers were the turnovers made with lemon juice, sugar, and just a pinch of salt. (I squeezed in the cinnamon by dusting the surface of the turnovers with a sugar/cinnamon mix.)

With the dough and filling now good to go, I turned to the last element, the proper oven temperature. I tested several options and found that turnovers baked at 375 degrees were the flakiest, with the nicest amount of rise. After 20 minutes in the oven and a 15-minute cool-down on a wire rack, the turnovers were ready to be eaten. Just make sure you're not wearing black—it doesn't sufficiently camouflage the flakes that are bound to dust your shirt on impact.

FLAKY APPLE TURNOVERS
MAKES NINE 5-INCH TURNOVERS

If at any point during rolling the dough becomes sticky and difficult to work with, transfer it to a cookie sheet or cutting board, wrap it in plastic, and chill until it becomes workable. The dough can be made through step 4, then wrapped tightly in plastic wrap and kept for up to 5 days in the refrigerator or 2 months in the freezer. Defrost frozen dough in the refrigerator 1 day before you plan to use it.

Quickest Puff Pastry
- 2 cups (10 ounces) all-purpose flour
- 1 tablespoon sugar
- 1 teaspoon salt
- 16 tablespoons (2 sticks) cold unsalted butter, cut into ¼-inch cubes
- 6 tablespoons ice water
- 1 teaspoon juice from 1 lemon

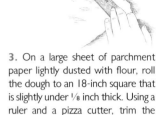

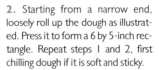

1. Place the dough onto a lightly floured large piece of parchment paper and roll into a 15 by 10-inch rectangle. Fold the dough lengthwise into thirds.

2. Starting from a narrow end, loosely roll up the dough as illustrated. Press it to form a 6 by 5-inch rectangle. Repeat steps 1 and 2, first chilling dough if it is soft and sticky.

3. On a large sheet of parchment paper lightly dusted with flour, roll the dough to an 18-inch square that is slightly under ⅛ inch thick. Using a ruler and a pizza cutter, trim the dough to a 15-inch square.

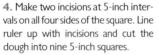

4. Make two incisions at 5-inch intervals on all four sides of the square. Line ruler up with incisions and cut the dough into nine 5-inch squares.

5. Grate the peeled apples on the large holes of a box grater, discarding the core and seeds.

6. With a fork dipped in flour, press to seal and crimp the edges.

Apple Filling
- 4 Granny Smith apples (about 1 pound)
- 1 cup sugar
- 2 teaspoons juice from 1 lemon
- ¼ teaspoon salt

Cinnamon Sugar
- ½ cup granulated sugar
- 2 teaspoons ground cinnamon

1. In workbowl of food processor fitted with steel blade, pulse to combine flour, sugar, and salt. Add one-quarter of the butter cubes and cut butter into flour until butter is in dime-sized pieces, four 1-second pulses. Add remaining butter to coat cubes with flour, two 1-second pulses. Transfer mixture to medium bowl.

2. Combine ice water and lemon juice in small bowl. Add 3 tablespoons liquid to flour and butter mixture and toss until just combined. Toss in remaining water, then turn dough out onto work surface. Follow illustrations 1 through 3 on page 22 to fraisage dough; wrap in plastic and refrigerate.

3. Unwrap dough and follow illustrations 1 and 2 in "Shaping the Turnovers" (above) to roll and fold dough twice. If dough is soft and sticky, wrap in plastic and refrigerate 30 minutes until workable, then repeat rolling and pressing. When second rolling and folding is complete, wrap dough in plastic and chill at least 30 minutes.

4. Following illustrations 3 and 4, roll, trim and cut dough into nine 5-inch squares. Slide parchment and dough onto cookie sheet or large cutting board and refrigerate while making filling.

5. Peel apples. Following illustration 5, grate on large holes of box grater. Combine grated apples, sugar, lemon juice, and salt in medium bowl. Line baking sheet with parchment paper; set aside. Working one at a time, remove dough squares from refrigerator and set on work surface. Place 2 tablespoons grated apple filling (squeezed of excess liquid) in center of dough. Moisten two adjoining edges of dough square with finger dipped in apple liquid, then fold top portion of dough over bottom, making sure to overlap the bottom portion by ⅛ inch. Follow illustration 6 to crimp edges of turnover with tines of fork. Using wide metal spatula, transfer turnover to prepared baking sheet. Repeat process with remaining dough squares. Refrigerate 30 minutes or cover with plastic wrap and refrigerate up to 24 hours.

6. While turnovers are chilling, adjust oven rack to upper-middle position and heat oven to 375 degrees. Combine sugar and cinnamon in small bowl.

7. Brush or mist turnovers lightly with water and sprinkle evenly with cinnamon sugar. Bake until golden brown, 18 to 22 minutes. Using wide metal spatula, transfer turnovers to wire rack to cool.

All-Purpose Chocolate Sheet Cake

For an easy, foolproof, last-minute cake that packs in great chocolate flavor, just whisk together a few ingredients and bake.

⇒ BY CHRISTOPHER KIMBALL ⇐

A sheet cake is like a two-layer cake with training wheels—it's hard to fall off. Unlike regular cakes, which often require trimming and decorating skills to make sure the cake doesn't turn out lopsided, domed, or altogether amateurish, sheet cakes are single-story and easy to frost. These are the sorts of cakes made for church suppers, old home days, bake sales, and Fourth of July picnics, decorated with red, white, and blue frosting.

But sheet cakes are still cakes. They can still turn out dry, sticky, or flavorless and, on occasion, can even sink in the middle. So we set out to find the simplest, most dependable recipe for a chocolate sheet cake, one that was moist yet also light and chocolatey.

First off, a sheet cake is nothing more than cake batter baked in one layer, usually in a square or rectangular pan. A basic chocolate sheet cake is used as the foundation for Mississippi mud cake (just add a layer of marshmallow cream and chocolate frosting) and is also referred to as a Texas sheet cake. We started with a test batch of five different recipes that required a variety of mixing techniques, everything from creaming butter to beating yolks, whipping whites, and gently folding everything together at the end. The best of the lot was the most complicated to make. But we were taken with another recipe that simply whisked together the ingredients without beating, creaming, or whipping. Although the recipe needed work, its approach was clearly a good match for the simple, all-purpose nature of a sheet cake.

The recipe called for 2 sticks of butter, 4 eggs, 1½ cups flour, 2 cups sugar, ½ cup cocoa, 1 teaspoon vanilla, and ⅛ teaspoon salt. Our first change was to add buttermilk, baking powder, and baking soda to lighten the batter, as the cake had been dense and chewy in its original form. To increase the chocolate flavor, we reduced the sugar and flour, increased the cocoa, and decreased the butter. To further deepen the chocolate taste, we also decided to use semisweet chocolate in addition to the cocoa.

With this revised recipe and our simple mixing method, we actually had a cake that was superior to those whose recipes called for creaming butter or whipping eggs.

The only significant problem came when we tested natural versus Dutch-processed cocoa and discovered that the cake fell a bit in the center when we used the former. A few tests later, we eliminated the baking powder entirely, relying instead on baking soda alone, and the problem was fixed. (Natural cocoa is more acidic than Dutch-processed, and when it was combined with baking powder, which also contains acid, it produced an excess of carbon dioxide gas. This in turn caused the cake to rise very fast and then fall like a deflated balloon that pops.)

Also of note is the low oven temperature—325 degrees—which, combined with a relatively long baking time of 40 minutes, produced a perfectly baked cake with a lovely flat top. Using a microwave oven rather than a double boiler to melt the chocolate and butter also saved time and hassle.

This cake can be frosted with almost anything—a buttercream, an Italian meringue, a sour cream or whipped cream frosting—but we developed a classic American milk chocolate frosting that pairs well with the darker flavor of the cake. Unlike a regular two-layer cake, this cake is a snap to frost. Even my 10-year-old did quite a respectable job (and an even better job licking the bowl).

SIMPLE CHOCOLATE SHEET CAKE
MAKES ONE 9 BY 13-INCH CAKE

Melting the chocolate and butter in the microwave is quick and neat, but it can also be done in a heatproof bowl set over a saucepan containing 2 inches of simmering water. We prefer Dutch-processed cocoa for the deeper chocolate flavor it gives the cake. The baked and cooled cake can simply be served with lightly sweetened whipped cream or topped with any frosting you like.

- ¾ cup cocoa, preferably Dutch-processed
- 1¼ cups (6¼ ounces) all-purpose flour
- ¼ teaspoon salt
- 8 ounces semisweet chocolate, chopped
- 12 tablespoons (1½ sticks) unsalted butter, plus extra for baking pan
- 4 large eggs
- 1½ cups sugar
- 1 teaspoon vanilla extract
- 1 cup buttermilk
- ½ teaspoon baking soda

1. Adjust oven rack to middle position and heat oven to 325 degrees. Coat bottom and sides of 9 by 13-inch baking pan with 1 tablespoon butter.

2. Sift together cocoa, flour, and salt in medium bowl; set aside. Heat chocolate and butter in microwave-safe bowl covered with plastic wrap 2 minutes at 50 percent power; stir until smooth. (If not fully melted, heat 1 minute longer at 50 percent power.) Whisk together eggs, sugar, and vanilla in medium bowl.

3. Whisk chocolate into egg mixture until combined. Combine buttermilk and baking soda; whisk into chocolate mixture, then whisk in dry ingredients until batter is smooth and glossy. Pour batter into prepared pan; bake until firm in center when lightly pressed and toothpick inserted in center comes out clean, about 40 minutes. Cool on wire rack until room temperature, at least 1 hour; serve, or ice with frosting, if desired.

CREAMY MILK CHOCOLATE FROSTING
MAKES ABOUT 2 CUPS, ENOUGH TO ICE ONE 9 BY 13-INCH CAKE

This frosting needs about an hour to cool before it can be used, so begin making it when the cake comes out of the oven.

- ½ cup heavy cream
  Pinch salt
- 1 tablespoon light or dark corn syrup
- 10 ounces milk chocolate, chopped
- ½ cup confectioners' sugar
- 8 tablespoons (1 stick) cold unsalted butter, cut into 8 pieces

Heat cream, salt, and corn syrup in microwave-safe measuring cup on high until simmering, about 1 minute, or bring to simmer in small saucepan over medium heat. Place chocolate in workbowl of food processor fitted with steel blade. With machine running, gradually add hot cream mixture through feed tube; process 1 minute after cream has been added. Stop machine; add confectioners' sugar to workbowl and process to combine, about 30 seconds. With machine running, add butter through feed tube one piece at a time; process until incorporated and smooth, about 20 seconds longer. Transfer frosting to medium bowl and cool at room temperature, stirring frequently, until thick and spreadable, about 1 hour.

Understanding and Using Yeasts

Months of kitchen tests revealed almost no difference in baking results when using different types and brands of yeast. It's how you use them that matters.

≥ BY KAY RENTSCHLER AND JULIA COLLIN ≤

Like many things that inspire awe through their magical properties, yeast inspires angst as well. Baking books old and new abound with yeasted recipes, and yet the single-celled spore that enlivens our breads still breeds confusion.

Some recipes, for example, say that fresh yeast is essential to the success of a sweet roll or that a dough cannot rise unless it is in a warm place. Some recipes call for two packets of yeast, others a fraction of a teaspoon. One hears that a special yeast is necessary for bread machines and that quick-rise yeast puts bread on the table fast. Which yeasts need to be proofed (activated by dissolving in liquid before use)? Refrigerated? If a dough rises sluggishly, is the yeast simply old? What has happened when dough rises like a hot air balloon but bakes up like a sneaker?

Yet another question worth asking is how to keep track of the commercial yeasts multiplying on grocery shelves in colorful profusion. Is one really any different from the other? But the first thing we wanted to know was this: Does the type of yeast—fresh, active dry, or instant—matter?

Armed with a stack of recipes and enough yeast to raise the dead, we went into the test kitchen to find out.

The Nature of Yeast

First, let's get a few basics in line. Yeast is a living organism. Its function in a bread dough is to consume sugars and starches in the flour and convert them into carbon dioxide and alcohol, which give bread its lift and flavor. This process is known as fermentation. Flavor compounds and alcohol—byproducts of fermentation—give a yeasted bread its characteristically irresistible aroma and flavor.

Yeast has changed over the centuries. Until the 1700s, bread was produced from bitter beer or brewer's yeast (called *barm*, referring to the liquid in which yeast grows) or from fermented solutions of grains, potatoes, malt, or sugar. Each method was problematic and unpredictable. In the late 1700s, Holland became the first country to produce a compressed baker's yeast from spirit distilleries. The Viennese refined the process shortly thereafter. In fact, it was an Austrian, Charles Fleischmann, who brought yeast manufacturing to America. By patenting a compressed yeast cake in the late 1860s, he made home baking far less frustrating and started an empire that thrives to this day. In response to the need to feed American troops abroad during World War II, Fleischmann's company went on to create active dry yeast. Active dry yeast requires no refrigeration and can be activated simply by adding warm water. In the 1970s, Europeans took the virtues and convenience of dry yeast one step further when they created instant yeast. Dry and long-lived, instant yeast requires no proofing.

Despite indications to the contrary—created by the commercial largesse of the yeast companies—there remain to this day only these three types of yeast: fresh, active dry, and instant. All are derived from the powerful brewer's yeast known as *Saccharomyces cerevisiae*, but each is processed from a slightly different strain of this protypical yeast.

The original commercial yeast, known as fresh or compressed, is about 70 percent water by weight and is composed of 100 percent living cells. It is soft and crumbly and requires no proofing—fresh yeast will dissolve if it is simply rubbed into sugar or dropped into warm liquid. Owing to qualities associated with its strain, fresh yeast will produce the most carbon dioxide of all three types of yeasts during fermentation. Fresh yeast is considered fast, potent, and reliable, but has somewhat of a drawback: it is perishable and must be refrigerated.

Active dry and instant yeasts arrive at their granular state by undergoing processes that reduce them to 95 percent dry matter. Traditional active dry yeast is exposed to heat so high that many of its cells are destroyed in the process. Because the spent outer cells encapsulate living centers, active dry yeast

---

Less Yeast, More Flavor

The United States is one of the few countries where yeast is sold in "single-serve" quarter-ounce envelopes. This apparently convenient packaging actually contains more yeast than many recipes require, and is one of the reasons it is difficult to make quality bread at home. In the test kitchen, we found we could produce better bread by reducing the amount of yeast and lengthening the rising times by hours or even overnight. Although most recipes call for one package of yeast, you can easily alter any recipe following these basic guidelines for using instant yeast.

TYPE OF DOUGH	PROPER YEAST/FLOUR RATIO
Lean (Without sugar or dairy) EXAMPLE: Baguette or Italian-style loaf	**By weight:** Yeast should be about 0.5 percent of flour by weight **By volume:** About ¼ teaspoon instant yeast for 1 cup flour
Lightly enriched (Small amount of sugar and/or dairy) EXAMPLE: American sandwich loaf	**By weight:** Yeast should be about 0.8 percent of flour by weight **By volume:** About ⅓ teaspoon yeast for 1 cup flour
Heavily enriched (Substantial amounts of sugar and/or dairy) EXAMPLE: Kuchen or brioche	**By weight:** Yeast should be about 1 percent of flour by weight **By volume:** About ½ teaspoon yeast for 1 cup flour

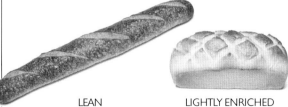

LEAN
Baguette

LIGHTLY ENRICHED
American Sandwich Loaf

HEAVILY ENRICHED
Kuchen

---

must first be dissolved in a relatively hot liquid (proofed) to slough off dead cells and reach the living centers.

Instant yeast, on the other hand, is subjected to a gentler drying process. As a result, every dried particle is living, or active. This means the yeast can be mixed directly with recipe ingredients without first being dissolved in water. It is in this context that the yeast is characterized as "instant." With one-third less instant yeast than active dry yeast required for the purposes of most recipes, instant yeast has earned a reputation as a stronger yeast. It combines the potency of fresh yeast with the convenience of active dry, and it is considered by some to have a cleaner flavor than active dry because it contains no dead cells. (In our months of testing, we found this to be true when we made a lean baguette dough but could detect no difference in flavor when using the two yeasts in doughs made with milk, sugar, and butter.)

Though instant yeast was not developed to create a quicker rise, it is often marketed and used as such in the United States. This is because it is more potent than active dry. When recipes call for yeast without distinguishing instant from active dry, the instant will rise more rapidly. But it is best used in judicious amounts, as we discovered in our kitchen tests.

Everything That Rises Must Converge
Given the apparent differences in the three types of yeast, we were shocked when our initial series of tests with an American sandwich bread recipe turned up nothing noteworthy. We had assumed that doughs made with different types of yeast would perform differently or produce breads with individual flavors or textures. But for all intents and purposes, the breads we baked were identical. Tasters had to literally bury their noses in the crumb of the bread to establish olfactory differences—but these differences did not translate to the tongue.

Proceeding one step further, we put individual brands of yeast into competition. After all, yeast companies themselves scramble to come up with proprietary formulas—of the hundreds of artificially created strains of yeast, some are even housed in a national repository—so there must be qualitative differences, right? Wrong. We found no perceptible differences in the breads baked with different brands of yeast. Realizing at this point that we had to rethink our testing strategy, we decided to advance to the second round by using only instant yeast—selecting it because it is widely available, convenient, and strong—and attempt to come up with some pointers for home bakers on how to make sense of and use these putty-colored granules.

Control Fermentation before It Controls You
As noted above, one misconception about instant yeast arises from the recommendations of the yeast companies themselves, which often call for quantities far in excess of what is required. When a recipe calls for instant yeast in amounts comparable with those of active dry (usually an envelope), the dough will rise faster because instant yeast contains no dead cells. But is that a good thing? The equation between less yeast and more flavorful bread has been long established in Europe. In her remarkable book *English Bread and Yeast Cookery* (Penguin Books, 1977), Elizabeth David cites Eliza Acton, writing in the 1845 book *Modern Cookery*, as having observed that rapid fermentation brought on by excess yeast is "by no means advantageous to the bread, which not only becomes dry and stale from it, but is of less sweet and pleasant flavor than that which is more slowly fermented." Unfortunately, many Americans over the years have come to associate raw yeasty smells and flavor with hearth and home—in a word, with homemade.

Understanding the relationship between yeast and fermentation, we learned, creates practical advantages for the baker. The less yeast employed, the longer the fermentation required. A long fermentation at a moderately cool temperature means the yeast can go about its business without being rushed. The fermentation flavors will improve. The bread will taste better. Instead of fearing that your dough will exhaust its resources if it rises slowly, relax—throw it in the fridge overnight if it suits you.

In embracing the axiom that a dough's rising time can be manipulated by adjusting the amount of yeast used and the temperature of the surrounding environment, one becomes considerably less time- and recipe-bound. Consider a bread recipe that uses a high proportion of yeast: the dough rises quickly. Offer this heavily yeasted dough a tropical rising spot, toss in a pinch of neglect by forgetting about it, and what will you get? In terms of the first rise, according to food scientist Shirley Corriher, bacteria produced in an excessively warm environment will create "short acid chains," which corrupt the bread's flavor. In terms of the final rise (once the dough is shaped), such a dough will be stretched to its limits. Gas will escape during baking, and the baked bread will resemble the above-mentioned sneaker—with an open grain and poor texture. Cool fermentation thus has the added advantage of reducing the margin of error if bread is left to rise for too long.

We tested these theories ourselves using the dinner roll recipe from the November/December 1999 issue of *Cook's*. We made two original recipes, each of which used one envelope of instant yeast (2¼ teaspoons) and 3½ cups of flour. We also made a recipe with only ¾ tea-

---

Which Is the Most Instant?

Many consumers are confused by the plethora of yeasts out there whose names suggest speed: fast rise, rapid rise, perfect rise, instant rise, quick rise, yeast for bread machines, and so on. Do they represent an advanced formula that kick-starts fermentation? No, says Maggie Glezer, a baker certified by the American Institute of Baking. These are all just instant yeasts to which different amounts of ascorbic acid have been added. (Ascorbic acid functions as an antioxidant and dough strengthener.) Translation: marketing fluff.—K.R.

Why Slow Is Good

Though we knew empirically that bread made with less yeast tasted better than bread made with lots, we wondered what was happening in the dough to account for superior flavor development during long fermentations. Our understanding of the process always screeched to a halt in the face of molecular formulas displayed in scientific baking books. So we asked Maggie Glezer, a baker certified by the American Institute of Baking, to walk us through this process at a layman's pace. "It is all about enzymes," she told us.

During the process of rising, Glezer explained, many reactions take place. In the initial phase of fermentation, which lasts one to two hours, the yeast feeds on readily available natural sugars found in the flour. These simple sugars require less enzymatic conversion and produce less interesting flavor byproducts, so it makes sense that doughs with lots of yeast (which in the aggregate create a great deal of carbon dioxide) will rise quickly and be ready to bake before much flavor has developed. The resulting baked bread will be dominated by the flavor of raw yeast.

When less yeast is used in a dough, on the other hand, the dough takes more time to rise and thereby allows more time for enzymatic activity. After easily fermented sugars are gone, the yeast sustains itself by fermenting "damaged starches," starch granules that have been crushed during the milling process and provide the next most accessible sugars after simple sugars. Damaged starches can sustain a dough for a significant period of time, Glezer said. Coming at the end of this long, very complicated fermentation process, enzymatic activity will produce the sugar maltose, which fuels the yeast once again. Thus, the amount of flavor in any given loaf of baked bread is directly related to the length of fermentation and the side reactions that occur over time. —K.R.

TASTING YEAST

We selected recipes for three yeasted breads, each quite different in character, to get a sense of each yeast's versatility: a quick all-purpose sandwich bread (from *Cook's*, May/June 1996), a lean baguette dough (March/April 2000), and a sweet, rich dough called Kuchen. Each of these doughs, we reasoned, would demand different things from the yeast: the American sandwich bread, which used milk and a fair amount of yeast and sugar, could in theory rise too rapidly; the baguette dough, with its modicum of yeast and overnight fermentation, demanded sustained energy from the yeast; and the Kuchen dough, heavy with butter, sugar, and eggs, would stress the yeast and slow the dough's fermentation considerably—a weak yeast might gorge itself quickly on the available sugars and simply give out.

Each of the four instant yeasts we tested performed very well; they are listed in terms of overall preference. Their "also known as" aliases, listed to the side, are different names for what amounts to the same product and can be used interchangeably. The tasting panel, called into duty over a period of several months, consisted of the *Cook's* editorial staff and, occasionally, participants from other departments of the company.

SAF Perfect Rise Gourmet Yeast (¼-oz. packets), SAF-Instant Yeast (1-lb. vacuum-packed brick), and SAF Perfect Rise Gourmet Yeast (3-oz. package)

Red Star Quick Rise Fast-Rising Yeast (¼-oz. packets), Red Star Instant Active Dry Yeast (1-lb. vacuum-packed brick), and Red Star Quick Rise Fast-Rising Yeast (4-oz. jar)

Fermipan Instant Yeast (1-lb. vacuum-packed brick)

Fleischmann's Rapid Rise Yeast (¼-oz. packets), Fleischmann's Instant Yeast (1-lb. vacuum-packed brick), and Fleischmann's Bread Machine Yeast (4-oz. jar)

SAF	RED STAR	Fermipan Instant	Fleischmann's
➤ **$5.50/pound**	➤ **$5.50/pound**	➤ **$4.50/pound**	➤ **$4.95/pound**
This yeast, the stepchild of the French company Lesaffre, is produced in Mexico and Belgium for use in the United States. It is available by mail order, in specialty stores, and, increasingly, in supermarkets.	This is an American yeast available by mail order, in specialty stores, and, increasingly, in supermarkets.	This Canadian yeast is available by mail order and in specialty stores.	This is an American yeast available in supermarkets.

SAF
COMMENTS
American Loaf Steady, predictable rise; "clean," "natural flavors"
Baguette Great oven spring, airy crumb, "clean aroma and flavor"; shattery crust
Kuchen Clean, "clear" flavor; "perfect" crumb

RED STAR
COMMENTS
American Loaf "Rustic" flavor
Baguette Medium oven spring; average crumb density; "unencumbered flavors"; chewy crust
Kuchen Flavor not quite as delicate as others; good crumb

Fermipan Instant
COMMENTS
American Loaf "Clean"; no noticeable flavors or aromas; "soft, delicate crumb"
Baguette Good oven spring; delicate; fresh, clean flavor
Kuchen "Clean, mild"; delicate crumb

Fleischmann's
COMMENTS
American Loaf Slightly uneven rising times; "cheesy smelling"; "sour dairy aroma"
Baguette Heady yeast aroma and flavor; crisp crust
Kuchen Uneven crumb

---

spoon instant yeast. We gave the dough with less yeast an initial two-hour rise at room temperature, followed by an overnight fermentation. As for the two original doughs, one was handled as the recipe instructed while the second was given twice as much time for the first rise (in a warm oven) as well as the second rise (after being formed). The results were instructive. Once baked, the orginal-recipe rolls that were left for double the usual rising time looked squat and dispirited, their interior was heavy, and their flavor frankly sour—"indescribably awful," one taster said. The regular rolls were as we remembered them: sweet, yeasty, and pillowy soft. One taster described them as "a yeast explosion in my mouth." But the rolls with less yeast and a long fermentation had improved height, a complex, lingering aroma, a fine interior crumb, and a richer flavor. "You can taste the yeast," one taster said, "but the flavor is developed and full, not so in your face."

And so we found ourselves at the end of the day with a handful of rough gems. First, we like instant yeast (to include those brands whose names imply haste—rapid rise, instant rise, and so on): it has a long shelf life, does not need to be activated by dissolving it in water, and is "stronger," which means you can use less. Second, we learned that less yeast makes better bread precisely because it takes longer to rise. We recognize that fermentation is something a baker can control by decreasing the amount of yeast and increasing the rising time. And, last but not least, we confirm that a kitchen that smells of just-baked bread will always draw a crowd.

Is It Dead Yet?

People who bake only occasionally, we've found, tend to buy yeast, put it in the refrigerator, and leave it for months, sometimes until after the expiration date. We were curious to know how an expired yeast would perform. Would it be totally ineffective, work but yield only a subpar loaf, or be just fine? In side-by-side tests with SAF (a brand name) instant yeast, we made a couple of basic breads, one with a yeast packet that had expired two months earlier and one with a yeast packet with a full year to go. Though the expired yeast was still capable of lift, the bread we made with it lacked the height and lightness of the bread made with the new yeast. So check that expiration date. –K.R.

How to Choose a Sauté Pan

Among pricey sauté pans, good performance is a pretty sure bet, but subtle design features distinguish the cream of the crop.

≥ BY ADAM RIED ≤

With some kitchen equipment, the difference between pricey and inexpensive models just isn't that big a deal—either will get the job done. But sauté pans are another story, primarily because of the very nature of sautéing. When you sauté, you cook food quickly, with minimal fat, in a very hot pan. As it cooks, the food develops a nice, dark, flavorful crust, which is the glory of sautéing.

But there is a thin line between crusty and burnt—and it's a line that you definitely don't want to cross. To sauté successfully, you need a pan that distributes heat evenly, without hot spots that can cause food to scorch or burn outright. Additional factors to consider include browning performance, ovenworthiness (can the pan be used in the oven?), heft (does it feel substantial without being too heavy?), and construction (does it feel solid, with the handles attached firmly?). A number of pans on the market claim to fit the bill, but, at well over $100, many of them are also quite expensive. We opened our wallet and chose eight popular models in the three-quart size, then headed off to the test kitchen for a two-week sauté-a-thon.

The popularity of nonstick pans compelled us to consider several in our tests. By and large, the nonsticks performed on a par with the other pans in our tests. Yet for all of their virtues, the nonsticks had, in our opinion at least, what amounted to a serious flaw: they resist the development of a *fond*, the sticky, brown, caramelized film and bits that form on the pan bottom as the food cooks. When released from the pan bottom with the addition of liquid, which is then boiled to dissolve those bits (in a process called *deglazing*), fond provides the savory underpinnings of sauces, stews, and braises. Fond develops because the drippings from the food stick to the pan; no sticking, no fond. As a result, when we used the nonsticks to make the sauce for a braised chicken dish, the sauce looked light and tasted weak.

In our view, then, nonstick pans almost impede the development of flavor in many of the dishes we typically prepare in a sauté pan. If you use your sauté pan for delicate foods that won't be dressed with a pan sauce, nonstick is a fine choice. But if you, like us, sauté in part to produce a pan sauce from the drippings, or if you braise or stew often, we advise you to stick with a traditional nonreactive cooking surface.

Pan Parade

Differences in the pans' sautéing and browning performance were not as significant as we had imagined they would be. All of the pans in our price range were thick enough to favor good conduction with no significant hot spots that could cause food to burn. Beyond that, each metal has a *thermoconductivity coefficient;* this refers to the amount of heat it can transfer over a centimeter of length in one second. Honors for best conductivity go to copper, at 0.94, and pure aluminum, at 0.53. At the other end of the spectrum is cast iron, which has a thermoconductivity coefficient of 0.12. This is the reason our enamel-covered cast-iron Le Creuset pan was so slow to heat up, especially when compared with the copper Mauviel.

To our surprise, though, we discovered that the superconductivity of copper was not for us, especially in light of its high price. In our view, pans that sauté reliably at a medium pace—meaning that they hedge the threat of burning by heating neither too hot nor too fast—are preferred. In our tests, the copper did its work a bit too fast. It cooled quickly when we turned the flame down, but we would just as soon avoid the need to adjust the heat in the first place.

While variations in the sautéing and browning performance of the pans turned out to be relatively undramatic, certain aspects of pan design made a much bigger difference to us than we had anticipated. For example, each pan was rated at or very close to three quarts, but their diameters varied by more than an inch, from about 11 inches for the Look and All-Clad pans (the surface area of the bottom of the Look pan is actually smaller because its sides slope inward) to about 10 inches for the KitchenAid, Analon, and Mauviel. A little larger diameter was a big advantage for the cook. For instance, the 11-inch All-Clads accommodated the chicken in our braised chicken test

The Sauté Pans We Tested

BEST OVERALL

All-Clad Stainless Steel
A winner in design and performance alike.

BEST NONSTICK

All-Clad Stainless Steel Nonstick
Top choice among nonsticks.

RECOMMENDED WITH RESERVATIONS

Calphalon Commercial
A solid performer with a lid we don't care for.

KitchenAid Stainless Steel
Slightly small diameter means snug fit for many foods.

Look Classic Cookware
Extra spacious, extra easy to clean.

Analon Anodized Nonstick
Suffers from the characteristic nonstick problem.

NOT RECOMMENDED

Mauviel Cuprinox
Expensive, heavy, and a blazing hot brass handle.

Le Creuset 10-Inch Deep
Gorgeous, but quirky and superheavy.

RATING SAUTÉ PANS

<table>
<tr><td>RATINGS
★★★
GOOD
★★
FAIR
★
POOR</td></tr>
</table>

Eight sauté pans, each available individually, and rated with a capacity of three quarts (or as close to it as we could find in that manufacturer's line), were tested and evaluated according to the following criteria. The pans are listed in order of preference within each category.

MATERIALS: The materials that go into the pan itself as well as the lids and handles.

PRICE: Prices as listed at Boston-area retail outlets or in mail-order catalogs, or manufacturer's suggested retail promotional price. Because cookware is often heavily discounted, you may see different prices for the same item in local stores.

WEIGHT: Measured with the lid.

MEASUREMENTS: Measurements listed include the diameter, measured across the top of the pan from outside rim to outside rim, and height, measured from the inside of the bottom surface to the top inside edge of the pan wall.

SAUTÉ SPEED: In this test, we started with a cold pan and sautéed 1½ cups chopped onions in 2 tablespoons olive oil over medium heat for 15 minutes. Pans that produced fully soft, medium gold onions with no burnt edges were rated good; pans that produced pale gold onions with any hint of undercooking were rated fair; and pans that produced onions that were dark brown, crisp, or burnt at the edges were rated poor.

PERFORMANCE: To determine overall performance, we conducted six separate everyday cooking tasks in each pan. We seared hamburgers; browned turkey cutlets; deglazed the drippings from the turkey cutlets; prepared a braised chicken dish with a whole 3½-pound chicken cut into eight serving pieces; boiled one quart of water in the pans, covered, for 15 minutes and measured the remaining water to determine how tightly the lids sealed; and covered the entire bottom surface of each pan with pancake batter to determine if any hot or cool spots were present. Scores of good, fair, or poor were assigned for each test, and the composite of those scores comprise the overall performance rating for each pan.

USER FRIENDLINESS: Factors evaluated included the pans' ability to accommodate eight serving pieces of chicken without overlap, whether their handles stayed cool enough to touch after browning and braising the chicken on the stovetop for 50 minutes, and the shapes of their lids. We favored pans that held all the chicken without overlap, whose handles stayed cool, and whose lids were deeply domed to maximize interior volume.

Brand	Price	Materials	Weight	Measurements	Sauté Speed	Performance	User Friendliness	Testers' Comments
BEST OVERALL **All-Clad** Stainless Steel Covered 3 Quart Sauté Pan, Model 5403	$165	Stainless steel exterior and interior with complete aluminum core; stainless steel lid and handle	4 lb. 7 oz.	11" diam./ 2½" deep	★★★	★★★	★★★	Promoted a beautiful crust on burgers, cutlets, and chicken alike, developed impressive fond, and handled batches with aplomb. Spacious, too.
BEST NON-STICK **All-Clad** Stainless Steel Nonstick Covered 3 Quart Sauté Pan, Model 5403-NS	$174	Stainless steel exterior and interior with complete aluminum core and interior nonstick coating; stainless steel lid and handle	4 lb. 12 oz.	11" diam./ 2½" deep	★★★	★★★	★★★	The same subpar fond as all the nonstick pans, but otherwise as good as its stainless steel brother, and it cleaned up more easily. Pan sauces will suffer, though.
RECOMMENDED WITH RESERVATIONS **Calphalon** Commercial Hard-Anodized 3 Quart Sauté Pan	$137	Anodized aluminum pan and lid; cast stainless steel handle	4 lb. 3 oz.	10⅜" diam./ 2½" deep	★★★	★★	★★★	Nice job at heavy browning of burgers and chicken, but it sautéed and simmered a hair slow. Flat lid rested on the food in the chicken braise, thereby limiting capacity and compromising seal.
KitchenAid Stainless Steel 3 Quart Covered Sauté Pan	$180	Stainless steel interior and exterior with complete aluminum core; stainless steel lid and handle	4 lb. 14½ oz.	10" diam./ 2⅜" deep	★★★	★★	★★★	Watch the heat on this one—it browned and sautéed a little fast. We adjusted heat to avoid burning drippings. Comfortable handle.
Look Classic Cookware 3.2 Quart Covered Sauté, Model #128	$87	Cast aluminum with triple-thick base; interior and exterior nonstick coating; vented glass lid; phenolic handle	5 lb. 9 oz.	11¼" diam./ 2½" deep	★★★	★★	★★★	Browned delicate turkey cutlets beautifully, burgers and chicken less so. Sauté speed was not perfectly consistent, so keep an eye on the heat.
Analon Anodized Nonstick 3 Quart Sauté	$80	Anodized aluminum with interior and exterior nonstick coating; glass lid, phenolic handle	4 lb. 7 oz.	9⅞" diam./ 2½" deep	★★★	★★	★★★	Sauté speed a tad slow; better at browning turkey cutlets than burgers. Chicken was fine. Phenolic handle stayed cool.
NOT RECOMMENDED **Mauviel Cuprinox** 3 Quart Covered Sauté Pan	$235	Copper with stainless steel interior; copper lid and brass handle	6 lb. 4 oz.	9⅞" diam./ 3" deep	★★	★★	★★★	Browned turkey cutlets and chicken well, but a little faster than we thought ideal. Likewise the sauté speed.
Le Creuset 10-Inch Deep Covered Sauté Pan	$119	Enameled cast-iron pan, lid, and handle	10 lb. 7 oz.	10½" diam./ 3" deep	★★★	★	★★	Sautés and browns on the slow side, but heat really builds so that burning drippings becomes a real possibility. Snug fit.

more comfortably than the smaller KitchenAid, Analon, and Mauviel, which were snug. This meant it was easier to slide tongs or a spatula into the All-Clads to move the chicken pieces without accidentally gouging or damaging them or splashing the sauce. It also meant more favorable conditions for sautéing turkey cutlets, which were wide and flat and needed space around them to brown properly.

Handles were another important difference. If we're removing a dish from the oven, we always remember to don oven mitts. But the same cannot be said before grabbing the handle of a hot pan on the stove. If that handle is hot, we're in for a rude surprise. Hot handles turned out to be a problem with only two of the pans,

the Le Creuset and the Mauviel copper. The stainless steel handles of the All-Clad and KitchenAid pans and the cast-steel handle of the Calphalon stayed cool (though KitchenAid tended to heat near the base), as did the phenolic (heat-resistant plastic) handles of the Look and Analon pans. Incidentally, the handles on all of the pans were ovenworthy, though up to only 350 degrees for the Analon and 500 degrees for the Look because of the phenolic material. All of the pans except for the Look and Mauviel have a "helper handle," usually consisting of a small loop opposite the long handle so that the cook can use two hands to lift the pan when desired. We find the helper handle especially useful when we're hoisting full pans in and out of the oven.

Based on our tests, the Le Creuset had distinct performance patterns you'd have to get to know well before this pan could be used at its best. Though none of these pans come cheap, the notoriously expensive copper (and our pan was not even the most expensive copper on the market) was not worth the extra money for the kind of cooking we do. For our money, then, the All-Clad pans, with a traditional cooking surface or nonstick, if you prefer it, provided the best combination of great design, ample proportions, and reliable performance. The Calphalon, KitchenAid, Analon, and Look pans all performed well, too, and some cost a few dollars less, but each had a design flaw that caused it to fall behind the All-Clads.

Bread Blankee

The test kitchen had a large bolt of thick-gauge natural canvas left over from a photo shoot. During our trials for the yeast tasting in this issue, it occurred to us that the fabric mimicked the bread *couches* in which the French place baguettes and country loaves to let them rise. The canvas also bore a resemblance to those wobbly wood-supported pastry cloths favored by our mothers (the ones that come with little stocking caps for the rolling pins). The canvas came out with a flourish. Treated to a fine film of flour, this cloth became our all-purpose bread blanket. We left loaves to rise on it, we shaped and rounded loaves on it. It needed little additional flour, and the dough never stuck. It worked well with doughs, rolls, coffee cakes, even biscuits. Rolled or folded, it can easily be tucked out of sight and then brought out for command performances. A double thickness of heavy canvas about 2 feet wide by 3 feet long is ideal. If you're especially handy, you can put a hem around it with a sewing machine.

All-Purpose?

Everyone knows what all-purpose flour is—except the flour itself. That is because the term *all-purpose*, rather than denoting a particular protein percentage, simply means "whatever you use it for most." In the southern United States, for instance, all-purpose flour has a lower protein content than all-purpose flour elsewhere. That is because southern cooks use flour mostly to produce tender biscuits, cakes, and pie doughs. Most all-purpose flour hovers at around 10 percent protein. King Arthur all-purpose flour, which we particularly like, has a protein content of 11.7 percent, which is high compared with that of other all-purpose flours. In the thin-crust pizza dough recipe featured in this issue, a softer all-purpose flour did a better job.

Sheets to the Wind

We are big fans of parchment paper and fans of big parchment paper as well. In fact, because we go through so much of it and value the large unrolled sheets made for commercial bakers and chefs, parchment paper is one of the few staples we order from a commercial purveyor. Common supermarket parchment paper is typically narrow in width and, being sold in a roll, often unruly about the edges. Just this year we learned that much of it isn't up to high temperatures, either. A reader wrote to tell us he had baked our baguettes using the parchment-paper-onto-stone transfer we recommend for ease of negotiation. His parchment paper had simply gone up in smoke. Because this had never happened to us, we figured our parchment sheets were more substantial than his, and we sent him a few sheets to try. His next batch of baguettes came off without a hitch. The good news is that some types of parchment paper available to consumers are as durable as the professional-grade paper. Assistant editor Shannon Blaisdell hunted the good stuff down. Details follow in Resources, page 32.

Whole Hog

There seems to be some confusion about the difference between fatback and salt pork, a confusion we experienced ourselves while shopping for salt pork to make beef Burgundy for our current issue. Salt pork comes from the belly of the pig and has been cured or preserved in salt. It has streaks of meat running through it and is rendered to make cracklings. Fatback, as its name implies, comes from the back of the animal. Unlike salt pork, fatback is not smoked or "cured"—it is simply fresh fat. Fatback is generally used to lard meat—that is, to run strips of fat through lean meat to improve its flavor when roasted.

Wrong Number

Those of you who purchase packaged fresh or frozen shrimp may have spotted mysterious codes printed on the box or bag and been perplexed by numbers such as 26/30 or 36/40. You may have requested a pound of large shrimp only to have the clerk inquire, "You want sixteen twenties or twenty-one twenty-fives?" Instead of mumbling "No, just a pound," remember that these codes refer to the number of shrimp per pound. To crunch these numbers precisely, we called Evie Hansen, author of five seafood cookbooks. She told us that the two numbers separated by a slash reflect the variable range of shrimp per pound within a given category. The largest, or colossal, shrimp are called u/15, which means "under 15 shrimp per pound." Thereafter, in the large category, the extrajumbo (16/20) and jumbo (21/25) shrimp are followed by shrimp ranging between 26 and 40 per pound. These large shrimp stand alone when stuffed or grilled and make handsome scampi or shrimp cocktail. Hanson recommends what the industry calls "medium-sized" shrimp, between 40 and 50 per pound, for batter dipping as well as for seafood stews like bouillabaisse or cioppino. Small shrimp, those in the range of 50, 60, or 70 per pound, work nicely in stuffed pasta dishes or gratins. The featherweights, at 200 per pound, look fetching on the end of a fish hook as well as on ice at a salad bar. So order with confidence—and avoid getting the wrong number.

Apple Foldovers

During an editorial meeting not long ago, associate editor Dawn Yanagihara posed a riveting question: "Why are they called turnovers," she asked, "when they aren't turned during baking?" Suspecting the name *turnover* had more to do with construction than baking technique, we decided to look into the matter. We thought turnovers were probably English in origin and duly leafed through a few food encyclopedias, looking under *pasties*. Pasties refer to the Cornish miner's pocket lunch, a portable savory pie pointed at both ends for easy pocketing and sealed for easy eating. In the course of our research, however, we realized that turnovers speak a universal language: they are *calzones* in Italy, *emapanadas* in Mexico, *samosas* in India, *pierogi* in Poland, and *piroshki* in Russia. There is clearly something appealing the world over about fillings sweet and savory wrapped in dough. As for the term *turnover*, the oldest eponymous reference we found was in *Cassell's Dictionary of Cookery*, published in England in 1892. It instructs the cook to cut out dough rounds, place a mound of filling in the center, and "turn the other half over." Modern recipes generally say to "fold the dough over."

Turnover

Restaurant Chefs and Home Cooks

Chef-written cookbooks routinely claim to contain "recipes for the home cook."
We chose two examples and went in the kitchen to try them out. BY CHRISTOPHER KIMBALL

I admit it: I would be thrilled to discover that a four-star chef eats Hamburger Helper at home. I suppose, like most restaurant-goers, that I have an appetite for seeing just how far the high and mighty can fall—or perhaps it's simply the need to peek behind the curtain to unmask the Great Culinary Oz. I know that James Beard had nothing against potato chips and that Julia Child, who is known for serving spectacular food at her home, once offered guests at a cocktail party miniature meatballs in tomato sauce. (Yes, the meatballs were delicious.)

So it was with great interest that the staff of *Cook's* cooked from two "casual" cookbooks put together by two of New York's fanciest chefs: Charlie Palmer (Aureole, Lenox Room, Alva, and Metrazur) and David Waltnuck, the founding chef at Chanterelle. Palmer's book, *Charlie Palmer's Casual Cooking*, is billed as cooking for "family and friends." Waltnuck has cleverly titled his book *Staff Meals*, the recipes being those he makes for staff dinners at his restaurant. Do they really eat hot dogs and beans or macaroni and cheese without adding five-spice powder and some rare dried mushroom? Is this food as good as the $30-a-plate fare they serve to their well-heeled customers? Or is it the same last-minute, ho-hum food that most of us consume during the week? We tested more than 20 recipes to find out. (Both books were reviewed in galley form.)

STAFF MEALS
David Waltnuck and Melicia Phillips
Workman Publishing, 432 pages

Chanterelle is a small jewel of a restaurant that opened in 1979 in Manhattan's SoHo district. (It has since moved to TriBeCa.) The printed menu is graced with works by famous artists, the dining room is spare and hushed, and the food is usually exquisite. This is about as far away from home cooking as one can imagine. A quick glance at *Staff Meals* makes it clear that while its food may be a few notches below the restaurant's fare, the cooking obviously benefits from a wide range of available ingredients and plenty of hands to help with preparation. Recipes for homemade sausage, 12 quarts of veal stock, and dishes that require kaffir lime leaves and lily buds don't qualify as home cooking to me. Yet, to be fair, there are also plenty of recipes that are within the scope of the home cook. These are staff meals at a famous, top-notch New York restaurant, after all, so a bit of fast-lane culinary sleight of hand is in order.

PROS: The recipes are all over the place in terms of both country of origin and complexity, a fact that gives this book much of its character. Italian-Style Meatloaf and David's Burgers share these pages with Red-Cooked Chicken and Chinese Eggplant with Black Beans and Pork. Waltnuck also includes some refreshingly simple yet elegant recipes, including cold boiled chicken served with a spicy Asian dipping sauce. Given the eclectic and global nature of the recipes, one gets the feeling that the staff meals at Chanterelle might have been influenced by the ethnic backgrounds of the entire kitchen staff. (I am waiting for them to put out their own cookbook—these are recipes I would kill for.)

CONS: OK, lots of these recipes are not well suited for home cooking. Although *Staff Meals* does deliver a good number of simple recipes, we were hoping for a higher percentage of fast and easy dishes.

RECIPE TESTING: Good news. About two-thirds of the recipes we tested were worth making again, a very high percentage indeed. A chilled avocado soup took just 10 minutes to prepare and was outstanding. Wild Turkey Glazed Ribs were good, the Vegetable Lo Mein was quick and easy (although our noodles stuck to the wok), and the pancakes lived up to their enthusiastic billing. But a fish stew, while excellent, took three hours to make. A leftover polenta dish with spicy tomato sauce made sense for a restaurant, but if you don't have leftover polenta (which needs to be cooled, cut into squares, and then baked), forget about it.

CHARLIE PALMER'S CASUAL COOKING
Charlie Palmer
Morrow Cookbooks, 236 pages

Palmer starts this book by making a few promises: the recipes will be suitable for the home cook, very few special ingredients will be required, and the food will be, well—he said it in the title—casual. Even a cursory glance at the recipe titles indicates that this is indeed casual food—from a tuna melt and hamburger to potato gratin and roast chicken. So the question immediately arises: "What is special about these recipes?" Are they the sort of recipes that are available anywhere, or has the author imbued them with his own particular culinary talents?

PROS: Here, at last, is a famous New York chef who seems like a regular guy on the weekends when he cooks at home. I can find the ingredients at Price Chopper or Stop & Shop (the tamarind pulp in the Grilled, Marinated Quail is an exception), and the cooking does not require first acquiring one's "chops" in one of Palmer's establishments. Some of these straightforward recipes do have an unusual twist, though, such as kimchee in cucumber soup and basil with crème fraîche for a dessert.

CONS: The recipe titles are not, in and of themselves, inspiring. We have all seen Mom's Chicken Noodle Soup before, as well as some variation on "Cheez Sammiches." If you are looking for a completely new take on home cooking, look somewhere else.

RECIPE TESTING: As with *Staff Meals*, a majority of the recipes turned out well, although a few called for restaurant-style accents that were not always well received in our test kitchen. The best recipe we tested was a watercress salad with baked goat cheese: it was both spectacular and simple. (Goat cheese is dipped in olive oil and bread crumbs and then baked and served with watercress.) Strawberry tarts were very good, but the basil added to the crème fraîche was not loved by our tasters. While the cucumber soup was wonderful, the addition of an odd ingredient—the kimchee—was interesting in theory but an acquired taste in practice. Both linguine with eggplant ragu and grilled scallop and onion brochettes were good, a lobster club sandwich was way over the top (too rich for our taste as the lobster was drenched in mayonnaise and served with a load of bacon), and the macaroni and cheese was afflicted with ingredients such as mascarpone and white wine. Sometimes simpler really is better.

Most of the ingredients and materials necessary for the recipes in this issue are available at your local supermarket, gourmet store, or kitchen supply shop. The following are mail-order sources for particular items. Prices listed below were current at press time and do not include shipping or handling unless otherwise indicated. We suggest that you contact companies directly to confirm up-to-date prices and availability.

Sauté Pans

Two All-Clads topped our sauté pan rating on page 27. An overall great performer, the spacious and user-friendly All-Clad Stainless Steel 3 Quart Sauté Pan, model 5403, with its long stay-cool handle and "helper handle," was our favorite. **A Cook's Wares (211 37th Street, Beaver Falls, PA 15010-9788; 800-915-9788; www.cookswares.com)** sells the pan (with cover) for $165, item #2712. The store also carries our favorite nonstick pan—the All-Clad Stainless Steel Nonstick 3 Quart Sauté Pan, model 5403-NS—for $175, item #2734.

Yeast

SAF Instant Yeast, Red Star Instant Active Dry Yeast, and Fermipan Instant Yeast may be hard to find in grocery stores, but they can be mail-ordered in one-pound, vacuum-packed bags—good for frequent bread bakers—from **The Baker's Catalogue (King Arthur Flour, P.O. Box 876, Norwich, VT 05055; 800-827-6836; www.kingarthurflour.com)**. SAF, the long-time industry leader in the production of instant yeast, sells for $4.50, item #1466; Red Star for $5.50, item #1468; and Fermipan for $4.50, item #1472.

Pizza Paraphernalia

Parchment paper, extrawide plastic wrap, and a lightweight French-style rolling pin will help you roll your thin-crust pizza dough out to the desired 14 inches. Floured lightly, a sheet of 16.4 by 24.4-inch, heavy-duty parchment paper is an ideal surface on which to roll and stretch the dough. **Bridge Kitchenware (214 East 52nd Street, New York, NY 10022; 800-274-3435; www. bridge kitchenware. com)** sells a box of 40 commercial-grade sheets for $4.00, item code ABKP-PS. Covering the dough lightly with plastic wrap eliminates the need to periodically dust the pin with flour, which would introduce more flour to the dough and possibly dry it out. Recently released to markets nationwide, Reynolds Extra Wide Plastic Wrap is a huge 18 inches in width and will keep the dough thoroughly covered until it reaches the expected 14 inches in diameter. We were able to purchase a box of 50 feet for $2.59.

A tapered French-style rolling pin is the perfect tool for rolling out the dough as thin as a credit card. **Kitchen Arts (161 Newbury Street, Boston, MA 02116; 617-266-8701)** sells a tapered beechwood rolling pin that is 20 inches long and 2 inches thick at its widest point. This lightweight pin, which is easier to manipulate than its standard, bulky cousin, sells for $14.00, including shipping within the United States.

After the dough has been rolled out and topped and the parchment trimmed, the next step is to transfer the pizza onto a baking stone that has been heating up in the oven. The best way to do this is with a baker's peel. The peel is easy to maneuver and keeps the cook a safe distance from the blazing hot pizza stone. The baking stone's capacity to absorb heat from the oven and transfer it to the dough is instrumental in the development of a crisp, shattering crust. **The Baker's Catalogue (P.O. Box 876, Norwich, VT 05055; 800-827-6836; www.kingarthurflour.com)** carries both a baker's peel (14-inch square aluminum blade and 12-inch wooden handle, item #5717, $16.95) and a baking stone (item #5236, $34.95).

Boning Knife

A boning knife is an excellent tool with which to remove the fat and silverskin from the meat for the beef Burgundy on page 13. Its slender shape, slightly curved design, and light weight make it easy to maneuver around these trouble spots. You can order our favorite, the Victorinox Fibrox 6-inch stiff boning knife from **Professional Cutlery Direct (242 Branford Road, North Branford, CT 06471; 800-859-6994; www.cutlery.com)**, item #1CI2F, for $18.10.

Fresh Dried Beans

While developing the Tuscan White Bean Soup recipe (page 21), test cook Bridget Lancaster ran into some trouble finding fresh dried beans. When dried beans are fully hydrated and cooked, they should be plump, with taut skin, and have creamy insides; spent beans will have wrinkled skin and a dry, almost gritty texture. If you think your local grocery store stocks old beans, you can mail-order a huge array (though only via the Internet) from **Woodland Foods (2011 Swanson Court, Gurnee, IL 60031; 847-625-8600; www.gourmetstore.com)**. A 12-ounce bag of cannellini beans, item #B09GA, costs $2.35. If you don't have Web access, call Woodland Foods to locate a distributor near you.

Bread Blankee

Duck cloth makes a great bread blanket (see Kitchen Notes, page 30). If you can't find any in your favorite fabric store, try **Jo-Ann Fabrics (841 Apollo Street, Suite 100, El Segundo, CA 90245; 800-525-4951; www.joann.com)**, a nationwide chain of fabric and craft stores with hundreds of retail outlets nationwide. Try the Web site or 800 number to locate a store near you. Jo-Ann's duck cloth, which costs roughly $7.00 per yard, is a bit lighter than our canvas, but it has the same overall texture and works just as well. We suggest buying a piece that is 4 by 6 feet and folding it to 2 by 3 feet for use.

United States Postal Service
Statement of Ownership, Management, and Circulation

1. Publication Title: Cook's Illustrated
2. Publication Number: 1068-2821
3. Filing Date: 10/1/00
4. Issue Frequency: Bi-Monthly
5. Number of Issues Published Annually: 6
6. Annual Subscription Price: $29.70
7. Complete Mailing Address of Known Office of Publication: Boston Common Press, 17 Station Street, Brookline, MA 02146
Contact Person
Telephone: 617-232-1000
8. Complete Mailing Address of Headquarters or General Business Office of Publisher: Same as above.
9. Full Names and Complete Mailing Addresses of Publisher, Editor, and Managing Editor
Publisher: Christopher Kimball, Boston Common Press, 17 Station St., Brookline, MA 024-
Editor: Same as Publisher
Managing Editor: Barbara Bourassa, Boston Common Press, 17 Station St., Brookline, MA 02445
10. Owner: Boston Common Press Limited Partnership, 17 Station Street, Brookline, MA 02 (Christopher Kimball)
11. Known Bondholders, Mortgagees, and Other Security Holders: None / N/A
12. Tax Status: Has Not Changed During Preceding 12 Months
PS Form 3526, September 1998

13. Publication Title: Cook's Illustrated
14. Issue Date for Circulation Data Below: Sept/Oct 2000

15. Extent and Nature of Circulation	Average No. Copies Each Issue During Preceding 12 Months	No. Copies of Single Issue Published Nearest to Filing Date
a. Total Number of Copies (Net press run)	477,055	470,615
b. Paid and/or Requested Circulation (1) Paid/Requested Outside-County Mail Subscriptions Stated on Form 3541	352,574	346,740
(2) Paid In-County Subscriptions	0	0
(3) Sales Through Dealers and Carriers, Street Vendors, Counter Sales, and Other Non-USPS Paid Distribution	56,488	55,200
(4) Other Classes Mailed Through the USPS	0	0
c. Total Paid and/or Requested Circulation	409,063	401,940
d. Free Distribution by Mail (1) Outside-County as Stated on Form 3541	4,529	4,676
(2) In-County as Stated on Form 3541	0	0
(3) Other Classes Mailed Through the USPS	0	0
e. Free Distribution Outside the Mail (Carriers or other means)	430	430
f. Total Free Distribution	4,959	5,106
g. Total Distribution	414,022	407,046
h. Copies not Distributed	63,034	63,569
i. Total	477,055	470,615
j. Percent Paid and/or Requested Circulation	98.8%	98.7%

16. Publication of Statement of Ownership: Publication required. Will be printed in the Jan/Feb 2001 issue of this publication.
17. Signature and Title of Editor, Publisher, Business Manager, or Owner
Date: 10/1/00

I certify that all information furnished on this form is true and complete.

PS Form 3526, September 1998 (Reverse)

Instructions to Publishers

RECIPES
January & February 2001

Beef Burgundy

Thin-Crust Pizza

Main Dishes
Beef Burgundy **13**
Chicken Piccata **7**
   with Black Olives **7**
   Peppery **7**
   with Prosciutto **7**
Crisp Thin-Crust Pizza **9**
Stir-Fried Shrimp,
   Aromatic **19**
   Cantonese-Style **19**
   Singapore Chili **19**
FOR STIR-FRIED SHRIMP:
   Simplest Shrimp Broth **19**

Soups and Sides Dishes
Roasted Carrots,
   Maple, with Browned Butter **15**
   with Ginger-Orange Glaze **15**
   Simple **15**
White Bean Soup,
   Quick **21**
   Tuscan **21**
   with Winter Vegetables **21**

Pestos and Sauces
Pesto,
   Arugula and Ricotta **11**
   Mushroom, with Parsley and
      Thyme **11**
   Roasted Red Pepper **11**
   Toasted Nut and Parsley **11**
Quick Tomato Sauce for Pizza **10**

Desserts
Apple Turnovers, Flaky **23**
Chocolate Sheet Cake,
   Simple **24**
FOR CHOCOLATE SHEET CAKE:
   Creamy Milk Chocolate
      Frosting **24**

Simple Roasted Carrots

Arugula and Ricotta Pesto

Chicken Piccata

PHOTOGRAPHY: CARL TREMBLAY AND VAN ACKERE (White Bean Soup)

www.cooksillustrated.com

If you enjoy *Cook's Illustrated* magazine, you should visit our Web site. Simply log on at www.cooksillustrated.com. Although much of the information is free, database searches are for site subscribers only. *Cook's Illustrated* readers are offered a 20 percent discount.

Aromatic Stir-Fried Shrimp

Tuscan White Bean Soup

Here's what you can do at our site:
Search Our Recipes: We have a searchable database of all recipes published in *Cook's Illustrated*.
Search Tastings and Cookware Ratings: You will find all of our reviews (cookware, food, wine, cookbooks) plus new material created exclusively for the Web site.
Find Your Favorite Quick Tips.
Get Your Cooking Questions Answered: Post questions for *Cook's* editors and fellow site subscribers.
Take a Cooking Course Online: Take online cooking courses from *Cook's* editors and receive personalized instruction.
Check Your Subscription: Check the status

of your subscription, pay a bill, or give gift subscriptions online.
Visit Our Bookstore: You can purchase any of our cookbooks, hardbound annual editions of the magazine, or posters online.
Subscribe to *e-Notes:* Our free e-mail companion to the magazine's Kitchen Notes offers cooking advice, test results, buying tips, and recipes about a single topic each month.
Find Out about Our New Public Television Show: Watch for *America's Test Kitchen*, to see the *Cook's Illustrated* staff at work in our test kitchen.
Get All the Extras: The outtakes from each issue of *Cook's* are available at Cook's Extra, including step-by-step illustrations.

Chocolate Sheet Cake

Apple Turnovers

Adzuki

Flageolet

Jacob's Cattle

Pinto

Garbanzo

Rice Bean

Steuben YellowEye

Scarlet Runner

Appaloosa

Kidney

Cannellini

Black-Eyed Pea

DRIED BEANS

©2000

COOK'S
ILLUSTRATED

Perfecting Pasta with Garlic and Oil
Use Both Raw and Cooked Garlic

Fresh Ham Roast
Brine and Then Roast at 500 Degrees

Crispy Chocolate Chip Cookies

Coconut Layer Cake
The Secret to Deep Coconut Flavor

Rating Supermarket Extra-Virgin Olive Oils
Can You Taste the Difference?

Do Garlic Presses Work?
We Test 10 Models to Find Out

Velvety Mushroom Soup
Quick Sauces for Asparagus
Refrigerator Rules
Really Good Fried Rice
Stuffed Peppers

$4.95 U.S./$6.95 CANADA

CONTENTS

March & April 2001

2 Notes from Readers
Readers ask questions and suggest solutions.

4 Quick Tips
Quick and easy ways to perform everyday kitchen tasks.

6 Stuffed Peppers
We discovered a technique for producing soft, tender peppers that are still firm enough to hold simple but flavorful fillings. BY JULIA COLLIN

8 Discovering Fresh Ham Roast
With the right brine, the right sequence of oven temperatures, and the right type of glaze, we transform an uncured ham into a pork roast with rich, moist meat and crackling crisp skin. BY RAQUEL PELZEL WITH JULIA COLLIN

11 Quick, Fresh Sauces for Asparagus
In fewer than 10 minutes, you can have both perfectly broiled asparagus and one of these four quick sauces.

12 Perfect Sautéed Turkey Cutlets
What's the difference between a juicy, flavorful turkey cutlet and a tough, dry one? Use just the right amount of heat and brown only on one side. BY ADAM RIED

14 Pasta with Garlic and Oil
The marriage of cooked and raw garlic as well as a generous splash of extra-virgin olive oil just before serving make this simple dish shout with flavor. BY KAY RENTSCHLER

16 Getting to Know Your Refrigerator
Is the meat drawer really cooler? Does the crisper really keep things crisp? BY RAQUEL PELZEL

18 Really Good Fried Rice
For fried rice that is light and flavorful rather than sodden and greasy, cook the ingredients in batches and forget about your fear of frying. BY BRIDGET LANCASTER

20 Velvety Mushroom Soup
Long, slow cooking turns ordinary supermarket mushrooms into deeply flavored, creamy mushroom soup. BY KAY RENTSCHLER

22 Thin and Crispy Chocolate Chip Cookies
Three sweeteners and one-sheet baking yield cookies with a satisfying crunch and praline-like texture. BY SHANNON BLAISDELL

24 Coconut Layer Cake
A triumvirate of coconut products puts maximum coconut flavor in this classic, tender cake. BY DAWN YANAGIHARA

26 Which Supermarket Extra-Virgin Olive Oil Is Best?
A blind tasting of nine supermarket olive oils reveals that the differences in brands are often minimal. BY RAQUEL PELZEL

28 Do Garlic Presses Really Work?
Once viewed as tools for culinary novices, garlic presses now come in models that can puree cloves—peeled or not—in just seconds. BY ADAM RIED

30 Kitchen Notes
Test results, buying tips, and advice related to stories past and present, directly from the test kitchen. BY KAY RENTSCHLER

31 Jewish Cooking
Two ambitious cookbooks tackle the subject of Jewish cooking. Each succeeds admirably, though in different ways. BY CHRISTOPHER KIMBALL

32 Resources
Products from this issue, why we like them, and where to get them.

COOK'S ILLUSTRATED

www.cooksillustrated.com

PUBLISHER AND EDITOR
Christopher Kimball

SENIOR EDITOR
John Willoughby

SENIOR WRITER
Jack Bishop

CORPORATE MANAGING EDITOR
Barbara Bourassa

TEST KITCHEN DIRECTOR
Kay Rentschler

ASSOCIATE EDITORS
Adam Ried
Dawn Yanagihara
Raquel Pelzel

RECIPE TESTING AND DEVELOPMENT
Bridget Lancaster
Julia Collin

ASSISTANT EDITOR
Shannon Blaisdell

CONSULTING FOOD EDITOR
Jasper White

CONTRIBUTING EDITOR
Elizabeth Germain

ART DIRECTOR
Amy Klee

COPY EDITOR
India Koopman

PROOFREADER
Jana Branch

EDITORIAL INTERNS
Tammy Inman
Matthew Card

SPECIAL PROJECTS
Barry Estabrook

ASSOCIATE EDITOR,
ONLINE EDUCATION
Becky Hays

ASSISTANT EDITOR, WEB SITE
Shona Simkin

MARKETING MANAGER
Pamela Caporino

SALES REPRESENTATIVE
Jason Geller

MARKETING ASSISTANT
Connie Forbes

CIRCULATION DIRECTOR
David Mack

CIRCULATION MANAGER
Larisa Greiner

PRODUCTS MANAGER
Steven Browall

DIRECT MAIL MANAGER
Robert Lee

CIRCULATION ASSISTANT
Jennifer McCreary

INBOUND MARKETING REPRESENTATIVES
Adam Dardeck
Jacqui Valerio

VICE PRESIDENT OPERATIONS
AND TECHNOLOGY
James McCormack

PRODUCTION MANAGER
Jessica Lindheimer

PRODUCTION ARTIST
Daniel Frey

PRODUCTION COORDINATOR
Mary Connelly

PRODUCTION INTERN
Christine Rizzo

SYSTEMS ADMINISTRATOR
Richard Cassidy

WEB MASTER
Nicole Morris

CONTROLLER
Mandy Shito

OFFICE MANAGER
Juliet Nusbaum

PUBLICITY
Deborah Broide

For list rental information, contact The SpecialLISTS, 1200 Harbor Blvd. 9th Floor, Weehawken, NJ 07087; 201-865-5800; fax 201-867-2450. Editorial office: 17 Station Street, Brookline, MA 02445; 617-232-1000; fax 617-232-1572. Editorial contributions should be sent to: Editor, *Cook's Illustrated*. We cannot assume responsibility for manuscripts submitted to us. Submissions will be returned only if accompanied by a large self-addressed envelope. Postmaster: Send all new orders, subscription inquiries, and change of address notices to: *Cook's Illustrated*, P.O. Box 7446, Red Oak, IA 51591-0446. PRINTED IN CHINA.

BRASSICA The highly useful *Brassica* family consists of many quite dissimilar varieties of cruciferous vegetables. The two most common, broccoli and cauliflower, have dense clusters of edible immature flower buds. Turnips and rutabagas, on the other hand, are grown for their fleshy, tender roots, while kohlrabi, which looks like a root, is actually a sweet, bulbous stem that grows above ground. Among the many cabbage varieties in the *Brassica* clan are commonplace head cabbages as well as Brussels sprouts, small cabbagelike buds that sprout from a thick stem. The strongly flavored and often bitter *Brassica* greens include the several varieties of kale and mustard greens. The many traits of this far-flung family come together in broccoli rabe, which features long, slender stalks and small clusters of immature buds along with dark, bitter greens.

COVER (*Artichokes*): ELIZABETH BRANDON, BACK COVER (*Brassica*): JOHN BURGOYNE

COOKING WITH JULIA

Julia Child and I live in neighboring towns, so once or twice a year we get together and cook. Some might find such an invitation daunting—after all, Julia is a formidable icon, the person one would least like to have stoveside after botching a soufflé—but my guess is that her expectations of my cooking skills are probably pretty low, so I never give it much thought. On one such occasion, she invited me over for an impromptu supper. I was to bring the makings of soup and dessert, and she would make the rest. The soup was a well-tested showstopper, a chowder that has never failed to please. The dessert would be a casual, last-minute peach tart.

In an age of $100,000 kitchens, Julia's is hardly worth a mention. It is small and packed with papers, pans, books, and tools. The center of the space is filled with a simple plastic-covered kitchen table. This is the spot where one dines with Julia unless the crowd is greater than six, at which point the dinner is moved to the more formal dining room. My introduction to Julia was in the early 1980s, when I interviewed her at this modest table, and she served me the world's best oyster stew. On this evening, however, I was there to cook.

I have learned over the years that if one needs to prepare food at Julia's, one is expected to fend for oneself. The kitchen is at your disposal, but Julia assumes that you have a sufficient degree of proficiency in culinary matters to choose your own saucepan or pick the right knife. She is also kind enough to present a casual indifference to your difficulties, as once happened while I was trying to shuck a dozen oysters. Used to chefs who manage this feat in seconds, Julia paid my belabored progress little attention until I began to endanger the progress of the meal, at which point she asked in her trademark high-pitched voice, "Have you ever tried using a can opener?" The implication was, of course, that only an incompetent cook would have to trade an oyster knife for a church key. I ignored the question and grimly made it through the full dozen, late but stalwart.

On the evening in question, two of Julia's old friends served a first course of freshly dug new potatoes from Maine, boiled and accompanied by caviar. Next up was my well-tested chowder. Julia approached it with curiosity before giving it a rather cursory rejection. For whatever reason, this dish did not meet with her approval, perhaps being a bit too rustic or lacking in some aspect of execution. I served a New Zealand Riesling with the briny chowder, which piqued her interest a bit, but only for a moment. She then turned her attention to politics and the main course.

Sitting on a stool at the old Garland stove, Julia ministered to duck parts in a large sauté pan. To my surprise, this was not a dish from *Mastering the Art of French Cooking* or some other, more recent work. She was experimenting with a new recipe and was eager to discover how it would turn out. Although a staunch liberal when it comes to politics, Julia is eminently flexible about the culinary arts (unless one is preparing some vulgar American road food such as

Christopher Kimball

canned cherry pie or sticky barbecue). Julia was curious, hopeful that she might learn something new about cooking duck, a dish she must have made a thousand times in her career. On this evening, the duck recipe was a triumph, the thin, crispy skin covering rich, tender meat.

Dinner was over, the dishes had been cleared, and it was now time to serve my thrown-together tart. Julia took one bite, and, as I held my breath and watched her closely for signs of approval, a smile gradually made its way onto her face, perhaps a memory of a long-ago lunch in Provence causing a happy association. Every bite was savored, every morsel of the crust consumed with relish.

Since that time, I have had my ups and downs when cooking with Julia. I have thrown caution to the wind and, on occasion, met with abject failure, but I have also had moments when a first bite leads to an unsolicited compliment. Cooking with Julia should be, if nothing else, an adventure, moments of uncertainty and improvisation that result in unpredictable outcomes. If Julia, at fourscore and more years, is still eager to grab hold of the train we are all riding, lean into the wind, and look into the distance searching for signs of the unfamiliar, we had best tag along. For we know that she will lead us to that undiscovered country where the sky is painted with dreams and smiles appear on the faces of angels.

ABOUT COOK'S ILLUSTRATED

Visit our expanded Web site The *Cook's* Web site features original editorial content not found in the magazine as well as searchable databases for recipes, equipment tests, food tastings, buying advice, step-by-step technique illustrations, and quick tips. The site also features our online bookstore, a question and answer message board, a sign-up form for *e-Notes*, our free newsletter on cooking, as well as infomation on *America's Test Kitchen*, our new television series currently airing on Public Television. Join us online today at www.cooksillustrated.com.

The Magazine *Cook's Illustrated* (ISSN 1068-2821) is published bimonthly (6 issues per year) by Boston Common Press Limited Partnership, 17 Station Street, Brookline, MA 02445. Copyright 2001 Boston Common Press Limited Partnership. Periodical postage paid at Boston, Mass., and additional mailing offices, USPS #012487. A one-year subscription is $29.70, two years is $55, and three years is $75. Add $6 postage per year for Canadian subscriptions and $12 per year for all other foreign countries. To order subscriptions in the U.S. call 800-526-8442; from outside the U.S. call 515-247-7571. Gift subscriptions are available for $24.95 each. Postmaster: Send all new orders, subscription inquiries, and change of address notices to *Cook's Illustrated*, P.O. Box 7446, Red Oak, IA 51591-0446.

Cookbooks and other products *Cook's Illustrated* offers cookbooks and magazine-related items for sale through its online bookstore. Products offered include annual hardbound editions of the magazine, an eight-year (1993–2000) reference index for the magazine, single-subject cookbooks from our How to Cook Master Series, as well as copies of *The Best Recipe, The Complete Book of Pasta and Noodles, The Dessert Bible, The Best Recipe: Grilling & Barbecue,* and many others. Prices and ordering information are available by calling 800-611-0759 inside the U.S. or 515-246-6911 from outside the U.S. or visiting our bookstore at www.cooksillustrated.com. Back issues of *Cook's Illustrated* are available for sale by calling 800-611-0759 inside the U.S. or 515-246-6911 from outside the U.S.

Questions about your book order? Visit our customer care page at www.cooksillustrated.com, or call 800-611-0759 inside the U.S. or 515-246-6911 from outside the U.S.

Reader submissions *Cook's* accepts reader submissions for Quick Tips. We will provide a one-year complimentary subscription for each tip that we print. Send your tip, name, address, and daytime telephone number to Quick Tips, *Cook's Illustrated*, P.O. Box 470589, Brookline, MA 02447. Questions, suggestions, or submissions for Notes from Readers should be sent to the same address.

Questions about your subscription? Visit our customer service page at cooksillustrated.com where you can manage your subscription, including changing your address, renewing your subscription, paying your bill, or viewing answers to frequently asked questions. You can also direct questions about your subscription to *Cook's Illustrated*, P.O. Box 7446, Red Oak, IA 51591-0446, or call 800-526-8442.

No Piccata Pedigree

I often see piccata on Italian menus, but when I search for a recipe in my many Italian cookbooks, I come up empty-handed. What is the reason for this?

GUS BURROWS
PASADENA, CALIF.

➤ *Senior writer Jack Bishop replies:* The term *piccata* appears on Italian restaurant menus as regularly as fettuccine Alfredo or spaghetti carbonara. When I see the word *piccata* after chicken, veal, or turkey, I assume that the meat will be sautéed and sauced with lemon and capers.

After researching this term in more than 50 Italian cookbooks, however, I was surprised to find that none of the books written by Italian-born authors contained a recipe for piccata. Yes, there were recipes for sautéed cutlets with lemon and capers, but none was called piccata. While some of the books written by Italian-Americans had piccata recipes, not one mentioned any specific connection to Italy, such as where the sauce originated or what the word *piccata* means. (I later found that the word derives from *piccare*, meaning "to prick or sting," perhaps a reference to the sharp flavors of lemon and capers.)

A quick check of several culinary dictionaries only confused matters further. According to several reliable tomes, the term *piccata* refers to the cut of meat, typically thin cutlets of veal. In fact, in my research I ran across piccata recipes that contained neither lemon nor capers—and these days, chicken and even turkey have supplanted the pricey, out-of-favor veal.

Based on my research, it is safe to say that the picatta with which most Americans are familiar is a product not of Italy but of the Italian-American kitchen.

Looking for Proof

I am confused about the meaning of the term *proof* in bread baking. Does it have to do with the yeast or the dough?

ABBY FRIEDMAN
RUMSON, N.J.

➤ The term *proof* has two meanings—one having to do with yeast and the other with dough.

Proofing yeast is a quick way for bakers to determine whether or not the yeast spores in dry yeast or cake yeast are active. If these types of yeast have an extended stint in the refrigerator or if their age is unknown, it is a good idea to test them before using them in a recipe. To do so, fill a glass bowl or measuring cup with the amount of lukewarm water (105 to 115 degrees Fahrenheit) called for in the recipe, add ½ teaspoon of sugar for each tablespoon of yeast, and whisk until dissolved. Now sprinkle the yeast granules over the surface of the sugar water and whisk again. If active, the yeast will feed on the sugar and begin to foam and swell in five to 10 minutes. At this point, it is safe to proceed with the recipe. If there is no activity, the yeast will not do its work in the recipe and should not be used. Instant active dry yeast, which is what we use in our test kitchen (see "Understanding and Using Yeasts," January/February 2001), does not require proofing. Each package is marked with an expiration date and, if used within the specified time, should be active.

The other use of the term *proof* usually denotes a stage in the rising of dough. After its first rise, dough is deflated, or punched down, and shaped into its final form. The shaped dough is then set out for its final rise and fermentation before baking; this is the step that is referred to as *proofing*. Fermentation allows flavors to develop for better- and fuller-tasting bread. Most bread recipes recommend proofing dough at room temperature under plastic wrap or a clean, slightly damp, lightweight towel to prevent dehydration. Not all doughs proof quickly; some (like that developed for the story "Ultimate Homemade Baguette," March/April 2000) proof overnight. A reliable way to test the dough's progress is to touch it lightly with a moistened finger. At first the dough will feel firm and will bounce back to the touch. At the halfway mark it will feel spongy on the surface but firm underneath. It is ready for the oven when it feels altogether spongy and when the indentation left in the dough fills in slowly. If the indentation doesn't fill in at all, the dough has overproofed and is in danger of collapsing in the oven.

Clove Conundrum

Many of my holiday recipes call for cloves, and I realized that all the while I have been using them in cooking and baking, I have had no idea what they really are. Can you help?

ISABELLE EDMUNDS
TORONTO, CANADA

➤ By virtue of their distinct appearance and smell, cloves are one of the most easily recognized spices in the cabinet. But we concur: very few people know what they actually are.

Cloves are the intensely aromatic flower buds of *Syzygium aromaticum* (sometimes called *E. caryophyllata*), a tropical evergreen tree native to the Spice Islands of Indonesia. The pale green and pink buds are harvested from the tree before the flowers open and are laid out on palm mats to dry in the sun, or over gentle heat, until they turn reddish-brown and become the scepter-shaped cloves with which we are familiar. The head rests on top of a shaft that varies in length from about ½ to ¾ inch, or can be slightly longer.

Cloves contain 14 to 20 percent essential oils, the principal component of which is the aromatic oil eugenol. Eugenol oil, which concentrates as the buds dry, is responsible for the clove's characteristically penetrating peppery aroma and sweet-hot flavor. Cloves have an unmistakable taste that marries well with saline flavors such as ham (see page 8), pork, and sausage, and they are commonly used in baked goods and traditional Christmas fare such as wassail and mincemeat.

Because their essential oils dissipate when they are ground, cloves should always be bought whole. If you need cloves in powder form, you can easily crush them with a mortar and pestle or spice grinder. Whole or ground, cloves should always be used with a light hand because their flavor and aroma can easily overwhelm a dish.

No-Pop Pop-Up Timer

I made your Roast Crisped-Skin Turkey (November/December 2000) for Thanksgiving, and it was wonderful—juicy and delicious with skin just as crisp as promised. However, I was wondering why my pop-up timer didn't pop by the time the breast and thigh meat reached the temperatures specified in the recipe. Do you think it was faulty? How do these timers work, anyway?

TRACY WOOD
ALBANY, GA.

➤ Almost 20 years ago, some poultry suppliers began inserting automatic pop-up timers in their birds. The technology behind this device is quite simple. A harmless compound with a known melting temperature is liquefied in the bottom of the timer device. A spring is compressed into the molten material as it cools and hardens. The timer is then inserted into the thickest part of the breast. When the material at the bottom of the timer melts again during cooking, the spring is free to expand, and the plastic stem pops up.

The failure of your timer is due to the one basic problem with pop-up timers. The largest supplier of the devices, Volk Enterprises in Turlok, Calif., calibrates its timers to "pop" at 178 degrees Fahrenheit, a temperature chosen to make sure that the legs, which take more time to cook than the breast, will be completely cooked through. Unfortunately, this also guarantees that the breast meat will be thoroughly overcooked. Since we recommend that you remove the bird from the oven when the breast temperature reaches 165 degrees, the popper in your bird never got hot enough to pop.

Sticky Situations

Are there differences between long-, medium-, and short-grain rice aside from their length? I am not a fan of sticky rice and wonder if the different grains have different degrees of stickiness.

NANCY TESTIN
HARRINGTON, DEL.

➤ There is in fact a correlation between length of grain and stickiness in rice. Generally speaking, the shorter the grain the stickier the rice.

The grain of any variety of rice is determined by the ratio of its length to its width. In long-grain rice, the grains are more than three times as long as they are wide. Well-known varieties include basmati, jasmine, and the American Carolina Gold. Both medium- and short-grain rice are often marketed and sold as short-grain to set them apart from long-grain—both have a fatter, more rounded look. Medium grains are 2½ to three times longer than they are wide, and short grains are less than twice as long as they are wide. Most varieties of Japanese rice are medium- to short-grain, as are Italian Arborio (used for risotto) and Spanish Valencia (used for paella).

The stickiness of rice, referred to as waxiness in the rice industry, is related to its relative amount of amylose, a starch that does not gelatinize during cooking. The less amylose, the stickier the rice. Short-grain rice consists of 15 to 20 percent amylose, making it the most waxy and sticky of all rice types. Medium-grain rice has an average amylose content of 18 to 26 percent, putting it right in the middle of the waxiness spectrum. Finally, long-grain rice consists of 23 to 26 percent amylose, causing it to cook up light and fluffy.

The Virtues of Pizza Stones

I recently made your thin-crust pizza (January/February 2001), and my family thought it was better than any pizza we had ever eaten. My children asked me why I had to use a pizza stone in the oven, and I didn't know quite what to tell them. What exactly is the role of the stone?

DIANNA HENDERSON
PORTSMOUTH, N.H.

➤ Most pizza kitchens are equipped with stone or tile-lined ovens that supply the steady, dry, intense heat necessary to make pizzas with crisp, cracker-like crusts. Pizza stones (also called baking stones) were created to simulate these conditions in home ovens.

Home ovens, whether electric or gas, are furnished with thermostats that switch on and off to maintain the oven's internal temperature. This, along with the opening and closing of the oven door, causes the temperature to fluctuate, which can be damaging to baked goods that require extremely high heat. Our thin-crust pizza required such an environment, so we turned to the pizza stone to rectify the situation. Preheating our oven with a pizza stone at 500 degrees for 45 minutes evened out the heat in the oven, and the stone's ability to absorb, retain, and radiate heat insulated the pizza from temperature swings that may have occurred during baking. Likewise, the high and dry heat of

the stone radiating directly into the pizza dough for a mere 10 minutes caused the dough to give up more moisture than it would otherwise and thereby encouraged the formation of a particularly crispy crust.

Baking stones intended for home use are usually made from clay or terra cotta. When purchasing, be sure to look for the thickest possible stone. Thickness is indicative of a stone's ability to retain heat; the better the heat retention, the more quickly the stone will come back up to temperature between successive bakes. Thick stones are also less likely to crack than their thinner, lighter counterparts.

Mirepoix Defined

I am interested in making some of the soups from "Improving Vegetable Soups" (Charter Issue) but need to clarify something before I start. What is *mirepoix*? The article doesn't clearly define it, and I can't find reference to it in my cookbooks.

WAYNE KIDD
FAIRPORT, N.Y.

➤ *Mirepoix* is a mixture of onions, carrots, and celery that serves as a flavor base for stocks, broths, sauces, braises, and other dishes. The three vegetables are sautéed (alone or with other ingredients) until their flavor is exhausted and are usually removed before the sauce or dish is finished and served. Many roasts are also cooked over a bed of mirepoix—the flavors leached from the vegetables in combination with the drippings from the roast make for excellent gravy. The classic ratio of ingredients is 2 parts onions, 1 part carrots, and 1 part celery.

Errata

➤ In the story "Improving Dutch Apple Pie" in our November/December 2000 issue, we discovered a discrepancy between the text and the recipe. In the text, we state that the filled pie was done after 20 minutes in the oven; in the recipe, however, our instructions call for only 10 minutes. The reason? The baking time varies depending on the crispiness you desire in your topping. If you prebake your streusel to get an extra-crispy topping, as directed in the recipe, then the filled, topped pie is baked for only 10 minutes. If you prefer a softer streusel topping, simply sprinkle the filled pie with the uncooked streusel and bake the pie for 20 minutes.

WHAT IS IT?

I found this among other cast-iron pans at a local flea market. I thought perhaps it was used to make biscuits, but the indentations are not quite the right depth or shape for that—they are somewhat deep and rounded. Any ideas as to what the pan is used for?

FRANK UDAL
MINNEAPOLIS, MINN.

You have found a Danish *aebleskive* pan. Aebleskive are rounded, puffed dumplings stuffed in some manner (varying from recipe to recipe) with apples. The pan is usually round or hexagonal in shape, measures 8 inches in diameter, and has seven depressions, 2¼ inches in diameter and 1 inch deep, that are responsible for the dumplings' characteristically domed shape. To make the aebleskive, the semispherical depressions are buttered, heated, and filled with a batter of flour, milk, eggs, a bit of sugar, and apples. When the underside is done, the dumplings are turned over to cook the other side. The finished dumplings are dusted with confectioners' sugar and served with tea or a regional spiced red wine.

In Thailand, the very same pan is called a *Kanom krok* and is used to make hotcakes of the same name, churned out daily in open-air markets. Kanom krok are sweet and savory cakes made with a batter of coconut milk and ground rice. They are cooked in the pan's depressions until crispy and hot and are topped with shrimp, cilantro, chilies, or even sugar. Some are stuffed with ingredients such as scallions, pumpkin, or shrimp. The popular treats are usually served for breakfast or as a snack.

Quick Tips

Potato Peeling Trick

Peeling raw potatoes can be a challenge, the peeled flesh making the potato slippery and difficult to grasp. This is particularly true of smaller spuds. Joel Smith of Chicago, Ill., avoids this problem by creating a handle for the potatoes with a corkscrew. Just lodge the corkscrew firmly in the potato as if it were a cork, then hold the potato by the corkscrew handle.

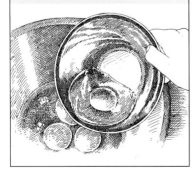

Safe Egg Separation

Loath though we are to dirty extra dishes, we're even more reluctant to risk contaminating a bowlful of good cracked eggs with a spoiled one. Once you've added a bad egg to the bowl, the whole lot is contaminated and has to be thrown away. To be on the safe side, Cheryl Weinstein of New London, N.H., sets up two bowls, one small and the other large. She then cracks one egg into the small bowl, inspects it, and, if it's OK, pours the egg into the large bowl, which will eventually contain all of the cracked eggs that have been inspected.

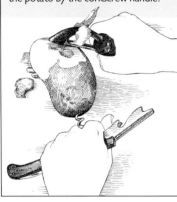

Storing and Measuring Brown Sugar

Pouring brown sugar out of its narrow box into a measuring cup can be a messy, frustrating chore. Sandra Biehl of Mesa, Ariz., has streamlined the task by transferring her brown sugar to a large, heavy-duty zipper-lock bag for storage. Not only does the sugar remain more moist during storage, but a cup measure fits inside the bag easily and can be loaded up by pressing the sugar into it through the plastic. No pouring, spilling, or sticky hands.

Using Up Fresh Herbs

Many cooks complain that fresh herbs such as parsley or basil are sold in bunches much larger than they need to make just one or two recipes. Often, the leftover herbs just rot in the refrigerator and have to be thrown out. Not one to let fresh herbs go to waste, Kimberly Apostol of Hoffman Estates, Ill., adds them to sandwiches in place of lettuce or other greens for an unexpected flavor boost.

Pie Weights Efficiency

Always on the lookout for ways to streamline her pie-baking efforts, Melanie Jones of Doylestown, Pa., stores her pie weights (or beans or rice used for the same purpose) in a doubled-up ovenproof cooking bag that can be used again and again. Because the bag can be lifted in and out of the pie plate, there's no need to line it with foil or transfer the weights from their storage container to the pie plate and back again.

Stabilizing Sandwiches

Be they grinders, hoagies, subs, or po' boys, overstuffed sandwiches in bulky rolls are an American favorite. But they can be pretty sloppy, with fillings spilling out every which way. Gregory Goodhart of Thurmont, Md., neatens up these sandwiches by pulling out some of the interior crumb in the top and bottom halves of the bread. This creates a trough in the bottom half for meat fillings and a cap on the top for toppings.

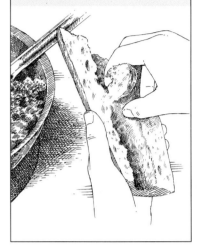

Clean Utensils at the Ready

Every cook knows the frustration of having to stop in the middle of dinner preparation to wash a utensil, such as a paring knife, which you've dirtied but need to use again. Ruthie Gershon of Virginia Beach, Va., eliminated this frustration when she thought to start her preparations by filling a glass or jar with hot, sudsy water. She slips a dirty utensil into the water to soak as soon as she's done with it, and, if she needs it again, just a quick rinse under the faucet makes it ready to go.

Send Us Your Tip We will provide a complimentary one-year subscription for each tip we print. See page 1 for information.

Sifter Coaster

When Gwen Brown of Forest Park, Ga., has to put down her sifter in the midst of a baking project, she usually places it on a sheet of wax or parchment paper to catch any flour that falls through. When she was out of wax paper one day, she devised an even better solution—she used the lid from her flour canister.

Collecting Zest Neatly

Tired of watching citrus zest fly off her Microplane zester and all over her work surface, Janice Montiverdi of Sugar Land, Texas, came up with a simple solution: she simply inverted the whole operation. When she turns the zester upside down, so that the teeth face down and the fruit is under the zester rather than above it, the shavings collect right in the trough of the zester.

Liberating Trapped Muffins

Every now and then, one muffin will stick tenaciously to its cup. In these cases, Michael Richards of Murrumbateman, NSW, Australia, uses a curved grapefruit knife to gently free the bottom of the muffin from the cup.

More Deviled Eggs Tricks

In the recipe for deviled eggs in our May/June 2000 issue, we suggested using a slotted spoon to transfer the hot eggs to their ice-water bath. One reader, Jennifer Ware from Austin, Texas, found that a poorly timed nudge or a shift in balance can easily send the eggs flying out of the shallow spoon and onto the floor. When she goes about this task now, her tool of choice is a pasta server, which has a deep bowl and is the ideal size to cradle an egg securely.

In our May/June 2000 Quick Tips, Lynn Cheesebrough of Laramie, Wyo., suggested a method for keeping already-filled deviled eggs stable when transporting them from home to their ultimate destination. John Allen of Sherman, Conn., sidesteps the problem of stabilizing the eggs by packing the prepared filling into a zipper-lock bag, then simply placing the egg white halves and the bag of filling in a cooler for transport. Just before serving the eggs, he snips the corner of the bag and pipes the filling into the halved whites, a technique we recommended in our recipe for deviled eggs.

Protecting a Roast's Brown Crust

For many of us, the crispy brown skin is the most sought after morsel of a roasted chicken or turkey. The same can be said of the crust that forms on the outside of a roast. But when the roast reposes before it is carved and served, the bottom crust is often softened by the juices that accumulate in the platter. Joseph Dillon III of Chicago, Ill., gets around this problem by letting the roast rest on a wire rack, thereby elevating the meat over the puddle of juices.

Tongs Caddy

Tongs are our tool of choice for a wide range of cooking projects. When Teri Pang of Honolulu, Hawaii, cooks with tongs, she keeps them at the ready by resting them in a heavy beer or coffee mug. This way, any juices on the tongs drip into the mug.

Opening Stubborn Jar Lids

Here's another way to remove stubborn jar lids, this time from Palmer Van Dyke of Murphys, Calif. Invert the jar so that it rests lid-down in about 1/2 inch of hot tap water in a shallow bowl or pie plate. After 30 seconds or so, the heat will break the vacuum seal and the lid will unscrew easily.

Unloading Simplified

Unloading the dishwasher is a dreaded chore. Lisa Van Sand of Gloucester, Mass., has found that a little extra care while loading the silverware makes unloading go faster. Separate the silverware as you go; all forks together, knives together, and so on. At unloading time, simply grab each bunch of silverware and store.

Stuffed Peppers

We discovered a technique for producing soft, tender peppers that are still firm enough to hold simple but flavorful fillings.

⇒ BY JULIA COLLIN ⇐

The first stuffed pepper I ever tasted was a U.S. Army green shell crammed with leftovers from the school cafeteria. I never gave this dish any credit after that. So when a colleague recently spoke fondly of stuffed peppers, I was surprised. Although her description of the classic 1950s sweet pepper—filled with aromatic rice and beef and topped with ketchup—sounded mediocre to me, she swore it was delicious. I also knew that this stuffed vegetable was highly valued in Middle Eastern cuisines. Wondering if I could possibly be missing out on something, I set out to find a stuffed pepper worth eating.

To get my palate going, I tried a few classic recipes. Although these trial runs produced nothing as bad as what I remembered from the school cafeteria, they were far from perfect. First off, the peppers themselves varied greatly in degree of doneness. Some were so thoroughly cooked that they slumped onto their sides, unable to support their stuffed weight. On the other end of the spectrum, barely cooked peppers added an unfriendly crunch and bitter flavor to the mix. To be a success, the stuffed peppers would have to yield a tender bite yet retain enough structure to stand up proudly on the plate.

None of the fillings hit home, either. An all-rice version was uninteresting, while another stuffed with all meat was leaden and greasy. One recipe called for small amounts of so many varied ingredients that it made me think its creator just wanted to clean out her refrigerator. I came away from this first round of tests wanting a simple yet gratifying filling, neither humdrum nor packed with odd ingredients.

The Ideal Venue

To start, I needed a solid pepper venue with minimal crunch. So I steamed, microwaved, roasted, and blanched a round of peppers and lined them up for my colleagues to examine. The steamed and microwaved examples were bland in both color and flavor. I tried roasting in an uncovered dish filled with a little water, an

When shopping for bell peppers to stuff, it's best to choose those with broad bases that will allow the peppers to stand up on their own.

uncovered dish with no water, and a covered dish. Each procedure produced a bitter, subpar pepper. I knew that if I allowed the peppers to roast a little longer, their sugars would eventually caramelize and the peppers would turn sweet. But at that point their texture would also have disintegrated into that of an Italian sandwich ingredient. My tasters unanimously preferred the vibrant color, sturdiness, and overall sweeter flavor of the blanched peppers; the hot water actually seemed to have washed away some of their bitterness.

Usually, a freshly blanched vegetable is plunged immediately into an ice cold water bath in a process known as shocking. The point is to halt the cooking process at just the right moment while stabilizing the vegetable's brightened color. I find water baths to be a real pain, especially in a kitchen where counter space is prime property. Although the shocked peppers had a slightly brighter hue than those that had been blanched but not shocked, they took much longer to heat through in the oven. So I abandoned shocking

and instead fussed with blanching times, being careful to remove the peppers a little early and allow the residual heat to finish their cooking. I found that a three-minute dip in boiling water followed by a cooling period on the countertop yielded the perfect balance of structure and chew.

Fill 'Er Up

Even with a pepper that's cooked to perfection, everyone knows that in this dish the stuffing is the real star of the show. The options for stuffing ingredients are many, including couscous, polenta, and a number of interesting and unusual grains. But I landed on rice. A universal pantry ingredient, it is a classic in the world of stuffed peppers and easily accommodates many cuisines and updated flavors.

Because I wanted these stuffed peppers to work as a quick mid-week meal, my goal was to keep the rice-based filling simple and satisfying, with a streamlined ingredient list and preparation method. My tasters did not care much for sausage, heavy seasonings, or a mix of too many ingredients. To my surprise, they were big fans of the classic, 1950s version of a pepper stuffed with rice and ground beef. Sautéed onions and garlic rounded out the flavors, while tomatoes added a fresh note and some color. Bound together with a little cheese and topped with ketchup, this retro pepper is not only a model of "make it from what you have in the pantry" simplicity, but it also can be updated easily just by switching a few ingredients.

Now I had a pepper, and I had a filling. All I had to do was figure out the best way to get them together. The first trick is to use the boiling water from the blanched peppers to cook the rice. While the peppers cool and the rice cooks, the onions, garlic, and beef can be sautéed quickly. Then filling and peppers can be assembled and heated through in the oven. The result? Stuffed peppers that take only 45 minutes from start to finish—and that are also truly worth eating.

Color Blind

Bell peppers spanning the colors of the rainbow are now commonly found sitting side by side in the grocery store, no matter what the season. Wondering if these cheerfully colored peppers actually had different flavors or were simply cultivated for eye appeal, I conducted a blind tasting. After masking my colleagues' eyes with scarves, I lined them up to taste both raw and blanched examples of red, yellow, orange, green, and purple peppers fresh from the market.

No one guessed all of the colors correctly, but the differences in taste were dramatic. The favorite colors turned out to be red and orange. Without exhibiting much of a pungent pepper flavor, they were both pleasantly sweet. The yellow pepper, with its mildly sweet and slightly tannic flavor, was also well liked. The green pepper, the most easily recognized, was universally disliked for its unripe bitterness. The absolute worst entry, however, was the thin-skinned purple pepper. Its slimy texture and singularly unpleasing flavor elicited comments such as "What I imagine a shoe tastes like" and "Did I just eat a slug?"

As it turned out, these comments weren't far off the mark. As a bell pepper ripens, it turns from green to yellow, orange, or red, depending on the variety. These bright peppers are sweeter simply because they are ripe, whereas the bitter green pepper is unripe. Purple peppers, too, are harvested when immature and would turn an uncommonly dark green if allowed to ripen fully. So unless you're fond of the tannic bitterness of the common green and the purple varieties, I suggest sticking with yellow, orange, or red. —J.C.

CLASSIC STUFFED BELL PEPPERS
SERVES 4 AS A LIGHT MAIN DISH OR SIDE DISH

Salt
4 medium red, yellow, or orange bell peppers (about 6 ounces each), 1/2 inch trimmed off tops, cores and seeds discarded
1/2 cup long-grain white rice
1 1/2 tablespoons olive oil
1 medium onion, chopped fine (about 1 cup)
12 ounces ground beef, preferably ground chuck
3 medium garlic cloves, minced
1 (14 1/2-ounce) can diced tomatoes, drained, 1/4 cup juice reserved
1 1/4 cups (about 5 ounces) shredded Monterey Jack cheese
2 tablespoons chopped fresh parsley leaves
Ground black pepper
1/4 cup ketchup

1. Bring 4 quarts water to boil in large stockpot or Dutch oven over high heat. Add 1 tablespoon salt and bell peppers. Cook until peppers just begin to soften, about 3 minutes. Using slotted spoon, remove peppers from pot, drain off excess water, and place peppers cut-sides up on paper towels. Return water to boil; add rice and boil until tender, about 13 minutes. Drain rice and transfer to large bowl; set aside.

2. Adjust oven rack to middle position and heat oven to 350 degrees.

3. Meanwhile, heat 12-inch heavy-bottomed skillet over medium-high heat until hot, about 1 1/2 minutes; add oil and swirl to coat. Add onion and cook, stirring occasionally, until softened and beginning to brown, about 5 minutes. Add ground beef and cook, breaking beef into small pieces with spoon, until no longer pink, about 4 minutes. Stir in garlic and cook until fragrant, about 30 seconds. Transfer mixture to bowl with rice; stir in tomatoes, 1 cup cheese, parsley, and salt and pepper to taste.

4. Stir together ketchup and reserved tomato juice in small bowl.

5. Place peppers cut-side up in 9-inch square baking dish. Using soup spoon, divide filling evenly among peppers. Spoon 2 tablespoons ketchup mixture over each filled pepper and sprinkle each with 1 tablespoon of remaining cheese. Bake until cheese is browned and filling is heated through, 25 to 30 minutes. Serve immediately.

STUFFED BELL PEPPERS WITH SPICED LAMB, CURRANTS, AND FETA CHEESE
SERVES 4 AS A LIGHT MAIN DISH OR SIDE DISH

Salt
4 medium red, yellow, or orange bell peppers (about 6 ounces each), 1/2 inch trimmed off tops, cores and seeds discarded
1/2 cup long-grain white rice
1 1/2 tablespoons olive oil
1 medium onion, chopped fine (about 1 cup)
12 ounces ground lamb
1 tablespoon ground cumin
1 teaspoon ground cardamom
1/2 teaspoon ground cinnamon
1/2 teaspoon red pepper flakes
3 medium garlic cloves, minced
1 (1-inch) piece fresh ginger, minced (about 1 tablespoon)
1/4 cup currants
1 (14 1/2-ounce) can diced tomatoes, drained
1 cup (about 6 ounces) feta cheese, crumbled
2 tablespoons chopped fresh cilantro leaves
Ground black pepper
1/3 cup roughly chopped salted, toasted cashews

1. Follow recipe for Classic Stuffed Bell Peppers through step 2.

2. Meanwhile, heat 12-inch heavy-bottomed skillet over medium-high heat until hot, about 1 1/2 minutes; add oil and swirl to coat. Add onion and cook, stirring occasionally, until softened and beginning to brown, about 5 minutes. Add ground lamb, cumin, cardamom, cinnamon, and red pepper flakes; cook, breaking lamb into small pieces with spoon, until no longer pink, about 4 minutes. Stir in garlic, ginger, and currants; cook until fragrant, about 30 seconds. Transfer mixture to bowl with rice; stir in tomatoes, cheese, cilantro, and salt and pepper to taste.

3. Continue with recipe for Classic Stuffed Bell Peppers from step 5, substituting chopped cashews for ketchup mixture and cheese topping.

STUFFED BELL PEPPERS WITH CHICKEN, SMOKED MOZZARELLA, AND BASIL
SERVES 4 AS A LIGHT MAIN DISH OR SIDE DISH

Salt
4 medium red, yellow, or orange bell peppers (about 6 ounces each), 1/2 inch trimmed off tops, cores and seeds discarded
1/2 cup long-grain white rice
1 1/2 tablespoons olive oil
1 medium onion, chopped fine (about 1 cup)
12 ounces ground chicken
3 medium garlic cloves, minced
1 (14 1/2-ounce) can diced tomatoes, drained
1 cup (about 4 ounces) shredded smoked mozzarella
2 tablespoons chopped fresh basil leaves
Ground black pepper
1/3 cup fresh bread crumbs

1. Follow recipe for Classic Stuffed Bell Peppers through step 2.

2. Meanwhile, heat 12-inch heavy-bottomed skillet over medium-high heat until hot, about 1 1/2 minutes; add oil and swirl to coat. Add onion and cook, stirring occasionally, until softened and beginning to brown, about 5 minutes. Add chicken and cook, breaking it into small pieces with spoon, until chicken becomes opaque, about 4 minutes. Stir in garlic and cook until fragrant, about 30 seconds. Transfer mixture to bowl with rice; stir in tomatoes, cheese, basil, and salt and pepper to taste.

3. Continue with recipe for Classic Stuffed Bell Peppers from step 5, substituting bread crumbs for ketchup mixture and cheese topping.

TECHNIQUE
FILLING THE PEPPERS

It is easier to fill the peppers after they have been placed in the baking dish, because they hold steady.

Discovering Fresh Ham Roast

The right brine, the right sequence of oven temperatures, and
the right glaze transform an uncured ham into a pork roast with rich,
moist meat and crackling crisp skin.

≥ BY RAQUEL PELZEL WITH JULIA COLLIN ≤

Looking for a new centerpiece roast to alternate with the more traditional turkey or leg of lamb, we asked some of our cooking friends for suggestions. Several offered up the idea of fresh ham. We had already heard about and been intrigued by this unusual but accessible pork roast, so we decided that it bore investigation.

Although this roast is called a ham, it gains much of its undeniable appeal from the fact that it's really not a ham at all—or at least not what most of us understand the term to mean. It's not cured in the fashion of a Smithfield ham or salted and air-dried like prosciutto. It's not pressed or molded like a canned ham, and it's not smoked like a country ham. In fact, the only reason this cut of pork is called a ham is because it comes from the pig's hind leg.

Getting to Great Ham

Overall, our path to a great ham roast was surefooted. In fact, after just one round of tests we had a good idea of how to achieve both moist meat and crackling skin. But that does not mean the road to success was completely free of obstacles. As we soon found out, you definitely can do wrong by a fresh leg of pig. That became clear with our first parade of roasts, a motley crew consisting of three duds and one lovely ham.

Even before we began roasting, we had decided that a full fresh ham, weighing in at about 20 pounds, was too much for all but the very largest feast. So we decided to use one of the two cuts into which the leg is usually divided—the sirloin, which comes from the top of the leg, or the shank, from the bottom of the leg (see illustration on page 9). We also decided that we wanted our ham skin-on (we couldn't see giving up the opportunity for cracklings, after all). Fortunately, this is how these roasts are typically sold.

From our experiences with other large roasts, we knew what the big problem would be: making sure the roast cooks all the way through while the meat stays tender and moist. In our first set of

Buying a fresh ham can be tricky, and we had the best results when we ordered straight from the butcher. When ordering, be sure to ask for the shank end with the skin on and unscored.

tests, then, we wanted to assess not only the relative merits of sirloin and shank but also the best oven temperature and cooking time.

Early on in this process, we determined that the roast needed to be cooked to a lower final internal temperature than some experts recommend. We found that we preferred the roast pulled from the oven at 145 to 150 degrees—at this point, the meat is cooked to about medium and retains a slight blush. While the roast rests, its residual heat brings the temperature up to approximately 155 to 160 degrees.

That determined, we started testing different oven temperatures. First to come out of the oven was a ham from the sirloin end of the leg that we had roasted at a high temperature, 400 degrees, for its entire stay in the oven. Carving this ham was

akin to whittling wood—Olympics-worthy agility with the carving knife was required to gut around the aitch-bone (part of the hip), the cracklings were more suited for tap shoes than consumption, and the meat was dry, dry, dry. We moved on to roasting a shank-end ham at a low heat the whole way through. This ham tasted like a wrung-out washcloth, with no cracklings in sight. What we did appreciate was the straightforward bone composition of the shank end, which simplified carving and convinced us to use this end of the fresh ham for the remainder of our tests.

Next we roasted a shank-end ham by starting it at a low temperature (325 degrees) and finishing it at a higher one (400 degrees), hoping to end up with both moist meat and crispy cracklings. To our dismay, this ham was also rather dry, which we attributed to the ham's long stay in the oven, made necessary by the low cooking temperature. What's more, the brief hike in the temperature at the end of cooking didn't help to crisp the skin.

Again, we figured we ought to try the opposite: starting the ham at a high temperature to give the meat a head start and get the skin on its way to crisping, then turning down the heat for the remainder of the roasting time. Although the meat cooked according to this method was slightly chalky and dry, the skin was close to our goal, crispy enough to shatter between our teeth yet tender enough to stave off a trip to the dentist. We decided that this would be our master roasting method.

Hoping to solve the dry meat dilemma, we brined a shank-end ham, immersing it in a solution of salt water and spices to tenderize and flavor it. More than slightly biased from positive results we've achieved in past brining experiments with turkey, chicken, shellfish, and other cuts of pork, we expected brining to make the meat incredibly juicy. The salt in a brine causes the protein structure in meat to unravel and trap water in its fibers; brining also encourages the unwound proteins to gel, forming a barrier that helps seal in moisture. Together, these effects allow the cook to increase the roasting temperature, thus speeding the roasting process, without fear of drying out the meat. We drew on our brining knowledge from past stories to establish the necessary quantity of salt and the brining time (overnight) as well as the flavors with which to infuse the pork. Our estimations proved accurate: the brined shank emerged from the oven succulent and flavorful, with meat tender enough to fall apart in your mouth.

Just when we thought the ham couldn't possibly get any better, we decided to try roasting one shank face-down on a rack set in a roasting pan rather than letting it sit directly in the pan. This adjustment kept the cut end from becoming tough and leathery from direct contact with the hot pan. Rack roasting also allowed the heat to circulate around the ham constantly, promoting faster and more even cooking.

Sage Decision, Tidy Ending

With our timing and temperature firmly in place, we turned to tweaking the flavor of the roast and obtaining the type of cracklings we had heard of but never really tasted. Not content with the infusion of flavor from the brine, we turned to spice rubs to further develop the flavor of the roast. Fresh thyme, sage, rosemary, garlic, brown sugar, cloves, dried mustard, juniper berries, peppercorns, and salt were all given an equal opportunity to complement the pork. We liked the combination of sage's earthy sweetness and garlic's pungent bite as well as the edge of fresh parsley, peppercorns, and kosher salt. Since our composed rub didn't lean strongly in the direction of any one particular spice, we were left with a wide-open field of glazing options.

While some recipes we tried called for simply basting the roast in its own drippings, we veered in the direction of sugary glazes, opting for sugar's ability to crisp, caramelize, and sweeten the skin. But the intermittent encounters between glaze, brush, and ham were still under negotiation: Exactly when should we glaze? Throughout the roasting period? If so, at what intervals? Since part of the beauty of this pork roast is that it can be left in the oven mostly unattended, we didn't want glazing to complicate the process. Starting the ham at 500 degrees negated glazing it at the outset—the sugary glaze would definitely char black before the roast had been in the oven for too long. We decided to let the roast cook unglazed at 500 degrees for the first 20 minutes. We then turned the oven temperature down to 350 degrees and began to brush it liberally with glaze. We continued to do so in

Where's the Ham?

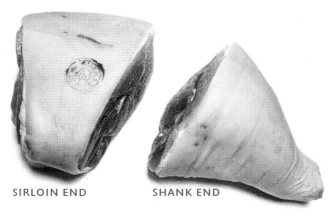

SIRLOIN END   SHANK END

Fresh ham comes from the pig's hind leg. Because a whole leg is too large for most occasions, it is usually cut into two sections. The sirloin, or butt, end, shown at left, is harder to carve than our favorite, the shank end, at right.

45-minute intervals, which amounted to three bastings during the roasting period. This ham was the one: flavorful meat with sweetened, crunchy skin.

Just as we thought the final rounds of testing were upon us, one more surprise was in store: when we opened a pork shipment from our butcher we discovered that our pork shank had been skinned. If it happened to us, we assumed it could also happen to others, so we tested our brining and glazing methods on the nude shank. Not only did the ham lack character and spine, but it shriveled up like a muscle gone into spasm. From this point on, when we order fresh ham, we will always ask for it with the skin on.

Now we really were in the homestretch. We cooked one more ham with our perfected method, let it rest under foil for about 30 minutes (imperative so that when the ham is sliced, the juices in

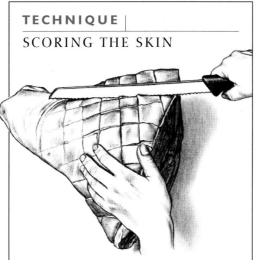

TECHNIQUE
SCORING THE SKIN

Without cutting into the meat, slice through the skin and fat with a serrated knife, making a 1-inch diamond pattern.

the meat stay there and do not run rampant across the work surface), then carved it using the method shown on page 10. The slices were moist and flavorful, the skin crimson and crispy.

More than one person at *Cook's* told me that this ham is the best roast pork they've ever eaten. Rich and tender, with an underlying hint of sweetness, the meat has the power to quiet a room full of vocal, opinionated cooks and editors. Perhaps even better is the sweet, slightly salty, crisp and crunchy skin that intensifies to a deep crimson by the time the roast is done. It was attacked with precision and proprietary swiftness during our trials in the test kitchen. Unbelievably succulent, tender, and uncomplicated, this culinary gem will leave you wondering how you could have gotten along so far without it.

ROAST FRESH HAM
SERVES 8 TO 10

If you don't have room in your refrigerator, you can brine the ham in a large insulated cooler or a small plastic garbage can; add five or six freezer packs to the brine to keep it well cooled.

Roast
- 1 bone-in fresh half ham with skin, 6 to 8 pounds, preferably shank end, rinsed

Brine
- 4 cups kosher salt or 2 cups table salt
- 3 cups packed dark or light brown sugar
- 2 heads garlic, cloves separated, lightly crushed and peeled
- 10 bay leaves
- 1/2 cup black peppercorns, crushed

Garlic and Herb Rub
- 1 cup lightly packed sage leaves from 1 large bunch
- 1/2 cup parsley leaves from 1 bunch
- 8 medium garlic cloves, peeled
- 1 tablespoon kosher salt or 1 1/2 teaspoons table salt
- 1/2 tablespoon ground black pepper
- 1/4 cup olive oil

Glaze
- 1 recipe glaze (see page 10)

1. Following illustration at left, carefully slice through skin and fat with serrated knife, making 1-inch diamond pattern. Be careful not to cut into meat.

2. In large (about 16-quart) bucket or stockpot, dissolve salt and brown sugar in 1 gallon hot tap water. Add garlic, bay leaves, black pepper, and 1 gallon cold water. Submerge ham in brine and refrigerate 8 to 24 hours.

3. Set large disposable roasting pan on baking sheet for extra support; place flat wire rack in roasting pan. Remove ham from brine; rinse under cold

water and dry thoroughly with paper towels. Place ham, wide cut-side down, on rack. (If using sirloin end, place ham skin-side up.) Let ham stand, uncovered, at room temperature 1 hour.

4. Meanwhile, adjust oven rack to lowest position and heat oven to 500 degrees. In workbowl of food processor fitted with steel blade, process sage, parsley, garlic, salt, pepper, and oil until mixture forms smooth paste, about 30 seconds. Rub all sides of ham with paste.

5. Roast ham at 500 degrees for 20 minutes. Reduce oven temperature to 350 degrees and continue to roast, brushing ham with glaze every 45 minutes, until center of ham registers 145 to 150 degrees on instant-read thermometer, about 2½ hours longer. Tent ham loosely with foil and let stand until center of ham registers 155 to 160 degrees on thermometer, 30 to 40 minutes. Carve, following illustrations at right, and serve.

APPLE CIDER AND BROWN SUGAR GLAZE
MAKES ABOUT 1⅓ CUPS, ENOUGH TO GLAZE HAM

- 1 cup apple cider
- 2 cups packed dark or light brown sugar
- 5 whole cloves

TECHNIQUE |
THERMOMETER PLACEMENT

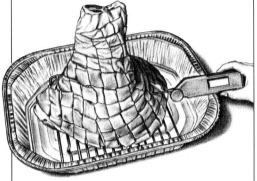

SHANK END With the ham placed cut-side down on a rack, insert the thermometer into the meat as illustrated to check its temperature.

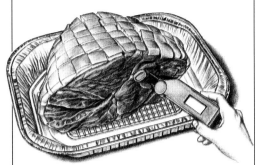

SIRLOIN END With the ham placed skin-side up on a rack, insert the thermometer into the narrow swath of meat as illustrated, alongside but not touching the bone, to check the temperature.

Bring cider, brown sugar, and cloves to boil in small nonreactive saucepan over high heat; reduce heat to medium-low and simmer until syrupy and reduced to about 1⅓ cups, 5 to 7 minutes. (Glaze will thicken as it cools between bastings; cook over medium heat about 1 minute, stirring once or twice, before using.)

SPICY PINEAPPLE-GINGER GLAZE
MAKES ABOUT 1⅓ CUPS, ENOUGH TO GLAZE HAM

- 1 cup pineapple juice
- 2 cups packed dark or light brown sugar
- 1 (1-inch) piece fresh ginger, grated (about 1 tablespoon)
- 1 tablespoon red pepper flakes

Bring pineapple juice, brown sugar, ginger, and red pepper flakes to boil in small nonreactive saucepan over high heat; reduce heat to medium-low and simmer until syrupy and reduced to about 1⅓ cups, 5 to 7 minutes. (Glaze will thicken as it cools between bastings; cook over medium heat about 1 minute, stirring once or twice, before using.)

ORANGE, CINNAMON, AND STAR ANISE GLAZE
MAKES ABOUT 1⅓ CUPS, ENOUGH TO GLAZE HAM

- 1 cup juice plus 1 tablespoon grated zest from 2 large oranges
- 2 cups packed dark or light brown sugar
- 4 pods star anise
- 1 (3-inch) cinnamon stick

Bring orange juice, brown sugar, star anise, and cinnamon to boil in small nonreactive saucepan over high heat; reduce heat to medium-low and simmer until syrupy and reduced to about 1⅓ cups, 5 to 7 minutes. (Glaze will thicken as it cools between bastings; cook over medium heat about 1 minute, stirring once or twice, before using.)

Cola Ham

Although cooking with Coke may seem humorous and unsophisticated, you haven't lived until you've tried cola pork. Cola pork was born when one of our staff members mentioned the southern tradition of Coca-Cola glaze and joked that we should try brining the meat in it. After giving this joke fair consideration, I dumped six liters of Coca-Cola Classic into a brine bucket, added 2½ cups of kosher salt, and let the ham soak in this foamy concoction overnight. The next day I cooked it according to our recipe. The outcome was the talk of the kitchen. It was juicy, it was unusual, it was fantastic. The Coke had added its own unique flavor to the ham while tenderizing the meat even more than our regular brine. The meat was falling off the bone and unbelievably tender throughout.

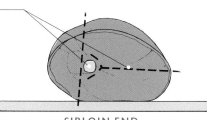

I turned to food scientist Dr. Eric Decker from the University of Massachusetts at Amherst to find out just what the Coke brine was doing. While Coke has about the same amount of sugar as orange or apple juice, he explained, it has roughly 27 times that of our brine. This higher sugar concentration flavors the meat. Coke is also considerably more acidic than our brine; it has a pH level of 3.3, while our brine is relatively neutral, hovering around 7. The acid helps to tenderize the roast by untangling (or denaturing) the protein strands, much like a marinade. Luckily, this sour, acidic flavor is balanced by the sugar and that unique Coca-Cola flavor, resulting in a ham you won't soon forget. —J.C.

COCA-COLA HAM
SERVES 8 TO 10

Follow recipe for Roast Fresh Ham, substituting six liters Coke Classic for both hot and cold water in brine, omitting sugar, and reducing salt to 3 cups Kosher salt or 1½ cups table salt.

TECHNIQUE | CARVING THE TWO CUTS OF HAM

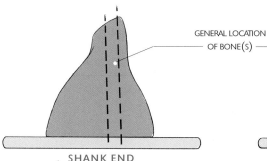

GENERAL LOCATION OF BONE(S)

SHANK END

1. Transfer the ham to a cutting board and carve it lengthwise alongside the bone, following the two dotted lines in the illustration above.
2. Lay the large boneless pieces that you have just carved flat on the cutting board and slice into ½-inch pieces.

SIRLOIN END

1. Transfer the ham to a cutting board and carve into three pieces around the bones along the dotted lines in the illustration above.
2. Lay the large boneless pieces that you have just carved flat on the cutting board and slice into ½-inch pieces.

Quick, Fresh Sauces for Asparagus

In fewer than 10 minutes, you can have both perfectly broiled asparagus and one of these four quick sauces.

You could, were you so inclined, call asparagus the double agent of the vegetable world. It has the feel and reputation of a fancy vegetable, much more uptown than, say, broccoli or carrots. Yet—and here is the great benefit for home cooks—it is arguably quicker and easier to cook than either of those more pedestrian choices. Better yet, asparagus goes well with almost any kind of sauce. We decided to capitalize on its easygoing nature and develop the quickest, lightest sauces we could—vinaigrettes.

Broiling was our cooking method of choice because it concentrates the flavor of the asparagus and lightly caramelizes its peels, thus making the most of its delicate taste. Broiling also keeps the stovetop free for other dishes. The two primary questions related to broiling concerned the thickness of the stalks and the distance they should be kept from the heat source during cooking.

In our tests with thicker asparagus, anywhere from ¾ inch to 1 inch in diameter, the peels began to char before the interior of the spears became fully tender. Another disadvantage of the thicker asparagus was that they often had to be peeled because their peels were generally thicker and tougher than those of more slender asparagus (with a maximum thickness of about ⅝ inch). Thinner asparagus not only let us skip the peeling step, they also tended to cook more evenly, without threat of burning.

Working now with thinner asparagus, we focused on how far to keep them from the heating element. At 3 inches, the asparagus charred a bit, just as the thicker spears had done. At 5 inches, the thinner asparagus took a little too long to cook, and they failed to develop enough caramelization for our taste. The middle ground, 4 inches, proved perfect for cooking speed, control, and browning.

While the asparagus speed along in the broiler, you need only whisk together some oil, an acid such as vinegar or lemon juice, and flavorings for a bright, simple sauce that beats the clock and keeps you free and clear of the stovetop.

SIMPLE BROILED ASPARAGUS

2   pounds (2 bunches) thin asparagus spears, tough ends trimmed (see illustration below)
1   tablespoon olive oil
    Salt and ground black pepper

1. Adjust oven rack to uppermost position and heat broiler.
2. Toss asparagus with oil and salt and pepper, then lay spears in single layer on heavy rimmed baking sheet. Broil about 4 inches from heating element, shaking pan halfway through to turn spears, until asparagus is tender and lightly browned, 8 to 10 minutes.
3. Cool asparagus 5 minutes and arrange on serving dish.

ASPARAGUS WITH SOY-GINGER VINAIGRETTE
SERVES 6 TO 8

2   medium scallions, white and green parts, minced
1   (1-inch) piece fresh ginger, minced (about 1 tablespoon)
2   small garlic cloves, pressed through garlic press or minced to puree (about 1½ teaspoons)
3   tablespoons Asian sesame oil
3   tablespoons soy sauce
¼   cup juice from 2 large limes
1   tablespoon honey
1   recipe Broiled Asparagus

Whisk scallions, ginger, garlic, sesame oil, soy sauce, lime juice, and honey in small bowl. Drizzle over asparagus and serve immediately.

ASPARAGUS WITH LEMON-SHALLOT VINAIGRETTE
SERVES 6 TO 8

1   large shallot, minced (about 2 tablespoons)
1   tablespoon juice plus 1 teaspoon grated zest from 1 lemon
1   tablespoon minced fresh thyme leaves
¼   teaspoon Dijon mustard
⅓   cup extra-virgin olive oil
    Salt and ground black pepper
1   recipe Broiled Asparagus

Whisk shallot, lemon juice and zest, thyme, mustard, and olive oil in small bowl; season to taste with salt and pepper. Drizzle over asparagus and serve immediately.

ASPARAGUS WITH TOMATO-BASIL VINAIGRETTE
SERVES 6 TO 8

1   medium ripe tomato, cored, seeded, and minced (about ½ cup)
1   medium shallot, minced (about 1½ tablespoons)
1½   tablespoons juice from 1 lemon
1   tablespoon minced fresh basil leaves
3   tablespoons extra-virgin olive oil
    Salt and ground black pepper
1   recipe Broiled Asparagus

Whisk tomato, shallot, lemon juice, basil, and olive oil in small bowl; season to taste with salt and pepper. Drizzle over asparagus and serve immediately.

ASPARAGUS WITH BACON, RED ONION, AND BALSAMIC VINAIGRETTE
SERVES 6 TO 8

6   slices bacon (about 6 ounces), cut into ¼-inch strips
2   tablespoons minced red onion
¼   cup balsamic vinegar
1   tablespoon minced fresh parsley leaves
¼   cup extra-virgin olive oil
    Salt and ground black pepper
1   recipe Broiled Asparagus

1. Fry bacon strips in medium skillet over medium heat until brown and crisp, about 6 minutes. Using slotted spoon, transfer bacon to paper towel–lined plate and set aside.
2. Whisk onion, vinegar, parsley, and oil in small bowl; season to taste with salt and pepper. Drizzle over asparagus, sprinkle with bacon, and serve immediately.

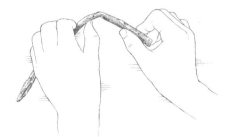

SNAPPING OFF THE TOUGH ENDS
Hold the asparagus about halfway down the stalk; with the other hand, hold the cut end between the thumb and index finger about an inch or so up from the bottom and bend the stalk until it snaps.

Perfect Sautéed Turkey Cutlets

What's the difference between a juicy, flavorful turkey cutlet and a tough, dry one?
Use just the right amount of heat and brown only on one side.

≥ BY ADAM RIED ≤

One quick look at the supermarket meat case will confirm it: Turkey has spread its wings far beyond Thanksgiving. There's ground turkey, smoked turkey, turkey parts, turkey sausage, and turkey burgers—to name just a few. But best of all for cooks in need of a light, quick, satisfying weeknight dinner, there are turkey cutlets.

Cutlets are thin slices of meat, usually no more than about ⅜ inch thick, cut from the breast. Sautéing is the ideal cooking method for cutlets because it's both fast and easy and can yield any number of delicious pan sauces. To sauté cutlets *well*, however, is something of a balancing act. You want to cook them just long enough, in a pan that is just hot enough to promote the formation of a flavorful crust. If the cutlets stay too long in a pan that's too hot, they can easily overcook or scorch, which will make them dry and hardly worth eating. To walk this sauté tightrope with confidence, I knew I would have to investigate the basic tenets of technique: cooking medium, temperature, and time.

The ideal turkey cutlet is of even thickness from end to end. It is cut across the grain of the breast so that its edges won't curl when it cooks and it won't be stringy when you eat it, and it is cut on the diagonal to increase surface area. I tried all the brands of cutlets I could get my hands on, both national and northeast regional, and found them to be inconsistent in terms of size, shape, and thickness. One regional brand, Shady Brook, was pretty good, while one national brand, Perdue Fit 'N Easy, was very disappointing. Short of butchering your own cutlets, which takes some practice and seriously curtails the speed and ease inherent to this dish, the best you can do is to inspect packages carefully before you buy and to sample the brands in your area systematically to identify the most uniform product. Use the photos of poorly and

Start with uniform, well-butchered cutlets to ensure even cooking.

well-butchered cutlets on the opposite page to help guide your purchase.

Sauté Specifics

Flouring delicate meat and fish before sautéing to protect them from dry, searing heat is a common practice—one we've used ourselves in the test kitchen. Floured turkey cutlets did develop a nice crust in spots, but I found I could achieve a similar crust using unfloured cutlets as long as the pan was properly preheated. After several rounds of testing, the balance tipped toward the unfloured cutlets for a couple of reasons. First, some of the *Cook's* staff who tasted the cutlets noticed that the crust on floured cutlets dissolved a bit once they were sauced, giving them a slightly pasty mouthfeel. Second, I found that residual flour from the cutlets burned in the pan when it was necessary to cook the cutlets in batches. This gave the drippings, as well as the pan sauce made from them, a faintly bitter edge. Last, eliminating the flouring step helped to streamline the recipe.

The next tests focused on the cooking medium—that is, the fat. Some sauté recipes call

for butter, which adds both color and flavor, in combination with oil, which can withstand higher temperatures before smoking or burning. While some tasters were fans of the butter-and-oil combination, I wasn't one of them. I had burned the butter more than once despite the presence of the oil and felt that plain olive oil offered a reasonable compromise, with its mild but pleasant flavor and better resistance to burning.

When it came to preheating the pan, I found three minutes over medium-high heat on our test kitchen stovetop to be perfect for the heavy-bottomed, 12-inch skillet we typically use (you may have to adjust the preheating time accordingly if using a pan that is larger or lighter or if cooking over a more modestly powered stovetop). The crust on the cutlets sautéed in our sturdy pan was well developed, and the fond (the caramelized meat drippings that form on the bottom of the pan) was bronzed and gorgeous. By comparison, the crust on cutlets sautéed in pans preheated for two minutes was light, while the fond in pans preheated for any more than three minutes burned some of the time. In the test kitchen, we use a sophisticated digital thermometer to measure surface temperatures in cookware, and it gave a reading of approximately 415 degrees Fahrenheit for the three-minute preheated pan. At this level of heat, the oil may smoke almost immediately upon contact with the pan, but it stops as soon as the cutlets are added—which is the very next step—because the temperature of the pan drops.

Tips for Perfect Cutlets

The usual intensive regimen of recipe testing we conduct at *Cook's* led me to a couple of tips that should help every cook turn out beautifully sautéed cutlets. First, brown the cutlets on one side only. At ¼ to ⅜ inch thick, turkey cutlets are simply too thin to brown well on both sides without overcooking and drying out. Letting the cutlets spend most of the cooking time, 2 to 2½ minutes, forming a good crust on one side, allowed me to protect them from overcooking. Turn the cutlets once just to finish cooking, for about 30 to 60 seconds, and then serve them browned-side up. It is also important to make sure the cutlets are dried well before cooking—not just dabbed, not just blotted, but dried thoroughly on both sides. Damp cutlets form poor crusts.

The T-Spot

One key to a successful sauté is making sure the pan is hot enough before you start to cook. But how can you tell exactly when your pan has reached that point? This very question has become the subject of an ongoing investigation in the test kitchen.

Until we are able to settle on a definitive answer, there is the T-Fal Thermospot. This line of nonstick cookware features a built-in heat indicator in the center of the cooking surface. According to the Thermospot packaging, "When the Thermospot pattern disappears [and the spot turns a solid brick red] your pan is perfectly pre-heated."

The directions recommend heating the pan and cooking over low to medium heat. After about 7 minutes over medium-low heat, the spot turned a solid brick red. We then followed our recipe, using half the amount of oil that we would in a pan with a regular cooking surface. The results were acceptable but not stellar. Over medium-low heat, the cutlets steamed more than we like, which compromised their browning.

T-FAL THERMOSPOT SAUTÉ PAN

As we have often found with nonstick pans, the fond was unimpressive, which meant that the finished pan sauce lacked the proper rich color and depth of flavor. In our view, then, the recommendation for modest heat essentially defeats the purpose of sautéing.

When we broke the manufacturer's rules and used the Thermospot over medium-high heat (which, warns T-Fal, can damage the pan); the results improved. In fact, they far exceeded our expectations. The textured cooking surface provided edges to which the fond could stick and develop. This did not seem to impede the pan's nonstick performance at all; in fact, our cutlets slid right out (as they do in any properly heated pan). But it did improve the browning of the cutlets and the fond, both of which were reasonably good.

Used over the high heat against which the manufacturer warns, the Thermospot might make a good training tool for new cooks. But know that you risk cutting your pan's lifespan short. For $39.99, the suggested retail price of the 12½-inch, hard enamel sauté pan we tried, the choice is yours. –A.R.

Cooked for just three minutes and complemented by an interesting pan sauce, this turkey dinner has the speed, ease, and flexibility that Thanksgiving birds can only dream of.

SAUTÉED TURKEY CUTLETS
SERVES 4

One cutlet per person makes a skimpy serving, so we call for a total of six to serve four people, with the two extra cutlets divided among diners. If you cannot fit all the cutlets in the pan without overlapping them, cook them in two batches, using 1½ tablespoons oil for each batch.

- 6 turkey cutlets (about 1½ pounds), rinsed and thoroughly dried
  Salt and ground black pepper
- 2 tablespoons olive oil

1. Adjust oven rack to middle position, set large heatproof plate on rack, and heat oven to 200 degrees. Sprinkle both sides of cutlets with salt and pepper.

2. Heat heavy-bottomed 12-inch skillet over medium-high heat until hot, about 3 minutes. Add oil to pan and swirl to coat pan bottom (oil will shimmer and probably smoke almost immediately). Lay cutlets in pan and cook, without moving them, until light golden brown, 2 to 2½ minutes (fat should sizzle but not smoke). Using tongs, flip cutlets and cook until meat feels firm when pressed, 30 to 60 seconds longer. Off heat, transfer cutlets to warmed plate, and return plate to oven to keep cutlets warm while preparing one of following sauce recipes.

HONEY-MUSTARD PAN SAUCE WITH TARRAGON
MAKES ABOUT ²/₃ CUP, ENOUGH FOR 6 CUTLETS

- 1 large shallot, minced (about 3 tablespoons)
- 1 cup dry white wine
- ½ cup chicken stock or canned low-sodium chicken broth
- 2 teaspoons honey
- 1 tablespoon Dijon mustard
- 3 tablespoons unsalted butter, softened
- 1 tablespoon chopped fresh tarragon leaves
  Salt and ground black pepper

After transferring cutlets to warmed plate, set now-empty skillet over medium-low heat (do not clean skillet or discard any fat); add shallots and cook, stirring constantly, until softened, about 1

SHOPPING | THE RIGHT CUTLET

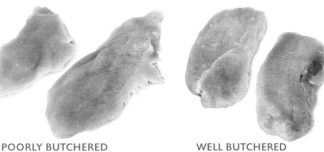

POORLY BUTCHERED   WELL BUTCHERED

Try to avoid buying packages with ragged, uneven, inconsistently sized cutlets, like those on the left. The even cutlets (right) will cook at the same rate and look better on the plate.

minute. Add wine, stock, and honey; increase heat to high and bring to boil, scraping skillet bottom with wooden spoon to loosen browned bits. Boil until liquid is reduced to about ⅓ cup, about 10 minutes, adding any accumulated turkey juices from plate after about 8 minutes. Off heat, whisk in mustard and butter until melted and sauce is slightly thickened. Stir in tarragon, season to taste with salt and pepper, spoon sauce over cutlets, and serve immediately.

WARM-SPICED PAN SAUCE WITH CURRANTS AND ALMONDS
MAKES ABOUT ²/₃ CUP, ENOUGH FOR 6 CUTLETS

- 2 teaspoons light or dark brown sugar
- ⅛ teaspoon cayenne (or more, to taste)
  Pinch ground cloves
  Pinch ground allspice
- 1 tablespoon olive oil
- 2 (3-inch) cinnamon sticks
- 1 large shallot, minced (about 3 tablespoons)
- 2 medium garlic cloves, minced or pressed through garlic press (about 2 teaspoons)
- 1 (¾-inch) piece fresh ginger, minced (about 2 teaspoons)
- 1 cup fruity red wine, such as Zinfandel
- ½ cup chicken stock or canned low-sodium chicken broth
- 3 tablespoons currants
- 3 tablespoons unsalted butter, softened
- 2 tablespoons chopped fresh parsley leaves
  Salt and ground black pepper
- ¼ cup sliced almonds, toasted in small dry skillet over medium heat until color deepens slightly, about 4 minutes

Mix brown sugar, cayenne, cloves, and allspice in small bowl; set aside. After transferring cutlets to warmed plate, set now-empty skillet over medium-low heat (do not clean skillet or discard any fat); add oil, spice mixture, and cinnamon sticks and cook, stirring constantly, until fragrant, about 1 minute. Add shallots and cook, stirring frequently, until softened, about 1 minute. Add garlic and ginger and cook, stirring constantly, until fragrant, about 30 seconds. Add wine, stock, and currants; increase heat to high and bring to boil, scraping skillet bottom with wooden spoon to loosen browned bits. Boil until liquid reduces to about ⅓ cup, about 10 minutes, adding any accumulated turkey juices from plate after about 8 minutes. Off heat, discard cinnamon sticks, whisk in butter until melted and sauce is slightly thickened; stir in parsley. Season to taste with salt and pepper, spoon sauce over cutlets, sprinkle with almonds, and serve immediately.

Pasta with Garlic and Oil

The marriage of cooked and raw garlic as well as a generous splash of extra-virgin olive oil just before serving make this simple dish shout with flavor.

⇒ BY KAY RENTSCHLER ⇐

Pasta with garlic and oil looks guileless. It reads: "tangle of spaghetti flecked with parsley." But its subtext shouts garlic: garlic in every register, in every pitch, a virtual manifesto of bright garlic and deep green oil. Twirled hot on a fork and eaten without restraint, this is among the most satisfying dishes on earth. It has the texture of innocence and a tyrant's bite.

At first, I wondered why anyone would need a recipe for this dish. You take spaghetti or capellini, perfume it straight from its bath with quality olive oil and as much fresh garlic as decency allows, add a dusting of red pepper flakes, a little fistful of parsley, and there it is, *pasta aglio e olio*. And yet, and yet. Who hasn't ordered it in a restaurant to find its fresh scent tormented by burnt garlic or its noodles gripped in a starchy skein dripping with oil? "I've never made a good one," I announced boldly to my colleagues, risking dishonor. "Neither have I," came several murmured responses. Clearly, there was much to learn.

Diving into Italian cookbooks, I found general agreement on ingredients: all those mentioned above, along with a splash of hot cooking water to keep the components in motion. Beyond the basics were regional variations that included a

Pasta forks effectively toss and combine the components of this dish.

selection of fresh herbs, savory accents such as capers and anchovies, and bread crumbs.

I first pursued the perfect garlic flavor, working down the list of possibilities from whole crushed cloves to grated raw garlic and using one pound of pasta for my tests. (None of the recipes I saw called for roasting the garlic whole.) *Cook's* editors didn't care for sautéed whole or slivered garlic, whether ultimately removed from the dish or

left in. In fact, no one cared for browned garlic at all—it was acrid and one-dimensional. Raw minced or grated garlic alone was zingy and metallic. We needed a third way.

I knew of a technique associated with Mexican cookery, in which a large amount of minced garlic is sautéed slowly until it turns golden and becomes mellow, which produces garlic flavor far more complex than does a simple sauté. I tried this with a full head of garlic (about a quarter cup minced) and was delighted to discover that given low heat and constant stirring, the garlic became sticky and straw-colored, with a flavor that was butter-nutty and rich, adding a pronounced depth to the dish. But alone this slow-sautéed garlic lacked brightness. I decided to combine the forces of cooked and raw by reserving a tablespoon of raw garlic, then stirring it into the fully cooked, candied garlic off heat to release its perfume and spicy sharpness. The effect of this one-two garlic punch was outstanding, causing waves of flavor to resonate within the dish.

Not All Garlics Are Alike

Technique aside, however, the fact remained that the garlic I was using—the standard supermarket variety—produced both some ethereal flavors and some that were rather fishy. My entire orientation to this subject was to change the moment I bought some farmer's market garlic just one month out of the ground: its waxy firm, pearly opaque cloves made improvements in flavor that none of us had anticipated. I began researching

Tasting the Dragon

Garlic falls into two primary categories, hardneck and softneck. The garlic that most of us cook with is softneck, so-called because its neck is soft and braidable. Softneck garlic contains a circle of reasonably sized cloves shrouding a second circle of smaller cloves, all enveloped by many papery layers. Because softneck is heat tolerant and produces and stores well, it has become the favored commercial garlic. Supermarket garlics are almost invariably softneck.

Hardneck, which is the original cultivated garlic variety, is distinguished by its stiff center staff, around which large uniform cloves hang. Hardneck garlic has a relatively sparse parchment wrapper that makes it easier to peel (and damage) than softneck. It is considered superior in flavor—more complex and intense than softneck. Its thinly wrapped cloves lose moisture quickly, however, and do not winter over, as do the cloves of the robust softneck.

Members of the *Cook's* editorial staff tasted a number of garlic varieties, softneck and hardneck, raw and cooked. Here's what we found. –K.R.

SOFTNECK GARLICS

⇒ **ARTICHOKE**
Inchelium Red
FILAREE FARMS
raw: Nice medium bite, slow low heat, lingering flavor
sautéed: Big bite, raw-tasting, hot and pungent, sour and bitter

⇒ **ARTICHOKE** *Polish*
BLUE WILLOW FARMS
raw: Mild, mellow, buttery, nutty
sautéed: Fishy and rancid, not sweet enough, dull and flat

⇒ **SILVERSKIN** *Silver White*
LOCAL GROCERY STORE
raw: Rough, "heartburn city" according to one taster, "garlic by Hasbro" according to another, sharp and metallic
sautéed: Very mellow, full garlic flavor, anchovy flavored, spicy

types of garlic and was astounded at the varieties and subvarieties available by mail. Their differences proved to be intriguing (see "Tasting the Dragon," pages 14–15).

While conducting garlic experiments, it became obvious that other ingredient ratios—for example, the amount of oil—needed to be established contiguously. Too much oil removed the silky mouthfeel I wanted for the pasta, but too little left the garlic mute. The amount of oil necessary varied with the diameter of the pasta as well—thicker strands, such as spaghetti, required more oil, even when the total weight of each batch of pasta was the same. In fact, the diameter of the pasta strands altered the behavior of the recipe to such a degree that I decided to work with just one type of pasta—spaghetti, which, unlike some thinner pastas, is available in every grocery store.

The olive oil contributes much of the freshness and verve to this dish: extra-virgin is a must. I settled on 6 tablespoons: 3 to sauté the garlic, 3 tossed into the pasta at the end for flavor. (Though we at *Cook's* generally do not recommend extra-virgin olive oil to sauté foods, preferring to experience its fruitiness raw, I thought it excessive to require two types in this one simple recipe.)

Little Things

Parmesan cheese is not conventional in this dish, but, heathens that we are, we liked the nutty depth of flavor it added. Resist, by all means, an urge to up-end the contents of a little green cylinder on this dish—it will be forever ruined. A very modest sprinkle of coarsely grated Parmigiano-Reggiano, on the other hand, won't do much harm. (Be sure to do your grating on the larger holes of a box grater; this will discourage the cheese from getting into a sticking contest with the pasta.)

We liked parsley for its freshness but didn't want much of it slipping around on the noodles like mower clippings; 3 tablespoons did the trick. Gentle seasoning improvements were effected with a touch of lemon juice and sea salt flakes—the bright citrus

notes and wee crunch made a big difference.

Finally, sequence and timing matter greatly with this dish. Perhaps to a larger degree than other pastas, pasta aglio e olio suffers from being dumped into cold serving bowls or waiting around for diners to make their way to the table. The most familiar pasta tool, a set of tongs, cannot be recommended for tossing: bits of garlic get stuck in its craw, right where you don't want them. I recommend that you toss the hot strands with a heatproof spatula or pasta rakes and use rakes or tongs only to transfer the pasta to bowls.

PASTA WITH GARLIC AND OIL (AGLIO E OLIO)
SERVES 4 TO 6

For a twist on pasta with garlic and oil, try sprinkling toasted bread crumbs over individual bowls, but prepare them before proceeding with the pasta recipe. We like Maldon sea salt flakes for this dish, but ordinary table salt is fine as well.

1	pound spaghetti
	Salt (see note above)
6	tablespoons extra-virgin olive oil
¼	cup minced garlic (about 30 small, 20 medium, 10 large, or 5 extralarge cloves) from 1 to 2 heads
¾	teaspoon red pepper flakes
3	tablespoons chopped fresh parsley leaves
2	teaspoons juice from 1 lemon
½	cup coarsely grated Parmesan (optional)

1. Adjust oven rack to lower-middle position, set large heatproof serving bowl on rack and heat oven to 200 degrees. Bring 4 quarts water to rolling boil, covered, in large Dutch oven or stockpot. Add pasta and 1½ teaspoons table salt to boiling water, stir to separate pasta, cover, and cook until al dente; reserve ⅓ cup pasta cooking water and drain pasta.

2. While water is heating, combine 3 tablespoons oil, 3 tablespoons garlic, and ½ teaspoon

see "Tasting the Dragon," pages 14–15

Crushed to Bits

Upon exploring three tools for rendering garlic small—a chef's knife, a mortar and pestle, and a garlic press—I found each equal to the task. The mortar and pestle were unexpectedly easy to use and released the most flavor from the garlic. The chef's knife took more time but produced good results, while the press rendered neat little garlic bits without leaving behind a smelly cutting board. Here are some recommendations on how to use each tool.

Mortar and Pestle: Slice the peeled cloves in half (or in quarters if large), add half the garlic and ½ teaspoon salt, and pound with the pestle, using a grinding motion to form a puree. When garlic begins to break down (it may even foam), add remaining cloves and continue pounding.

Garlic Press: Leave the peeled cloves whole (or halve if large), and press them directly into the skillet. Use the blade of a sharp paring knife to cut off any extruded garlic left hanging on the press. Discard the inner garlic membrane and proceed with the recipe.

Chef's Knife: Slice the peeled garlic thinly, sprinkle it with ½ teaspoon salt, and alternate chopping and sliding the blade across the garlic's surface until a very fine minced product is obtained. —K.R.

table salt or sea salt flakes in heavy-bottomed nonstick 10-inch skillet; cook over low heat, stirring constantly, until garlic foams and is sticky and straw-colored, 10 to 12 minutes. Off heat, add remaining tablespoon raw garlic, red pepper flakes, parsley, lemon juice, and 2 tablespoons pasta cooking water to skillet and stir well to keep garlic from clumping.

3. Transfer drained pasta to warm serving bowl; add remaining 3 tablespoons olive oil and remaining reserved pasta cooking water and toss to coat. Add garlic mixture and ¾ teaspoon table salt or 1 teaspoon sea salt flakes to pasta; toss well to combine. Serve immediately, sprinkling individual bowls with portion of Parmesan, if desired.

HARDNECK GARLICS

★ OVERALL FAVORITE ★

PORCELAIN *Zemo*
FILAREE FARMS
raw: Sweet top note, turns into a pleasing bite, garlic flavor without heat, lingering, complex, no bitterness on finish, very nice
sautéed: Strong yet balanced, spicy bite, mild, mellow, nice

PORCELAIN *Music*
BLUE WILLOW FARM
raw: Fragrant, floral, deep round garlic flavor, peppery but sweet, quite a sting
sautéed: Mild, perfumed, buttery, almond, toasty, caramel-like, sweet

PORCELAIN *German White*
BLUE WILLOW FARM
raw: Stinging red-hot-candy heat, strongly spicy, vegetal and green, tannic and metallic
sautéed: Hot and raw, light bitter finish, lots of high and low notes, complex, astringent

ROCAMBOLE *Carpathian*
FILAREE FARMS
raw: Burns roof of mouth but has good flavor, starts mild, turns hot, long biting, bitter aftertaste
sautéed: "Yummy," mild, fragrant, perfumed, upfront flavor dissolves fast, no lingering flavor

PURPLE STRIPE *Chesnok Red*
FILAREE FARMS
raw: Sweet, caramel-like, nutty, no heat upfront, fleeting, piquant
sautéed: Lifeless, spineless, "old gym socks," "garlic muzak"

Getting to Know Your Refrigerator

Proper storage techniques are the key to longer lasting fruits, meats, and vegetables.

BY RAQUEL PELZEL

Although we don't often think about it, every refrigerator has hot, cold, and humid spots. Together they create a complex food storage matrix inside a basic three-shelf refrigerator. You can make the temperature flux in your refrigerator work to your advantage by learning a few facts about storing fruits, vegetables, and meats. Of course, conditions inside individual refrigerators do vary somewhat. But experts agree on certain general trends in terms of which areas are warmer or cooler. We spent some time verifying what the refrigeration experts told us, and when we were finished we had a much better idea of how best to use a refrigerator. Follow the tips and guidelines shown here to keep your meat, dairy, and produce fresh and flavorful.

REFRIGERATOR TEMPERATURE BASICS

To verify the information we gathered from refrigeration experts, we hooked up a test kitchen refrigerator to a piece of equipment called a chart scan data recorder. The recorder was connected to a laptop computer as well as several temperature monitors placed in strategic locations on the shelves and drawers inside the refrigerator. The refrigerator was then closed and left undisturbed for 24 hours while the interior temperatures were monitored.

Keeping in mind that a refrigerator goes through many cooling cycles throughout a 24-hour period (that is, at times the temperature may be well above or below 34 degrees Fahrenheit, the optimal temperature for a home refrigerator), our results provided some interesting information. For example, the butter compartment was not the warmest spot in the fridge, as we had expected. Instead, the middle shelf on the door and the front portion of the bottom cabinet shelf registered the highest readings—all the way up to 43 degrees. Not a place where you would want to store your milk or eggs, each of which should be kept at 40 degrees or below. The meat compartment remained the coolest area of the refrigerator (on average, 33 degrees), making it perfect for storing what it is supposed to store: meat.

If you'd like to find the hot and cold spots in your home refrigerator, you can purchase a couple of inexpensive refrigerator temperature gauges (available at most kitchenware stores) and place them on the top, middle, and bottom shelves of your refrigerator, recording the temperature every couple of hours. Generally, though, you can expect your readings to follow the trends shown in the diagram on page 17.

ILLUSTRATION: JOHN BURGOYNE

THREE CATEGORIES OF FRUITS AND VEGGIES

When it comes to refrigeration, produce can be divided into three basic categories: items that should not be refrigerated at all, those that should be refrigerated at a moderately cool temperature, and those that can be stored in the coolest part of the refrigerator without injury.

CHILL-INJURY PRONE
These items should not be refrigerated. If they are, they could be subject to dehydration, internal browning, or internal and external pitting.

➤ tropical fruits (mangoes, pineapples—may be refrigerated up to two days when fully ripe)
➤ avocados
➤ tomatoes
➤ bananas
➤ pickling cucumbers

CHILL-INJURY SENSITIVE
These items should not be stored below 37 degrees Fahrenheit.

➤ any snap beans
➤ berries
➤ citrus fruits (grapefruit, limes, oranges)
➤ melons
➤ fresh corn on the cob

NOT PRONE TO CHILL INJURY
These items can be stored at the refrigerator's coldest temperature without injury (provided the temperature does not freeze the item).

➤ lettuces
➤ other leafy greens
➤ apples
➤ asparagus
➤ broccoli

REFRIGERATOR STORAGE TIPS

Storing Meat
Storing meat on a rimmed baking sheet helps keep refrigerator shelves sanitary and allows other food items, such as fruits and vegetables, to be stored on the same shelf without risk of cross-contamination.

Storing Cheese
Because cheese should not be exposed to too much oxygen, it's best to wrap it first in parchment paper and then in foil. Store the wrapped cheese in the crisper or in an airtight plastic bag or container.

Storing Greens
To prevent bacterial growth, greens must be completely dried before being stored. If you own a salad spinner, store your washed and dried greens in it with a bit of water in the bottom to create a humid environment. (The water should not touch the greens.)

HOW LONG WILL IT KEEP?

BEEF

steaks, roasts	3–5 days
ground	2 days
defrosted	2–3 days
cooked	2–3 days

LUNCHMEATS

sliced to order	3–5 days
prepackaged	I week

POULTRY

fresh, whole	2 days
fresh, pieces	2 days
defrosted	2 days
cooked	2–3 days

PORK

fresh chops, roasts	3 days
smoked ham, bacon	2 weeks, after opened

FISH AND SEAFOOD

fresh	I–2 days
cooked	3–4 days
bisques, chowders	I–2 days
fresh crab, in shell	2 days
other fresh shellfish	I day

WHERE TO STORE WHAT

TOP SHELF, FRONT
TEMPERATURE: moderate
- eggs in the carton
- butter stored in a butter dish

DOOR, BUTTER COMPARTMENT
TEMPERATURE: moderate
- herbs

MIDDLE SHELF, FRONT
TEMPERATURE: moderate
- chill-sensitive fruits and vegetables, such as melons and beans (green beans, wax beans)

DOOR, MIDDLE COMPARTMENT
TEMPERATURE: warm
- beverages
- condiments

BOTTOM SHELF, FRONT
TEMPERATURE: warm
- chill-sensitive fruits and vegetables, such as subtropical fruits, mushrooms (stored in original packaging or a zipper-lock bag, with air holes), and corn (wrapped in a wet paper bag and placed in a plastic bag)

DOOR, BOTTOM COMPARTMENT
TEMPERATURE: cool
- milk (gallon-sized containers may be stored on the back portion of the top shelf)
- sour cream
- yogurt

TOP SHELF, BACK
TEMPERATURE: cool
- refrigerator-safe fruits, such as apples and grapes
- lunch meats stored in zipper-lock bags

MEAT COMPARTMENT
TEMPERATURE: cool
- ground meat
- chops
- cutlets
- steaks
- chicken parts

MIDDLE SHELF, BACK
TEMPERATURE: cool
- prepared foods and leftovers

BOTTOM SHELF, BACK
TEMPERATURE: cool
- whole birds, roasts wrapped in original wrapper or placed in plastic bags
- fish and shellfish, placed on top of zipper-lock bags of ice inside a deep plastic container

CRISPER(S)
TEMPERATURE: moderate to cool
- leafy greens (completely dried) in a plastic container or salad spinner
- celery
- asparagus
- broccoli
- cheese wrapped in parchment paper and then foil

Are You Really Seeing Red?

If you associate red meat with freshness, you shouldn't. What gives meat its bright color, according to Duane Wulf, professor of meat science at South Dakota State University, is oxygen. "When you buy ground beef in the store, it is bright red on the surface, but when you break the meat up, it is darker in the center," explained Wulf. "This means that the center was not exposed to as much oxygen." This is also why ground meat is more perishable than an intact muscle—a steak, for example.

Furthermore, the packaging of meat in a supermarket or even a meat factory is specifically designed to let oxygen in, transforming the natural purple hue of a muscle to a more desirable red color. But don't get the purple color of fresh unoxygenated meat confused with the brownish-gray color of older meat—this means that the myoglobin (the pigment that makes meat red) has converted to metmyoglobin (meaning that the iron atom in the pigment has lost an electron), which is caused by age and enhanced bacterial activity.

A Rain Forest in Your Crisper

Have you ever wondered how your crisper works, or if it works at all? Steve Benton, general manager and vice president of refrigeration for Maytag, explained that all a crisper or humidity compartment does is allow more or less cold air in through small vents located by the slide control. (If your crisper doesn't have a slide control, it is always at the highest humidity level of which it is capable.) The more cold air that is let in, the less humid the environment. But why do you want to have humidity in your crisper, anyway?

A humid environment provides vegetables with water, without which they would shrivel and rot. But the key is balance. If the humidity is too high, water can build up on the surface of the food, explains Dr. Richard Gladon, professor of horticulture at Iowa State University. The water then condenses, giving fungi and bacteria the incentive to grow, compromising the quality and safety of your food. One way to control this process is to store humidity- and chill-sensitive foods like lettuce, berries, and mushrooms inside the crisper in a refrigerator storage bag that has been punctured. This allows carbon dioxide to escape while still providing moisture for the humidity-sensitive produce.

Really Good Fried Rice

For fried rice that is light and flavorful rather than sodden and greasy, cook the ingredients in batches and forget about your fear of frying.

⇒ BY BRIDGET LANCASTER ⇐

Leftovers are an incredible boon to the busy cook, as long as you know what to do with them. Some are obvious, like transforming that turkey or ham into sandwiches. Some are a bit more obtuse, like turning leftover mashed potatoes into potato pancakes. But when faced with the question of what to do with leftover rice, I say, "Fry it."

A trip to the local suburban Chinese restaurant, though, might make you pause. There the norm is often greasy, soggy fried rice doused with so much soy sauce that you can hardly tell the mushrooms from the chicken. But this is no more representative of the virtues of this dish than a fast-food burger is of a great home-grilled version. I wanted fried rice with firm, separate grains, a dish so clean and light that I could distinguish the many different flavors in every bite. I also knew that the success of the dish would depend on the answers to four questions: what to add, how much to add, when to add it, and when to leave it alone.

Getting the Rice Right

Fried rice was created as a way to turn leftover rice into a delicious dish. But since many American cooks are unlikely to have leftover rice, I decided to experiment with making the dish from freshly cooked, still warm rice. It was a disaster. The grains gelled together in large clumps, and the whole dish was very wet. Rice freshly cooked and then allowed to cool to room temperature fared little better, still coming out wet and unappealing. Cold rice produced by far the best fried rice. The grains were more separate and evenly coated with oil, and the overall dish much drier.

Still, I wanted to find out if I could avoid overnight refrigeration. I tried spreading the cooked rice on a sheet pan to cool it down to room temperature rapidly, then placed the pan in the refrigerator to chill completely. The fried rice was drier and the clumps of rice much smaller. This, then, offers an option for cooks who want to make fried rice as quickly as possible from freshly cooked rice.

Leftover rice is still the best option, as I found when I tried refrigerating cooked rice for different amounts of time. While rice kept in the refrigerator for four hours was acceptable, a whole night in the refrigerator produced the driest, most separate grains and therefore the best fried rice.

Adding the ingredients in batches ensures a bright, flavorful fried rice that is never mushy.

I tested various types of rice, including extra long, long, medium, and short grain. All are suitable for cooking after an overnight stay in the refrigerator. But don't try making fried rice with store-bought rice that has been precooked, parboiled, or converted. These processed rices become too soggy and wet, and the grains quickly begin to break down and disintegrate during frying.

Sauce and Eggs

Despite the preference of many Chinese-American restaurants for large quantities of soy sauce in their fried rice, a quick look through many Chinese cookbooks revealed salt as the preferred seasoning. When tested, this rice tasted very clean and light, but tasters longed for a more substantial flavor. I went back to the soy sauce, but the large amount (nearly six tablespoons) needed to season the dish well caused

the rice to turn soggy and ugly. I wanted to find a seasoning with enough flavor intensity to be used sparingly.

The answer was oyster sauce. More appropriately referred to as oyster-*flavored* sauce, this condiment is a highly concentrated combination of soy sauce, brine, and oyster extracts. It is very thick, salty, and potent. Fried rice made with this sauce was well seasoned and full of distinctive flavor but not soggy.

In the process of all this testing, I also figured out how best to add the usual egg and vegetable to the rice. To get the eggs to the right texture, I scrambled them lightly, then removed them from the pan to be added at the end of cooking for a quick warm-up. Similarly, I found that moisture from vegetables such as peas, mushrooms, green beans, or asparagus caused the rice to clump when added to the pan along with it. Sautéing the vegetables alone in oil first allows

No Fear of Frying

The odd thing about fried rice is that it's not truly fried. When food is fried, it is cooked in a large amount of fat, usually enough to cover. What we call fried rice is actually pan-fried or sautéed, which means it is cooked over relatively high heat in a much smaller amount of fat (in this case, oil). I needed to figure out exactly how much oil and knew that the pan I used would determine the amount. I wanted to make a large quantity of fried rice, and I limited my testing to large (12-inch) skillets—nonstick and regular—and as a 14-inch wok.

The wok held plenty of rice, but the sloped sides and small 6-inch bottom allowed only a small portion of the rice to cook at once. Also, a great deal of oil was necessary when cooking with the wok. The rice on the bottom continually absorbed what was added. The flat surface of the skillet provided a larger cooking surface, and the rice sautéed more quickly and evenly. Choosing between regular and non-stick was easy. The regular skillet required much more oil to keep the rice from sticking, making the dish too greasy. I preferred the nonstick skillet for the lighter rice it produced.

Even using a nonstick pan, I found that a moderate amount of oil was required to keep the rice grains separate. Too little oil will cause the rice grains to clump together during sautéing. —B.L.

sufficient moisture to cook off, producing a drier dish with better-flavored vegetables. More tender vegetables, such as sprouts and scallions, along with herbs, hold their texture and flavor better if added at the end of the cooking process.

FRIED RICE WITH PEAS AND BEAN SPROUTS

MAKES ABOUT 8 CUPS, SERVING 4 TO 6

1/4	cup oyster sauce
1	tablespoon soy sauce
3	tablespoons peanut or vegetable oil
2	large eggs, beaten lightly
1	cup frozen peas, preferably baby peas, thawed
2	medium garlic cloves, minced (about 2 teaspoons)
6	cups cold cooked white rice, large clumps broken up with fingers
1	cup (about 2 1/2 ounces) bean sprouts
5	medium scallions, sliced thin (about 1/2 cup)

1. Combine oyster sauce and soy sauce in small bowl; set aside.

2. Heat 12-inch nonstick skillet over medium heat until hot, about 2 minutes; add 1 1/2 teaspoons oil and swirl to coat pan bottom. Add eggs and cook without stirring until they just begin to set, about 20 seconds, then scramble and break into small pieces with wooden spoon; continue to cook, stirring constantly, until eggs are cooked through but not browned, about 1 minute longer. Transfer eggs to small bowl and set aside.

3. Return skillet to burner, increase heat to high, and heat skillet until hot, about 2 minutes. Add remaining 2 1/2 tablespoons oil and swirl to coat pan bottom. Add peas and cook, stirring constantly, 30 seconds; stir in garlic and cook until fragrant, about 30 seconds. Add rice and oyster sauce mixture; cook, stirring constantly and breaking up rice clumps, until mixture is heated through, about 3 minutes. Add eggs, bean sprouts, and scallions; cook, stirring constantly, until heated through, about 1 minute. Serve immediately.

FRIED RICE WITH SHRIMP, PORK, AND PEAS

MAKES ABOUT 8 CUPS, SERVING 4 TO 6

1/4	cup oyster sauce
1	tablespoon soy sauce
3 1/2	tablespoons peanut or vegetable oil
2	large eggs, beaten lightly
8	ounces small shrimp, peeled and deveined
1	cup frozen peas, preferably baby peas, thawed
1/2	ounce (5 to 6 medium) dried shiitake mushrooms, rehydrated in 1 cup hot water until softened, about 15 minutes, then drained, trimmed of stems, and sliced into 1/4-inch strips
2	Chinese sausages (lop cheong) (about 4 ounces), halved lengthwise and cut crosswise into 1/2-inch pieces, *or* 8 ounces sliced smoked ham, cut into 1/2-inch pieces (optional)
4	ounces Chinese roast pork, cut into 1/2-inch chunks
2	medium garlic cloves, minced (about 2 teaspoons)
5	cups cold cooked white rice, large clumps broken up with fingers
5	medium scallions, sliced thin (about 1/2 cup)

1. Combine oyster sauce and soy sauce in small bowl; set aside.

2. Heat 12-inch nonstick skillet over medium heat until hot, about 2 minutes. Add 1 1/2 teaspoons oil and swirl to coat pan bottom. Add eggs and cook without stirring, until they just begin to set, about 20 seconds, then scramble and break into small pieces with wooden spoon; continue to cook, stirring constantly, until eggs are cooked through but not browned, about 1 minute longer. Transfer eggs to small bowl and set aside.

3. Return skillet to medium heat and heat until hot, about 1 minute; add 1 1/2 teaspoons oil and swirl to coat pan bottom. Add shrimp and cook, stirring constantly, until opaque and just cooked through, about 30 seconds. Transfer to bowl with eggs and set aside.

4. Return skillet to burner, increase heat to high and heat skillet until hot, about 2 minutes; add remaining 2 1/2 tablespoons oil and swirl to coat pan bottom. Add peas, mushrooms, sausage or ham, and pork; cook, stirring constantly, for 1 minute. Stir in garlic and cook until fragrant, about 30 seconds. Add rice and oyster sauce mixture; cook, stirring constantly and breaking up rice clumps, until mixture is heated through, about 3 minutes. Add eggs, shrimp, and scallions; cook, stirring constantly, until heated through, about 1 minute. Serve immediately.

THAI-STYLE CURRIED CHICKEN FRIED RICE

MAKES ABOUT 8 CUPS, SERVING 4 TO 6

1	tablespoon dark brown sugar
3	tablespoons fish sauce
1	tablespoon soy sauce
2	small (about 8 ounces) boneless skinless chicken breasts, cut into 1-inch chunks
1/2	teaspoon salt
3 1/2	tablespoons peanut or vegetable oil
2	large eggs, beaten lightly
1	teaspoon plus 1 tablespoon curry powder
1	large onion, sliced thin
2	medium garlic cloves, minced (about 2 teaspoons)
5	Thai green or 3 jalapeño chiles, seeded and minced (about 2 tablespoons)
6	cups cold cooked white rice, large clumps broken up with fingers
5	medium scallions, sliced thin (about 1/2 cup)
2	tablespoons minced fresh cilantro leaves
	Lime wedges for serving

1. Dissolve sugar in fish and soy sauces in small bowl; set aside. Season chicken with 1/2 teaspoon salt; set aside.

2. Heat 12-inch nonstick skillet over medium heat until hot, about 2 minutes. Add 1 1/2 teaspoons oil and swirl to coat pan bottom. Add eggs and cook without stirring, until they just begin to set, about 20 seconds, then scramble and break into small pieces with wooden spoon; continue to cook, stirring constantly, until eggs are cooked through but not browned, about 1 minute longer. Transfer eggs to small bowl and set aside.

3. Return skillet to burner, increase heat to high and heat skillet until hot, about 1 minute; add 1 1/2 teaspoons oil and swirl to coat pan bottom. Add 1 teaspoon curry and cook until fragrant, about 30 seconds; add chicken and cook, stirring constantly, until cooked through, about 2 minutes. Transfer to bowl with eggs and set aside.

4. Return skillet to high heat and heat until hot, about 1 minute; add remaining 2 1/2 tablespoons oil and swirl to coat pan bottom. Add onion and 1 tablespoon curry and cook, stirring constantly, until onion is softened, about 3 minutes. Stir in garlic and chiles; cook until fragrant, about 30 seconds. Add rice and fish sauce mixture; cook, stirring constantly and breaking up rice clumps until mixture is heated through, about 3 minutes. Add eggs and chicken, scallions, and cilantro; cook, stirring constantly until heated through, about 1 minute. Serve immediately with lime wedges.

Velvety Mushroom Soup

Long, slow cooking turns ordinary supermarket mushrooms into deeply flavored, creamy mushroom soup.

≥ BY KAY RENTSCHLER ≤

Mushrooms are the meatiest vegetable: substantial, distinctive, rich. That is why I am constantly surprised at the number of mushroom soups that, given such promising material, offer so little in return. Yet a superb mushroom soup is simple to achieve if you know what you're doing.

I believe a soup must be purposefully chunky or decidedly smooth. None of this lazy in-between stuff. In this case, I opted for a pureed soup finished with a splash of cream. To my mind, a mushroom soup of this type should be like a fine warm sweater—not cashmere, but not nubby fisherman knit, either; richly textured and hued, not too thick, not too thin; not casual, but not dressy. Merino, perhaps—or alpaca.

The starting point was clear. Traditional French mushroom soups (and mushroom soups are traditionally French) use white button mushrooms sautéed in butter with onions or shallots. The sautéed mushrooms are simmered in a white veal or chicken stock, pureed, and then finished with cream and sherry. Nutmeg or thyme provide the narrow range of flavoring options.

Given this history, I did not feel constricted by the uniformity of the recipes I found in my initial research—I had expected as much. A mushroom soup is obliged to have a faultlessly smooth texture and to taste of mushrooms. That's it. Additional "stuff" would simply bring the soup off course. I also decided to rule out any combination of fresh wild mushrooms for the base of the soup: they are expensive and occasionally difficult to find. Instead, I wanted to develop a recipe that would call on the very real virtues of the white mushroom, a readily available ingredient that is often underestimated. On the other hand, a soupçon of dried mushrooms seemed a reasonable option if the flavor needed encouragement.

Slicing and Roasting

I began my testing with the mushrooms themselves. Coaxing forth their flavor would be the premier issue. In the past I had "sweated" sliced mushrooms in butter in a covered pan to soften them up and release their juices. But I was interested in seeing how roasting would affect their flavor in a soup. Roasted mushrooms appealed to me not only because they are a sublime eating experience but also because I saw them as a means

To dress this soup up for company, and to satisfy those looking for a bit of chew, garnish it with lightly sautéed strips of wild mushrooms.

of losing the chop-chop segment of the recipe altogether. Though I enjoy slicing mushrooms and pretending I am Jacques Pépin, some people chafe at the idea of using a knife for what it was designed to do and are always on the lookout for a mechanical shortcut of some sort. I hoped that the roasting and subsequent shrinkage would reduce the mushrooms to manageably sized pieces that could be simmered in broth until spent and then pureed.

So against 2 pounds of roasted mushrooms I sliced and sautéed 2 pounds of raw mushrooms. Both batches were simmered in chicken stock and pureed, finished with cream, and tasted. To my surprise, the roasted mushroom soup was less flavorful than the soup made with sautéed mushrooms: juices released during the roasting process had browned on the sheet pan and were, for all intents and purposes, irretrievable.

My next attempt to minimize chopping was more mundane. A cook who once worked for me also hated chopping mushrooms (though, to be fair, she was dealing with 10 or 15 pounds) and so one day made a soup by pulsing the mushrooms in

a food processor before sautéing them. The unevenly sliced scraps became bruised and watery, and the resulting soup neither looked nor tasted good. Just to be sure, I repeated her effort; sure enough, the soup made with food-processed mushrooms had a blackish hue and an unfulfilled flavor. Though I cannot precisely say why this is the case, I can only assume that the food processor brings out the juices in a manner aggressive enough to do some damage to subsequent flavor and that the unevenly pulsed bits do not sauté at the same rate.

Putting It All Together

Butter was the obvious fat to go with here, earning high marks for flavor transport while requiring no application of high heat (which might have supported a call for olive oil, since it burns less easily). Six tablespoons of butter did the trick, an amount that shouldn't induce cardiac arrest in someone reading the ingredient list. Shallots were more delicate in flavor and more supportive of the mushroom flavor than onions, though I did find two small, minced garlic cloves to be like a bright little room at the end of a corridor. Nutmeg, yes; thyme, no.

The sliced mushrooms required an initial toss in hot melted butter (which bore the translucent shimmer and perfume of the sautéed shallots and garlic and had been dusted with ground nutmeg), followed by prolonged cooking over low heat in a covered Dutch oven. This half-moist/half-dry heat in close quarters brings out flavors in the way a sweat lodge can, and it is far superior to boiling a vegetable away in broth or water until softened. The technique is similar to cooking a chicken in a clay pot with only its juices to moisten it—what the French call *poêler*—and it brings forth intense flavor. In contrast, a soup made with sliced mushrooms that were sautéed in an uncovered skillet, and thus stripped of their liquid and browned, suffered in much the same way as the roasted mushrooms.

After the initial cooking of the button mushrooms, I added chicken stock and a pinch of dried porcini mushrooms, which torqued up the flavor a notch or two. (Water alone, I discovered, would not produce the trophy flavor that even watery canned broth managed to impart.) Fifteen minutes of measured simmering drained every last bit of fiber and flavor from the mushrooms and fused the small family of flavors together.

Once run through the blender, the soup took on a beautiful deep taupe, provoking tasters to fantasize about paint colors and loveseat sofa fabric (a stark contrast with the institutional flecked beige that blights most mushroom soups). With no thickening to mar its innocence, the texture of the soup was light, but it had body from the puréed mushrooms and heavy cream. The cream and the splash of Madeira added with it at the close of business rounded out the flavors and added just the right touch of sweetness.

CREAMY MUSHROOM SOUP
MAKES 8 CUPS, SERVING 6 TO 8

To make sure that the soup has a fine, velvety texture, puree it hot off the stove, but do not fill the blender jar more than halfway, as the hot liquid may cause the lid to pop off the jar.

- 6 tablespoons unsalted butter
- 6 large shallots, minced (about ¾ cup)
- 2 small garlic cloves, minced (about 1½ teaspoons)
- ½ teaspoon freshly grated nutmeg
- 2 pounds white button mushrooms, wiped clean and sliced ¼ inch thick
- 3½ cups chicken stock or canned low-sodium chicken broth
- 4 cups hot water
- ½ ounce dried porcini mushrooms, rinsed well
- ⅓ cup Madeira or dry sherry
- 1 cup heavy cream
- 2 teaspoons juice from 1 lemon
   Salt and ground black pepper
   Sautéed wild mushrooms for garnish (optional)

1. Melt butter in large, heavy-bottomed Dutch oven over medium-low heat; when foaming subsides, add shallots and sauté, stirring frequently, until softened, about 4 minutes. Stir in garlic and nutmeg; cook until fragrant, about 1 minute longer. Increase heat to medium; add sliced mushrooms and stir to coat with butter. Cook, stirring occasionally, until mushrooms release liquid, about 7 minutes. Reduce heat to medium-low, cover pot, and cook, stirring occasionally, until softened and mushrooms have released all liquid, about 20 minutes. Add chicken stock, water, and porcini mushrooms; cover and bring to simmer, then reduce heat to low and simmer until mushrooms are fully tender, about 20 minutes longer.

2. Rinse and dry Dutch oven. Puree soup in batches in blender until smooth, filling blender jar only halfway for each batch. Return soup to Dutch oven; stir in Madeira and cream and bring to simmer over low heat. Add lemon juice, season to taste with salt and pepper, and serve with sautéed mushroom garnish, if desired. (Can be cooled to room temperature and refrigerated up to 4 days.) If making ahead, add cream at serving time.

SAUTÉED WILD MUSHROOM GARNISH
MAKES 1 TO 1½ CUPS,
ENOUGH TO GARNISH 6 TO 8 SERVINGS SOUP

- 8 ounces shiitake, chanterelle, oyster, or cremini mushrooms, stems trimmed and discarded, mushrooms wiped clean and sliced thin
- 2 tablespoons unsalted butter
   Salt and ground black pepper

Heat butter in medium skillet over low heat; when foam subsides, add mushrooms and sprinkle with salt and pepper. Cover and cook, stirring occasionally, until mushrooms release their liquid, about 10 minutes for shiitakes and chanterelles, about 5 minutes for oysters, and about 9 minutes for cremini. Uncover and continue to cook, stirring occasionally, until liquid released by mushrooms has evaporated and mushrooms are browned, about 2 minutes for shiitakes, about 3 minutes for chanterelles, and about 2 minutes for oysters and cremini. Sprinkle a portion of mushrooms over individual bowls of soup and serve.

Don't Slight Buttons

With more than 300 edible mushroom varieties, it's surprising that until recently most supermarkets carried only one type of fresh mushroom consistently: the white button (*Agaricus bisporus*). The primary reason? Availability.

But the "everyday" nature of this mushroom should not blind us to its virtues. In fact, until the turn of the 20th century, even this mushroom was considered rare and exotic. The French were the first to discover how to cultivate white mushrooms when 17th-century Parisian melon growers discovered that compost from their melon crops provided a favorable growing medium for white button mushrooms. Soon mushrooms, now grown in specially prepared caves, dotted the city, earning them the nickname *champignon de Paris*.

In the United States, florists in Pennsylvania first utilized the dark spaces under their greenhouse shelves for mushroom cultivation in the late 19th century. These efforts were followed in the 20th century with the manufacture of mushroom "houses," which, by providing a stable, controlled environment similar to that of the French caves, made cultivation easier. Although other types of mushrooms are now cultivated (oyster, shiitake, and portobello, to name a few), the white button has become the world's most commonly cultivated fungus, with the United States leading global consumption. Whereas wild mushrooms enjoy only seasonal availability, mushroom cultivation ensures a consistent supply of that unique, meaty mushroom flavor. –Tammy Inman

Garnishing the Soup

To sprinkle this soup with a bit of textural interest, we chose four mushroom varieties to sauté: shiitake, oyster, cremini, and chanterelle. The first three are cultivated mushrooms available year-round. The chanterelle is a wild mushroom available in the spring. Though stems from white button mushrooms are perfectly useable, the stems of the wild mushrooms we used were tough, so we removed them. In each case, 8 ounces of untrimmed, uncooked mushrooms yielded between 1 and 1½ cups of sautéed mushrooms, just the right amount to garnish a pot of our soup. You can use any one variety of mushroom as a garnish, or you can mix the varieties. Because each variety has a distinct cooking time, it should be sautéed separately even if you plan to mix varieties for the garnish.

SHIITAKE is an esteemed mushroom of Japan and China, tan to dark brown in color. Tasters described them as woody, with earthy lower notes, savory, and meaty.

OYSTER mushrooms are beige, cream, or gray in color. They are delicate and best cooked only briefly. Tasters described them as redolent of fried oysters, delicate and briny.

CREMINI mushrooms have the same shape as white button mushrooms but are brown in color and more intensely flavored than their pale cousins. Tasters described them as rich and sweet, like a caramelized button mushroom.

CHANTERELLE mushrooms are bright yellow to pale orange in color and grow under oak trees. Tasters found them nutty and fruity. –K.R.

Thin and Crispy Chocolate Chip Cookies

Three sweeteners and a slow but effective baking technique yield cookies with a satisfying crunch and a praline-like texture.

⋝ BY SHANNON BLAISDELL ⋜

It's best to use a small ice cream scoop to turn out the dough for these delicately crispy cookies.

Rich and buttery, with their soft, tender cores and crispy edges, Toll House cookies are the American cookie jar standard. As such, they serve as the springboard for all other versions of the chocolate chip cookie. The two most popular variations, thick and chewy and thin and crispy, embody the Toll House cookie's textural extremes. We developed a thick and chewy chocolate chip cookie for *Cook's* January/February 1996 issue. Now, we decided, it was time to tackle the other end of the textural spectrum: thin and crispy.

I could see these cookies clearly in my mind's eye. They would be very flat, almost praline in appearance, and would pack a big crunch without either breaking teeth or shattering into a million pieces when eaten. They'd have the simple, gratifying flavors of deeply caramelized sugar and rich butter, along with agreeable amounts of salt and vanilla. The chips—always tender and super-chocolatey—would not overwhelm but leave plenty of room for enjoyment of the surrounding cookie. Finally, these cookies would be resilient enough for pantry storage and worthy of five consecutive appearances in a school lunchbox.

Taking Inventory

To get my bearings, I first surveyed a handful of recipes for thin and crispy chocolate chip cookies, taking inventory of the ingredient lists and ratios. I was hoping to find the key to what might make these cookies thinner and crispier than the classic Toll House. My collection of test recipes featured the same basic ingredients—butter, flour, sugar, flavorings, and chocolate chips—but widely varying ratios and yields. As a result, the cookies were all quite different when baked. While all of the cookies tasted good, tasters were dissatisfied with the various textures, which they found too brittle, too crumbly, too dense, or too greasy. Believe it or not, I was pleased with the mixed reactions. The ingredients I had to work with held promise; I just needed to understand the role of each one and tweak the proportions to arrive at a cookie with the texture I wanted.

The Sweet Stuff

Whether chewy or crispy, nearly all chocolate chip cookies contain a mixture of granulated and brown sugars. Aside from contributing sweetness, sugar also affects the texture, flavor, and color of cookies. Doughs high in granulated sugar yield crispy cookies. As the cookies cool, the sugar crystallizes and the cookies harden. Brown sugar is quite different from granulated. It contains 35 percent more moisture and is also more hygroscopic (that is, it more readily absorbs moisture from the atmosphere). Consequently, cookies made with brown sugar come out of the oven tender and pliable and often soften further as they stand. These characteristics were the opposite of what I was looking for. Nevertheless, I knew the recipe had to include brown sugar, because it alone is responsible for the irresistible butterscotch flavor I associate with chocolate chip cookies.

With this understanding, I went on to test various proportions of sugar. Too much granulated sugar produced cookies with no butterscotch flavor. Too much brown sugar produced cookies that were delicious but too soft. Desperate to retain the flavor of the brown sugar, I shifted from dark brown to light brown. Light brown sugar, I knew, had the potential to crisp the cookies because it contains half the molasses that dark brown sugar does and, therefore, less moisture. But I was skeptical because its flavor is weaker. I needn't have worried; the cookies were much improved, producing a flavor that fully satisfied my tasters. After a little more tinkering, I settled on ⅓ cup light brown sugar and ½ cup granulated sugar, yielding cookies with a notable butterscotch flavor and sufficient crunch.

Flatter than Pancakes

Satisfied with the crispness of the cookies, I turned my attention to their thickness. Throughout earlier testing, I hadn't been totally happy with the cookies' "spread" in the oven—they never became thin enough to achieve that praline-like look I sought. This was important not just for appearance but because, in my experience, the flatter these cookies were, the more delicate and tender they became; I wanted them crisp, without being tough.

After some research, I returned to the kitchen armed with the understanding that a cookie's spread is determined largely by the type, treatment, and melting properties of fat in the dough. Butter, which is key in this recipe, has both a low melting point and outstanding flavor. Initial test recipes advised creaming butter and sugar, but I noticed that cookies made with this technique came out of the oven with a slight lift. I was certain that creaming was the culprit.

When butter and sugar are creamed, rigid sugar crystals cut into the butter's fat solids and create air cells. As the remaining ingredients are incorporated into the airy mixture, the air cells get locked up in the dough and capture moisture from the butter (and other ingredients) as it vaporizes in the oven. The cells expand, and the cookies rise.

My other option, melting the butter, was much more successful. Because melted butter, unlike creamed, does not accommodate air cells, the moisture from various ingredients has nowhere to go except out. Working my way down from 12 tablespoons, I found that the cookies spread evenly and effortlessly at 8 tablespoons (one stick) of melted butter. To get them thinner still, I added a couple tablespoons of milk, working on a tip from Shirley Corriher, author of *Cookwise* (Morrow, 1997). As Corriher explains, adding a small amount of liquid to a low-moisture dough thins the dough and enhances its spread. The cookies were flatter than pancakes.

Looking Good

Having spent all of my time thus far perfecting the cookies' texture and spread, I was surprised to notice that they were looking slightly pallid and dull. The light brown sugar I had introduced to the recipe was the problem: it has less browning power than dark brown sugar. Knowing that corn syrup browns at a lower temperature than sugar, I tried adding a few tablespoons. As it happened, the corn syrup made the surface of the cookies shiny and crackly. Despite their new spiffy, dressed-up look, though, they remained a little on the pale side. I rectified the situation by adding a bit of baking soda, which, as Harold McGee explains in *On Food and Cooking* (Simon and Schuster, 1984), enhances browning reactions in doughs. With only a few tests at various amounts, the cookies went from washed out to a beautiful deep, golden brown.

Finally, after a few last-minute adjustments in amounts of salt and vanilla, I turned the full amount of my final dough onto two parchment-lined baking sheets and tested baking times and temperatures. After a few batches, I found that these cookies, like Greta Garbo, wanted to be alone, baked one sheet at a time. In 12 uninterrupted minutes at 375 degrees, they spread, flattened, caramelized, and came out to cool into thin, crispy, and delicious chocolate chip cookies.

Measuring Up Morsels

Because these cookies were to be dainty and delicate, my choice of chocolate morsel was of utmost importance. I tried three varieties. First were the nation's best-selling Nestlé Toll House Semi-Sweet Morsels. These chips were ultragooey even when cooled, which made them seem out of place in such a crispy cookie. Tropical Source Semi-Sweet Chocolate Chips, winner of our September/October 1998 chocolate chip tasting and typically sold in natural food stores, softened but held their shape nicely. After storing the cookies for a week, these chips were still tender and delicious. Then the idea of using Nestlé's Semi-Sweet Mini Morsels was brought to my attention. Well, as cute as the idea seemed (you know, small cookie, tiny chip), the mini morsels completely changed the dynamic of the cookie. The more morsels per square inch, the more the dough held together and the less it spread. The cookies were dense and had a distinctive store-bought look. —S.B.

NESTLÉ MORSELS
Ultra gooey, even when cooled

TROPICAL SOURCE
Still tender and delicious after a week

NESTLÉ MINI MORSELS
Smaller spread and store-bought look

Now I just had to find out if these cookies had staying power. I stored a batch of the finished cookies in an airtight container for a week to test their longevity. After the wait, my tasters gathered to give them a final critique. To my delight (and relief), the cookies were still a hit, as crisp and flavorful as they had been on day one. In fact, some commented that the crunch had improved with time. At last, I had met all my cookie goals.

THIN, CRISPY CHOCOLATE CHIP COOKIES
MAKES ABOUT 4 DOZEN 2-INCH COOKIES

The dough, en masse or shaped into balls and wrapped well, can be refrigerated up to 2 days or frozen up to 1 month. Be sure to bring it to room temperature before baking.

1 ½	cups (7 ½ ounces) unbleached all-purpose flour
¼	teaspoon salt
¾	teaspoon baking soda
8	tablespoons (1 stick) unsalted butter, melted and cooled
½	cup granulated sugar
⅓	cup packed light brown sugar
3	tablespoons light corn syrup
1	large egg yolk
2	tablespoons milk
1	tablespoon vanilla extract
¾	cup (about 4 ½ ounces) semisweet chocolate chips

1. Adjust oven rack to middle position and heat oven to 375 degrees. Line 2 baking sheets with parchment paper; set aside. Sift flour, salt, and baking soda onto large sheet of parchment paper; set aside.

2. In bowl of standing mixer fitted with paddle attachment, beat melted butter, granulated sugar, brown sugar, and corn syrup at low speed until thoroughly blended, about 1 minute. Add yolk, milk, and vanilla; mix until fully incorporated and smooth, about 1 minute, scraping bottom and sides of bowl with rubber spatula as necessary. With mixer running on low speed, fold up 3 edges of parchment around dry ingredients to form a pouch (see illustrations below) and slowly shake dry ingredients into bowl; mix on low speed until just combined, about 2 minutes. Do not overbeat. Add chips and mix on low speed until distributed evenly throughout batter, about 5 seconds.

3. Leaving about 2 inches between each ball, scoop dough onto parchment-lined baking sheets with 1¼-inch (1 tablespoon capacity) ice cream scoop. Bake 1 sheet at a time, until cookies are deep golden brown and flat, about 12 minutes.

4. Cool cookies on baking sheet 3 minutes. Using wide metal spatula, transfer cookies to wire rack and let sit until crisped and cooled to room temperature. (Can be stored in airtight container for up to 1 week.)

FOLD

NEAT MIXING
To neatly add dry ingredients to the dough mixture, fold the sides of the parchment up and around the ingredients. Then pour into bowl.

POUR

Coconut Layer Cake

A triumvirate of coconut products puts maximum coconut flavor in this classic, tender cake.

⇒ BY DAWN YANAGIHARA ⇐

To me, coconut cake should be perfumed inside and out with the cool, subtle, mysterious essence of coconut. Its layers of snowy white cake should be moist and tender, with a delicate, yielding crumb, and the icing a silky, gently sweetened coat covered with a deep drift of downy coconut. So it's irksome and disappointing that coconut cakes are often frauds, no more than plain white cakes with plain white icing slapped with shredded coconut. I decided to find a coconut cake that lived up to my dreams.

With a roundup of cakes baked according to different recipes, likes and dislikes among the members of my tasting panel surfaced. Cakes baked in a 9 by 13-inch baking dish defied the archetypal sky-high layer cake form. Coarse, crumbly textured cakes did not fit the bill, nor did cakes tinted yellow from yolks or whole eggs. Light, spongy, cottony cakes were too dry and too toothsome for a coconut cake. Doctored with coconut milk and a bit of coconut extract and tweaked ever so slightly, a basic white cake dating back to the May/June 1995 issue of *Cook's* garnered the most praise for its buttery flavor and its tender, fine crumb.

The cake doctored with coconut milk and extract was good, but it wasn't perfect. I was finding that from batch to batch, coconut milk could produce mystifyingly different results—sometimes a flat cake, sometimes a mounded cake, sometimes a heavy, greasy cake. I discovered that the source of the problem was variation in the fat content of coconut milk, which can be as much as 33 percent from brand to brand. Cream of coconut, a sweetened coconut product that contains a few inscrutable emulsifiers, seemed to be a more consistent product, perhaps because there appear to be fewer brands, Coco López being the best known. So I cut back on some of the sugar that went into the batter and used cream of coconut instead of coconut milk. These cakes baked up beautifully, their exteriors an appealing burnished brown color that the coconut milk versions lacked, and they tasted more strongly of coconut as well.

Unfortunately, these cakes also baked up with a giant mound at their centers, which made them

Be vigilant when toasting the cocnut that covers the cake—it can go from golden to burnt very quickly.

look more like desert turtles than dessert. Because the batter was a very thick one that could use gentler heat (which would facilitate a more even rise in the oven), I was able to lower the mounds by reducing the oven temperature to 325 degrees. The resulting cakes were significantly improved. Then, to level things out even more, I manipulated the quantity of eggs. During these trials, I discov-

ered that one yolk in addition to six egg whites gave the cake a richer, fuller flavor without tainting its saintly color. This did nothing to alleviate the remaining slight mounding problem, however, so I tried scaling back on the cream of coconut and diluting the batter with a bit of water. This thinner batter baked into a nice, even cake.

And then there was the icing polemic. Cream cheese frosting—not uncommon on coconut cakes—was unanimously rejected for its heavy texture and a distinct, distracting tang that obscured the delicate coconut flavor. Whipped cream met with just as much opposition; lifeless and uninteresting, it was patently unsuited to a coconut cake. Most tasters acknowledged that a seven-minute meringue icing is what they'd expect, but I found this icing to be painfully sweet and devoid of appealing texture, and many of my tasters agreed. So I assembled one coconut cake with a butter and confectioners' sugar icing and one with an egg white buttercream that was an offshoot of the whole-egg buttercream devised for our devil's food cake (see *Cook's*, March/April 2000). Both icings garnered applause, but the egg white buttercream was the favorite. Not only was it incredibly lithe, but it was also less sweet, significantly more silky and smooth, and much more fluffy and light than its competitor. In some ways, it was reminiscent of the traditional seven-minute icing, just not as sweet or as sticky, and with a creamier consistency.

This buttercream begins life as a meringue, with softened butter eventually beaten in. I tried two

Ain't Nothing Like the Real Thing

Pure extracts are essential oils extracted from natural flavoring agents such as fruit rinds, nuts, and herbs and then dissolved in alcohol. Imitation extracts are fabricated from chemical compounds that mimic natural flavors; these compounds are then also dissolved in alcohol. As with most things natural and synthetic, natural products cost more. When it came to coconut extract, we wanted to know whether "pure" was worth the price. So we made our buttercream frosting (see recipe, page 25) using three extracts—McCormick Imitation Coconut Extract, Spices Etc. Natural Coconut Flavoring, and LorAnn Gourmet Coconut Flavor—and put them to the test.

LorAnn Gourmet Coconut Flavor was uniformly rejected, bringing new meaning to the word *artificial*. One taster commented, "I feel like I'm eating suntan lotion." McCormick Imitation Coconut Extract came in second. Tasters didn't note any off flavors and considered this extract "subtle" and "good." Spices Etc. Natural Coconut Flavoring, made from the pulp of coconuts, was the most "deeply coconutty" and highly praised of the group. Ringing in at $3.25 for a 1-ounce bottle compared with $2.42 for the McCormick, the natural is worth the extra 80 cents. –Shannon Blaisdell

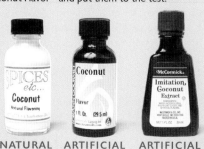

NATURAL ARTIFICIAL ARTIFICIAL

approaches to building the meringue. In the first, the whites and sugar are simply beaten to soft peaks in a standing mixer. In the second, the whites and sugar are whisked together over a hot water bath until the sugar dissolves and the mixture is warm to the touch. The former straightforward meringue fell quickly as the butter was added, and the resulting buttercream was incredibly heavy and stiff, almost no better than the butter and confectioners' sugar icing. The meringue that went over heat was much more stable. Although it did fall when butter was added, the completed icing was soft, supple, and dreamy. (Note that this temperature is not hot enough to eliminate the unlikely presence of salmonella bacteria.)

The textural coup de grace of a coconut cake is its woolly coconut coat. Indeed, pure white shredded coconut straight from the bag makes for a maidenly cake. Toasted coconut, however, has both chew and crunch as well as a much more intense flavor. And when toasted not to the point of even brownness but to that where it resembles a toss of white and bronze confetti, it dresses this cake to be belle of the ball.

STEP-BY-STEP | ASSEMBLING THE CAKE

1. With a long serrated knife, cut both cakes in half horizontally so that each cake forms two layers.

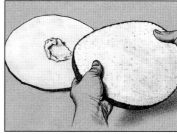

2. Put a dab of icing on a cardboard round cut just larger than the cake. Center one cake layer on the round.

3. Place a large blob of icing in the center of the layer and spread it to the edges with an icing spatula.

4. Hold the spatula at a 45-degree angle to the cake and drag it across the surface to level the icing. Repeat steps 3 and 4 with remaining cake layers.

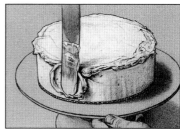

5. To ice the sides of the cake, scoop up a large dab of icing with the tip of the spatula and spread it on the sides with short side-to-side strokes.

6. Sprinkle the top of the cake with coconut. Then press the coconut into the sides, letting the excess fall back onto a baking sheet.

COCONUT LAYER CAKE
MAKES ONE 9-INCH, 4-LAYER CAKE, SERVING 8 TO 10

Cream of coconut is often found in the soda and drink-mix aisle in the grocery store. One 15-ounce can is enough for both the cake and the buttercream; make sure to stir it well before using because it separates upon standing.

Cake
- 1   large egg plus 5 large egg whites
- ¾   cup cream of coconut
- ¼   cup water
- 1   teaspoon vanilla extract
- 1   teaspoon coconut extract
- 2¼ cups (9 ounces) cake flour, sifted
- 1   cup sugar
- 1   tablespoon baking powder
- ¾   teaspoon salt
- 12 tablespoons (1½ sticks) unsalted butter, cut into 12 pieces, softened, but still cool

- 2   cups packed (about 8 ounces) sweetened shredded coconut

Buttercream
- 4   large egg whites
- 1   cup sugar
-     Pinch salt
- 1   pound (4 sticks) unsalted butter, each stick cut into 6 pieces, softened, but still cool
- ¼   cup cream of coconut
- 1   teaspoon coconut extract
- 1   teaspoon vanilla extract

1. FOR THE CAKE: Adjust oven rack to lower-middle position and heat oven to 325 degrees. Grease two 9-inch round cake pans with shortening and dust with flour.

2. Beat egg whites and whole egg in large measuring cup with fork to combine. Add cream of coconut, water, vanilla, and coconut extract and beat with fork until thoroughly combined.

3. Combine flour, sugar, baking powder, and salt in bowl of standing mixer fitted with paddle attachment. Mix on lowest speed to combine, about 30 seconds. With mixer still running on lowest speed, add butter 1 piece at a time, then beat until mixture resembles coarse meal, with butter bits no larger than small peas, 2 to 2½ minutes.

4. With mixer still running, add 1 cup liquid. Increase speed to medium-high and beat until light and fluffy, about 45 seconds. With mixer still running, add remaining 1 cup liquid in steady stream (this should take about 15 seconds). Stop mixer and scrape down bowl with rubber spatula, then beat at medium-high speed to combine, about 15 seconds. (Batter will be thick.)

5. Divide batter between cake pans and level with offset or rubber spatula. Bake until deep golden brown, cakes pull away from sides of pans, and toothpick inserted into center of cakes comes out clean, about 30 minutes (rotate cakes after about 20 minutes). Do not turn off oven.

6. Cool in pans on wire racks about 10 minutes, then loosen cakes from sides of pans with paring knife, invert cakes onto racks and then re-invert; cool to room temperature.

7. TO TOAST THE COCONUT: While cakes are cooling, spread shredded coconut on rimmed baking sheet; toast in oven until shreds are a mix of golden brown and white, about 15 to 20 minutes, stirring 2 or 3 times. Cool to room temperature.

8. FOR THE BUTTERCREAM: Combine whites, sugar, and salt in bowl of standing mixer; set bowl over saucepan containing 1½ inches of barely simmering water. Whisk constantly until mixture is opaque and warm to the touch and registers about 120 degrees on an instant-read thermometer, about 2 minutes.

9. Transfer bowl to mixer and beat whites on high speed with whisk attachment until barely warm (about 80 degrees) and whites are glossy and sticky, about 7 minutes. Reduce heat to medium-high and beat in butter 1 piece at a time. Beat in cream of coconut and coconut and vanilla extracts. Stop mixer and scrape bottom and sides of bowl. Continue to beat at medium-high speed until well-combined, about 1 minute.

10. TO ASSEMBLE CAKE: Follow illustrations above. Cut into slices and serve. (Wrap leftover cake in plastic and refrigerate; bring to room temperature before serving.)

Which Supermarket Extra-Virgin Olive Oil Is Best?

Blind tastings of nine supermarket olive oils reveal that the differences in brands are often minimal.

⇒ BY RAQUEL PELZEL ⇐

When you buy a supermarket extra-virgin olive oil, you're not buying a boutique oil produced and bottled in the small production plant of an olive grower just outside a quaint Tuscan village. You are buying a big-name producer's mass-marketed extra-virgin brand, usually made from olives shipped into Italy from different countries—or even different continents—for bottling. (An extra-virgin oil can be called "Italian" even if it is only bottled in Italy.)

This leads to differences not only in price and quality but in what you may or may not know about the oil. When you purchase an artisanal oil in a high-end shop, certain informational perks are expected (and paid for). These typically include written explanations of the character and nuances of the particular oil as well as knowledgeable staff who can assist you in your purchase. But in a supermarket, it's just you and a price tag. How do you know which supermarket extra-virgin oil best suits your needs? To provide some guidance, we decided to hold a blind tasting of the extra-virgin oils typically available in supermarkets.

What Is Extra-Virgin?

Owing to the spike in the popularity of extra-virgin olive oil over the past 20 years (olive oil imports have more than quadrupled to 358 million pounds since 1982), the average American supermarket now offers several varieties. The first step in selecting one of them is understanding just what defines a quality extra-virgin oil.

The label "extra-virgin" denotes the highest quality of olive oil, with the most delicate and prized flavor. (There are three other grades, including "virgin," "pure," and "olive pomace." "Pure" oil, often labeled simply "olive oil," is the most commonly available.) To be tagged as extra-virgin, an oil must meet three basic criteria. First, it must contain less than 1 percent oleic free fatty acids per 100 grams of oil. Second, the oil must not have been treated with any solvents or heat. (Heat is used to reduce strong acidity in some nonvirgin olive oils to make them palatable. This is where the term *cold pressed* comes into play, meaning that the olives are pressed into a paste using mechanical wheels or hammers and are then kneaded to separate the oil from the fruit.) Third, it must pass taste and aroma standards as defined by groups such as the International Olive Oil Council (IOOC), a Madrid-based intergovernmental olive oil regulatory committee that sets the bar for its member countries.

Despite these criteria, not all extra-virgin oils are what they claim. The IOOC can regulate only those olive oils produced or labeled in countries that are members of the organization, a category that includes all European and some North African countries but not the United States. If a U.S.-based company purchases olive oil in bulk from Italy and bottles and labels the oil in its U.S. plant, that company could call the oil "Italian extra-virgin" even if it is not a true extra-virgin oil. While some grass-roots organizations, such as the California Olive Oil Council, have willingly adopted IOOC guidelines to try to regulate the quality of domestically produced oils, U.S. producers are not required to belong to any such organization. Of the nine extra-virgin olive oils included in our tasting, all but one—Pompeian—are harvested, produced, bottled, and labeled in an IOOC-member country.

Tasting the Oil

Tasting extra-virgin olive oil is much like tasting wine. The flavors of these oils range from citrusy to herbal, musty to floral, with every variable in between. And what one taster finds particularly attractive—a slight briny flavor, for example—another person might find unappealing.

Also like wine, the flavor of a particular brand of olive oil can change from year to year. For instance: If Italy has a poor harvest, it also has fewer olives to sell to olive oil producers. The short supply raises the price of Italian olives, making them more expensive than those from other countries, such as Tunisia and Spain. In such a situation, a company that blends oils from a number of countries might choose to use fewer Italian olives and more olives from the other countries to keep the price of its oil competitive. A producer committed to using only Italian olives and maintaining quality, however, would have to either buy its usual volume of olives and raise prices or blend this year's oil with some extra-virgin oil from a previous year. All of this means that the quality of a given brand of oil may vary quite a bit from year to year.

Because we wanted to make sure that the oils in our tasting would be widely available to readers, we contacted the Chicago-based market research firm Information Resources and selected the most popular extra-virgin olive oils based on their statistics. Our tasting panel was composed of staff members and olive oil experts alike. To help the panel describe what they were tasting, we used vocabulary recommended by the IOOC for judging extra-virgin olive oil.

Whereas in a typical *Cook's* tasting we can identify a clear "winner" and "loser," this time around we could not draw such a distinct line. In fact, the panel seemed to quickly divide itself into those who like a gutsy olive oil with bold flavor and those who prefer a milder, more mellow approach. Nonetheless, in both camps one oil clearly had more of a following than any other—the all-Italian-olive Davinci brand. Praised for its rounded and buttery flavor, it was the only olive oil we tasted that seemed to garner across-the-board approval with experts and in-house staff alike. Consequently, it is the only supermarket extra-virgin olive oil we could rate as "highly recommended."

Because tasting olive oil is an esoteric endeavor, we decided to group our results in a manner different from that in other tastings. Instead of the usual "highly recommended" and "not recommended" categories (with the exception of the Davinci brand), we grouped the oils according to their primary defining feature as either "full-bodied, bold, and ripe" or "mild, delicate, and approachable." Since an olive oil's character can change with each harvest, it's safe to say that your favorite extra-virgin olive oil of 2001 may not be your favorite oil from 1998 (which may explain why Colavita performed very well in this tasting but not so well in the 1996 tasting conducted at *Cook's*). Use the scorecard from this tasting as a guide to match your preferences with the description of the oil, keeping in mind that it's really a matter of your own personal taste.

TASTING SUPERMARKET EXTRA-VIRGIN OLIVE OILS

We chose to taste extra-virgin olive oil in its most pure and unadulterated state: raw. Tasters were given the option of sampling the oil from a spoon or on neutral-flavored French bread and were then asked to eat a slice of green apple—for its acidity—to cleanse the palate between oils. We'd like to thank the magazine staff and the several Boston-based olive oil aficionados who joined us for the tasting: Albert Capone of Capone Foods, Peter Gondolfo of the California Olive Oil Company, Jonathan Imes of the Agawam-Hunt Country Club, Thor Iverson of the *Boston Phoenix*, Jeannie Rogers of Il Capriccio, and Michele Topor of L'arte di Cucinare. The olive oils were evaluated for color, clarity, viscosity, bouquet, depth of flavor, and lingering of flavor. All of the extra-virgin olive oils we tested are categorized as either "bold" or "mild" and are listed within their respective group in order of how agreeable they were to tasters.

HIGHLY RECOMMENDED

DAVINCI Extra Virgin Olive Oil
➤ **$7.99 for 34 ounces**

BOTTLED AND LABELED IN ITALY
Made exclusively from Italian olives

Our only highly recommended oil garnered top marks from both professional and lay tasters. Described as rich, deep, and beautifully green, Davinci olive oil was clearly triumphant. Tasters described it as "very ripe and buttery," with "leafy" and "herbaceous" qualities. They also noted that while Davinci has a slightly bitter edge, it is very balanced. One taster found the oil "interesting and complex," with a "big olive nose."

FULL-BODIED AND BOLD

COLAVITA Extra Virgin Olive Oil
➤ **$9.99 for 34 ounces**

BOTTLED AND LABELED IN ITALY
Made exclusively from Italian olives

This olive oil was deemed heavy on the tongue, complex, and "organic," with "high-toned and full" qualities and "excellent acidity." Its nose was called strong and briny. Several tasters commented that the oil was just a little too harsh.

FILIPPO BERIO Extra Virgin Olive Oil
➤ **$11.69 for 51 ounces**

BOTTLED AND LABELED IN ITALY
Blended from oils of Italy, Greece, Spain, and Tunisia

The Berio brand was slightly cloudy, with a gray-green color. Although tasters found the oil somewhat greasy on the palate, they said that it still managed to build a full, solid flavor that ended in a soft, peppery finish.

CARAPELLI Extra Virgin Olive Oil
➤ **$5.99 for 25.5 ounces**

BOTTLED AND LABELED IN ITALY
Blended from oils of Italy, Greece, Spain, and Tunisia

This oil had what tasters called a "classic olive oil color." While the nose of the oil was perceived as woody and oaky, the flavor was deemed "unpleasantly harsh," with fishy and smoky nuances and a soapy finish that was very heavy on the palate.

MILD AND DELICATE

POMPEIAN Extra Virgin Olive Oil
➤ **$7.99 for 32 ounces**

BOTTLED AND LABELED IN BALTIMORE, MD.
Blended from various Mediterranean oils

Even though this was the only oil in our tasting that was bottled outside IOOC jurisdiction, tasters found the flavor "clean, round, and lingering." One taster said it had a golden "sunny" hue and brought forth nutty flavors such as hazelnut and walnut; an expert, however, described Pompeian's flavor as "too light for an extra-virgin oil."

WHOLE FOODS Extra Virgin Olive Oil
➤ **$5.99 for 33.8 ounces**

BOTTLED AND LABELED IN ITALY
If the label reads "Product of Italy," the oil was made exclusively from Italian olives; if the label reads "Packed in Italy," the oil is blended from various Mediterranean oils.

The Whole Foods brand was described as "clear, light, and golden," with a "light mouthfeel" and "buttery finish." One taster described the flavor as "mild and pleasant" but said that it "dissipates quickly," without much of an initial bouquet.

STAR Extra Virgin Olive Oil
➤ **$4.69 for 17 ounces**

BOTTLED AND LABELED IN SPAIN
Blended from oils of Spain, Italy, Greece, and Tunisia

Characterized by a light, peaked yellow color that reminded one taster of vegetable oil, Star extra-virgin was criticized for the strong, peppery burning sensation it produced at the back of the throat, which quickly overpowered the initial subtle artichoke and cucumber flavors. And while the aroma was described as "delicate" and "discreet," the finish of the oil was considered abrupt, with strong metallic flavors and harsh qualities.

GOYA Extra Virgin Olive Oil
➤ **$4.59 for 17 ounces**

BOTTLED AND LABELED IN SPAIN
Blended exclusively from Spanish oils

"Shockingly yellow" is how one taster described this oil, while another called it "canary" colored with a faint green cast. Many tasters agreed its flavor was reminiscent of bitter lemons. Another taster added that while the bouquet was pleasant and complex, "upon tasting, the acidity seemed to build," while the herbaceous "oregano and mint" qualities vanished.

BERTOLLI Extra Virgin Olive Oil
➤ **$11.69 for 51 ounces**

BOTTLED AND LABELED IN ITALY
Blended from oils of Italy, Greece, Spain, and Tunisia

Tasters admired this oil's color—"golden, with flecks of copper"—but not its "flat," "boring" flavor. There were some bitter almond undertones, but the peppery harshness killed any subtleties. One taster complained, "the acid killed my throat."

Do Garlic Presses Really Work?

Once viewed as a tool for culinary novices, some new models can puree garlic cloves, peeled or not, in just seconds.

≥ BY ADAM RIED ≤

Let's start with a given: Most cooks dislike the chore of mincing garlic. First, its texture is defiantly sticky, so that little bits cling tenaciously to your cutting board, knife blade, and fingers. Second, despite the garlic clove's diminutive size, mincing a couple of them finely and evenly is a time- and labor-intensive proposition. So how do we solve this dilemma? The garlic press is one good possibility.

We know that many cooks sneer at this tool, but we have a different opinion. In hundreds of hours of use in our test kitchens, we have found that this little tool delivers speed, ease, and a comfortable separation of garlic from fingers. And there are other advantages. First is flavor, which changes perceptibly depending on how the cloves are broken down. The finer a clove of garlic is cut, the more flavor is released from its broken cells in the guise of an enzyme called *allicin*. Fine mincing or pureeing, therefore, results in a fuller, more pungent garlic flavor. A good garlic press breaks down the cloves more than an average cook would with a knife. Second, a good garlic press should also ensure a consistently fine texture, which in turns means better distribution of the garlic throughout the dish.

The question for us, then, was not whether garlic presses work but which of the many available presses work best. Armed with 10 popular models, we pressed our way through a mountain of garlic cloves to find out.

Price and Design

Garlic press prices can vary by as much as a shocking 800 percent, from about $3 up to $25. Some are made from metal and others from plastic. Some offer devices to ease cleaning, and most show subtle differences in handle and hopper design.

Most garlic presses share a common design, comprising two handles connected by a hinge. At the end of one handle is a small perforated hopper; at the end of the other is a plunger that fits snugly inside that hopper. The garlic cloves in the hopper get crushed by the descending plunger when you squeeze the handles together, and the puree is extruded through the perforations in the bottom of the hopper.

Some presses employ a completely different design. In our group, both the Chef'n "Garlic Machine" and the Genius Garlic Cutter consisted of relatively large cylindrical containers with tight-fitting screw-down plungers. These presses were designed for large capacity—we fit 10 medium cloves in the Chef'n "Garlic Machine"—and to serve as a container for refrigerator storage of the unused portion of garlic. This unusual design failed to impress us. Both the "Garlic Machine" and the Genius Garlic Cutter struck our testers as cumbersome because their screw-type plungers required both pressure and significant repetitive motion, which we felt contributed to hand fatigue. This seemed like a lot of work just to press garlic. Matters did not improve when the hoppers were loaded with multiple garlic cloves. Even greater effort was required to twist down the plungers, and the texture of the garlic puree produced by the "Garlic Machine" was coarse and uneven. Likewise, the mince created by the Genius Garlic Cutter was larger than we like. Based on these tests, we'll pass on this design.

Press Check

A good garlic press should not only produce a smooth, evenly textured garlic puree but should also be easy to use. To us, this means that different users should be able to operate it without straining their hands. With several notable exceptions, all of

The Presses We Tested

RECOMMENDED

BEST GARLIC PRESS

Zyliss
Classic design is light, effective, and easy to handle.

Bodum
Beautiful design blurs the line between gadget and art.

Kuhn Rikon
Well-designed swing-out plate makes cleaning supereasy.

Henckels
Effective, but expensive and annoying to some.

Oxo
Bulky rubber handle and heavy weight drew mixed reviews.

NOT RECOMMENDED

Endurance
Designed to process especially large garlic cloves.

Chef'n
More tedious to use than traditional design.

Bradshaw International
Narrow handle provided little grip or leverage.

Farberware
Flimsy and largely ineffective.

Genius
Poor handle design; minces rather than presses garlic.

RATING GARLIC PRESSES

RATINGS
★★★
GOOD
★★
FAIR
★
POOR

With each of the 10 garlic presses listed below, we performed four tests: pressing single, medium-sized garlic cloves, both with and without their skin; pressing several peeled, medium-sized garlic cloves at once; and pressing 1-inch pieces of peeled fresh ginger. The degree of effort required to press the garlic (which we call ease of use), grip comfort, and the texture of the pressed garlic (we preferred finely and evenly mashed garlic—essentially, a puree) were equally important considerations. The design category comprises our assessment of the presses' cleaning device (attached, separate, or none at all), weight, and relative sturdiness or flimsiness. Additional observations are noted in the testers' comments.

Brand	Price	Materials	Ease of Use	Grip Comfort	Design	Garlic Texture	Dishwasher Safe	Testers' Comments
BEST GARLIC PRESS **Zyliss** SUSI DeLuxe Garlic Press	$12.99	Metal with nonstick coating	★★★	★★★	★★★	★★★	YES	Comfortable and easy for all users, this press also produced very finely pureed garlic. Can crush three cloves at once, but two is easier. Separate cleaner attachment stores cleverly in handle.
RECOMMENDED **Bodum** Allium Garlic Press No. 6760	$11.98	Teflon-coated aluminum	★★★	★★★	★★★	★★★	YES	Perforated plate swings out for cleaning access. Mashed garlic is uniform, but not as fine as Zyliss. Has a tough time with three cloves. Loose cleaner does not store on unit, and so it can be lost easily.
Kuhn Rikon Garlic Press	$11.95	Plastic	★★★	★★★	★★★	★★	YES	Plastic handles have a bit too much "give" for maximum pressing efficiency, so the mashed garlic was slightly uneven in texture, though certainly acceptable. Worked well on multiple (three) cloves, less so on unpeeled cloves.
Zwilling J. A. Henckels Garlic Press	$25.00	Stainless steel with polypropylene handles	★★★	★★★	★★	★★★	YES	Includes fine and coarse removable hopper inserts, which can be lost as easily as loose cleaners. When filled with garlic, the removable hopper had the annoying tendency to lift out of position when the handles were separated.
Oxo Good Grips Garlic Press	$11.99	Metal with soft rubber grip	★★★	★★	★★	★★★	YES	Felt heavy and somewhat awkward to users with small hands. Some users' fingers were pinched repeatedly between the handles when shut.
NOT RECOMMENDED **Endurance** Large Garlic Press	$11.98	18/8 Stainless Steel	★★	★★	★★	★	YES	Requires near-Herculean hand strength to process several cloves at once. Texture of mashed garlic was coarse and uneven, but it did process unpeeled cloves well. Depth of hopper makes it difficult to clean.
Chef'n "The Garlic Machine," Model GGMD-12	$7.99	Plastic	★★	★★	★	★	YES	We were not fans of this design. Though not difficult to use, the repetitive twisting motion was tedious and promoted hand strain. Must disassemble completely to clean, which is a nuisance.
Bradshaw International Good Cook Garlic Press	$3.99	Cast aluminum with nonstick coating	★	★	★★	★	YES	Most users found they needed a great deal of hand strength to use this press. Lots of garlic pulp and juice ooze out around the plunger. No cleaner means extra cleaning effort.
Farberware Garlic Press and Cleaner with Microban, Model #87039	$3.49	Plastic	★	★	★★	★	YES	So much flex in the handles that garlic cloves barely got crushed. Cloves were juiced more than pureed. Cleaner stores in handle.
Genius Garlic Cutter	$19.99	Plastic	★	★	★	★	YES	We found the handle slick, difficult to grasp, and difficult to turn. Promoted hand fatigue quickly. Garlic mince was uniform, but too large for our tastes. Holds six cloves easily but will not work with unpeeled cloves or ginger.

our presses performed reasonably well in this regard. We did find, however, that squeezing both the Bradshaw Good Cook and the Farberware presses required a good deal of effort and that the texture of the extruded garlic was unacceptably coarse. In fact, the Farberware, which felt flimsy in our hands because of its all-plastic construction, barely crushed the clove at all.

Several *Cook's* editors wondered if we could make an easy task even easier by putting the garlic cloves through the presses without first removing their skins. Instructions on the packaging of the Zyliss and Bodum presses specified that it was OK to press unpeeled cloves, and our tests bore out this assertion. Though the directions for several other presses did not address this issue specifically, we found that the Oxo and the Endurance also handled unpeeled garlic with ease. We did note, however, that the yield of garlic puree was greater across the board when we pressed peeled cloves. While we were at it, we also

tried pressing chunks of peeled, fresh ginger. The Zyliss, Kuhn Rikon, and Oxo were the only three to excel in this department, and we found that smaller chunks, about ½ inch, were crushed much more easily than larger, 1-inch pieces.

Though all the presses were dishwasher-safe, you first had to remove the remains of the clove from the hopper. To help with this task, the Oxo featured an attached cleaning mechanism. The Zyliss and Farberware had detachable cleaners that could be stowed in the handle. Both the Bodum and Kuhn Rikon featured swing-out perforated plates for easier cleaning access (the Bodum also included a separate cleaner), and the Henckels had removable hopper plates. But you know what? To us, none of these aids mattered much. While the cleaning devices were slightly helpful, all of the presses required a bit of digging to release the garlic remnants. We found the Kuhn Rikon the easiest to clean because we could run the tip of a paring knife along the full area of its

gently curved swing-out plate. In our view, both the "Garlic Machine" and the Genius Garlic Cutter were particularly onerous to clean because they had to be completely disassembled.

Indeed, using a good garlic press really can spare your cutting board, knife, and fingers lingering garlic odor. It also spares your food the indignity of using garlic powder to avoid the task of mincing it fresh, and your arm much of the work therein. Despite some grumbles about cleanup, we now routinely reach for our garlic press to make quick work of the clove or two called for in many recipes.

When all was said and pressed, the traditionally designed, moderately priced Zyliss turned out to be comfortable and consistent, and it produced the finest, most even garlic puree. In addition, it handled unpeeled garlic and small chunks of fresh ginger without incident. While all of the presses in the Recommended category on the accompanying chart get the job done, the Zyliss just edged out the others in terms of both performance and design.

≥ BY KAY RENTSCHLER ≤

Tying the Knot

Practiced butchers make it look easy when they tie a roast. Over, under, and around—whoosh-whoosh, done. You want to stick a bow on it. But for many of us at home, binding a roast with butcher's twine makes holiday gift-wrapping look easy. Getting started without slippage is the toughest part—next to understanding the near nautical logic of a true butcher's knot. But while working on the stuffed pork loin for our November/December 2000 issue, we pulled this decent opening move out of our hats (and you won't need a spare finger to hold the string because it holds itself tight).

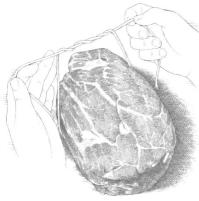

Begin by tying an overhand knot as if tying a bow, but loop the free end around the other end once more, then pull the ends to tighten the twine around the meat.

Rescuing Buttercream

Given proper proportions and supervision when its sugar base is cooked, a buttercream can be made quickly and easily. (See our coconut cake recipe, page 25.) But cooks are inclined to read catastrophe into their finished efforts if the icing appears curdled or broken. Generally, though, this phenomenon reflects, vicissitudes of temperature—a buttercream, after all, is a delicate mass—that are easily corrected. A buttercream that has become too warm may appear soupy and slippery. Plunge the bowl into an ice bath and whisk briskly until the icing becomes silky and cohesive again. A finished buttercream that is

too cold, on the other hand (from cold butter or a chilly ambient temperature), will resemble fine-curd cottage cheese and slide about in the bowl. The solution to this problem is also simple: a steaming hot dish towel, wrapped turbanlike around the bowl, will begin to melt the sides of the buttercream a bit, and subsequent whisking or stirring with a wooden spoon will bring the icing back to its shiny, satiny self.

Commercial Puff Pastry

While we are frankly partial to the quick puff pastry featured with our apple turnover recipe in the January/February 2001 issue (page 23), we realize that even a quick puff pastry takes time. In a nod to our busy readers, we took two nationally distributed, ready-made brands of puff pastry—Pepperidge Farm Puff Pastry Sheets and Classic Puff Pastry from Dufour Pastry Kitchens—into the kitchen to try them with our raw, grated apple filling. Commercial puff pastry, which comes frozen and ready to use, also comes folded and has a tendency to tear when it is unfolded. We find it best to transfer the frozen dough onto a large parchment sheet as soon as it comes out of the package, then work with the dough directly on the paper. That way potential tears can be repaired with a rolling pin.

One package of Pepperidge Farm dough (a little over a pound in weight) contains two pastry sheets each of which can be cut into four 4½-inch squares, one fewer than our recipe. The package directions do not specify oven temperatures or times, so we followed our own. (One thing we did discover is that Pepperidge Farm dough is best left at the thickness it arrives in—rolling it thinner to match our own specifications did not produce high, flaky turnovers.) The turnovers we made with this dough were handsome and barrel-chested, with

a neutral, unobjectionable taste (this product contains no butter).

The Dufour puff pastry weighs 14 ounces and will also make eight turnovers. This dough, made exclusively with butter, is available in specialty and gourmet stores. Though not as rich and buttery as a real puff pastry, it puffed admirably and tasted pretty good. (Unlike the Pepperidge Farm dough, it can be rolled thinner.) To use the Dufour puff pastry in

our apple turnover recipe, unfold the dough to obtain a 12-inch square dough block. Follow the tears in the dough to cut four 6-inch squares. Next, use a rolling pin to roll each dough square into a 6- by 12-inch rectangle, then cut two 5-inch squares from each rectangle. Fill and bake as we direct (package directions suggest an oven temperature of 375 degrees—just as we do in our recipe).

Rice Cooker Roundup

Although we conducted an extensive testing of rice cookers in our March/April 1995 issue, in the process of doing the story on fried rice we decided to check up on genre. We found that nowadays even most basic models in the practical 5-cup range, such as the $50 National SR-W10NA Rice Cooker/Steamer, have nonstick pans and automatic warming functions. Next step up in price are chunky jar-style rice cookers, such as the $95 Sanyo ECJ-5104PF Electric Rice Cooker/Warmer. Finally, there are the new futuristic "neuro fuzzy logic" rice cookers, such as the $170 Zojirushi NS-JCC10 Neuro Fuzzy Rice Cooker and Warmer. These cookers come equipped not only with bells and whistles but even with little electronic brains.

To put these three machines through their paces, we cooked 3 cups of long-grain rice, 3 cups of short-grain rice, and 1 cup of short-grain rice according to the manufacturers' specifications; we kept the rice warm for three hours using the warming functions; and we assessed cleanup. The basic National and medium-priced Sanyo models turned out evenly cooked rice, although some minor browning occurred on the bottom of the rice when the larger quantity of short-grain rice was tested. (This didn't mar the texture or flavor of the rice, only the color.) The warming function also worked well on both, but at three hours, the bottom rice in the National had begun to take on some color. The expensive Zojirushi cooked each batch of rice perfectly and did a nice job of keeping it warm, too, with no bottom browning at all. The dizzying array of options on this cooker include variable settings for "regular," "softer," and "harder" rice; settings for brown rice and rice porridge; a special extended warming function that kicks in after eight hours; and a reheating function.

We were left to conclude that a basic rice cooker does the job just fine; that a more costly jar-style rice cooker has a few more appealing features, such as longer warming cycles and a rice paddle holder; and that an ultrafancy neuro fuzzy logic rice cooker is for well-to-do, very serious rice eaters. —Dawn Yanagihara

Zojirushi Neuro Fuzzy Rice Cooker and Warmer

Sanyo Electric Rice Cooker/Warmer

National Rice Cooker/ Steamer

Jewish Cooking

Two ambitious cookbooks tackle the subject of Jewish cooking.
Each succeeds admirably, though in different ways. BY CHRISTOPHER KIMBALL

Writing a book on Jewish cooking is a seemingly limitless undertaking. At first it might appear that such a book could simply be divided into two parts: one for the Ashkenazim (from Europe and Russia) and the other for the Sephardim (from the Mediterranean region and Asia). But as Claudia Roden points out in her *Book of Jewish Food*, this is only the beginning. As Jews emigrated all over the world during the Diaspora (which dates back more than two millennia), each new community began to develop its own cuisine. Even a single city—Venice, for example—had four different styles of Jewish cooking, including Spanish, Levantine, German, and Italian. So how does one research, organize, and publish a comprehensive cookbook and also get the recipes right? To answer this question, we tested a total of 36 recipes, culled from Roden's *Book of Jewish Food* and Faye Levy's *1,000 Jewish Recipes*.

THE BOOK OF JEWISH FOOD
Claudia Roden
Knopf, 668 pages

The Book of Jewish Food was first published in 1996 and is being included in this review because of the breadth of its coverage, which would have to be considered definitive. After just a quick glance at the book, you get the sense that Claudia Roden is first and foremost a writer and researcher. Placed before the recipes are 57 pages of introduction and discussion, all of which are interesting and well written. Not content with simply dividing Jewish cooking into European and Mediterranean cuisines, Roden recognizes its huge variety by including information on Jewish cooking in France, Israel, Georgia, Greece, Yemen, India, Iraq, Tunisia, Persia, Turkey, Ethiopia, and more. **PROS:** The huge diversity of Jewish cuisine is well represented, and the book reads more like a captivating anthropological narrative than a cookbook. One could argue that Jewish cuisine tells the story of the Diaspora better than any history book. In addition, much of the book is presented as a personal journey, which makes the text compelling. **CONS:** The mix of recipes, history, and personal narrative makes this volume somewhat less accessible as a cookbook. In addition, some of the recipes are not as well suited to the modern kitchen and taste preferences as they might be. (A

Bukharan tea made with 4 cups of liquid and 1 teaspoon of salt was interesting, but much too salty for the modern American palate.) **RECIPE TESTING:** We tested a whopping 23 recipes from this tome and found slightly more than half to be worth making again, although many needed a bit of adjustment. The successes were a Yemeni chili relish (although, contrary to the author's notes, its flavor faded quickly in the refrigerator); a great Moroccan ratatouille; Pumpkin Tzimmes (savory-sweet cooked pumpkin); a wonderful rice pudding; light and fluffy matzo balls; a good but not stellar Djaj Mahshi

(stuffed chicken), in which the stuffing is cooked outside the bird; Lamb with Red Chiles and Tamarind; and Pumpkin Kofta Curry.

When recipes didn't work, however, they were very problematic. These included Pumpkin Soup so sweet that it tasted like an ice cream base. Other recipes had promise but would have benefited from some revision, including a bland meat and cracked wheat pie, pickled cucumbers that needed more flavor, a bread pudding that was too eggy, and a celeriac and fennel salad for which the cooking time was too long.

1,000 JEWISH RECIPES
Faye Levy
IDG Books Worldwide, 625 pages

Faye Levy is a seasoned cook, food columnist, and cookbook author, having trained at La Varenne in Paris and written a number of award-winning books, including the *International Vegetable Cookbook*. Her latest work, *1,000 Jewish Recipes* (2000), is first and foremost a cookbook, not a work of history. The preliminary pages contain only perfunctory remarks about the history of Jewish cooking; it is clear that Levy wants you to skip the reading and get into the kitchen and

cook her food. The chapters include the usual suspects (fish, poultry, meat, and so forth), while also covering Jewish holidays such as Passover, Sukkot, and Hanukkah. The recipes are coded with an *M* for meat, a *D* for dairy, or a *P* for pareve (which denotes foods such as fish, eggs, and grains that can be eaten with either meat or dairy). **PROS:** Levy's recipes are clear, well written, and easy to follow. She is clearly writing and testing recipes for the American market, and this shows in the recipe names as well as the recipes themselves. **CONS:** The context given for the recipes is rather perfunctory compared with that provided by Roden, who shows a more detailed and intimate command of the subject. The book's production quality is much lower than that of the *Book of Jewish Food*, and the copy is printed in royal blue, which makes the small type hard to read. **RECIPE TESTING:** Levy's kitchen skills shine through in the recipes—the vast majority were easy to make and delicious. The winners included Classic Potato Latkes (both gentiles and Jews gave them thumbs up), fruit poached in wine, Cajun Corn Latkes, a cinnamon-apple cake (that was a delight), Rice with Butternut Squash, Artichokes with Spicy Lemon-Herb Dressing, an avocado and arugula salad, and Israeli Baked Chicken with Potatoes and Onions. A few recipes disappointed, including Israeli Doughnuts, which turned out as promised but had almost no flavor; Mushroom and Matzo Kugel (a noodle dish), which looked curdled and had the mouthfeel of lumpy oatmeal; and zucchini and onion patties that were soggy on the outside and mushy on the inside.

Corrections

➤ In the January/February 2001 issue, we misspelled the name of chef and cookbook author David Waltuck. We apologize for any confusion.

➤ In the same issue our review of *Charlie Palmer's Casual Cooking* attributed three recipes to Mr. Palmer that were, in fact, from another "Charlie"—Charlie Trotter. All three of these recipes were well liked, but we noted that two of them had odd combinations of flavors. We hereby restore Mr. Palmer's reputation for down-to-earth home cooking with nary a hint of culinary extremism. As we stated in the original review, *Charlie Palmer's Casual Cooking* has solid, home-style recipes that are well worth the price of the book.

Most of the ingredients and materials necessary for the recipes in this issue are available at your local supermarket, gourmet store, or kitchen supply shop. The following are mail-order sources for particular items. Prices listed below were current at press time and do not include shipping or handling unless otherwise indicated. We suggest that you contact companies directly to confirm up-to-date prices and availability.

Garlic Presses
Topping the list of presses in our testing is the Zyliss SUSI DeLuxe Garlic Press. If you can't find one in your favorite kitchen store, it can be mail-ordered from **Cook's Corner (836 South 8th Street, Manitowoc, WI 54220; 800-236-2433; www.cookscorner.com)**, item #12018, for $11.99. The Bodum Allium Garlic Press, no. 6760, is also a great performer; it is sold exclusively at **Zabar's (2245 Broadway, New York, NY 10024; 800-697-6301; www.zabars.com)** for $11.98. The ergonomically designed third-place Kuhn Rikon Garlic Press can be purchased from **Cooking.com (2850 Ocean Park Boulevard, Suite 310, Santa Monica, CA 90405; 800-663-8810; www.cooking.com)**, item #102920, for $11.95.

Pasta with Garlic and Oil
To avoid tainting your hands with the pungent and lasting smell of garlic when removing its skin, we recommend using a rubber garlic peeler. Just toss the cloves inside the tube, roll it on a hard surface, and out comes the garlic, perfectly peeled. You can mail-order this handy gadget from **Sur La Table (1765 Sixth Avenue South, Seattle, WA 98134-1608; 800-243-0852; www.surlatable.com)** for $7.95 in a choice of two colors: natural (item #2266) or green (item #23260). Mashing the garlic with a mortar and pestle is both easy and effective, and it also keeps hands odor-free. The best mortar and pestle we used was a sturdy marble model with a 6-ounce capacity. **A Cook's Wares (211 37th Street, Beaver Falls, PA 15010; 800-915-9788; www.cookswares.com)** sells the mortar and pestle, item #8481, for $15.

We found that a 10-inch, stainless steel non-stick All-Clad fry pan was the best pan in which to cook the garlic. The pan, item #2732, costs $115 and can also be ordered from **A Cook's Wares**. A heatproof spatula was useful in keeping the garlic moving. The Williams-Sonoma Clear Large Silicone Spatula was the winner of a recent test conducted for our Web site. You can order the spatula, item #3482668, for $9 from **Williams Sonoma (P.O. Box 7456, San Francisco, CA 94120-7456; 877-812-6235; www.williams-sonoma.com)**.

We found that seasoning with Maldon Sea Salt adds superb flavor and a light crunch. If you can't find this specialty sea salt in your local gourmet grocery store, you can mail-order an 8.82-ounce bottle for $5.75 from **Pasta & Co. (2640 NE University Village, Seattle, WA 98105; 800-943-6362; www.pastaco.com)**. Finally, serving the pasta is a snap when using wooden pasta rakes. **Kitchen Arts (161 Newbury Street, Boston, MA 02116; 617-266-8701)** sells a pair for $14 including shipping.

Mail-Order Garlic
If you are interested in using any of the soft- or hardneck varieties of garlic we tasted (see page 14), they can be mail-ordered from **Blue Willow Farm (5288 Ely Road, Wooster, OH 44691; 330-264-8167; www.bluewillowfarm.com)** or **Filaree Farm (182 Conconully Highway, Okanogan, WA 98840; 509-422-6940; www.filareefarm.com)**. Contact the farms directly for pricing and shipping costs.

Fresh Ham
When it came to scoring the skin on our fresh ham (see page 9), the most convenient tool was the LamsonSharp Offset Bread Knife, model 39556, the runner-up in our July/August 2000 bread knife testing. Its sharp 10-inch offset blade provided just enough muscle and leverage to tackle the tough skin. **Professional Cutlery Direct (242 Branford Road, North Branford, CT 06471; 800-859-6994; www.cutlery.com)** sells the knife, item code 1CI4L, for $39.99.

The ham brine uses a lot of bay leaves, which can be quite expensive when purchased in small quantities. To save money, we ordered a ½-ounce bag of Turkish bay leaves, item #30391, for $1.79 from **Penzeys Spices (P.O. Box 933, W19362 Apollo Drive, Muskego, WI 53150; 800-741-7787; www.penzeys.com)**. The bag contains 30 to 40 very fresh leaves—more than enough for the brine—that will last for months if stored in an air-tight container.

When roasting the ham, we found that elevating it slightly on a rack, allowing the heat to circulate constantly around the ham, promoted even cooking. A 10 by 11¼-inch rack does the trick. **Bridge Kitchenware (214 East 52nd Street, New York, NY 10022; 800-274-3435)** sells a sturdy, elevated rack, item code ABBR-56, for $5.95.

Pure Coconut Extract
When developing the recipes for coconut cake and buttercream frosting, we preferred pure coconut extract over imitation. It is worth the extra expense. By far the best we tasted was the Natural Coconut Flavoring made by **Spices Etc. (1209 East Highway 80, Pooler, GA 31322; 800-827-6373)**. A 1-ounce bottle can be mail-ordered for $3.25.

Chocolate Chip Cookies
When turning out the cookie dough for our chocolate chip cookies (page 23) onto the parchment-lined cookie sheet, it's best to form the small dough balls with a 1¼-inch stainless steel ice cream scoop. You can mail-order the scoop from **Bridge Kitchenware (214 East 52nd Street, New York, NY 10022; 800-274-3435)**, item code BICS-I-100, for $16.95.

Fried Rice
If you are making the Fried Rice with Shrimp, Pork, and Peas on page 19 and are feeling adventurous, seek out the lop cheong Chinese sausages. If your local Asian grocer doesn't carry them (they come in vacuum-sealed packages), you can mail-order a 16-ounce package from **The Oriental Pantry (423 Great Road, Acton, MA 01720; 978-264-4576; www.orientalpantry.com [search for *lap chung*—spelling varies])**, item #1122, for $5.19. Fish sauce, a Southeast Asian staple made from pressed, salted, and aged anchovies, enhances the flavor of the Thai-Style Curried Chicken Fried Rice. We used Thai Kitchen Premium Fish Sauce, which is available in supermarkets. Call the manufacturer at **800-967-8424, ext. 103**, to locate a merchant near you that carries it.

Rice Cookers
Based on our tests (see page 30), we found that there is a rice cooker out there to fit just about anyone's needs. Rice cookers are available in many fine kitchen stores but can also be mail-ordered. **Appliances.Com (11558 State Route 44, Mantua, Ohio 44255; 888-543-8345; www.appliances.com)** sells both the basic, all-around good performer, the 5-cup National SR-W10NA ($50), and the ultrafancy 5-cup Zojirushi NS-JCC10 ($169). The Sanyo ECJ-5104PF 4-Cup Jar-Type Electronic Rice Cooker and Warmer can be ordered from **Global Mart (909 South Main Street, Suite D, Logan, UT 84321; 800-758-8245; www.globalmart.com)**, item #APSN5104, for $94.95.

Thermospot Sauté Pan
The 12½-inch T-Fal Thermospot Hard Enamel Sauté Pan (see page 13 for our testing of this pan) can be mail-ordered from **Kitchen Etc. (32 Industrial Drive, Exeter, NH 03833; 800-232-4070; www.kitchenetc.com)**, item #683466, for $29.99.

RECIPES
March & April 2001

Stuffed Bell Peppers

Creamy Mushroom Soup

Main Dishes
Fried Rice
   with Peas and Bean Sprouts 19
   with Shrimp, Pork, and Peas 19
   Thai-Style Curried Chicken 19
Pasta with Garlic and Oil 15
Roast Fresh Ham 10
Roast Fresh Ham, Cola-Brined 10
Sautéed Turkey Cutlets 13
Stuffed Bell Peppers,
   Classic 7
   with Chicken, Smoked Mozzarella,
      and Basil 7
   with Spiced Lamb, Currants, and
      Feta Cheese 7

Soups and Side Dishes
Asparagus,
   Simple Broiled 11
   with Bacon, Red Onion, and
      Balsamic Vinaigrette 11
   with Lemon-Shallot Vinaigrette 11
   with Soy-Ginger Vinaigrette 11
   with Tomato-Basil Vinaigrette 11
Mushroom Soup, Creamy 21

Sauces, Glazes, and Garnishes
FOR CREAMY MUSHROOM SOUP:
   Sautéed Wild Mushroom
      Garnish 21
FOR ROAST FRESH HAM:
   Apple Cider and Brown Sugar
      Glaze 16
   Orange, Cinnamon, and Star Anise
      Glaze 10
   Spicy Pineapple-Ginger Glaze 10
FOR SAUTÉED TURKEY CUTLETS:
   Honey-Mustard Pan Sauce with
      Tarragon 13
   Warm-Spiced Pan Sauce with
      Currants and Almonds 13

Desserts
Chocolate Chip Cookies, Thin and
   Crispy 23
Coconut Layer Cake 21

Sautéed Turkey Cutlets

Fried Rice

Broiled Asparagus with Tomato-Basil Vinaigrette

PHOTOGRAPHY: CARL TREMBLAY

www.cooksillustrated.com

If you enjoy *Cook's Illustrated* magazine, you should visit our Web site. Simply log on at www.cooksillustrated.com. Although much of the information is free, database searches are for site subscribers only. *Cook's Illustrated* readers are offered a 20 percent discount.

Here is what you can do on our site:

Search Our Recipes: We have a searchable database of all the recipes from *Cook's Illustrated*.

Search Tastings and Cookware Ratings: You will find all of our reviews (cookware, food, wine, cookbooks) plus new material created exclusively for the Web site.

Find Your Favorite Quick Tips.

Get Your Cooking Questions Answered: Post questions for *Cook's* editors and fellow site subscribers.

Check Your Subscription: Check the status of your subscription, pay a bill, or give gift subscriptions online.

Visit Our Bookstore: You can purchase any of our cookbooks, hardbound annual editions of the magazine, or posters online.

Subscribe to *e-Notes*: Our free e-mail companion to the magazine offers cooking advice, test results, buying tips, and recipes about a single topic each month.

Find Out about Our New Public Television Show: Watch *America's Test Kitchen* to see the *Cook's Illustrated* staff at work in our test kitchen. Check www.americastestkitchen.com for program times in your area.

Get All the Extras: The outtakes from each issue of *Cook's* are available at Cook's Extra, including step-by-step illustrations.

Roast Fresh Ham

Pasta with Garlic and Oil

Coconut Layer Cake

Thin and Crispy Chocolate Chip Cookies

Kale

Rutabaga

Dinosaur Kale

Cabbage

Turnip

Brussels Sprouts

Cauliflower

Broccoli Rabe

White Kohlrabi

Broccoli

Purple Kohlrabi

Mustard Greens

BRASSICA

©2000 John Rollinette

NUMBER FIFTY

MAY & JUNE 2001

COOK'S
ILLUSTRATED

Crispy Fried Chicken
Brine, Air-Dry, Then Fry

Perfect Cheese Omelets
Finish Cooking Off-Heat

The Best Tuna Salad
Lively Taste, Light Texture

Chocolate Cream Pie
Rich Flavor, Easy-Slice Crust

Rating Cutting Boards
Is Plastic Better Than Wood?

Filet Mignon at Home
Sear, Then Roast

Peanut Butter Taste Test
Spicy Sichuan Noodles
Fresh Rhubarb 'Fool'
Vegetable Soup Refined
How to Grill Vegetables
Bok Choy Basics

$4.95 U.S./$6.95 CANADA

CONTENTS
May & June 2001

2 Notes from Readers
Readers ask questions and suggest solutions.

4 Quick Tips
Quick and easy ways to perform everyday kitchen tasks, from grinding pepper to cleaning microwaves to storing flour.

6 Sichuan Noodles Demystified
Choose the right noodle and sauté, rather than fry, the ground pork. BY DAWN YANAGIHARA

8 Filet Mignon at Home
For a well-crusted steak with a quick pan sauce, sear on the stovetop (in the right size pan) and finish in the oven. BY ADAM RIED

10 The Ultimate Crispy Fried Chicken
To solve the problem of dry, leathery fried chicken, we brined and then air-dried the chicken parts before frying.
BY KAY RENTSCHLER AND BRIDGET LANCASTER

13 Tuna Salad Done Right
Three simple steps eliminate the twin problems of tuna salad: watery texture and bland flavor. BY ADAM RIED

14 Vegetable Soup Refined
For a quick, light soup we use only four vegetables plus souped-up commercial chicken broth. BY JULIA COLLIN

16 Great Grilled Vegetables
An illustrated guide to quickly cutting, seasoning, and grilling vegetables with no precooking.

18 The Perfect Cheese Omelet
Melting the cheese without overcooking the eggs is just one problem we solved in producing an almost foolproof recipe for moist, creamy cheese omelets. BY BRIDGET LANCASTER

20 How to Cook Bok Choy
Stir-frying and quick braising are superior to blanching and steaming for best flavor and texture. BY JACK BISHOP

22 Fresh Rhubarb 'Fool'
How do you tame rhubarb's tartness without losing its true flavor? We cooked 50 pounds of it to find out.
BY RAQUEL PELZEL

23 Chocolate Cream Pie
Two kinds of chocolate and Oreo cookies produce a pie with rich chocolate flavor and an easy-to-slice crust. BY KAY RENTSCHLER

26 Conventional Peanut Butters Cream 'Natural' Varieties
Skippy Creamy Peanut Butter beat other supermarket brands as well as freshly ground peanuts in a tasting of cookies, sauces, and raw peanut butter. BY RAQUEL PELZEL

28 Cutting Boards: Wood versus Plastic
Steer clear of gimmicky designs and hard materials when choosing cutting boards—and, if space permits, keep more than one board in circulation. BY ADAM RIED

30 Kitchen Notes
Test results, buying tips, and advice related to stories past and present, directly from the test kitchen. BY KAY RENTSCHLER

31 Voices of Authority
Two chef-written cookbooks deliver good food and a large measure of personality. BY CHRISTOPHER KIMBALL

32 Resources
Products from this issue, plus Dutch ovens, whipped cream siphons, and 16-inch tongs.

COOK'S
ILLUSTRATED
www.cooksillustrated.com

PUBLISHER AND EDITOR
Christopher Kimball

SENIOR EDITOR
John Willoughby

EXECUTIVE EDITOR
Catherine O'Neill Grace

SENIOR WRITER
Jack Bishop

CORPORATE MANAGING EDITOR
Barbara Bourassa

TEST KITCHEN DIRECTOR
Kay Rentschler

ASSOCIATE EDITORS
Adam Ried
Dawn Yanagihara
Raquel Pelzel

RECIPE TESTING AND DEVELOPMENT
Bridget Lancaster
Julia Collin

ASSISTANT EDITOR
Shannon Blaisdell

CONSULTING FOOD EDITOR
Jasper White

CONTRIBUTING EDITOR
Elizabeth Germain

ART DIRECTOR
Amy Klee

COPY EDITOR
India Koopman

PROOFREADER
Jana Branch

ASSOCIATE EDITOR,
ONLINE EDUCATION
Becky Hays

ASSISTANT EDITOR, WEB SITE
Shona Simkin

EDITORIAL INTERNS
Matthew Card
Meg Suzuki

VICE PRESIDENT MARKETING
David Mack

MARKETING MANAGER
Pamela Caporino

SALES REPRESENTATIVES
Jason Geller
Karen Shiffman

MARKETING ASSISTANT
Connie Forbes

CIRCULATION MANAGER
Larisa Greiner

PRODUCTS MANAGER
Steven Browall

DIRECT MAIL MANAGER
Robert Lee

CIRCULATION ASSISTANT
Jennifer McCreary

CUSTOMER SERVICE MANAGER
Jacqueline Valerio

INBOUND MARKETING REPRESENTATIVE
Adam Dardeck

VICE PRESIDENT OPERATIONS
AND TECHNOLOGY
James McCormack

PRODUCTION MANAGER
Jessica Lindheimer

PRODUCTION ARTIST
Daniel Frey

PRODUCTION COORDINATOR
Mary Connelly

SYSTEMS ADMINISTRATOR
Richard Cassidy

WEB MASTER
Nicole Morris

CHIEF FINANCIAL OFFICER
Sharyn Chabot

CONTROLLER
Mandy Shito

OFFICE MANAGER
Juliet Nusbaum

PUBLICITY
Deborah Broide

For list rental information, contact The SpeciaLISTS, 1200 Harbor Blvd. 9th Floor, Weehawken, NJ 07087; 201-865-5800; fax 201-867-2450. Editorial office: 17 Station Street, Brookline, MA 02445; 617-232-1000; fax 617-232-1572. Editorial contributions should be sent to: Editor, *Cook's Illustrated*. We cannot assume responsibility for manuscripts submitted to us. Submissions will be returned only if accompanied by a large self-addressed stamped envelope. Postmaster: Send all new orders, subscription inquiries, and change of address notices to: *Cook's Illustrated*, P.O. Box 7446, Red Oak, IA 51591-0446. PRINTED CHINA.

FRESH CHILES

CHILES The pungent members of the genus *Capsicum* contain capsaicin, the compound responsible for the mouth-burning, nose-running, sweat-inducing sensations associated with hot peppers. The level of capsaicin in peppers is measured in Scoville units on a scale from a mild zero to a fiery 50,000 (nonscientists use a scale of 0 to 10). The peppingers—habaneros (10), Jamaican hots (9 to 10), and Scotch bonnets (9 to 10)—are three of the hottest. The small but mighty green and red machos (9 to 10) have a sharp, hot flavor that sweetens with ripening. Ajís (7 to 8) have a taste of tropical fruit; amatistas (7) are earthy and sweet; cylindrical serranos (7) are highly acidic; jalapeños (5.5) have a distinct vegetal flavor. Poblano (3) is the perfect pepper to stuff (think chiles rellenos). Sweet, mild cherry peppers (1 to 3) are often pickled. The pimento (1) is most commonly used in this country in its powdered form, paprika.

COVER (*Strawberries and Blueberries*): ELIZABETH BRANDON. BACK COVER (*Chiles*): JOHN BURGOYNE

REQUIEM FOR A PIG

I grew up on a farm. Not the modern, industrial sort of place with 2,000 cows and a barn as long as a football stadium. I mean a small mountain farm where, on rainy afternoons, I'd shoot at rats in the hay barn and flick the metal tops of cream soda bottles for sport. We had no more than 20 milkers on any given day, and our meat was never store-bought; it was slaughtered out back and then brought down to the meat locker to be cut up and wrapped in pale green butcher paper.

But that was years ago, and now I shop at a supermarket, just like you. I buy milk in plastic containers and purchase antiseptic, shrink-wrapped pieces of meat with names like *rib eye* or *top round*, labels that mean about as much as *brougham* or *cabriolet* to the average car buyer.

Last year, I decided it was about time that my family knew something about where meat comes from. I have always believed that unless one opts for the vegetarian lifestyle (which I have done upon occasion), eating meat carries with it a certain responsibility that should not be casually avoided. The taking of a life is serious business and—as is the practice in kosher slaughterhouses—this process should be accorded time, attention, and thoughtfulness. My plan was simple. I would buy two pigs to raise at the farm in Vermont. Then, after the first frost, when my kids were safely back at school, the animals would be slaughtered and brought down to the local meat locker.

Plenty of farm animals were missing in action when the brains were handed out. The list includes cows, oxen, and even horses, which are large, skittish, and unpredictable. But pigs, contrary to their cartoon image, are actually intelligent animals who prefer clean living to rolling in the mud. Our two young ones were long and black, of a breed chosen for the flavor of the meat, not for quick weight gain or pink-faced good looks.

Keenly aware of the endgame, my wife and I tried to avoid naming the pigs, but the kids were soon calling them Daisy and Boris. Around August, my oldest daughter was spending more and more time down at the pen, having fully accepted the pigs as pets. This was to be expected, I told myself. This project was going to teach everyone a thing or two about country living, and if that included a dose of reality, so be it.

Labor Day came and went and our family had moved back to Boston for the winter. In late October, the pigs had hit 180 pounds each, so I called Porky, a local farmer who used to do all of the butchering when I was a kid. He showed up at 6:30 one Saturday morning in a blue Ford pickup. We filled a 55-gallon drum with water, and he pulled out a furnace blower to heat it up. When it reached 160 degrees, I started up the tractor and moved the drum to the pen.

It was a glorious fall day, cold, but the sun had risen over Tate Mountain and was beginning

Christopher Kimball

to clear the frost. Porky loaded his .22 rifle, culled out the sow, and dispatched her quickly. The carcass was dipped in the hot water, scraped, trimmed, and loaded onto the truck. The whole process had taken about an hour.

I was taking this pretty well, having seen my share of butchering as a kid. But the sow's brother, Boris, had become agitated and was scurrying back and forth in the small pen. He couldn't see what we were doing, but he knew that on this perfect October day, some connection had been broken with his sister. It reminded me of a duck I'd once seen in the middle of the road. Its mate had been run over, and it was dazed, waddling in circles around the body, stunned and lonely.

When winter came, we ate the meat. It was tender, juicy, and flavorful—vastly better than the supermarket variety. Although my oldest daughter had lost her taste for pork, her siblings soon developed an appetite for the bacon, chops, and sausage.

We had made the effort to confront the ultimate truth about consuming meat, but, to my surprise, I had taught myself, rather than my kids, a lesson. Death is common, but love is fleeting. Love today, not tomorrow. Don't forget to kiss your kids goodnight, and when things are finally going just right, keep a keen eye out for a farmer in a blue pickup.

ABOUT COOK'S ILLUSTRATED

Visit our expanded Web site The *Cook's* Web site features original editorial content not found in the magazine as well as searchable databases for recipes, equipment tests, food tastings, buying advice, step-by-step technique illustrations, and quick tips. The site also features our online bookstore, a question and answer message board, a sign-up form for *e-Notes*, our free newsletter on cooking, as well as information on *America's Test Kitchen*, our new television series currently airing on public television. Join us online today at **www.cooksillustrated.com.**

The magazine *Cook's Illustrated* (ISSN 1068-2821) is published bimonthly (6 issues per year) by Boston Common Press Limited Partnership, 17 Station Street, Brookline, MA 02445. Copyright 2001 Boston Common Press Limited Partnership. Periodical postage paid at Boston, Mass., and additional mailing offices, USPS #012487. A one-year subscription is $29.70, two years is $55, and three years is $75. Add $6 postage per year for Canadian subscriptions and $12 per year for all other foreign countries. To order subscriptions in the U.S. call 800-526-8442; from outside the U.S. call 515-247-7571. Gift subscriptions are available for $24.95 each. Postmaster: Send all new orders, subscription inquiries, and change of address notices to *Cook's Illustrated*, P.O. Box 7446, Red Oak, IA 51591-0446.

Cookbooks and other products *Cook's Illustrated* offers cookbooks and magazine-related items for sale through its online bookstore. Products offered include annual hardbound editions of the magazine, an eight-year (1993–2000) reference index for the magazine, single-subject cookbooks

from our How to Cook Master Series, as well as copies of *The Best Recipe, The Complete Book of Pasta and Noodles, The Dessert Bible, The Best Recipe: Grilling & Barbecue,* and many others. Prices and ordering information are available by calling 800-611-0759 inside the U.S. or 515-246-6911 from outside the U.S. or visiting our bookstore at www.cooksillustrated.com. Back issues of *Cook's Illustrated* are available for sale by calling 800-611-0759 inside the U.S. or 515-246-6911 from outside the U.S.

Questions about your book order? Visit our customer service page at www.cooksillustrated.com, or call 800-611-0759 inside the U.S. or 515-246-6911 from outside the U.S.

Reader submissions *Cook's* accepts reader submissions for Quick Tips. We will provide a one-year complimentary subscription for each tip that we print. Send your tip, name, address, and daytime telephone number to Quick Tips, *Cook's Illustrated*, P.O. Box 470589, Brookline, MA 02447. Questions, suggestions, or submissions for Notes from Readers should be sent to the same address.

Questions about your subscription? Visit our customer service page at www.cooksillustrated.com, where you can manage your subscription, including changing your address, renewing your subscription, paying your bill, or viewing answers to frequently asked questions. You can also direct questions about your subscription to *Cook's Illustrated*, P.O. Box 7446, Red Oak, IA 51591-0446, or call 800-526-8442 inside the U.S.; from outside the U.S. call 515-247-7571.

Wondering About Wondra

While visiting a friend I wanted to bake a cake but couldn't find regular, all-purpose flour in her pantry. Instead, my friend uses Wondra flour and explained that it could be used as a substitute. I wasn't convinced—the texture is so different from normal flour. I have heard of using Wondra for gravies and sauces, but can it be used for baking?

NEENA SIMON
BASKING RIDGE, N.J.

➤ Wondra is a granulated form of flour that was developed in the 1960s in response to homemakers' complaints about flour dust and lumping. Unlike soft and silky regular flour, Wondra has a grainy texture, like fine sand (or pixie-stick sugar), and, as promised, it does not produce dust or lump when added to liquid. These characteristics are the product of a process called agglomeration that turns regular flour into what the manufacturer calls "instant" flour. The process was derived from technology that had been used for years to produce instant coffee, powdered milk, and powdered gelatin.

To help us understand the process of agglomeration, and the nature of granulated flour itself, we contacted Kevin Ryan, food chemist at the University of Illinois. According to Ryan, the process involves placing all-purpose flour on a vibrating conveyor belt that moves through a very fine mist of water. Next, the flour is agitated to evenly disperse the water and break apart any clumps that may have formed. It then undergoes spray-drying. As the wet flour is subjected to a jet of hot air, the water evaporates, leaving dried particles of flour behind. These are passed through a sieving machine to get rid of any wayward clumps.

But let's look a little deeper. An individual particle of normal flour has two main parts: a starch and a protein. Standard milling breaks up some of these particles, shearing off bits of both starch and protein. The result is a jumble of whole flour particles (containing both starch and protein), broken bits of starch, and protein particles. When this motley crew is sprayed with water, the starch particles swell, become sticky, and glue all the particles back together. Spray-drying the mix re-separates the individual flour particles, but this time they are a uniform size and shape. According to a General Mills representative, the

preswelled flour particles are hollow and thus receptive to instant rehydration when introduced to liquid, eliminating clumping. Also, because the particles are of equal size, Wondra is pourable and, unlike regular flour, weighs the same no matter how it is measured (no need for *Cook's* preferred dip-and-sweep method here). It requires no sifting and is dust-free. General Mills asserts that Wondra "can be used cup-for-cup in your favorite recipes."

Armed with two of our favorite recipes—Quick and Easy Cream Biscuits (May/June 2000) and Rich and Tender Yellow Layer Cake (March/April 1999)—each of which requires a different kind of flour, we put Wondra to the test. When our two batches of the biscuits, one made with all-purpose flour and one with Wondra, came out of the oven, they looked identical. Both had the same 1½-inch rise and were lightly browned. The differences—though subtle—were in texture and taste. The Wondra biscuits were dense, mildly chalky, bland, and had a slightly sour aftertaste. The biscuits made with all-purpose flour were light, flaky, and toothsome, and they tasted sweet, creamy, and nutty. The yellow layer cake, which calls for cake flour, was a different story. The cake-flour version had a moist, tight crumb, was tender and soft, and had a sweet, clean butter flavor. The Wondra cake had a loose, dry crumb, was cottony, and tasted of raw flour. It wasn't something we'd choose to eat.

According to Ryan, our results have much to do with the protein content of the flours. When protein comes in contact with water and is subjected to mechanical action it forms gluten, which is partly responsible for the structure of baked goods. When regular flour is agglomerated, the protein content is not altered and the proteins themselves are not physically changed. So it makes sense that Wondra would perform adequately in place of all-purpose flour because both flours have the same protein content (10–11 percent). Cake flour, on the other hand, contains approximately 8 percent protein, resulting in less gluten formation—and baked goods with a delicate, velvety texture. The verdict? In a pinch, Wondra will do in place of all-purpose. But if your recipe calls for cake flour, use the real thing.

Cream of the Crop

I recently tried pasteurized heavy cream instead of ultrapasteurized heavy cream. What a difference! It whipped up instantly and tasted unbelievably

good. Can you tell me how the two differ in preparation? Pasteurized heavy cream is clearly harder to find. Is there an advantage to using ultrapasteurized?

JUDY YOUNG
NEW YORK, N.Y.

➤ Pasteurization, developed in the 1860s by French scientist Louis Pasteur, is the process of applying heat to a food product to destroy pathogenic (disease-producing) microorganisms and to disable spoilage-causing enzymes.

Because cow's milk is highly perishable and an excellent breeding ground for bacteria, yeast, and molds, it and other dairy products are among the most highly regulated and monitored foods in the United States. There are a handful of different temperature and timing treatments associated with milk and milk-product pasteurization. According to Dr. Barry Swanson, food scientist at Washington State University, the two most common are low-temperature–long-time (LTLT) and high-temperature–short-time (HTST) pasteurization. In the LTLT process, milk is heated to 145 degrees Fahrenheit for 30 minutes; in the HTST process it is heated to 161 degrees Fahrenheit for 15 seconds. Both processes are followed by a rapid cool-down to 38–40 degrees. Heating the milk kills 100 percent of existing pathogenic bacteria, yeast, and molds and 95 to 99 percent of other, nonpathogenic bacteria. Rapid cooling and subsequent refrigeration retard the growth of the survivors, which eventually cause spoilage. Today, most milk is pasteurized by the HTST method because it causes less damage to nutrients and flavor than the LTLT treatment.

Ultrapasteurization was developed to solve the problem of slow-selling items such as eggnog, lactose-reduced products, and cream. Ultrapasteurized products are heated to 280 degrees Fahrenheit or higher for at least two seconds and packaged in an aseptic atmosphere in sterilized containers. This process destroys not only all pathogenic organisms but also those that cause spoilage. Combined with sterile packaging techniques, ultrapasteurization extends shelf life. Ultrapasteurized dairy products last about 14 to 28 days after opening if properly refrigerated. Pasteurized cream is hard to come by these days, having been all but replaced by the ultrapasteurized variety.

We managed to get our hands on some pasteurized heavy cream at our local natural food store and pitted it against two ultrapasteurized creams: organic and a run-of-the-mill supermarket brand. We initially held a blind tasting of the three creams side by side, straight out of the carton. The regular pasteurized cream was the favorite for its unadulterated, natural flavor; it tasted sweet, fresh, and mild. But tasters were surprised by its comparatively thin texture. The two ultrapasteurized creams, while thick and rich, had a mildly cooked taste; the organic cream was quite buttery, while by comparison the supermarket brand was nearly flavorless.

After taking the supermarket brand out of the running, we whipped the two that remained. Again, the regular pasteurized cream was the victor. One cup of the thin cream yielded a surprising 2 cups of smooth and delicate whipped cream. The superthick ultrapasteurized organic cream—despite its superthick consistency—fell just short of 2 cups when whipped, and the taste was noticeably inferior.

The reason for our findings? The high temperature required for ultrapasteurization destroys some of the proteins and enzymes that promote whipping. The higher heat also leaves the cream with the slightly cooked taste our tasters detected, eliminating the more complex, fresh taste of pasteurized cream.

If you take cream in your coffee, or need to keep cream around for a few days, reach for ultrapasteurized (organic, if available). Mixed with coffee's strong taste, its flavor deficit will go unnoticed, and the cream will last much longer in your refrigerator. But if you plan to use cream on its own, whether whipped or poured over berries, seek out the pasteurized version—you'll be glad you did.

Curious About Currants
I was recently told that the currants in my favorite scones are not the same as the currants used to make jelly. Dried and fresh currants are two different fruits. Is this true?

PETER BENSLEY
BERKELEY, CALIF.

☞ Though it may seem surprising, it is true. The currants in your scone are not the same as those used to make preserves, syrups, and liqueurs. The two distinctly different fruits just happen to have the same name.

The tiny currants in your scone are dried Zante grapes. The deeply purple and highly sweet Zante grape is minuscule (⅛ to ¼ inch in diameter), seedless, and most often encountered in its dry form. Zante refers to the Greek island where these grapes first grew, and the word *currant* is presumably a distortion of Corinth, the Greek city from which the minute raisin grapes were originally shipped. Seldom eaten out-of-hand like normal raisins, currants are commonly used in baking and often in savory sauces (see "Perfect Sautéed Turkey Cutlets," in March/April 2001).

The second type of currant is a relative of the gooseberry. This tiny, piquant, acidic berry grows on a shrubby bush in clusters and has taut, translucent skin. There are black, red, and white currants. Black currants are used primarily to make preserves, syrups, and liqueurs (Cassis); red and white currants are eaten out-of-hand or with cream and sugar and are used in preserves as garnishes or in savory sauces. Black, red, and white currants, though unrelated to the Zante grape, resemble it in size, and it is said that this is how they acquired the name. They are often called English currants.

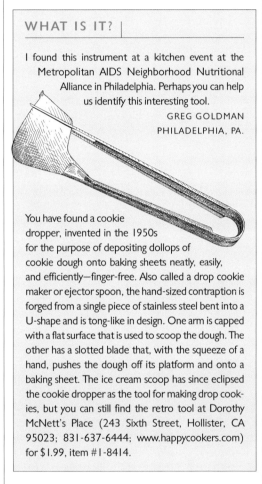

WHAT IS IT?

I found this instrument at a kitchen event at the Metropolitan AIDS Neighborhood Nutritional Alliance in Philadelphia. Perhaps you can help us identify this interesting tool.

GREG GOLDMAN
PHILADELPHIA, PA.

You have found a cookie dropper, invented in the 1950s for the purpose of depositing dollops of cookie dough onto baking sheets neatly, easily, and efficiently—finger-free. Also called a drop cookie maker or ejector spoon, the hand-sized contraption is forged from a single piece of stainless steel bent into a U-shape and is tong-like in design. One arm is capped with a flat surface that is used to scoop the dough. The other has a slotted blade that, with the squeeze of a hand, pushes the dough off its platform and onto a baking sheet. The ice cream scoop has since eclipsed the cookie dropper as the tool for making drop cookies, but you can still find the retro tool at Dorothy McNett's Place (243 Sixth Street, Hollister, CA 95023; 831-637-6444; www.happycookers.com) for $1.99, item #1-8414.

Wine Woes
I have been getting severe headaches when I drink red wine lately. Is this common? What is the cause?

HANNAH WHITE
BOSTON, MASS.

☞ Getting a headache after drinking wine is usually the result of one of three factors: sulfites, amines, or overindulgence. It's easy to pinpoint a hangover—but the cause of a throbbing head after one glass of wine has been the subject of numerous studies.

Grape skins not only host the yeast that ferments grapes into wine, they also contain vinegar bacteria that can spoil new wine. Adding sulfites (sulfur dioxide and its salts) helps to prevent the spoilage. Used in preserving a wide variety of foods, sulfites inhibit the growth of molds and bacteria, curtail oxidation (browning), and also preserve wine's natural flavor.

Many people incorrectly blame sulfites for their wine headaches. According to the Food and Drug Administration, only 1 percent of the general population and 5 percent of asthmatics are affected by sulfites. If you were allergic to sulfites, you would know it. You would be sensitive to a long list of common foods, including—but not limited to—crackers, pizza crust, canned tuna, pickles, olives, shrimp, and dried fruit. If your headaches are severe only when you drink red wine, you can rule out sulfites as the culprit. White wines contain more of the additives.

The other suspect is a group of chemicals called amines, which occur naturally in fermented foods and beverages. Wine contains two kinds: histamines and tyramines. A study conducted by Mark Daeschel, professor of food science and technology at Oregon State University, confirmed that histamines dilate blood vessels in the brain, while tyramines constrict them. Either effect may cause headaches in people sensitive to one or both of the chemicals. But here, too, the reaction occurs only in a small percentage of people. If you experience headaches when you consume foods such as cheese, sauerkraut, salami, flour tortillas, sourdough breads, horseradish, or maraschino cherries, all high in histamines, you will have trouble with wine, too—particularly reds. Both red and white wines contain amines, but reds generally have a higher content.

Persillade
I have come across the word *persillade* a few times in my French cookbooks and wonder if you can explain what it means.

JULIE RUSSO
TOWSON, MD.

☞ *Persil* is French for parsley, and *persillade* is the French term for a simple mixture of finely chopped parsley and garlic. The duo is commonly used to flavor or garnish meat or vegetable dishes at the last minute. The word *persillé* is used to denote dishes finished off with the mixture. A typical use is to toss persillade with boiled potatoes.

Errata
On the back-cover illustration of *Brassica* in our March/April 2001 issue we inadvertently transposed the labels identifying the rutabaga and the turnips. Additionally, the pictures of the oyster and chanterelle mushrooms on page 21 were mistakenly swapped. We apologize for the confusion.

Quick Tips

Storing and Measuring Flour

Bakers who make cakes infrequently may not have a covered storage container especially for cake flour. Rather than simply storing her cake flour as it came in the box, Mereda Metz of Honolulu, Hawaii, transfers it to a zipper-lock bag and stores the bag in the original box. Then she just lifts the bag out of the box, opens it up wide, and dips the cup measure right in. No more spills from pouring flour out of the box.

Adding Eggs One at a Time

Catherine Vodrey of East Liverpool, Ohio, who wishes to be extra careful when handling raw eggs, found cracking and mixing eggs into a batter one at a time to be terribly tedious because she stopped to wash her hands after every egg. Now she simply cracks all the eggs for a recipe into a Pyrex measure with a pouring spout and washes her hands just once. Then she pours slowly and carefully to let the eggs slip out one at a time.

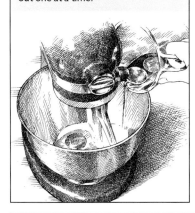

Preparing Picture-Perfect Peas

Stuffed snow peas make a pretty and fresh springtime appetizer, but neatly opening each pod, one by one, can be tiresome. Katrina Moore of Littleton, Colo., was in the midst of this process when she pressed the seam ripper from her sewing box into action. It was perfect for the job.

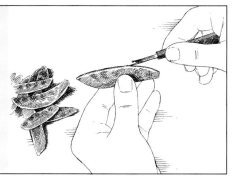

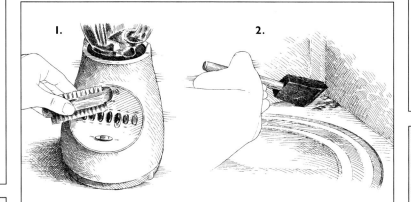

1.   2.

Cleaning Blenders and Microwaves

Nooks, crannies, and crevices on kitchen appliances can be a particular cleaning challenge, so we'll take all the help we can get. Here are two good suggestions.
1. The buttons on a blender are situated very close together, so it's a chore to clean between them when something spills. Katharine Morsberger of Claremont, Calif., uses a nail brush to get into the tight spaces.
2. The corners of a microwave oven pose another cleaning problem. Rosemary Marino of Hershey, Pa., found that a small, disposable, tapered foam paintbrush can be used to brush away crumbs and other residue with ease.

Streamlining Crostini

Both crostini and bruschetta derive flavor and color from a brushing with olive oil. But not everyone has a spare pastry brush on hand for savory applications. In these instances, Grace Won of San Francisco, Calif., uses the heel of the loaf of bread from which she's cut slices. Just dip the cut surface into the olive oil until it has a generous coating, then press it onto the surface of the slice you want to oil. Repeat the process until all of the slices are oiled.

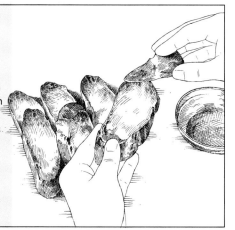

Reconstituting Hardened Almond Paste

Almond paste is expensive and seldom used, which means that leftovers often sit around and harden before they can be used up. When faced with rock-hard almond paste, Gloria Smith of Cedar Rapids, Iowa, used the old trick for softening brown sugar: she placed the paste in an airtight plastic bag along with a slice of bread. When she returned to the almond paste a couple of days later, it had been restored to its normal, pliable state.

Impromptu Candlestand

In the January/February 1999 article on French onion soup, we tested every which way to staunch the tears that flow when chopping onions. The most practical method turned out to be chopping near a flame from a lit gas burner (if you have a gas stove) or a candle (if you have electric burners). Tina Velte of Boston, Mass., figured that if one candle was good, three or four would be better. To make a cheap, easy candle holder, she puts about two cups of kosher salt (sugar would be fine, too) in a bowl and plants the candles right in the salt, which keeps them upright and stable.

Send Us Your Tip   We will provide a complimentary one-year subscription for each tip we print. See page 1 for information.

Pennies for Pie Weights

We prefer ceramic or metal pie weights to those old standbys, rice and beans. Knowing this but having neither ceramic nor metal weights on hand, Ursula Edwards-Howells of Crestline, Calif., improvised by emptying the contents of her penny jar into a foil liner. The pennies lie flat and conduct heat beautifully.

Measuring Water Accurately

Accurate measurement of water in a liquid measuring cup requires that the cup rest on a flat surface so the water is level. Fran Miller of North Granby, Conn., found that setting the cup on the counter and filling it with the sink sprayer is a particularly quick and easy means to a level measurement.

Closing the Bread Bag Tight

The twist ties that seal bread bags have an uncanny ability to disappear. When this happens to Rosemary Parker of Ostego, Mich., she secures the bag by twisting it shut and folding the excess back on itself, over the remaining bread. This works best after a few slices have been eaten.

Homemade Power Pepper Grinder

At one time or another, many cooks face the task of seasoning a huge quantity of meat with salt and ground black pepper while preparing for a large dinner party or big outdoor barbecue. Glen Nuckolls of Bethesda, Md., was not even halfway through peppering 16 pounds of beef when his arm began to tire from all that manual grinding. His solution? He used his cordless power driver/drill to motorize his pepper mill. Two tips make the whole operation run smoothly: First, make sure the driver/drill is scrupulously clean. Second, use only the slower driver settings—the higher speed settings might overheat the pepper mill.

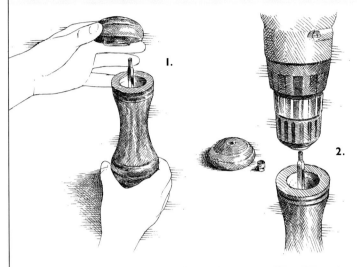

1. Unscrew the finial at the top of the mill to reveal the tip of the square shaft that runs down the center.
2. Insert the shaft into the chuck of a power driver/drill and off you go. Changing the tension in the connection between shaft and driver/drill controls the grind size, from fine to coarse.

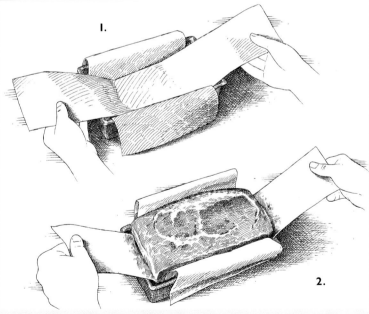

Quick Bread Sling

For extra assurance that her quick breads will release intact from their pans, Amanda Johnson of Sonoma, Calif., not only sprays the pan thoroughly with cooking spray, she also borrows this classic technique for working with French pastry dough.
1. Make a sling for the loaf by laying long, wide strips of parchment paper across the length and width of the pan so that the paper overlaps the edges.
2. Use the overlap as a handy grip when it's time to remove the loaf from the pan.

Warming the Bowl

It is always nice to serve food from a warm dish, but it's particularly nice with mashed potatoes, which otherwise cool off quickly. Helen Sukunda of Colonia, N.J., warms her mashed potato bowl by draining the water in which the potatoes have boiled into the bowl and letting it warm up while she mashes. Just make sure the bowl is heatproof.

Weighing Out Flour

Many bakers weigh out their flour in a bowl or on a piece of parchment paper, but not Rachel Pomerantz of Brooklyn, N.Y. She finds it easier to use a brown paper lunch bag to hold the flour, particularly if the quantity is large. The bag stands open on the scale, is deep enough to hold a lot with no overflow, and pours neatly.

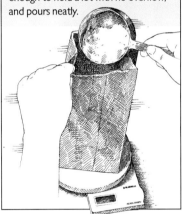

Goat Cheese at the Ready

Rather than rewrapping her log of fresh goat cheese every time she uses a portion, Theresa Cross of Corrales, N.M., stores it in a covered butter dish. That way the cheese is neatly protected and easy to use.

Sichuan Noodles Demystified

This rich, flavorful Chinese dish can be made without exotic ingredients.

⋛ BY DAWN YANAGIHARA ⋜

Years ago, in the kitchen of a university apartment, my Taiwanese roommate taught me to create a simple noodle dish that involved no more cooking than boiling the noodles. It was a cheap, quick, meatless meal on which a student tired of Salisbury steak could subsist.

During a recent phase of cooking all things Chinese, I stumbled across a recipe for *dan dan mian,* or spicy Sichuan noodles, and was reminded of those noodles from my college years. Could I create something that recalled that satisfying dish, yet was a bit more substantial—more suited to a weeknight dinner? Spicy Sichuan noodles are a meal in a bowl. To make them, you top the noodles with a rich, savory sauce—a mélange of browned ground pork, aromatic ginger and garlic, salty soy sauce, and nutty peanut butter in a chicken broth base. All this is set ablaze by the heat of chiles and finished with a sprinkling of sliced scallions and bean sprouts.

I am no stranger to cooking ethnic food—or to going far afield to find unusual ingredients—but I appreciate the fact that this dish can be made with supermarket staples. As an added benefit, it awakens a noodle-loving palate that may have grown weary of pasta with tomato sauce.

This dish is absent from restaurant menus. By all accounts it is street food in China, the equivalent of sausage and onions from a curbside cart in New York. Because I could not sample prepared versions, I researched Sichuan noodles in cookbooks, but turned up only a handful of recipes. Ground pork, peanut butter or sesame paste, chiles (in the form of oil, paste, or flakes), chicken broth, and soy sauce were common denominators. Other flavorings and ingredients, such as oyster sauce, were a tossup. Wanting to add Sichuan noodles to my repertoire, I decided to explore the range of possibilities and realize this dish's full potential.

Sauced Up

The sauce for spicy Sichuan noodles is built simply. Ground pork, marinated briefly in soy sauce and sherry, is browned either by sautéing it in a skillet with just a little oil or by deep-frying it in a cup or so of oil. The pork is then removed from the skillet, the oil drained off, and the ginger and garlic briefly cooked. Next the chicken broth is added, then peanut butter or sesame paste. In a simpler rendition, the ginger and garlic are omitted and the other sauce ingredients are simmered

A sprinkling of bean sprouts adds a refreshing crunch to this surprisingly rich-tasting dish.

right in the skillet with the pork. In both versions, the mixture of pork and sauce is simply poured over noodles and served.

I quickly determined that deep-frying the pork was not worth the trouble or waste of oil. Browning could be accomplished easily in only 1 tablespoon of oil. Next I concluded that once the pork was browned, there was no need to remove it from the skillet. It was fine to build the sauce on top of it. Having decided on these two simplifications, I began weeding through the different ingredients called for in different recipes. I had one clear goal in mind—to create a rich, complex sauce in which the powerful flavors of garlic, ginger, and soy were well balanced.

Fresh ginger and garlic spike the dish with aromatic piquancy, but in equal amounts their potencies vied for dominance, and the pairing was not harmonious. Tasters voted garlic to the fore, relegating ginger to second position. Soy sauce brought a savory quality, while oyster sauce added depth and sweetness that rounded out the flavors. Rice vinegar cut the richness of the sauce and livened things up. Asian sesame paste (not Middle Eastern tahini sesame paste) is typically called for in spicy Sichuan noodle recipes, with peanut butter a

recommended substitute. I was inclined to use peanut butter because of its availability, and it produced perfectly good results. Two tablespoons, the amount recommended in many recipes, was too little to contribute much flavor or to thicken the amount of chicken broth needed to coat a pound of cooked fresh noodles. I doubled the amount to 4 tablespoons, enough to add rich nutty flavor and to adequately thicken the sauce. Any more and the sauce became intolerably rich as well as overly thick.

Next I tried Asian sesame paste in place of peanut butter. Its flavor is mysterious, and it yields an intriguing sauce with an earthy, smoky flavor and a faintly bitter edge. If an Asian grocer is nearby, I recommend seeking out sesame paste. The consistency varies from brand to brand—some are thin and pourable, like honey, while others are spreadable—so I found it necessary to compensate by making minor adjustments in the amount of chicken broth in the sauce.

While you're shopping for sesame paste, look for Sichuan peppercorns. These berries from a prickly ash tree native to Asia bring to the dish a woodsy flavor, with a hint of star anise.

Use Your Noodle

Chinese grocery stores are stocked with a dizzying array of noodles, fresh as well as dried. A couple of recipes recommended fresh egg noodles, so I thought that this is where I would begin. In the refrigerator sections of the major Chinatown markets, the only fresh noodles I found that would qualify as egg noodles (because they listed eggs in their ingredient lists) were "wonton" noodles. Cooked and sauced, these noodles were clearly not right. They were far too delicate. As a result, they wilted under the weight of the sauce, clumped together into a ball, and ended up as listless as a pile of wet rags.

Back in the refrigerated-food aisle, I chose two more types of fresh noodles, lo mein and the descriptively named "plain noodles." From the local supermarket, I purchased—for nearly twice

The Tao of Noodles

With everything from bean threads to rice sticks, the noodle aisle of a Chinese grocery store is more mysterious and perplexing than the shelves of pasta at the supermarkets. When shopping, bear in mind that the ideal noodles for *dan dan mian* are wider than linguine but narrower than fettuccine.

DRIED NOODLES

Straight These plain, straight noodles are typically available in different widths—go for medium (about ³⁄₈ inch). They cook up with good chew and without mushiness, providing a great match for the sauce.

Nested These noodles are much like the boxed dried noodles above, but they're sold in smaller quantities and are packaged in loosely wound nests.

STRAIGHT   NESTED

FRESH NOODLES

Plain If you think you'd like very heavy noodles with a chewy, gummy texture (some tasters did, some didn't), look for noodles like these in the refrigerator section of your Chinese grocery store. Their spaghetti-like shape is not ideal, but the sauce will cling nicely to their sticky surface.

"Asian-Style" Noodles like these can be found in the produce departments of well-stocked supermarkets across the country. They are sometimes packaged in very odd weights, so be sure to read the label and be prepared to buy two packages. The noodles cook up chewy and tender and are a nice match for the sauce.

PLAIN   ASIAN-STYLE

the cost—a few packages of "Asian-style noodles" in wide-cut and narrow-cut versions. Cooked, these three types of noodles were different from one another, but all were a better match for the sauce than the wonton noodles. The spaghetti-shaped lo mein didn't give the sauce much noodle surface to cling to, and their very yielding texture was unremarkable. The plain noodles, shaped like fat, squared-off strands of spaghetti, were as soft and gummy as a piece of Bazooka;

this pleased some and annoyed others. The wide-cut Azumaya noodles had good chew, too, but to a lesser degree. Their fettuccine-like shape was perfect for the sauce; the broad surfaces were easily sauced and could buoy up bits of pork.

Fresh noodles are not always an option, so I also looked into dried. I focused on those having a flat shape sized between linguine and fettuccine. What was true of fresh noodles was also true of dried: the egg and the imitation egg noodles were too delicate for the sauce. Sturdier non-egg noodles, with their chewy and more substantial presence, were a superior match. In fact, for those who prefer noodles with a lesser "mush" quotient, dried noodles are better than fresh.

And for those for whom neither fresh nor dried Asian noodles are an option, dried linguine is an acceptable substitute. Most tasters polished off an entire bowl. One note: If you're using pasta, abandon the notion of "al dente"—Asian noodles are cooked until they submit readily to the tooth. When I cooked them al dente and dressed them, the combination was unpleasant. Once the noodles are cooked and drained, it's best to serve them immediately; give them a few idle minutes and they will fuse together. The only remedy is a hot-water rinse to help disentangle the mass.

Common practice with Italian pasta is to toss the sauce with the cooked and drained pasta in the pot in which the pasta was cooked, giving the mix a little additional heat to help form a loose union. Noodles for *dan dan mian*, however, look and hold up better when simply divided among bowls, ladled with sauce, and then sprinkled with a garnish. It is then up to the diner to toss, swirl, and slurp down the noodles with chopsticks... or a fork.

SPICY SICHUAN NOODLES (DAN DAN MIAN)

SERVES 4 AS A MAIN COURSE

If you cannot find Asian noodles, linguine may be substituted. If you are using natural peanut butter or Asian sesame paste that has a pourable rather than spreadable consistency, use only 1 cup of chicken stock. Also note that the amount of sauce will coat 1 pound of fresh noodles but only 12 ounces of dried noodles, which bulk up during boiling.

8	ounces ground pork
3	tablespoons soy sauce
2	tablespoons dry sherry
	Ground white pepper
2	tablespoons oyster-flavored sauce
4	tablespoons peanut butter or Asian sesame paste
1	tablespoon rice vinegar
1–1¼	cups chicken stock or canned low-sodium chicken broth (see note)
1	tablespoon peanut oil
1	(1-inch) piece fresh ginger, minced (about 1 tablespoon)
6	medium garlic cloves, minced or pressed through garlic press (about 2 tablespoons)
¾	teaspoon red pepper flakes
1	tablespoon Asian sesame oil
12	ounces dried Asian noodles or 1 pound fresh Asian noodles (width between linguine and fettuccine—see "The Tao of Noodles") or 12 ounces linguine
3	medium scallions, sliced thin (about ⅓ cup)
2	cups (about 6 ounces) bean sprouts (optional)
1	tablespoon Sichuan peppercorns, toasted in small dry skillet until fragrant, and ground (optional)

1. Combine pork, 1 tablespoon soy sauce, sherry, and pinch white pepper in small bowl; stir well with fork and set aside while preparing other ingredients. Whisk together oyster-flavored sauce, remaining soy sauce, peanut butter or sesame paste, vinegar, and pinch white pepper in medium bowl. Whisk in chicken stock and set aside.

2. Bring 4 quarts water to boil in large stockpot over high heat.

3. Meanwhile, heat 12-inch skillet over high heat until hot, about 2 minutes. Add peanut oil and swirl to coat pan bottom. Add pork and cook, scraping along pan bottom and breaking up pork into small pieces with wide metal or wooden spatula, until pork is in small well-browned bits, about 5 minutes. Stir in ginger, garlic, and red pepper flakes; cook until fragrant, about 1 minute. Add peanut butter/chicken stock mixture; bring to boil, whisking to combine, then reduce heat to medium-low and simmer to blend flavors, stirring occasionally, about 3 minutes. Stir in sesame oil.

4. While sauce simmers, add noodles to boiling water and cook until tender (refer to package directions, but use them only as a guideline and be sure to taste for doneness). Drain noodles; divide noodles among individual bowls, ladle a portion of sauce over noodles, sprinkle with scallions, bean sprouts, and ground Sichuan peppercorns, if using; serve immediately.

SPICY SICHUAN NOODLES WITH SHIITAKE MUSHROOMS

Soak 8 small dried shiitake mushrooms in 1 cup boiling water until softened, 15 to 20 minutes; drain, reserving ½ cup soaking liquid. Trim and discard stems; cut mushrooms into ¼-inch slices and set aside. Follow recipe for Spicy Sichuan Noodles, substituting reserved mushroom liquid for an equal amount of chicken stock and stirring sliced mushrooms into sauce along with sesame oil.

Filet Mignon at Home

For a well-crusted steak with a quick pan sauce, sear on the stovetop
(in the right size pan) and finish in the oven.

⇒ BY ADAM RIED ⇐

W hen it comes to steak, Americans prize tenderness above all—and filet mignon is the most tender steak there is. It is also expensive, and both factors may drive its perennial popularity as a grand, splashy, celebratory restaurant meal. You've probably noticed that in a restaurant, filet mignon (also known as tenderloin steak or simply as filet) is usually served rare, with a deeply seared crust, and adorned with a rich, luxurious pan sauce or flavored butter.

Well, there is no reason to limit the fun to restaurants. Filets are available in any supermarket with a meat case, and they are not difficult to cook. We wanted to replicate the best restaurant filets at home, which meant developing a deeply browned, rich crust on both sides of each steak without overcooking the interior or scorching the drippings in the pan, which would go on to serve as the basis for a luscious sauce. To that end, we investigated the fine points of both the steaks themselves and the cooking process. Is it worth paying top dollar for superthick steaks, or would supermarket filets of any size do? And what about the best cooking method, temperature, and pan?

Selecting the Steaks

Filets are thick (usually 1¼ to 2 inches), boneless steaks, cut from the slender, supertender, ultra-lean tenderloin muscle, which rests under the animal's spine. The muscle remains tender because the animal doesn't use it to move about, and it is both lean and mildly flavored because it has little marbling (ribbons of intramuscular fat that melt during cooking to provide flavor and juiciness).

We shopped for filets at six local supermarkets and were not satisfied with the butchering job from a single one. The steaks were usually cut unevenly, with one end noticeably thicker than the other (see "Making the Cut," page 9). Beyond that, different steaks in the same package were different sizes and weights. This was far from ideal for expensive, premium steaks. Consistency of size and thickness was important for even cooking within each steak, as well as from steak to steak, in the pan. With that in mind, we took to purchasing a small, roughly two-pound section of the tenderloin, called a tenderloin roast, and cutting our own steaks from it. The process was easy, taking less than

To protect filet mignon's natural tenderness, it's best to cook it no further than medium-rare.

two minutes, and our hand-cut filets were uniform. Tenderloin roasts were available wherever we shopped, so if you can get them, too, we recommend this practice. Alternatively, ask the butcher to cut the steaks for you.

To determine the optimal thickness for filets, we cooked steaks cut 1 and 2 inches thick and at ¼-inch intervals in between. Tasters preferred the 1½-inch cut, which made for a generous (but not over-the-top) portion.

Cooking the Steaks

Grilling is a good option for filets, but because we also wanted to make a pan sauce, we decided to cook our filets in a pan. The recipes we looked at suggested a couple of alternatives, including broiling, high-roasting (oven-roasting at high heat), and pan-searing (stovetop cooking over high heat), all of which we tried. Pan-searing was our approach of choice because it developed the deep brown, caramelized crust critical to the flavor of both the meat and the sauce. Right off the bat we confirmed our suspicion that filets are best cooked rare to medium-rare. In our opinion, cooking them to medium begins to compromise

their tenderness, which is, after all, their raison d'être.

Our next tests involved searing well-dried filets in a dry pan and in a pan filmed with oil. (Drying the steaks thoroughly with paper towels aids development of a crust.) Not surprisingly for such lean meat, the oil was necessary to produce a deep, dark, satisfying crust, and we found that rubbing the oil right into the steaks reduced the spattering a little.

In our tests of different heat levels, we found that a crust formed over a consistently high heat was better developed than that produced by a medium-high flame. But this approach also created a problem. Over such high heat, the fond (the browned bits left in the pan after the steaks were cooked) was often scorched by the time the meat reached medium-rare, giving the sauce a bitter flavor. We tried a couple of things to remedy the problem.

First, we switched from the 12-inch skillet we'd been using (for four steaks) to a smaller, 10-inch model. The decreased surface area between the steaks helped protect the fond. (A heavy-bottomed or cast-iron skillet is essential here; the All-Clad 10-inch skillets we use in the test kitchen weigh about 2½ pounds. Smaller or lighter pans, we found, overheat too easily.) Second, we revisited the high-roasting method, combining it with our searing method by finishing the seared steaks in a hot oven. This approach offered the double advantage of protecting the fond from direct heat and giving us a head start on the pan sauce while the steaks finished cooking.

Throughout testing, the oven time needed to achieve a given degree of doneness varied continually, as did our thermometer readings. While internal temperature guidelines for varying stages of doneness certainly do exist, it can be difficult to achieve an accurate reading in such a small piece of meat. The reading could be way off depending on where the thermometer probe hits, and it's surprisingly easy to miss dead center when you're working fast and juggling tongs and a hot steak in one hand and a thermometer in the other. In some of the steaks we cooked for this story, for instance, we had readings as low as 117 degrees and as high as 140 degrees in the same steak. It all depended on the exact position of the thermometer probe.

So what's a cook to do? We agree with Chris Schlesinger and John Willoughby, authors of *How to Cook Meat* (Morrow, 2000), that it's far more reliable to "nick, peek, and cheat." Just make a small nick in the steak with the tip of a paring knife and look inside. Be sure to remove the steaks from the heat just before they are done to your liking, as they will continue to cook a little, which should give them a perfect finish. This method never failed to produce steaks cooked just the way we like them.

PAN-SEARED FILET MIGNON
SERVES 4

Determining when the meat is cooked to your liking is key, so pay close attention to the visual cues in step 3. If you choose to serve the steaks with one of the sauces below, have all the sauce ingredients ready before searing the steaks. Begin the sauce while the steaks are in the oven. To cook six steaks instead of four, switch to a 12-inch pan and use 6 teaspoons of olive oil.

- 4   center-cut filets mignon, 1 1/2 inches thick, 7 to 8 ounces each, dried thoroughly with paper towels
- 4   teaspoons olive oil
     Salt and ground black pepper

1. Adjust oven rack to lower-middle position, place rimmed baking sheet on oven rack, and heat oven to 450 degrees. When oven reaches 450 degrees, heat 10-inch heavy-bottomed skillet (not nonstick) over high heat on stovetop until very hot, about 3 minutes.

2. Meanwhile, rub each side of steaks with 1/2 teaspoon oil and sprinkle generously with salt and pepper. Place steaks in skillet and cook, without moving steaks, until well-browned and a nice crust has formed, about 3 minutes. Turn steaks with tongs and cook until well-browned and a nice crust has formed on second side, about 3 minutes longer. Remove pan from heat, and use tongs to transfer steaks to hot baking sheet in oven.

3. Roast 2 to 4 minutes for very rare (center of steaks will appear cherry red and feel very soft and loose when cut with tip of paring knife), 4 to 6 minutes for rare (centers will appear red and soft), 6 to 8 minutes for medium-rare (centers will appear pink and feel firm but juicy), or 8 to 10 minutes for medium (centers will appear light pink and feel firm and compact). (After transferring steaks to oven, proceed with pan sauce.) Transfer steaks to large plate; loosely tent with foil, and let rest about 5 minutes before serving.

BACON-WRAPPED FILET MIGNON

Wrap 1 slice bacon around circumference of each filet, overlapping ends and securing to meat with toothpick. Follow recipe for Pan-Seared Filet Mignon, holding the filets two or three at a time on their sides briefly with tongs in skillet to crisp bacon slightly before transferring to oven.

MADEIRA PAN SAUCE WITH MUSTARD AND ANCHOVIES
MAKES 2/3 CUP, ENOUGH FOR 4 STEAKS

This sauce was inspired by one served in a Paris bistro, where the menu includes steak frites and nothing else. If you do not have Madeira on hand, sherry makes a fine substitute.

- 1   large shallot, minced (about 3 tablespoons)
- 1   cup Madeira
- 2   anchovy fillets, minced to paste (about 1 teaspoon)
- 1   tablespoon chopped fresh parsley leaves
- 1   tablespoon chopped fresh thyme leaves
- 1   tablespoon Dijon mustard
- 1   tablespoon juice from 1 lemon
- 3   tablespoons unsalted butter, softened
     Salt and ground black pepper

After transferring steaks to oven, set skillet over medium-low heat; add shallot and cook, stirring constantly, until softened, about 1 minute. Add Madeira; increase heat to high, and scrape pan bottom with wooden spoon to loosen browned bits. Simmer until liquid is

POORLY BUTCHERED FILET   WELL-BUTCHERED FILET

It is not uncommon to find supermarket-butchered filets mignon that are thick at one end and thin at the other, like the steak on the left, which promotes uneven cooking. Well-cut filets, like the one on the right, are even from edge to edge.

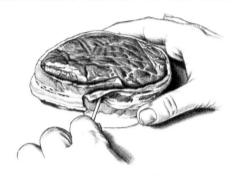

Wrap a slice of bacon around the filet, overlapping ends slightly. Secure the ends by pushing a toothpick through them and into the meat. Remember to remove the toothpick before saucing and serving the cooked filet.

reduced to about 1/3 cup, 6 to 8 minutes. (If steaks are not yet out of oven, set skillet off heat and wait for steaks to come out of oven and rest for 2 minutes before proceeding.) Add accumulated juices from baking sheet and reduce liquid 1 minute longer. Off heat, whisk in anchovies, parsley, thyme, mustard, lemon juice, and butter until butter has melted and sauce is slightly thickened. Season with salt and pepper to taste, spoon sauce over steaks, and serve immediately.

ARGENTINIAN-STYLE FRESH PARSLEY AND GARLIC SAUCE (CHIMICHURRI)
MAKES 1 GENEROUS CUP

Like a loose, fresh salsa in consistency, this mixture is a common accompaniment to sautéed, roasted, and grilled meat in South America. For best results use flat-leaf parsley.

- 1   cup (packed) fresh parsley leaves, washed and dried, from one large bunch
- 5   medium garlic cloves, peeled
- 1/2 cup extra-virgin olive oil
- 1/4 cup red wine vinegar
- 2   tablespoons water
- 1/4 cup finely minced red onion
- 1   teaspoon salt
- 1/4 teaspoon red pepper flakes

Process parsley and garlic in workbowl of food processor fitted with steel blade, stopping as necessary to scrape down sides of bowl with rubber spatula, until garlic and parsley are chopped fine (20 one-second pulses); transfer to medium bowl. Whisk in remaining ingredients until thoroughly blended. Spoon about 2 tablespoons over each steak and serve. (Sauce tastes best when used fresh but can be refrigerated, with plastic wrap pressed directly on surface, up to 3 days.)

The Ultimate Crispy Fried Chicken

To solve the problem of leathery, underseasoned fried chicken, we brined and then air-dried the chicken parts before frying.

⇒ BY KAY RENTSCHLER AND BRIDGET LANCASTER ⇐

Fried chicken is so patently American, so perennially "in," that it travels with a band of icons. It's not possible to think of biscuits or gravy, coleslaw or ham, or of Grandma without thinking of fried chicken.

But what makes fried chicken great? First come, first served: the crust. Crisp and crackling with flavor, the crust must cleave to the chicken itself, not balloon away or flake off in chips like old radiator paint. In addition, it should carry a deep, uniform mahogany without spots or evidence of greasiness. As for the chicken itself, tender, seasoned, and flavorful are the descriptors of the day. Served hot, it should be demonstrably juicy; served room temperature, it should be moist. On no account should it be punishingly dry or require a salt shaker as a chaperone.

The truth is, though, that those with a knack for frying chicken are about as rare as hen's teeth. Frying chicken at home is a daunting task, a messy tableau of buttermilk dip and breading, hot fat, and splatters one hopes will end at the stove's edge. The results are often tantamount to the mess: greasy, peeling chicken skin and dry, unseasoned meat that's a long way from Grandma's.

At this magazine, we first examined the subject of fried chicken back in June 1994. A few years on, we now wanted to see if a couple of the techniques for cooking poultry that we had adopted in the intervening years might enhance our earlier efforts. In the course of this investigation we would, of course, revisit every variable, beginning inside out with the chicken itself.

The Chicken before the Egg

It was no surprise to us that the chicken we were frying had to be premium quality to be worth the effort. Packaged chicken parts were irregular and disappointing, containing mismatched pieces in shabby dress with tattered skin, cut with no nod to basic anatomy. Given this situation, we ended up buying whole 3- to 3½-pound naturally raised or free-range broilers (Bell and Evans being our top choice for good flavor) and spending a few minutes cutting each one into 12 manageable pieces (see "Cutting It Down to Size," page 12). Now we were ready to fry.

In our first stove-side excursion we fried up several batches of chicken with different coatings, oils, and so on. But our real interest resided beneath the skin: half of the chickens had been

For the home cook, pan-frying works better than deep-frying.

brined for two hours; the other half had not. The tasting results were unequivocal: however glorious the crust, however perfectly fried the piece, the unbrined chicken earned marks far below its brined competition. The reason? Seasoning. Seasoned food has more flavor. Who wants to bite through a crisp, rich, seasoned crust only to hit white Styrofoam? Brined meat is also juicy, and the benefits of this moisture cushion extend to the pan. Our brined chicken parts fried at equal rates, relieving us of the need to baby-sit the white meat or pull the wings out of the fat early.

Those of you hoping to forsake brining by frying a kosher chicken will regret the results of our next tests: the kosher fried chicken meat was slippery, its skin loose and extensible. In the koshering process, a chicken is subjected to multiple ice baths and a dry salt rub, and the latter, according to food scientist Dr. Joe Regenstein of Cornell University, changes the composition of the surface layer, loosening the skin. Kosher chickens, in our experience, benefit from dry heat cookery, such as roasting, in which some surface evaporation occurs, but not from an insulating breading and exposure to hot, steam-producing fat.

Soaking chicken pieces in some kind of liquid

before breading—a practice not to be confused with dipping chicken in buttermilk or egg during breading—is traditional in fried chicken recipes. This process is thought to tenderize the meat (a mistaken assumption) and add flavor. Our earlier article examined a number of soaking solutions and found the bright acidic flavor and clinging viscosity of buttermilk to produce the best flavor accents and richest browning during cooking.

Appreciating the tang of a buttermilk soak but unwilling to forgo the succulence of brined chicken, we were whispering—well before the first drum roll—"buttermilk brine." Instead of soaking the chicken in buttermilk alone, why not add the saline blast of a brine, doubling the rewards and minimizing the number of steps? To get a leg up on the idea, we made it a flavored brine, adding a mountain of crushed garlic, a couple of crushed bay leaves, and some sweet paprika.

This remarkable "twofer" won high marks indeed, well above those garnered by a unilateral soak or brine. The buttermilk and paprika showed spirit, garlic and bay crept into the crust, and the meat was tender and seasoned. Time considerations persuaded us to up the saline concentration to 1¼ cups kosher salt per 2 quarts of buttermilk. This concentration delivered maximum brining benefits within two hours. We also spiked the brine with ¼ cup of sugar—not enough to sweeten but enough to bring other flavors out of hiding.

A Coat of Many Crumbs

Fried foods taste irresistibly good when dressed in crumbs or flour, not only because their insides are protected from damaging temperatures but because hot, enveloping fat performs minor miracles on the flavor of the flour or crumbs. But what kind of coating is best?

To find out, we tested straight flour against a panoply of contenders: matzo crumbs, ground saltines, cornflakes, Melba toast, cornmeal, and panko bread crumbs. Cornflakes and Melba toast fared badly, burning and becoming tough.

Cornmeal was also a loser; even a negligible amount mixed with flour betrayed a carbon grittiness. Matzo, saltines, and panko all elicited initial favorable reviews from several northern tasters who were raised on the Colonel's Extra Crispy, but these coatings shared one common liability: they chipped. They were *on* the skin, not *of* it. Plain flour—requiring in this instance no seasoning whatsoever since the chicken had been brined—surpassed all other options for the integrity and lightness of the crust it produced. "Fried chicken skin should peel off in one piece," our Texas colleague said over and over. "It's not supposed to crumble." We had to agree.

Many fried chicken recipes use a single breading process in which the chicken is dipped first into beaten egg, then into flour or crumbs. A double, or *bound*, breading dips the chicken into flour first, then into egg, and finally into flour or crumbs. In side-by-side tests we were surprised to discover that single breading was actually messier than double, lacking the latter's dry, talcum-smooth first flouring, which maintains tidiness and establishes control before the egg dip. The double breading offered a superior base coat—more tenacious in its grip, more protective in its bearing—without being overly thick or tough. In terms of the egg wash, whole eggs provided the best balance; yolks alone were too fatty, coating the flour and creating a gritty finish on the crust; whites lacked body, and the resulting crusts were thin and meager.

Air Play

Another practice that has made its way into many fried chicken recipes is that of air-drying breaded chicken before frying it. Rather than becoming soggy in the refrigerator, as might be expected, the breading toughens up over time to produce a fried chicken of superior crispiness.

We were also curious about the effect of air-drying on unbreaded chicken. We have come to favor the laser-crisp and taut skin of roasted birds that have been air-dried and wanted to see if an analogous effect could be achieved by refrigerating our brined unbreaded chicken on a rack for a couple of hours. We were reasonably confident this would allow the buttermilk to dry just enough to maintain a protective and flavorful posture and the chicken to bread nicely without first being dabbed or dried, frying up dry and crisp.

We tested the effects of air-drying the chicken before and after breading and compared the results with chicken that underwent no air-drying. Both air-dried versions were superior in terms of crust, but each was distinctly different from the other. The breaded air-dried chicken had a heartier, more toothsome crust—crunchy to some, hard to others. The previously air-dried, just-breaded chicken, on the other hand, was lighter and crispier, flaky, more shattery. We preferred this traditionally southern crust. Though it initially seemed ideal, we noticed that its delicate crispiness succumbed to sandiness and porosity over the course of a few hours. This was not acceptable.

The memory of a particularly light but resilient crust on a chicken-fried steak recipe we had made persuaded us to add baking soda and baking powder to an egg wash bolstered with buttermilk. We hoped the sandiness in the crust that developed over time might thus be offset. Stirred into the wash, 1/2 teaspoon of soda and 1 teaspoon of powder produced just enough carbon dioxide to lighten the breading to perfection. Not only did it bronze to a shattery filigree in the hot fat, it also remained crisp as it cooled.

Fry Time

The road to perfect execution did not prove as circuitous as our other adventures. We performed all initial tests using Crisco shortening—winner of the fat test in the magazine's original recipe—at temperatures and in amounts commensurate with pan-frying: 375 degrees, with the fat halfway up the chicken.

One of the most important requirements of fat as a frying medium is that it offer nothing of its own flavor—and, in fact, have none to offer. This means that the oil must be refined—in other words, cleansed and sanitized. Another requirement is that the oil perform at temperatures below its smoke

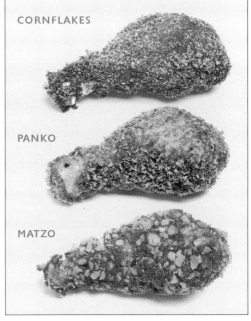

Flour Power

Our experiments with coatings proved that a crunchy snack does not a good breading make. The crunchier the original, the tougher the coating. Flour is best.

CORNFLAKES

PANKO

MATZO

point (the temperature at which it emits smoke and acrid odors) to maintain thermal stability. With the relatively moderate temperatures required by our recipe, all refined vegetable oils stayed well below their smoke points. In the end, peanut oil edged out Crisco shortening by virtue of its marginally more neutral and clean flavor.

Some commercial enterprises favor deep-frying, wherein the chicken pieces are completely submerged in fat. But on a home stove, fat cannot reach the temperature it does in a commercial fryolater, and the chicken often turns out tough and overdone. For a crisp coating and juicy skin, we found it much better to pan-fry the chicken, immersing only one half of each piece in hot fat at a time.

Though a cast-iron skillet seemed the obvious choice for pan-frying, splatters were dramatically reduced when we used a Dutch oven. In fact, a cast-iron Dutch oven maintained temperature

Testing Pots and Pans for Frying

Though a skillet would seem the natural choice for frying chicken, the deeper sides of a Dutch oven—or its first cousin, the stockpot—solve the splatter problem and create a humid veil of condensation that rains down on the chicken to make it tender.

Cast-iron skillet	**Lodge cast-iron Dutch oven**	**All-Clad Dutch oven**	**Le Creuset enameled Dutch oven**
The lid for this squat skillet basically sat on top of the chicken, giving the hot, moist air nowhere to go. After turning, the top of the chicken became soggy.	The 1/4-inch-thick walls of this pot took 10 minutes or more to heat, but once they did, it maintained its oil temperature and fried the chicken to perfection.	This sturdy entry took on heat quickly but lost it, and failed to recover it, once the chicken entered the fat. The chicken did not color easily.	A rather pricey version of the Lodge pan, the thinner cast-iron walls of this beauty heated up fast and stayed that way. Cleanup was a cinch with its slick enamel surface.

significantly better than anything else we tried. A cast-iron Dutch oven covered during the first half of the frying did everything one better. It reduced splatters to a fine spray, maintained oil temperature impeccably, and fried the chicken through in about 15 minutes total versus the 20 minutes *per side* recommended in many recipes. This time-efficient frying method made up for the fact that our chicken needed to be fried in two batches. As much as we would have liked to find a way to fit 12 pieces into a 12-inch Dutch oven all at once, success eluded us. But it was really no big deal. It simply meant that by the time the second batch was fried up, the first batch was cool enough to eat.

Drying the gleaming, bronzed statuettes was the most satisfying test. We would lift them out of the oil and admire their rugged beauty, turning them this way and that on paper towels, paper bags, and bare racks. We would try not to eviscerate them as they reposed and cooled a bit. Bottom line: paper bags are simply not porous enough to keep the chicken out of a gathering pool of grease. We found that paper towels absorbed excess fat quickly and that rolling the pieces over onto a bare rack thereafter kept them crisp.

THE ULTIMATE CRISPY FRIED CHICKEN
SERVES 4 TO 6

Maintaining an even oil temperature is key to the success of this recipe. An instant-read thermometer with a high upper range is perfect for checking the temperature (our favorite is the Thermapen; see Resources, page 32); a clip-on candy/deep-fry thermometer is fine, though it can be clipped to the pot only for the uncovered portion of frying.

1¼	cups kosher salt or ½ cup plus 2 tablespoons table salt
¼	cup sugar
2	tablespoons paprika
3	medium garlic heads, cloves separated
3	bay leaves, crumbled
2	quarts low-fat buttermilk
1	whole chicken (about 3½ pounds), giblets discarded, cut into 12 pieces (see illustrations, right)
4	cups all-purpose flour
1	large egg
1	teaspoon baking powder
½	teaspoon baking soda
3–4	cups refined peanut oil or vegetable shortening

1. In large zipper-lock plastic bag, combine salt, sugar, paprika, garlic cloves, and bay leaves. With rubber mallet or flat meat pounder, smash garlic into salt and spice mixture thoroughly. Pour mixture into large plastic container or non-reactive stockpot. Add 7 cups buttermilk and stir until salt is completely dissolved. Immerse chicken and refrigerate until fully seasoned, 2 to 3 hours. Remove chicken from buttermilk brine

and shake off excess; place in single layer on large wire rack set over rimmed baking sheet. Refrigerate uncovered for 2 hours. (After 2 hours, chicken can be covered with plastic wrap and refrigerated up to 6 hours longer.)

2. Measure flour into large shallow dish. Beat egg, baking powder, and baking soda in medium bowl; stir in remaining 1 cup buttermilk (mixture will bubble and foam). Working in batches of 3, drop chicken pieces in flour and shake pan to coat. Shake excess flour from each piece, then, using tongs, dip chicken pieces into egg mixture, turning to coat well and allowing excess to drip off. Coat chicken pieces with flour again, shake off excess, and return to wire rack.

3. Adjust oven rack to middle position, set second wire rack over second rimmed baking sheet, and place on oven rack; heat oven to 200 degrees. Line large plate with double layer paper towels. Meanwhile, heat oil (oil should have 2½-inch depth in pan) to 375 degrees over medium-high heat in large 8-quart cast-iron Dutch oven with a diameter of about 12 inches. Place half of chicken pieces skin-side down in oil, cover, reduce heat to medium, and fry until deep golden brown, 6 to 8 minutes; after about 3 minutes, lift chicken pieces with tongs to check for even browning; rearrange if some pieces are browning faster than others. (Spot-check oil temperature; after first 6 minutes of frying, oil should be about 325 degrees. Adjust burner if necessary.) Turn chicken pieces over and continue to fry, uncovered, until chicken pieces are deep golden brown on second side, 6 to 8 minutes longer. Using tongs, transfer chicken to paper towel–lined plate; let stand 2 minutes to drain, then transfer to rack in warm oven. Replace paper towel–lining on plate. Return oil to 375 degrees and fry remaining pieces, transferring pieces to paper towel–lined plate to drain, then transferring to wire rack with other chicken pieces. Cool chicken pieces on wire rack about 5 minutes and serve.

STEP-BY-STEP | CUTTING IT DOWN TO SIZE

1. With a sharp chef's knife, cut through the skin around the leg where it attaches to the breast.

2. Using both hands, pop the leg joint out of its socket.

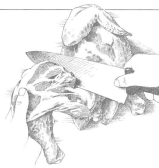

3. Use a chef's knife to cut through the flesh and skin to detach the leg from the body.

4. A line of fat separates the thigh and drumstick. Cut through the joint at this point. Repeat steps 1 through 4 with the other leg.

5. Bend the wing out from the breast and use a boning knife to cut through the joint. Repeat with the other wing.

6. Cut through the cartilage around the wing tip to remove it. Discard the tip. Cut through the joint to split. Repeat with the other wing.

7. Using poultry shears, cut along the ribs to completely separate the back from the breast. Discard backbone.

8. Place the knife on the breastbone, then apply pressure to cut through and separate the breast into halves.

9. Cut each breast in half crosswise into two pieces.

Tuna Salad Done Right

Three simple steps eliminate the twin problems of tuna salad: watery texture and bland flavor.

Grade-school lunches, hospital cafeterias, and second-rate delis have given tuna salad a bad name with mixtures that are typically mushy, watery, and bland. But these poor examples should not cause cooks to lose hope for this old standard. We recently tackled tuna salad in the test kitchen and came up with three simple preparation and flavoring tricks that guarantee a tuna salad that is evenly moist, tender, flaky, and well-seasoned every time.

A first-rate tuna salad begins with the best canned tuna. Luckily, *Cook's* July/August 1998 rating of canned, water-packed tuna had taken care of that for us. All comers favored solid white tuna over chunk light for its meaty texture and delicate flavor. Among the five brands we tried, StarKist reigned supreme, so we made it the basis of all our subsequent testing.

In a dish as simple as tuna salad, the finer points of preparation make a real difference. For instance, most cooks simply squeeze out a bit of the packing water by pressing the detached can lid down lightly on the fish. Tasters consistently deemed all of the salads made with tuna prepared in this manner as "soggy" and "watery." Taking the minor extra step of draining the tuna thoroughly in a colander before mixing it gave the salads a toothsome, less watery texture.

Breaking the tuna apart with a fork was another standard procedure we dumped. In salads made with tuna prepared this way, we'd invariably bite into a large, dry, unseasoned chunk that the fork had missed. With the tuna in the colander, we decided to break down the larger chunks with our fingers until the whole amount was fine and even in texture. This gave the finished salad a smooth, even, flaky texture that all of our tasters appreciated.

Seasoning was the last problem we addressed. All too often, tuna salad tastes dull and lifeless because of careless seasoning or, even worse, no seasoning at all. Salt and pepper were critical to making the most of tuna's delicate flavor. An acidic seasoning, such as lemon or lime juice or vinegar, was equally important, adding some much needed brightness to the flavor. We also found that the order in which we mixed the ingredients made a difference. We first tried mixing the basic seasoning and garnishes with the tuna alone before adding the mayonnaise. Next

Light, separate, seasoned flakes of fish give our tuna salad a noticeable advantage in both texture and flavor.

we tried adding the seasonings, garnishes, and mayonnaise all at once. Our tasters agreed that preseasoning the tuna resulted in a more deeply flavored, lively tuna salad.

After settling on these three basic techniques, we were unanimous in finding mayonnaise to be the binder of choice and found other salad ingredients to be largely a matter of taste. We nonetheless agreed that trace amounts of garlic and mustard added dimension to the overall flavor and that a modest amount of minced pickle provided a touch of piquancy, not to mention a link to tradition. (In fact, tuna takes well to a wide range of flavorings; see some of our variations for inspiration.)

So forget the sopping, mushy salad you ate in your last beleaguered, institutional tuna sandwich. The next time the cold cuts run out, or even before, reach for the canned tuna that graces even the emptiest pantry, take a little extra care with the contents, and find out how satisfying a well-made tuna salad sandwich can be.

CLASSIC TUNA SALAD
MAKES ABOUT 2 CUPS, ENOUGH FOR 4 SANDWICHES

- 2 (6-ounce) cans solid white tuna in water
- 2 tablespoons juice from 1 lemon
- 1/2 teaspoon salt
- 1/4 teaspoon ground black pepper
- 1 small rib celery, minced (about 1/4 cup)
- 2 tablespoons minced red onion
- 2 tablespoons minced dill or sweet pickles
- 1/2 small garlic clove, minced or pressed through garlic press (about 1/8 teaspoon)
- 2 tablespoons minced fresh parsley leaves
- 1/2 cup mayonnaise
- 1/4 teaspoon Dijon mustard

Drain tuna in colander and shred with fingers until no clumps remain and texture is fine and even. Transfer tuna to medium bowl and mix in lemon juice, salt, pepper, celery, onion, pickles, garlic, and parsley until evenly blended. Fold in mayonnaise and mustard until tuna is evenly moistened. (Can be covered and refrigerated up to 3 days.)

TUNA SALAD WITH BALSAMIC VINEGAR AND GRAPES

Follow recipe for Classic Tuna Salad, omitting lemon juice, pickles, garlic, and parsley and adding 2 tablespoons balsamic vinegar, 6 ounces halved red seedless grapes (about 1 cup), 1/4 cup lightly toasted slivered almonds, and 2 teaspoons minced thyme leaves to tuna along with salt and pepper.

CURRIED TUNA SALAD WITH APPLES AND CURRANTS

Follow recipe for Classic Tuna Salad, omitting pickles, garlic, and parsley and adding 1 medium firm, juicy apple, cut into 1/4-inch dice (about 1 cup), 1/4 cup currants, and 2 tablespoons minced fresh basil leaves to tuna along with lemon juice, salt, and pepper; mix 1 tablespoon curry powder into mayonnaise before folding into tuna.

TUNA SALAD WITH LIME AND HORSERADISH

Follow recipe for Classic Tuna Salad, omitting lemon juice, pickles, and garlic and adding 2 tablespoons juice and 1/2 teaspoon grated zest from 1 lime and 3 tablespoons prepared horseradish to tuna along with salt and pepper.

TUNA SALAD WITH CAULIFLOWER, JALAPEÑO, AND CILANTRO

Follow recipe for Classic Tuna Salad, omitting pickles, garlic, and parsley and adding 4 ounces cauliflower florets cut into 1/2-inch pieces (about 1 cup), 1 medium jalapeño chile, minced (about 2 tablespoons), 2 medium scallions, minced (about 1/4 cup), and 2 tablespoons minced fresh cilantro leaves to tuna along with lemon juice, salt, and pepper.

PHOTOGRAPHY: CARL TREMBLAY

Vegetable Soup Refined

For a quick, fresh-tasting soup, we use only four vegetables and souped-up commercial chicken broth.

⇒ BY JULIA COLLIN ⇐

Vegetable soup is a welcome supper any time of year. But as warm weather arrives in spring, I find myself hungry for vegetable soup that, unlike the hearty stew-like soups of winter, offers a light broth filled with delicate vegetables.

Vegetable soup has many interpretations. Some consider it inherently vegetarian, while others depend on beef bones and meat for flavor. Many recipes go for something clear and brothy, while others aspire to a thickened puree. Some note the importance of cutting the vegetables into tiny, perfect cubes for the ultimate presentation.

As I began to research and cook up some of these recipes, problems arose. The purees turned out too heavy, and the lighter soups had the tinny taste of the canned broth I used to make them. The vegetarian soups were sweet and bland, while the addition of beef bones muscled all fresh flavors out of the way. As for the vegetables, most recipes simply packed in the standard, year-round varieties without paying much attention to fresh greens. What ultimately emerged from these many disappointments was a clear idea of the kind of soup I was after: It should be simple and clean tasting, and it should make use of tender greens. It should be light and fresh, yet substantial enough to serve as supper on a chilly night.

Broth Revisited

While most other soups rely on their main ingredients for flavor, character, and overall heft, I soon found that some vegetables, including leeks, peas, and fresh spinach, are simply too delicate to carry this load alone. They are easily overcooked if simmered for too long, and their flavors can be overpowered at the drop of a hat. To make a good soup, these tender vegetables would need the support of a broth that was rich

Light broth, fresh baby spinach, peas, leeks, and potatoes create a delicate vegetable soup.

and multidimensional, not characterized by any single, distinctive flavor. To maintain the vegetables' delicate character, I focused on how to build a flavorful broth base that was not overly assertive.

I knew that one solution to this problem would be to make a rich, savory vegetable stock, but I couldn't justify the amount of time that would take. I tried using canned vegetable stocks, but they were incredibly thin and sweet, with an overwhelming taste of celery. Beef stocks and broths gave the soup some heft, but they also imparted an unwanted meaty flavor that couldn't be quieted. Canned chicken broth, while not perfect, was promising, with a mellow and sturdy character. On its own it wasn't nearly balanced or flavorful enough, but I figured it would work well with a little doctoring. Looking for a quick way to give the chicken broth a rounder, fuller vegetable flavor, I decided to

borrow some techniques from previous *Cook's* recipes for stock.

To start, I looked at our recipe for quick homemade chicken soup (March/April 1996), which begins by cooking onions and chicken pieces covered, over low heat, to encourage them to release their flavor. Not wanting any more chicken flavor, I tried adding onions alone. The resulting broth was better, but still not there. Looking to our vegetable stock recipe (September/October 2000), with its diverse selection of ingredients, I began to realize that it would take more than just onions to help out this canned broth. Not wanting to cut or cook anything unnecessarily, I worked my way one-by-one through a variety of other vegetables, from carrots and celery to dried mushrooms and cauliflower. In the end, I found a core group of vegetables to be key. The hallowed trio of carrot, celery, and onion, with some extra help from shallots, leeks, and garlic, turned the boring canned chicken broth into something rich and satisfying. Parsley stems, a branch of thyme, and a bay leaf also helped to reinforce the overall flavor change from canned to fresh.

Now that I had decided on the vegetables for the broth, I wanted to streamline the process of making it. I tried using a food processor to cut the vegetables, but it produced a wholly inferior broth. The processed vegetables had a harsher edge and rougher flavor than those cut by hand. The blades of the food processor made for battered and torn vegetables, eliciting an off, acidic flavor from the onions, leeks, and shallots. After going back to chopping by hand, I realized how important it is to cut these vegetables into small pieces so they can cook and release their flavors more quickly. It may take a couple minutes longer to cut the vegetables by hand into petite pieces, but the resulting flavor and speedy cooking time is worth the extra effort.

Taking a cue from our other stock recipes, I

Give Peas a Chance

Throughout the testing of this soup, I came to depend on frozen peas. Not only are they more convenient than their fresh, in-the-pod comrades, but they taste better. Test after test, I found frozen peas to be tender and sweet while fresh peas tasted starchy and bland. Trying to understand this curious finding, which defied common sense, I looked to the frozen food industry for some answers.

Green peas are one of the oldest vegetables known to humankind. Yet despite this long history, they are relatively delicate; fresh peas have little stamina. Green peas lose a substantial portion of their nutrients within 24 hours of being picked. This rapid deterioration is the reason for the starchy, bland flavor of most "fresh" peas found at the grocery store. These not-so-fresh peas might be several days old, depending on where they came from and how long they were kept in the cooler. Frozen peas, on the other hand, are picked, cleaned, sorted, and frozen within several hours of harvest, which helps to preserve their delicate sugars and flavors. When commercially frozen vegetables began to appear in the 1920s and 1930s, green peas were one of the first among them.

Finding good frozen peas is not hard. After tasting peas from the two major national frozen food purveyors, Birdseye and Green Giant, along with some from a smaller organic company, Cascadian Farm, my panel of tasters found little difference between them. All of the peas were sweet and fresh, with a bright green color. So unless you grow your own or can stop by your local farm stand for fresh picked, you're better off cruising up the frozen food aisle for a bag of frozen peas. –J.C.

Just Spray It

Cooking sprays, most often used in low-fat cooking or to coat bakeware, have been around since the late 1950s. The convenient sprays consist of oil, soy lecithin, propellants, and sometimes silicone or grain alcohol. Under pressure, this combination of ingredients creates a stick-resistant spray that evenly distributes a minuscule amount of fat on a surface. We found that a light mist of oil made all the difference when sweating vegetables for soup broth.

Larger amounts of oil turned the broth cloudy, and smaller amounts were difficult to measure and work with. Although we were wary of food that comes packaged in an aerosol can, the convenient spray made quick work of coating vegetables with a negligible amount of fat.

There are several types of cooking spray on the market, as well as self-serve pumps like the Quick Mist that allow you to dispense your oil of choice. While all of the sprays we tried worked well with our vegetable soup, we recommend avoiding any that are "flavored." –J.C.

Canola   Olive Oil   Pam   Quick Mist

---

tried cooking the vegetables lightly on their own first, in a process known as sweating, before covering them with the canned broth. The difference in flavor between this sweated broth and a broth in which the vegetables were simply simmered was dramatic. Once strained, the sweated vegetable broth had a full, round flavor, while the simmered broth tasted thin and one-dimensional. Sweating allows the vegetable cells to break down and release their flavor into the pot before the broth is even added. This process is a good way to get flavor into the broth without taking the time for a long simmer.

Going Green

Now that I had a flavorful broth, I could focus on the main characters of this soup: the vegetables. Not wanting to clutter the soup with vegetables that were inessential, I steered toward a simple, clean soup with tender green vegetables. Leeks, green peas, and baby spinach all made the cut quickly. Their delicate flavors, different shapes, and varying shades of green made for a balanced and elegant lineup. Although chard, arugula, and asparagus are brightly colored and flavorful, their spicy, overpowering flavors and sulfuric aroma took over the otherwise delicate soup. Small, new red potatoes were a nice addition, giving the soup some body and a little variety in color. Scallions, celery, and carrots, on the other hand, managed only to crowd and distract.

Cooking the four finalists—leeks, peas, baby spinach, and red potatoes—was easy enough. The broth, still warm after being doctored and strained, was at just about the perfect temperature to poach this somewhat fragile foursome. The leeks and potatoes went in first, the spinach, peas, and herbs just before serving. The vegetables took well to this gentle cooking process, as

the simmering broth brought out and reinforced the flavor of each. Garnished only with some chopped parsley and tarragon, the soup's fresh flavor is unmistakable.

FOUR-VEGETABLE SOUP
MAKES ABOUT 2 QUARTS, SERVING 6

This soup uses canned chicken broth as its base, but the broth is first doctored with vegetables and herbs to brighten and improve its flavor.

Broth

1	medium carrot, minced (about 1/3 cup)
1	celery rib, minced (about 1/4 cup)
2	medium onions, minced (about 1 1/2 cups)
1	large shallot, minced (about 2 1/2 tablespoons)
1	medium leek, white and light green parts only, minced (about 1 cup)
3	garlic cloves, unpeeled and crushed Vegetable cooking spray
7	cups (four 14 1/2-ounce cans) canned low-sodium chicken broth
1/4	teaspoon black peppercorns, crushed
1	bay leaf
1	sprig fresh thyme
5	parsley stems

Soup

2	medium leeks, white and light green parts only, halved lengthwise, cut into 1-inch lengths, washed and drained thoroughly
6	small red potatoes, unpeeled and cut into 3/4-inch chunks (about 1 1/2 cups, or 9 ounces)
1	cup frozen peas (about 5 ounces)
2	cups packed baby spinach (about 3 ounces)
2	tablespoons chopped fresh parsley leaves
1	tablespoon chopped fresh tarragon leaves Salt and ground black pepper

1. FOR THE BROTH: Combine carrot, celery, onions, shallot, leek, and garlic in large heavy-bottomed stockpot or Dutch oven; spray vegetables lightly with cooking spray and toss to coat. Cover and cook vegetables over medium heat, stirring frequently, until slightly softened and translucent, about 6 minutes. Add broth, peppercorns, bay leaf, thyme sprig, and parsley stems; increase heat to medium-high and bring to simmer. Simmer until broth is flavorful, about 20 minutes. Strain broth through fine-mesh sieve; discard solids in sieve. (Broth can be cooled to room temperature, covered, and refrigerated up to 3 days.)

2. FOR THE SOUP: Bring broth to simmer in large saucepan over medium heat; add leeks and potatoes, and simmer until potatoes are tender, about 9 minutes. Stir in peas, spinach, parsley, and tarragon; season to taste with salt and pepper and serve immediately.

Great Grilled Vegetables

Here's how to cut, season, and grill vegetables without precooking.

Once considered something of a novelty, grilling vegetables is now a common practice in backyards across the country. Not only do grilled vegetables give you side dishes with bright, intense flavors, but they are also quick and easy to make. We tested many vegetables to find the best grilling methods and discovered certain common problems: they burned, they cooked unevenly, they fell through the grill grate. Fortunately, these problems are easily overcome. In the tips below, we present our findings and recommend the best way to prepare a number of vegetables. To keep things simple, we considered only those vegetables that will cook through on the grill without any precooking.

General Guidelines

➤ To avoid scorching or over-cooking, you want the grill fire to be medium-hot.

➤ Test the temperature by holding your hand 5 inches above the grill grate; if you can hold your hand there for only three to four seconds, the fire is medium-hot.

➤ When grilling a variety of vegetables at once, be prepared to take each off the grill at a different time. Serving mixed vegetable dishes warm or at room temperature rather than piping hot makes complicated timing and sequencing unnecessary.

Preparing Vegetables for Grilling

In general, vegetables should be cut to expose the maximum surface area to the grill, which helps them cook quickly and thoroughly. Smaller vegetables, such as cherry tomatoes and button mushrooms, need to be skewered to keep them from falling through the grill, as do slices of some larger vegetables like onions. Thin metal skewers are best for the job since they will neither burn (as bamboo skewers can) nor tear delicate vegetables (as broad, flat metal skewers can). Just before grilling, brush the vegetables with olive oil or, for more flavor, one of the flavored oils on page 17, then season with salt and pepper.

ZUCCHINI OR SUMMER SQUASH
COOKING TIME:
8 to 10 minutes, turning once
The intense heat of grilling evaporates excess moisture and concentrates the delicate flavor of these squash. The goals in grilling them are to cook the interior thoroughly without burning the exterior and to keep slices from falling through the grate. The trick to solving both problems is to cut the squash lengthwise into half-inch slices.

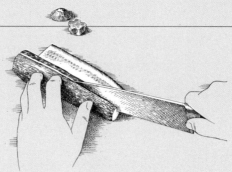

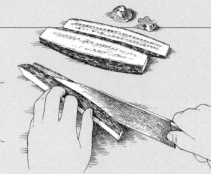

1. Trim the ends off the zucchini or summer squash. Slice lengthwise into ½ inch thick planks.

2. You may want to trim the peel from the outer slices. Besides creating more attractive grill marks, the flesh cooks better when directly exposed to the heat.

ENDIVE
COOKING TIME:
5 to 7 minutes, turning once

RADICCHIO
COOKING TIME:
4½ minutes, turning every 1½ minutes
The bitterness of endive and radicchio is tempered by the grill. Slicing each endive head in half lets it cook evenly while allowing the core to hold the leaves together. Radicchio leaves tend to separate as they cook. Cutting the head into thick wedges keeps the leaves together. Brush the pieces with a fair amount of olive oil before grilling.

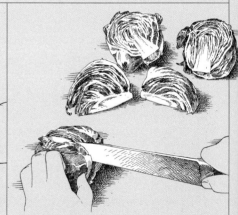

FOR ENDIVE: With a knife, shave off the discolored end of the endive. Cut the endive in half lengthwise, through the core end.

FOR RADICCHIO: Remove any browning outer leaves. Cut the radicchio in half through the core. Cut each half again through the core to make four wedges.

ONIONS
COOKING TIME:
10 to 12 minutes, turning once
We found that onion slices tend to separate and fall through the grate during grilling. A thin skewer inserted crosswise through each slice anchors it sufficiently and makes for easy turning. Large onions may require two parallel skewers.

1. Cut thick slices from large onions, then skewer them all the way through with a thin metal skewer.

2. The skewered onion slices remain intact as they grill, and, best of all, they can be flipped easily with tongs.

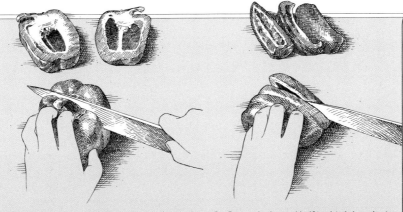

BELL PEPPERS

COOKING TIME:

7 to 9 minutes, turning once
A quick grilling can bring out the natural sweetness of peppers and soften their tough flesh, but overcooking results in bitter skins that may become partially detached. We found that the best way to ensure that the peppers cook quickly and don't fall through the grate is to cut them into "steaks," as shown.

1. Cut each pepper in half lengthwise (through the stem end). Remove the core, seeds, and ribs.

2. Cut each cleaned half in thirds lengthwise.

CORN ON THE COB

COOKING TIME:

8 to 10 minutes, turning every 1½ to 2 minutes
While grilling husk-on corn delivers great pure corn flavor, it lacks the smokiness of the grill; essentially, the corn is steamed in its protective husk. By leaving on only the inner-most layer, we were rewarded with perfectly tender corn graced with the grill's flavor. Prepared in this way, corn does not need basting with oil.

1. Remove all but the inner-most layer of the husk. The kernels should be covered by, but visible through, the last husk layer.

2. Use scissors to snip off the tassel, or long silk ends, at the tip of the ear.

FENNEL

COOKING TIME:

7 to 9 minutes, turning once
Fennel caramelizes beautifully on the grill. The trickiest part is cutting it so that it does not fall through the grate. We found that slicing it into cross sections ¼-inch thick, with a piece of the core still attached, keeps the layers intact.

1. Cut off the stems and feathery fronds.

2. Trim a very thin slice from the base and remove any tough or blemished outer layers.

3. Slice the bulb vertically through its base into ¼-inch-thick pieces that resemble fans.

BUTTON OR CREMINI MUSHROOMS

COOKING TIME:

8 to 12 minutes, turning every 3 minutes
It is important to skewer small button and cremini mushrooms to keep them from falling through the grate during grilling.

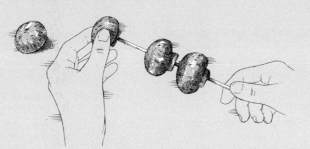

Once these small mushrooms have been cleaned and any dry ends trimmed from the stems, they should be skewered through the cap and stem so they are less likely to rotate when turned on the grill.

Illustrations: John Burgoyne

Seasoning the Vegetables

The best way to season vegetables is to brush them with flavored oil just before grilling. Add fresh herbs, garlic, and/or grated citrus zest to the oil for more flavor. Seasoning with salt and pepper both before and after grilling maximizes flavor.

Garlic Basting Oil

1   cup extra-virgin olive oil
1   medium garlic clove, minced to a paste or pressed through garlic press

Combine ingredients in a small bowl; let stand to infuse flavors, about 10 minutes. Use while fresh and discard any unused oil.

Lemon-Rosemary Basting Oil

1   cup extra-virgin olive oil
2   teaspoons minced fresh rosemary leaves
2   teaspoons grated zest plus 2 tablespoons juice from 1 lemon

Combine ingredients in a small bowl; let stand to infuse flavors, about 10 minutes.

Essential Grilling Equipment

- Kitchen tongs—stainless steel locking tongs are best, ideally 16 inches long
- Thin metal skewers
- Soft-bristled pastry brush for basting
- Oven mitts
- Paper towels
- Rimmed sheet pan to hold utensils
- Spray/mister filled with water to control flare-ups

The Perfect Cheese Omelet

Melting the cheese without overcooking the eggs is just one problem we solved in producing an almost foolproof recipe for a moist, creamy cheese omelet.

≥ BY BRIDGET LANCASTER ≤

With their quick preparation and cooking time—under 10 minutes—omelets are the perfect solution for a fast and easy dinner that is satisfying and delicious. But for all their attractive convenience, cheese omelets are fraught with problems. First and foremost is the issue of how to achieve perfect texture. Just a few seconds too long in the pan can turn an omelet from light, soft, and creamy to dark, tough, and rubbery. But you can't skimp too much on cooking time, either, because the cheese must melt completely before the omelet leaves the pan. And, speaking of cheese, I wanted to know if there was a way to make sure that none of that delicious filling would creep out of its egg casing during cooking. In short, I wanted to develop a foolproof method for cooking a cheese omelet with a tender, supple mouthfeel, a creamy interior filled with completely melted cheese—and no leaks.

Be sure that your diners are ready at the table, because a perfect omelet waits for no one.

Let's Get Cracking

In "Omelets Revisited," an article in the September/October 1993 issue of *Cook's*, the test kitchen developed a simple and consistent method for turning out omelets. I retested the findings and agreed with them. A good-quality, nonstick skillet with gently sloped sides is the superior implement for the production of a great omelet. It is neither impractical (traditional iron or steel omelet pans must be seasoned regularly, like cast iron) nor unusual (there's probably one in your kitchen). I concurred, too, that beating the eggs thoroughly ensures uniform texture for the exterior and interior of the omelet, a quality that is particularly important for filled omelets. I also agreed that the texture of an omelet is improved by stirring the eggs once they are in the pan; eggs cooked without stirring produced an uneven, loose omelet.

Further testing confirmed that a good omelet needs no added liquid. Heavy cream, half-and-half, milk, and water diffused the delicate flavor of the eggs. Medium-high heat (and a little practice) created an omelet that was neither over- nor undercooked. Finally, I agreed that butter added rich flavor, and its capacity to sizzle made it easy to gauge how hot the pan was.

Now that I had the basics, I set out to find the most foolproof technique. I began cooking three-egg cheddar omelets for anyone who came within range of the stove. Popular demand stated that skimping on the cheese was a no-no. In fact, tasters liked best the omelets filled with 3 table-spoons of cheese. But with this large amount of cheese, I found that my trusty 8-inch skillet was no longer big enough. When I opted for a 10-inch skillet, the eggs spread out to a thinner shell that was much easier to wrap around the cheese. Sprinkling the cheese all over the cooked eggs, as many recipes suggested, produced an unsatisfying, uneven filling. The cheese, I found, must be placed down the center of the omelet, perpendicular to the handle of the pan.

I also discovered that merely folding or rolling the eggs around the cheese was insufficient to contain it. The cheese inevitably found a way out. The perfect method turned out to be the classic French style, in which a pan is used to shape the omelet. (See "Preparing an Omelet," page 19.)

Handling the Heat

Even after making several omelets with this method, I noticed that they were all a little too well-done and brown for my taste. I played around with the idea of reducing the heat after the eggs set up, but working within a timeframe of only a few seconds, I found it impractical to have to readjust the flame. I also considered that cooks making omelets on an electric stove, where temperature reduction occurs at a much slower rate, would be unable to use this method. Reluctantly, I went back to the beginning and added a little oil to the pan along with the butter, hoping to discourage any coloring that might originate from that source. The resulting small improvement was tempered greatly by the sacrifice in flavor.

Finally, I realized that every stove has one universal temperature setting: no heat. I started the omelet with the same technique that I had been using: waiting for the butter to sizzle, pouring in the eggs, scrambling the eggs slightly, pulling the cooked edges in toward the center of the pan while tilting the pan to redistribute the uncooked eggs, and adding the cheese. But this time, I turned the flame off completely, hoping that the residual heat in the pan would be sufficient to finish cooking the omelet.

Oddly enough, even with the flame off, the omelet colored a little too much. Next I tried taking the pan off the heat completely. Let me emphasize, this meant not just turning off the heat but physically removing the pan from the burner. This time my omelet was perfect. As it turns out, once the cheese has been added, the pan retains enough residual heat to continue cooking the omelet. This new method produced perfectly colored, blond omelets, no matter the stove, no matter the cook.

Melting the Cheese

The on-burner, off-burner technique had one drawback. The cheese, which had melted perfectly until this point, now melted only partially. I hoped this could be remedied with a finer grating of cheese. I threw my box grater back in the drawer and pulled out the fine grater we often use for Parmesan. This time the cheese melted throughout.

It was now time to see which cheeses worked best in the omelet. Only the harder cheeses (Pecorino Romano, Asiago, Parmesan) failed to melt completely within the small window of time open to them. Many other cheeses worked well. The only rule of thumb is to use a cheese that can be grated and that (obviously) pleases your palate.

For those times when a plain cheese omelet just won't do, I developed a few more substantial variations. I limited the amount of filling to a maximum of ¼ cup—anything more and the omelet burst open and spilled into the pan. Just about any ingredient must be sautéed beforehand; the less-than-a-minute cooking time of the eggs is not sufficient to properly cook the filling. I also found that herbs packed a flavor punch when stirred right into the filling at the very end of cooking.

PERFECT CHEESE OMELET
SERVES 1

Making perfect omelets takes some practice, so don't be disappointed if your first effort fails to meet your expectations. If using an additional filling, be sure to prepare it before you begin making the omelets.

- 3 large eggs
  Salt and ground black pepper
- ½ tablespoon unsalted butter, plus melted butter for brushing finished omelet
- 3 tablespoons very finely grated Gruyère, cheddar, Monterey Jack, or other cheese of your choice
- 1 recipe filling, optional (recipes follow)

1. Beat eggs and salt and pepper with fork in small bowl until thoroughly combined.
2. Heat butter in 10-inch nonstick skillet over medium-high heat; when foaming subsides and butter just begins to color, pour in eggs. Cook until edges begin to set, 2 to 3 seconds, then, with rubber spatula, stir in circular motion until slightly thickened, about 10 seconds. Following illustration 1, above, use spatula to pull cooked edges in toward center, then tilt pan to one side so that uncooked eggs run to edge of pan. Repeat until omelet is just set but still moist on surface, about 20 to 25 seconds. Sprinkle cheese and filling, if using, down center of omelet, perpendicular to handle of skillet.

TECHNIQUE | PREPARING AN OMELET

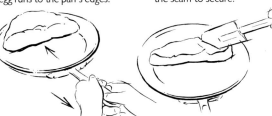

1. Pull the cooked eggs in along the edges of the pan toward the center, tilting the pan so that any uncooked egg runs to the pan's edges.

2. Remove the pan from the burner. Fold the lower third of the eggs over the filling, as illustrated. Press the seam to secure.

3. Pull the pan sharply toward you so that the omelet slides up the lip of the far edge of the pan.

4. Fold the far edge of the omelet toward the center. Press to secure the seam. Invert onto a plate.

3. Remove skillet from burner. Following illustration 2, use rubber spatula to fold lower third (nearest you) of omelet to center; press gently with spatula to secure seams, maintaining fold.
4. Run spatula between outer edge of omelet and pan to loosen. Following illustration 3, jerk pan sharply toward you a few times to slide omelet up far side of pan. Jerk pan again so that 2 inches of unfolded edge folds over itself, or, following illustration 4, use spatula to fold edge over. Invert omelet onto plate. Tidy edges with spatula, brush with melted butter, and serve.

SAUTÉED MUSHROOM FILLING WITH THYME
MAKES ABOUT ½ CUP, ENOUGH TO FILL 2 OMELETS

This filling is particularly good when paired with Gruyère.

Heat 1 tablespoon butter in medium skillet over medium heat until foaming; add 1 small shallot, minced (about 1 tablespoon), and cook until softened and just beginning to color, about 2 minutes. Add 2 medium white mushrooms (about 2 ounces), cleaned and cut into slices ¼ inch thick. Cook, stirring occasionally, until softened and lightly browned, about 3 minutes. Off heat, stir in 1 teaspoon fresh minced thyme leaves and salt and pepper to taste; transfer mixture to small bowl and set aside until ready to use.

BACON, ONION, AND SCALLION FILLING
MAKES ABOUT ½ CUP, ENOUGH TO FILL 2 OMELETS

Smoked Gouda is a good match for this filling.

Fry 2 slices bacon, cut crosswise into ½-inch strips, in medium skillet over medium heat until crispy, about 3 minutes; with slotted spoon, transfer bacon to paper towel–lined plate. Discard all but 1 tablespoon fat from skillet; set skillet over medium heat and add ½ small onion, chopped fine, to skillet. Cook, stirring frequently, until golden brown, about 3 minutes. Off heat, stir in 1 scallion, sliced thin. Remove paper towel from under bacon and transfer onion mixture to plate with bacon; set aside until ready to use.

SAUTÉED RED BELL PEPPER FILLING WITH MUSHROOM AND ONION
MAKES ABOUT ½ CUP, ENOUGH TO FILL 2 OMELETS

Monterey Jack is our choice for this filling.

Heat 1 tablespoon butter in medium skillet over medium heat until foaming; add ½ small onion, chopped fine, and cook, stirring occasionally, until softened but not browned, about 2 minutes. Add 1 medium (about 1 ounce) white mushroom, cleaned and sliced ¼ inch thick. Cook, stirring occasionally, until softened and beginning to brown, about 2 minutes. Add ¼ red bell pepper (about 2 ounces), seeds discarded, cut into ½-inch dice; cook, stirring occasionally, until softened, about 2 minutes. Off heat, stir in 1 teaspoon minced fresh parsley leaves. Transfer mixture to small bowl and season with salt and pepper to taste; set aside until ready to use.

TESTING | BROWN OUT

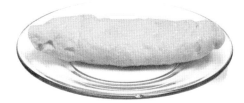

Overcooking damages an omelet's taste and texture. The omelet at left has dry, dense curds and a tough, chewy exterior. The one on the right, which was allowed to finish cooking off heat, has soft, moist curds and a tender, blond exterior.

How to Cook Bok Choy

For best flavor, stir-fry or braise—don't blanch or steam.

≥ BY JACK BISHOP ≤

There are dozens of Chinese cabbages, but only two—Napa and bok choy—are widely available in American supermarkets. Napa cabbage has frilly, pale green leaves. Although it can be cooked, I find this rather bland cabbage is best shredded and used raw in spicy Asian-style slaws. Bok choy is another story entirely. Although a member of the cabbage family, this vegetable resembles leafy greens, especially chard. Its crisp, ivory stalks and crinkly, dark green leaves are easy to recognize.

Unlike so many leafy greens, bok choy doesn't shrink down to nothing when cooked. The stalks are crisp and fleshy—like celery, but not stringy. In fact, when cooked fully they become creamy, with an almost meatlike texture and an underlying sweetness. In contrast, the leaves become tender and soft, having an earthy, robust flavor similar to that of chard or even spinach.

But for all of its virtues, there are some issues to look at when cooking this vegetable, especially for American cooks who are not familiar with its characteristics. If not prepared properly, bok choy can turn mushy and pallid, losing its considerable appeal. My goal was simple: to devise a cooking method that would produce perfectly cooked (and seasoned) bok choy—both the leaves and stems.

I combed through several dozen cookbooks looking for recipes. A few non-Chinese sources suggested cooking the stalks and greens together. I was skeptical, since all of the Chinese sources I consulted called for separating the stalks and leaves so that the stalks could be cooked longer. Nonetheless, I went ahead and tried stir-frying roughly chopped bok choy stalks and greens together. Rather predictably, I was disappointed. If I cooked the bok choy briefly, the greens were fine but the stalks were much too crunchy. Increasing the stir-fry time softened the stalks, but the leaves turned limp and unappealing.

I now knew that I was going to have to separate the white stalks and green leaves before cooking. I started by trimming and discarding the bottom inch of the stalks, which is often tough and blemished. This also served to separate the leaves so that each one could be washed and patted dry individually.

With my bok choy prepped, it was time to start testing cooking methods. Most methods I uncovered in my research made some effort to deal with the fact that the stalks require a longer cooking time than the greens. After a few tests, I quickly dismissed blanching or steaming the stalks. Steaming was better than blanching

(which washed away too much flavor), but both methods made the bok choy watery.

I had better luck stir-frying bok choy in a large nonstick skillet—the test kitchen's preferred vessel for stir-frying because of its wide, flat surface area. Throwing the sliced stalks into the pan first gave them the necessary head start. After stir-frying for five minutes, the stalks were crisp-tender and beginning to brown. I could then add the leaves and continue stir-frying for another minute or so until the leaves wilted.

Some sources suggested covering the pan after adding the leaves. But because I had also decided to add a sauce to the pan at the same time, covering the stir-fry made it a bit soupy; the sauce couldn't evaporate and thicken. I decided it was better just to leave the cover off for the entire cooking time.

This stir-fry method has plenty of advantages. It's simple, and the seasonings can be changed endlessly. The stalks, however, were still crisp-tender (increasing the stir-frying time didn't seem to help much) and not as creamy as some of the bok choy dishes I've eaten in Chinese restaurants. I liked stir-fried bok choy, but I wondered if there was another option.

Several recipes I consulted suggested braising bok choy in a covered pan with some liquid, as

Bok Choy Basics

Although most American supermarkets carry only one kind of bok choy—the green-leaved, white-stalked variety—in Asian markets you might see three or four different vegetables all labeled "bok choy."

Baby bok choy In addition to the varietal differences, bok choy also comes in various sizes, from diminutive baby bok choy that weigh just four ounces to mammoth heads that weigh more than two pounds. Any variety of bok choy (with either white or green stems) picked at an early age can be called baby bok choy. Most heads weigh just three or four ounces and will fit in your hand. Because of their small size, the stalks are fairly tender, so there's no need to cook them separately. Baby bok choy are best halved and seared.

Shanghai bok choy has jade-colored stalks that are

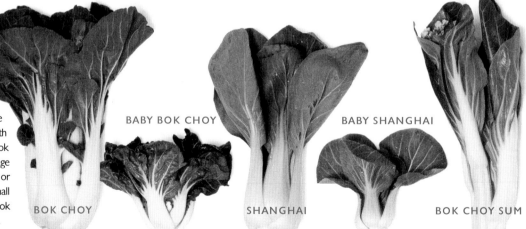

BABY BOK CHOY   BABY SHANGHAI

BOK CHOY   SHANGHAI   BOK CHOY SUM

slightly wider than the ivory stalks on regular bok choy and are shaped like Chinese soup spoons. Shanghai bok choy can be handled like regular bok choy.

Bok choy sum has small yellow flowers sprouting from the center of its dark green leaves. As with broccoli rabe, the flowers are edible. To keep the flowers bright, slice and cook them with the leaves and stir-fry rather than braise.

What you're likely to find in the supermarket are medium or large heads of regular bok choy. In general, heads between 1½ and 1¾ pounds are your best bet—one head yields four side-dish servings, but the stalks are still thin enough to cook up tender. In testing, I found that the stalks on larger heads (weighing two pounds or more) can be spongy and woody in the center. In terms of appearance, make sure the leaves are bright green and crisp. Leaves that are wilted or yellow are a sign of aging. The stalks should be bright white. If the stalks are covered with tiny brown spots, the bok choy is past its prime. Once you get bok choy home, it should be stored like other leafy greens—in a loosely sealed plastic bag in the refrigerator for up to two or three days. Don't wash bok choy until you are ready to cook it. I found that prewashing accelerated the decay process.

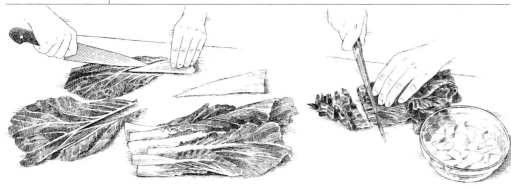

1. Trim the bottom inch from the head of bok choy. Wash the leaves and pat them dry. With a chef's knife, cut the leafy green portion away from either side of the triangular white stalk.

2. Cut each white stalk in half lengthwise and then crosswise into thin strips. Stack the leafy greens and then slice them crosswise into thin strips. Keep the sliced stalks and leaves separate.

you might do with kale or another tough green. I first stir-fried the stalks to give them color (and flavor from the browning), then added the greens and some stock and let the bok choy simmer away. After 10 minutes the stalks were soft but not mushy. Their texture was creamy and delicious. The leaves were completely tender. Best of all, the flavor of the bok choy seemed more robust and earthy.

Both stir-frying and braising have their advantages. Stir-frying results in a fairly dry dish, making bok choy a good partner on most dinner plates. Braising, which is not much more work than stir-frying, makes bok choy very moist and soft, an ideal partner for lean meat, fish, or chicken.

STIR-FRIED BOK CHOY WITH SOY SAUCE AND GINGER
SERVES 4 AS A SIDE DISH

Stir-frying preserves some of the texture of the bok choy, especially the stalks.

- 2 tablespoons soy sauce
- 1 teaspoon sugar
- 2 tablespoons peanut oil
- 1 medium head bok choy (1 1/2 to 1 3/4 pounds), prepared according to illustrations above (about 5 cups each sliced stalks and sliced greens)
- 1 (1-inch) piece fresh ginger, minced (about 1 tablespoon)

1. Combine soy sauce and sugar in small bowl.
2. Heat large nonstick skillet over high heat until hot, about 2 minutes. Add oil, swirl to coat pan bottom. Add bok choy stalks and cook, stirring frequently, until lightly browned, 5 to 7 minutes. Add ginger and cook, stirring frequently, until fragrant, about 30 seconds. Add bok choy greens and soy sauce mixture; cook, stirring frequently, until greens are wilted and tender, about 1 minute. Serve immediately.

STIR-FRIED BOK CHOY WITH OYSTER SAUCE AND GARLIC
SERVES 4 AS A SIDE DISH

If you prefer, hoisin sauce can be substituted for the oyster-flavored sauce.

Follow recipe for Stir-Fried Bok Choy with Soy Sauce and Ginger, substituting 2 tablespoons oyster-flavored sauce and 1 tablespoon rice vinegar for soy sauce, and adding 2 garlic cloves, minced or pressed, along with ginger.

BOK CHOY BRAISED WITH GARLIC
SERVES 4 AS A SIDE DISH

This dish is fairly saucy, making it an excellent accompaniment to seared pork chops, sautéed chicken breasts, or a firm fish like cod.

- 2 tablespoons peanut oil
- 1 medium head bok choy (1 1/2 to 1 3/4 pounds), prepared according to illustrations above (about 5 cups each sliced stalks and sliced greens)
- 4 medium garlic cloves, minced or pressed through garlic press
- 3/4 cup chicken stock or canned low-sodium chicken broth
  Salt and ground black pepper
- 1 teaspoon rice vinegar

1. Heat large nonstick skillet over high heat until hot, about 2 minutes. Add oil, swirl to coat pan bottom. Add bok choy stalks and cook, stirring frequently, until lightly browned, 5 to 7 minutes. Add garlic and cook, stirring frequently, until fragrant, about 30 seconds. Add bok choy greens, chicken stock, and salt and pepper to taste. Cover, reduce heat to medium-low, and cook, stirring twice, until bok choy is very tender, 8 to 10 minutes.
2. Remove cover, increase heat to medium-high, and cook until excess liquid evaporates, 2 to 3 minutes. (Bok choy should be moist but not soupy.) Stir in rice vinegar and adjust seasonings with salt and pepper; serve immediately.

BOK CHOY BRAISED WITH SHIITAKE MUSHROOMS
SERVES 4 AS A SIDE DISH

Soak 6 dried shiitake mushrooms in 1 cup boiling water until softened, 15 to 20 minutes; drain, reserving soaking liquid. Strain liquid through paper towel–lined strainer and reserve. Trim and discard mushroom stems; cut mushroom caps into 1/4-inch slices. Follow recipe for Bok Choy Braised with Garlic, substituting 1 tablespoon minced fresh ginger for 2 garlic cloves and substituting mushroom liquid and sliced mushrooms for chicken stock.

SESAME-SOY-GLAZED BABY BOK CHOY
SERVES 4 AS A SIDE DISH

This recipe works best with baby bok choy weighing no more than 4 ounces each. If your market sells larger baby bok choy, remove a layer or two of the large outer leaves.

- 2 tablespoons soy sauce
- 2 tablespoons chicken stock or canned low-sodium chicken broth
- 1 tablespoon rice vinegar
- 2 teaspoons Asian sesame oil
- 1 teaspoon sugar
- 3 tablespoons peanut oil
- 4 baby bok choy (about 4 ounces each), each head halved lengthwise
- 3 medium garlic cloves, minced or pressed through garlic press (about 1 tablespoon)
- 1 (1-inch) piece fresh ginger, minced (about 1 tablespoon)
- 2 medium scallions, sliced thin
- 1 tablespoon sesame seeds, toasted in small dry skillet over medium heat until lightly browned and fragrant, about 4 minutes

1. Combine soy sauce, stock, vinegar, sesame oil, and sugar in small bowl.
2. Heat large nonstick skillet over high heat until hot, about 2 minutes. Add 2 tablespoons peanut oil, swirl to coat pan bottom. Place bok choy in skillet, cut-side down, in single layer. Cook, without moving, until lightly browned, about 2 minutes. Turn bok choy and cook until lightly browned on second side, about 1 minute longer; transfer to large, warm platter.
3. Add garlic, ginger, and scallions to now-empty pan and drizzle with remaining 1 tablespoon peanut oil. Cook, stirring constantly, until fragrant, about 20 seconds. Add soy sauce mixture and simmer until reduced and thickened, about 20 seconds. Return bok choy to pan and cook, turning once, until glazed with sauce, about 1 minute. Sprinkle with sesame seeds and serve immediately.

Fresh Rhubarb 'Fool'

How do you tame rhubarb's tartness without losing its true flavor? We cooked 50 pounds of it to find out.

⇒ BY RAQUEL PELZEL ⇐

Fool is a quick, everyday dessert that just so happens to have a quaint and quirky British name. When we decided to try our hand at this simple dessert—essentially cooked fruit with sweetened whipped cream folded in—we sided with tradition and used rhubarb as the cooked fruit foundation. Although fool is in itself no culinary feat, working with rhubarb can prove tricky. First, its sourness can be overpowering. Second, if boiled, or cooked too hard and fast, it breaks down into a watery, porridge-like mass. Finally, its vivacious red color leaches out easily, leaving the rhubarb a drab gray. I knew that before I could finalize a fool, I would have to tame the rhubarb.

To begin my testing I tried baking the rhubarb, stewing it for a long time, sautéing it in butter, and simmering it for a short time. Baking and sautéing turned the rhubarb pulpy, chalky, and bland, while stewing produced a watery cream-of-rhubarb soup. And in each case the rhubarb lost its attractive red color, presenting instead hues that varied from gray-lavender in the baked version to pale, watery yellow in the stewed. The simmered batch, on the other hand, had a nice pinkish red color, a sweet/tart flavor, and a thick, toothsome texture.

The simmered rhubarb was not ideal, though; it was still too tart for most tasters. Looking further, I found an interesting pre-cooking approach that purported to subdue its acidity: soaking 6-inch pieces in cold water for 20 minutes prior to cutting and simmering. When I gave this trick a try, I was surprised to find the rhubarb much less acidic, with a flavor that was more round and full. But this approach had one drawback: the color had dulled to a pale mauve.

To figure out what happened, I called Barry Swanson, a confirmed rhubarb enthusiast who is a professor of food science at Washington State University in Pullman. Swanson explained that a water-soluble pigment called anthocyanin is responsible for rhubarb's somewhat chalky, tannic mouthfeel as well as its bright pinkish red color. When I presoaked the rhubarb, a portion of the anthocyanin escaped from the rhubarb's cut ends into the water, muting the color as well as the harsh bite.

Swanson also explained that anthocyanin is sensitive to the acidity of its environment. When the pH is high (low acidity), the color shifts to the bluish gray range; when the pH is low (high acidity), the color is red. Thinking about this, I wondered what would happen if I reintroduced an acid with no bitter or tannic qualities, such as the citric acid in orange juice, while the rhubarb simmered. This test was successful. The juice added just enough acidity to retain the rhubarb red without having any ill effects on flavor.

Now I turned my attention from the rhubarb to the whipped cream and the assembly of the fool. I tried whipping the cream to various degrees of stiffness, and my colleagues and I concurred that a soft-to-medium peak was just right. It gave the fool just enough body without making it sliceable and stiff.

Fool-making tradition dictates that the cream be folded into the fruit, but this gave the dessert a somewhat dull, monochromatic texture and flavor. Arranging the fruit and cream in layers produced a more interesting result. The natural tanginess of the rhubarb played off the sweetness of the cream, and the alternating texture of fruit and cream made for a pleasing contrast.

This parfait-like arrangement, unusual for a fool, enhances flavor and adds visual appeal.

RHUBARB FOOL
SERVES 8

2¼	pounds rhubarb, trimmed of ends and cut into 6-inch lengths
⅓	cup juice from 1 large orange
1	cup plus 2 tablespoons sugar
	Pinch salt
2	cups cold heavy cream

1. Soak rhubarb in 1 gallon cold water for 20 minutes. Drain, pat dry with paper towels, and cut rhubarb crosswise into slices ½-inch thick.

2. Bring orange juice, ¾ cup sugar, and salt to boil in medium nonreactive saucepan over medium-high heat. Add rhubarb and return to boil, then reduce heat to medium-low and simmer, stirring only 2 or 3 times (frequent stirring causes rhubarb to become mushy), until rhubarb begins to break down and is tender, 7 to 10 minutes. Transfer rhubarb to nonreactive bowl, cool to room temperature, then cover with plastic and refrigerate until cold, at least 1 hour or up to 24.

3. Beat cream and remaining sugar in bowl of standing mixer on low speed until small bubbles form, about 45 seconds. Increase speed to medium; continue beating until beaters leave a trail, about 45 seconds longer. Increase speed to high; continue beating until cream is smooth, thick, and nearly doubled in volume and forms soft peaks, about 30 seconds.

4. To assemble fool, spoon about ¼ cup rhubarb into each of eight 8-ounce glasses, then spoon in a layer of about ¼ cup whipped cream. Repeat, ending with dollop of cream; serve. Can be covered with plastic wrap and refrigerated up to 6 hours. (To make one large fool, double the recipe and layer rhubarb and whipped cream in a 12-cup glass bowl.)

STRAWBERRY-RHUBARB FOOL
SERVES 8

Clean and hull 2 pints strawberries; quarter each berry. Follow recipe for Rhubarb Fool, substituting strawberries for 1¼ pounds rhubarb.

BLUEBERRY-RHUBARB FOOL WITH FRESH GINGER
SERVES 8

Follow recipe for Rhubarb Fool, reducing rhubarb to 1½ pounds, adding 1 teaspoon grated fresh ginger to orange juice along with sugar and salt, and gently stirring 1 pint blueberries into rhubarb after it has simmered 2 minutes.

Chocolate Cream Pie

Two kinds of chocolate and Oreo cookies produce a pie with
rich chocolate flavor and an easy-to-slice crust.

⊰ BY KAY RENTSCHLER ⊱

Despite its grand flourishes and snow-capped peaks, a chocolate cream pie is but a pudding or pastry cream whose substance has been given form. Comprising very basic ingredients—milk or cream, eggs, sugar, flour or cornstarch, butter, vanilla, and chocolate—it is cooked on the stove in a matter of minutes, chilled in a baked pie shell for a couple of hours, then topped with whipped cream. This pie, while looking superb, can be gluey or gummy, too sweet, even acrid. I wanted a filling of voluptuous creaminess that was reasonably sliceworthy, with a well-balanced chocolate flavor somewhere between milkshake and melted candy bar.

In our out-of-the-starting-gate tradition, I began by making a number of versions of this pie. Ingredient ratios were fairly stable, white sugar was standard, and about half the recipes used butter. But within ingredient margins, options abounded. I got to work.

Getting to Perfect Pastry Cream

A pastry cream, while in essence a quick, simple production, will form tapioca-like lumps of varying diameter in the presence of sloppiness or inattention—something I was well aware of, having seen the results of poor technique and preparation firsthand. Sequencing is pretty standard: while the milk or cream is brought to a boil with most of the sugar, a small portion of the sugar is held back, combined with the starch, and mixed thoroughly with the yolks. This yolk mixture is then tempered, or warmed with a fraction of the simmering milk or cream, allowing the starch molecules to expand gently. (That small amount of reserved sugar is important; as it is stirred with the yolks, it begins to dissolve, making the emulsion more fluid and easing the integration of the simmering milk or cream.) The warmed emulsion is reintroduced to the simmering milk or cream, and the whole is brought rapidly to a boil under constant stirring or whisking. Despite the fact that it contains eggs, a pastry cream can and must boil if the starch molecules are to expand and thicken.

I began by assessing my favorite pastry cream recipe—4 egg yolks, ½ cup sugar, 3 tablespoons cornstarch, 2 cups milk, 1 teaspoon vanilla extract, and 2 tablespoons butter—realizing that the proportions might require substantial modification for a chocolate filling. I wanted first to settle on the ingredient base and ran some comparative

Oreo cookie crumbs for the crust and an ounce of unsweetened chocolate in the filling lend intense flavor to this classic pie.

tests, most of which left me true to my original candidates. Egg yolks, for example, produced a cream of unsurpassed texture and flavor, far superior to one made with whole eggs. Cornstarch tasted lighter and cleaner than flour. Whole butter stirred into the finished cream effected tremendous improvements in texture and flavor, making the pastry cream supple and lush. One ingredient was to change: half-and-half provided enhanced mouthfeel and textural support for the chocolate; it was markedly better than milk or cream.

Through multiple trials and tweakings I developed a basic recipe that contained all of the ingredients mentioned above, along with more half-and-half to increase overall volume. It also called for higher proportions of egg yolks (6) and butter (6 tablespoons) than a standard pastry cream. Testing had convinced me that the texture of a chocolate cream filling benefits immeasurably when fats are used as thickeners while basic starch is minimized. Butter, egg yolks, and half-and-half render a silky texture and provide most of the requisite thickening with greater finesse than just flour or cornstarch. Well padded with fat, these ingredients are also staunch chroniclers of flavor.

Put another way, stingy fillings made with milk, a minimum of eggs, and no butter require far more base thickener to set up. The job gets done—but at the expense of texture and taste.

Chocolate Shopping

The chocolate options before me were three: semisweet (or bittersweet, which is quite similar), unsweetened, or a mixture of the two. Tasters felt that fillings made exclusively with semisweet or bittersweet chocolate lacked flavor depth, while those made with unsweetened chocolate alone hit a sour note. Without exception, tasters wanted the filling to land on the dark, intense bittersweet side and the cream topping to be sweet and pure.

The roundest, most upfront chocolate flavor, with lingering intensity at the finish, came in the form of 6 ounces semisweet and 1 ounce unsweetened chocolate. The apparently negligible amount of unsweetened chocolate contributed hugely to the flavor; semisweet or bittersweet chocolate on its own left the palate unsatisfied. We wondered why, so we called Thalia Hohenthal, a food scientist with Guittard Chocolate. According to Hohenthal, bittersweet chocolate has been processed more than unsweetened chocolate and has therefore lost some of its raw, "native" chocolate flavor. Unsweetened chocolate, which does not undergo the kneading, grinding, and smoothing process known as conching, retains all of its strong and sometimes bitter flavors that translate well in desserts.

This was not the only advantage of the small amount of unsweetened chocolate. Because it further thickened the cream (see "Constitutional Differences," page 24), I was able to reduce the cornstarch from 3 tablespoons to 2.

Next I moved on to compare fancy imported chocolates with domestic grocery store brands. The first test, pitting the widely available Baker's unsweetened chocolate against several unsweetened chocolates with European pedigrees, confirmed my fears that the supermarket stuff would be no match for its European competition. (Of the imported chocolates, all tasters preferred Callebaut.) Even at 1 ounce, the Baker's chocolate contributed an "off" flavor and rubberiness of texture that everyone noticed. But the next round of testing brought unexpected good news: Hershey's Special Dark chocolate was a consistent winner in the semisweet category, beating out not only a premium American semisweet entry but also its European competitors—and you can buy it in a drugstore! Hershey's unsweetened chocolate, while not as refined in flavor and texture as Callebaut unsweetened, placed a respectable second to Callebaut and was miles ahead of Baker's.

Technique Pulls It All Together

In the course of making versions of my pastry cream with all these different chocolates, I found that this filling requires as much care in its execution as a standard pastry cream, perhaps more. Because it is 3 standing inches of pure chocolate, a texture less than faultlessly smooth will deliver an experience less than ethereal. Temperature, timing, and technique are important.

On occasions when I didn't combine the eggs adequately with the sugar and starch (which meant mixing almost until the yolks ribbonned) or when I left the emulsion to sit around awaiting the simmering half-and-half, the sugar began to denature (break down) the yolks and made the finished texture of the cream grainy. For the pastry cream to attain a flawless texture, the half-and-half in the pan had to be simmering and left to simmer, rather than pulled off the stove, while the yolks were tempered. This way the introduction of the warmed yolks barely registered on the half-and-half, which quickly came back to a boil and was finished. Cold butter, whisked into the

bright-hot, nearly finished pastry cream, made a finer finished texture than soft butter. The chocolate, stirred in at the end in finely chopped bits, gave the finish sheen and body.

This was now a splendid pastry cream. Three hours of refrigeration gave it just enough wherewithal to slice up under a cloud of whipped cream and remain creamy on the tongue. It was deep in flavor and shy enough in sweetness to set up a lovely counterpoint to its topping.

Bottoms Up

As for the crust, I prepared every imaginable crumb variant, from graham to zwieback and back, as well as a standard pastry dough. Without exception, tasters swooned over a crumb crust made with chocolate cookie crumbs to the exclusion of all others.

While easier to make than rolled pastry dough and arguably better suited to chilled pudding fillings, crumb crusts are not altogether seamless enterprises. Sandy and insubstantial at one extreme, tough and intractable at the other, they can be a serving nightmare. While no one expects a slice of cream pie to hold up like a slab of marble, it isn't expected to collapse on a bed of grit or lacerate a cornea with airborne shrapnel, either. At the outset, the powers that be offered me a single crust mandate: It's got to slice, they said. Roger.

The standard cookie used to make a chocolate crumb crust is of course Nabisco Famous Chocolate Wafers. I duly recruited these veterans for early tests, using around a cup and a half of crumbs and a quarter cup melted butter along with a couple tablespoons of sugar and a bit of salt. We didn't care for the flavor of these crusts

Deconstructing Oreos

I was not one of those kids who pried Oreos apart and made a big spectacle of licking and scraping. I was greedy and had no time for ritualistic folly. For this crust, too, I ground the Oreos whole, just as a set of molars might. That the dazzling white sandwich cream plays a major role in an Oreo's appeal is obvious; that it is pure fat, less so. But it is. Oreo centers are sweetened hydrogenated shortening, like the Crisco icing on an inexpensive wedding cake. Hydrogenation refers to a process in which hydrogen gas is forced under pressure into the molecules of a vegetable oil, expanding, or "saturating," them into a semisolid state. Harold McGee, in *On Food and Cooking* (Scribners, 1984) terms this "a modern oil that is conveniently pre-creamed"—in other words, whipped. It is this quality in an Oreo filling that gives Oreo crumb crusts their edge over crusts made with plain chocolate cookies and melted butter. The fat in a hydrogenated shortening encases millions of air pockets. When the fat melts during baking, the air pockets remain, creating small empty spaces between the crumbs, thereby making the crust register as light and agreeably crisp—not hard—to the teeth. —K.R.

unbaked and found them somewhat tough (if sliceable) baked. I began rooting around for additions, vowing to avoid ground nuts, which I felt would mitigate the chocolate authority I wanted this pie to have.

After trying without much success to soften the crust with a percentage of fresh white bread crumbs, I made a leap of faith to Oreo cookies pulverized straight up with their filling. I hoped that the creaminess of the centers would lend flavor and softness to the finished crust and that their pure fat would eliminate the need for additional butter. No luck there. The crust was grainy and porous without butter and stubbornly linoleum-like when fortified with water or egg white. I tried again, this time dressing the crumbs with 2 tablespoons of melted butter. Now I had a hit on my hands. The Oreo flavor came through loud and clear, and the creamy, hydrogenated centers, along with a bit of butter, prevented the baked crumbs from becoming tough. No additional sugar or even salt was required.

In terms of technique, I discovered that while a crumb crust adheres nicely to a pie plate that has been buttered first, it does not release as well after baking. Many recipes recommend chilling the crumb-lined plate for 20 or 30 minutes before baking, and this is a recommendation that I generally support (the melted butter becomes firm and keeps everything from shifting). Still, on the occasions when I baked the crust straight off, it did remain in place. Ten minutes at 350 degrees did the trick—higher temperatures burned the cocoa. The crisp salty-sweet chocolate crumbs

Constitutional Differences

Everyone knows that bittersweet and unsweetened chocolates have different flavors and levels of sweetness. But their dissimilarities do not end there. As we developed our chocolate cream pie recipe, we discovered that ounce-for-ounce, unsweetened chocolate has more thickening power. We were aware of chocolate's starchy properties (cocoa solids are rich in starches), but we were not prepared for the dramatic differences in texture that awaited us in side-by-side pie fillings made with each type. Though both fillings had roughly the same amount of cocoa solids by volume, the unsweetened chocolate filling was significantly stiffer and also had a viscous, gummy quality. Its counterpart made only with bittersweet chocolate had a pleasantly smooth and creamy texture.

To find out why the two chocolates produced such different results, we made numerous phone calls to scientists and chocolate aficionados and received many answers—but no consensus. Varied ratios of cocoa solids, cocoa butter, and additives in chocolate, and different production methods from brand to brand are some of the factors that make it difficult to isolate a single cause.

While many cookbook substitutions fail to take into account the higher starch concentration of unsweetened chocolate, cooks should be mindful of its thickening power. Comparable amounts of bittersweet or semisweet chocolate and unsweetened chocolate plus sugar will not produce identical results. While a direct swap might work well enough in fudgy brownies, it could wreak havoc on a delicate custard or airy cake.

So why did we decide to include unsweetened chocolate in our filling if it can produce such unappealing results? The chocolate's intensity is essential to the filling's character. By using just a single ounce of unsweetened chocolate in our recipe, we were able to attain the perfect balance of nuanced chocolate flavor and pleasing, velvety texture. —Matthew Card

give the rich filling voice and definition. Cloaked with whipped cream, as a composite, this piece moves as one.

CHOCOLATE CREAM PIE
MAKES ONE 9-INCH PIE, SERVING 8 TO 10

For the best chocolate flavor and texture, we recommend either Callebaut semisweet and unsweetened chocolates or Hershey's Special Dark and Hershey's unsweetened chocolates. Do not combine the yolks and sugar in advance of making the filling—the sugar will begin to denature the yolks, and the finished cream will be pitted.

Chocolate Cookie Crumb Crust
- 16   Oreo cookies (with filling), broken into rough pieces, about 2¹/₂ cups
- 2   tablespoons unsalted butter, melted and cooled

Chocolate Cream Filling
- 2¹/₂   cups half-and-half
-   Pinch salt
- ¹/₃   cup sugar
- 2   tablespoons cornstarch
- 6   large egg yolks, room temperature, chalazae removed (see photo, below right)
- 6   tablespoons cold unsalted butter, cut into 6 pieces
- 6   ounces semi- or bittersweet chocolate, finely chopped
- 1   ounce unsweetened chocolate, finely chopped
- 1   teaspoon vanilla extract

Whipped Cream Topping
- 1¹/₂   cups cold heavy cream
- 1¹/₂   tablespoons sugar
- ¹/₂   teaspoon vanilla extract

TECHNIQUE
FORMING THE CRUST

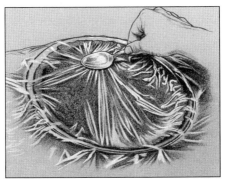

Press the crumbs evenly into the bottom and sides of the pie pan. Once the crumbs are in place, line the pan flush with a large square of plastic wrap, and use a spoon to smooth the crumbs into the curves and sides of the pan.

STEP-BY-STEP | MAKING THE PASTRY CREAM

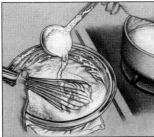

1. Add half cup simmering cream to the yolk mixture, stirring well to temper the yolks, and scraping down the sides of the bowl to incorporate.

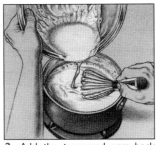

2. Add the tempered eggs back into the simmering cream all at once, whisking vigorously with the other hand.

3. Bring the cream quickly back to a simmer, whisking vigorously.

4. Off heat, whisk in the cold butter, one piece at a time.

5. Add the chopped chocolate and whisk well to combine.

6. Pour the filling into the baked and cooled shell.

1. FOR THE CRUST: Adjust oven rack to middle position and heat oven to 350 degrees. In bowl of food processor fitted with steel blade, process cookies with 15 one-second pulses, then let machine run until crumbs are uniformly fine, about 15 seconds. (Alternatively, place cookies in large zipper-lock plastic bag and crush with rolling pin.) Transfer crumbs to medium bowl, drizzle with butter, and use fingers to combine until butter is evenly distributed.

2. Pour crumbs into 9-inch Pyrex pie plate. Following illustration at left, press crumbs evenly onto bottom and up sides of pie plate. Refrigerate lined pie plate 20 minutes to firm crumbs, then bake until crumbs are fragrant and set, about 10 minutes. Cool on wire rack while preparing filling.

3. FOR THE FILLING: Bring half-and-half, salt, and about 3 tablespoons sugar to simmer in medium saucepan over medium-high heat, stirring occasionally with wooden spoon to dissolve sugar. Stir together remaining sugar and cornstarch in small bowl, then sprinkle over yolks and whisk, scraping down sides of bowl, if necessary, until mixture is glossy and sugar has begun to dissolve, about 1 minute. Whisk yolks thoroughly in medium bowl until slightly thickened, about 30 seconds. When half-and-half reaches full simmer, drizzle about ¹/₂ cup hot half-and-half over yolks, whisking constantly to temper; then whisk egg yolk mixture into simmering half-and-half (mixture should thicken in about 30 seconds). Return to simmer, whisking constantly, until 3 or 4 bubbles burst on the surface and mixture is thickened and glossy, about 15 seconds longer.

4. Off heat, whisk in butter until incorporated; add chocolates and whisk until melted, scraping pan bottom with rubber spatula to fully incorporate. Stir in vanilla, then immediately pour filling into baked and cooled crust. Press plastic wrap directly on surface of filling and refrigerate pie until filling is cold and firm, about 3 hours.

5. FOR THE TOPPING: Just before serving, beat cream, sugar, and vanilla in bowl of standing mixer on low speed until small bubbles form, about 30 seconds. Increase speed to medium; continue beating until beaters leave a trail, about 30 seconds more. Increase speed to high; continue beating until cream is smooth, thick, and nearly doubled in volume and forms soft peaks, about 20 seconds. Spread or pipe whipped cream over chilled pie filling. Cut pie into wedges and serve.

Removing the *chalazae*—strands of protein attached to the yolk that harden when cooked—precludes the need to strain the pastry cream after cooking.

Conventional Peanut Butters Cream 'Natural' Varieties

Skippy Creamy Peanut Butter squeaks past other supermarket brands in a tasting of cookies, sauces, and raw peanut butter.

≥ BY RAQUEL PELZEL ≤

Peanut butter is a cupboard staple, used for everything from peanut butter and jelly sandwiches to Sichuan noodles (see recipe on page 7). In the United States alone, peanut butter accounts for more than $630 million in sales annually, which is pretty amazing considering that just 150 years ago the peanut was thought fit only as fodder for pigs. Since we are constantly turning to peanut butter as a flavor booster for cookies, sauces, and sandwiches, we decided to find out which brand is best.

To do so, we first took a look at how all those brands got onto our supermarket shelves. Early peanut butters were (like today's "natural" versions) essentially just nuts ground into a paste. Because of the peanut's high fat content, these butters turned rancid easily and so were basically local products, with most producers supplying only their home city. In the early 1920s, Swift & Company introduced the first emulsified peanut butter, E. K. Pond, to American consumers. Emulsification involves the addition of hydrogenated oils and/or mono- and diglycerides, stabilizers that help prevent the separation of nut oil and nut mass. This process not only makes for a smoother, more spreadable product but also increases peanut butter's shelf life. As a result, E. K. Pond became the first nationally available brand of peanut butter. In 1928, Swift changed the E. K. Pond label to Peter Pan; in 1932, a disgruntled Swift employee left the company to make his own brand of peanut butter, which he called Skippy; in 1958, Procter & Gamble lined market shelves with its new brand, Jif.

Since then, the peanut butter scene hasn't changed much. Shoppers can choose natural, or "old-fashioned," peanut butter, or they can opt for a smooth emulsified peanut butter with a long shelf life.

We decided to focus this tasting on the top-selling peanut butters in grocery stores nationwide. This decision led us to include both natural and emulsified peanut butters, but only in their "creamy" form, since "crunchy" peanut butter accounts for only 26 percent of peanut butter sales. In addition, our tasting would confine itself to "real" peanut butters as defined by the Food and Drug Administration: those that

contain at least 90 percent peanuts. We tasted the peanut butters raw, in a sauce, and in a baked peanut butter cookie. After many long hours of tasting, we concluded that the peanut butter you choose might well depend on how you plan to use it.

When sampling the peanut butters straight from the jar, tasters chose Reese's as their favorite, with Jif only one point behind and Skippy trailing a distant third. When we checked the labels to try to explain this, we found that Reese's and Jif were the only two brands to include molasses. This, it seemed, added a caramel-like facet to their flavor profiles—an attribute tasters valued.

In the peanut sauce tasting, emulsified peanut butter once again stole the show. The rather grainy texture of the natural peanut butters was at odds with what should be the silky mouthfeel of the sauce. But this time Skippy took the lead, getting twice as many votes as the runner-up, Jif. Both the Jif and Reese's sauces were described by tasters as "very sweet" and "rather unbalanced." We deduced this to be the result of combining the already sweet ingredients in the sauce, which included coconut milk, with the molasses in the peanut butter.

It was in the cookie category, though, that we observed the most dramatic differences from brand to brand. The textures of the cookies were quite distinct. The cookies made with Teddie's and Smucker's and those made with freshly ground peanut butter were hearty and thick, just what you would expect of a "natural" cookie. The cookies made with Reese's and Simply Jif (a version of Jif with reduced salt, molasses, and sugar) were sandy and delicate, while those made with regular Jif were of medium build with soft, chewy centers and crisp edges. We attributed the semipliant character of the cookies made with regular Jif to the presence and amount of molasses, a hygroscopic substance that helps to retain moisture, giving the cookie its chewy quality. But if the Jif cookie was slightly soft, why wasn't the Reese's cookie, which also contains a significant amount of molasses?

We once again compared the ingredient lists

of Jif and Reese's and found our answer: Reese's contains cornstarch and less fat (1 gram). Robert Parker, a professor in the division of nutritional sciences at Cornell University, explained that the cornstarch in the peanut butter bound the water in the dough, leading to a dry cookie.

When it came to flavor, tasters slightly preferred the cookie made with Skippy, which they described as "tender and crisp." But the cookies made with natural peanut butters (one of which earned second and another third place in the cookie tasting) were consistently called more "peanutty" in flavor. The reason, according to University of Maryland lipids expert Elizabeth Boyle-Roden, is that natural peanut butters have not been doctored with hydrogenated oils, starches, sweeteners, or mono- or diglycerides, which can interfere with the peanut flavor in a cookie after it is baked.

Given all this information, what peanut butter should you buy? If you're looking for an all-purpose peanut butter, you can't go wrong with Skippy—and regular Jif comes in a close second. But if you eat your peanut butter on crackers, in sandwiches, or on an apple more often than you cook with it, you might prefer Reese's for its molasses-enhanced, caramel-like sweetness.

Separation Anxiety

The first few steps in making any type of peanut butter are essentially the same. Raw, shelled peanuts are roasted, cooled by industrial-strength suction fans, skinned, and ground. After being ground, natural peanut butters are immediately jarred and shipped.

When emulsified peanut butters are made, the peanuts must be ground once more, this time with salt, sweeteners, and hydrogenated stabilizers. During this grinding, the stabilizers trap the oil that is extracted from the peanuts in what scientists call a beta-prime polymorph. In layman's terms, this is a lattice-like structure that holds the peanut oil in its weave, suspending it throughout the creamed mass and protecting it from exposure to oxygen, which is the cause of rancidity. This is why hydrogenated peanut butters have a longer shelf life than natural peanut butters. —R.P.

TASTING PEANUT BUTTER

After consulting the most recent sales data, we assembled the most popular national peanut butters, including one sample of peanut butter made from freshly ground roasted peanuts, two "natural" peanut butters made only from ground roasted peanuts and salt, and five stabilized peanut butters with added emulsifiers, various oils (cottonseed, peanut, rapeseed, and soybean), and a host of other ingredients such as cornstarch, molasses, salt, and granulated sugar.

We tasted these peanut butters in peanut butter cookies, in peanut sauce (using a recipe from our book *How to Make Quick Appetizers*, 2000), and, of course, straight from the jar. The tasting was attended by 20 *Cook's* staff members, who were asked to evaluate the peanut butters and the sauces for intensity of peanut flavor and mouthfeel (mealy, smooth, pasty, gritty, and the like). The cookies were evaluated for peanut flavor, texture, and appearance. The peanut butters are listed below in the order of tasters' preferences.

HIGHLY RECOMMENDED

Skippy Creamy Peanut Butter ➤ $2.09/17.3 ounces

RAW: 3rd place
SAUCE: 1st place
COOKIE: 1st place
Overall, tasters felt that Skippy had a "good sweet/salty balance" and "tasted just like peanut butter should." Skippy made a tender and crisp cookie and a satisfying peanut sauce.

RECOMMENDED

Jif Creamy Peanut Butter ➤ $1.99/18 ounces

RAW: 2nd place
SAUCE: 2nd place
COOKIE: 4th place
Many tasters described second-place Jif as having the "perfect thickness" and being "sweet, but not obnoxiously so." Its texture was "silky and smooth," and it produced cookies with brown sugar undertones that were soft in the middle and crisp around the edge. In the peanut sauce, however, Jif was relatively sweet.

Teddie Smooth Old Fashioned Peanut Butter ➤ $2.39/16 ounces

RAW: 5th place
SAUCE: 3rd place
COOKIE: 3rd place
Teddie Old Fashioned was the only natural peanut butter to rank in the upper echelons of the tasting. In its raw state, one taster complained that she "couldn't even swallow" it, while others criticized Teddie for its mealy and pasty texture. A couple tasters defended Teddie for being "real and true." In the cookie, it was described as having "peanutty perfection."

Reese's Creamy Peanut Butter ➤ $1.88/18 ounces

RAW: 1st place
SAUCE: 7th place
COOKIE: 6th place (tie)
Even though Reese's didn't fare too well in either sauce (tasters found it "unbalanced") or cookie (it was deemed "gritty," with a "loose, shattery crumb"), tasters loved it raw. Most found it sweet and silky smooth, with a delicious flavor.

RECOMMENDED (continued)

Simply Jif Creamy Peanut Butter ➤ $1.99/17.3 ounces

RAW: 4th place
SAUCE: 4th place
COOKIE: 5th place
With only two-thirds of the sugar and less than half of the sodium per serving of other brands, Simply Jif scored surprisingly well. Many tasters thought it was very peanutty (albeit a little bland), with a smooth consistency that bordered on pasty. In the sauce, it was called "fairly peanutty," but in the cookie this peanut butter failed to impress.

Freshly ground peanuts from a natural food store ➤ $1.99/16 ounces

RAW: 8th place
SAUCE: 5th place
COOKIE: 2nd place
Tasters found the cookie made with this product to be "meaty," with "lots of peanut flavor," which was enough to put it in the "Recommended" category for those of you making cookies. But that's about all that can be said for it. When tasted raw, it was thought very bland, with a "cardboard" mouthfeel, and the sauce made with it lacked character.

NOT RECOMMENDED

Peter Pan Creamy Peanut Butter ➤ $1.95/18 ounces

RAW: 6th place
SAUCE: 6th place
COOKIE: 7th place
Peter Pan was criticized for its "artificial" and "unbalanced" flavor. It gave the sauce a bitter, "fake" flavor, while it made a cookie that was sandy, dry, and generally unpleasant.

Smucker's Natural Creamy Peanut Butter ➤ $2.79/16 ounces

RAW: 7th place
SAUCE: 8th place
COOKIE: 6th place (tie)
Finishing last or next to last in all three categories, Smucker's Natural was the loser of the tasting. Tasters just couldn't get past the mouthfeel when it came to eating the peanut butter raw, calling it "gritty," "grainy," and "pasty." In the sauce it was criticized for being too salty, and the cookie made with it was described as "dense," "tough," and very dry.

Cutting Boards: Wood versus Plastic

No-frills plastic and a wood composite—both dishwasher-safe—
are a cut above the competition.

⇒ BY ADAM RIED ⇐

Home cooks and chefs alike usually name knives as their most important kitchen tools. But what's a knife without its unsung partner, the cutting board? A good board feels spacious and secure. A bad one can impede the efficiency of any cook.

But what separates the good boards from the bad? Is it material? Size, thickness, or weight? Whether the board warps or retains odors with use? Do special features—wells to catch juices, feet to elevate the board or limit skidding, backstops to prevent cut food from scattering—make a difference? And what about the issue of bacteria retention? To sort all of this out, we gathered boards made from wood, polyethylene (plastic), acrylic, glass, and Corian (the hard countertop material), with a wide range of features, and used them daily in our test kitchen work for eight weeks. With every cut, we observed, noted, and debated the boards' merits and shortcomings to determine our favorites.

We found the two most important factors in cutting boards to be material and size. Material is important primarily in terms of the way the board interacts with the knife, but it is also relevant to odor retention and warping.

Large boards provide ample space for both cutting and pushing aside cut foods and waste. The disadvantage of really large boards is that they may not fit in the dishwasher. We are willing to make that sacrifice for the extra workspace, but if you are loath to wash your board by hand in the sink, as many cooks are, then buy the largest board that will fit in your dishwasher, which is what we did for this test. A board should be heavy enough for stability but not so heavy (or thick and bulky) that it is difficult to move around the kitchen or to store. To us, boards in the range of 3 to 4 pounds are ideal.

As for material, we discovered that we dislike cutting on the hard acrylic, glass, and Corian boards because they absorb none of the shock of the knife strike. Without exception, every tester's reaction was visceral, as if someone scraped their fingernails across a blackboard. Plastic and wood are softer and therefore cushion the knife's blow, making for a better controlled, more pleasant cutting experience. The pebbly surface texture of the acrylic and glass boards was another point against them. We found that a rough texture promotes a bit of knife slide.

On the other hand, the boards made from harder materials did not retain odors noticeably during the course of our testing, while the softer plastic and wood boards did. Our preference is not to use the harder boards but to keep several boards—three, if space allows—in circulation simultaneously: one board for garlic and onions and the like, another for raw poultry and meat, and a third for other foods.

Another reason to keep separate boards for separate purposes is to protect against the possibility of residual bacteria from a contaminated product. The debate over whether wood or plastic is safest in this regard is ongoing. What's important—no matter what material you choose—is to keep your boards clean. Researchers and government officials recommend washing every board well after each use, in the dishwasher, if possible, or by hand with hot soapy water, and then sanitizing with a light bleach solution (1 tablespoon of bleach to 1 gallon of water).

Many cutting boards, especially those made from wood or plastic, warp with time and cleaning. Makers of wood boards advise consumers to season the boards with mineral oil to build water resistance and, thereby, warp resistance. (Wood boards should not be washed in the dishwasher.) But none of the cooks we interviewed went this extra mile, and many, as a result, had warped wood boards. Because plastic boards can also warp with overexposure to heat, Keith Ohmart, president of Joyce Chen Products, recommends placing plastic boards away from the heating element of the dishwasher. The hard acrylic, glass, and Corian boards did not warp, but that benefit was not enough to change our minds about their shortcomings in the knife-strike department.

The real surprise in our testing was the dishwasher-safe wood board. Like a regular wood board, it softened the blow of the knife, but it also resisted warping after 50 runs through the dishwasher, even though we neglected to treat it with oil. A representative from Bemis Manufacturing, the producer of this board, explained that it was made by mixing wood composite (think particle board) with waterproof phenolic resin and then compressing the materials with thousands of pounds of pressure. The top and bottom surfaces are covered with wood veneer and the sides sealed with a waterproof coating.

Flex or Vex

The boards in our test had a wide range of features, only one of which offered much advantage. The New Age Products Chop & Chop Flexible Cutting Mat, which cost just $2.99, turned out to be a useful kitchen tool. It's light, thin, and flexible enough to pick up and fold so you can pour the cut food right from the mat, thereby eliminating spills and tedious transfers made with the help of a knife or your hands. The mat is best for light-duty mincing and slicing—heavy knife work will cut right through it—and it must be used on an even surface, but even with those limitations it's an incredibly useful supplement to a regular cutting board. In addition, it's dishwasher safe (though you shouldn't place it too close to the heating element lest the mat sustain damage from melting, which happened to the mat owned by one of our editors) and reusable. Our test mat showed signs of deterioration after four weeks of heavy use, but another editor has used the same mat at home, in lighter duty, for six months.

Special features on other boards—including built-in backstops, counter grips, and rinsing baskets—failed to impress us.

Juice Well A well around the outer edge of the board to capture meat juices as you carve gets in the way when sweeping cut food off the board. You can, in fact, mimic the effect of the well by placing a regular board in a rimmed baking sheet when carving.

Over-the-Sink All of the "over-the-sink" type boards we tested were wobbly; this is a design we'd avoid.

Feet Several of the boards had feet. This was OK if they were "no-skid" but disastrous if not because the feet made the board difficult to stabilize on the work surface. —A.R.

Where does this leave us? Essentially, with plastic. Plastic boards are dishwasher-safe and therefore easy to clean, they don't need the extra maintenance (oiling) that wood boards need, they come in innumerable sizes and weights to suit your preference, and they provide stability, control, and a pleasant cutting surface. Equally advantageous but harder to find is the Bemis dishwasher-safe wood board, which, if you don't mind oiling it occasionally, combines the benefits of plastic with the handsome appearance of wood.

CUTTING BOARD SURVEY

We gathered 10 cutting boards, made from various materials and with an array of features, and used them daily in the test kitchen over an eight-week period. While manufacturers tend to offer many types of boards with different features in a wide range of materials, sizes, shapes, and prices, to keep the testing manageable we chose to focus on materials and features instead of brand. For instance, we wanted to assess boards made of wood versus Corian versus plastic as opposed to looking at different brands of wood boards.

Recommended

	Price	Size	Weight	Dishwasher-Safe	Testers' Comments
MATERIAL: Polyethylene **FEATURES:** "Spot 'n Chop" color disc system with a red disc for the meat side, and a green disc indicating vegetables	$14.99	17 1/8" long by 9 3/4" wide by 1/2" thick **BRAND NAME: Joyce Chen** Spot 'n Chop Cutting Board	3 lb. 1 oz.	YES	Appreciated for cushioning the knife strike in the way that wood does. We'd rather have altogether separate boards for meat and other foods, which limits the usefulness of the color discs.
MATERIAL: Wood composite/phenolic resin/natural hardwood **FEATURES:** Dishwasher-safe	$13.99	15" long by 11" wide by 1/2" thick **BRAND NAME: Bemis** Dishwasher Safe Wood Large Utility Board	3 lb. 2 oz.	YES	Stable, sturdy, and comfortable to cut on because the wood absorbs the shock of the knife. Resisted warping after 50 runs in the dishwasher. Handsome, too.

Recommended with Reservations

	Price	Size	Weight	Dishwasher-Safe	Testers' Comments
MATERIAL: Polypropylene **FEATURES:** Flexible and thin for easy lifting/bending/pouring, antibacterial treatment	$2.99	15" long by 11 1/2" wide by .022" thick **BRAND NAME: New Age Products** Chop & Chop Flexible Cutting Mat	2 1/2 oz.	YES	Useful, clever design, and an excellent supplement to a regular board, but we wouldn't want this as our only cutting surface.
MATERIAL: Wood **FEATURES:** Juice well	$17.50	18 3/4" long by 12 3/4" wide by 3/4" thick **BRAND NAME: Catskill Craftsmen** Carving/Pastry Food Preparation Board	4 lb. 1 oz.	NO	The juice well drew mixed reactions. We neglected to oil the board, so it split in several places upon prolonged contact with water.

Not Recommended

	Price	Size	Weight	Dishwasher-Safe	Testers' Comments
MATERIAL: Wood **FEATURES:** Feet, thickness of 1 1/4"	$37.99	17 1/2" long by 12 1/2" wide by 1 1/4" thick **BRAND NAME: Snow River Wood Products** Traditional End Grain Tagliere Hardwood Cutting Board	6 lb. 10 oz.	NO	Without oiling, thickness did not prevent warping with use and cleaning. The feet made it difficult to secure on the work surface. Quite heavy.
MATERIAL: Acrylic **FEATURES:** Feet, doubles as serving tray	$12.99	15" long by 11" wide by 3/8" thick **BRAND NAME: US Acrylic** Clear Acrylic Cutting Board	1 lb. 13 oz.	YES	We disliked the feel of the pebbly textured surface and the acrylic material itself for chopping—the knife hits hard and then tends to slide a little bit. Low-skid feet keep board reasonably stable.
MATERIAL: Laminated tempered glass **FEATURES:** Heatsafe (can be used as trivet), protective safety backing	$13.99	15" long by 12" wide by 1/8" thick **BRAND NAME: Vance Industries** The Surface Protector	2 lb. 6 oz.	NO	The same problems as acrylic, only more pronounced. A knife blade against textured glass is like fingernails against a chalkboard. Resists odors and warping.
MATERIAL: Corian **FEATURES:** Nonskid rubber feet, juice well, built-in handle	$35.00	15" long by 9 3/4" wide by 1/2" thick **BRAND NAME: Eraz Corian Designs** Solid Surface Kitchenware Cutting Board	4 lb. 3 oz.	YES	Exceptionally hard surface makes for especially harsh knife strikes. Blade tends to slide a little. Nonskid feet keep the board stable. The handle is handy. Resists odors and warping.
MATERIAL: Polyethylene **FEATURES:** No-slip corners, backstop to catch food, counter grip, draining slope with collection pool at backstop	$19.99	14" long by 11 3/4" wide by 5/8" thick **BRAND NAME: Progressive International** Pro Grip Ultra Z Board	2 lb. 13 oz.	YES	No-slip corners are effective, but the backstop was irritating because the knife constantly bumped into it. The counter grip forced us to work closer to the work surface's edge than was comfortable. Board warped slightly with use.
MATERIAL: Polyethylene **FEATURES:** Rinse basket, adjustable arm for suspension over sink, drainage channel, antibacterial treatment	$15.99	16 3/4" long by 11 7/8" wide by 1/2" thick **BRAND NAME: Farberware** Over the Sink Cutting Board	3 lb. 2 oz.	YES	Adjustable arm was so loose that we feared it could slip out and cause the board to collapse into the sink as we worked. Rinse basket means board can't be used on a flat surface.

Fat Tactics

We fried dozens of chickens during the development of the Ultimate Crispy Fried Chicken recipe featured in this issue. What remained, after the final crumbs were swept away and everyone had wiped their fingers? Fat. Over time we amassed buckets of it, prompting us to wonder whether it could be reused. Turns out the answer is yes. We found that careful straining of either warm solid shortening or peanut oil removed bits of residue, leaving the fat perfectly suitable for a rerun. A fine-mesh conical strainer, such as a chinois, traps the tiniest particles, which would burn if not removed. Dampened layers of cheesecloth or even a paper coffee filter lining a sieve or strainer also get the job done. We found that the fat can be reused three times before it begins to develop off flavors. But be sure to refrigerate the fat between engagements.

Electric Knife Scores Again

The diamond grid we scored into the skin of the fresh ham featured in the March/April 2001 issue is a pleasing optical design as well as a means of obtaining crisp, pluckable cracklings—pieces of sweet, crisp, roasted skin padded with meltingly flavorful fat. Along the way, we discovered yet another use for electric knives, tested in our November/December 2000 issue. Held aloft like a miniature chain saw, an electric knife will race right through the skin, making the lacerations almost effortlessly. Scoring the pattern first with shallow punctuations ensures symmetry of design.

Chocolate Pie-ticulars

When we first began the research for our chocolate cream pie recipe on page 25, we learned that not any chocolate pie qualifies as a cream pie. A chocolate cream pie (which contains milk, flour or cornstarch, egg yolks, sugar, chocolate, and butter) is cooked, indeed boiled, on the stove to thicken. It has the finished texture of chilled, lush, creamy pudding. A chocolate custard pie derives its thickness exclusively from eggs and is baked gently until firm. Its finished texture is delicate, quivering, and glassine. A chocolate mousse pie derives its thickness from whipped whole eggs (often in the context of a boiling sugar syrup) or egg whites, melted chocolate, and lightly whipped cream. Its finished texture is plushly rich on the tongue and substantial. A chocolate chiffon pie experiences no real cooking at all. Thickened with gelatin, egg whites, and whipped cream, it has an ethereally light and airy finished texture.

Pan-Handling

Cookware manufacturers suggest the need for a variety of skillets for stovetop cookery. Omelets and crêpes, for instance, are each thought to require a different type. We have found that although pricey, specialized skillets often do little to enhance the products they produce, omelets and crêpes do benefit from different pan surfaces. Because omelets require constant, gentle movement and only a glancing acquaintance with the bottom of the pan, a 10-inch nonstick skillet works best for cooking them. In recent tests, the omelets we made in an All-Clad nonstick were fine-pored, delicately pale, and—unlike those cooked in the skillet's specialized counterparts—incapable of sticking. A crêpe, on the other hand, tastes better when a sticking point or two yields a few brown spots; we found pale crêpes to be uninteresting in flavor and texture, rather omelet-like, in fact. This makes traditional pans (without a nonstick surface) a must for crêpes. A heavy, All-Clad skillet performed as capably as a French crêpe pan—in some regards even better, as the heat was more even.

The Right Stuff

Two of the dishes in this issue—the Sichuan noodles on page 6 and the bok choy on page 20—are flavored with roasted sesame oil, which is widely used in culinary applications throughout Asia and the Middle East. Generally referred to as dark, or Asian, sesame oil, it is produced from deeply roasted seeds, which give it a dark brown color and rich, perfumed flavor. It should not be confused with cold-pressed sesame oil, which is produced from raw seeds and has a very light color and little aroma or flavor. Whereas cold-pressed sesame oil may be used interchangeably with other vegetable oils—indeed, even to cook foods—roasted sesame oil, which has a low smoke point (it burns easily), is used not to cook foods but as a flavoring agent to give them a distinctive character. Because roasted sesame oil is particularly prone to damage from heat and light, it should be purchased only in tinted glass and stored in the refrigerator.

Blushing Beauty

The rhubarb plant, an herbaceous perennial—botanically a vegetable, but used as a fruit—comes in more than 100 varieties, only a handful of which have responded to the efforts of commercial growers. Nevertheless, rhubarb turns up in many different colors and sizes during spring and early summer (and, increasingly, at other times of year as well). Our extensive use of rhubarb during development of the rhubarb fool on page 22 prompted us to offer this informal buyer's guide. By far the best rhubarb stalks we used were deeply colored, firm, crisp, and tender. In our experience, deeply colored stalks invariably possessed superior flavor (an observation supported by the U.S. Department of Agriculture). Mature rhubarb, which has been left in the ground too long before being harvested, is likely to be tough and stringy—even peeling didn't improve the sinewy stalks. In fact, we found peeling to be superfluous; crisp, medium-sized stalks—about the size of a regular celery stalk—were not improved by peeling. Peeling also removes the lovely blush color from the stalks.

Palm Pilot for Grill Cooks

How does a frenzied cook working the grill or broiler on busy Saturday nights bring your rib eye or filet to a perfect medium-rare? You can bet it's not by sawing past the grill marks with a knife to check color. No, it is the finely honed skill of palpation that makes the call: the firmer the meat, the more well done it is. To help inexperienced grill cooks develop fingertip precision, chefs train them literally by hand: different points on a relaxed, open palm replicate the texture of rare, medium-rare, and well-done meats. We offer the following rules of thumb to help you develop your own *Fingerspitzengefühl* (literally, "feeling in the tips of the fingers"). Once mastered, these guidelines will help you recognize the doneness of fish, chicken, pork, and lamb as well as steak.

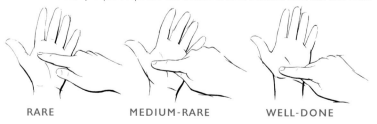

RARE   MEDIUM-RARE   WELL-DONE

Voices of Authority

Two personable chefs bring strong voices to their cookbooks.
We decided to see if their food speaks as clearly. BY CHRISTOPHER KIMBALL

Good cookbook writers, like good novelists, have a voice. Some are persnickety, others are enthusiastic, but the really good ones exude a thoughtful command of their material while also informing the recipes with a strong sense of their own style. Like a good operatic tenor, a successful cookbook author exhibits a convincing blend of technical skill and passion for the role without hitting any off notes.

The two cookbooks reviewed here could not be more different, at least at first glance. One is written by America's leading authority on Mexican cooking, Rick Bayless, who is also a successful Chicago restaurateur, and the other is penned by a young, fresh-faced Brit who last summer left London's famous River Café to take over the kitchen at Monte's, a private club. They are, however, both a bit larger than life, having their own television shows, and also produce prose infused with a strong sense of self. We knew we liked their personas—we went into the test kitchen to see if we also liked their food.

THE NAKED CHEF
Jamie Oliver

Hyperion, 250 pages, $34.95

I am told by some of the test cooks here at *Cook's Illustrated* that Jamie Oliver is seriously cute. As I am at least 40 years beyond the point at which anyone would use that adjective to describe me (the last time may have been before matriculating from kindergarten), I have to put aside that aspect of his appeal and judge his cookbook on its own merits. However, his image and personality are integral to this endeavor since, for example, he describes what lies under chicken skin as "a little bit of tissuey-type stuff," an indication that his recipes will not sound a bit like a textbook from La Varenne or Cordon Bleu. *The Naked Chef* is full of mouthwatering full-page color photos (of Oliver and, oh, his food, too) as well as the occasional rasher of color step-by-step photos. It's bright; it's simply designed; it's modern.

PROS: Oliver's cooking is straightforward, and it's produced in a second-rate home kitchen. A high percentage of modern cookbooks are aiming for this same hallowed ground—quick and easy home cooking with big flavors—but Oliver's casual prose and the clean, friendly book design carry it off exceptionally well. The color photos make the food look both simple and great.

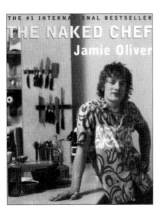

CONS: As with the Emeril cult, Oliver is selling himself and his personal style as much as his food. The recipe directions are cheerful and chatty but would benefit from more precision. In keeping with his loose, easygoing style, he leaves out what would have been helpful information on preparation, ingredients, and cooking instructions.

RECIPE TESTING: Out of 13 recipes tested, nine were considered worth making again. Among the winners were a Cranberry Bean, Pancetta, and Rosemary Risotto (we could do without the crunchy celery); Pork Chops with Thyme, Lemon, and Pesto (the pesto was easy to make and would also be excellent with chicken); Pan-Seared Scallops with Crispy Bacon and Sage, Green Lentils, and Green Salad (nice dish, but it isn't quick to make since it calls for two other recipes to finish it); Kedgeree (a dish of smoked haddock, rice, and boiled egg, which sounded awful but tasted good); and Roasted Asparagus with Cherry Tomatoes, Black Olives, and Basil (this combination was excellent although not quite "orgasmic," as the author promised). Some recipes we tested were less successful. The focaccia was tasteless (he uses a basic bread recipe for all of his breads, which in this case seems a mistake), and Fragrant Green Chicken Curry had vague directions (knowing which type of green chile to use would be helpful). Chickpea and Leek Soup looks terrific in full color, but the texture was a bit too sludge-like for our taste.

MEXICO ONE PLATE AT A TIME
Rick Bayless

Scribner, 374 pages, $35.00

Bayless is a hard guy not to like. The food at the Frontera Grill in Chicago is good, really good, and Bayless, much like Alice Waters, has a strong sense

of community, with an emphasis on locally grown food. He also knows what he is talking about, a rare commodity in cookbooks these days. Nonetheless, we at *Cook's Illustrated* have been chary of reviewing his books because authentic Mexican cooking requires both lots of time and ingredients that many American home cooks may be hard-pressed to find. Perhaps sophisticated Mexican cooking makes a great deal of sense for a restaurant but little sense for the home cook. To find out, we tested 13 recipes from *Mexico One Plate at a Time* (the book is based on the public television series).

PROS: With color and black-and-white photographs throughout, high-quality paper, and a clever use of flat color with the recipes, this is one cookbook for which the publisher spared no expense. In addition, recipes have a question-and-answer section that provides useful advice from the author's many hours of kitchen testing. Make-ahead information is included as well as icons indicating whether a recipe is traditional or contemporary.

CONS: This book has many graphic elements that might have been better organized. The small black-and-white photos from Mexico are interesting but could have been put to better use, and the ingredient shots are nice but not nearly as appealing as the finished dishes, which are drop-dead gorgeous. This is not a book for the Tuesday night dinner crowd; given the complexity of the recipes, you need to make a commitment to this sort of cooking.

RECIPE TESTING: If you have any interest in Mexican cooking, buy this book. Most of this food was terrific—worth the serious investment of time and effort—and the directions were clear. We tested 13 recipes and would definitely make 10 of them again. Cheese-and-Mushroom Quesadillas were crisp and hot, and the filling was nicely spiced; Roasted Lobster Tails with Mojo Mayonnaise was nearly perfect—sweet, garlicky, and bright with lime juice; Tequila-Flamed Mangoes paired with vanilla ice cream were outstanding (although the ¼ cup butter was on the rich side); and Quick-Fried Shrimp were devoured instantly by all. The filling for Zucchini Tacos was a bit runny, Red Tomato Rice was bland although eye-catching, and Creamy Enchiladas tasted good, but the texture was on the mushy side.

Most of the ingredients and materials necessary for the recipes in this issue are available at your local supermarket, gourmet store, or kitchen supply shop. The following are mail-order sources for particular items. Prices listed below were current at press time and do not include shipping or handling unless otherwise indicated. We suggest that you contact companies directly to confirm up-to-date prices and availability.

Cutting Boards

After eight weeks of mincing, chopping, butchering, washing, and generally manhandling cutting boards, we found dishwasher-safe wood composite and polyethylene (plastic) to be our cutting board materials of choice. When shopping for a board, material and size should be your first consideration—brand, we found, has little bearing on the matter. There is no mail-order source for the Bemis Dishwasher Safe Wood Large Utility Board, Model 7502, but, according to a company representative, Bemis products are sold at Wal-Mart, Ace Hardware, and Publix stores. (Note that these stores may not carry this particular board—inventory varies from store to store.) The Bemis board retails for $13.99. The polyethylene and dishwasher-safe wood boards we found on the shelves of our local kitchen stores were good performers. Joyce Chen's Spot 'n Chop Cutting Board features a handy color-coding system, and its surface works like wood to cushion the knife strike. **Cooks Corner (836 South 8th Street, Manitowoc, WI 54220; 800-236-2433; www.cookscorner.com)** sells the 17 by 9-inch board for $14.99, item #103010. The cheap, flexible, and versatile New Age Products Chop & Chop Flexible Cutting Mat is sold at **Kitchen Etc. (32 Industrial Drive, Exeter, NH 03833; 800-232-4070; www.kitchenetc.com)** for $2.99, item #454822.

Fried Chicken

Frying chicken in a Le Creuset enamel-coated, cast-iron Dutch oven instead of a cast-iron skillet eliminated oil splatters, maintained the frying temperature, and allowed for extremely easy cleanup. **A Cook's Wares (211 37th Street, Beaver Falls, PA 15010; 800-915-9788; www.cookswares.com)** sells the 8¾-quart round oven we preferred. It costs $239.00 and comes in six different colors (each with a different item number). **Lehman's (P.O. Box 41, Kidron, OH 44636; 877-438-5346; www.lehmans.com)** carries the less expensive Lodge 7-quart cast-iron Dutch oven for $45.00, item #1810D02. Cleanup is a bit cumbersome, but it is a great performer.

Cooking with large amounts of oil can be tricky. In the fried chicken recipe, the temperature

of the oil must be monitored. While long thermometers with clips are designed specifically for gauging the temperature of oil and sugar syrups, we found the Thermapen thermometer to be a much better, safer alternative. It has a wide reading range (50 degrees Fahrenheit to 572 degrees Fahrenheit), is highly accurate (within 0.5 degrees Fahrenheit), is easy to read (½-inch LCD characters), and it's fast (five seconds for a reading). The Thermapen has a sharp, stainless steel probe with a needle-thin tip (also great for testing the temperature of meats and breads) that folds back (turning off the thermometer automatically) and locks in place when not in use. This is the ultimate kitchen thermometer. **The Baker's Catalogue (P.O. Box 876, Norwich, VT 05055; 800-827-6836; www.kingarthurflour.com)** sells the highly useful Thermapen for $79.95, item #4325.

Chocolate Cream Pie

If you find it time-consuming to spread or pipe whipped cream on top of our Chocolate Cream Pie (page 23), try using a whipped cream siphon to speed things up. Siphons function like cans of whipped cream from the grocery store, but fresh ingredients are added at home. Pour in the cream mixed with sugar and vanilla extract, attach the charger (which helps to expel the cream from the siphon), point, and shoot. Whipped cream comes out effortlessly, and the pie is covered in no time. The contents will keep for up to two weeks if stored in the refrigerator. **Sur La Table (1765 Sixth Avenue South, Seattle, WA 98134-1608; 800-243-0852; www.surlatable.com)** carries two siphons, white (item #8386) and red (item #5303), for $44.95 each. They also sell a box of 10 chargers for $8.95.

Ultra-Flex spatulas, which are thin, superflexible, and easy to maneuver, will help you serve up clean slices of pie. **The Baker's Catalogue (P.O. Box 876 Norwich, VT 05055; 800-827-6836; www.kingarthurflour.com)** sells a triangular Ultra-Flex Pie Spatula for $3.95, item #5046.

Omelets

Getting the cheeses in our omelets (page 18) to melt perfectly meant abandoning chunky cuts of cheese from the box grater for something a bit finer. The "coarse" (by its own standards) Microplane grater became our grater of choice. Its handled design makes the grater easy to maneuver, and its sharp teeth turn out mounds of beautifully grated cheese with minimal effort. **Williams-Sonoma (P.O. Box 7456, San Francisco, CA, 94120-7456; 800-541-2233; www.williams-sonoma.com)** carries the Microplane Coarse Grater for $16.50, item #16-3720679.

Sichuan (aka Szechuan) Ingredients

If you feel inspired to take the authentic route when making the Spicy Sichuan Noodles (page 7), you'll need to begin with a trip to your local Asian grocer to find three of the ingredients: sesame paste, dried Asian noodles, and Sichuan peppercorns. Alternatively, you can order all three from **The Oriental Pantry (423 Great Road, Acton, MA 01720; 978-264-4576; www.orientalpantry.com)**. Using sesame paste made from toasted sesame seeds in place of peanut butter will impart an earthy, smoky flavor to the final dish. It comes in an 8-ounce jar for $3.49. And if Italian linguine doesn't cut it for you, try Chinese Style Lo Mein Noodles ($1.59 for a 12-ounce package). Flat, relatively broad, and soft yet sturdy when cooked, the noodles really stand up to the sauce. Finally, highly aromatic Sichuan peppercorns ($1.99 for a 4-ounce bag) lend a woodsy flavor and heighten the piquancy of the dish.

Veggie Grilling Gear

Grilling vegetables requires attention to technique and the right tools. Basting or oiling veggies with a soft-bristled pastry brush keeps them from sticking to the grill. **Kitchen Etc. (32 Industrial Drive, Exeter, NH 03833; 800-232-4070; www.kitchenetc.com)** carries a 2-inch pastry brush for $7.99 (item #592626) with bristles that are soft enough to keep from bruising or damaging the vegetables.

Spring-loaded tongs are a must-have when it comes to grilling. We prefer 16-inch tongs because the added length protects your hands from the heat whether you use the tongs to add coals to the fire, turn food, or transfer food to and from the grill. You can order a set of 12-inch and 16-inch tongs for $9.99, item #0506, from **The Chef's Catalog (P.O. Box 620048, Dallas, TX 75262; 800-884-2433; www.chefscatalog.com)**.

Steadying veggies like button mushrooms, cherry tomatoes, and sliced onions to keep them from falling through the grill grate is best done with thin stainless steel skewers. You can mail-order a set of four 11-inch skewers from **A Cook's Wares (211 37th Street, Beaver Falls, PA 15010; 800-915-9788; www.cookswares.com)** for $5.00, item #8068. These thin rods won't burn or split your veggies in two, and they will last for many barbecues. Alternatively, small veggies can be laid atop a finer grate (a wire mesh cooling rack will do) or sheet of perforated steel to keep them from slipping through the cracks. **Bridge Kitchenware (214 East 52nd Street, New York, NY 10022; 800-274-3435)** sells a heavy-duty piece of perforated steel with a porcelain coating (also great for seafood) for $12.95, product code BSRK.

RECIPES
May & June 2001

Perfect Cheese Omelet with Red Pepper, Mushroom, and Onion

Four-Vegetable Soup

Main Dishes
Filet Mignon,
    Bacon-Wrapped **9**
    Pan-Seared **9**
Fried Chicken, The Ultimate Crispy **12**
Spicy Sichuan Noodles
    (Dan Dan Mian) **7**
    with Shiitake Mushrooms **7**

Soups, Salads, and Side Dishes
Bok Choy
    Baby Bok Choy, Sesame-
      Soy-Glazed **21**
    Braised with Garlic **21**
    Braised with Shiitake
      Mushrooms **21**
    Stir-Fried, with Oyster Sauce
      and Garlic **21**
    Stir-Fried, with Soy Sauce
      and Ginger **21**
Four-Vegetable Soup **15**
Tuna Salad
    Classic **13**
    with Apples and
      Currants, Curried **13**
    with Balsamic Vinegar and
      Grapes **13**
    with Cauliflower, Jalapeño, and
      Cilantro **13**
    with Lime and Horseradish **13**

Sauces
FOR FILET MIGNON:
    Argentinian-Style Fresh Parsley and
      Garlic Sauce (Chimichurri) **9**
    Madeira Pan Sauce with Mustard
      and Anchovies **9**

Omelets and Omelet Fillings
Bacon, Onion, and Scallion Filling **19**
Cheese Omelet, Perfect **19**
Sautéed Mushroom Filling with
    Thyme **19**
Sautéed Red Bell Pepper Filling with
    Mushroom and Onion **19**

Desserts
Blueberry-Rhubarb Fool with
    Fresh Ginger **22**
Chocolate Cream Pie **25**
Rhubarb Fool **22**
Strawberry-Rhubarb Fool **22**

PHOTOGRAPHY: CARL TREMBLAY

The Ultimate Crispy Fried Chicken

Classic Tuna Salad

Pan-Seared Filet Mignon

www.cooksillustrated.com

If you enjoy *Cook's Illustrated* magazine, you should visit our Web site. Simply log on at www.cooksillustrated.com. Although much of the information is free, database searches are for site subscribers only. *Cook's Illustrated* readers are offered a 20 percent discount.

Here is what you can do on our site:

Search Our Recipes: We have a searchable database of all the recipes from *Cook's Illustrated*.

Search Tastings and Cookware Ratings: You will find all of our reviews (cookware, food, wine, cookbooks) plus new material created exclusively for the Web site.

Find Your Favorite Quick Tips.

Get Your Cooking Questions Answered: Post questions for *Cook's* editors and fellow site subscribers.

Check Your Subscription: Check the status of your subscription, pay a bill, or give gift subscriptions online.

Visit Our Bookstore: You can purchase any of our cookbooks, hardbound annual editions of the magazine, or posters online.

Subscribe to *e-Notes*: Our free e-mail companion to the magazine offers cooking advice, test results, buying tips, and recipes about a single topic each month.

Find Out about Our New Public Television Show: Watch *America's Test Kitchen* to see the *Cook's Illustrated* staff at work in our test kitchen. Check www.americastestkitchen.com for program times in your area.

Get All the Extras: The outtakes from each issue of *Cook's* are available at Cook's Extra, including step-by-step illustrations.

Spicy Sichuan Noodles

Sesame-Soy-Glazed Baby Bok Choy

Rhubarb Fool

Chocolate Cream Pie

Serrano

Amatista

Jalapeño

Jamaican Hot

Cherry Pepper

Pimento

Poblano

Scotch Bonnet

Ají

Habanero

Macho Green

Macho Red

FRESH CHILES

NUMBER FIFTY-ONE

JULY & AUGUST 2001

COOK'S
ILLUSTRATED

Juicy Grilled
Chicken Cutlets
Brine the Meat and Cook It Fast

Backyard
Potato Salad
Skewer, Boil, and Grill

Better Gazpacho
Chunky Texture Preferred

Perfect Kebabs
Juicy Meat, Tender Vegetables

Best Cherry Cobbler
Fresh Flavor, Light Biscuits

Balsamic Vinegar
Taste-Test
$3.49 Supermarket Brand Wins

Pepper Mill Kitchen Test
Summer Fruit Salads
Knife Sharpening 101
Grilled Chilean Sea Bass
Fruit Tarts at Home
Smoky, Creamy Eggplant Dip

$4.95 U.S./$6.95 CANADA

CONTENTS

July & August 2001

2 Notes from Readers
Readers ask questions and suggest solutions.

4 Quick Tips
Quick and easy ways to perform everyday kitchen tasks, from pouring charcoal to loading pepper mills.

6 Grilled Chicken Cutlets
Boneless chicken can turn dry and leathery on the grill. For tender, juicy cutlets that won't dry out, brine the meat, then cook it quickly over high heat. BY BRIDGET LANCASTER

8 Really Good Gazpacho
For summer in a bowl, hand-cut the vegetables and marinate them in seasoned vinegar. BY ADAM RIED

10 Backyard-Grill Potato Salad
Potatoes cooked on the grill deliver smoky flavor, but they are usually either charred or undercooked in the center. Here is how to do it right. BY RAQUEL PELZEL

12 The Secret of Chilean Sea Bass
Undercooked, this fish is inedible. Buy thick fillets and cook them a long, long time. BY JACK BISHOP

14 Perfect Shish Kebab
To avoid the raw lamb and charred vegetables that cooking on skewers often delivers, we cut the meat into 1-inch cubes and narrowed the vegetable field. BY JULIA COLLIN

16 Sharpening Knives by Hand
Sharp knives are essential to smooth and precise chopping, slicing, and carving. With two simple tools—and a little elbow grease—you can keep your knives in professional trim at home. BY MATTHEW CARD

18 The Best Baba Ghanoush
Scorching eggplant on the grill produces a smoky, creamy dip far superior to the wan, tasteless fare that is the bane of many dinner parties. BY KAY RENTSCHLER

20 Summer Fruit Salads
Good fruit salads aren't overwhelmingly sweet. We found that a sweet-tart dressing brightens flavors rather than cloaking them.

21 Fresh Fruit Tarts Worth Eating
Bakery tarts look elegant but are often tasteless and rubbery. Here's a step-by-step guide to making your own pâtisserie creation that will taste as good as it looks. BY DAWN YANAGIHARA

24 Solving the Problems of Cherry Cobbler
Most cherry cobblers are no more than canned pie filling. We wanted fresh cherry flavor paired with a light biscuit topping. BY KAY RENTSCHLER

26 $3.49 Balsamic Vinegar Wins Tasting
In the $15-and-under category, the lack of artificial sweetener and coloring makes a cheap brand a winner. BY RAQUEL PELZEL

28 Testing Pepper Mills
Extensive trials reveal that grind quality, capacity, ease of filling, and rate of output distinguish the best mills. BY ADAM RIED

30 Kitchen Notes
Test results, buying tips, and advice related to stories past and present, directly from the test kitchen. BY KAY RENTSCHLER

31 Recipes from the Pacific Rim
A stunning, Southeast Asian–inspired cookbook moves comfortably from coffee table to home kitchen. A Hawaiian offering seems more at home in a restaurant kitchen. BY CHRISTOPHER KIMBALL

32 Resources
Products from this issue and where to get them, including pepper mills, tart pans, and fresh sour cherries.

COOK'S ILLUSTRATED

www.cooksillustrated.com

PUBLISHER AND EDITOR
Christopher Kimball

EXECUTIVE EDITOR
Catherine O'Neill Grace

SENIOR WRITER
Jack Bishop

FOOD EDITOR
Kay Rentschler

MANAGING EDITOR
Dawn Yanagihara

ASSOCIATE EDITORS
Adam Ried
Raquel Pelzel

RECIPE TESTING AND DEVELOPMENT
Bridget Lancaster
Julia Collin

ASSISTANT EDITOR
Shannon Blaisdell

CONSULTING FOOD EDITOR
Jasper White

CONTRIBUTING EDITOR
Elizabeth Germain

ART DIRECTOR
Amy Klee

COPY EDITOR
India Koopman

PROOFREADER
Jana Branch

ASSOCIATE EDITOR,
SPECIAL PROJECTS
Rebecca Hays

ASSISTANT EDITOR, WEB SITE
Shona Simkin

EDITORIAL INTERNS
Matthew Card
Meg Suzuki

VICE PRESIDENT MARKETING
David Mack

MARKETING MANAGER
Pamela Caporino

MARKETING SPECIALIST
Barbara Bourassa

SALES REPRESENTATIVES
Jason Geller
Karen Shiffman

MARKETING ASSISTANT
Connie Forbes

CIRCULATION MANAGER
Larisa Greiner

PRODUCTS MANAGER
Steven Browall

DIRECT MAIL MANAGER
Robert Lee

CIRCULATION ASSISTANT
Jennifer McCreary

CUSTOMER SERVICE MANAGER
Jacqueline Valerio

INBOUND MARKETING REPRESENTATIVE
Adam Dardeck

VICE PRESIDENT OPERATIONS
AND TECHNOLOGY
James McCormack

PRODUCTION MANAGER
Jessica Lindheimer

PRODUCTION ARTIST
Daniel Frey

PRODUCTION COORDINATOR
Mary Connelly

PRODUCTION INTERN
Lisa Leonard

SYSTEMS ADMINISTRATOR
Richard Cassidy

WEBMASTER
Nicole Morris

CHIEF FINANCIAL OFFICER
Sharyn Chabot

CONTROLLER
Mandy Shito

OFFICE MANAGER
Juliet Nusbaum

RECEPTIONIST
Henrietta Murray

PUBLICITY
Deborah Broide

For list rental information, contact The SpeciaLISTS, 1200 Harbor Blvd. 9th Floor, Weehawken, NJ 07087; 201-865-5800; fax 201-867-2450. Editorial office: 17 Station Street, Brookline, MA 02445; 617-232-1000; fax 617-232-1572. Editorial contributions should be sent to: Editor, *Cook's Illustrated*. We cannot assume responsibility for manuscripts submitted to us. Submissions will be returned only if accompanied by a large self-addressed envelope. Postmaster: Send all new orders, subscription inquiries, and change of address notices to: *Cook's Illustrated*, P.O. Box 7446, Red Oak, IA 51591-0446. PRINTED IN CHINA.

HERBES DE PROVENCE The fresh herbs that, when dried, constitute *herbes de Provence* flourish in the Provence region of southern France. Though there is no definitive formula for this savory mélange, most include all or some of the herbs illustrated, including lavender, with its fragrant, edible blue-violet flowers; marjoram, a member of the mint family with sweet notes and a slight taste of oregano; peppery, pungent summer savory; rosemary, a highly aromatic and strong-flavored evergreen; and spicy-sweet basil. Sage adds a warm, musty flavor, while thyme is earthy and woodsy. Fennel seeds contribute a strong anise flavor. All together, or in various combinations, herbes de Provence is generally used to flavor meats, stews, and sauces.

HERBES DE PROVENCE

COVER (*Collards and Watermelon*): ELIZABETH BRANDON, BACK COVER (*Herbes de Provence*): JOHN BURGOYNE

SAP HOUSE RULES

If you know what to look for, you can see the remains of ancient sap houses dotting the Vermont landscape like rusted hulks of antique cars, doors askew, creepers headed up toward the eaves. Unlike hunting camps, which are found deep in the woods, sap houses are usually built near roads for easy access, so they are readily discovered, even by a casual observer. Many of these tumble-down shacks still come alive in late February and March, when the nights are cold but the days push up over freezing and the sap runs freely from the sugar maples to fill galvanized buckets and holding tanks to overflowing.

This arrangement may sound crude, but, as in much cooking, there is a science to the art of sugaring. Each day begins with a measurement of barometric pressure. This will affect the temperature at which the sap boils—some days it boils at 212 degrees, other days at 210—and therefore the temperature at which the syrup is done, which is always 7 degrees above the boiling temperature. Sugarers also measure the density of the syrup. This is done with the help of a hydrometer, which consists of a narrow metal cylinder and a glass tube that floats inside it when the cylinder is filled with hot syrup. This is the best gauge of when the syrup is ready for canning.

Things get started when the cold sap is run into pans, and the arch—the assemblage of evaporator pans, firebox, and smokestack—is fired up. Within 15 minutes, the sap is bubbling, and great clouds of steam head skyward through the open louvers on top of the building.

The process sounds simple enough, but there are rules. First, you never start a boil unless you have enough sap. It takes a wood fire a long time to cool down, and if you run out of sap, the pans will scorch or even melt. The second rule is to burn hot and quick, reducing 50 or 60 gallons of sap to 1 gallon of syrup as quickly as possible. This requires dry wood that has been split into small pieces. Finally, you have to pay keen attention. The sap can boil over in seconds (a dab of butter on the surface of boiling sap will instantly stop a boil-over); stepping out, even to grab a cold beer from a snowbank, often has serious consequences.

Boiling sap, for most Vermonters, is about passion, not profit. The wife of one committed sugarer figured out that her husband earned about 6 cents an hour. She offered him a raise to 25 cents if he would do some work around the house, but he knew what all sap boilers know. Sitting around a hot arch on a cold March day, and sometimes boiling through the night, is not about economics. The hot steam swirls, the pulsing wood coals blast enough heat

Christopher Kimball

to cause a sunburn, the sap jumps and froths in the pans, and neighbors swap stories, some of them true. We are refugees, huddled in the dark around fires, sitting in lawn chairs like lesser kings of New England, convinced that we live in a world of our own making.

In my sap house, I sit with my 5-year-old son, Charlie, in front of our own small arch, watching the boil, making maple snowcones, throwing 2-inch bits of wood onto the hot fire every few minutes. Just down the dirt road, my neighbor Tom sugars with his now grown-up son, Nate, checking the taps, collecting the sap, and adjusting the float. Here we are, fathers and sons, sitting in shacks in late winter, working side by side, distilling memories into thick syrup. We follow the rules, boiling hot and fast, trying to prepare for the future. But as we stoke the fires, we sense that this easy partnership burns brightly for only a short while. Even summer tourists can see that in time, all sap houses turn wild, roof lines sagging, stinging nettles pushing up around the foundations. That is why Vermonters know to pay attention when it matters. In these sweet short years, even a moment's inattention can have serious consequences.

ABOUT COOK'S ILLUSTRATED

Visit our Web site The *Cook's* Web site features original editorial content not found in the magazine as well as searchable databases for recipes, equipment tests, and food tastings. The site also features our online bookstore, a question-and-answer message board, and a sign-up form for *e-Notes*, our free newsletter on cooking.

America's Test Kitchen television series. Look for our series currently airing on public television. For information visit www.americastestkitchen.com.

The Magazine *Cook's Illustrated* (ISSN 1068-2821) is published bimonthly (6 issues per year) by Boston Common Press Limited Partnership, 17 Station Street, Brookline, MA 02445. Copyright 2001 Boston Common Press Limited Partnership. Periodical postage paid at Boston, Mass., and additional mailing offices, USPS #012487. A one-year subscription is $29.70, two years is $55, and three years is $75. Add $6 postage per year for Canadian subscriptions and $12 per year for all other foreign countries. To order subscriptions in the U.S. call 800-526-8442; from outside the U.S. call 515-247-7571. Gift subscriptions are available for $24.95 each. Postmaster: Send all new orders, subscription inquiries, and change of address notices to *Cook's Illustrated*, P.O. Box 7446, Red Oak, IA 51591-0446.

Cookbooks and other products *Cook's Illustrated* offers cookbooks and magazine-related items for sale through its online bookstore. Products offered include annual hardbound editions of the magazine, an eight-year (1993–2000) reference index for the magazine, single-subject cookbooks from our How to Cook Master Series, as well as copies of *The Best Recipe, The Best Recipe: Grilling & Barbecue*, and many others. Prices and ordering information are available by calling 800-611-0759 inside the U.S. or 515-246-6911 from outside the U.S. or visiting our bookstore at www.cooksillustrated.com. Back issues of *Cook's Illustrated* are available for sale by calling 800-611-0759 inside the U.S. or 515-246-6911 from outside the U.S.

Questions about your book order? Visit our customer service page at www.cooksillustrated.com, or call 800-611-0759 inside the U.S. or 515-246-6911 from outside the U.S.

Reader submissions *Cook's* accepts reader submissions for Quick Tips. We will provide a one-year complimentary subscription for each tip that we print. Send your tip, name, address, and daytime telephone number to Quick Tips, *Cook's Illustrated*, P.O. Box 470589, Brookline, MA 02447. Questions, suggestions, or submissions for Notes from Readers should be sent to the same address.

Questions about your subscription? Go to www.cooksillustrated.com and visit our customer service page, where you can manage your subscription, including changing your address, renewing your subscription, paying your bill, or viewing answers to frequently asked questions. You can also direct questions about your subscription to *Cook's Illustrated*, P.O. Box 7446, Red Oak, IA 51591-0446, or call 800-526-8442 inside the U.S.; from outside the U.S. call 515-247-7571.

Meringues Defined

In baking books I've seen different names for meringues and different techniques for making them. Can you tell me how each is made and used?

LOUISE ABBOTT
LANCASTER, PA.

➤ Meringues are defined by their ingredients—egg whites and sugar—and distinguished by the techniques used to produce them. Known colloquially as French, Swiss, and Italian, the three types of meringues are made differently and have different applications.

For a French meringue, the raw egg whites are whipped with sugar (generally twice their weight) until they double in volume and become shiny and hold stiff peaks. Often in French meringues half the sugar is granulated and beaten in with a mixer; the other half is confectioners' sugar, folded in by hand at the end. A French meringue is particularly delicate and will deflate quickly if it is not used right away. It is spooned or piped into different shapes and baked. (It is interesting to note that a meringue is called a meringue when it is raw as well as baked.) A baked French meringue has a light, crisp texture, whether it is used for a dessert shell filled with ice cream or fruit or a cake layer sheathed with buttercream.

A Swiss meringue is prepared by whisking egg whites and sugar together over simmering water until they are quite warm to the touch (120 to 130 degrees) and the sugar has dissolved. At that point the mixture is transferred to an electric mixer and given a vigorous beating until the volume has doubled and the meringue is cool and stiff. More smooth and dense than a French meringue, a Swiss meringue is nevertheless fragile and must be used quickly after it is made. One of its best applications is as a base for buttercream frostings.

An Italian meringue is made by drizzling boiling sugar syrup (238 degrees, or at the softball stage) into whipped egg whites, which are then beaten in a mixer until they are cool and stiff. Because Italian meringues are the most stable of the three (the eggs are in effect poached, or stabilized, by the sugar syrup), they have a wide application and can be used in frostings, mousses, frozen parfaits, and buttercreams.

Professional pastry chefs rely on Italian meringues when constructing elaborate desserts.

The stability of each type of meringue is in part a function of the degree to which it is cooked. In the case of the French meringue, for instance, the meringue achieves stability only after it has been baked. Sugar, which attracts water molecules, stabilizes a French meringue in the oven by delaying the evaporation of water until after the egg whites have coagulated, or cooked. An Italian meringue, on the other hand, is given a dose of hot sugar syrup that raises the temperature of the whites to more than 160 degrees. It is completely cooked when it comes off the mixer. It can be used straight out of the bowl. In terms of stability, a Swiss meringue falls between the two.

In a Jam

I make your refrigerator jams (see "Quick Refrigerator Fruit Jams," July/August 1998) every summer and my family loves them. In the winter, however, we buy commercial jams. It occurred to me recently that I don't really know what makes jellies, jams, and preserves different. Can you explain?

LYNN JACOBS
GRAND RAPIDS, MICH.

➤ Commercial jellies, jams, and preserves are all made in the same basic manner: by cooking fruit down with sugar and an acid. What differentiates the trio, according to the standards of identity regulated by the U.S. Food and Drug Administration (FDA), are the size and structure of the fruit products used. Jellies are made with fruit juices and cook up into thick, clear, homogeneous mixtures. Jams contain fruit pieces (crushed, chopped, sliced, or pureed) and have a slightly chunky, slightly firm texture. Preserves are made with large chunks or even whole fruits and are usually described as fruit suspended in thick syrup.

To meet FDA requirements, all three products must be prepared with at least 45 percent fruit and no more than 55 percent sugar by weight. Compared with *Cook's* refrigerator jams, which call for as little as 33 percent sugar, the standardized ratio may seem sugar-heavy. It's true that commercial jellies, jams, and preserves can be exceedingly sweet, but the sugar is there for more than flavor. When sugar and water molecules bond, the water is no longer available to microorganisms, such as bacteria and some molds and yeasts, which need water to survive. The sugar, along with airtight packaging, makes these products nonperishable until opened.

Another FDA regulation associated with the trio dictates the amount of pectin they may contain. Pectin is a high-fiber carbohydrate with thickening properties that occurs naturally in the cell walls of various fruits. According to law, to obtain optimal spreading consistency manufacturers are allowed to add an amount of pectin sufficient to compensate for a deficiency, if any, in the natural pectin content of a particular fruit—and no more.

Getting to Know Garlic

I enjoyed your article on pasta with garlic and oil (March/April 2001) and understand the importance of fresh garlic in a recipe like this. But are there dishes in which I can get away with using garlic powder or dry minced garlic? What are the differences between these products?

WADE JEFFERS
DENVER, COLO.

➤ Tasting and discerning the subtle and delicate flavor ranges of fresh garlic was an odoriferous undertaking that had us breathing fire for days. Happily, explaining the differences between garlic powder and dehydrated minced garlic is an easier endeavor. Garlic powder comes from cloves of garlic that have been dehydrated and then pulverized to form a powder. Dehydrated minced garlic, as the name implies, is minced while fresh and then dehydrated and packaged as is. Garlic powder and dehydrated minced garlic have essentially the same potency—¼ teaspoon of each is equivalent to 1 fresh clove—but their flavor overall is much more subdued than that of fresh garlic. That's because the dehydration process mellows the sharp, acidic flavors of raw garlic—a plus for those who find fresh garlic too pungent, a minus for those of us who love it.

According to Pamela Penzey of Penzeys Spices in Muskego, Wis., the primary difference between garlic powder and dehydrated minced garlic is the speed at which their flavor develops when added to a recipe. The flavor of garlic powder comes out immediately because its tiny grains hydrate instantly in the presence of moisture, making it perfect for sprinkling on meat, poultry, fish, pasta, or vegetables. Dehydrated minced garlic needs a little more time to rehydrate and thus works best in braises, stews, and soups. Penzey adds that it is imperative to mix dehydrated minced garlic with a small amount of water before adding it to a dish with acidic ingredients. Otherwise, the acid will inhibit the flavor from developing.

In our opinion, when it comes to garlic, there's nothing like the real thing. But if you're in a pinch, or don't care for the naturally intense, sometimes biting flavor of fresh garlic, garlic powder and dehydrated minced garlic are acceptable substitutes. But do go the extra mile and buy—mail-order if you must—high-quality dehydrated garlic products. They cost only a little more than grocery store brands, but their taste is far superior.

Buttermilk
My family loves your Coleslaw with Bacon and Buttermilk Dressing (September/October 1999), especially with barbecue in the summer. When I made it recently, I realized that I was using "cultured nonfat buttermilk" as opposed to the "cultured reduced-fat buttermilk" I normally use. We didn't notice a flavor difference, but it made me wonder exactly what buttermilk is and how nonfat buttermilk differs from reduced fat. Is one of them better in the coleslaw dressing?

SAMANTHA SMITH
RICHMOND, VA.

☛ *Buttermilk* is a misleading word. Many assume the product is infused with butter and high in fat, when the truth is quite the opposite. The name refers to the watery end product of butter making—the "milk" left behind after the solid fat has been removed through the process of churning cream into butter. Years ago buttermilk was a popular beverage, esteemed for its light, watery consistency and crisp, tangy flavor. Like most things modern, however, buttermilk is no longer the simple liquid just described.

Today, buttermilk is a fermented product made by adding lactic acid–producing bacteria (usually *Streptococci* or *Lactobacilli*) to pasteurized or ultrapasteurized milk (for an explanation of pasteurization see "Pasteurized Cream" in Notes from Readers, May/June 2001). The milk is heated to 72 degrees, and the harmless bacteria convert lactose (milk sugar) to lactic acid, which gives the final product a slightly thickened, rich texture and tangy, somewhat salty flavor. The ripening process is complete within 14 hours, at which point the milk is cooled to 45 degrees to halt fermentation. Sometimes butter flakes (also called liquid butter) are added to give the velvety liquid a "churned" look and feel. More often than not, salt and/or citric acid is added to enhance flavor.

There are several kinds of buttermilk in the dairy case these days: cultured buttermilk, cultured reduced-fat buttermilk, and cultured skim (nonfat or fat-free) buttermilk. The first is made with whole milk, and the others, as their names imply, with reduced fat and skim milks. Fat content correlates directly with the type of milk used and can vary from producer to producer, but it is never higher than 3.25 percent, the percentage of fat in whole milk. Markets north of the Mason-Dixon line generally carry only reduced-fat and nonfat buttermilk. Whole milk buttermilk is extremely hard to come by unless you are in the South. It's so scarce up North that we couldn't get our hands on any to test it. The difference in fat content between the reduced-fat and nonfat brands we found in our local market was a mere 0.5 percent. In our opinion, there is little difference between them. Tasted side by side, we noticed a slight difference in texture—the nonfat buttermilk was just a tad runnier than the reduced fat—but they both had an equally tangy flavor. When we made our Coleslaw with Bacon and Buttermilk Dressing with each one, we could discern no difference in texture. So use whichever you can find. The dressing will be tasty with either one.

Measuring Grill Temperature
My charcoal grill doesn't have a thermometer, and I have a hard time figuring out if my fire is hot, medium-hot, and so on. Is there a simple way to test the fire's intensity?

CANDICE ELMORE
SAN DIEGO, CALIF.

☛ There is an easy way to determine the intensity of a fire's heat, and it works for both charcoal and gas grills. With charcoal, once you have started the coals (*Cook's* recommends lighting the coals in a chimney to start the fire quickly) and they are covered with a layer of gray ash, distribute the coals on the grill bottom, put the cooking grate in place, and allow the grate to heat up for about five minutes. On a gas grill, preheat with the lid down and all burners on high for about 15 minutes. Take the temperature of either type of fire by holding your hand 5 inches above the cooking grate and counting the number of seconds you can leave it there comfortably. With a hot fire, you'll be able to hold your hand above the grate for only 2 seconds. With a medium-hot fire, you'll be able to keep your hand there for 3 to 4 seconds; a medium fire, 5 to 6 seconds; and a medium-low fire, 7 seconds. When using a gas grill, you may just as well ignore the built-in thermometer with its general readings of medium, medium-high, or high in favor of the hand-testing method, which is much more accurate.

Dutch Oven Clarification
While developing our Ultimate Fried Chicken recipe for the May/June 2001 issue of the magazine, we tested various pots and pans, including a cast-iron skillet and three so-called Dutch ovens. One of these three, the All-Clad, turned out to be a source of confusion for some readers because we referred to it as a Dutch oven while the All-Clad company itself sells it as a "stockpot." All-Clad does indeed manufacture a pot that it sells as a Dutch oven, but it looks and behaves very differently from its stockpot.

In our January/February 1998 testing of Dutch ovens, we defined the Dutch oven as a wide, deep pot with a lid and used this definition to determine which pots we would test. We preferred straight-sided pots with 6- to 8-quart capacities and large interior cooking surfaces. The All-Clad 8-quart stockpot was included in this testing.

What All-Clad calls its Dutch oven has a capacity of only 5½ quarts and sloping sides that taper at the base to make for a bottom surface area that is much smaller than that of its stockpot. When faced with frying chicken, we chose to test the All-Clad stockpot instead of the Dutch oven because its shape and size were better suited to the task. In the fried chicken story we mistakenly labeled the stockpot as a Dutch oven. We regret any confusion this may have caused.

WHAT IS IT?

I found this contraption in a basket labeled "miscellaneous kitchen gadgets" at a tag sale. Can you tell me what miscellaneous function it performs?

PETER MURRAY
LOUISVILLE, KY.

The small plastic gadget you discovered is an orange peeler. A hot item at orange stands in Florida and in kitchen stores with extensive gadgetry sections, this inexpensive, snail-like little tool is an excellent alternative to the typical fingernail-dig or bite-start technique used to start peeling an orange. To use it, slip your pointer finger through the ring and press the curved surface against the top of the orange, letting the sharp tooth pierce the skin. When the tooth is firmly in place, move the contraption over the skin with a downward motion, making a clean slice. Repeat the motion across sections of the orange, and the skin will easily peel free from the fruit.

Quick Tips

Corn on the Kebab

Grill cooks who like pieces of corn on the cob on their kebabs know how difficult it can be to impale them on the skewer, especially when using bamboo. Christine Lins of Apple Valley, Minn., starts by running a corkscrew through the cob pieces before skewering them. The puncture makes it easier to run the skewer through, and the coiled hole helps ensure a snug fit.

Draining Hot Boiled Corn

Boiled corn on the cob is a backyard summer staple, but how to drain all those bulky ears at once when a colander is too small? Rather than juggling ear after ear in a cramped colander, Dwight Collin of Mt. Riga, Conn., puts all the corn into a clean, empty dish rack as he removes them from the pot. The rack accommodates many more ears than a colander.

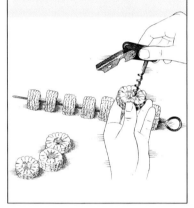

Improvising in a Summer Rental Kitchen

With summer in full swing, *Cook's* readers often find themselves cooking in unfamiliar and meagerly equipped kitchens in all manner of rented cottages, cabins, condos, and shanties by the sea, lake, mountain, or farm. Here are some improvisations a few clever readers came up with when they didn't have exactly what they needed.

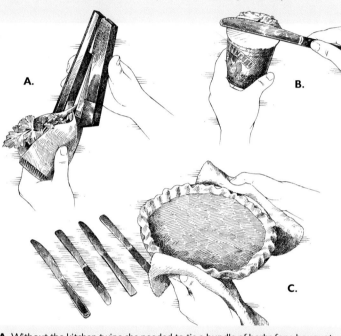

A. Without the kitchen twine she needed to tie a bundle of herbs for a bouquet garni, Katherine Failing of Indianola, Miss., made an herb sachet by placing the herbs in a cone-shaped paper coffee filter, folding the top over, and stapling it to seal.
B. Ernest Zickrick of St. Cloud, Minn., found that the kitchen in his vacation rental lacked a set of measuring cups. He substituted cleaned yogurt containers: the 4-ounce size for ½ cup, the 6-ounce size for ¾ cup, and the 8-ounce size for a full cup.
C. With a pie to cool and no rack to cool it on, Emily Lewis of Loveland, Ohio, jury-rigged a cooling rack by laying four dinner knives on the counter, alternating the direction of the blades and spacing them more than an inch apart. The knives were stable, and they elevated the pie as much as most racks would.

Another Way to Transport Knives Safely

Inspired by a July/August 1998 Quick Tip on wrapping knives in cone-shaped paper coffee filters for safe transport to picnics and cookouts, Eric Sutphin of San Francisco, Calif., offered his own twist on the same trick. Since he always brings a roll of paper towels to picnics anyway, he simply inserts the knife blade into the paper towel roll. Most rolls easily accommodate the blade of an 8- or 10-inch chef's knife.

Easiest Grill Cleaning

No matter how you do it, emptying a kettle grill of cool ashes is a messy procedure. Don Camp of Philadelphia, Pa., neatens things up by fashioning a grill scoop out of a plastic one-quart or half-gallon milk jug with a handle.

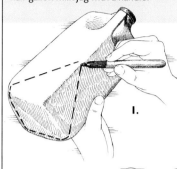

1. Cut off a bottom corner of the jug to form a scoop.
2. The plastic conforms to the curve of the grill bottom, which makes it easier to collect more ashes with a single sweep.

Easier Pepper Mill Loading, Redux

Anyone who has filled a pepper mill using a funnel knows how frustrating it is when the peppercorns jam in the neck. In a January/February 2001 Quick Tip, Darcie O'Grady proposed her solution: substitute a rubber garlic peeler for the funnel. Diane Hazen of Jackson, Wyo., devised another solution. Cut out the bottom of a small plastic soda or water bottle. A bottle neck is small enough to fit easily into the mouth of a pepper mill but is wider than a funnel neck, so no jamming will occur.

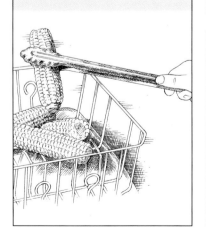

Send Us Your Tip We will provide a complimentary one-year subscription for each tip we print. See page 1 for information.

Impromptu Basting Brush

Not many households stock extra pastry brushes to use just for basting, especially for foods on the grill. When John Abbattemateo of Pembroke, Mass., is short of a brush to apply marinades and sauces, he gets the job done with a large lettuce leaf.

Brushless Grill Rack Cleaning

Food that is being grilled is much less likely to stick to a clean grate. We recommend cleaning the hot grate with a wire brush designed for that purpose specifically. When Marianne Somolik of Scottsdale, Ariz., recently found herself without a brush, she improvised with a pair of tongs and a crumpled wad of aluminum foil, which cleaned the grate beautifully.

Slashing the Loaf Neatly

Often when you slash the top of a proofed loaf of bread prior to baking it, the blade will snag a bit of dough and drag it out of shape. To avoid this small annoyance, Jon Paul Tilley of Philadelphia, Pa., sprays the blade lightly with cooking spray so it will travel through the dough smoothly.

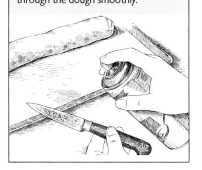

Restarting a Grill Fire

When a charcoal fire peters out before it really gets started, you can douse it with lighter fluid and toss on a match, which creates a thrilling ball of flame. Some grillers, including Lucas Price of Telluride, Colo., prefer a tamer, safer approach. Assuming the grill is placed close enough to an outdoor power outlet, simply turn an electric hair dryer to high and aim it toward the base of the pile of coals. The air flow acts as a bellows to get the fire going again in just a few minutes—without a dangerous ball of flames.

Charcoal Prep

Hoisting a huge bag of charcoal to pour some into a chimney starter can be messy and difficult, especially when you are dressed nicely for a summer dinner party. To get around this sloppy situation, try this tip submitted by Jim Matfiak of Manhattan Beach, Calif.

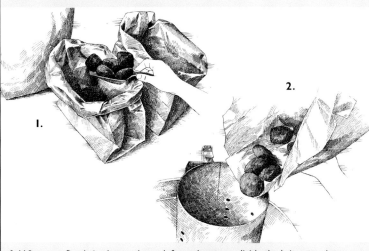

1. When you first bring home the sack from the store, divide the briquettes into smaller bags, about 4 quarts (50 briquettes) to a bag.
2. When you need to build a fire, just cut a large hole in the bottom of an individual bag, and the charcoal flows right into the chimney without mess or strain.

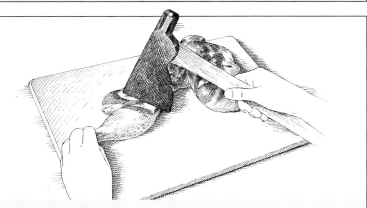

Cleaver Substitute

In our recipe for Hearty Chicken Noodle Soup (March/April 1996), we recommend hacking chicken parts into 2-inch pieces with a meat cleaver, heavy chef's knife, or heavy-duty kitchen shears. With none of those tools on hand, Jodie Wright of Paonia, Colo., made do with a new hatchet from the hardware store. It not only worked beautifully but also cost under $10.

Better Vase for Herbs

A good way to store fresh herbs such as basil or parsley is stems down in a water-filled glass, with the leaves covered by a plastic bag. But the leaves and the bag make the setup top-heavy and prone to tips and spills in the refrigerator.

Daphne Keller of Red Bank, N.J., suggests making a more stable container from a one-quart or half-gallon plastic milk jug.

Summer Flour Storage

Readers who live in humid climates probably know firsthand that flour absorbs moisture from the air, which in turns adds weight when you weigh it out for a recipe.
A. Bonnie Famely of Lexington, Mass., limits the rate of moisture absorption by storing her flour in the freezer. This method also eliminates the possibility of bug infestation in her flour.

B. Those who may not have enough freezer space to take Bonnie Famely's advice can try this tip from Linda Sapp of Cross Lanes, W. Va. She stores her flour in a microwave oven. When she needs to use the microwave, she just removes the flour, replacing it when she's finished.

Grilled Chicken Cutlets

Boneless chicken can turn dry and leathery on the grill. For tender, juicy cutlets that won't dry out, brine the meat, then cook it quickly over high heat.

≳ BY BRIDGET LANCASTER ≲

Cut from the breast and stripped of bones and skin, chicken cutlets are the essence of convenience. Unfortunately, that convenience comes at a price. With no skin or bones to protect and flavor the meat, chicken cutlets can cook up into tasteless, dry pieces of leather in no time flat. Throwing the cutlets on the grill only compounds the problem. In the time it takes to say "briquette," the cutlets can overcook into a carbon-flavored nightmare. Then there's the shape of the chicken breast: thick at one end, thin at the other. The meat never seems to cook evenly. But during hot summer days I'll try anything to avoid turning on the oven. I wanted to find a trouble-free way to grill cutlets that were tasty and tender, with plump, juicy meat and an attractive seared exterior. That would mean negotiating a truce between fire and flavor.

Playing with Fire

When it comes to grilling, temperature is key. Texture, moistness, and flavor are all affected by the degree of fire. So I hauled out bags of charcoal, lit the chimney starter, and began the testing.

Just about every cookbook offers a way to grill boneless chicken breasts, and I tried them all. My tests fell into three categories: single-level fires, in which the grill cooks at one constant temperature; two-level fires, in which the grill is set up to cook at two different temperatures; and covered cooking, in which the meat is cooked under the cover of the grill or tented with an aluminum pan.

From the start I had very good luck with single-level fires, especially at high heat. Medium and low heat did not provide a good sear; without any fat from the skin, the interior overcooked in the time necessary to color the exterior. High heat produced the most attractive chicken breasts, turning them a deep golden brown. At this temperature the chicken cooked up in only three minutes per side and produced the least dry meat. Unfortunately, the breasts did not cook evenly; the thin tapered end was almost inedible. I wanted to find a way to cook the breasts evenly, but grilling the unevenly shaped pieces at any temperature was bound to produce uneven results. Playing around with different grilling times provided no relief.

I decided to remove the tenderloins and then pound the breasts to an even thickness. Once

Perfect for salad, our chicken cutlets cook in only four minutes.

again, I threw the chicken breasts on the hot grill, this time pounded to within ½ inch of their lives. These cutlets cooked evenly, and now the grilling time was reduced to two minutes per side. Talk about fast food! Another benefit of the cutlets' now-flat surface was that they browned evenly. The interior was relatively juicy although not as moist as I had hoped. But I was headed in the right direction.

Next I tried working with a two-level fire, a method that we use with much success at *Cook's*. Building a high heat on one side of the grill, I tested medium and low heat on the other side. Although both batches colored relatively well from the initial sear over high heat, the meat overcooked and started to toughen when left to finish cooking on the cooler side of the grill. It was now clear that the less time the chicken spent on the grill—no matter what the temperature—the better the texture of the meat.

Hoping to further expedite the process, I tried cooking the chicken under the grill cover. It cooked in record time, but the flavor of carbon from the charcoal briquettes was overwhelming. I decided to try a method we had used in our story "How to Grill Bone-In Chicken Breasts"

(July/August 1997). Working with a two-level fire, I started the breasts over direct heat to get a good sear and then moved them to an area with no coals, covered them with a disposable aluminum pan, and let them finish cooking in this makeshift oven. This method is great when the concern is cooking the meat through to the bone, but for boneless breasts it had no advantage over the simpler direct-fire, high-heat method.

Finding the Flavor Within

Grilled or not, chicken breasts are decidedly mild-tasting. My next round of tests included methods to add flavor—marinating, basting, using spice rubs and pastes, and brining.

Marinating proved the most disappointing. Although the meat was pounded relatively thin, it took several hours of soaking in an oil and lemon juice marinade to make any flavor difference. I tried poking holes in the chicken breasts, but this caused no appreciable improvement in flavor. In addition, the appearance of the marinated chicken suffered greatly from the frequent flare-ups caused by the dripping oil. Basting the chicken breasts with flavored oils and vinaigrettes was inconvenient; in the four minutes it took to grill the cutlets, little flavor was imparted, but flames again leaped up from the coals. I had high hopes for the spice rubs and pastes but these, too, disappointed. Though well suited to more robust cuts of meat and poultry, the rubs and pastes all but decimated the flavor of the cutlets.

Finally, I tested brining, a method used often in *Cook's* test kitchen, in which poultry is soaked in a saltwater solution to promote flavor and juiciness. In conjunction with the quick, high-heat fire, this turned out to be the key to perfect grilled chicken breasts. After experimenting with different salt ratios and soaking times, I found that a high concentration of salt penetrates the thin cutlets in a short amount of time—30 minutes, to be exact, about the same amount of time it takes to fire up the grill. These cutlets were well seasoned, juicy, and very tender. I added sugar to the brine, which not only improved the flavor of the cutlets but also their appearance as the sugar caramelized on the exterior, adding more color. These cutlets were ready to step up to the plate as the basis for quick, satisfying salads and sandwiches or to be served with a salsa, relish, or chutney accompaniment.

CHARCOAL-GRILLED CHICKEN CUTLETS
SERVES 6 TO 8

To save time, the chicken cutlets are brined while the fire gets going. Try them in our salad recipe or with our relish or salsa (recipes follow). They're also great served simply with lemon or lime wedges.

- 8 boneless, skinless chicken breasts (about 6 ounces each), trimmed of excess fat, tenderloins removed (see illustration, right) and reserved for another use
- 1/2 cup kosher salt or 1/4 cup table salt
- 1/2 cup sugar
  Ground black pepper
  Vegetable oil

1. Pound chicken breasts to even 1/2-inch thickness.

2. In gallon-sized zipper-lock plastic bag, dissolve salt and sugar in 1 quart cold water. Add chicken and seal bag, pressing out as much air as possible; refrigerate 30 minutes. Remove from brine, dry thoroughly with paper towels, and sprinkle with pepper.

3. While chicken is brining, ignite about 6 quarts (1 large chimney, or about 6 pounds) charcoal briquettes and burn until completely covered with thin coating of light gray ash, 20 to 30 minutes. Spread coals evenly over grill bottom, then spread additional 6 quarts unlit briquettes over lit coals. Position grill rack over coals and heat until very hot, about 15 minutes (you can hold your hand 5 inches above grill surface no longer than 2 seconds).

4. Lightly brush both sides of chicken breasts with vegetable oil. Grill uncovered until light brown, 2 to 3 minutes on each side.

GAS-GRILLED CHICKEN CUTLETS

Follow steps 1 and 2 of Charcoal-Grilled Chicken Cutlets. While chicken is brining, turn all burners on gas grill to high, close lid, and heat until hot, 10 to 15 minutes. Continue with recipe from step 4, grilling chicken breasts uncovered, 3 to 4 minutes on each side.

CUCUMBER AND MANGO RELISH WITH YOGURT
MAKES 1 3/4 CUPS

- 1 large cucumber (about 8 ounces), peeled, seeded, and cut into 1/4-inch cubes

---

TECHNIQUE | GETTING EVEN

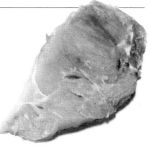

Tenderloin Attached
Most chicken breasts are packaged with their tenderloins attached.

Tenderloin Removed
For a more uniform piece, detach the tenderloin. Use your fingers to pull it away from the breast.

Pounded Cutlet
Pounding the breasts to uniform thickness will ensure even cooking.

- 1 large mango (about 1 pound), peeled and cut into 1/4-inch cubes
- 1 medium jalapeño chile, seeded and minced
- 1/4 cup plain yogurt
- 1/2 teaspoon sugar
- 1/4 teaspoon ground cardamom
- 1 tablespoon chopped fresh mint leaves
  Salt

In small bowl, combine cucumber, mango, jalapeño, yogurt, sugar, cardamom, and mint; season to taste with salt. Cover and refrigerate at least 30 minutes to blend flavors.

SPICY TOMATILLO AND PINEAPPLE SALSA
MAKES 2 CUPS

Be sure to use a ripe pineapple. Tomatillos are very tart—blanching softens their texture and their sour edge.

- 6 small tomatillos (about 8 ounces), husked
- 1/2 large pineapple, cut into 1/2-inch cubes (about 3 cups)
- 1 chipotle chile en adobo, minced (about 1 teaspoon)
- 1 teaspoon juice from 1 lime
  Salt

1. Bring 1 quart water to boil in small saucepan over high heat; boil tomatillos until skins start to pucker, about 5 minutes. With slotted spoon, remove tomatillos to bowl of ice water to stop cooking. When cool enough to handle, core tomatillos and cut into 1/2-inch cubes.

2. Toss tomatillos, pineapple, chipotle chile, lime juice, and salt to taste in medium bowl. Cover and refrigerate at least 30 minutes to blend flavors.

GRILLED CHICKEN SALAD WITH SESAME-MISO DRESSING
SERVES 4 TO 6 AS A LIGHT MAIN COURSE

This recipe uses a half recipe of the grilled chicken cutlets. Halve the brine ingredients, but brine for the same length of time.

- 2 tablespoons white miso
- 1 tablespoon honey
- 1 tablespoon soy sauce
- 2 tablespoons peanut oil
- 2 tablespoons sesame seeds, toasted and crushed
- 1 scallion, sliced thin
- 1/2 recipe Charcoal- or Gas-Grilled Chicken Cutlets, cut crosswise into 1/2-inch wide strips
- 10 cups mesclun, washed and dried

Whisk together miso, honey, soy sauce, and 2 tablespoons water in medium bowl; gradually whisk in peanut oil, then stir in sesame seeds and scallion. Toss chicken with 2 tablespoons dressing in large bowl. Add mesclun and remaining dressing; toss to combine. Divide salad among individual plates; serve immediately.

TECHNIQUE | DIAMOND-PATTERN GRILL MARKS

1. Place each cutlet on grill so its length runs at a diagonal to the grate bars.

2. With tongs, turn each cutlet 45 degrees to achieve a diamond pattern.

3. Flip each cutlet over and repeat.

Really Good Gazpacho

Hand-cut vegetables marinated in seasoned vinegar make the difference.

⋺ BY ADAM RIED ⋹

azpacho is high summer in a bowl. Popular on both sides of the Atlantic, this ice-cold uncooked vegetable soup, made principally of tomatoes (whole and juice), cucumbers, bell peppers, and onion and seasoned with olive oil and vinegar, is sometimes referred to as "liquid salad" in its native Spain. That expression may be more apt on these shores, though, where many recipes simply instruct the cook to puree all the vegetables together in the blender. Needless to say, the resulting mixture is a thin porridge with an anonymous vegetal flavor. I was looking for a soup with clearly flavored, distinct pieces of vegetable in a bracing tomato broth.

It's little wonder, then, that texture is one key to a great gazpacho. As you might imagine, philosophies about what is the right texture and how to achieve it vary considerably. Traditionally, gazpacho was thickened with water-soaked bread for extra body, but a number of the recipes I looked at skipped the bread altogether. Some called for putting the mixture through a fine sieve to create a silky smooth texture, while others left it chunky. Clearly, thickening, method of manufacture (as it relates to both texture and flavor), and seasoning were important questions to explore.

Through Thick and Thin

In deference to tradition, I started by trying a number of bread-thickened gazpachos. No matter what kind of bread was used or how long it was soaked, my tasters and I consistently favored breadless brews. The consensus was that the bread-thickened soups had a subtle but inescapable pastiness. It was the same with the gazpachos that were passed (rather laboriously, I might add) through a sieve. Their texture was too uniform for a soup that featured fresh vegetables. Like me, my tasters called for an interplay between recognizable pieces of vegetable and a light tomato broth.

With our preference for a chunky-style soup established, we had to figure out the best method for preparing the vegetables. Although it was a breeze to use, the blender broke down the vegetables beyond recognition, which was not at all what I wanted. The food processor fared somewhat better, especially when I processed each vegetable separately. This method had distinct pros and cons. On the pro side were ease and the fact that the vegetables released some juice as they broke down, which helped flavor the soup. The cons were that no matter how I finessed the pulse feature, the vegetable pieces were neither neatly

A brisk tomato broth studded with small, uniform chunks of summer vegetables makes our ideal gazpacho.

chopped nor consistently sized. This was especially true of the tomatoes, which disintegrated into pulp. The texture of the resulting soup was more along the lines of a vegetable slushy—acceptable, but far from ideal. (On balance, though, the food processor is a decent option, especially if you favor speed and convenience, so we've included a recipe based on its use.)

And so I pressed on to the old-fashioned, purist method: chopping the vegetables by hand. The benefits to the gazpacho's texture were dazzling. Because the vegetable pieces were consistent in size and shape, they not only retained their individual flavors but also set off the tomato broth beautifully,

adding immeasurably to the whole. This was just what we were after.

One last procedural issue to investigate was the resting time. Gazpacho is best served ice cold, and the chilling time also allows the flavors to develop and meld. We tasted every hour for eight hours and found that four hours was the minimum time required for the soup to chill and the flavors to blossom.

Investigating Ingredients

Several of gazpacho's key ingredients and seasonings also bore some exploration. Tomatoes are the star player, and we preferred beefsteak to plum because they were larger, juicier, and easier to chop. Gazpacho is truly a dish best made when local tomatoes are plentiful. I made several batches using handsome supermarket tomatoes, but the flavor paled in comparison. When it came to peppers, tasters preferred red to green for their sweeter flavor. But red was unpopular in the onion department; tasters rejected red onions—as well as plain yellow—as too sharp. Instead we favored sweet onions, such as Vidalia or Maui, equally with shallots. To ensure thorough seasoning of the whole mixture, I marinated the vegetables briefly in the garlic, salt, pepper, and vinegar before adding the bulk of the liquid. These batches had more balanced flavors than the batches that were seasoned after all the other ingredients had been combined.

The liquid component was also critical. Most recipes called for tomato juice, which we sampled both straight and mixed in various amounts with water and low-sodium canned chicken broth. The

TASTING: **Tomato Juice**

To drown vine-ripened vegetables in inferior tomato juice and call it gazpacho is a travesty. So we blind-tasted seven leading brands. The lineup included tomato juices from R. W. Knudsen, Muir Glen, Campbell's, and Welch's and vegetable juices from V-8, Muir Glen, and Fresh Samantha, a small East Coast company working its way toward national distribution. Tasters assessed the color, flavor, and viscosity of each juice, straight up and in gazpacho. Juices perceived to be too thick, acidic, or salty were downgraded, and those thought to taste more tomatoey or fresh were favored. V-8, Knudsen, and both Muir Glen entries were judged too thick; the Knudsen and Muir Glen tomato juices were deemed too acidic; and V-8 was considered too salty. While Campbell's did not receive uniformly negative comments, neither was it among most tasters' top choices. The juices that were rated tops, Fresh Samantha and Welch's, had distinctly different flavor profiles. Fresh Samantha was termed spicy and peppery but fresh tasting, Welch's straightforward, tomatoey, and mellow. Neither of these juices was judged "pasty," a criticism that felled some other juices. –A.R.

THE WINNERS

Welch's   Fresh Samantha

winning ratio was 5 cups of tomato juice thinned with 1 cup of water. The water cut the viscosity of the juice just enough to make it brothy and light but not downright thin. Given our preference for ice-cold gazpacho, I decided to add ice cubes instead of straight water. The ice helped chill the soup while providing water as it melted.

Finally, a word about gazpacho's two primary seasonings, vinegar and olive oil. With Spain being a noted producer of sherry, it follows that sherry vinegar is a popular choice for gazpacho. When we tasted it, along with champagne, red wine, and white wine vinegars, the sherry vinegar was the favorite by far, adding not only acidity but richness and depth as well. If you find that your stock of sherry vinegar has run dry, try white wine vinegar, our runner-up. Olive oil contributes both flavor and a lush mouthfeel to this simple soup, and only extra-virgin will do. Liquid or not, would you dress a beautiful summer salad with anything less?

GAZPACHO
MAKES ABOUT 3 QUARTS, SERVING 8 TO 10

Traditionally, diners garnish their gazpacho with more of the same diced vegetables that are in the soup, so cut some extra vegetables when you prepare those called for in the recipe. Additional garnish possibilities include simple garlic croutons (see recipe), chopped pitted black olives, chopped hard-cooked eggs, and finely diced avocados. For a finishing touch, serve in chilled bowls.

- 3 ripe medium beefsteak tomatoes (about 1 1/2 pounds), cored and cut into 1/4-inch cubes following illustrations, right (about 4 cups)
- 2 small red bell peppers (about 1 pound), cored, seeded, and cut into 1/4-inch cubes following illustrations, right (about 2 cups)
- 2 small cucumbers (about 1 pound), one peeled and the other with skin on, both seeded and cut into 1/4-inch cubes following illustrations, right (about 2 cups)
- 1/2 small sweet onion (such as Vidalia, Maui, or Walla Walla) or 2 large shallots, peeled and minced (about 1/2 cup)
- 2 medium garlic cloves, minced
- 2 teaspoons salt
- 1/3 cup sherry vinegar
  Ground black pepper
- 5 cups tomato juice, preferably Welch's
- 1 teaspoon hot pepper sauce (optional)
- 8 ice cubes
  Extra-virgin olive oil for serving

Combine tomatoes and their juices, bell peppers, cucumbers, onion, garlic, salt, vinegar, and pepper to taste in large (at least 4-quart) nonreactive bowl; let stand until vegetables just begin to release their juices, about 5 minutes. Stir in tomato juice, hot pepper sauce, if using, and ice cubes; cover tightly and refrigerate to blend flavors, at least 4 hours.

BLENDED Too much time in the blender yields tomato slush.

OVER-PROCESSED Overpulsing creates uneven, pulpy vegetable bits.

HAND-CHOPPED Hand-chopping retains vibrant color and firm texture.

Adjust seasonings with salt and pepper, remove and discard any unmelted ice cubes, and serve cold, drizzling each portion with about 1 teaspoon extra-virgin olive oil and with desired garnishes (see note). (Can be covered and refrigerated up to 2 days.)

QUICK FOOD PROCESSOR GAZPACHO

Using the same ingredients and quantities as for Gazpacho, core and quarter tomatoes and process in workbowl of food processor fitted with steel blade until broken down into 1/4- to 3/4-inch pieces, about 12 one-second pulses; transfer to large bowl. Cut cored and seeded peppers and seeded cucumbers into rough 1-inch pieces and process separately until broken down into 1/4- to 3/4-inch pieces, about 12 one-second pulses; add to bowl with tomatoes. Mince onion and garlic by hand, then add to bowl with vegetables along with salt, vinegar, and ground black pepper to taste; continue with recipe.

GARLIC CROUTONS
MAKES ABOUT 3 CUPS

- 2 large garlic cloves, finely minced or pressed through garlic press
- 1/4 teaspoon salt
- 3 tablespoons extra-virgin olive oil
- 3 cups 1/2-inch white bread cubes (from baguette or country loaf)

Adjust rack to middle position and heat oven to 350 degrees. Combine garlic, salt, and oil in small bowl; let stand 20 minutes, then pour through fine-mesh strainer into medium bowl. Add bread cubes and toss to coat. Spread bread cubes in even layer on rimmed baking sheet and bake, stirring occasionally, until golden, about 15 minutes. Cool on baking sheet to room temperature. (Can be covered and stored at room temperature up to 24 hours.)

TECHNIQUE | CHOPPING THE VEGETABLES

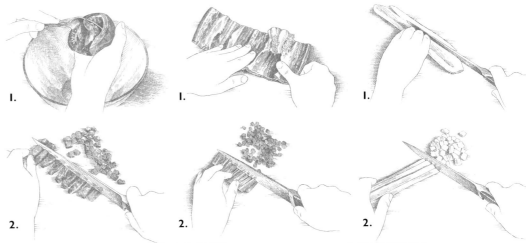

TOMATOES

1. Core tomatoes, halve them pole to pole, and, working over a bowl to catch all the juices, scoop out the inner pulp and seeds. Chop the tomato pulp into 1/4-inch cubes.
2. Cut tomato halves into 1/4-inch slices. Turn slices 90 degrees, so they are parallel with the edge of the work surface, and cut into 1/4-inch cubes.

PEPPERS

1. Slice a 3/4-inch section off both the tip and stem ends of the peppers. Make one slit in the trimmed shells, place skin-sides down, and open the flesh.
2. Scrape off seeds and membranes. Cut flesh into 1/4-inch strips. Turn the strips 90 degrees, so they are parallel with the work surface edge, and cut into 1/4-inch cubes.

CUCUMBERS

1. Cut a 3/4-inch section off both ends of cucumbers. Halve cucumbers lengthwise and scoop out seeds with a spoon. Cut each seeded half lengthwise into 1/4-inch strips.
2. Turn strips 90 degrees, so they are parallel with the work surface edge, and cut into even 1/4-inch cubes.

Backyard-Grill Potato Salad

Potatoes cooked on the grill deliver smoky flavor, but they are usually either charred or undercooked in the center. Here is how to do it right.

⇒ BY RAQUEL PELZEL ⇐

Grilled potato salad is the perfect backyard-barbecue dish. But grilling potatoes can be a challenge, requiring a deft hand and a good dose of patience on the part of the grill master. If the fire is too hot, all you're going to get is a raw-on-the-inside, burnt-on-the-outside spud. But if you're nursing a modest, low-fire grill, your potatoes are more likely to be served alongside tomorrow's bacon and eggs than with your burger.

When researching different ways to grill potatoes, I was confronted time and time again with the order to blanch the potatoes in boiling water first and then transfer them to the grill just long enough to char slightly. The advantage to this is that the potatoes finish cooking on the grill in the same time it takes for the skin to color. I wondered if it would be possible to cook the potatoes entirely on the grill.

I grilled two different types of potatoes—russets and Yukon Golds—in three different ways: diced and then skewered, cut into rounds, and diced and grilled on a grill pan (a perforated pan that allows you to grill small items without risk of their falling through the grill grate). I used a medium-hot grill. After I took the potatoes off the grill, I immediately dressed each with a simple vinaigrette. To my dismay, all of the potatoes were starchy, mealy, and dry. *Cook's* 1994 story "Perfect Potato Salad" explained why: Starchy potatoes like russets (and even medium-starchy ones like the Yukon Golds) absorb more dressing than lower starch varieties. The lack of moisture on the surface of the dressed spuds makes them seem mealy when eaten.

These findings led me to trade in the russets and Yukon Golds for Red Bliss potatoes (also known as red creamers or simply as red potatoes). I repeated the tests. Even though red potatoes are known for their high-moisture, low-starch content, they, too, turned out dry. While they're smaller than russets, they still had to be cut into smaller segments that

exposed too much flesh to the fire. I tried new red potatoes—smaller still—which seemed to have it all: the high-moisture, low-starch characteristics of their larger cousins plus a higher skin-to-flesh ratio. I hoped the skin would protect the potatoes from being bullied by the flame.

I slid the cut potatoes onto skewers, figuring

Skin-on, new potatoes cut into eighths are the perfect size for grilling.

this would allow me to rotate them more easily when it came time to turn them for browning. While my assumption proved correct and the potatoes were much more moist, by the time the insides were tender, the skins were charred and ashy. I tried wrapping the skewered spuds in foil, and while this kept the skins from turning to carbon, the potatoes didn't pick up enough smoky flavor.

After these setbacks, I had to admit that the solution was only to be found in a pot of boiling water. I dropped a platoon of cut potatoes into boiling water, cooking them until slightly underdone. Now I faced another problem: Many of my parboiled chunks split as I tried to thread them onto skewers. A colleague came up with a brilliant solution—skewer the potatoes first, boil them on the skewers, and *then* transfer them to the hot

grill. So I threaded my raw potatoes on skewers and submerged them in boiling water until they were just tender. With tongs, I easily transferred the skewers from pot to baking sheet to grill. About 5 minutes later, I had perfectly browned potatoes that were tender, moist, and really smoky. But they still needed a bit of spunk. For the next round, I brushed the skewered potatoes with some olive oil and sprinkled them with salt and pepper before putting them on the fire. When these potatoes came off of the grill, I had to hide them from my coworkers if I wanted to save any for a salad—they were just too tempting to eat on their own as a snack.

Now that I had finally found a grilling method for the potatoes, I tried a few with mayonnaise-based dressings. Horrid! Dressing the potatoes with mayonnaise required me to chill them first, which added more time to the salad preparation. While chilling, the potatoes became tough and rubbery. Even worse, the delicate smoky nuance I had worked so hard to get was overpowered by the tanginess of the mayonnaise. I concluded that grilled potatoes were much better suited to a simple oil and vinegar dressing. Still, the smoky flavor of these potatoes is so satisfying that one taster remarked, "Why dress them at all? I'd serve them plain."

GRILLED POTATOES FOR SALAD
SERVES 4 TO 6

When buying potatoes for these salads, the color is less important than the size; make sure they are no longer than 3 inches. You will need about fifteen 10-inch metal or bamboo skewers. Prepare the other salad ingredients while the water heats so that the salad can be made with potatoes that are hot off the grill. Because the potatoes are precooked, they need only brown on the grill; you can grill them alongside your main dish over a charcoal- or gas-grill fire of any intensity.

1 1/2   pounds new potatoes, 2 to 3 inches long, scrubbed and unpeeled, cut into eighths
1 1/2   teaspoons salt
2   tablespoons olive oil
1/4   teaspoon ground black pepper

1. In large Dutch oven or stockpot, bring 4 quarts water to boil over high heat; add 1 teaspoon salt.

2. Following illustrations 2 and 3, skewer potato pieces. Drop skewers into boiling water and boil until paring knife slips in and out of potato easily, about 10 minutes.

3. While potatoes boil, line rimmed baking sheet with paper towels. With tongs, remove skewers to paper towel–lined baking sheet; pat potatoes dry with additional paper towels. Discard paper towels (potatoes can be cooled to room temperature, covered with plastic wrap, and kept at room temperature for up to 2 hours); brush all sides of potatoes with olive oil and sprinkle with remaining ½ teaspoon salt and pepper.

4. Place skewers on hot grill; cook, turning skewers twice with tongs, until all sides are browned, 2 to 3 minutes per side over high or medium-high heat (you can hold your hand 5 inches above grill grate no longer than 2 seconds for high heat or 3 to 4 seconds for medium-high heat) or 4 to 5 minutes per side over medium or medium-low heat (you can hold your hand 5 inches above grill grate 5 to 6 seconds for medium or 7 seconds for medium-low heat).

5. Slide hot potatoes off skewers into medium bowl and use immediately in one of the following recipes.

GAS GRILL VARIATION FOR GRILLED POTATOES

Follow recipe for Grilled Potatoes for Salad through step 3. Set gas grill temperature to desired heat setting. Heat grill, covered, for approximately 15 minutes. Continue with recipe from step 4.

GRILLED POTATO AND ARUGULA SALAD WITH DIJON MUSTARD VINAIGRETTE
SERVES 4 TO 6

If you prefer, watercress can be substituted for arugula.

1	recipe Grilled Potatoes for Salad
1½	teaspoons rice vinegar
	Salt
½	teaspoon ground black pepper
3	tablespoons chives, finely chopped
1	large bunch arugula, washed, dried, stems trimmed (about 3 cups)
1	medium yellow bell pepper, halved, seeded, deveined, and cut into ½-inch squares
1	teaspoon Dijon mustard
1	small shallot, minced (about 1½ tablespoons)
2	tablespoons olive oil

1. Toss hot potatoes with 1 teaspoon vinegar, ¼ teaspoon salt, and pepper. Add chives, arugula, and yellow pepper; toss to combine.

2. Combine mustard, shallot, remaining ½ teaspoon vinegar, olive oil, and salt to taste in small bowl. Pour over potatoes; toss to combine. Serve immediately.

SPICY GRILLED POTATO SALAD WITH CORN AND POBLANO CHILES
SERVES 4 TO 6

We prefer to use corn kernels cut from grilled corn on the cob, but boiled corn works, too. Poblano chiles are relatively mild; to alter spiciness, decrease or increase the quantity of jalapeños.

1	recipe Grilled Potatoes for Salad
1	teaspoon white wine vinegar
	Salt
¼	teaspoon ground black pepper
1	cup cooked corn kernels cut from 2 ears grilled or boiled corn
2	medium poblano chiles, roasted, peeled, seeded, and cut into ½-inch pieces
2	jalapeño chiles, seeded and minced
3	tablespoons juice from 1 large lime
½	teaspoon sugar
4	tablespoons olive oil
3	scallions, white parts only, sliced thin
3	tablespoons minced fresh cilantro leaves

1. Toss hot potatoes with vinegar, salt, and pepper. Add corn, poblanos, and jalapeños; toss to combine.

2. Whisk lime juice and sugar in small bowl until sugar dissolves; whisk in olive oil and salt to taste. Pour mixture over potatoes and add scallions and cilantro; toss to combine. Serve. (Can be covered with plastic wrap and kept at room temperature up to 30 minutes; toss before serving.)

GERMAN-STYLE GRILLED POTATO SALAD
SERVES 4 TO 6

1	recipe Grilled Potatoes for Salad
1	tablespoon yellow mustard seeds, toasted in small dry covered skillet until lightly browned, added to red wine vinegar while still hot
3	tablespoons red wine vinegar
	Salt
½	teaspoon ground black pepper
4	slices bacon (about 4 ounces), cut crosswise into ¼-inch strips
2	small shallots, minced (about 3 tablespoons)
⅓	cup chicken stock or canned low-sodium chicken broth
1	rib celery, chopped fine (about ¼ cup)
2	tablespoons minced fresh parsley leaves

1. Toss hot potatoes, 2 tablespoons vinegar with mustard seeds, ¼ teaspoon salt, and pepper.

2. Fry bacon in medium skillet over medium-high heat until brown and crisp, about 6 minutes; with slotted spoon, transfer bacon to bowl with potatoes. Reduce heat to medium, add shallots to fat in skillet and cook, stirring occasionally, until softened, about 3 minutes. Add

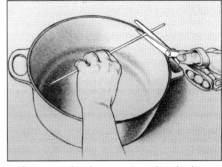

1. If using wooden skewers, trim to lengths that can be submerged in the Dutch oven you will be using.

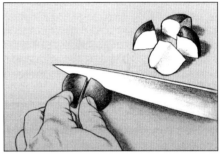

2. Halve each potato and quarter each half.

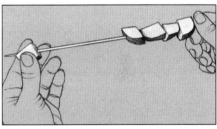

3. Skewer through the center of each potato with the skin facing out.

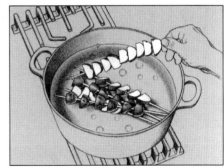

4. Lower skewers into boiling water and cook potatoes until just tender, about 10 minutes.

chicken stock and bring to boil; stir in remaining 1 tablespoon vinegar. Pour mixture over potatoes, add celery, parsley, and salt to taste; toss to combine. Serve. (Can be covered with plastic wrap and kept at room temperature up to 30 minutes; toss before serving.)

The Secret of Chilean Sea Bass

Undercooked, this fish is inedible. Buy thick fillets and cook them a long, long time.

⇒ BY JACK BISHOP ⇐

Every once in a while a "new" fish suddenly appears on restaurant menus and at fish counters. Monkfish, mahi mahi, and orange roughy are past examples of this phenomenon. The current darling is Chilean sea bass.

What makes Chilean sea bass the fish of the moment? Like salmon, it has a rich flavor, but it's milder and not as "fishy." When seared or grilled, the snow-white flesh develops a beautiful golden brown crust that's crunchy. Also like salmon, Chilean sea bass separates into large flakes, but the fish is firmer and meatier. Best of all, this fish is said to be easy to cook.

Chilean sea bass contains more than twice as much fat as farmed Atlantic salmon—16.1 grams of fat per 3.5-ounce serving versus just 6.3 grams of fat in a similar portion of salmon. (That may sound like a lot, but it's a lot of "good" fat, packed with omega-3 fatty acids, which have been found to be beneficial to coronary health.) All that oil means the fish won't dry out, so grilling it should be a simple proposition. At least I thought so when I started testing recipes. I figured I could cook the fish just as I would salmon. Boy, was I wrong on several counts.

I massaged olive oil into skin-on sea bass fillets (to prevent sticking) and grilled them the way I grill salmon—until the center is barely warm and still translucent. Although the fish looked pretty good, it tasted awful. This wasn't the great Chilean sea bass I've eaten out so many times. The problems were numerous.

I usually like fish skin, but not in this case. The skin was thick, chewy, and unappetizing. As for the flesh, it was soft and fishy. I bought more fish (at a different store), tried again, and it still tasted fishy. I figured the problem had to be my cooking method, not the sea bass.

Chilean sea bass skin is too thick and fatty to eat. It reminds me of halibut skin rather than salmon or snapper skin, which I love. But without skin, would the fish stick to the grill? Massaging oil into the fish was clearly a mistake—the last thing Chilean sea bass needs is more fat. I found

To keep the fish from sticking to the grill, apply a light coating of vegetable spray to the surface of the fillets before cooking.

that coating the fish with a thin film of oil (I used nonstick cooking spray) combined with oiling the grill (I wiped the hot rack with a wad of paper towels dipped in vegetable oil) guaranteed good results. In addition, I found that having the fishmonger cut individual pieces across the grain ensured that the fish would not flake or stick. (See "Fillet o' Fish," page 13.)

The fishy flavor proved more perplexing. I kept telling myself that I liked Chilean sea bass, but test after test I couldn't finish a single portion. I tried marinating the fish in lemon juice and oil, but that just made it taste greasy. I tried brining the fish in a solution of water, salt, sugar, and sliced lemons, hoping that the salt, sugar, and acidity would cut the fishy flavor. Brining helped a bit, but it seemed like an odd way to handle my problem. Salting the fish before cooking and serving it with lemon wedges was equally (and only moderately) effective.

A colleague suggested that I reexamine the cooking time. Most experts cite the so-called Canadian method for cooking fish—10 minutes per inch of thickness. In the past, the test kitchen has found that this guideline usually results in overcooked fish. For instance, we grill 1½-inch-

thick salmon fillets and tuna steaks for just six or seven minutes—any longer and the fish will be dry and tasteless. Salmon and tuna are best cooked medium-rare, and I was assuming that Chilean sea bass would be the same. Not so.

I realized that I liked the edges of the fish I had grilled, which were completely opaque, rather than the center, which was still translucent. I was cooking 1¼-inch-thick pieces for eight minutes. I decided to start increasing the cooking time. At 10 minutes the fish was better but not perfect. At 12 minutes it began to taste right, but I was encountering another problem—the surface was burning. It was time to switch tracks and use a two-level fire.

A two-level fire—with all the coals piled up on one side of the grill and the other side empty—allowed me to sear the fish until golden brown and then move the pieces over to the cool side to finish cooking through. After repeated tests, I found that 1¼-inch-thick fillets could be kept over hot coals for eight to 10 minutes. They then required another three to six minutes on the cool side to finish cooking through from a combination of their residual heat and the glow of the nearby coals. I had finally found a case where the Canadian method held true. On average, I was cooking

---

Not Your Average Bass

Despite its name, the Chilean sea bass is not a member of the true bass family. Its scientific name is *Dissostichus eleginoide*, and until its recent popularity with chefs, it was better known by the common name Patagonian toothfish. It is a large, slow-growing fish found in the cold, deep waters of the Southern hemisphere and is actually more similar to the sablefish, or black cod, than the sea bass in terms of texture and cooking properties. When you see "sea bass" on a menu or in a fish market, the fish is likely to be one of several varieties of saltwater bass. Black sea bass, pulled from the Atlantic, is the most common. During the summer, you may also see wild striped bass in many fish markets, especially in the Northeast. This fish has pinkish white flesh and is meaty and extremely tasty. (Don't confuse farmed striped bass with wild. Farmed striped bass is a cross between freshwater bass and wild striped bass and is not nearly as flavorful.) Because of differences in texture and fat content between the Chilean sea bass and "real" sea bass, recipes intended for one type of fish cannot be used for the other.

1¼-inch-thick pieces for 13 or 14 minutes, slightly longer than the 12½ minutes predicted by the Canadian method.

One chef friend told me that he loved Chilean sea bass because it's nearly impossible to overcook. I decided to test this proposition by leaving the fish on the cool side of the grill for 10 minutes. After 20 minutes on the grill, the fish was still delicious and not in the least dry. While I see no benefit in *overcooking* Chilean sea bass, it must be *fully cooked* to taste right.

CHARCOAL-GRILLED CHILEAN SEA BASS FILLETS
SERVES 4

- 4 Chilean sea bass fillets, skinned, about 8 ounces each and 1¼ inches thick (see "Fillet o' Fish")
  Salt and ground black pepper
  Nonstick cooking spray
  Vegetable oil
  Lemon or lime wedges for serving (optional)

1. Ignite about 6 quarts (1 large chimney, or about 6 pounds) charcoal briquettes and burn until covered with thin coating of light gray ash, 20 to 30 minutes. Spread coals over one half of grill bottom to create 2-level fire. Position grill rack over coals, cover grill with lid, and heat rack until hot, about 5 minutes. Scrape hot grill rack clean with wire brush.

2. Sprinkle fish generously with salt and pepper; spray both sides lightly with cooking spray. Dip small wad of paper towels in vegetable oil; holding wad with tongs, wipe grill rack.

3. Place fish directly over coals and grill until golden brown on first side, 4 to 5 minutes. Flip fish onto second side and continue to grill until golden brown on second side, 4 to 5 minutes longer. Move fish to cool part of grill and continue cooking until center of fillets is opaque and cooked through, 3 to 6 minutes longer. Serve immediately, with lemon or lime wedges if desired.

GAS-GRILLED CHILEAN SEA BASS FILLETS

Turn all burners on gas grill to high, close lid, and heat until hot, 10 to 15 minutes. Scrape hot grill rack clean with wire brush. Follow step 2 of recipe for Charcoal-Grilled Chilean Sea Bass Fillets. Turn 1 burner down to medium-low and leave other burner(s) on high. Place fish over burner(s) set on high and grill until golden brown on first side, about 5 minutes. Flip fish and continue to grill until golden brown on second side, about 5 minutes longer. Move fish to cooler part of grill and cook until center of fillets is opaque and cooked through, 3 to 6 minutes longer. Serve immediately, with lemon or lime wedges if desired.

Fillet o' Fish

Many restaurants serve towering hunks of Chilean sea bass that are 2 or even 2½ inches thick. When testing recipes for this article, I often saw (and sometimes purchased) individual portions of Chilean sea bass that were 2 inches thick, about 2 inches across, and maybe 4 inches long. In most instances, these pieces were sold skinless.

Because of their thickness, these nearly block-like chunks were difficult to grill. (If your fish market offers only superthick pieces, increase the cooking time on the cool part of the fire by about five minutes and make sure to oil the grill well.) For home grilling, I prefer thinner fillets—1¼ inches is ideal—that resemble halibut or tuna steaks. You have more surface area on this cut, so you get more browning, and it's easier to cook the fillets through to the center.

A side of Chilean sea bass can be enormous—sometimes weighing 10 pounds or more. Many markets cut the side of fish in half lengthwise and then into long, torpedo-like pieces that are shaped like monkfish fillets. When these long pieces are cut into individual portions, you get those restaurant-style block-like chunks.

Other markets take the huge side of a Chilean sea bass, cut it in half lengthwise, turn each piece on its side, and then slice the fish crosswise into steak-like slabs. Because the fish has been cut across the grain, it doesn't flake or fall apart on the grill. In addition, the fishmonger can vary the thickness of each piece. This is how I like to buy sea bass. When Chilean sea bass is caught at a weight of 10 pounds or fewer, the fishmonger will simply slice the whole side across the grain into fillets about 1¼ inch thick, which is how a side of salmon is cut up. These traditional fillets, with skin on the bottom, not the side, are harder to maneuver on the grill than the steak-like pieces I prefer. —J.B.

BLOCK   STEAK   TRADITIONAL

ORANGE AND SOY MARINADE FOR GRILLED CHILEAN SEA BASS FILLETS

This marinade creates an especially thick, brown crust on the grilled fish. Do not marinate the fish longer than suggested or the flavors will become too strong.

- ¼ cup juice from 1 large orange
- 2 tablespoons soy sauce
- 1 tablespoon dry sherry
- 2 medium garlic cloves, minced
- 2 teaspoons minced fresh ginger
  Ground black pepper

Combine orange juice, soy, sherry, garlic, and ginger in shallow dish just large enough to hold fish in single layer; place fish in marinade and turn to coat. Marinate 20 minutes, turning fish over after 10 minutes. Remove fish from marinade, sprinkle with pepper, and continue with recipe for Charcoal- or Gas-Grilled Chilean Sea Bass Fillets.

BLACK OLIVE AND CITRUS RELISH
MAKES ABOUT 1½ CUPS

Use only the segmented fruit in the relish, not the juices, which will water down the flavor and texture.

- 2 medium oranges, segmented (pith and membrane removed) and cut into ½-inch pieces
- 1 medium pink grapefruit, segmented (pith and membrane removed) and cut into ½-inch pieces
- ½ teaspoon ground cumin

- ½ teaspoon paprika
- 10 kalamata olives, pitted and chopped (about ¼ cup)
- 2 tablespoons minced fresh parsley leaves
  Cayenne pepper
  Salt

Combine oranges, grapefruit, cumin, paprika, olives, parsley, cayenne, and salt to taste in medium nonreactive bowl. Serve relish at room temperature with grilled fish. (Can be covered and set aside up to 1 hour.)

SPICY FRESH TOMATO SALSA
MAKES ABOUT 1¼ CUPS

The acidity of the tomatoes and lime juice complements the richness of the fish.

- 2 medium tomatoes, cored, seeded, and diced small
- 2 tablespoons minced red onion
- 4 teaspoons juice from 1 lime
- 1 small fresh serrano chile, stemmed, seeded, and minced
- 1 tablespoon minced fresh cilantro leaves
  Salt

Combine tomatoes, onion, lime juice, chile, cilantro, and salt to taste in medium bowl. Cover and set aside for 1 hour to allow flavors to blend. Serve salsa at room temperature with grilled fish. (Can be covered and set aside up to 3 hours.)

Perfect Shish Kebab

To avoid the raw lamb and charred vegetables that cooking on skewers often delivers, we cut the meat into 1-inch cubes and narrowed the vegetable field.

≥ BY JULIA COLLIN ≤

Shish kebab is the star of many a backyard barbecue. But its components cook at different rates—either the vegetables are still raw when the meat is cooked perfectly to medium-rare, or the lamb is long overdone by the time the vegetables have been cooked properly. My efforts to resolve this dilemma led me to explore which cut of lamb and which vegetables serve the kebab best. Getting the grill just right was another challenge. Too hot, and the kebabs charred on the outside without being fully cooked; too cool and they cooked without the benefit of flavorful browning.

The Right Cut

Lamb is expensive, so I was on a search for a cut that would give me tender, flavorful kebabs without breaking the bank. I immediately ruled out expensive cuts like loin or rib chops, which fetch upward of $14.99 per pound. These chops are just too pricey to cut up for a skewer and yield little meat. I had better luck with sirloin and shoulder chops, which are meatier and more reasonable at $4.99 per pound. Each of these, however, requires cutting the meat off the bone before trimming and cubing. The best cut turned out to be the shank end of a boneless leg of lamb. It requires little trimming, yields the perfect amount of meat for four to six people, and can be purchased for about $6.99 per pound.

Lamb has a supple, chewy texture that behaves best when cut into small, dainty pieces. I found 1-inch pieces of lamb to be the optimal size for kebab. With the meat cut and ready to go, I could now focus on the vegetables.

All too often, shish kebab vegetables end up being passed to the dog under the table (and even the dog may turn up his nose at them). Many vegetables don't cook through by the time the lamb reaches the right temperature. This can be particularly ugly if you're using eggplant, mushrooms, or zucchini. I tried precooking the vegetables, but they turned slimy and were difficult to skewer. I thought about cooking them separately alongside the lamb on the grill, but that's just not shish kebab. Other vegetables, such as cherry tomatoes, initially looked great on the skewer but had a hard

A brief stay on a sizzling hot grill cooks the kebabs perfectly.

time hanging on once cooked. Some burst open and took a dive onto the coals below.

As I worked my way through various vegetables, I came up with two that work well within the constraints of this particular cooking method. Red onions and bell peppers have a similar texture and cook through at about the same rate. When cut into smallish sizes, these two were the perfect accompaniments to the lamb, adding flavor and color to the kebab without demanding any special attention.

'Tis the Seasoning

What these handsome kebabs needed now was a little seasoned help, so I tried a variety of spices, dry rubs, and marinades on the meat. Spice rubs tasted good but left the surface of the meat chalky and dry; kebabs just aren't on the fire long enough for their juices to mix with the dried spices and form a glaze. Marinades, on the other hand, added a layer of moisture that kept the kebabs from drying out on the grill while their flavors penetrated the meat. I was not surprised to find that the

flavors that worked best with the lamb kebabs came from regions in or neighboring their ancient culinary home: the Middle East, India, Africa, and the Mediterranean. Ginger, cardamom, garam masala, cumin, and cinnamon brought the kebabs to life. Two hours in the marinade was sufficient time to achieve some flavor, but it took a good eight hours for these flavors to really sink in. Marinating for 12 hours, or overnight, was even better.

The Perfect Flame

I was aware of the pitfalls of a mismanaged grill. The trick was to get a nice caramelization around the edges of the kebab without overcooking the small, delicate pieces of lamb. A medium fire didn't work, turning the lamb an unappealing gray while leaving no grill marks behind. By the time the medium-hot fire turned out some decent grill marks, the meat was overcooked and a bit dry. A direct, single-level, hot fire turned out to be the ticket. I found this sizzling, fast fire cooked the kebabs perfectly in only seven to eight minutes, about two minutes per side for medium-rare to medium. My tasters and I agreed that these kebabs tasted best when the meat was cooked to medium-rare, whereas well-done lamb tasted "too muttony."

Finally, I had perfectly cooked lamb kebabs, with tender meat kissed by the grill, crisp vegetables charred around the edges, and authentic flavor. This is not just any old food on a stick; this is shish kebab.

CHARCOAL-GRILLED SHISH KEBAB
SERVES 6

1	recipe marinade (recipes follow)
2¼	pounds boneless leg of lamb (shank end), trimmed of fat and silver skin and cut into 1-inch pieces
3	medium bell peppers, 1 red, 1 yellow, and 1 orange (about 1½ pounds), each cut into twenty-four 1-inch pieces
1	large red onion (about 12 ounces), cut into thirty-six ¾-inch pieces (see page 15)
	Lemon or lime wedges for serving (optional)

1. Toss marinade and lamb in gallon-sized zipper-lock plastic bag or large, nonreactive bowl; seal bag, pressing out as much air as possible, or cover bowl and refrigerate until fully seasoned, at least 2 hours and up to 24 hours.

TESTING EQUIPMENT: **The Same Old Tong**

While the Middle and Near Eastern originators of shish kebab needed only an open fire and a sword to cook their dinner (loosely translated from Turkish, *shish kebab* means skewered meat), grilling today can be a lot more complicated. Each grilling season brings with it a truckload of snazzy, new barbecue utensils. We wondered if any were worth a second look.

Using all manner of tongs, we groped and grabbed kebabs, asparagus, chicken drumsticks, and 3-pound slabs of ribs and found tong performance differed dramatically. Grill tongs by Progressive International, Charcoal, Lamson, Oxo Good Grips, and AMC Rosewood were heavy and difficult to maneuver, and their less delicate pincers couldn't get a grip on asparagus. Other problems included sharp, serrated edges that nicked the food, flimsy arms that bent under the strain of heavy food, and pincers whose spread could not even accommodate the girth of a chicken leg. A new tong on the scene, the Lamson multipurpose, had a spatula in place of a pincer, rendering its grasp almost useless.

The winner was a pair of 16-inch stainless steel kitchen tongs by Amco. Not only did they grip, turn, and move food around the grill easily, but they also were long enough to keep the cook a safe distance from the hot coals. So forget about all those flashy new grill utensils and simply bring your kitchen tongs outside. —J.C.

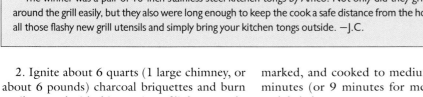

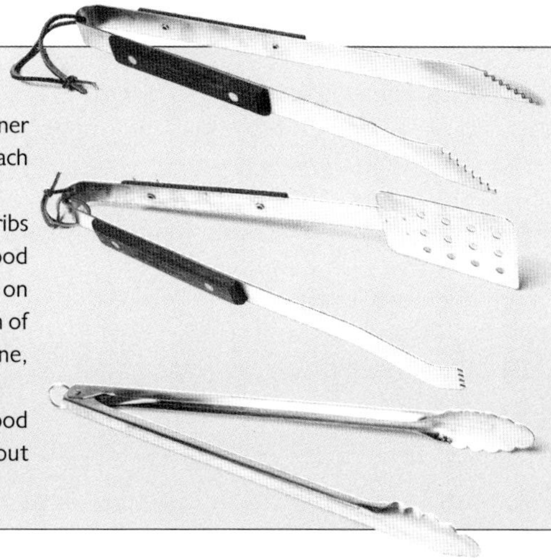

2. Ignite about 6 quarts (1 large chimney, or about 6 pounds) charcoal briquettes and burn until covered with thin coating of light gray ash, 20 to 30 minutes. Spread coals evenly over grill bottom, then spread additional 6 quarts unlit briquettes over lit coals. Position grill rack over coals and heat until very hot, about 15 minutes (you can hold your hand 5 inches above grill surface no longer than 2 seconds).

3. Meanwhile, starting and ending with meat, thread 4 pieces meat, 3 pieces onion (three 3-layer stacks), and 6 pieces pepper in mixed order on 12 metal skewers.

4. Grill kebabs, uncovered, until meat is well browned all over, grill-marked, and cooked to medium-rare, about 7 minutes (or 8 minutes for medium), turning each kebab one-quarter turn every 1¾ minutes to brown all sides. Transfer kebabs to serving platter, squeeze lemon or lime wedges over kebabs if desired, and serve immediately.

GAS-GRILLED SHISH KEBAB

Follow step 1 of Charcoal-Grilled Shish Kebab. Turn all burners on gas grill to high, close lid, and heat grill until hot, 10 to 15 minutes. Continue with recipe from step 3, grilling kebabs covered, until well browned, grill-marked, and cooked to medium-rare, about 8 minutes (or 9 minutes for medium), turning each kebab one-quarter turn every 2 minutes to brown all sides.

GARLIC AND CILANTRO MARINADE WITH GARAM MASALA

- ½ cup (packed) fresh cilantro leaves
- 3 medium garlic cloves, peeled
- ¼ cup dark raisins
- ½ teaspoon garam masala
- 1½ tablespoons juice from 1 lemon
- ½ cup olive oil
- 1 teaspoon salt
- ⅛ teaspoon ground black pepper

Process all ingredients in workbowl of food processor fitted with steel blade until smooth, about 1 minute, stopping to scrape sides of workbowl with rubber spatula as needed.

WARM-SPICED PARSLEY MARINADE WITH GINGER

- ½ cup (packed) fresh parsley leaves
- 1 jalapeño chile, seeded and chopped coarse
- 1 (2-inch) piece fresh ginger, peeled and chopped coarse

- 3 medium garlic cloves, peeled
- 1 teaspoon ground cumin
- 1 teaspoon ground cardamom
- 1 teaspoon ground cinnamon
- ½ cup olive oil
- 1 teaspoon salt
- ⅛ teaspoon ground black pepper

Process all ingredients in workbowl of food processor fitted with steel blade until smooth, about 1 minute, stopping to scrape sides of workbowl with rubber spatula as needed.

SWEET CURRY MARINADE WITH BUTTERMILK

- ¾ cup buttermilk
- 1 tablespoon juice from 1 lemon
- 3 medium garlic cloves, minced
- 1 tablespoon brown sugar
- 1 tablespoon curry powder
- 1 teaspoon crushed red pepper flakes
- 1 teaspoon ground coriander
- 1 teaspoon chili powder
- 1 teaspoon salt
- ⅛ teaspoon ground black pepper

Combine all ingredients in gallon-sized zipper-lock plastic bag or large, nonreactive bowl in which meat will marinate.

ROSEMARY-MINT MARINADE WITH GARLIC AND LEMON

- 10 large fresh mint leaves
- 1½ teaspoons chopped fresh rosemary
- 2 tablespoons juice and ½ tablespoon zest from 1 lemon
- 3 medium garlic cloves, peeled
- ½ cup olive oil
- 1 teaspoon salt
- ⅛ teaspoon ground black pepper

Process all ingredients in workbowl of food processor fitted with steel blade until smooth, about 1 minute, stopping to scrape sides of workbowl with rubber spatula as needed.

STEP-BY-STEP | ONION PREP

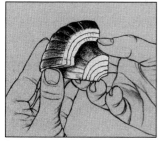

1. Trim away stem and root end and cut the onion into quarters. Peel the three outer layers of the onion away from the inner core.

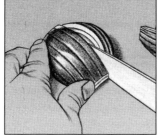

2. Working with the outer layers only, cut each quarter—from pole to pole—into 3 equal strips.

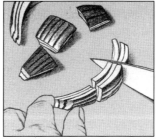

3. Cut each of the 12 strips crosswise into 3 pieces. (You should have thirty-six, 3-layer stacks of separate pieces of onion.)

Sharpening Knives by Hand

Sharp knives are essential to smooth and precise chopping, slicing, and carving. With two simple tools—and a little elbow grease—you can keep your knives in professional trim at home. BY MATTHEW CARD

Razor-sharp knives make cooking a pleasure, putting perfect cubes, ribbon-thin strips, and meticulous minces well within reach of the home cook. But many kitchen knives are poorly maintained. When knives are dull, they drag and tear their way through even the most basic tasks. More important, blunt knives are dangerous. Their blades slide off onions or carrots rather than cutting through them. The good news? Home sharpening is possible—and relatively inexpensive.

Most cooks are familiar with the iron rods known as steels. But steels are only half the story. Steeling doesn't sharpen a knife; it maintains the edge. To *put* an edge on a truly dull knife, a stone is essential. Stones are abrasive blocks that remove metal from a knife's blade to re-create and thin its edge. By following the steps recommended here, you can achieve professionally sharp knives in as little as five minutes.

IS IT SHARP?

Unless you are starting with a brand new knife, you will need a steel and sharpening stone. In the test kitchen, we use a couple of simple tests to see if our knives need to be steeled or ground on a sharpening stone. If your knife fails either test, first try steeling. If the knife still fails, it needs to be ground on a stone. Note: If your knives have been hopelessly neglected, it might be good idea to send them out for professional sharpening (see Resources, page 32). You can maintain their edges at home thereafter.

THE EDGE (MICROSCOPIC VIEW): With use, a knife blade develops nicks and microscopic bumps. Steeling removes irregularities and bumps and restores the knife's true edge.

THE EDGE (CLOSE-UP): In addition to developing microscopic bumps, the fine razor edge of the knife actually bends over with use.

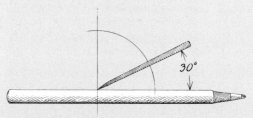

PEN TEST: Rest the edge of a blade on the barrel of a plastic pen at a 30-degree angle—if it fails to catch, the knife needs attention. A sharp edge, on the other hand, will bite into the pen's barrel.

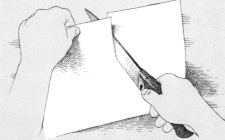

PAPER TEST: Hold a sheet of paper by one end and try slicing clean ribbons from it. If the knife snags or fails to cut the paper, it needs to be steeled or sharpened.

To Lube or Not to…?

With the help of the test kitchen's supply of blunted 8-inch chef's knives, we set out to find the most efficient way to sharpen on a stone. We tested two conventional methods: sweeping the blade straight across the stone and grinding the blade in a circular motion. With each method, we tried three variations: lubricating the stone with water, lubricating with vegetable oil, and leaving it completely dry. Each knife was ground on the coarse side of the stone until it would catch on the barrel of a plastic pen. We then ground the knife on the finer side until it could slice ribbons from a free-hanging sheet of paper. We found the circular method on the dry stone to be the fastest. Depending on the knife's dullness, sharpening took about five to 10 minutes. Extremely dull knives, or thick-bladed knives like cleavers, took longer. It took significantly longer to achieve a sharp edge on oil- or water-lubricated stones. And with oil, the knife blade became quite slippery, making sharpening treacherous—the knife actually slipped out of one tester's hands.

EQUIPMENT

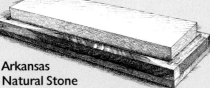

Arkansas Natural Stone
Arkansas, or novaculite, stones are relatively expensive and often considered too fine-gritted for sharpening kitchen knives.

Synthetic sharpening stone
Stones are available in a variety of shapes and prices. We chose a double-sided (coarse and fine grit) Norton brand "India" synthetic stone. At around $25, it is economical, and it's widely available at hardware stores.

Traditional steel
Traditional steels are lightly grooved, magnetized iron rods.

Diamond steel
Relatively new to the market are diamond steels—hollow, oval tubes coated with diamond dust. Unlike traditional steels, diamond steels simultaneously sharpen and straighten the blade, extending the period between sharpenings. We pitted a traditional steel against a diamond steel and were impressed with how quickly the diamond steel put an edge back on knives we thought were ready for the sharpening stone.

USING A STONE

The only way to sharpen a really dull knife is to use a stone. Begin with the coarse side and fine-tune the edge with the smooth side.
Most kitchen knives need sharpening every three or four months. Once sharp, knives must be steeled routinely between uses to maintain their edges.

I. SHARPENING ON THE COARSE SIDE OF THE STONE

Hold the knife by the handle with your index finger on top of the blade and your thumb running up the spine. Fan the fingers of your other hand out across the length of the blade. Place the knife at a 20-degree angle to the stone. Let the edge of the knife blade be your guide.

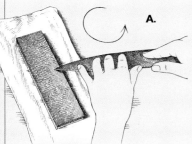
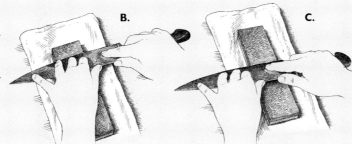

A.

B.

C.

A. With the edge of the blade facing away from you, grind one side of the knife in a counterclockwise motion, starting at the tip.

B. Exerting consistent pressure, continue grinding in a circular motion, moving the blade across the stone from tip to bolster.

C. As you grind, the edge of the knife will form a burr, a ridge that curls up from the ground side of the blade (see step 2, above right).

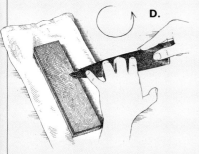
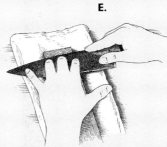
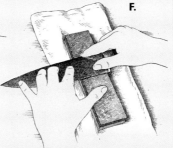

D.

E.

F.

D. Flip the knife over and repeat, this time with the blade edge facing toward you. Grind the other side of the knife counterclockwise.

E. Continue grinding counterclockwise from tip to bolster, exerting consistent pressure until the edge forms another burr.

F. Continue grinding until the knife is ready for the fine side of the stone (see "Pen Test," page 16). Expect to grind about two minutes per side.

2. DETECTING THE BURR

You can feel the burr by running your fingernail down the edge of the blade on the side that has not been ground. If your nail catches, the burr has formed and the second side of the blade is ready to be ground. Check to make sure a burr has formed along its entire length.

3. USING THE FINE SIDE OF THE STONE

Turn the stone fine-side up and grind the knife. Alternate sides of the blade every four strokes or so to polish and refine the edge. Continue grinding until the blade can slice a free-hanging sheet of paper. Steel the knife to remove debris.

USING A STEEL

Steeling removes debris after grinding or can restore a knife's edge and remove irregularities that have formed along the blade. A knife that feels dull may need only a few light strokes on a steel to correct its edge and regain its sharpness. In fact, when cutting gristly meat, bony chicken, or other tough foodstuffs, occasional swipes on the steel may be called for. Wipe the knife clean before using it again.

I. Hold the steel perpendicular to the work surface, with the metal end resting on a cutting board. Place the heel of the blade against the top of the steel and point the tip upward slightly. Hold the blade at a 20-degree angle away from the steel.

2. Maintaining light pressure and a 20-degree angle, slide the blade down the length of the steel in a sweeping motion. As the knife glides down the steel, pull the back of the knife toward your body so that the middle of the blade is in contact with the middle of the steel.

3. Finish the motion by passing the tip of the blade over the bottom of the steel. Repeat the motion on the other side of the blade. Four or five strokes on each side of the blade (a total of eight or 10 alternating passes) should true the edge.

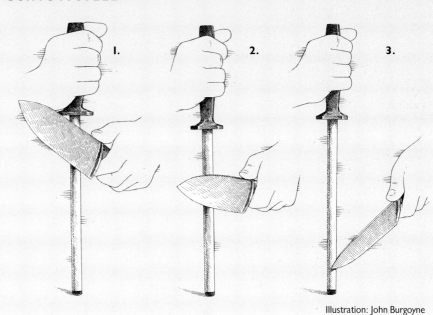

I.

2.

3.

Illustration: John Burgoyne

The Best Baba Ghanoush

Scorching eggplant on the grill produces a smoky, creamy dip far superior
to the wan, tasteless fare that is the bane of many dinner parties.

BY KAY RENTSCHLER

Baba ghanoush is not just another pretty face. In fact, baba ghanoush is not really pretty at all. But, honestly, who cares? It has sex appeal, magnetism, complexity, and allure without being beautiful, by being, well—just a dip. The driving force behind baba ghanoush is grill-roasted eggplant, sultry and rich. Its beguiling creaminess and haunting flavor come from sesame tahini paste, cut to the quick with a bit of garlic, brightened with lemon juice, and flounced up with parsley. In Middle Eastern countries baba ghanoush is served as part of a *meze* platter—not unlike an antipasto in Italy—which might feature salads, various dips, small pastries, meats, olives, other condiments, and, of course, bread.

There is no doubt that the eggplant is a majestic fruit—shiny, sexy, brilliantly hued. But its contents can be difficult to deal with. Baba ghanoush often turns up as a plate of gray matter intersected by pita triangles. Its taste can be bitter and watery, green and raw, metallic with garlic, or occluded by tahini paste.

A tireless advocate of eggplant, I was determined to take up its cause in pursuit of a fresh, balanced baba ghanoush and to file complaints about it where they belong: with the cook. The eggplant would be innocent of all charges.

Transformed by Fire

The traditional method for cooking eggplant for baba ghanoush is to scorch it over a hot, smoky grill. There the purple fruit grows bruised, then black, until its insides fairly slosh within their charred carapace. The hot, soft interior is scooped out with a spoon and the outer ruins discarded. Having eaten my share of baba ghanoush that had not experienced the thrill of the grill, I was amazed at what an improvement live coals made. The smokiness of the fire induced other ingredients to relate to one another in a more interesting way.

Another thing I realized is that baba made with eggplant not cooked to the sloshy soft stage simply isn't as good. Undercooked eggplant, while misleadingly soft to the touch (eggplant has, after all, a yielding quality), will taste spongy-green and remain unmoved by additional seasonings.

Another question was whether a decent baba ghanoush could be made without a grill. Taking

When fresh, an eggplant has firm, shiny skin and a short, shiny section of stem. Don't buy eggplant with wrinkled skin and spongy flesh.

instruction from the hot fire I had used, I roasted a few large eggplants in a 500-degree oven. It took about 45 minutes to collapse the fruit and transform the insides to pulp. Though the babas made with grill-roasted eggplant were substantially superior to those made with oven-roasted, the latter were perfectly acceptable. My efforts to replicate the smokiness of the grill with a couple of drops of eau de Liquid Smoke, however, were not well received.

Bitter Fruit?

Eggplant suffers from persistent rumors that it is bitter. Some say it is the seeds that are bitter, some the skins; others hold an eggplant's maturity accountable. Most baba ghanoush recipes call for discarding the seedbed. During the time I worked on this recipe, a colleague—himself in the throes of eggplant passion fired by a trip to Turkey—mentioned that Middle Eastern eggplant

is a different variety altogether, being both squatter and fleshier. Its seedbed is traditionally removed. "Try that with an eggplant around here," he remarked, "and there's nothing left."

Indeed, it was true. The insides of the eggplants I was roasting were veritably paved with seeds. I thought it impractical and wasteful to lose half the fruit to mere rumor, so I performed side-by-side tests comparing versions of the dip with and without seeds. I found no tangible grounds for seed dismissal. The dip was not bitter. The seeds stayed.

Another antibitterness clause in baba recipes tells cooks to accord the scooped pulp some downtime in a colander to expel bitter juices. I tried this technique, but the juices never tasted bitter to me. I continued draining the pulp in a colander in case I one day encountered bitter juices and because I didn't want the finished dip to be watery (though in truth the dip went together so quickly once the eggplant was scooped that dripping time was minimal).

A Turkish chef had told my colleague that scooped, roasted eggplant must be rinsed and doused with lemon juice to prevent discoloring. I was pleasantly surprised to find that my baba ghanoush remained a pale golden green without rinsing or dousing—nothing like the gray, pulpy matter I had been served in the past. In fact, I never learned what transgression occasions that color transformation, although I suspect it has to do with oxidation, or, to put it bluntly, age. Prepared in small quantities (this recipe makes 2 cups), my baba ghanoush never sat around long enough to fade to gray. Two cups may sound skimpy, but this stuff goes a long way. If you're serving a crowd, the recipe can easily be doubled or tripled. Time does nothing to improve the flavor of baba ghanoush, either. An hour-long stay in the refrigerator for a light chilling is all that's needed.

Once the eggplant is roasted and scooped, you are about five minutes away from removing your apron and heading for the cocktail trolley. The eggplant can be mashed with a fork, but I prefer the food processor, which makes it a cinch to add the other ingredients and to pulse the

COOK'S ILLUSTRATED

18

1. Place the eggplants on a hot grill rack. Turn as soon as their skins begin to darken and wrinkle.

2. Grill until the eggplant walls have collapsed and the insides feel sloshy when pressed with tongs.

3. Slice off top and bottom ends, then slit eggplants lengthwise. Scoop flesh and seeds into a colander.

eggplant, leaving the texture slightly coarse.

As for the proportions of said ingredients, my tests indicated that less was always more. Minced garlic gathers strength on-site and can become aggressive when added in abundance. Many recipes I saw also called for tahini in amounts that overwhelmed the eggplant. Likewise with lemon juice: liberal amounts dash the smoky richness of the eggplant with astringent tartness.

The Color Purple

The shining months of August and September bring a plenitude of eggplant types to stores and farmer's markets. I made baba ghanoush with standard large globe eggplant, with compact Italian eggplant (similar to the kind found in Turkey), and with long, lithe Japanese eggplant. All were surprisingly good. The globe eggplant made a baba that was slightly more moist. The Italian eggplant was drier and contained fewer seeds. The Japanese eggplant was also quite dry. Its very slenderness allowed the smoke to permeate the flesh completely, and the resulting dip was meaty and delicious. (Given a choice, I would definitely select Italian or Japanese eggplant.)

While several eggplant varieties purchased from the neighborhood farmer's market produced baba ghanoush of exceptional quality, batches of baba I made later in the season with eggplant from a local grocery store produced dull, flavorless fare. I could not believe this was my recipe! Because the quality of a dish like baba ghanoush relies directly on the freshness of the eggplant selected, I wondered what methods, if any, were available to shoppers for hand-selecting eggplant.

According to Dr. Mian Riaz of Texas A&M University, eggplant is harvested immature for shipping purposes and has between one and two weeks of peak freshness once in stores. Dull or wrinkled skin, a brownish tint, or a truncated, dried-out stem end all indicate that the eggplant is past its prime. Similarly, if when slicing eggplant to be sautéed your knife encounters brown or spongy flesh, the eggplant is too old to use.

BABA GHANOUSH, CHARCOAL-GRILL METHOD
MAKES 2 CUPS

When buying eggplant, select those with shiny, taut, and unbruised skins and an even shape (eggplant with a bulbous shape won't cook evenly). We prefer to serve baba ghanoush only lightly chilled. If yours is cold, let it stand at room temperature for about 20 minutes before serving. Baba ghanoush does not keep well, so plan to make it the day you want to serve it. Pita bread, black olives, tomato wedges, and cucumber slices are nice accompaniments.

- 2 pounds eggplant (about 2 large globe eggplants, 5 medium Italian eggplants, or 12 medium Japanese eggplants), each eggplant poked uniformly over entire surface with fork to prevent it from bursting
- 1 tablespoon juice from 1 lemon
- 1 small garlic clove, minced
- 2 tablespoons tahini paste
  Salt and ground black pepper
- 1 tablespoon extra-virgin olive oil, plus extra for serving
- 2 teaspoons chopped fresh parsley leaves

1. Ignite about 6 quarts (1 large chimney, or 6 pounds) charcoal briquettes and burn until completely covered with thin coating of light gray ash, 20 to 30 minutes. Spread coals evenly over grill bottom, then spread additional 6 quarts unlit briquettes over lit coals. Position grill rack and heat until very hot (you can hold your hand 5 inches above the grill grate for only 2 seconds), about 20 minutes.

2. Following illustration 1, set eggplants on grill rack. Grill until skins darken and wrinkle on all sides and eggplants are uniformly soft when pressed with tongs (illustration 2), about 25 minutes for large globe eggplants, 20 minutes for Italian eggplants, and 15 minutes for Japanese eggplants, turning every 5 minutes and reversing direction of eggplants on grill with each turn. Transfer eggplants to

rimmed baking sheet and cool 5 minutes.

3. Set small colander over bowl or in sink. Trim top and bottom off each eggplant. Following illustration 3, slit eggplants lengthwise and use spoon to scoop hot pulp from skins and place pulp in colander (you should have about 2 cups packed pulp); discard skins. Let pulp drain 3 minutes.

4. Transfer pulp to workbowl of food processor fitted with steel blade. Add lemon juice, garlic, tahini, ¼ teaspoon salt, and ¼ teaspoon pepper; process until mixture has coarse, choppy texture, about eight 1-second pulses. Adjust seasoning with salt and pepper; transfer to serving bowl, cover with plastic wrap flush with surface of dip, and refrigerate 45 to 60 minutes. To serve, use spoon to make trough in center of dip and spoon olive oil into it; sprinkle with parsley and serve.

BABA GHANOUSH, GAS-GRILL METHOD

Turn all burners on gas grill to high, close lid, and heat grill until hot, 10 to 15 minutes. Follow recipe for Baba Ghanoush, Charcoal-Grill Method, from step 2.

BABA GHANOUSH, OVEN METHOD

Adjust oven rack to middle position and heat oven to 500 degrees. Line rimmed baking sheet with foil, set eggplants on baking sheet and roast, turning every 15 minutes, until eggplants are uniformly soft when pressed with tongs, about 60 minutes for large globe eggplants, 50 minutes for Italian eggplants, and 40 minutes for Japanese eggplants. Cool eggplants on baking sheet 5 minutes, then follow recipe for Baba Ghanoush, Charcoal-Grill Method, from step 3.

BABA GHANOUSH WITH SAUTÉED ONION

Sautéed onion gives the baba ghanoush a sweet, rich flavor.

Heat 1 tablespoon extra-virgin olive oil in small skillet over low heat until shimmering; add 1 small onion, chopped fine, and cook, stirring occasionally, until edges are golden brown, about 10 minutes. Follow recipe for Baba Ghanoush, Charcoal-Grill, Gas-Grill, or Oven Method, stirring onion into dip after processing.

ISRAELI-STYLE BABA GHANOUSH

Replacing the sesame paste with mayonnaise makes this baba ghanoush pleasantly light and brings out the smoky flavor of charcoal-grilled eggplant.

Follow recipe for Baba Ghanoush, Charcoal-Grill, Gas-Grill, or Oven Method, substituting an equal amount of mayonnaise for tahini.

Summer Fruit Salads

Good fruit salads shouldn't taste like sugary desserts. We found that sweet-tart dressings brighten flavors rather than cloaking them.

Making a good, fresh fruit salad in the summer is not that hard. Nor is it very hard, we found, to make a truly *great* summer fruit salad, complemented by a simple, sweet-tart dressing that enhances the fruit and adds layers of interest and flavor.

Fruit salads can be dressed with yogurt or sugar syrup or simply be served plain. We felt that yogurt dressings fell short because they mask the colors, shapes, and jewel-like beauty of cut fruit. And the inescapable truth is that no matter what sort of flavoring you add, yogurt dressing always tastes like, well, yogurt. The fruit almost falls by the wayside. Sugar syrup can be insipidly sweet, and plain cut-up fruit can be boring.

So we chose another route, adapting a classic French dressing called *gastrique*. The definition of *gastrique* varies cookbook to cookbook, but we agree with the renowned culinary encyclopedia *Larousse Gastronomique* (Crown Publishers, 1984) that a gastrique is a reduction of an acidic liquid, usually vinegar, and sugar; it typically accompanies savory dishes made with fruit, such as duck à l'orange. The process of reducing the liquid over high heat couldn't be simpler, and, after some experimentation, we found that 1 cup of acidic liquid reduced with ¼ cup of sugar produced just the right balance of tart and sweet. The mixture complemented all the fresh fruits we wanted to use.

This technique worked beautifully with citrus juice, wine, and spirits, allowing us to introduce complex flavors beyond the traditional vinegar. We also got great results from infusing the gastriques with additional flavors, such as cinnamon in the brandy mixture for plums and figs. Our last step was to add some high, bright flavor notes with both lemon juice and zest. With that, we achieved a complex layering of flavors in 16 minutes flat.

STRAWBERRIES AND GRAPES WITH BALSAMIC AND RED WINE REDUCTION
MAKES 6 CUPS

An inexpensive balsamic vinegar is fine for use in this recipe. Save your more costly, high-quality balsamic for other preparations in which the vinegar is not cooked.

- ¾ cup balsamic vinegar
- ¼ cup dry red wine
- ¼ cup sugar
- Pinch salt
- 3 cloves
- 1 tablespoon grated zest plus 1 tablespoon juice from 1 lemon
- ¼ teaspoon vanilla extract
- 1 quart strawberries, hulled and halved lengthwise (about 4 cups)
- 9 ounces large seedless red or black grapes, each grape halved pole to pole (about 2 cups)

Simmer vinegar, wine, sugar, and salt in small, heavy-bottomed nonreactive saucepan over high heat until syrupy and reduced to ¼ cup, about 15 minutes. Off heat, stir in cloves, lemon zest and juice, and vanilla; steep 1 minute to blend flavors, and strain. Combine strawberries and grapes in medium bowl; pour warm dressing over fruit and toss to coat. Serve immediately at room temperature or cover with plastic wrap, refrigerate up to 4 hours, and serve chilled.

NECTARINES, BLUEBERRIES, AND RASPBERRIES WITH CHAMPAGNE-CARDAMOM REDUCTION
MAKES 6 CUPS

Dry white wine can be used as an alternative to champagne.

- 1 cup champagne
- ¼ cup sugar
- Pinch salt
- 1 tablespoon grated zest plus 1 tablespoon juice from 1 lemon
- 5 cardamom pods, crushed
- 3 medium nectarines (about 18 ounces), cut into ½-inch wedges (about 3 cups)
- 1 pint blueberries
- ½ pint raspberries

Simmer champagne, sugar, and salt in small, heavy-bottomed nonreactive saucepan over high heat until syrupy, honey-colored, and reduced to ¼ cup, about 15 minutes. Off heat, add lemon zest and juice and cardamom; steep 1 minute to blend flavors, and strain. Combine nectarines, blueberries, and raspberries; pour warm dressing over fruit and toss to combine. Serve immediately at room temperature or cover with plastic wrap, refrigerate up to 4 hours, and serve chilled.

RED PLUMS AND FIGS WITH BRANDY-CINNAMON REDUCTION
MAKES 6 CUPS

- 1 cup brandy
- ¼ cup sugar
- Pinch salt
- 1 (3-inch) stick cinnamon
- 1 tablespoon grated zest plus 1 tablespoon juice from 1 lemon
- 4 red plums (about 1¼ pounds), pitted and cut into ½-inch-thick wedges (about 4 cups)
- 12 fresh black mission figs (about 12 ounces), quartered lengthwise (about 2 cups)

Simmer brandy, sugar, and salt in small, heavy-bottomed nonreactive saucepan over high heat until syrupy, honey-colored, and reduced to ¼ cup, about 15 minutes. Off heat, add cinnamon and lemon zest and juice; steep 1 minute, and strain. Combine plums and figs in medium bowl; pour warm dressing over fruit and toss to combine. Serve immediately at room temperature or cover with plastic wrap, refrigerate up to 4 hours, and serve chilled.

HONEYDEW, MANGO, AND BLUEBERRIES WITH LIME-GINGER REDUCTION
MAKES 6 CUPS

- 1 cup juice plus 1 tablespoon grated zest from 4 limes (zest limes before juicing)
- ¼ cup sugar
- Pinch salt
- 1 (1-inch) piece fresh ginger, peeled and minced (about 1 tablespoon)
- 1 tablespoon juice from 1 lemon
- ½ small honeydew melon, seeds and rind removed, cut into 1-inch pieces (about 2 cups)
- 1 mango (about 10 ounces), peeled and cut into ½-inch pieces (about 1½ cups)
- 1 pint blueberries

Simmer lime juice, sugar, and salt in small, heavy-bottomed nonreactive saucepan over high heat until syrupy, honey-colored, and reduced to ¼ cup, about 15 minutes. Off heat, add lime zest, ginger, and lemon juice; steep 1 minute, and strain. Combine fruit in medium bowl; pour warm dressing over and toss. Serve immediately at room temperature or cover with plastic wrap, refrigerate up to 4 hours, and serve chilled.

Fresh Fruit Tarts Worth Eating

Bakery tarts look elegant but are often tasteless and rubbery. Here's a step-by-step guide to making your own pâtisserie creation that will taste as good as it looks.

⇒ BY DAWN YANAGIHARA ⇐

Glistening in the windows and glass cases of pâtisseries, fresh fruit tarts are things of beauty. Gemlike berries and fruits of ruby, sapphire, and emerald brilliance set in princely designs make for breathtaking displays. But these fruit tarts are tarts indeed. They draw you in with their beguiling looks—but venture beneath the surface and you are quickly disappointed with their substance. Most often, the pastry cream filling is an institutional pudding with either a goopy, overstarched texture or a stiff, rubbery demeanor. Its flavor is bland or, even worse, tainted by artificial flavorings. Even when it is not odious in itself, a pastry cream filling typically infects the crust with a different malaise: If the tart has been sitting pretty long enough (and you can bet it has), the crust has gotten soggy. Or, in the worst case, juices have begun to seep out of the fruit to form a sticky puddle in which the tart wallows. To add insult to injury, the fruit, though beautiful, is underripe and has the flavor and texture of wet cardboard.

Somehow, though, even a feeble fruit tart can provide a glimpse into what it could be. The perfect fresh fruit tart has components working in concert to produce complementary textures and flavors. Its crust is buttery and sweet, crisp and sugar-cookie-like, not flaky like a pie pastry. The pastry cream filling is creamy and lithe, just sweet enough to counter the tartness of fresh fruits and just firm enough to support their weight. A finish of jellied glaze makes the fruits sparkle and keeps them from drying out. With each forkful, you experience the buttery crumbling of crust, the chill of cool, rich, silky pastry cream, and the juicy explosion of lusty ripe fruit.

So in high summer, with beautiful fruit tumbling into farmer's markets, I set out to create the perfect fresh fruit tart myself at home, knowing I could not find it in a bakery or pâtisserie.

Crust and Cream

The pastry for a fresh fruit tart is called pâte sucrée, or sweet pastry. The tart shell is baked

Use quick, sharp motions to drizzle, dab, and flick the hot glaze on the tart. Avoid direct brushing to leave the fruit undisturbed.

empty (aka prebaked, blind-baked, or baked au blanc) until it reaches a deep golden hue. It is then cooled completely, filled with pastry cream, topped with fruit, glazed, *et voilà*. *Cook's* already had a very good recipe for sweet pastry in its repertoire, developed alongside a classic lemon tart (see the January/February 2000 issue). It bakes into a sturdy, buttery, tender pastry that is crisp and just a little crumbly. With even the oven temperature for prebaking determined for me, I immediately turned to the insides.

Pastry cream is cooked in a saucepan on the stovetop like a homemade pudding. Making it is really not difficult, but making it just right, I knew, would mean finding the perfect balance of ingredients—milk (or cream), eggs, sugar, and starch (usually either cornstarch or flour). I gathered and then prepared a number of recipes for pastry cream and even included a couple of atypical fruit tart fillings—whipped cream and crème anglaise (stirred custard), both stabilized with gelatin. These anomalies were quickly and

unanimously rejected by tasters for being uninteresting and Jell-O-like, respectively. I also included basic pastry creams stabilized with gelatin and lightened with egg whites or whipped cream (both often called crème chiboust in the French pastry vernacular), but these more labor-intensive preparations turned out not to be worth the effort. Moreover, despite the fact that it is called "flavorless," the gelatin forced itself on and swallowed up the subtle cream, egg, and vanilla flavors, leaving the pastry cream with a hollow trademark gelatin flavor. It was evident from this tasting that a simple, basic pastry cream was the one to pursue.

With the information gleaned from this first round, I was able to formulate a working recipe from which I could test components systematically. I sought to determine which was preferable: milk, half-and-half, or heavy cream. Milk was lean on flavor, and cream was superfluous in its fat. Half-and-half was the dairy of choice; the pastry cream made with it was silky in texture and agreeably, not overly, rich. To fill a 9- to 9½-inch tart shell, I needed 2 cups, sweetened with only ½ cup of sugar.

Egg yolks—and sometimes whole eggs—help thicken and enrich pastry cream. A whole egg pastry cream was too light and flimsy. An all-yolk cream was richer, fuller flavored, and altogether more serious. Three yolks were too few to do the job, four (a very common proportion of yolks to dairy) was fine, but with five yolks, the pastry cream was sensational—it was like smooth, edible silk, with a remarkable glossy translucency much like that of mayonnaise.

Thickener was up next. I knew from sauce making that flour yields a dull, cloudy sauce (think beef stew). Cornstarch leaves a sauce shiny and glossy, with a slicker look and feel (think Chinese food). I made four batches of pastry cream, using 3 or 4 tablespoons of cornstarch or flour in each one. Four tablespoons of either starch made gummy, chewy, gluey messes of the pastry creams. Three tablespoons was the correct amount; any less would have resulted in soup. In equal amounts, cornstarch and flour were extremely close in flavor and texture, but cornstarch inched out in front with a slightly lighter, more ethereal texture and a cleaner and purer flavor; flour had a trace of graininess and gumminess. That a cornstarch pastry cream is marginally easier to cook than one made with flour was a bonus. Once a cornstarch cream reaches a boil, it is done. A pastry cream with flour must cook for a few minutes for the raw flour flavor to cook out and the cream to reach maximum viscosity.

Most pastry cream recipes finish with a whisking of butter into the just-made cream. As fine-grained sandpaper removes the smallest burrs and gives wood a velveteen finish, butter, I found, rounds out the flavor of pastry cream and endows it with a smooth, silken texture. Usually, only 1 tablespoon of butter is added per cup of liquid, but I found that amount to be shy. I doubled the amount—to 4 tablespoons per 2 cups of half-and-half—to make a superbly rich, satiny pastry cream. This relatively generous amount of butter also helped the chilled cream behave better when it came time to slice; it resisted sliding and slipping much more than it had without the extra butter. When the tart was well chilled, the pastry cream held its own.

As for timing, I found it best to prepare the pastry cream before beginning the pastry shell. In fact, it can be made a day or two in advance. This gives the cream adequate time to chill, and I did find a fruit tart with filling that is cool on the tongue much more thrilling to eat. And since it is best to fill the pastry fairly close to serving time lest it become soggy, the cream must be cold when it goes into the shell and is topped with fruit.

Tarted Up

Small, soft, self-contained fruits—in other words, berries—are ideal atop fresh fruit tarts. Raspberries, blackberries, and blueberries require no paring and no slicing. That means no breaking of fruit skin to release juices that can ruin a tart. Strawberries are certainly acceptable. They do need to be hulled, and sliced strawberries can make an attractive display if arranged, glazed, and served swiftly. While fruits like mangoes and papayas, with their juicy, soft, creamy textures, might seem inviting, they aren't good candidates for a tart because they quickly send their juices flowing. What's more, their irregular and awkward shapes can be difficult to slice and make attractive. Kiwis, however, work well and are gorgeous complements to the berry reds and blues. But use kiwis sparingly, as they, too, can water things down. I do not wash berries that are destined to grace a fruit tart. They need to be utterly dry and completely bruise- and blemish-free. Any excess water can cause the tart to weep, which ultimately results in a soggy bottom. (If you are concerned about pesticide residues on your fresh fruit, buy organic.)

The "simpler is better" precept applies to fruit arrangement on a fresh fruit tart. In the test kitchen, the tarts that met with the most flattery were the simple ones that showed restraint, not the over-designed ones with lots of fanfare. If you are not inclined to create your own design, follow one of those suggested, below. If you are so inclined, bear in mind that one goal is to arrange the fruit in a tight design so that very little to none of the ivory-toned pastry cream peeks out of the spaces between the fruit. Also, the nicest designs are those in which the tallest points are at the center of the tart, with a gradual and graceful descent to the edges.

The finishing touch on a fruit tart is the glaze. For tarts that are covered only with berries of red and blue hues, garnet-colored red currant jelly is perfect. For tarts covered with kiwi and other fair-colored fruits (for instance, golden raspberries), apricot jam is the norm because of its neutral tones, but I took to using apple jelly because it eliminated the need to strain out chunks of fruit and then reheat.

Fresh fruit tarts are often displayed with a shellacked armor of glaze painted on the fruit. After glazing dozens of tarts, I can vouch that sticky brush bristles can ensnare and dislodge bits of fruit, wrecking a design. Instead, I adopted a technique of dabbing/drizzling/flicking the glaze on the tart with a pastry brush. The result is not a smooth, even coat but something more dazzling—a sheath of droplets that catch light and

---

Three Fruit Tart Designs

MIXED BERRY TART

TO ARRANGE FRUIT: Sort ½ pint of blueberries, ½ pint of blackberries, and two ½ pints of raspberries, discarding any blemished berries. Place all the berries in a large plastic bag, then very gently shake the bag. Empty the berries on top of the tart, distributing them in an even layer. Then, using your fingers, adjust the berries as necessary so that they cover the entire surface and the colors are evenly distributed. Use red currant jelly to glaze this tart.

TIP: Place the berries in a large plastic bag. Hold the bag closed with one hand and, with the other, gently jostle the berries about to combine them.

STRAWBERRY TART

TO ARRANGE FRUIT: Try to buy ripe berries of medium, uniform size. With a pastry or mushroom brush, brush off any dirt from about 3 quarts strawberries, then slice off the tops with a paring knife. Sort the berries by height and place the tallest and largest strawberry in the center of the tart. Using the nicest and most evenly shaped ones, arrange the berries in tight rings around the center, placing them in descending height to the edge of the pastry. Quarter the remaining berries lengthwise and, beginning at the center, place one quarter between each whole berry, leaning its tip toward the center, to cover gaps. Use red currant jelly to glaze this tart.

TIP: To fill the gaps between the whole berries, place quarters of berries between them, pointed side up and skin-side out, leaning them toward the center of the tart.

KIWI, RASPBERRY, AND BLUEBERRY TART

TO ARRANGE FRUIT: Peel 2 large kiwis, halve lengthwise, and cut into half-moon slices about ⅜ inch thick. Arrange them cut-side down in an overlapping circle propped up against the inside edge of the pastry. Sort two ½ pints of raspberries by height, discarding any blemished berries, and arrange them in 2 tight rings just inside of the kiwi, using the taller berries to form the inner ring. Sort ½ pint of blueberries, discarding stems and blemished berries, and mound them in the center. Use apple jelly to glaze this tart.

TIP: To peel kiwi, cut off the ends, then slip a wide, shallow spoon between skin and flesh. Rotate the kiwi while pushing the spoon into the fruit, freeing flesh from skin.

glisten like dewdrops. The caveat is that the glaze must have the correct consistency. Too thin and the glaze will run off the fruit and pool in valleys; too thick and it falls from the brush in heavy globules. I found it helpful to bring the jelly to a boil, stirring it occasionally to ensure that it melts entirely, then use it straight off the stove. Be prepared to put your pan back on the stove if the glaze begins to gel as you use it. A quick reheating and a teaspoon of water gets it flowing again. (See Kitchen Notes, page 30, for more information.)

Lengthy cogitation and intense labor frequently result in food that at the end of cooking is neither visually appealing nor very palatable—at least that is the case for me. But the fruit tarts I had been making were so spectacular that they held even me in their grip, and they never failed to make admirers of passers-by. These are honest fruit tarts, not showpieces aiming to dupe. They live up to their good looks.

TESTING EQUIPMENT: **Tart Pans**

Tart pans with removable bottoms are available in three types of finishes. The traditional tinned steel tart pan is silver and reflective. Then there is the nonstick version coated with a brown finish inside and out. The third type, a black steel tart pan (also sometimes called blue steel), is quite difficult to find, at least in this country.

A tinned steel pan is what I used throughout recipe development of the fruit tart—without incident. So I wondered what a nonstick tart pan—at 2½ times the cost—could possibly improve upon. The answer is nothing, really. Tart pastry is brimming with butter and is not likely to stick to flypaper, so a nonstick tart pan is superfluous. And despite its darker finish, it browned the pastry at the same rate as the tinned steel pan.

The black steel pan was another matter. Colored to absorb heat and encourage browning, it did just that, actually taking the pastry a bit past even my preference for very deeply browned. This pan would be fine for baking a filled tart (the filling slows down the baking), but for unfilled pastry, it was a bit impetuous. If you own one and are using it to prebake tart pastry, try lowering your oven temperature by about 25 degrees. –D.Y.

TINNED STEEL   NONSTICK   BLACK STEEL

CLASSIC FRESH FRUIT TART

MAKES ONE 9- TO 9½-INCH TART, SERVING 8 TO 10

Chalazae are cordlike strands of egg white protein that are attached to the yolks—removing them with your fingers is easy and eliminates the need to strain the pastry cream after cooking. The pastry cream can be made a day or two in advance, but do not fill the prebaked tart shell until just before serving. Once filled, the tart should be topped with fruit, glazed, and served within half an hour or so.

Pastry Cream

- 2 cups half-and-half
- ½ cup sugar
- Pinch salt
- 5 large egg yolks, chalazae removed (see note)
- 3 tablespoons cornstarch
- 4 tablespoons cold unsalted butter, cut into 4 pieces
- 1½ teaspoons vanilla extract

Tart Pastry (Pâte Sucrée)

- 1 large egg yolk
- 1 tablespoon heavy cream
- ½ teaspoon vanilla extract
- 1¼ cups (6¼ ounces) all-purpose flour
- ⅔ cup (about 3 ounces) confectioners' sugar
- ¼ teaspoon salt
- 8 tablespoons (1 stick) very cold unsalted butter, cut into ½-inch cubes

Fruit and Glaze

- Fruit, unwashed
- ½ cup red currant or apple jelly (see "Three Fruit Tarts Designs," page 22)

1. **FOR THE PASTRY CREAM:** Heat half-and-half, 6 tablespoons sugar, and salt in medium heavy-bottomed saucepan over medium heat until simmering, stirring occasionally to dissolve sugar.

2. Meanwhile, whisk egg yolks in medium bowl until thoroughly combined. Whisk in remaining 2 tablespoons sugar and whisk until sugar has begun to dissolve and mixture is creamy, about 15 seconds. Whisk in cornstarch until combined and mixture is pale yellow and thick, about 30 seconds.

3. When half-and-half mixture reaches full simmer, gradually whisk simmering half-and-half into yolk mixture to temper. Return mixture to saucepan, scraping bowl with rubber spatula; return to simmer over medium heat, whisking constantly, until 3 or 4 bubbles burst on surface and mixture is thickened and glossy, about 30 seconds. Off heat, whisk in butter and vanilla. Transfer mixture to medium bowl, press plastic wrap directly on surface, and refrigerate until cold and set, at least 3 hours or up to 48 hours.

4. **FOR THE TART PASTRY:** While pastry cream is chilling, whisk together yolk, cream, and vanilla in small bowl; set aside. Pulse to combine flour, sugar, and salt in bowl of food processor fitted with steel blade. Scatter butter pieces over flour mixture; pulse to cut butter into flour until mixture resembles coarse meal, about fifteen 1-second pulses. With machine running, add egg mixture and process until dough just comes together, about 25 seconds. Turn dough onto sheet of plastic wrap and press into 6-inch disk. Wrap in plastic and refrigerate at least 1 hour or up to 48 hours.

5. Remove dough from refrigerator (if refrigerated longer than 1 hour, let stand at room temperature until malleable). Unwrap and roll out between lightly floured large sheets of parchment paper or plastic wrap to 13-inch round. (If dough is soft and sticky, slip onto baking sheet and refrigerate until workable, 20 to 30 minutes.) Transfer dough to tart pan by rolling dough loosely around rolling pin and unrolling over 9- to 9½-inch tart pan with removable bottom. Working around circumference of pan, ease dough into pan corners by gently lifting dough with one hand while pressing dough into corners with other hand. Press dough into fluted sides of pan. (If some edges are too thin, reinforce sides by folding excess dough back on itself.) Run rolling pin over top of tart pan to remove excess dough. Set dough-lined tart pan on large plate and freeze 30 minutes (can be sealed in gallon-sized zipper-lock plastic bag and frozen up to 1 month).

6. Meanwhile, adjust oven rack to middle position and heat oven to 375 degrees. Set dough-lined tart pan on baking sheet, press 12-inch square of foil inside frozen tart shell and over edges and fill with metal or ceramic pie weights. Bake until golden brown, about 30 minutes, rotating halfway through baking time. Remove from oven and carefully remove foil and weights by gathering edges of foil and pulling up and out. Continue to bake until deep golden brown, 5 to 8 minutes longer. Set baking sheet with tart shell on wire rack to cool to room temperature, about 30 minutes.

7. **TO ASSEMBLE AND GLAZE THE TART:** When tart shell is completely cool, spread cold pastry cream over bottom, using offset spatula or large spoon. (Can press plastic wrap directly on surface of pastry cream and refrigerate up to 30 minutes.) Arrange fruit on top of pastry cream, following a design on page 22, if desired.

8. Bring jelly to boil in small saucepan over medium-high heat, stirring occasionally to smooth out lumps. When boiling and completely melted, apply by dabbing and flicking onto fruit with pastry brush; add 1 teaspoon water and return jelly to boil if it becomes too thick to drizzle. (Tart can be refrigerated, uncovered, up to 30 minutes.) Remove outer metal ring of tart pan, slide thin metal spatula between bottom of crust and tart pan bottom to release, then slip tart onto cardboard round or serving platter; serve.

Solving the Problems of Cherry Cobbler

Most cherry cobblers are no more than canned pie filling.
We wanted fresh fruit flavor paired with a tender biscuit topping.

> BY KAY RENTSCHLER <

No more than a fleet of tender biscuits on a sea of sweet fruit, good cobblers hold their own against fancy fruit desserts. But unlike fancy fruit desserts, cobblers come together in a couple of quick steps and can be dished up hot, ready to hit the dance floor with a scoop of vanilla ice cream. Picking fresh sour cherries one summer in Vermont and cooking them up into a compote for crêpes acquainted me with their virtues: Sour cherries have sufficient acidity to cook up well and become truly expressive with a touch of sugar and some heat. (Sweet eating cherries, like Bings, lose their flavor when cooked.) Until then, the only sour, or baking, cherries I had known of were the canned variety. And however plump and lacquered their depictions on the label, those which slid from under a lattice were so pale, so limp and exhausted, that their flavor barely registered. But I knew sour cherries would feel at home in a cobbler—if I could find some good ones.

Vanilla ice cream or whipped cream is the perfect accompaniment for the light "cobbles" and warm fruit.

A Tart Response

Though sour cherries are grown in relatively large quantities in Michigan, here in the Northeast our grocery shelves are bereft of sour cherry products, save the crayon-red canned gravy with lumps called "pie filling." So I was grateful to find two different kinds of jarred sour cherries at my local Trader Joe's during the off season (all 11 months of it). In addition, the Cherry Marketing Institute of Michigan provided variously processed sour cherries—frozen, canned, and dried. Since it would be months before I could try making cobbler with fresh cherries, I began my testing with processed.

Early tests in which I prepared quick fruit fillings elicited unenthusiastic comments from tasters. While frozen Michigan sour cherries maintained their color well, flavor was left largely to the imagination. Both canned and jarred sour cherries from Michigan were flaccid and developed an anemic pallor when cooked. Adding a handful of dried cherries did little to heighten their impact. Only Trader Joe's jarred Morello cherries drew a crowd: deep ruby red, plump,

meaty, and tart, they delivered bracing flavor and a great chew right out of a jar.

The experience prompted me to do a little research. Sour cherries, I learned, are classified in two groups, amarelles and griottes. The former have lighter flesh—tan on the inside—and clear juices; the latter are dark—even black—with deep red juice. The best known examples of each group are Montmorency (an amarelle) and Morello (a griotte). Most tart cherries grown in the United States are Montmorency. Those from Eastern Europe are Morello. Remembering stellar cherries I had tasted in baked goods in Germany, I decided to base my recipe on jarred Morellos.

A cobbler should be juicy, but not swimming in juice, and it should taste like the fruit whose name it bears. Jarred and canned cherries come awash in juices, which I would use to produce the sauce. Since jarred and canned cherries have already been processed, they are already cooked: the less heat they're exposed to thereafter the better. Straining the juice off, I dumped the drained contents of four 24-ounce jars of Morellos into a 9 by 13-inch baking dish, then thickened and sweetened 3 cups

of the juice. The resulting flavor was a bit flat. I replaced 1 cup of the cherry juice with red wine and added a cinnamon stick, a pinch of salt, and a whiff of almond extract. Much better. Red wine and sour cherries have a natural affinity; the cinnamon stick added a fragrant woody depth, and, as with all fruits, salt performed its usual minor miracle. The almond extract brought the entire flavor experience up a couple of notches. For thickener I resolved to go with cornstarch. It could be mixed in with the sugar and brought directly to a simmer with the reserved cherry juices, then poured over the waiting cherries and baked. Lightly thickened fruit is best; a cobbler shouldn't be thick enough to spread on toast.

Stir, Scoop, Bake

I also had some requirements for the cobbles. I wanted them feather-light but deeply browned and crisp. This said a number of things to me. The first was: no eggs. Eggs would make my biscuits too heavy and substantial. (After working for years with *Cook's* scone recipe, a light and tender English biscuit that uses no eggs, I felt supported in that expectation.) The second thing it said was buttermilk. Buttermilk biscuits are famously light and tender. The third precept came by way of a number of southern recipes, which said a wet dough made a nice light biscuit. I baked several biscuit variations to confirm these notions, settling on all-purpose flour, a moderate amount of butter, small amounts of baking powder and soda, a touch of sugar (plus more on top for crunch), a wave of buttermilk, and a nice hot oven. Dispensing with rolling altogether, I simply dropped the biscuits onto the fruit with an ice cream scoop. The biscuits had a buttery lightness, a mild tang, and a crunchy, sugary top.

Not quite satisfied with their pale bellies touching the fruit, I undertook to bake the biscuits for 15 minutes on a sheet pan while the filling was coming together on the stove. I then wedded them to the fruit for only 10 minutes in the oven. By then the fruit (already hot from the cooked sauce) was bubbling around the biscuits, which were deeply browned on top and baked through

The Mighty Balaton

In 1984, well before unrestricted travel and commerce in Eastern Bloc countries became commonplace, Dr. Amy Iezzoni, professor of horticulture at Michigan State University, traveled extensively throughout Hungary to locate a vigorous sour cherry cultivar she could bring home to Michigan. Having spent years hybridizing local sour cherry seedlings, Hungarian breeders were prepared to release new cultivars with improved characteristics.

Sure enough, Iezzoni returned home with a dazzling Morello cultivar, which she named Balaton (after a lake in its native environs). She enlisted it in her breeding program, currently the only sour cherry breeding program in the United States. Under her care, the Balaton has thrived in its new climate. Cherry trees prefer long winters, Iezzoni told me, as well as cooler spring and summer temperatures, which favor normal fruit and flower development and lower the incidence of disease. The moderating winds of Lake Michigan reduce the probability that cherry flowers will be killed by an early freeze—much as Europe's continental climate buffers harsh weather.

Unlike the fragile and perishable Montmorency (a 400-year-old cultivar that has not been subject to crossbreeding to make it more vigorous), Balaton cherries are robust enough once harvested to endure shipping well. They are not only larger and plumper than Montmorency cherries but their dark juices are also beautiful and mysterious. (For information on purchasing Balaton or other Michigan sour cherries, see Resources, page 32.) —K.R.

THE BALATON CHERRY

underneath. Heaven in about a half-hour.

Jarred Morellos made a fine cobbler. But I wanted more, and finally, summer came. Searching for fresh cherries, I made an exciting discovery: Morello cherries had made their way to the United States (see "The Mighty Balaton"). I got to work. To test available varieties, I used both Morellos and the more delicate Montmorency cherries.

And how were the fresh cobblers? Both varieties of fresh cherries graced the recipe, yielding cobblers with plump, gorgeous, deeply flavorful fruit. The Montmorency cherries bore a candy apple red and a flavor resonant with almond accents; the fresh Morellos were transcendent, with a smooth richness and complex flavor notes. If you can get your hands on fresh sour cherries during their brief season in July, buy them—quickly—and start baking. And take heart. When the brief sour-cherry season is over, jarred Morello cherries will create a cobbler that is almost as wonderful.

SOUR CHERRY COBBLER
SERVES 12

Use the smaller amount of sugar in the filling if you prefer your fruit desserts on the tart side and the larger amount if you like them sweet.

Biscuit Topping
- 2 cups (10 ounces) all-purpose flour
- 6 tablespoons sugar plus additional 2 tablespoons for sprinkling
- 1/2 teaspoon baking powder
- 1/2 teaspoon baking soda
- 1/2 teaspoon salt
- 6 tablespoons cold unsalted butter, cut into 1/2-inch cubes
- 1 cup buttermilk

Cherry Filling
- 4 (24-ounce) jars Morello cherries, drained (about 8 cups drained cherries), 2 cups juice reserved
- 3/4–1 cup sugar
- 3 tablespoons plus 1 teaspoon cornstarch Pinch salt
- 1 cup dry red wine
- 1 (3-inch) stick cinnamon
- 1/4 teaspoon almond extract

1. Adjust rack to middle position and heat oven to 425 degrees. Line baking sheet with parchment paper.

2. In workbowl of food processor fitted with steel blade, pulse flour, 6 tablespoons sugar, baking powder, baking soda, and salt to combine. Scatter butter pieces over and process until mixture resembles coarse meal, about 15 one-second pulses. Transfer to medium bowl; add buttermilk and toss with rubber spatula to combine. Using a 1 1/2- to 1 3/4-inch spring-loaded ice cream scoop, scoop 12 biscuits onto baking sheet, spacing them 1 1/2 to 2 inches apart. Sprinkle biscuits evenly with 2 tablespoons sugar and bake until lightly browned on tops and bottoms, about 15 minutes. (Do not turn off oven.)

3. Meanwhile, spread drained cherries in even layer in 9 by 13-inch glass baking dish. Stir sugar, cornstarch, and salt together in medium nonreactive saucepan. Whisk in reserved cherry juice and wine, and add cinnamon stick; set saucepan over medium-high heat, and cook, whisking frequently, until mixture simmers and thickens, about 5 minutes. Discard cinnamon stick, stir in almond extract, and pour hot liquid over cherries in baking dish.

4. Arrange hot biscuits in 3 rows of 4 over filling. Bake cobbler until filling is bubbling and biscuits are deep golden brown, about 10 minutes. Cool on wire rack 10 minutes; serve.

FRESH SOUR CHERRY COBBLER

Morello or Montmorency cherries can be used in this cobbler made with fresh sour cherries. Do not use sweet cherries. If the cherries do not release enough juice after macerating for 30 minutes, cranberry juice makes up the difference.

1. Pit 4 pounds fresh sour cherries (about 8 cups), reserving juices. Stir together 1 1/4 cups sugar, 3 tablespoons plus 1 teaspoon cornstarch, and pinch salt in large bowl; add cherries and toss well to combine. Pour 1 cup dry red wine over cherries; let stand 30 minutes. Drain cherries in colander set over medium bowl. Combine drained and reserved juices (from pitting cherries); you should have 3 cups. If not, add enough cranberry juice to equal 3 cups.

2. While cherries macerate, follow steps 1 and 2 of recipe for Sour Cherry Cobbler to make and bake biscuit topping.

3. Spread drained cherries in even layer in 9 by 13-inch glass baking dish. Bring juices and one 3-inch cinnamon stick to simmer in medium nonreactive saucepan over medium-high heat, whisking frequently, until mixture thickens, about 5 minutes. Discard cinnamon stick, stir in 1/4 teaspoon almond extract, and pour hot juices over cherries in baking dish.

4. Continue with recipe from step 4.

TASTING | 'PROCESSED' CHERRIES

CANNED CHERRY PIE FILLING

FROZEN MICHIGAN SOUR CHERRIES

DRIED SOUR CHERRIES

JARRED MORELLO CHERRIES

In our tests, canned and frozen cherries were colorful but lacked flavor—even with dried cherries added. Jarred Morellos packed true cherry flavor.

$3.49 Balsamic Vinegar Wins Tasting

In the $15-and-under category, the lack of artificial sweetener and coloring makes an inexpensive brand a winner.

⪈ BY RAQUEL PELZEL ⪇

You can buy a decent bottle of nonvintage French table wine for $8, or you can invest in a bottle of 1975 Château Lafite Rothschild Bordeaux for $300—but no one would ever compare the two. They are two different beasts. The same holds true for balsamic vinegars. There are balsamic vinegars you can buy for $2.50 and ones that nudge the $300 mark. The more expensive vinegars bear the title *tradizionale* or *extra-vecchio tradizionale aceto balsamico* (traditional or extra-old traditional). According to Italian law, these "traditional" vinegars must come from the northern Italian provinces of Modena or Reggio Emilia and be created and aged in the traditional time-honored fashion.

Unfortunately, there is no way for American consumers to really be sure that the industrial-style balsamic vinegar they purchase in their grocery or specialty foods store is a quality product. Unlike the makers of trademark-protected products of Italy, including tradizionale balsamico, Parmigiano-Reggiano, and Prosciutto di Parma (all from the Reggio Emilia region), Italian producers of commercial balsamic vinegars failed to unite before market demand for their products ballooned in the United States in the early 1980s. The result has been high consumer demand with little U.S. regulation—the perfect scenario for some producers to take advantage of the system by misleading consumers about the integrity of their products.

For hundreds of years, tradizionale balsamico vinegar has been made from Trebbiano grapes found in the Modena or Reggio Emilia regions of northern Italy. The grapes are crushed and slowly cooked over an open flame into *must*. The must begins mellowing in a large wooden barrel, where it ferments and turns to vinegar. The vinegar is then passed through a series of barrels made from a variety of woods. To be considered worthy of the tradizionale balsamico title, the vinegar must be moved from barrel to barrel for a minimum of 12 years. An extra-vecchio vinegar must be aged for at least 25 years.

Because of its complex flavor and high production cost, tradizionale balsamico is used by those in the know as a condiment rather than an ingredient. The longer the vinegar ages, the thicker and more intense it becomes, maturing from a thin liquid into a spoon-coating, syrupy one—perfect for topping strawberries or cantaloupe. This is the aristocrat of balsamic vinegars.

The more common varieties, those with a price tag under $30, are categorized as commercial or industrial balsamic vinegars. These vinegars are what most Americans are familiar with and often use to complete a vinaigrette or flavor a sauce. The flavor profile of commercial balsamic vinegars ranges widely from mild, woody, and herbaceous to artificial and sour, depending on the producer and the style in which the vinegar was made. Commercial balsamic vinegar may or may not be aged and may or may not contain artificial caramel color or flavor.

We wondered how bad—or good—inexpensive, commercial balsamic vinegars would be when compared in a blind tasting. To level the playing field—and ease the burden on our budget—we limited the tasting to balsamic vinegars that cost $15 and under. We included some vinegars from supermarkets (we had held a preliminary supermarket balsamic vinegar tasting and included the three most favored by our tasters in the final tasting) and some from mail-order sources and specialty foods stores. We also included samples of the many different production styles, including some aged in the traditional fashion, some with added caramel color and flavor, and some made from a blend of aged red wine vinegar with added grape must.

We found that a higher price tag did not correlate with a better vinegar. Less expensive (under $5) and more expensive (more than $10) vinegars earned places in all three final categories (see chart on page 27). In addition, age seemed to play a less important role than we had expected. There were young vinegars in the top category as well as older vinegars in the bottom category.

Across the board, tasters found balsamic vinegars containing caramel color or flavor "sour" and "uninteresting." The top four brands from our tasting contain no artificial colors or flavors whatsoever. Our findings led us to believe that much as *fond* (the browned bits left in a pan after food has been sautéed) is instrumental in creating a quality pan sauce, must is paramount to making a full-flavored balsamic vinegar. As the must ages, it becomes thick and sweet, contributing an almost sherry- or port-like character to the vinegar. Producers

who substitute artificial color and flavor for must end up with a shallow sort of product that was routinely derided by our tasters. Some connoisseurs might argue that the only balsamic vinegars worth buying are aged ones, but we found that age didn't make nearly as big a difference as artificial additives did.

So how can consumers figure out what type of balsamic vinegar to buy? The easy answer is to check the label. If it discloses that artificial ingredients have been added, don't buy it. Unfortunately, it's not only commonplace but legal for the ingredient label to skirt the issue and completely avoid publishing the contents of the vinegar. This is because Italian law dictates that "Balsamic Vinegar of Modena," which is how nine out of 10 vinegars are labeled, is itself considered an ingredient and product, so no further description of the vinegar's contents is required. Label specifications from the U.S. Food and Drug Administration require only that the producer identify whether or not the vinegar contains sulfites, a preservative that produces a severe allergic reaction in some people.

"Whatever you want to call a balsamic vinegar, you can call a balsamic vinegar," says John Jack, vice-president of sales and marketing for Fiorucci Foods in Virginia. "It's become very much of a commodity-oriented business." Even if a vinegar is labeled "Balsamic Vinegar of Modena," a title that conveys the idea of quality to consumers, it may not have been produced in, or even near, Modena. In fact, several manufacturers bottle their vinegar right here in the United States. Young vinegars can bear the "balsamic" title, too. As a result of the less-than-stringent regulations, many producers and importers look forward to the passage of a new regulation in Italy that would make it illegal to label a vinegar younger than three years of age a balsamic.

According to an article on a balsamic vinegar tasting conducted by *Cook's* in 1995, these same regulations were pending six years ago. U.S. consumers are still left in the lurch, because even a white wine vinegar with added caramel color and flavor can legally be labeled as balsamic. So check the label. If the vinegar contains artificial color or sweetener, look further—or follow the guidelines of our tasters.

COOK'S ILLUSTRATED
26

TASTING BALSAMIC VINEGAR UNDER $15

The balsamic vinegar tasting was attended by 21 members of the *Cook's* staff. Tasters were asked to rate the vinegars for color, bouquet, flavor, body, and density. The balsamic vinegars were tasted in their natural state, with bread and water provided to cleanse the palate between samples. The balsamic vinegars were also evaluated by administrators and chef-instructors at Johnson & Wales University in Providence, R.I., as well as by local chefs and restaurateurs. We would like to thank the following Johnson & Wales attendees: Jack Chiaro, Marc DeMarchena, Paula Figoni, Karl Guggenmos, Ed Korry, Steven Shipley, and Miriam Weinstein. We also thank Providence chefs Steven Constantino of Venda Ravioli and Kevin Millonzi of Prov Restaurant. The balsamic vinegars listed below are ranked according to tasters' preferences. For purchasing information, see Resources on page 32.

HIGHLY RECOMMENDED

365 EVERY DAY VALUE
➤ **$3.49 for 500 milliliters**
MADE IN MODENA

Started from must; blend of older (up to five years) and younger balsamic vinegars. Tasters described this vinegar as chocolate brown, with a medium thickness. They loved its vanilla, fruit, and caramel-like underpinnings as well as its "balanced acidity."

MASSERIE DI SANT'ERAMO
➤ **$10.95 for 250 milliliters**
MADE IN MODENA

Started from must; aged a minimum of five years.
This vinegar was dark reddish-brown in color. Our tasters liked the fruit and honey notes in this sample as well as its "balanced spice and acidity." One taster called it "demure" and "floral"; another found it "sherry-like."

FIORUCCI RISERVA
➤ **$8.99 for 250 milliliters**
MADE IN MODENA

Aged wine vinegar blended with must; aged six years.
Described as "translucent brown," the Fiorucci vinegar was called "mellow" and "tangy-sweet" in flavor, reminding some tasters of plums and apples.

RECOMMENDED

CAVALLI BALSAMIC SEASONING
➤ **$15.00 for 250 milliliters**
MADE IN REGGIO EMILIA

Started from must; aged three years. This was an interesting, "enormously complex" sample, scoring either as a favorite or as a most detested balsamic—which lands it in the middle of the rankings. It had big vanilla and honey attributes, but some tasters couldn't get past the "strange but alluring" cedar/balsam notes.

FINI
➤ **$10.50 for 250 milliliters**
MADE IN MODENA

Started from must; aged two years.
NOTE: Contains caramel color.
Tasters called this sample "cloudy" and "muddy," with many objecting to the presence of sediment. It was characterized as having a fermented flavor somewhat reminiscent of soy sauce or raisins.

COLAVITA
➤ **$2.99 for 500 milliliters**
MADE IN MODENA

Aged wine vinegar blended with must; aged one year.
NOTE: Contains caramel color and flavor. Although this vinegar wasn't considered very complex, tasters were fond of its "fig," "burnt nut," and "tobacco" flavors. It was downgraded for being overly harsh, acidic, and "fleeting."

NOT RECOMMENDED

REGINA
➤ **$2.79 for 350 milliliters**
GRAPES FROM MODENA
BOTTLED IN U.S.

Wine vinegar blended with must; aged two to four years.
NOTE: Contains caramel color and flavor.
Called a "thin, mousy, unassuming little vinegar," Regina was disliked for its "artificial" qualities.

GIUSEPPE GIUSTI
➤ **$11.95 for 250 milliliters**
MADE IN MODENA

Started from must; aged approximately six years.
NOTE: May contain caramel color and flavor (an industry representative was unable to confirm or deny their presence in this product).
Tasters called it "salty," "harsh," and "sharp."

GREY POUPON
➤ **$4.49 for 500 milliliters**
MADE IN MODENA

Started from must; aged up to three years.
The color of "light cola," Grey Poupon was disliked for its "harsh" and "astringent" notes. One taster reported that it "leaves a bit of a sting."

MANICARDI
➤ **$9.00 for 250 milliliters**
MADE IN MODENA

Wine vinegar blended with must; aged six years.
NOTE: Contains caramel color and flavor. "Deep garnet" in color with a "spicy" and "burning" aftertaste, this sample was overwhelmingly harsh and oaky. One taster commented, "It tastes like a number 2 pencil."

Are All Pepper Mills Created Equal?

No! Some have large capacities, are easy to fill, and grind fast and furious.
Other models are worthless for kitchen use.

≥ BY ADAM RIED ≤

Season with salt and freshly ground pepper. Almost every savory recipe out there contains some variation of the phrase. Of course, rendering whole peppercorns fine requires a pepper mill, a kitchen tool for which function usually follows fashion. Pepper mills come in a vast range of styles and materials, but what really matters to us and other serious home cooks is performance. Is the fine-ground pepper truly fine? Is the medium grind really medium, or are there coarse particles mixed in? And how about output? Will you have to turn and turn and turn until your arm needs a brace to produce a teaspoon of ground pepper?

Though the pepper-mill market is flooded with handsome mills fit for a dining room table, in this test we sought out top performers that would make great kitchen partners; appearance was pretty much beside the point. Prices ranged from a high of $45 to a low of $14.99. But would that $45 actually buy you a three-fold improvement in performance?

Mill Work

Most pepper mills work by similar means. Peppercorns are loaded into a central chamber, through which runs a metal shaft. Near the bottom of the mill, the shaft is connected to a grinding mechanism that consists of a rotating, grooved "male" head that fits into a stationary, grooved "female" ring. Near the top of the male piece, the grooves are larger to crack the peppercorns and feed the smaller pieces downward to be ground between the finer grooves, or teeth, of the male and female components.

To a reasonable point, the finer the grind, the more evenly the pepper will be distributed throughout a dish. Thus the quality of a pepper mill's fine grind is more important than options for an endless range of grinds beyond fine, medium, and coarse. All of the mills in both "recommended"

categories did a decent job in terms of grind quality as well as output.

The industry experts we queried explained that the specifics of the grinding mechanism are key to grind quality. Jack Pierotti, president of Chef Specialties, maker of the Windsor mill, named the size, number, and angle of teeth in both male and

The Pepper Mills We Tested

RECOMMENDED

Unicorn
Huge capacity, awesome speed.

EHI
Unusual looks, but all the right moves.

Oxo (Grind It)
Odd looking, but a great performer.

Zyliss
Huge capacity and excellent grind quality.

RECOMMENDED WITH RESERVATIONS

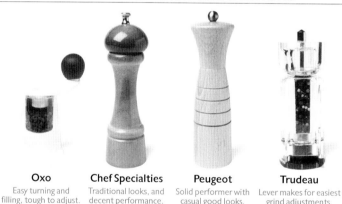

Oxo
Easy turning and filling, tough to adjust.

Chef Specialties
Traditional looks, and decent performance.

Peugeot
Solid performer with casual good looks.

Trudeau
Lever makes for easiest grind adjustments.

NOT RECOMMENDED

William Bounds
Handsome, but cranky to use.

Mr. Dudley
Limited settings, slow speed.

Zassenhaus
Fine grind is too coarse and coarse is too fine.

Chef'n
Irksome design makes this difficult to refill.

female grinder components as factors in performance. A related consideration, according Tom David, president of Tom David, Inc., maker of the Unicorn Magnum Plus mill, is how well the male and female grinding pieces are machined (the process used to cut the grooves). Sharper teeth combined with a very tight tolerance between the pieces yield a better grind, which to us means finer fine-ground pepper. Unfortunately, none of these details are evident upon inspecting a pepper mill in a kitchen store.

In addition to having an excellent grind quality, Unicorn Magnum Plus managed an awesome output. In one minute of grinding, the Magnum produced an incredible average of 7.3 grams, or about 3½ teaspoons, of fine-ground pepper. By comparison, honors for the next highest average output went to the Oxo Grind It, at 5.1 grams, while about half the pack hovered around the two-grams-or-less mark (which, at roughly one teaspoon in volume, is perfectly acceptable). We surmised, and Tom David confirmed, that the size of the grinding mechanism makes the difference. The Magnum Plus's mechanism measures a little more than one inch across; most of the others measure around three-quarters of an inch, making them about 25 percent smaller.

Fill 'Er Up

Grind quality and speed are only half the battle—especially if most of your peppercorns land on the floor when you try to fill the mill. So we appreciated mills with wide, unobstructed filler doors that could accommodate the tip of a wide funnel or, better yet, the lip of a bag or jar so that we could dispense with the funnel altogether. The filler openings on most of the mills measured about one inch, and they were often obstructed by the shaft. The easiest-to-fill mills had wider openings, often without the obstruction. The EHI Peppermate took high honors, with a lid that snaps off to create a gaping 3-inch opening, followed by the Zyliss

RATING PEPPER MILLS

RATINGS
★★★
GOOD
★★
FAIR
★
POOR

We rated 12 pepper mills, each one as close as possible to 8 inches in height if different sizes were available, and evaluated them according to the criteria below. The mills are listed in order of preference. All tests were performed using India Malabar peppercorns purchased from Penzeys Spices.

PRICE: Prices paid in Boston-area stores, in national mail-order catalogs, and at Web sites, with one exception. We tested the Oxo Good Grips Grind It prior to its market release, so the price listed is manufacturer's suggested retail.

CAPACITY: Volume of peppercorns hopper accommodates.

GRIND QUALITY: Our most important test. We preferred mills that produced fine-ground pepper that was uniformly powdery with no large pieces of peppercorn. If the fine-ground pepper was uneven or there was little visible or tactile difference between pepper ground at the medium and coarse settings, the mill was downgraded. Likewise, if the mill did not offer any grind adjustments, it was downgraded.

GRIND SPEED: Each mill was adjusted to its finest setting and operated at a consistent rate for one minute. Then the gram-weight of the resulting ground pepper was measured. Faster-grinding mills were preferred.

EASE OF FILLING: For each mill, we measured the opening through which it received peppercorns and filled the hopper with the help of a flexible rubber garlic peeler. Mills with unobstructed openings of 2 inches or more, which could be filled without spilling any peppercorns, were preferred.

EASE OF USE: The ease of using each mill was assessed based on a combination of factors, including the ease with which the mill could be filled and operated and the grind adjusted. Mills that required the least effort to operate or adjust and that had the most comfortable grip were preferred. Additional observations are noted in the Testers' Comments column of the chart.

Brand	Price	Capacity	Grind Quality	Grind Speed	Ease of Filling	Ease of Use	Testers' Comments
RECOMMENDED							
Unicorn Magnum Plus Restaurant Use Peppermill	$45.00	15 tablespoons	★★★	★★★	★★	★★★	In looks, at least, the Darth Vader of pepper mills. Very easy to adjust the grind, and dazzlingly effective.
East Hampton Industries (EHI) Peppermate Pepper Mill, Model 623	$40.00	7 tablespoons	★★★	★★	★★★	★★★	Detachable cup captures pepper to make measuring easy. Huge opening makes this mill easiest of all to fill. Among the fastest grinders.
Oxo Good Grips Grind It Pepper Mill, Model 41202	$19.99	8 tablespoons	★★★	★★★	★★	★★★	Part of a new spice grinder series. Difficult to determine grind setting, but lightning-fast grind speed.
Zyliss Large Pepper (and Salt) Mill	$27.50	16 tablespoons	★★★	★	★★★	★★★	That it is ample and easy to fill while also having exemplary grind quality helps forgive its slower, but still acceptable, grind speed.
RECOMMENDED WITH RESERVATIONS							
Oxo Good Grips Pepper Mill, Model 32180	$14.99	6 tablespoons	★★★	★★	★★	★★	Comes with a coaster/base to catch spills. Excellent grind quality and easy to use in many respects, but adjusting the grind can be a challenge.
Chef Specialties Windsor 8-Inch Pepper Mill	$22.99	5 tablespoons	★★★	★	★★	★★★	Most traditional of all in terms of design. Grind quality is good, if a hair behind the Peugeot model.
Peugeot Menton 20 cm Pepper Mill	$26.98	3 tablespoons	★★★	★	★★	★★★	All grind adjustments seem to be on the fine side, which is better for the fine-ground pepper than it is for the coarse-ground.
Trudeau Iceberg Adjustable Pepper Mill, Model 071-7005	$16.98	2 1/2 tablespoons	★★	★	★★	★★★	Head with flat sides provides good grip (surer than those with round heads) for easier turning. Smallest capacity of the lot, but grind adjustment system is well designed.
NOT RECOMMENDED							
William Bounds Shake 'n Twist Salt and Pepper Grinder	$27.99	6 1/2 tablespoons	★★	★	★★	★★★	Fine grind is OK, but coarse and medium are uneven. Especially poor output.
Mr. Dudley Saturn Battery-Operated Peppermill, Model 6003W	$21.99	5 1/2 tablespoons	★	★	★★	★★★	Gimmicky mill couldn't be easier to use, but how can you leave out something as basic as grind adjustment? Medium grind only.
Zassenhaus Pepper Mill, Model #4	$34.95	3 tablespoons	★★	★★	★★	★	Exceptionally difficult to crank in the two units we sampled. Finial has a tiny spring that pops out the moment the finial is unscrewed.
Chef'n "The Pepper Ball," Model APG-66CBK	$14.99	6 1/2 tablespoons	★	★	★	★★	Looks more comfortable to use than it actually is; fatigued the hands of several users. No grind settings between fine and coarse.

with a 2-inch opening and the Oxo Grind It with a wide-open 1⅜-inch mouth. Two other mills were easy to fill: the other Oxo, with its chute-style door, and the Unicorn Magnum Plus, with its sliding collar door. Along the same lines, the more peppercorns a mill could hold, the less often it has to be filled. Large capacity—about one-half cup or more—is an asset. The Zyliss held a full cup, and the Unicorn Magnum Plus trailed behind by just 1 tablespoon.

The ease of adjusting the grind was another factor we considered. Changing the grind from fine to coarse involves changing the tolerances of, or distances between, the male and female grinding components. The more space between them, the larger the pepper particles and the coarser the grind. Traditionally, a knob at the top of the mill called the finial is used to adjust the grind. This was our least favorite design for two reasons. First, the finial must be screwed down very tight for a fine grind, which not only requires significant finger strength but also makes the head (or the crank) of the mill more difficult to turn. Second, the finial usually has to be removed entirely to fill the mill, which means you have to readjust the grind with each filling. We preferred mills like the Unicorn Magnum Plus, which use a screw or dial at the base of the grinding mecha-

nism. Even easier to use were the lever system on the Trudeau Iceberg and the adjustment ring on the William Bounds Shake 'n Twist.

More than half of the mills tested did their jobs well, but the Unicorn Magnum Plus is a superstar. Its grind quality is exemplary, its output astounding, and its capacity huge. If that weren't enough, it's also easy to fill and comfortable to use. At $45, however, this mill was one of the two most expensive in the test (the second-place EHI Peppermate was $40). If your budget is a bit more restricted, bear in mind that both the Oxo Grind It and the Zyliss, at about half the cost of the winning mills, are also recommended.

⇒ BY KAY RENTSCHLER ⇐

Weighting for Pies

Most recipes that call for prebaking, or "blind baking," a pie or tart dough with pie weights or dried beans recommend baking the pastry shell just until it is set—generally 20 minutes—before removing the weights to let the inner crust firm and brown. With tender or fragile doughs, getting the weighted parchment or foil out of the shell without damaging the still-virgin dough can be challenging. We discovered that pie crusts bake just as well—better, in fact—if they are baked most of the way through with weights. The crust firms up and browns beneath the weights, and the dough remains intact when the weights are lifted out. Check both timer and crust frequently after about three-quarters of the projected baking time has elapsed. If the crust is still very blond and producing a lot of steam, leave the weights in place another five or 10 minutes. Our recipe for sweet pastry dough in this issue (page 23) bakes the crust for 30 minutes with pie weights and five minutes without.

Tips for Tarts

Glazing a fruit tart is not like painting woodwork; it's like dabbling on canvas. Such an artistic endeavor requires proper tools and supplies. Don't touch that greasy, round basting brush! A good pastry brush will feature graduated rows of bristles ending in a fine edge, essential for placement of the glaze without disturbing the fruit. Also crucial is the temperature and viscosity of the jelly. All fruits contain pectin, a carbohydrate that consists of chains of sugar molecules called polysaccharides. When fruits are boiled during jelly making, the evaporating water crowds pectin polysaccharides and additional sugars together to form tangled chains. When the jelly cools, these tangled chains hold the remaining water in suspension, making a semisolid gel. When heated to make a glaze, the jelly returns to a liquid state. Because a glaze needs to be blasting hot to mold itself to the arranged fruit, it must come boiling off the stove. That's rule number one. Let too much water boil away, and you'll have a sticky, elastic mess. That brings us to rule number two: As soon as the glaze boils, get it off the stove. We went into the test kitchen to see if we could come up with real temperature and texture predictors of the perfect glaze. We brought a half cup each of red currant and apple jelly to a boil, whisking all the while. (Boiling and whisking together are necessary to eliminate lumps.) At 225 degrees, the texture is perfect for glazing. After two minutes the jellies were about 165 degrees—still hot as all get out and holding steady with consistency. At 150 degrees the jellies were too cool and sluggish to glaze correctly. When we added a teaspoon of water and brought them back over heat to 225 degrees, they were as good as new.

Eau de Shallots

The most delicate member of the allium clan, the shallot, gets most of its culinary mileage in sauce reductions and sautés. But the shallot offers equally impressive aromatic results when used raw—like an ordinary onion. In vinaigrettes, egg, tuna, chicken, or seafood salads, the shallot gives off subtle flavor notes unavailable to the blunt, outspoken onion. Biting into a raw shallot is another matter. Lacking the water content of onions, shallots lack onions' bright apple-crispness as well. A shallot's crunch is pure, stubborn cellulose. In the past we have addressed the problem of crunch by mincing shallots as finely as possible. But grating shallots is even better, getting at their essence, while leaving the crunch behind. Using a fine box grater, we discovered that about half the amount of raw grated shallots can be substituted for raw minced shallots in a recipe.

Caramel Sauce Update

Our caramel sauce recipe (September/October 2000) produces a no-fuss, luxurious sauce that glides over a couple of scoops of vanilla ice cream like a velvet stole over a starlet's shoulders. But reheated leftovers, we learned from one of our readers, got a bit thick. Though the sauce warmed beautifully, it recoiled when it hit the ice cream and hung on like chewy candy. We headed back to the kitchen for some follow-up tests. Sure enough, after a couple of microwave rewarmings, the same thing happened to us. We fixed the problem quickly: A tablespoon or two of warm cream or hot water, a bit of a stir, and 10 seconds of microwave heat (or a bit longer on the stove) restored the caramel's fluidity.

Parsing Parsley

Some of it is curly, some of it straight. What's the difference? We're talking about *Pertoselinum crispum* here. That's right—parsley. Though curly and flat-leaf parsley have the same name, they are far from identical. Curly parsley is the old-fashioned corsage propped up next to your steak, a flouncy garnish. Beyond that—being practically flavorless—it's not much use. Even so, restaurants often favor curly parsley for chopping because its upright carriage and drier nature make the going easier. Flat-leaf, or Italian, parsley, on the other hand, with its big green flavor, achieves the culinary status of any fresh herb. Salads like Middle Eastern tabbouleh and sauces like the chimichurri featured in our May/June 2001 issue (page 9) depend on it. So shop wisely: Go for the big taste, forget the frills.

Boarding School

Though the jury is still out on whether wooden or plastic cutting boards best discourage germs, our age of bacterial vigilance has made us aware of cross-contamination. Everybody knows, for example, that it is an alarming breach of hygiene to cut a strawberry on the surface just used to cut up a chicken. If you have only one board, what should you do? Sanitation experts agree that rigorous and constant cleaning is imperative, citing a hot soapy scrub and thorough drying as one way to clean boards between tasks.

While nothing can replace a hot soapy scrub when chicken remains are stuck to your board, there is a quick way to sanitize cutting boards and other work surfaces whose good hygiene is in doubt. Simply apply straight 3 percent bleach and plain white or cider vinegar. These nontoxic disinfectants can be sprayed full strength from individual plant misters onto cutting boards (the order of the spray does not influence efficacy). According to research by Dr. Susan Sumner of Virginia Polytechnic Institute and State University, spraying one mist right after the other is more effective than using either alone and is also better than using the two mixed together. We were very pleased to use these mists on our cutting boards and countertops—residues from neither are harmful.

For large, smelly, or stained plastic boards that don't fit into the dishwasher, our favorite cleaning method is the overnight bleach bath. One tablespoon bleach per quart of water and a sink free of dishes will afford your cutting board an opportunity to detox. Immerse the board fouled-side up. When the board rises to the surface, drape a clean kitchen towel or two over its surface, and splash the towel with about a quarter cup additional bleach. A pristine board will await you in the morning.

Recipes from the Pacific Rim

A stunning, Southeast Asian–inspired cookbook moves comfortably from coffee table to home kitchen. A Hawaiian offering seems more at home in a restaurant kitchen. BY CHRISTOPHER KIMBALL

HOT SOUR SALTY SWEET
Jeffrey Alford and Naomi Duguid
Artisan, 346 pages, $40

There are travel books, coffee-table books, and cookbooks—and sometimes all three merge into one, as is the case with *Hot Sour Salty Sweet*. Jeffrey Alford and Naomi Duguid began traveling to Southeast Asia back in the 1970s, using the Mekong Delta as the organizing principle of their culinary adventures. Although the Vietnam War circumscribed their earliest outings, by the late 1980s they were traveling to Laos, Vietnam, and Cambodia, often crisscrossing parts of China as well. The authors have divided this area into seven culinary regions, although the book is organized by recipe type rather than geography. The book is richly illustrated, combining top-notch, *National Geographic*–style photography by Mr. Alford with gorgeous studio shots of food and stunning monochromatic chapter openers.

PROS: Although British publishers evidence a healthy lust for the well-designed, well-printed book, most American publishers seem to have little appetite for anything other than lowering unit costs. Artisan, an imprint owned by Workman Publishing, is one exception to that rule. This book is drop-dead gorgeous from the paper to the printing, design, and photography. The recipes appear reasonable in length and are well suited to the American kitchen, although trips to Asian markets will be in order.

CONS: Having spent a considerable amount of time with this work, I slowly realized that *Hot Sour Salty Sweet* is two genres joined at the hip. One is a personal travelogue by two very interesting folks with a spare, nicely honed writing style. Short anecdotes and observations from their travels are sprinkled among the recipes—including tales of almost getting run over by an elephant and traveling for two days through the jungle only to encounter, in the middle of nowhere, a small rock group singing a slow, bluesy variation of "Home on the Range." Although Mr. Alford is an exceptional photographer, I found the "real" story of the authors' travels more compelling than the Disney World version that the pictures promote. The authors experienced a grittier, more complex Southeast Asia than indicated by the happy folk in brightly colored costumes who people the photographs. I, for one, am hungry for the real thing.

RECIPE TESTING: The general rule of cookbook reviews at *Cook's Illustrated* is to test a dozen recipes. The staff found the recipes from *Hot Sour Salty Sweet* so compelling that we made 30 of them before we were finished. Of that group, an impressive 25 were worth making again. These are recipes that pair a simple approach with a bit of culinary adventure, a large percentage being soups, rice dishes, stir-fries, sauces, vegetable dishes, and simple salads. Among the outstanding offerings were Stir-Fried Cabbage with Dried Chiles and Ginger; Fried Bananas; Rice Paper Roll-Ups with Shrimp and Herbs; Tom Yum Pa (hot-and-sour soup with fish); Buddhist Sour Soup; Chinese Greens, Thai Style; and Grilled Chicken with Hot and Sweet Dipping Sauce. Although most of the recipes were quick and relatively easy, with a keen eye toward American home cooking, we did have to make a few substitutions (try finding cilantro with the roots attached). We also came across a few recipes that required other recipes, such as Green Curry Paste, the odd recipe that required a lot of preparation, and a couple of dishes that were a bit bland. Although Asian aficionados will no doubt recognize many of the recipes in *Hot Sour Salty Sweet*, no other cookbook on this subject has done such a good job of adapting the recipes to the American market. Our advice is to run out and purchase your own copy of this remarkable work along with a jumbo bottle of Thai fish sauce.

THE HALI'IMAILE GENERAL STORE COOKBOOK
Beverly Gannon
Ten Speed Press, 204 pages, $35

This cookbook is based on the Hali'imaile General Store in Maui, which started life as a plantation store in 1927 and was then converted to a takeout restaurant/catering headquarters/gourmet shop in 1988 by the Gannon family, who moved from Dallas to Maui in 1980. The store quickly became a full-fledged restaurant, one that has become a sought-after destination for visitors from around the world. The book is well packaged, with plenty of color photographs of the food, the restaurant, and local scenery.

PROS: Instead of buying the T-shirt, you can buy the cookbook! If you have fond memories of Hali'imaile, this book will rekindle them.

CONS: The prose has the slight odor of self-promotion and boosterism, which is, I suppose, not out of character for a chef/owner. The recipes are clearly restaurant recipes meant to impress—over-the-top in terms of both time invested and flavor for the home cook.

RECIPE TESTING: The test kitchen had a hard time finding a dozen recipes that would be worth the time and effort. For example, a seared duck breast recipe requires 28 ingredients and three separate recipes (the marinade, the compote, and the wild rice pancakes). On the whole, the recipes we did test turned out fine, although many of them required a sous-chef. Piña Colada Cheesecake went over the top by incorporating a white chocolate ganache and Pineapple Shortbread Cookies (we skipped the cookies), but tasters loved it. The Warm Gingerbread with Mascarpone Filling and Sautéed Pears was also excellent and had clear directions. Less successful dishes included the Sesame-Crusted Mahi-Mahi with Coconut-Curry Cabbage and Rum-Baked Bananas and the Szechuan Barbecued Salmon—good food, but fussy.

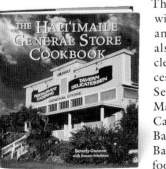

Most of the ingredients and materials necessary for the recipes in this issue are available at your local supermarket, gourmet store, or kitchen supply shop. The following are mail-order sources for particular items. Prices listed below were current at press time and do not include shipping or handling unless otherwise indicated. We suggest that you contact companies directly to confirm up-to-date prices and availability.

Balsamic Vinegar

Three brands of balsamic vinegar came in highly recommended as a result of our tasting (page 26). The 365 Every Day Value Balsamic Vinegar, sold exclusively at Whole Foods Market stores around the country, may be the hardest to come by. It can be ordered online at **www.gaiam.com** but only if ordered in combination with 365-brand oils. To find a Whole Foods Market store near you, check the store locator on the company's Web site at **www.wholefoodsmarket.com.** An 8½-ounce bottle of Masserie di Sant'Eramo vinegar is available for $10.95 from **La Cucina Rustica (P.O. Box 115, Wayne, IL 60184-0115; 800-796-0116; www.cybercucina.com)**, item #M1112B. An 8½-ounce bottle of Fiorucci Riserva can be mail-ordered for $8.99 from **Dorothy McNett's Place (243 Sixth Street, Hollister, CA 95023; 831-637-6444; www.happycookers.com)**, item #3-4583. Our recommended vinegars include Colavita, available in supermarkets nationwide, and Fini and Cavalli, both found in specialty foods stores. If your supermarket doesn't carry them, Fini can also be found at Williams-Sonoma, and Cavalli can be mail-ordered from La Cucina Rustica, item #CAV1106B, for $32.50, although it retails for $15 in stores.

Pepper Mills

Grind quality, hopper capacity, ease of use, and price were the pepper-mill characteristics we considered for our testing on page 28. The sleek, 9-inch Unicorn Magnum Plus Restaurant Use Peppermill was the best performer of the lot and can be mail-ordered from **Bridge Kitchenware (214 East 52nd Street, New York, NY 10022; 800-274-3435; www.bridgekitchenware.com)**, item code APMM-C, for $45. The East Hampton Industries Peppermate Pepper Mill, Model 623, has a clear base that collects ground pepper for easy measurement. **A Cook's Wares (211 37th Street, Beaver Falls, PA 15010; 800-915-9788; www.cookswares.com)** carries the handy mill in black (item #6030B) and white (item #6030), each for $40. Although not yet available as we went to press, the Oxo Good Grips Grind It Pepper Mill, Model 41202, was another great performer. According to an Oxo representative,

Amazon.com and **Cooking.com** will carry the mill at a suggested retail price of $19.99.

Fruit Tart

After testing nonstick and black steel against traditional tinned steel tart pans for the fruit tart on page 21, we were convinced that the original is still the best. Use a 9- or 9½-inch pan with a removable bottom for best results. **Sur La Table (1765 Sixth Avenue South, Seattle, WA 98134-1608; 800-243-0852; www.surlatable.com)** carries a 9½-inch tart pan, item #3557, for $6.95. When blind baking the pastry, it is imperative to weigh down the dough to avoid bubbling and shrinkage. Either ceramic or metal pie weights will do the trick. **The Baker's Catalog (King Arthur Flour, P.O. Box 876, Norwich, VT 05055-0876; 800-827-6836; www.kingarthurflour.com)** carries ceramic pie weights in 13-ounce packages for $5.95, item #9238. We recommend buying two packages. Instead of brushing the glaze onto the fruit, use a soft-bristled pastry brush to dab, drizzle, and flick it in beautiful droplets. **Kitchen Etc. (32 Industrial Drive, Exeter, NH 03833; 800-232-4070; www.kitchenetc.com)** carries a 2-inch pastry brush, item #592626, for $7.99, that is perfect for the job.

Grilled Potato Salad and Shish Kebabs

Using bamboo or thin metal skewers to thread cubed potatoes for parboiling and grilling makes them easy to handle. Ten-inch bamboo skewers, in a package of 100, can be mail-ordered from **The Oriental Pantry (423 Great Road, Acton, MA 01720; 978-264-4576; www.orientalpantry.com)** for $1.29, item #9609. For lamb kebabs, we prefer metal skewers. You can mail-order a set of four 11-inch skewers from **A Cook's Wares (211 37th Street, Beaver Falls, PA 15010; 800-915-9788; www.cookswares.com)**, item #8068, for $5. It is helpful to use spring-loaded tongs when transferring the speared potatoes from stovetop to grill and when turning the kebabs. We prefer 16-inch tongs for all grilling needs. You can order a pair of 16-inch Amco tongs for $6.50, item #450700, from **Kitchen Etc. (32 Industrial Drive, Exeter, NH 03833; 800-232-4070; www.kitchenetc.com)**.

Cherry Cobbler

Jarred Morello cherries turned out an amazing cobbler. You may be able to find them in your local specialty store; if not, Trader Joe's stores carry their own brand—and they are delicious. To find a store near you, check the online locator at **www.traderjoes.com.** Likewise, **German Deli (500 North Kimball Avenue, Suite 105, Southlake, TX 76092; 877-437-6269; www.germandeli.com)**

carries 24-ounce jars for $5.59. Click "fruits and syrups" at the bottom of the Web page, and Gundelsheim Schattenmorellen (aka Dark Morello Cherries) will appear. Fresh Balaton cherries will be available by mail order from mid-July through August from **Sleeping Bear Fresh Fruit Growers (6754 Yura Road, Williamsburg, MI 49690; 866-955-4555; www.michiganbalaton.com)** and **Wheeler Farms (2748 North 144th Avenue, Hart, MI 49420; 231-873-3753; www.wheelerfarms.com)**. The farms will be selling 5-pound boxes of fresh-picked cherries for $23.95.

Knife Sharpening

If you can't find the affordable Norton "India" combination sharpening stone at your local hardware store, check with **Stoddard's (50 Temple Place, Boston, MA 02111; 617-426-4187)**. It carries the synthetic stone, item code IB-8, for $25. While traditional sharpening steels help maintain a knife's edge, the Ultimate Edge Diamond Sharpening Steel can bring back an edge and lengthen the interval between thorough sharpenings. A diamond steel is made from an oval, lightweight steel shaft with a 600-grit diamond mesh bond that provides a hard surface to clean metal off a dulled knife and renew its edge. A 10-inch Ultimate Edge diamond steel will fit into most knife blocks and sells for $25 by mail order from **Professional Cutlery Direct (242 Branford Road, North Branford, CT 06471; 800-859-6994; www.cutlery.com)**, item #1CI7UE.

If you'd rather send your knives out to be sharpened and cannot locate a professional knife sharpener in your area, Kitchen Arts, a Boston kitchen equipment store, will accept knives by mail for sharpening service. If you choose this option, use common sense when packaging to protect the knife's edge—and the mail carrier. Do not tape up your blade. If you still have it, use the original plastic or cardboard sheath in which the knife was sold. Wrap in newspaper and pack in a sturdy corrugated box in such a way that the knife won't shift position. If your blade edge is not badly dulled, you can expect to be charged the following for sharpening: $2.00 for blades shorter than 5½ inches, $3.00 for all longer blades, and $4.00 for serrated blades. Mail to **Kitchen Arts (161 Newbury Street, Boston, MA 02116; 617-266-8701)**, and enclose your name, address, phone number, and credit card information. The store will bill you for sharpening and return shipment. Allow up to seven days for servicing. Don't be alarmed if your knife comes back with a few scuffs on the blade. That's normal.

RECIPES
July & August 2001

Grilled Chilean Sea Bass

Grilled Chicken Salad

Main Dishes
Grilled Chicken Cutlets 7
Grilled Chicken Salad
   with Sesame-Miso Dressing 7
Grilled Chilean Sea Bass Fillets 13
Shish Kebab 14

Soups and Side Dishes
Baba Ghanoush 19
   Israeli-Style 19
   with Sautéed Onion 19
Gazpacho 9
   Quick Food Processor 9
Grilled Potatoes for Salad 10
Grilled Potato Salad
   and Arugula, with Dijon Mustard
      Vinaigrette 11
   German-Style 11
   Spicy, with Corn and Poblano
      Chiles 11

Fruit Salads
Honeydew, Mango, and Blueberries
   with Lime-Ginger Reduction 20
Nectarines, Blueberries, and
   Raspberries with Champagne-
   Cardamom Reduction 20

Red Plums and Figs with Brandy-
   Cinnamon Reduction 20
Strawberries and Grapes with
   Balsamic and Red Wine
   Reduction 20

Salsas, Relishes, and Marinades
FOR GAZPACHO:
   Garlic Croutons 9
FOR GRILLED CHICKEN CUTLETS:
   Cucumber and Mango Relish with
      Yogurt 7
   Spicy Tomatillo and Pineapple
      Salsa 7
FOR GRILLED CHILEAN SEA BASS FILLETS:
   Black Olive and Citrus Relish 13
   Orange and Soy Marinade 13
   Spicy Fresh Tomato Salsa 13
FOR SHISH KEBAB:
   Garlic and Cilantro Marinade with
      Garam Masala 15
   Rosemary-Mint Marinade with
      Garlic and Lemon 15
   Sweet Curry Marinade with
      Buttermilk 15
   Warm-Spiced Parsley Marinade
      with Ginger 15

Desserts
Classic Fresh Fruit Tart 23
Sour Cherry Cobbler 25

PHOTOGRAPHY: CARL TREMBLAY

Gazpacho

Baba Ghanoush

Grilled Potato and Arugula Salad with Dijon Mustard Vinaigrette

Fruit Salad

Shish Kebab

www.cooksillustrated.com

If you enjoy *Cook's Illustrated* magazine, you should visit our Web site. Simply log on at www.cooksillustrated.com. Although much of the information is free, database searches are for site subscribers only. *Cook's Illustrated* readers are offered a 20 percent discount.

Here is what you can do on our site:
Search Our Recipes: We have a searchable database of all the recipes from *Cook's Illustrated*.
Search Tastings and Cookware Ratings: You will find all of our reviews (cookware, food, wine, cookbooks) plus new material created exclusively for the Web site.
Find Your Favorite Quick Tips.
Get Your Cooking Questions Answered: Post questions for *Cook's* editors and fellow site subscribers.
Check Your Subscription: Check the status of your subscription, pay a bill, or give gift subscriptions online.

Visit Our Bookstore: You can purchase any of our cookbooks, hardbound annual editions of the magazine, or posters online.
Subscribe to *e-Notes:* Our free e-mail companion to the magazine offers cooking advice, test results, buying tips, and recipes about a single topic each month.
Find Out about Our New Public Television Show: Watch *America's Test Kitchen* to see the *Cook's Illustrated* staff at work in our test kitchen. Check www.americastestkitchen.com for program times in your area.
Get All the Extras: The outtakes from each issue of *Cook's* are available at Cook's Extra, including step-by-step illustrations.

Sour Cherry Cobbler

Classic Fresh Fruit Tart

Rosemary

Marjoram

Lavender

Fennel Seeds

Basil

Summer Savory

Sage

Thyme

HERBES DE PROVENCE

NUMBER FIFTY-TWO

SEPTEMBER & OCTOBER 2001

COOK'S
ILLUSTRATED

Spaghetti alla Carbonara
Lighter, Brighter, Better

Quick, Pan-Fried Chicken Cutlets
Thick, Crunchy Coating

Steak au Poivre
The Peppercorns Stay On

Blueberry Muffins
Rich but Dainty

Bittersweet Chocolate Sauce
Best Sauce in 10 Minutes

Tasting Vanilla Ice Creams
Famous Brands Disappoint

Testing Colanders
Improving Ratatouille
Mustard Vinaigrette
Best Apple Cake
Measuring Tricks
Homemade Bouillabaisse

$4.95 U.S./$6.95 CANADA

62805

10>

0 232817 1

CONTENTS

September & October 2001

2 Notes from Readers
Readers ask questions and suggest solutions.

4 Quick Tips
Quick and easy ways to perform everyday kitchen tasks, from serving hard frozen ice cream to using an empty Pringles can to fill a pastry bag.

6 Spaghetti alla Carbonara
Restaurant carbonara is often an unctuous, congealed mass of cheese, eggs, and bacon. We set out to rediscover the beauty in the beast. BY BRIDGET LANCASTER

8 Steak au Poivre
Steak au poivre is often nothing more than uninspired skillet steak. We were after the real thing—a silky sauce married to a well-seared crust of pungent, cracked peppercorns.
BY DAWN YANAGIHARA

10 Better Breaded Chicken Cutlets
Most chicken cutlets deliver a flimsy, thin crust. We set out to make cutlets with crunch from a thick, flavorful coating that won't peel off like a bad sunburn. BY ADAM RIED AND BRIDGET LANCASTER

12 Beefing Up Mustard Vinaigrette
To make an assertive but well-balanced vinaigrette, choose the mustard carefully, match it with the right vinegar, and leave the extra-virgin olive oil on the shelf.
BY BRIDGET LANCASTER WITH ADAM RIED

13 Bouillabaisse Goes Home
Could we make a richly scented seafood stew at home in two hours with supermarket fish and no sous-chef? BY KAY RENTSCHLER

16 Measuring 101
Accurate measuring is the first step to successful cooking. We define the basics, show you some shortcuts, and explain why careful measuring is so important. BY RAQUEL PELZEL

18 Rethinking Ratatouille
How do you transform an oily, bland vegetable stew into a brightly flavored ratatouille? For starters, heat your oven to 500 degrees.
BY BRIDGET LANCASTER

20 The Best Blueberry Muffins
Some like them big, bland, and coarse. We like them rich, moist, and dainty, without the bother of creaming butter or finding great fresh berries. BY KAY RENTSCHLER

22 Apple Cake
Some apple cakes turn out shellacked and inedible while others are eggy and sodden. Fifty apple cakes later, we discovered a better way. BY RAQUEL PELZEL

24 Bittersweet Chocolate Sauce
A simple, foolproof technique and the right chocolate make the richest, most flavorful chocolate dessert sauce.
BY JULIA COLLIN

25 Big-Name Vanilla Ice Creams Fail to Sweep Tasting
Our panel favors "fresh," "clean" taste over "overwhelmingly vanilla" flavors. BY RAQUEL PELZEL

28 Are Expensive Colanders Worth the Dough?
In a word, no. A $25 colander performs as well as a $115 model.
BY ADAM RIED

30 Kitchen Notes
Test results, buying tips, and advice related to stories past and present, directly from the test kitchen. BY KAY RENTSCHLER

31 First-Class to New York and Seattle
Two chef cookbooks travel first-class from Italy to New York and from the Chesapeake Bay (via Asia) to Seattle. Can they make the trip to the home kitchen as well? BY CHRISTOPHER KIMBALL

32 Resources
Products from this issue and where to get them, including ice cream scoops, colanders, and measuring gear.

www.cooksillustrated.com

PUBLISHER AND EDITOR
Christopher Kimball

SENIOR EDITOR
Jack Bishop

FOOD EDITOR
Kay Rentschler

MANAGING EDITOR
Dawn Yanagihara

SENIOR WRITER
Adam Ried

EDITORIAL MANAGER
Barbara Bourassa

TEST KITCHEN DIRECTOR
Bridget Lancaster

ASSOCIATE EDITORS
Julia Collin
Raquel Pelzel

ASSISTANT EDITOR
Shannon Blaisdell

COPY EDITOR
India Koopman

MANAGING EDITOR,
BOOKS AND WEB SITE
Rebecca Hays

ASSISTANT EDITOR, WEB SITE
Shona Simkin

EDITORIAL INTERNS
Matthew Card
Meg Suzuki

PROOFREADER
Jana Branch

VICE PRESIDENT MARKETING
David Mack

SALES REPRESENTATIVES
Jason Geller
Karen Shiffman

MARKETING ASSISTANT
Connie Forbes

CIRCULATION MANAGER
Larisa Greiner

PRODUCTS MANAGER
Steven Browall

DIRECT MAIL MANAGER
Robert Lee

CIRCULATION ASSISTANT
Jennifer McCreary

CUSTOMER SERVICE MANAGER
Jacqueline Valerio

INBOUND MARKETING REPRESENTATIVE
Adam Dardeck

VICE PRESIDENT OPERATIONS
AND TECHNOLOGY
James McCormack

ART DIRECTOR
Amy Klee

PRODUCTION MANAGER
Jessica Quirk

PRODUCTION ARTIST
Daniel Frey

PRODUCTION COORDINATOR
Mary Connelly

PRODUCTION INTERNS
Ron Bilodeau
Kazumi Hashi
Lisa Leonard

SYSTEMS ADMINISTRATOR
Richard Cassidy

WEBMASTER
Nicole Morris

CHIEF FINANCIAL OFFICER
Sharyn Chabot

CONTROLLER
Mandy Shito

OFFICE MANAGER
Juliet Nusbaum

RECEPTIONIST
Henrietta Murray

PUBLICITY
Deborah Broide

For list rental information, contact The SpecialLISTS, 1200 Harbor Blvd. 9th Floor, Weehawken, NJ 07087; 201-865-5800; fax 201-867-2450. Editorial office: 17 Station Street, Brookline, MA 02445; 617-232-1000; fax 617-232-1572. Editorial contributions should be sent to: Editor, *Cook's Illustrated*. We cannot assume responsibility for manuscripts submitted to us. Submissions will be returned only if accompanied by a large self-addressed envelope. Postmaster: Send all new orders, subscription inquiries, and change of address notices to: *Cook's Illustrated*, P.O. Box 7446, Red Oak, IA 51591-0446. PRINTED IN CHINA.

DRIED PASTA

DRIED PASTA Dried pasta is nothing more than water and durum wheat flour, called semolina in Italy. When made commercially, the high-protein flour and water are kneaded in huge mixers to create a strong, elastic dough. The dough is then extruded through brass forms into one of a bewildering number of shapes. When cooking dried pasta, one general rule applies: A balanced serving of pasta and sauce should be provided in each bite. This requires a perfect marriage between the consistency of the sauce and the shape of the pasta. Long strands are nicely coated by smooth, creamy sauces that cling, such as Alfredo and carbonara. Short, tubular pasta such as cavatappi, gigli, mostaccioli, rotelle, and the bow-tie-like farfalle trap small bits of vegetables and meat. Larger tubular pasta such as pennoni, gomitoni, and castellane are best tossed with large chunks of meat or vegetables, while diminutive radiatore, gemelli, and orecchiette work best with smooth sauces or finely diced ingredients. COVER (*Tomatoes*): ELIZABETH BRANDON, BACK COVER (*Dried Pasta*): JOHN BURGOYNE

HOME MOVIES

Years ago I took piano lessons from John Mehegan, a well-known jazz musician who played at local night clubs, the chords building, the dog-house-bass drumming, and then a cascade of notes flying from his right hand, ducking and weaving through the melody, transforming it, condensing it, drawing it out until the audience was breathless. My very first lesson was indeed given by John, the keys of his black Yamaha baby grand discolored by cigarettes having burned too low, a tumbler of "tomato juice" sitting nearby. (I always suspected that it contained its share of vodka.) It was a painful, dull-witted hour on my part, a perfect match of physical and mental deficiencies merging quickly into despair and incompetence. The magic of John's music was being reduced to mathematical formulas, to inversions and conversions, to minor sevenths, to the wheel of fifths, to relative minors, to just plain repetition and hard work to build physical dexterity. It was difficult, perhaps impossible, for me to imagine that one day I would play "Satin Doll" in a fluid, recognizable form.

Much like musicians, farmers develop proficiency, even artistry, over a lifetime. They develop a natural rhythm, whether plowing a field in one continuous pattern of ovals or simply launching a 60-pound bale of hay from the ground to the top of a pickup in a smooth arc. That is why my incompetence has been the source of so much amusement in our town. I have watched helplessly as my tractor ran down an embankment and into the crotch of a sturdy black birch. (I had

to chainsaw the tree to free the tractor.) I was assured that deer don't eat pumpkin, so I didn't fence my patch the first year. (The local herd was well-fed.) My first attempts at an apple orchard were disastrous. If the trees didn't die, most of the apples fell off in June, the scabby survivors wormy and discolored by October. Every year I would bog down my tractor in exactly the same spot in the lower field; for the townsfolk, it was a sign that spring had arrived. And more than once I have tapped an oak, a red maple, or even an elm during the sugaring season instead of sugar maple.

Not all of us are musicians or farmers, but many of us are parents. Like dilettante musicians, we start off with our first child knowing little, having yet to master a natural rhythm of parenting. My wife and I have left our first daughter, Whitney, in her plastic car seat on top of the dining room table. (She rocked herself off the table onto the floor. We were panic-stricken; Whitney was fine.) I've yelled when I should have remained silent. I've negotiated when I ought to have laid down the law. I've been an ungrateful recipient of childhood alms (poems, welcome-home banners, and priceless bits of crayon art) when I should have counted myself the luckiest man alive.

Yet there is hope for all of us. I now walk a wet corner of a field before plowing it. I fence my pumpkin patch. I tap only sugar maples. The

Christopher Kimball

apple crop is a good one, the result of weekly organic sprays, scented bug traps, and a decent job of winter pruning.

This summer, I gathered our four kids together to watch home movies. Like Scrooge, I watched the past from a ghostly distance: kids hunting for frogs, telling stories on the front porch, lighting sparklers by the sap house on a moonless night, loading goats onto the pickup, and scrubbing apples for the cider press. I also saw moments of uncertainty and loneliness, times when I should have been out in front of the camera holding a hand or just paying attention. I remember one scene in particular. Our 3-year-old, Emily, was floating away from shore in a canoe, her face convulsed in tears, having been launched alone into deeper waters by a taunting older sister. Perhaps, in parenting, there is no perfection. I pray that it is the mistakes—and getting past them—that bond a family more than sparklers in the night, the fire illuminating the faces of hopeful children before the camera records their return to darkness.

Before bed, I took a walk through the orchard. I looked up and saw a moon bright with forgiveness. Home movies record the past, I thought, they don't predict the future. After all, the apple trees had finally borne large, red fruit and my kids were safe and sound, the wild things tamed by dreams of frogs and homemade cider.

ABOUT COOK'S ILLUSTRATED

Visit our Web site The *Cook's* Web site features original editorial content not found in the magazine as well as searchable databases for recipes, equipment tests, and food tastings. The site also features our online bookstore, a question-and-answer message board, and a sign-up form for *e-Notes,* our free newsletter on cooking. Go to www.cooksillustrated.com.

America's Test Kitchen television series. Look for our series currently airing on public television. For information visit www.americastestkitchen.com.

The Magazine *Cook's Illustrated* (ISSN 1068-2821) is published bimonthly (6 issues per year) by Boston Common Press Limited Partnership, 17 Station Street, Brookline, MA 02445. Copyright 2001 Boston Common Press Limited Partnership. Periodical postage paid at Boston, Mass., and additional mailing offices, USPS #012487. A one-year subscription is $29.70, two years is $55, and three years is $75. Add $6 postage per year for Canadian subscriptions and $12 per year for all other foreign countries. To order subscriptions in the U.S. call 800-526-8442; from outside the U.S. call 515-247-7571. Gift subscriptions are available for $24.95 each. Postmaster: Send all new orders, subscription inquiries, and change of address notices to *Cook's Illustrated,* P.O. Box 7446, Red Oak, IA 51591-0446.

Cookbooks and other products *Cook's Illustrated* offers cookbooks and magazine-related items for sale through its online bookstore. Products offered include annual hardbound editions of the magazine, an eight-year (1993–2000) reference index for the magazine, single-subject cookbooks from our How to Cook Master Series, as well as copies of *The Best Recipe, The Best Recipe: Grilling & Barbecue,* and many others. Prices and ordering information are available by calling 800-611-0759 inside the U.S. or 515-246-6911 from outside the U.S. or by visiting our bookstore at www.cooksillustrated.com. Back issues of *Cook's Illustrated* are available for sale by calling 800-611-0759 inside the U.S. or 515-246-6911 from outside the U.S.

Questions about your book order? Visit our customer service page at www.cooksillustrated.com, or call 800-611-0759 inside the U.S. or 515-246-6911 from outside the U.S.

Reader submissions *Cook's* accepts reader submissions for Quick Tips. We will provide a one-year complimentary subscription for each tip that we print. Send your tip, name, address, and daytime telephone number to Quick Tips, *Cook's Illustrated,* P.O. Box 470589, Brookline, MA 02447. Questions, suggestions, or submissions for Notes from Readers should be sent to the same address.

Questions about your subscription? Go to www.cooksillustrated.com and visit our customer service page, where you can manage your subscription, including changing your address, renewing your subscription, paying your bill, or viewing answers to frequently asked questions. You can also direct questions about your subscription to *Cook's Illustrated,* P.O. Box 7446, Red Oak, IA 51591-0446, or call 800-526-8442 inside the U.S.; from outside the U.S. call 515-247-7571.

Pasteurized Eggs

I recently came across a carton of pasteurized eggs in the market. Not knowing anything about how eggs are pasteurized or if the process changes the flavor or cooking properties of the eggs, I passed them up for ordinary eggs. Was this a wise decision?

THELMA WILLIAMS
CLEVELAND, OHIO

➤ When we first reported on the topic a few years ago (see Notes from Readers, January/February 1997), the only pasteurized egg products on the market consisted of shelled eggs (whole eggs with shells removed) that came in liquid, frozen, or dried form and were used primarily in the food service and manufacturing industries—as they still are. At that time, however, the egg industry was already testing the pasteurization of "shell" eggs (whole eggs in their shells) to address concerns about salmonella contamination. (The pasteurization process removes nearly all traces of bacteria, including salmonella.) Pasteurized shell eggs were approved for consumer use by the U.S. Food and Drug Administration (FDA) in 1995 and by the U.S. Department of Agriculture (USDA) in 1997. We contacted Davidson's Pasteurized Egg Corporation, a leading producer of pasteurized shell eggs, to learn more about the process. While the specifics are proprietary information, we learned from company representative Jenny Bartholdi that the process involves passing Grade-A eggs (the USDA classification for eggs with undamaged shells and high-quality yolks and whites) through a series of warm water baths. The combination of time and temperature heats the eggs enough to kill potentially harmful bacteria but not enough to cook the eggs. The eggs are then chilled and coated with an all-natural, nonanimal-based, FDA-approved wax sealant to prevent recontamination and to maintain freshness.

Because pasteurized eggs are slowly but surely appearing in grocery stores across the country, we decided to see how they measure up to ordinary supermarket eggs when put through the paces of frying, scrambling, baking, and whipping. Except for a little insignia (which varies from brand to brand) identifying them as pasteurized, the pasteurized eggs looked just like ordinary eggs. But when we cracked them open to fry and scramble them, we immediately noticed significant differences. Whereas the shells of the ordinary eggs were brittle and cracked cleanly, with little effort, the shells of the pasteurized shells were harder to crack—almost malleable—a result of the wax sealant holding the pieces together. More surprising were the cloudy, watery, pasteurized whites that poured out of the cracked shells. They did not have the body or jelly-like texture of ordinary eggs. Even so, once in the pan, the pasteurized eggs fried and scrambled at the same rate as ordinary eggs and cooked up in just the same way. In a tasting, a few tasters said the regular scrambled eggs were "creamier" and "more fragrant" than the pasteurized, but the distinction was slight. Most tasters could not detect a difference.

Next we baked two génoise sponge cakes—cakes leavened by whole egg foam—to see how the pasteurized eggs would perform in the batter and in the oven. The pasteurized eggs whipped up in the same manner and amount of time as the ordinary eggs, and the batters made with each type of egg were identical (though only the batter made with pasteurized eggs could be safely licked off a spoon). The final products, however, were not the same. The génoise made with ordinary eggs had a better rise and a springier, softer crumb than the cake made with pasteurized eggs, which was a bit sunken and dry. Tasters also found the latter cake slightly less rich tasting, but overall they thought the pasteurized-egg sponge cake tasted fine.

The results of the two remaining tests—for which we made a French meringue (eggs whites whipped with granulated sugar) and mayonnaise—would serve as our gold standard for performance and flavor. Getting fragile, finicky egg whites to whip up into a lustrous meringue can be tricky, and we doubted the runny, cloudy pasteurized whites would be up to the task. While the whites from the pasteurized eggs did take about twice the amount of time to whip into soft peaks (Bartholdi had warned us that this would happen), once they "came to," they were fine: voluminous, light, and airy. After sugar was folded into the foams and the meringues were baked in a moderate oven, the appearance of the pasteurized meringue suffered some, with a slight crackling on the surface, but there was no difference in taste. Both batches of mayonnaise were complete successes. The mixtures emulsified in the food processor with speed and little effort, and there were no noticeable taste differences. Both were creamy, silky smooth, and delicious.

Our conclusion? We still prefer and continue to use ordinary eggs for most recipes, especially those for baked goods. But if you are wary of making mayonnaise, eggnog, or dressing for Caesar salad using raw eggs, pasteurized eggs are a safe and acceptable option.

Scallop Scandal

About a year ago, while working in a popular local restaurant, I noticed that the "sea scallops" being served tasted nothing like the sweet, meaty scallops I knew and loved. I mentioned this to the chef, and he told me the restaurant's "scallops" probably came from another kind of seafood that had been cut to look like sea scallops. Have you heard of this practice? Is there a way to distinguish a real scallop from an imposter before buying and tasting it?

JAMES F. ELLISON
HAZELHURST, WIS.

➤ Though it is nearly impossible to determine how and where the practice of passing off other kinds of seafood for sea scallops began, we have heard the same rumor. No one on the staff at *Cook's* has ever seen a faux scallop (we hope we'd know one when we see one), but some research turned up plenty of information.

According to the New York Seafood Council, the two fish most often used to make faux scallops are skate (or ray) and shark, each of which has a simple central bony cartilage and contains no true bones. While skate and shark do have firm, whitish meat, we were surprised to hear that they pass for scallops because their grainy, striated texture isn't at all similar to the soft, supple, creamy flesh of the sea scallop. Nonetheless, it seems that some unscrupulous restaurateurs and fishmongers do in fact use round cookie cutters to stamp pieces from less expensive seafood and call them scallops, selling them for a profit. We assume that restaurants would serve them breaded or battered and deep-fried or doused in a heavy sauce to disguise their un-scallop-like qualities.

The best way to avoid being duped into buying faux scallops is to know what to look for when purchasing the real thing. Fishmongers usually lay out sea scallops on a tray in their display cases. Look for scallops that vary in color from ivory to pinkish beige to tan or a very pale, dull orange. They may sometimes even be slightly gray, depending on where they were dredged, but they should not be white. Raw fresh scallops feel sticky to the touch, are flabby, and should have a light, clean smell of the sea. You should see only a small amount—if any—of the scallops' natural juices in the tray. If you still suspect that what you have in front of you are not scallops, check for a small, tough white muscle adhering to the side of the scallops. This is where the scallop was attached to its shell. While this muscle is often removed before the scallops are sold, it should still be attached to at least a few in the bunch. It's a sure sign that what you've got is a real scallop.

Almost as bad as fake scallops are "processed" scallops—that is, scallops that have been dipped for a short time in a phosphate and water mixture that also may contain citric and sorbic acids. A whopping 90 percent of fish retailers "dip" scallops to extend their shelf life—they last on average four days longer than undipped scallops (called "dry" in the industry). Processed scallops are bright white and are generally displayed in a pool of milky liquid. Swollen with water (which makes them weigh and thereby cost more), these slippery scallops are impossible to brown and have an inferior flavor to dry scallops. By federal law, processed scallops must be identified at the wholesale level, but there is no regulation at the retail level, so the uninformed consumer is unprotected.

Frosting versus Icing

Is there a difference between frosting and icing?

ANN LEE
LOS ANGELES, CALIF.

➤ *The Food of the Western World* (Quadrangle/The New York Times Book Co., 1976), a major food encyclopedia, defines *frosting* as the American word for *icing*, and a handful of culinary dictionaries state that frosting and icing are one and the same, but most other sources differentiate the two. They define frostings as relatively thick, sometimes fluffy confections that are spread over a cake or used to fill it. Icings are considered to have a thinner consistency and are usually poured or drizzled over baked goods as opposed to spread. They form a smooth, shiny coating. Also commonly noted about icings is that they are typically white.

Pine Nuts

A friend told me that all pine trees produce pine nuts. Is this true? If so, are all of them edible?

FRANCESCO TERZANNI
NEW YORK, N.Y.

➤ Pine nuts are actually seeds from the pine cone, and about 80 varieties of pine tree, from the genus *Pinus*, produce edible pine nuts. Edible pine nuts grow on trees all over the world, including Europe, Asia, Africa, and North America, but the variety most familiar to Americans is the delicate, sweet, almost buttery Mediterranean pine nut. Also called pignoli, these pine nuts come from the *P. pinea*, or stone

pine, found in Italy, Spain, and North Africa. Cream colored and a mere half-inch in length, the torpedo-shaped pignoli do indeed look more like large seeds than nuts. They may be eaten out of hand and are often toasted to a golden brown before being added to a dish. They're perhaps best known as a component of pestos and pilafs but are also used in ravioli (often with spinach and ricotta), in stuffings for poultry, in salads, and in cakes and cookies. Though once carried mostly in specialty and gourmet shops, pignoli are now available in many supermarkets.

The second most popular variety is the Chinese pine nut, *P. koraiensis*, which has a more pungent, pine-like flavor than its Mediterranean cousin and a less graceful shape, being more bulbous and squat. Usually toasted or fried, these

WHAT IS IT?

This tool—which seems to be from the spoon family—has been in my family's catchall drawer for years, but none of us knows what it is for. Can you enlighten us?

BEN AFROOZ
JEFFERSON CITY, MICH.

The sharp, pointy "spoon" that lives in your drawer is commonly known as a peach pitter, though it can be used to pit any stone fruit and can be put to other uses. To remove pits from free- and cling-stone fruits, firmly grasp the handle and pierce the fruit's skin with the inflexible 2-inch spiked blade. Once the "spoon" reaches the core, twist the pitter to loosen and capture the pit, and then pull it out, leaving the fruit intact. The peach pitter can often be found among the tools of peach and plum tree growers. Before the advent of pitting machines, commercial growers and jam makers used it to ready their fruit for preserving. Home cooks may still find it handy when putting up preserves or jams.

The elliptical blade, with its close hand proximity, can also be used to make precise, shallow cuts; eyeing and coring even the toughest thick-skinned fruits and vegetables is a piece of cake. You can mail-order a peach pitter from Dorothy McNett's Place (243 Sixth Street, Hollister, CA 95023; 831-637-6444; www.happycookers.com), item #1-4212, for $5.99.

pine nuts are used to garnish a variety of stir-fries and are added to some cookies and tea cakes. Chinese pine nuts can be found almost exclusively in Asian markets. In most cases, Mediterranean pine nuts can be substituted for the Chinese variety.

Less accessible still are the pine nuts of the American Southwest and Mexico, produced by the pinyon pine, *P. edulis,* and some other species. These pine nuts, also called piñons or Indian nuts, rarely appear in markets outside their growing region and were for thousands of years a staple in the diet of several American Indian tribes, who ate them raw, boiled, mashed, and ground and baked into cakes. Similar in quality to Mediterranean pine nuts, piñons have a rich, slightly sweet taste.

Because extraction of the seeds from the cones is a labor-intensive process, all pine nuts tend to be expensive, with prices ranging from about $8 to $14 per pound. Highly nutritious and rich in both protein and fat, pine nuts need to be stored with care to prevent rancidity. They are best transferred to an airtight container as soon as their original packing is opened. They will keep in the refrigerator for up to three months or in the freezer for up to nine months.

Chipotle Chiles en Adobo

My family and I love your recipes for grilled hamburgers (July/August 2000). The variations really liven up the sometimes ordinary standard. I want to try the Grilled Hamburgers with Garlic, Chipotles, and Scallions, but I have no idea what chipotles are, let alone "chipotle chiles en adobo." Can you help me out here?

RICHARD MOYER
ALLENTOWN, PA.

➤ Strictly speaking, the word *chipotle* can refer to any smoked chile pepper, but in the mainstream American market, the chipotle is the smoke-dried, red-ripe jalapeño. Chipotles are dry, have wrinkly, leathery, brownish red skin, and are considered to have a medium level of heat. (They rank from about 5,000 to 15,000 Scoville units, the standard measure of the heat in chile peppers. Peppers range from 0 Scoville units for mild bell peppers to 300,000 or more for the hottest habaneros. Raw jalapeños are milder than dried, registering at 2,500 to 5,000 units.) The distinctly smoky flavor of chipotles correlates directly with the wood used to smoke them. They are usually smoked slowly over the branches of fruit trees or hardwoods such as hickory, oak, and pecan. Their smoky flavor is accompanied by undertones of sweetness and even hints of chocolate. *Adobo* is a tangy, oily, tomato- and herb-based sauce that customarily serves as a marinade for the dried peppers. The sauce reconstitutes the brittle chiles (making it possible to mince them easily, as directed in our recipe) and contributes a sharp, piquant flavor to the mix. Cans of chipotles en adobo are readily available in the Mexican food section of most supermarkets. Give them a try. Your burgers will have an extra dimension of flavor, smokiness, and heat. In most recipes you will not use an entire can. Refrigerate extra chiles in a small airtight container for up to two weeks.

Quick Tips

Pastry Bag Stand

It's always easier to fill a pastry bag when it is propped up and open. In the past, we have suggested using a blender jar (May/June 1997) or a Pilsner glass (September/October 1996) for that purpose. Susan Brooks of Fairfax, Va., recently offered her own suggestion: an empty Pringles potato chips can. A Pringles can is the ideal size and shape, and if you fold an inch or two of the bag over the rim of the can, the bag remains perfectly stable.

Measures at the Ready

To make sure that she always has dry measures on hand for baking projects and the like, Patricia Guzzo of Grand Rapids, Mich., recently bought a new set of dry measures and divided her old set among her dry ingredient canisters. With the 1/2-cup measure right in with the flour, for instance, she never wants for a clean, dry measure.

CAKE FLOUR

Easiest "Story Stick" for Accurate Reductions

Two readers, Linda Doyne of Seattle, Wash., and Scott Weingart of New York, N.Y., had the same response when they read the quick tip on using a story stick to mark the progress of a reduction in our January/February 2001 issue. Rather than marking up a wooden chopstick to measure the changing level of the liquid, they prefer to use a stainless steel ruler. Simply dip the ruler into the pot to measure the level of the initial volume of liquid, then check periodically to determine when it has reduced to the point where you want it. The ruler is cheap, heatproof, easy to clean, and reusable.

Serving Rock-Hard Ice Cream

Taken fresh from the freezer, small pint-sized containers of premium ice cream often are frozen too hard to scoop easily, and who can remember to pull them out in time to soften before serving? Adina Kagan of New York, N.Y., and Elissa Lorber of Los Angeles, Calif., solve this problem by slicing the ice cream right in the container.

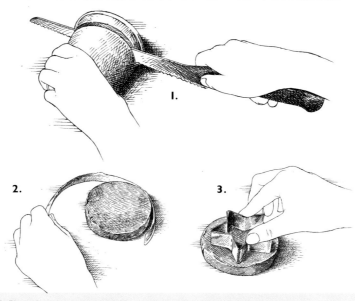

1.

2.   3.

1. Place the container on its side on a cutting board and cut off slices, right through the cardboard, with a serrated or an electric knife.
2. Peel the cardboard off the sides of the ice cream disk and serve. The lid will sit flush up against the ice cream left in the container for easy storage.
3. The slice-and-serve method lends itself to some artful presentations. Adina Kagan sandwiches each disk between two large cookies for easy ice cream sandwiches, and Elissa Lorber cuts the disks into interesting shapes using cookie cutters.

Dotting Baked Goods with Butter

From sweet potato casseroles to seasonal fruit pies to rich gratins of potato or other root vegetables, many recipes direct the cook to dot the surface of a dish with butter just before putting it in the oven. After losing patience with the soft, sticky pieces of butter that clung to her fingers, Sue Miller of Cleveland Heights, Ohio, decided to try frozen butter and a vegetable peeler. Shaving thin curls off the surface of a frozen stick of butter is infinitely neater—and easy, too.

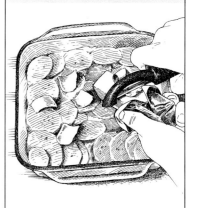

Protecting Nonstick Pan Surfaces, Redux

In many home kitchens space is at a premium, so pans are often stacked for compact storage. But this treatment can scratch a nonstick surface. In past Quick Tips (September/October 1997 and March/April 1998), we have suggested several means of protecting nonstick finishes, such as slipping sheets of paper towel or the plastic lids from supermarket coffee cans between the pans. Laura Rowe of Lexington, Ky., added the following idea to that list.

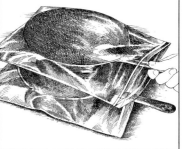

Before stacking the pans, slide them into large plastic zipper-lock bags (the 2-gallon size for 10-inch pans and the 1-gallon size for 8-inch pans). The plastic protects the nonstick surface.

Send Us Your Tip We will provide a complimentary one-year subscription for each tip we print. See page 1 for information.

ILLUSTRATION: JOHN BURGOYNE

Preventing Sticky Jar Lids

The lids of jars with sticky contents such as jelly, honey, or molasses often stick as if they were cemented in place. Instead of struggling with sticky lids, Rita Smith of Essexville, Mich., covers the tops of these jars with plastic wrap before screwing on the lids. The plastic prevents any serious sticking, so the lids always unscrew easily.

Juicing Fruits for Jam

When making jams and jellies from fresh summer fruits such as grapes, cherries, and plums, it's usually necessary to juice some of the fruit. Lori Trimpe of Ada, Mich., makes quick work of juicing by fitting her food processor with the short plastic dough blade. It breaks down the fruit without nicking the seeds or pits, which, when cut, release bitter flavors into the fruit.

Getting a Grip on Chicken

Raw chicken is slippery, which means that halving whole breasts can be a hazardous job. Karen Kennan of North Brookfield, Mass., gives herself a firmer grip on chicken by using a folded wad of paper towels to hold it in place as she cuts.

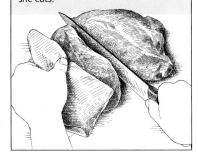

Stuffed Peppers That Sit Up

As we learned over and over while developing the recipe for them in our March/April 2001 issue, stuffed peppers have an annoying tendency to topple toward disaster in the roasting pan. Lynn Toscano of San Diego, Calif., and Tom Pawlowski of Brooklyn, Mich., have unique methods for keeping their peppers upright.

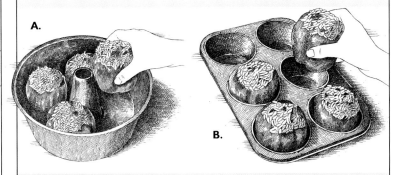

A. Instead of cooking the peppers in the baking dish or roasting pan specified in most recipes, put them in a tube pan. The snug fit makes the peppers sit right up.
B. Alternatively, place the peppers in the cups of a muffin tin. This also gets the job done nicely.

Giving Gnocchi Their Ridges

When making gnocchi, it is customary to give each piece distinct ridges using a butter paddle or the tines of a fork. Natalia Rizzo of Holmes Beach, Fla., likes to use a whisk for that job. She simply lines up the gnocchi pieces on the work surface, then rolls the whisk over them to create deep, even ridges.

Easy Apple Coring

Come fall, many cooks like to use fresh-picked apples and pears in crisps, cakes, and other desserts. One well-known trick for coring and seeding the halved fruit is to use a melon baller. Of course, that doesn't mean all cooks have one at the ready when they need it. What they're more likely to have is a sturdy, rounded metal 1/2-teaspoon measure. That's what Winston Braman of Jamaica Plain, Mass. uses. As he promised, it works beautifully.

Reserving Pasta Water to Thin a Sauce

In that last flurry of activity before saucing the pasta and getting dinner on the table, it's easy to overlook small details. It's no wonder, then, that many cooks forget to save a bit of pasta cooking water to thin the sauce when the recipe recommends it. Gayle Clow of Pickering, Ontario, no longer forgets, because she has figured out this foolproof reminder. Before cooking the pasta, set up the colander for draining it in the sink, then place a measuring cup inside the colander. It's sure to nudge your memory at the appropriate moment.

Mess-Free Glazing

A simple glaze of powdered sugar mixed with milk or lemon juice adds a flavorful finish to quick breads, muffins, cinnamon buns, and the like. While some cooks find mixing and applying the glaze to be a messy process, Michael Ritchie of Yuma, Ariz., avoids the mess altogether by using a zipper-lock bag.

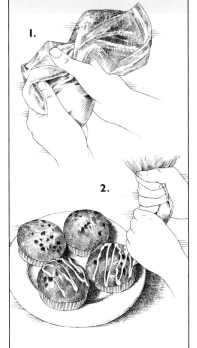

1. Add the powdered sugar and liquid to a zipper-lock sandwich bag, seal it, and knead the ingredients into a soft glaze.
2. To apply the glaze with precision, just snip off a small corner of the bag and squeeze.

Safeguarding Cream Pies

The whipped cream or meringue topping on a pie can be marred easily when covered directly with plastic wrap. Kerry Kelly of Syracuse, N.Y., keeps the surface of her pies neat by standing a few strands of uncooked spaghetti or linguini in the pie. She then suspends the wrap on the pasta.

Spaghetti alla Carbonara

Restaurant carbonara is often an unctuous, congealed mass of cheese, eggs, and bacon.
We set out to rediscover the beauty in the beast.

≥ BY BRIDGET LANCASTER ≤

A pasta dish quintessentially Roman in nature, carbonara taunts us with food taboos. It begins with a sauce made from eggs and cheese that cooks to velveteen consistency only from the heat of the just-drained pasta that it drapes. Shards of Italian bacon punctuate the dish with enough presence to make one give silent thanks to the pig. And just when you think that it can't get any better, the bright punch of hot garlic kicks in. The indulgent nature of carbonara is just one reason it is featured on every trattoria menu.

Far from this heavenly marriage of sauce and pasta, the run-of-the-mill carbonara is a lackluster dish of spaghetti smothered in a heavy, dull, cream-laden sauce that makes you wonder if you ordered Alfredo by mistake. Still worse are variations loaded with cheese that refuses to melt and sticks to the pasta in dry, abrasive pieces. Even a well-made carbonara can be destroyed by a waitperson. If the dish is not brought to the table immediately, the sauce congeals and the carbonara turns sticky and rubbery.

Searching Italian cookbooks for solutions to these problems provided little help. Most recipes deviated little in the ingredient list, and the technique was similar throughout: Make a raw sauce with eggs and cheese, render (melt the fat from) bacon, cook pasta, add hot pasta to the sauce and bacon, and toss until the mixture is hot and creamy. The only noticeable difference I found was in the ratio of ingredients, especially the eggs and cheese. That ratio, I reasoned, must be the key to a successful carbonara.

Eggs and Cheese

Eggs form the base of the lush, silky sauce that binds the other ingredients to the slender strands of pasta. Only the heat from the cooked pasta is necessary to cook the eggs to the right consistency, so I knew a precise amount of egg would be critical to both the texture and the richness of the dish. Basing my recipe on 1 pound of pasta, I started out with two eggs. Mixed with 1 cup

Pouring the cheese and eggs over the hot pasta, tossing, and then adding the bacon ensures that none of the sauce gets left in the bowl.

grated cheese, this sauce was thick and clumped when introduced to the hot pasta. Four eggs made a sauce too soupy and wet to stick to the pasta. Three eggs were just right. The sauce was silky in texture, had the fortitude to cling to the spaghetti, and was moist and rich.

Next, the cheese. In Rome, the cheese of choice is Pecorino Romano, an aged sheep's milk cheese with a distinctly sharp, tangy flavor. On its own, 1 cup of Pecorino proved too strong for our taste. But reducing the amount of cheese in hopes of buffering the strong flavor yielded a dish that lacked richness.

I tried substituting a cup of Parmigiano-Reggiano for the Pecorino. While the Parmigiano-Reggiano gave the dish a sweet, nutty flavor that was well received, tasters now longed for a little of the potency from the Pecorino. I found that a blend of cheeses—¼ cup Pecorino and ¾ cup Parmesan—brought out just the right amount of flavor from both. It also made for a perfect ratio of cheese to eggs to create the smooth, creamy sauce I'd been looking for.

Many carbonara recipes dictate the addition of ½ cup heavy cream to the sauce. Our tasters immediately rejected this lack of restraint. The

heavy cream dulled the mouth with a fatty coating, and it deadened the flavor of the cheeses. Tablespoon by tablespoon, I reduced the amount of cream in the recipe, but tasters were satisfied only when the cream was omitted altogether.

On the other hand, the punch of garlic was a welcome addition. At first I sautéed a few minced cloves in a little olive oil before adding them to the sauce, but this sautéed garlic lacked the strength to shoulder the weight of the eggs and cheese. Adding raw garlic to the mixture did the trick. With just a brief introduction to heat from the hot pasta, the garlic flavor bloomed.

Bring Home the Bacon

In Rome, carbonara is traditionally made with *guanciale,* also known as salt-cured pork jowl. I couldn't get my hands on it here in the United States, so I centered the testing around available bacons—pancetta (Italian bacon) and American bacon. Pancetta, like American bacon, comes from the belly of the pig, but rather than being smoked, pancetta is cured only with salt, pepper, and spice, usually cloves. American bacon is recognizably smoked and has a distinct sweetness from the sugar that's added during the curing process.

The pancetta gave the carbonara a substantial pork flavor. It was distinctly seasoned with the salt and pepper of the cure. But tasters weren't crazy about its meaty texture. Even though the pancetta was thinly sliced and fried until crisp, the pieces became chewy after a short time in the sauce. The American bacon managed to retain much of its crisp texture, and it added a pleasantly sweet and smoky flavor to the dish that tasters overwhelmingly preferred.

Brightening Up

In Italy, you can start a heated argument over whether or not to use wine in carbonara. In an effort to find the absolutely best carbonara, I tried a dry red wine (a common ingredient in authentic recipes), dry vermouth (which appeared in only one recipe but piqued my

TECHNIQUE |

SAVE THE PASTA WATER

If the sauce is to spread evenly, the pasta must be moist. Add up to ⅓ cup reserved pasta cooking water if the pasta is dry or sticky.

interest), and a dry white wine, which was favored in the majority of the recipes I had found.

The red wine wasn't unpleasant, but the overall flavor wasn't bright enough to stand up to the smoky flavor of the bacon. The vermouth offered a distinct herbal flavor that tasters voted down. White wine created the most impact and resonance. It was full-flavored, and the acidic nature of the wine cut through the taste of the bacon, brightening the flavor of the dish. When testing how much to add, I found that a modest amount wouldn't do. To bring the wine's full presence to the table, I needed to use at least ½ cup. I also found that adding the white wine to the bacon as it sautéed deepened the flavor of the dish overall.

Bottom Dwellers

Up to this point, I had been making the carbonara in the traditional method. I mixed the eggs and cheese in the bottom of the serving bowl along with the fried bacon, then dumped the hot, drained pasta on top and tossed the mixture thoroughly. But this method had flaws. It was difficult to distribute the egg and cheese mixture evenly throughout the pasta, and, try as I might to keep the bacon pieces afloat, gravity pulled them back to the bottom of the bowl.

Mixing the eggs and cheese together in a separate bowl and then pouring the mixture over the hot pasta ensured the even coverage I was

Getting the Texture Right

| CLOTTED | CREAMY |

A badly made carbonara appears knotted and gummy. Our recipe has a silky, translucent sauce.

looking for. In addition, by removing the eggs and cheese from the bottom of the serving bowl, I was able to preheat the bowl—a step that keeps the pasta warm. Finally, I found that tossing the hot pasta with the egg mixture first, then gently tossing in the bacon, worked best. The bacon adhered nicely to the sticky coating of sauce.

SPAGHETTI ALLA CARBONARA
SERVES 4 TO 6

Add regular table salt to the pasta cooking water, but use sea salt flakes, if you can find them, to season the dish. We like the full flavor they bring to the carbonara. Note that while either table salt or sea salt can be used when seasoning in step 3, they are not used in equal amounts.

- ¼ cup extra-virgin olive oil
- ½ pound bacon (6 to 8 slices), slices halved lengthwise, then cut crosswise into ¼-inch pieces
- ½ cup dry white wine
- 3 large eggs
- ¾ cup finely grated Parmesan (about 2 ounces)
- ¼ cup finely grated Pecorino Romano (about ¾ ounce)
- 3 small garlic cloves, pressed through garlic press or minced to paste
- I pound spaghetti
  Salt (see note) and ground black pepper

1. Adjust oven rack to lower-middle position, set large heatproof serving bowl on rack, and heat oven to 200 degrees. Bring 4 quarts water to rolling boil in large Dutch oven or stockpot.

2. While water is heating, heat oil in large skillet over medium heat until shimmering, but not smoking. Add bacon and cook, stirring occasionally, until lightly browned and crisp, about 8 minutes. Add wine and simmer until alcohol aroma has cooked off and wine is slightly reduced, 6 to 8 minutes. Remove from heat and cover to keep warm. Beat eggs, cheeses, and garlic together with fork in small bowl; set aside.

3. When water comes to boil, add pasta and 1 tablespoon table salt; stir to separate pasta. Cook until al dente; reserve ⅓ cup pasta cooking water and drain pasta for about 5 seconds, leaving pasta slightly wet. Transfer drained pasta to warm serving bowl; if pasta is dry, add some reserved cooking water and toss to moisten. Immediately pour egg mixture over hot pasta, sprinkle with 1 teaspoon sea salt flakes or ¾ teaspoon table salt; toss well to combine. Pour bacon mixture over pasta, season generously with black pepper, and toss well to combine. Serve immediately.

TASTING:

This Spaghetti's Still a Winner

Expensive packages of imported pasta may look tempting, but when we conducted our first spaghetti tasting for the May/June 1994 issue of *Cook's*, we liked American-made Ronzoni best. Since then, two other brands of pasta have become widely available, so we decided to pit them against the contestants from 1994. We tasted eight brands of pasta straight from the pot, unseasoned, unsauced, and al dente. Just as in 1994, Ronzoni was the tasters' favorite, followed by De Cecco, Mueller's, and Barilla. The two newcomers, Rienzi and 365 Brand (Whole Foods), received fair scores, while the expensive, imported brands of Martelli and Delverde came in last.

Ronzoni Ronzoni won tasters over with its firm "rockin'" texture and its "nutty," "buttery," "classic" flavor. "Tastes most like pure pasta," said one taster.

De Cecco "Chewy" came to mind for more than a couple of tasters when sampling this pasta. Perhaps "a tad chewy for some," said one, "but great for me." Some tasters detected a distinctive wheat flavor, though others found it a bit "bland" or "plasticky."

Mueller's Several tasters remarked on this pasta's "clean" and "wheaty" flavor. Most agreed that its texture was firm, but some found it "a little rubbery."

Barilla Tasters favored pasta with some chew, and several found chew to be lacking in Barilla, calling it too "soft" and "yielding." While a few tasters also found Barilla lacking in flavor, others noted a pleasant "wheaty" and "toasty" flavor.

Rienzi While a few tasters picked up on a favorable egg flavor, most characterized this pasta as "bland." "Gummy" was another word that kept popping up.

365 Brand Tasters faulted this pasta for having too much flavor. Comments included: "Strong egg flavor." "Too-over-the-top nutty/smoky flavor." "A little bitter—like burnt toast." "Sour." Some liked this brand for being thick and firm, but others described it as grainy and rubbery.

Martelli Tasters struggled to articulate the presence of any flavor in this pasta, which was repeatedly called "bland." Some noted an artificial flavor. The texture didn't win many fans either, with tasters labeling it "mealy," "gritty," "starchy," and "mushy."

Delverde Several tasters described this pasta as having a "raw" and "artificial" flavor. Comments on the texture ranged from "not cooked" to "spongy" and "gummy." —Julia Collin

Steak au Poivre

Steak au poivre is often nothing more than uninspired skillet steak. We were after the real thing—a silky sauce married to a well-seared crust of pungent, cracked peppercorns.

⋟ BY DAWN YANAGIHARA ⋞

There's nothing complicated about steak au poivre. When well-executed, the slightly sweet, smooth sauce has more than a hint of shallots and brandy, the steak is well-browned on the outside and cherry-red on the interior, and the crust of cracked peppercorns provides a pungent, slow burn, adding fire and depth to an otherwise simple steak.

That's the good news. A third-rate steak au poivre has peppercorns that fall off the steak only to reveal underbrowned meat. What's more, the peppercorn coat prevents the steak from forming drippings in the skillet that are the foundation of a rich sauce, and few home cooks have roasted beef or veal stock on hand to give the sauce the substance and backbone it needs. Since almost all steak au poivre recipes make no attempt to solve these problems, the home cook is left aghast at the end result: wan, tasteless steaks covered in an insipid sauce made in a blackened skillet that is headed straight for the trash.

My first few tests were useful only in determining the best cut of steak for au poivre. Filets were tender but too mild-flavored. Rib-eyes, always my favorite, have abundant fat pockets and pronounced veins of gristle that separate two differently textured muscles. A peppercorn crust obscures these imperfections, requiring scrutiny and maneuvering on the part of the diner to eat around these parts. Strip steaks, however, have

Pressing peppercorns into only one side of the steak allows the cook to sear the other side, providing a *fond* to use as a base for a full-flavored sauce.

external lines of gristle that are easily trimmed before cooking, and their neat, tight, even grain makes them particularly suited to steak au poivre.

I quickly determined peppercorn type. Among black, white, and a four-peppercorn blend of green, pink, black, and white, plain old black was the favorite in the test kitchen. Tasters extolled it for its sharp bite, rich and intense flavor, and elusive smokiness.

The steaks I cooked early on were crusted with a scant teaspoon of peppercorns on each side. Loose pepper fell off the steaks and scorched pitifully in the skillet. The pepper that did stick shielded the surface of the steaks, preventing browning and thereby the formation of a *fond* (the sticky browned bits left in a pan after sautéing) on which to build the sauce. In addition, most tasters thought I was far too liberal in my peppercorn allotment—the heat was vicious and incendiary. My first thought was to cut back on the peppercorns, but then a light bulb went on. What if the steaks were coated on only one side? The unpeppered side would brown nicely, producing more fond for the sauce, and there would be no peppercorns on that side to singe.

Typically, steaks cook over intensely high heat. But for this new approach, I placed the skillet over medium heat until it was hot, and, after laying the steaks in the skillet—

unpeppered-side down—turned up the heat to medium-high. This technique gave the steaks six minutes to brown on the first side and form a fond. Then the steaks were flipped onto their peppered side and given only three to five minutes (depending on desired doneness) to complete their cooking, this time without scorching the pepper. It worked like a charm.

The steak was done, so I turned my attention to the sauce. All steak au poivre sauces contain beef or veal stock and brandy. Most contain cream, though some get their richness from butter only. The stock was the first problem. Most home cooks have only canned chicken and beef broth on hand, and the latter has long been considered either artificial tasting or weakly flavored by the *Cook's* test kitchen. Therefore, using chicken broth, I cooked down the liquid to concentrate its flavor, but the sauce still lacked meatiness and depth. I tried to doctor it with dried porcini mushrooms, but the mushroom flavor was too distinct. I tried commercial veal

The Right Grind

For steak au poivre, grind or crush whole peppercorns (left) to a very coarse, not fine, texture (right).

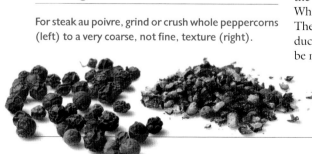

TECHNIQUE

CRUSHING PEPPERCORNS

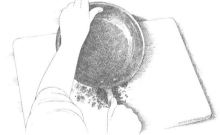

SAUTÉ PAN Chefs frequently use the back of a heavy pan and a rocking motion to grind peppercorns.

ROLLING PIN Spread the peppercorns in an even layer in a zipper-lock plastic bag and whack them with a rolling pin or meat pounder.

ADHERING THE PEPPER

Pressing the steaks with a cake pan or flat pot lid promotes browning and ensures that the peppercorns adhere.

demi-glace (superconcentrated veal stock), but the tomato paste–laden demi-glace looked and tasted unnatural. Finally, I tried low-sodium beef broth straight from the can and reduced it. This sauce was beefier, more substantial, and deeper in color—but it was plagued by the tinny flavor characteristic of canned beef broth.

On the verge of giving up, I finally hit upon a solution. I reduced almost equal amounts of chicken and beef broths with sautéed shallots to about one-quarter of their original volume. Finally—a terrific, full-flavored sauce. But the long simmering time threw a wrench in the works. A typical pan sauce for steak is made by deglazing the skillet in which the steaks were cooked. This usually takes no longer than a few minutes and can be accomplished while the steaks repose. My sauce took well over 10 minutes, much longer than you'd want the meat to rest. The solution was straightforward: Reduce the broth mixture before cooking the steaks, then use the resulting liquid to deglaze the skillet.

Introducing brandy to the sauce was no trivial matter. I tried reducing it with the broth mixture to concentrate its flavor. This worked, but because I was also concentrating the sugar in the brandy, the resulting sauce tasted as sweet as butterscotch pudding, with no spirited bite. If I held off adding the brandy until much later in the sauce-making process, it tasted hot and raw, like cough syrup. The time to add it was when the reduced broth mixture went into the skillet to deglaze it; the mixture simmers for about five minutes, just long enough for the brandy to reduce a bit, shake its alcoholic harshness, and meld with the broth.

Tasters voted to enrich the sauce with both cream and butter, not just butter alone. Cream made the sauce luxurious and sophisticated and gave its texture substance. Only ¼ cup was needed, and, when added at the same time as the brandy, the cream had a chance to cook down and lend body to the sauce. To finish, butter whisked in at the end brought silkiness, a bit of raw brandy

gave nice bite and fresh brandy flavor, and a teaspoon of lemon juice or champagne vinegar brightened things up.

STEAK AU POIVRE WITH BRANDIED CREAM SAUCE
SERVES 4

To save time, crush the peppercorns and trim the steaks while the broth mixture simmers. Many pepper mills do not have a sufficiently coarse setting. In that case, crush peppercorns with a sauté pan or rolling pin (see illustration, page 8).

Sauce
- 4 tablespoons unsalted butter
- 1 medium shallot, minced
- 1 cup canned low-sodium beef broth
- ¾ cup canned low-sodium chicken broth
- ¼ cup heavy cream
- ¼ cup plus 1 tablespoon brandy
- 1 teaspoon juice from 1 lemon or 1 teaspoon champagne vinegar
  Salt

Steaks
- 4 strip steaks (8 to 10 ounces each), ¾ to 1 inch thick and no larger than 3 inches at widest points, trimmed of exterior gristle
  Salt
- 1 tablespoon black peppercorns, crushed (see "The Right Grind," page 8)

1. Heat 1 tablespoon butter in 12-inch heavy-bottomed skillet over medium heat; when foaming subsides, add shallot and cook, stirring occasionally, until softened, about 2 minutes. Add beef and chicken broths, increase heat to high, and boil until reduced to about ½ cup, about 8 minutes. Set reduced broth mixture aside. Rinse and wipe out skillet.

2. Meanwhile, sprinkle both sides of steaks with salt; rub one side of each steak with 1 teaspoon crushed peppercorns, and, using fingers, press peppercorns into steaks to make them adhere.

3. Place now-empty skillet over medium heat until hot, about 4 minutes. Lay steaks unpeppered-side down in hot skillet, increase heat to medium-high, firmly press down on steaks with bottom of cake pan (see illustration, left), and cook steaks without moving them until well-browned, about 6 minutes. Using tongs, flip steaks, firmly press down on steaks with bottom of cake pan, and cook on peppered side, about 3 minutes longer for rare, about 4 minutes longer for medium-rare, or about 5 minutes longer for medium. Transfer steaks to large plate and tent loosely with foil to keep warm.

4. Pour reduced broth, cream, and ¼ cup brandy into now-empty skillet; increase heat to high and bring to boil, scraping pan bottom with wooden spoon to loosen browned bits. Simmer until deep golden brown and thick enough to heavily coat back of metal tablespoon or soup spoon, about 5 minutes. Off heat, whisk in remaining 3 tablespoons butter, remaining 1 tablespoon brandy, lemon juice or vinegar, and any accumulated meat juices. Adjust seasonings with salt.

5. Set steaks on individual dinner plates, spoon portion of sauce over steaks, and serve immediately.

TESTING EQUIPMENT: **Is a Set of Steak Knives Worth $150?**

If you've ever shopped for steak knives, you might have noticed that sets of four (and sometimes six) can range in price from as little as $40 to as much as $150. We wondered if price really makes a difference when it comes to the performance of these knives, so we cooked up some steaks to find out.

Our Favorite: HENCKELS

Another Top Choice: WÜSTHOF-TRIDENT

Great Value: CHICAGO CUTLERY

Our favorites were pricey. Henckels Four Star Steak Knives and Wüsthof-Trident Classic Steak Knives each fetch between $140 and $150 for a set of four. Manufactured in the same manner as the other kitchen knives in their high-quality lines, these knives justly demand a high price. Fresh from their boxes, they had razor-sharp blades that sliced effortlessly through crusts and glided through meat, and their handles made them comfortable to use (Henckels got top honors here). But if you are lax in the upkeep of your knives, beware—these knives require regular honing and sharpening to be kept in tip-top shape.

Right behind these big shots were Chicago Cutlery Steak Knives, Walnut Tradition. At $40 for a set of four, it's easy to overlook their slightly less comfortable handles and somewhat flimsier feel and rank them right in with the best. These knives were also sharp, and the gently curved angle of the blades made for simple and smooth slicing. And they look like they belong in a butcher shop—or in the fist of a serious steak eater. Don't forget to steel these knives as well to keep them sharp.

Our least favorite knife sets contained knives with serrated blades. Henckels Gourmet Steak Knives, $40 for a set of four, and Dexter Russell Steakhouse Steak Knives, $30 for a set of four, required a good deal of sawing to cut through a steak, which resulted in rather ragged pieces (not that your taste buds care). The Henckels Gourmet knives felt insubstantial in their construction, whereas the Dexter Russell knives were of mammoth proportions. Neither of these require steeling for upkeep. —D.Y. and Shona Simkin

Better Breaded Chicken Cutlets

Most chicken cutlets deliver a flimsy, thin crust. We set out to make cutlets with crunch from a thick, flavorful coating that won't peel off like a bad sunburn.

≥ BY ADAM RIED AND BRIDGET LANCASTER ≤

Tender boneless chicken breast pan-fried with a cloak of mild-flavored crumbs has universal appeal, yet this simple dish can fall prey to a host of problems. The chicken itself may be rubbery and tasteless, and the coating—called a bound breading, or *panade*, and arguably the best part of the dish—often ends up uneven, greasy, blond (undercooked), or even burnt. Since cutlets prepared here in the test kitchen have on occasion suffered such indignities, we recently took up the cause of the perfect breaded chicken cutlet.

The Cutlet

For a breaded chicken cutlet to be great, the chicken itself better hold up its end of the bargain. We tasted three kinds of cutlets: a common national supermarket brand; a naturally raised, or premium, brand; and a kosher chicken cutlet. Tasters preferred the firm texture and comparatively rich flavor of the premium chicken to the supermarket brand. The kosher chicken, although well seasoned because of the salt used in the koshering process, did not quite measure up to the premium sample when it came to texture.

The deeply seasoned kosher chicken did, however, send us another message loud and clear. In a dish this simple, thorough seasoning is paramount. Without it, the chicken tasted flat and uninteresting. This being *Cook's*, a test kitchen fiercely devoted to the benefits of brining poultry, the natural next step was to brine the supermarket and premium cutlets briefly in a salt and sugar solution, cook them, and then compare them with the kosher cutlets. It was no surprise that the brined cutlets were a hit, exceptionally juicy and seasoned all the way to the center. Also predictable was the fact that the supermarket brand lost out to the premium chicken cutlets, which tasted fresh, clean, and more deeply flavored. Still more interesting was our conclusion that the brined cutlets were superior to the kosher; it seems the sugar in our brine had made a valuable contribution to flavor. We confirmed this idea by trying a salt-only brine; we much preferred the chicken brined in a solution of salt and sugar. Were we unnecessarily complicating the recipe? Well, brining takes just 30 minutes, during which time you can pull together the rest of the recipe. Rarely does so little work yield such big benefits.

These crispy chicken cutlets have an unusally thick crust because they are coated in flour, eggs, and homemade bread crumbs.

Throughout this first series of tests, we noticed that the thin tip of the cutlet and the more plump opposite end cooked at different rates. This problem was easy to fix. All we had to do was pound the chicken breasts gently to an even ½-inch thickness with a meat pounder or the bottom of a small pan. Any thinner, and the chicken tended to overcook before the breading was sufficiently browned. Of course, thicker cutlets had the opposite problem. The chicken was underdone at the point when the coating was just right.

A Crisp Coat

The ideal breading should taste mild and comforting, but not dull and certainly not greasy. To explore the possibilities, we pan-fried cutlets coated with fine, fresh bread crumbs (made from fresh, sliced white sandwich bread ground fine in the food processor), dry bread crumbs, and Japanese panko crumbs. The dry bread crumbs had an unmistakably stale flavor, while the panko crumbs rated well for their shattering crispness and wheaty flavor. But the fresh bread crumbs, with their mild, subtly sweet flavor and light crisp texture, swept the test. We went on to test crumbs made from different kinds of white bread,

including premium sliced sandwich bread, Italian, French, and country-style. The sliced bread was the sweetest and, therefore, the favorite. (Pepperidge Farm white bread works fine.)

During the crumb testing, we made several important observations about the breading process. First, we learned that the cutlets had to be thoroughly dried after brining and that we could not dispense with the coating of flour that went onto the chicken before the egg wash and crumbs. If the cutlets were even slightly moist, or if we skipped the flour, the breading peeled off the finished cutlets in sheets. Dry cutlets also allowed for the thinnest possible coating of flour, which precluded any floury taste from persisting once the cutlets were cooked. In addition, we found that it was essential to press the crumbs onto the cutlets with our fingers to ensure an even, thorough cover. Finally, we discovered that it was best to let the breaded cutlets rest for about five minutes before frying them; this, too, helped bind the breading to the meat.

The bread crumbs are attached to the floured cutlets by means of a quick dip into beaten egg. But beaten eggs are thick and viscous, and they tended to form too heavy a layer on the meat, making the breading too thick, even for us. Thinning the egg with oil, water, or both is a common practice that allows excess egg to slide off the meat more easily, leaving a thinner, more delicate coat. We tried all three routines and honestly couldn't detect much difference between them in terms of the flavor or texture of the finished breading; each did a good job of thinning the egg wash. In repeated tests we did notice that the breading made with oil-thinned egg wash seemed to brown a little more deeply than that made with water-thinned wash, so we added a tablespoon of oil to our two beaten eggs.

Last we explored the details of pan-frying. For even, thorough browning in any breaded preparation, the oil must reach one-third to one-half of the way up the food being cooked. Because it's also important for the breading to brown gently and evenly, the oil should not be as hot as it is for a sauté, in which there is no breading and instant browning is critical. We put pure olive oil up against vegetable oil, and top billing went to the vegetable oil for its light, unobtrusive presence. The olive oil offered up too much of its own flavor. For the cutlets to brown evenly and become crisp, there must be sufficient space between them in the pan; ½ inch is ideal. To cook four cutlets comfortably, then, we needed a 12-inch skillet. In test after test, however, we found the breading on cutlets cooked four at a time got a bit greasy and browned unevenly. When the cutlets were cooked in two batches of two, in a 10-inch skillet, less steam was created. The result was cutlets with a crisp, well-browned breading every time. We would have preferred to avoid batch cooking, but repeated tests proved that it was worth the minimal extra time and effort.

CRISP BREADED CHICKEN CUTLETS
SERVES 4

If you'd rather not prepare fresh bread crumbs, use panko, or Japanese, bread crumbs, which cook up extracrisp. The chicken is cooked in batches of two because the crust is noticeably more crisp if the pan is not overcrowded. Finally, because the tenderloins, the small strips of meat on the underside of the breast, are likely to become detached during cooking, they must be removed at the outset. These cutlets can be served on their own, with lemon wedges, or used in sandwiches.

4	boneless, skinless chicken breasts (5 to 6 ounces each), preferably a premium brand, tenderloins removed and reserved for another use
½	cup kosher salt or ¼ cup table salt
½	cup sugar
5–8	slices high-quality white bread, such as Pepperidge Farm, crusts removed and torn into rough 1½-inch pieces
	Ground black pepper
¾	cup all-purpose flour
2	large eggs
1	tablespoon plus ¾ cup vegetable oil
	Lemon wedges for serving

1. Pound chicken breasts to even ½-inch thickness (see illustration at right). Dissolve salt and sugar in 1 quart cold water in gallon-size zipper-lock plastic bag. Add cutlets and seal bag, pressing out as much air as possible; refrigerate 30 minutes. Line rimmed baking sheet with triple layer of paper towels.

2. Remove cutlets and lay in single layer on baking sheet; cover with another triple layer of paper towels and press firmly to absorb moisture.

1. Coat the dry chicken breast liberally and evenly with flour before spanking the excess off, leaving only the barest film.

2. Using tongs, dip the floured breast in the egg wash, taking care to coat the entire surface before letting the excess drip back into the pan.

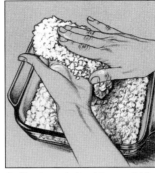

3. Good crumb depth is essential for an even, dry coating. Toss the chicken in the crumbs to coat and then press with fingers for even distribution.

Allow cutlets to dry for 10 minutes. Process bread in food processor until evenly fine-textured, 20 to 30 seconds (you should have about 1½ cups fresh bread crumbs). Transfer crumbs to baking dish. Carefully peel paper towels off cutlets, sprinkle cutlets with pepper, and set aside.

3. Adjust oven rack to lower-middle position, set large heatproof plate on rack, and heat oven to 200 degrees. Spread flour in baking dish. Beat eggs with 1 tablespoon oil in second baking dish. Spread bread crumbs in third baking dish.

4. As shown in illustrations 1–3 above, bread the cutlets, one at a time. Dredge cutlet in flour, shaking off excess. Using tongs, dip both sides of cutlet in egg mixture, allowing excess to drip back into baking dish to ensure very thin coating. Dip both sides of cutlet in bread crumbs, pressing crumbs with fingers to form even, cohesive coat. Place breaded cutlets in single layer on wire rack set over baking sheet and allow coating to dry for about 5 minutes.

5. Meanwhile, heat 6 tablespoons remaining oil in heavy-bottomed 10-inch nonstick skillet over medium-high heat until shimmering but not smoking, about 2 minutes. Lay two cutlets gently in skillet; cook until deep golden brown and crisp on first side, gently pressing down on cutlets with wide metal spatula to help ensure even browning, about 2½ minutes. Using tongs, flip cutlets, reduce heat to medium, and continue to cook until meat feels firm when pressed gently and second side is deep golden brown and crisp, 2½ to 3 minutes longer. Line warmed plate with double layer of paper towels and set cutlets on top; return plate to oven.

Pounded Flat

It is essential to pound boneless chicken breasts to an even ½-inch thickness to ensure quick and even cooking.

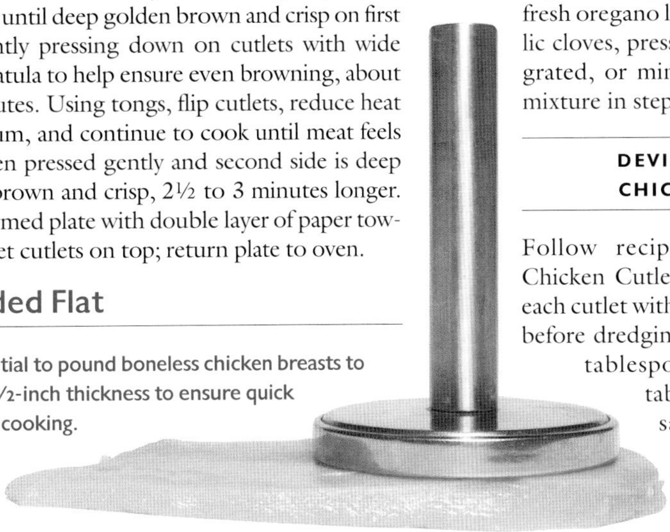

6. Discard oil in skillet and wipe skillet clean using tongs and large wad of paper towels. Repeat step 5 using remaining 6 tablespoons oil and now-clean skillet to cook remaining cutlets; serve along with first batch with lemon wedges.

BREADED CHICKEN CUTLETS WITH PARMESAN
(CHICKEN MILANESE)

Though Parmesan is the traditional cheese to use in this dish, feel free to substitute Pecorino Romano cheese if you prefer a stronger, more tangy flavor. The cheese is quite susceptible to burning, so be sure to keep a very close eye on the cutlets as they cook.

Follow recipe for Crisp Breaded Chicken Cutlets, substituting ¼ cup finely grated Parmesan cheese for an equal amount of bread crumbs.

BREADED CHICKEN CUTLETS WITH GARLIC AND OREGANO

Follow recipe for Crisp Breaded Chicken Cutlets, beating 3 tablespoons very finely minced fresh oregano leaves and 8 medium garlic cloves, pressed through garlic press, grated, or minced to puree, into egg mixture in step 3.

DEVILED BREADED CHICKEN CUTLETS

Follow recipe for Crisp Breaded Chicken Cutlets, rubbing each side of each cutlet with generous pinch cayenne before dredging in flour and beating 3 tablespoons Dijon mustard, 1 tablespoon Worcestershire sauce, and 2 teaspoons very finely minced fresh thyme leaves into egg mixture in step 3.

Beefing Up Mustard Vinaigrette

To make an assertive but well-balanced vinaigrette, choose the mustard carefully, match it with the right vinegar, and leave the extra-virgin olive oil on the shelf.

⋟ BY BRIDGET LANCASTER WITH ADAM RIED ⋞

There are two kinds of mustard vinaigrette. Many classic preparations use just a whisper of mustard to help blend and balance the other ingredients in the dressing. Such mild vinaigrettes are a good choice when dressing salads of tender greens and mildly flavored steamed vegetables. Then there is a bolder version, which we pursue here, that uses enough of its namesake ingredient to make you stand up and take notice. A mustardy mustard vinaigrette complements salads of hearty greens like romaine and bitter greens like frisée. It also does right by the concentrated flavors of grilled, roasted, or broiled vegetables, chicken, and fish.

We wanted to cast the mustard in a starring role, with its distinct flavor playing off a balance of oil and vinegar. But we also wanted to avoid introducing the harsh flavor that plagues some mustard vinaigrettes, a result of the fact that mustard tastes sharp in and of itself even before the tart vinegar enters the picture. To come up with a pungent, balanced vinaigrette, we'd have to thoroughly examine each component—the mustard, vinegar, and oil—as well as their proportions.

We started at square one, with mustard. From the many possibilities we selected three contestants: English mustard, which has a particularly strong bite; whole grain mustard, which features intact mustard seeds and a coarse texture; and Dijon mustard, which is made with white wine. The English and whole grain mustards both bombed, the English being too harsh for this purpose and the whole grain destroying the smooth texture we were after. Dijon mustard was the clear winner, producing a softly creamy vinaigrette that tasted bold and piquant without overpowering the oil and vinegar.

Up next was the vinegar. We prepared and tasted vinaigrettes made with six vinegars: cider, white wine, red wine, champagne, rice, and balsamic. Tasters found the cider, white and red wine, and champagne vinegars too fruity. The rice vinegar was appreciated for its subtle sweetness and low acidity (about 4 percent, versus 6 or 7 percent for the others). But the real winner was balsamic vinegar, which contributed a deep caramel sweetness that countered the mustard beautifully.

We got a real surprise when we tested different oils. Like most cooks, we always reach for the fruity extra-virgin olive oil when making vinaigrette, but when we tasted two vinaigrettes, one

made with extra-virgin and the other with milder pure olive oil, tasters shocked us with their unanimous preference for the version with pure olive oil. The fruity, peppery flavor of the extra-virgin olive oil competed with the flavor of the mustard, throwing the vinaigrette out of balance. The pure olive oil was rich tasting but unobtrusive.

The last critical variable was the ratio of oil to vinegar to mustard. Traditional vinaigrettes rely on a ratio of 3 parts oil to 1 part acid (vinegar). In our test kitchen, we've consistently preferred the flavor and texture of vinaigrettes with 4 parts oil to 1 part acid. This vinaigrette was no exception. The higher proportion of oil softened the tartness introduced by the extra mustard.

MUSTARD AND BALSAMIC VINAIGRETTE
MAKES ABOUT ⅓ CUP

We prefer a rasp-style grater for the shallot, but the small holes of a box grater work, too. The vinaigrette can be used immediately, but the flavors develop if it is left to stand at room temperature for about 1 hour before use. This vinaigrette is well matched with bitter salad greens such as radicchio and frisée.

- ¼ cup olive oil
- 1 tablespoon balsamic vinegar
- 2 teaspoons Dijon mustard
- ½ small shallot, finely grated (about 1 teaspoon)
- 1 teaspoon finely minced fresh tarragon or chives
- ¼ teaspoon salt
- ⅛ teaspoon ground black pepper

Whisk all ingredients in small nonreactive bowl until blended and creamy. Alternatively, combine all ingredients in small jar, seal tightly with lid, and shake until mixture is blended and creamy. (Can be covered and refrigerated for up to 1 week; return to room temperature before using.)

MUSTARD AND ROASTED GARLIC VINAIGRETTE
MAKES ABOUT ½ CUP

A little water is added to this vinaigrette to counter the thickening effect of the roasted garlic. Use the vinaigrette over grilled or roasted vegetables.

- 1 garlic head (about 2½ ounces), intact
- ½ teaspoon plus ¼ cup olive oil

- ½ teaspoon salt
- 1 tablespoon balsamic vinegar
- 2 teaspoons Dijon mustard
- ½ teaspoon minced fresh thyme leaves
- ⅛ teaspoon ground black pepper
- 2 tablespoons hot tap water

1. Adjust oven rack to middle position and heat oven to 400 degrees. Remove outer papery skins from head of garlic; cut ½ inch off top to expose most cloves. Place garlic head cut-side up in center of 8-inch-long piece of foil; drizzle cut surface with ½ teaspoon olive oil and ¼ teaspoon salt. Gather corners of foil and twist to seal. Roast garlic until cloves are soft and golden, about 45 minutes. When cool enough to handle, squeeze cloves from skins into small nonreactive bowl; using a fork, mash garlic to paste.

2. Add remaining ¼ cup olive oil, remaining ¼ teaspoon salt, vinegar, mustard, thyme, pepper, and water to bowl with garlic; whisk until blended and creamy. (Can be covered and refrigerated for up to 1 week; return to room temperature before using.)

MUSTARD VINAIGRETTE WITH LEMON AND FINES HERBES
MAKES ABOUT ⅓ CUP

The lemon and herbal flavors of this vinaigrette make a nice dressing for grilled, roasted, or broiled vegetables, chicken, and fish.

- ¼ cup olive oil
- 1 tablespoon juice from 1 lemon
- 2 teaspoons Dijon mustard
- ½ small shallot, finely grated (about 1 teaspoon)
- 1 teaspoon minced fresh parsley leaves
- 1 teaspoon minced fresh chervil leaves
- 1 teaspoon minced fresh tarragon leaves
- 1 teaspoon minced fresh chives
- ¼ teaspoon salt
- ⅛ teaspoon ground black pepper

Whisk all ingredients in small nonreactive bowl until blended and creamy. Alternatively, combine all ingredients in small jar, seal tightly with lid, and shake until mixture is blended and creamy. (Can be covered and refrigerated for up to 1 week; return to room temperature before using.)

Bouillabaisse Goes Home

Could we make a richly scented seafood stew at home in two hours
with supermarket fish and no sous-chef?

≥ BY KAY RENTSCHLER ≤

This streamlined American version of the French classic works just fine with any of a dozen widely available fish and is often topped by a garlic-rubbed crouton and a red pepper puree.

The rise of bouillabaisse from a stew of sea scraps fishermen cooked on the beach to the well-clad restaurant celebrity we know today is a classic rags-to-riches tale. Bouillabaisse is heady, powerful stuff—a jeweled tapestry of fish and shellfish in a briny-sweet broth with tomato, wine, garlic, and saffron. The base of this soup should have enough melted collagen from its fish frames to leave a sticky varnish on the lips that only a big hit of white Côtes de Provence and a fine linen napkin can remove. Its name alone suggests concentration and flavor: *bouillir* (to boil), *abaisser* (to reduce). And, indeed, bouillabaisse requires a good rollicking boil to emulsify the oils into its broth, making it thicker. Boldly colored and steaming in its plate, bouillabaisse is interrupted by a slab of toasted or stale baguette brushed with olive oil and garlic and anointed with a spicy, luxuriant red pepper aioli called rouille. It gives you more bang for your bite than anything else in the world.

On its way up the social ladder, bouillabaisse developed something of an attitude problem. For a while there was even talk that Americans couldn't make this dish. Why? The humble fish responsible for its origins (principally the firm, white-fleshed rascasse, among others) are native only to Mediterranean waters. The American home cook was also put off by the notion of creating a full-flavored fish stock from scratch, a crucial step in producing a first-class bouillabaisse. Finally, great bouillabaisse is predicated on the notion of finesse in cooking the fish to perfection, flavoring the broth delicately, and balancing a host of diverse ingredients, from orange zest to Pernod, saffron to fennel, mussels to sea bass. I expected the testing process to be more a matter of refinement and balance than one of making radical new discoveries.

Casting About

At the outset of this investigation, I tested a substantial number of bouillabaisse recipes and found that although the extended family of famous fish soups, both Gallic and Italian, reflect minor regional and cultural differences, there were few rogue upstarts or egregious bastardizations. That being said, seemingly minor variations in the recipes made an enormous impact on the finished dish. What is the best method for creating a homemade stock quickly and easily? How does one infuse this liquid with a complex range of flavors without producing a dull, oily stew? Which combination of fish provides just the right texture and flavor, and how does one prevent overcooking? How does one make a superior rouille? Finally, are there any shortcuts—bottled clam juice and frozen fish came to mind—that have a place in a great bouillabaisse?

I quickly dispensed with the obvious shortcuts. A couple of quarts of bottled clam juice will not stand in the stead of real fish stock, just as a couple boxes of frozen fish fillets cannot replace a selection of good, fresh fish. Although there is nothing technically or procedurally difficult about making it, a superior bouillabaisse was going to require a reasonable investment of time and attention. The good news is that bouillabaisse constitutes a one-pot, three-course meal—soup, fish, and bread. You won't need to put another thing on the table. My goal was to simplify whenever possible and enhance flavor at every turn to make bouillabaisse a frequent guest at the table.

Four Steps to Greatness

A bouillabaisse has four preparatory phases. The first is marinating the cut-up fish in olive oil and other flavorings. The second is making the fish stock. The third is preparing the soup, where the fish stock bows to the supporting cast of flavors—tomatoes, leeks, fresh fennel, and so on—and welcomes the fish. The fourth is preparing the rouille and crouton.

Fish destined for the bouillabaisse pot are generally cut, then splashed with olive oil and other herbs or aromatics and left to repose before being poached. This flavor marinade brightens the underwater landscape of the stew in ways that plain fish chunks cannot. Fish, with its delicate raw flesh, is capable of absorbing flavors nicely. In terms of specifics, green, fruity extra-virgin olive oil got the better of the fish—milder stuff was better. I found that 4 tablespoons serviced the 3 pounds of fish very well (mussels are not marinated because they hide in their shells, refusing to absorb new flavors; scallops and shelled shrimp can be marinated with the rest of the crew). Taste tests determined that minced garlic, saffron threads, fresh chopped basil, and Pernod, along with sea salt and a tiny bit of red pepper flakes, made the ideal marinade and that four hours were

PHOTOGRAPHY: CARL TREMBLAY

necessary to reach full flavor penetration. The more interesting discovery, however, was made when the marinade was poured into the boiling stock with the fish. The oil and other liquids emulsified into the stock, lending it more of its customary richness. This method was superior to simply adding olive oil directly to the stew later, as was the common practice in the recipes I tested.

Taking Stock

I had discarded the notion of bottled clam juice and also found that canned chicken broth just wasn't going to do the trick. So I visited an obliging fishmonger up the street who put together packages of cleaned fish heads and frames for me to begin preliminary tests on fish stock. Though home cooks may be tempted to freeze whatever fish bones and scraps are left from dinner to make a stock, this is not a good idea. I found that not only are the bones from salmon and the like too oily to produce a clean-tasting stock (white fish is essential), but leftover scraps and bits from any fish are likely to lack the essential levels of collagen required to produce a rich, flavorful stock. Fish heads are particularly collagen-rich, so it is important to buy some of them as well. (Don't worry about catching the fish's eye and cringing—the fishmonger will have scraped it out.) Ask the fishmonger to remove the fish's gills and organs as well, and, while he's at it, have him cut the frames into manageable 5- or 6-inch slabs.

One of two techniques is often used in making fish stock. Some recipes simply simmer the ingredients, whereas others "sweat" the aromatics in butter or olive oil, then add the bones with wine, and, finally, water to simmer. To determine which method was best, I used 3 pounds of fish bones, carrots, celery, onions, leeks, garlic, mushrooms, parsley stems, white wine, and water and made side-by-side fish stocks, one sweated and simmered, the other merely simmered. The resulting 2-plus quarts were robust and flavorful in the sweated version, watery and wanting in the simmered. While not as flawlessly clear as the simmered stock, the sweated stock was translucent, finished, and ready to move on; the simmered stock would have needed a

Simmering versus Sweating

Some stocks are made by simmering fish bones and vegetables in water (left). Others begin by sweating (cooking fish bones and vegetables in butter or oil in a covered pot, right) and then add water. We found that sweating, then simmering, releases more flavor from the bones and vegetables than simmering alone.

reduction by 50 percent to reach comparable flavor and texture. As for simmering time, an hour extracted every drop of flavor and liquid protein the soft, porous bones had to relinquish.

My second interesting discovery came when customizing the stock for this recipe. Most bouillabaisse recipes add sautéed chunks of leeks, tomatoes, and fennel slices to the stew along with the fish. I found the physical presence of these vegetables an encumbrance when served up with the fish, so I decided to add them to the stock, not the stew (which also saved me the bother of having to sauté them). Their flavor was rendered, and then they were summarily discarded so that the key players—the fish and shellfish—could shine undisturbed.

Now I had to choose just the right ingredients to make a fish stock perfectly suited for bouillabaisse. I dashed a quarter cup olive oil into a Dutch oven to sweat the vegetables: Onions and carrots remained in the lineup, but mushrooms brought nothing to the sultry flavors to come. I replaced celery with a Mediterranean native, fresh fennel—same clean flavor with a licorice twist. A signature player, the garlic was doubled to reach critical mass (three full heads). After 30 minutes under cover, these vegetables were exhausted. In went 3 pounds of fish frames and heads, sea salt, peppercorns, and a nice bottle of white Côtes de Provence. The bones were simmered and prodded (the prodding is useful in extracting collagen from the bones so that it can dissolve in the stock). Next came leeks, canned tomatoes and their juices, fresh thyme, bay leaves, and 4 cups of water. At the end of an hour I added a half teaspoon of saffron threads and large strips of zest from two oranges. Strained, this stuff was in-your-face-intense, its color a hot, tropical sunset.

Daily Catch

With the stock in an advanced state of readiness, it was time to throw some fish in the pot. Nearly all bouillabaisse recipes emphasize that a variety of fish and shellfish are essential to bring character to the stew. They support the call for firm-fleshed fish and caution against using fish that are too delicate in constitution or too strong in flavor to complement any of the others.

I went back to the local fishmonger, hunting down everything from the top-billed red snapper (a warm water fish not native to New England) to lobster (certainly not an original, but would it work?). Boston is obviously not a bad place to be when looking for fish, and I was fortunate to be able to test upward of 20 different varieties. Certain fish simply have no place in a bouillabaisse, among them bluefish and mackerel—these guys lacked the politesse not to upstage

everybody else. Others weren't worth the trouble required to get them suited up; besides being pricey and cumbersome, lobster failed to match any number of other entrants for flavor; squid was a nuisance to clean, and its chewy texture put it at odds with the group. Cod, Boston's great white hope, was too flaky and cooked too fast—it dissolved in the mouth.

Other fish fell out for the simple reason that their cooking times were too different. Sole was so thin that it overcooked right off. Clams required a separate pot to steam open. Once they had, their buff-colored shells and rubbery mollusk insides brought little to the party. Though many recipes suggest layering the fish in the pot, with longer cooking varieties going in first, the more delicate topping the stack, I wanted the liberty of adding fish to the boiling stock en masse and letting them poach to completion. (This "everyone-into-the-pool" simmer had one other advantage. It was easier to produce perfectly cooked fish since the timing was easier to control.)

In the end I found a lot to like, and, by grouping favored fish in "flaky" and "firm" camps, was able to put together some winning combinations (see "Choosing Seafood for Bouillabaisse," page 15). I concluded that at least six types of combined fish and shellfish were necessary to produce a first-class bouillabaisse and that 8 ounces per type of fish were required to satisfy 8 to 10 hungry diners.

Finishing Up

As if bouillabaisse weren't already a glorious synthesis of flavors, two additions dive into the fray: a roasted red pepper and garlic mayonnaise, known as a rouille, and a large garlic crouton. The crouton is a raft on the stew; the rouille its passenger.

The croutons can be cut from a baguette or French country loaf, any bread that is rustic and honest—just not sourdough. The French typically use stale bread; I preferred mine broiled lightly on each side. In fact, I preferred my crouton brushed with olive oil and rubbed with raw garlic as well. The favored texture was crunchy on both exposed surfaces, with a light golden band along the edge of the crust and a yielding center.

For the rouille, I started with a large grill-roasted red pepper. Recipes use egg yolks and/or bread to bind the roasted pepper and create a thick sauce. I tested three preparations: 2 egg yolks and no bread, 1 egg yolk and 1 ounce bread, and 2 ounces bread and no egg yolk. The procedure is simple: The roasted pepper is seeded and divested of its burnt skin, then ground up in the food processor with 2 garlic cloves and the egg and/or bread. With the processor running, 1/2 cup olive oil is drizzled in. Tasters preferred the rouille made with bread alone. It had a note of sweetness that brushed up against the red pepper and melted potently into the broth when it slid off the crouton.

Now I had found what I was looking for: a richly scented homemade fish stock with complex flavors, just the right combination of readily available and perfectly cooked fish, a salmon-colored dollop of garlicky rouille, and a recipe that, although not simple, was well within the grasp of any cook eager to bring the clean, briny taste of the ocean to the table. It doesn't get much better than this.

BOUILLABAISSE-STYLE FISH STEW
SERVES 8 TO 10

If you decide to make the fish stock ahead, it must be used within 2 days or frozen and defrosted. Use only the freshest fish. Monkfish, sea bass, and ocean perch or red snapper make up our favorite combination, but you can create your own according to the guidelines in the chart at right. The chopped vegetables for the stock must be fairly small (no larger than 1 inch in diameter) and evenly cut. The rouille must be made the day you are planning to serve the bouillabaisse.

Fish and shellfish marinade
- 8 ounces small (41/45) shell-on shrimp, peeled and shells reserved for fish stock
- 8 ounces large sea scallops, side muscles removed and each scallop halved
- 1 1/2 pounds fish fillets, cut into 1- to 1 1/2-inch cubes (see chart at right)
- 2 teaspoons sea salt or table salt
- 1/4 teaspoon red pepper flakes
- 3 garlic cloves, minced or pressed through garlic press
- 1/2 teaspoon saffron threads
- 1/3 cup shredded basil leaves
- 4 tablespoons olive oil
- 3 tablespoons Pernod

Fish stock
- 1 small fennel bulb, chopped medium (about 2 cups)
- 1 large carrot, chopped medium (about 1 cup)
- 2 medium onions, chopped medium (about 2 cups)
- 4 tablespoons olive oil
- 3 heads garlic, outer papery skin removed, but heads intact
- 1 (750-ml) bottle dry white wine (preferably white Côtes de Provence)
- 2 (28-ounce) cans diced tomatoes with juice
- 2 large leeks (white and green parts included), split lengthwise, then chopped, washed thoroughly, and drained (about 4 cups)
- 3 pounds fish frames, gills removed and discarded, frames rinsed and cut into 6-inch pieces
  Reserved shrimp shells
  Stems from 1 bunch fresh parsley
- 5 sprigs fresh thyme
- 2 bay leaves
- 2 teaspoons whole black peppercorns
- 2 teaspoons sea salt or table salt
  Zest from 2 medium oranges removed in large strips with vegetable peeler
- 1/2 teaspoon saffron threads

Stew
- 2 pounds mussels, shells scrubbed and beards removed
  Salt and ground black pepper

1. Combine all fish and shellfish marinade ingredients in large nonreactive bowl; toss well, cover flush with plastic wrap, and refrigerate 4 hours.

2. Meanwhile, stir fennel, carrot, onions, and oil together in 8-quart heavy-bottomed stockpot or Dutch oven. Cover pot and set over medium-low heat; cook, stirring frequently, until vegetables are fragrant, about 15 minutes. Place garlic in large heavy-duty plastic bag and seal. Smash garlic with rolling pin or meat pounder until flattened. Add smashed garlic to vegetables and continue to cook, stirring frequently, until vegetables are dry and just beginning to stick, about 15 minutes more. (Take care not to let garlic burn.) Add wine and stir to scrape pot bottom, then add tomatoes and their juices, leeks, fish frames, shrimp shells, parsley stems, thyme, bay leaves, peppercorns, salt, and 4 cups water. Bring to simmer over medium-high heat, reduce heat to medium-low, and simmer, pressing down on fish bones occasionally with wooden spoon to submerge, until stock is rich and flavorful, about 1 hour.

3. Strain stock through large fine-mesh strainer or chinois into large bowl or container (you should have about 9 cups); rinse and wipe out stockpot and return strained stock to pot. Bring stock to boil over high heat and simmer briskly until reduced to 8 cups, about 10 minutes. Off heat, add orange zest and saffron. Let stand 10 minutes to infuse flavors. Strain stock through mesh strainer and set aside.

4. Return fish broth to clean 8-quart stockpot and bring to rolling boil over high heat. Stir in marinated fish and shellfish along with mussels, cover pot, and return to simmer; simmer for 7 minutes, stirring a few times to ensure even cooking. Remove pot from heat, cover, and let stand until fish is cooked through and mussels have opened, about 2 minutes. Season to taste with salt and pepper; ladle into bowls, and float one garlic-rubbed crouton topped with dollop of rouille in each bowl. Serve immediately.

GARLIC-RUBBED CROUTONS

- 1 loaf (about 1 pound) country-style French bread, cut into ten 1/2-inch thick slices, remainder reserved for Rouille
- 6 medium garlic cloves, peeled and halved
- 3 tablespoons olive oil

Choosing Seafood for Bouillabaisse

Over the last couple of months I threw a ton of fish into my kettle. I wanted to see what worked, what didn't work, and what worked together. I also wanted to come up with textural combinations that pleased the palate and skated across the tongue. The fun of bouillabaisse is that one mouthful can contain buttery flakes of ocean perch, the bite of monkfish, the chew of a little mollusk, and the slippery firmness of shrimp. A tasting determined that a combination of three groups of seafood was best: firm-fleshed fish, flaky fish, and shellfish. Three fish and three shellfish make a great combination— or go with four fish and two shellfish if you prefer. Doubtless many freshwater fish would work well in this recipe, but I limited my testing to saltwater fish in the interest of time. — K.R.

RECOMMENDED

For best results, choose at least one fish from each category:

Firm	Flaky	Shellfish
Chilean sea bass	hake	mussels
grouper	ocean perch	sea scallops
haddock	red snapper	shrimp
halibut	Thai snapper	
John Dory		
monkfish		
striped bass		
tilapia		

NOT RECOMMENDED

Too Oily	Incompatible Cooking Rates	Too Meaty
bluefish	clams	mahi-mahi
mackerel	cod	swordfish
salmon	sole	tuna

Adjust oven rack (or broiler) to highest position and heat broiler. Arrange bread slices in single layer on baking sheet; broil until lightly toasted, about 1 1/2 minutes. Flip slices and rub second side of each slice with raw garlic, then brush with olive oil. Broil until light golden brown, about 1 1/2 minutes longer. Serve with bouillabaisse.

ROUILLE

- 1 large red bell pepper (about 9 ounces), roasted, peeled, seeded, and cut into large pieces (about 2/3 cup)
- 2 ounces reserved bread, trimmed of crust and cut into large cubes (about 2 cups)
- 2 medium garlic cloves, minced finely or pressed through garlic press (about 2 teaspoons)
- 1/8 teaspoon cayenne pepper
- 1/2 cup olive oil
  Salt

In workbowl of food processor fitted with steel blade, process roasted pepper, bread cubes, garlic, and cayenne until smooth, about 20 seconds. With machine running, drizzle olive oil through feed tube; process until rouille has thick, mayonnaise-like consistency. Season to taste with salt. Serve with bouillabaisse.

Measuring 101: Techniques & Shortcuts

Accurate measuring is the first step to successful cooking. We define the basics, show you some shortcuts, and explain why careful measuring is so important. BY RAQUEL PELZEL

Proper measuring can make or break a recipe. Take flour, for example. In baked goods such as cakes, cookies, and breads, adding too little flour can make the end product flat, wet, or lacking in structure. Many home cooks measure flour by spooning it into a cup, then leveling it off. This method of measuring dry ingredients can yield 20 percent less flour than the method we use in the test kitchen: dip and sweep (illustrated below, at left). In helping you to measure accurately, the tips and techniques we present here will help you achieve consistently good results whenever you cook or bake.

DRY OR LIQUID MEASURING CUP— WHAT'S THE DIFFERENCE?

Dry ingredients like flour and sugar should always be measured in dry measuring cups, never in liquid cups. Although liquid and dry measuring cups hold the same volume, in a liquid measuring cup, there is no way to level the surface of the contents to obtain an exact measurement.

While it is possible to measure liquids in a dry measuring cup, it's hard to fill the cup to the rim and decant it without spills. A liquid measuring cup has headroom so that it needn't be filled to the brim.

DRY MEASURING (DIP AND SWEEP) Dip a dry measuring cup into the ingredient and sweep away the excess with a straight-edged object such as an icing spatula.

LIQUID MEASURING To get an accurate reading in a liquid measuring cup, set the cup on a level surface and bend down to read it at eye level. Read the measurement at the bottom of the concave arc at the liquid's surface, known as the meniscus line.

DRY MEASURING CUPS
The Good, the Bad, and the Useless

For both measuring spoons and dry measuring cups, we prefer heavy, well-constructed stainless steel models with long, sturdy, well-designed handles. Plastic spoons and cups feel flimsy, have rims prone to developing nicks and bumps, can warp in the dishwasher, and will melt if placed too close to a heat source.

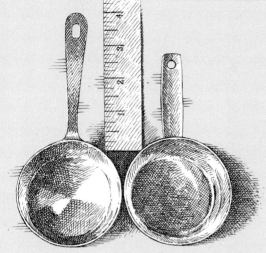

OUR FAVORITE An extra-long 4-inch handle makes dipping into a bin of flour a clean endeavor.

Three Problematic Handle Styles

short handle

STICKY FINGERS The short, awkward handle on this cup makes dipping and sweeping difficult. It can also be hard to keep your thumb out of the ingredients.

flexible handle

NO BACKBONE This flimsy, flexible handle bends under the slightest pressure.

heavy handle

TOPSY-TURVY This handle-heavy cup tilts when set down, increasing the chance that ingredients will spill out.

WHY AND HOW TO SIFT FLOUR

When a recipe calls for sifted flour, it is important to take the time to sift even if the flour you're using is labeled "presifted." In addition to eliminating lumps, sifting aerates the flour, making it easier to incorporate the flour into a batter. Sifted flour thus also weighs 20 to 25 percent less per cup than unsifted. We found that an additional ounce of flour caused an otherwise moist and perfectly level cake to bake up into a drier cake with a domed top.

SIFT AND LEVEL If a recipe reads "1 cup sifted flour," sift the flour directly into a measuring cup (set on top of parchment paper for a hassle-free cleanup) and level off the cup.

DIP, SWEEP, AND SIFT If a recipe reads "1 cup flour, sifted," first dip into the flour and sweep off the excess, then sift it onto a piece of parchment paper. This method yields the same amount of flour by weight as if you had simply dipped and swept, but the flour is now aerated and lump free.

MEASURING TIPS AND SHORTCUTS
Here are some ideas to help you deal with hard-to-measure ingredients.

MEASURING BUTTER ACCURATELY We've noticed that the tablespoon increment measures on butter wrappers often don't line up correctly with the stick of butter. If this is the case, unwrap the butter, mark the halfway point in the stick and then mark the midpoint of each half, dividing the stick into quarters (each quarter is equal to 2 tablespoons, or 1 ounce). If necessary, mark the midpoint of each quarter, dividing the stick into eighths (each eighth is equal to 1 tablespoon, or 1/2 ounce). Alternatively, use a scale to weigh the butter, keeping in mind that 1 tablespoon equals 1/2 ounce.

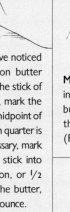

HANDLING HONEY AND MOLASSES When measuring sticky ingredients like honey and molasses, spray the measuring cup with nonstick cooking spray before filling it. When emptied, the liquid will slip right out of the cup.

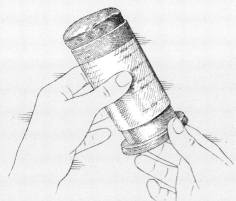

MEASURING PEANUT BUTTER Great for measuring semisolid ingredients like sour cream and peanut butter, this push-up-style cup allows you to scoop in the ingredient, level it off, and then push it right out. (For buying information, see Resources, page 32.)

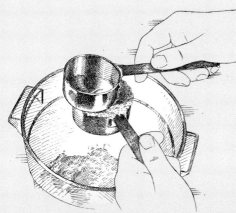

PACKING BROWN SUGAR Brown sugar is tacky and lumpy; packing it into a measuring cup compacts the sugar and presses out any air pockets (the difference in weight between 1 cup of packed brown sugar and 1 cup of unpacked can be as much as 2 ounces). A neat way to pack brown sugar is to use the bottom of a smaller cup to tamp and press the sugar into a larger cup.

MEASURING SHORTENING When measuring messy, malleable ingredients like shortening, line the measuring cup with plastic wrap, scoop in the shortening, and level it off. To retrieve it, simply lift out the plastic liner and the contents come with it. ILLUSTRATION: JOHN BURGOYNE

MEASURING FLOUR, SIMPLIFIED

Recipe reads:	then you:	to get a weight of:
➤ 1 cup all-purpose flour ➤ 1 cup cake flour	measure flour with dip-and-sweep method	➤ about 5 ounces ➤ about 4 ounces
➤ 1 cup sifted all-purpose flour ➤ 1 cup sifted cake flour	sift flour directly into measuring cup and level off	➤ about 4 ounces ➤ about 3 ounces
➤ 1 cup all-purpose flour, sifted ➤ 1 cup cake flour, sifted	measure flour with dip-and-sweep method, then sift	➤ about 5 ounces ➤ about 4 ounces

Rethinking Ratatouille

How do you transform an oily, bland vegetable stew into a brightly flavored ratatouille?
For starters, heat your oven to 500 degrees.

≥ BY BRIDGET LANCASTER ≤

Think, for a moment, of ratatouille as French soul food. A well-made ratatouille embodies the essence of flavors from the South of France, including firm eggplant, zucchini, caramelized onions, heady garlic, and garden-fresh herbs. Bringing the mixture together are the ripest of tomatoes, cooked just enough to lend their sweet juices to the mix.

Now think of the last time you had ratatouille for brunch at a second-rate local eatery. The ingredients were indistinguishable in taste, color, and texture. That's because each of the vegetables has its own set of cooking problems. If each is not handled properly, the resulting dish is a mess. Eggplant soaks up oil and leaches liquid into the pan. Zucchini's problem is lack of flavor. Cooked too little, it is pretty to look at but tastes like nothing; cooked enough to become flavorful, it turns into army mush. Ripe and juicy tomatoes break down to a runny sauce in minutes, especially when mixed with other vegetables.

The name ratatouille is derived from the French *touiller*, meaning "to stir." When it comes to interpretation of the method, there are two schools of thought. Included in the testing were the classic French preparation, in which vegetables are sautéed in olive oil in batches and combined at the last minute with minimal stirring, and a typical American ratatouille, in which everything is tossed into the pot at once and stewed until tender. In American-style ratatouille, it was difficult to distinguish eggplant from zucchini, and the whole amalgamation tasted like watery tomatoes. The batch-cooked ratatouille fared much better, although it was oily from the more than 1 cup of olive oil needed to keep the vegetables from sticking to the pan. On the plus side, the vegetables remained relatively intact, and the stew carried the flavors particular to each component. So I set out to deal with each vegetable individually, hoping to maximize texture and flavor while minimizing the amount of oil.

Good ratatouille features caramelized onions, heady garlic, and perfectly cooked eggplant and zucchini, all bound with tomatoes and perfumed by fresh herbs.

The Problem with Sautéing

I quickly discovered that sautéing eggplant has its problems. Eggplant is mostly water, which turns to steam and bursts through the cell walls, causing them to collapse in the process. The result is a soggy, soupy mess. Eggplant is also extremely absorbent, thanks to millions of air pockets built into its cell walls, and will soak up as much oil as you give it. To avoid these problems, cooks typically salt eggplant and allow it to drain before cooking. Using this method, however, the eggplant in our test kitchen still soaked up 1 cup of oil when sautéed. The next time around I pressed the eggplant chunks firmly with paper towels after salting to extract most of the moisture and to rid the pieces of their oil-absorbing air pockets. This time the eggplant was dense and firm, and it soaked up ¾ cup oil, still a large amount.

I performed the same procedure with zucchini and found that it was much less resilient than the eggplant. Under the duress of salting and pressing, it became mushy and flat. It was better to leave well enough alone and omit the salting/pressing altogether.

I then went on to make a batch of ratatouille using these preparation methods, complete with sautéed onions, tomatoes, and garlic. While this stew was a vast improvement over the previous batches, I still was not happy with the amount of oil necessary to cook each vegetable individually. I had to find a method for cooking the eggplant and zucchini that highlighted their natural flavors, provided good texture, and did not require an obscene amount of olive oil.

Because high heat draws out liquid and intensifies flavor, my next stop was the broiler. Still using the salting/pressing preparation for the eggplant, I tossed the chunks with a little oil and slipped them under the broiler. The results were less than satisfying. The extreme heat from the broiler caused the eggplant to burn before the pieces were sufficiently dehydrated. Then I turned to a high-heat oven set at 500 degrees, thinking that it would present no direct threat from the broiler element. Eureka! The eggplant was firm and toothy, with no sign of sponginess, and the flavor was rich and intense. Next I tried the zucchini (which was simply cut into chunks and lightly oiled) and found that it also benefited from the oven-roasting method. It was toothsome and flavorful. Left undisturbed in the oven, the zucchini retained its shape, and the chunky pieces gave the stew a fresh appearance.

No small advantage of using the oven to roast the eggplant and zucchini was the now-minuscule amount of oil that was required. Batch-cooking

The Effects of Salting Eggplant

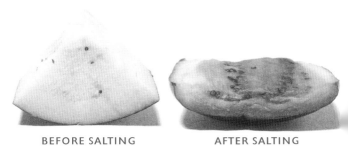

BEFORE SALTING	AFTER SALTING

Salting and pressing eggplant collapses the cell walls, eliminating air pockets that would otherwise soak up fat during cooking.

Any Eggplant Will Do

ITALIAN   JAPANESE   GLOBE

Some ratatouille recipes call for Japanese or Italian eggplant, each of which is thought to be superior to globe eggplant in flavor and texture. In a head-to-head comparison of the three in our recipe, we found that neither the Japanese nor the Italian eggplant had anything on the common globe eggplant.

the stew entirely on the stovetop had necessitated at least ¾ cup of oil, mostly for the eggplant. Now, a total of only 2 tablespoons was needed to coat both the zucchini and the eggplant, and they could be spread and roasted on sheet pans at the same time.

Roasting Isn't for Everybody

Any hopes of making this an entirely in-oven operation came to a screeching halt when I tested roasting the onions, garlic, and tomatoes. If the onions were to roast evenly, they would have to be sliced rather than chopped, and tasters found the long strands texturally unappealing. Chopping and then sautéing them until caramel-colored and soft gave them a delicate flavor that blended well with the sweet tomatoes. Garlic also performed better in the sauté pan. But rather than subject it to the same slow caramelization as the onions, I found that a quick blast of heat best allowed the flavor to bloom. There was no mistaking its presence in the ratatouille. Finally, the roasted plump tomatoes turned to mush well before any increase in flavor occurred. I found that it was much better to add the tomatoes near the end of cooking, giving them just enough time to start breaking down and supply a bit of moisture to hold the stew together.

Although the *Cook's* test kitchen usually prefers canned tomatoes to most produce aisle specimens, this is one recipe in which the real thing is mandatory, for authenticity as well as for texture and flavor. In fact, buying the right tomato and preparing it correctly can make or break a ratatouille. First I tried the compact Roma tomato, but its lack of liquid gave the stew the appearance of thick chutney. Round tomatoes, especially the rugged beefsteak variety, worked exceptionally well. Their robust flavor, substantial size, and abundance of fleshy meat added just the right amount of texture and freshness to the mélange.

I found it necessary to first peel the tomatoes, a process that goes quickly by dropping them in boiling water for a few seconds, followed by shocking them in ice water. But no matter what kind of tomato I used, I found that it was better to leave the seedbed in place. The seeds carry quite a bit of liquid, so removing them resulted in a dry ratatouille.

At last, I tested the herbs. Fresh herbs are an important part of Provençal cookery, and this dish is no exception. Basil is by far the herb called for most often in ratatouille, due in no small part to its growing schedule, which is simultaneous with that of the other ingredients. In the end, I chose to combine chopped fresh basil with bright green parsley and woody flavored thyme. I also found that the full-flavored vegetables demanded a bounty of herbs —a whopping 5 tablespoons in total. Adding the herbs just before serving ensures that they will remain bright in color and flavor and complement the intensely flavored vegetables perfectly.

RATATOUILLE
MAKES 7 CUPS, SERVING 4 TO 6 AS A SIDE DISH

For the best-flavored ratatouille, we recommend very ripe, beefsteak tomatoes.

- 2 large eggplants (about 2–2½ pounds), cut into 1-inch cubes
  Salt
- 2 large zucchini (about 1½ pounds), scrubbed and cut into 1-inch cubes
- ¼ cup olive oil
- 1 large onion, chopped large
- 2 medium garlic cloves, minced
- 3 medium ripe tomatoes (about 1 pound), peeled and cut into 2-inch cubes
- 2 tablespoons chopped fresh parsley leaves
- 2 tablespoons chopped fresh basil leaves
- 1 tablespoon minced fresh thyme leaves
  Ground black pepper

1. Place eggplant in large colander set over large bowl; sprinkle with 2 teaspoons salt and toss to distribute salt evenly. Let eggplant stand at least 1 hour or up to 3. Rinse eggplant well under running water to remove salt and spread in even layer on triple thickness of paper towels; cover with another triple thickness of paper towels. Press firmly on eggplant with hands until eggplant is dry and feels firm and compressed.

2. Adjust one oven rack to upper-middle position and second rack to lower-middle position; heat oven to 500 degrees. Line 2 rimmed baking sheets with foil.

3. Toss eggplant, zucchini, and 2 tablespoons oil together in large bowl, then divide evenly between prepared baking sheets, spreading in single layer on each. Sprinkle with salt and roast, stirring every 10 minutes, until well-browned and tender, 30 to 40 minutes, rotating baking sheets from top to bottom halfway through roasting time. Set aside.

4. Heat remaining 2 tablespoons oil in heavy-bottomed Dutch oven over medium heat until shimmering. Add onion; reduce heat to medium-low and cook, stirring frequently, until softened and golden brown, 15 to 20 minutes. Stir in garlic and cook until fragrant, about 30 seconds. Add tomatoes and cook until they release their juices and begin to break down, about 5 minutes. Add roasted eggplant and zucchini, stirring gently but thoroughly to combine, and cook until just heated through, about 5 minutes. Stir in parsley, basil, and thyme; adjust seasonings with salt and pepper and serve. (Can be covered and refrigerated for up to 3 days.)

TECHNIQUE
SALTING AND PRESSING

1. Place the cubed eggplant in a colander set over a large bowl. Sprinkle with salt and toss well to coat.

1. Use layers of paper towels to press the eggplant cubes until dry and compact.

The Best Blueberry Muffins

Some like them big, bland, and coarse. We like them rich, moist, and dainty, without the bother of creaming butter or finding great fresh berries.

≥ BY KAY RENTSCHLER ≤

The *Oxford Companion to Food* defines American muffins as "small, squat, round cakes." Yet today's deli muffins are big and buxom, inflated by chemical leavening and tattooed with everything from chocolate chips to sunflower seeds. Throwback that I am, I wanted a blueberry muffin with a daintier stature—a moist, delicate little cake that would support the blueberries physically, and, if I may say so, spiritually (in terms of flavor).

Despite the easy promise of a gingham-lined basket of warm, cuddly blueberry muffins, much can go wrong from kitchen to table. My panel of tasters sampled a half-dozen recipes, tasting muffins that ranged from rough and tough to dense, sweet, and heavy to lackluster—the typical coffee-shop cake, which has too few blueberries and too little flavor. It was clear that blueberry muffins came in no one style, flavor, or size, so I asked tasters which basic style of muffin they fancied: round tea cake or craggy biscuit? Of the 15 tasters, all but one said tea cake.

Finding the Formula

Because very minor fluctuations in ingredients had occasioned seismic differences in the muffins we tested, I thought it best to hold fast to a recipe whose proportions landed in between the two extremes in the original tests. That meant I would work with 1 stick of butter, 1 cup sugar, 2 cups flour, and ½ cup milk. It was not a perfect recipe but a serviceable springboard for future testing.

The two principal methods available to the muffin baker are mixing and creaming. The mixing method is a one-two-three-done courtship in which dry ingredients go in one bowl, liquid in another, and both then join up under a light touch. The creaming method is standard procedure for butter cakes. Everyone knows the drill: Beat butter with sugar until light and fluffy, add eggs one at a time, then alternately stir in dry ingredients and milk or cream. By aerating butter and sugar together, creaming produces a mousseline-light batter, a fine crumb, and admirable height.

But creaming is a nuisance when you want to whip up muffins for breakfast. It's a bother to soften butter and haul out a mixer. In side-by-side tests using the control recipe mentioned above, we got a first-hand taste of both methods. Had we been merely licking batter off our fingers, there would have been no contest. The creamed

Dip just-baked muffins in lemon syrup and then in lemon sugar to create tender, sugar-tufted cakes.

version was like a cake batter you wanted to suck through a straw. But the two baked muffins were nearly identical. Though the mixed muffin was slightly squatter than its creamed companion, its texture was not inferior. I was pretty sure this was the technique I could work with—or around.

For flour I remained true to unbleached all-purpose, since cake flour produced a batter that was too light to hold the blueberries aloft. Bleached flour lacked the flavor spectrum of unbleached. I set off next in pursuit of the perfect amount of butter needed to turn out a more moist and rich-tasting muffin, more like the tea cake my tasters had preferred. Increasing the butter simply weighed down the crumb without making the muffins any more moist. I also increased the liquid (testing both milk and buttermilk) and added extra egg yolks. Neither approach brought improvement. When I substituted yogurt for milk, the muffins had the

springiness of an old camp mattress.

Knowing that sour cream is often used in quick breads such as muffins, I decided to give it a try. At the same time, I wondered if the egg white protein from two eggs might be too much of the wrong type of liquid—adding structure rather than tenderness. My new recipe, then, called for 1 egg, 1 cup sour cream, no milk, and only half a stick of butter. It was a great success. The muffin was tender and rich, and the sour cream played up to the blueberries' flavor. An additional ¼ cup sour cream made even nicer muffins.

Through additional testing I discovered that this rather heavy batter required a full tablespoon of baking powder to rise and shine, but tasters noted no off chemical flavor. (Too much baking powder often results in leftover chemical leavener in the baked good, which imparts a bitter, soapy flavor.)

Next I refined the mixing method. Hoping to get more lift into the picture, I whisked the egg and sugar together by hand until the sugar began to dissolve, whisked in the melted butter, then the sour cream, and poured them into the dry ingredients. I folded everything together using the gentlest strokes possible. (Muffins become tough when overmixed.) This modified technique produced lovely muffins with a nice rise and beautifully domed crowns.

Almost Blue

Until now, the major player in this muffin had been not only off-stage but out of season as well. My winter testing left me with a choice between pricey fresh blueberries the size of marbles or tiny frozen wild berries. The flavor and sweetness of the frozen berries gave them a big edge over the puckery, flavorless fresh berries. In addition, the tiny wild berries distributed themselves in the batter nicely, like well-mannered guests, whereas the cultivated berries took the muffins by storm, leaving huge pockets of sour fruit pulp. So impressed was I by the superiority of these little berries that I resolved to offer them top billing in the recipe. (You shouldn't have to be vacationing

Don't Overfill Your Tin

Our batter is heavy and thick and should be mixed just until it comes together. Some small sprays of flour will be visible in the raw dough. We use an ice cream scoop to portion out the dough into a greased muffin tin. For moist, delicate muffins, don't overfill the cups.

CORRECT DOUGH PORTIONS

BAKED MUFFINS

Perfectly baked muffins have high domed crowns that do not spill over onto the top of the tin.

in Maine to make a decent blueberry muffin.) I came across one last trick. Frozen blueberries tend to be bleeders—and gummy when tossed with flour—so it's important to keep them completely frozen until they are stirred into the batter. The maximum amount of tiny berries my batter could support was 1½ cups.

These were perfect workaday muffins, but I wanted to give them a chance to play dress-up, to be more like little cakes. With that in mind, I considered a couple of options. A big fan of pebbly streusel topping dusted with confectioners' sugar, I picked up the topping recipe from our Dutch apple pie article (November/December 2000), and pared it down to meet the demands of a dozen

muffins. The streusel weighed heavily on the muffins and diminished their lift. Even after raising the oven temperature to 375 degrees (up from 350 degrees) and increasing baking time by five minutes, this topping was too heavy and dry.

My next topping idea came from Marion Cunningham's *Breakfast Book* (Knopf, 1987), in which she rolls whole baked muffins in melted butter and then dries them in cinnamon-sugar. Though my squeamish New England tasters objected to wiping their fingers off between bites (I obligingly restricted the festivities to the top of the muffin), the concept was a winning one. The melted butter seeped into the muffin's crown, the sugar stuck, and the muffin was transformed into a tender, sugar-crusted little cake.

I also made a simple syrup glaze with lemon juice. When brushed on the muffin tops it made a nice adhesive for the granulated sugar (which I mixed with either finely grated lemon zest or fresh ginger). Finally, muffins to take to the ball.

BEST BLUEBERRY MUFFINS
MAKES 12 MUFFINS

This recipe does not require a standing mixer, but when making the batter, be sure to whisk vigorously in step 2, then fold carefully in step 3. There should be no large pockets of flour in the finished batter, but small occasional sprays may remain. Do not overmix the batter. These muffins are great unadorned, but for an extra flourish, give them a dip in sugar by following one of the variations.

2	cups (10 ounces) unbleached all-purpose flour
1	tablespoon baking powder
½	teaspoon salt
1	large egg
1	cup (7 ounces) sugar
4	tablespoons unsalted butter, melted and cooled slightly
1¼	cups (10 ounces) sour cream
1½	cups frozen blueberries, preferably wild

1. Adjust oven rack to middle position and heat oven to 350 degrees. Spray standard muffin tin with nonstick vegetable cooking spray.

2. Whisk flour, baking powder, and salt in

medium bowl until combined. Whisk egg in second medium bowl until well-combined and light-colored, about 20 seconds. Add sugar and whisk vigorously until thick and homogenous, about 30 seconds; add melted butter in 2 or 3 steps, whisking to combine after each addition. Add sour cream in 2 steps, whisking just to combine.

3. Add frozen berries to dry ingredients and gently toss to combine. Add sour cream mixture and fold with rubber spatula until batter comes together and berries are evenly distributed, 25 to 30 seconds (small spots of flour may remain and batter will be thick). Do not overmix.

4. Use ice cream scoop or large spoon to drop batter into greased muffin tin. Bake until light golden brown and toothpick or skewer inserted into center of muffin comes out clean, 25 to 30 minutes, rotating pan from front to back halfway through baking time. Invert muffins onto wire rack, stand muffins upright, and cool 5 minutes. Serve as is or use one of the toppings below.

CINNAMON-SUGAR-DIPPED BLUEBERRY MUFFINS

Follow recipe for Best Blueberry Muffins; while muffins are cooling, mix ½ cup sugar and ½ teaspoon ground cinnamon in small bowl and melt 4 tablespoons butter in small saucepan. After baked muffins have cooled five minutes, working one at a time, dip tops of muffins in melted butter and then cinnamon-sugar. Set muffins upright on wire rack; serve.

GINGER-GLAZED OR LEMON-GLAZED BLUEBERRY MUFFINS

Follow recipe for Best Blueberry Muffins; while muffins are baking, mix 1 teaspoon grated lemon zest or grated fresh ginger and ½ cup sugar in small bowl. Bring ¼ cup lemon juice and ¼ cup sugar to simmer in small saucepan over medium heat; simmer until mixture is thick and syrupy and reduced to about 4 tablespoons. After muffins have cooled 5 minutes, brush tops with glaze, then, working one at a time, dip tops of muffins in lemon-sugar or ginger-sugar. Set muffins upright on wire rack; serve.

Muffin but Trouble

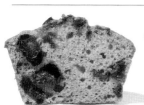 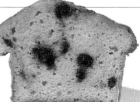 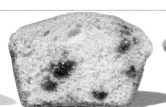 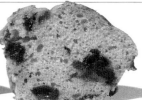 

(1) MASHED BERRIES   (2) STICKY SURFACE   (3) ARTIFICIAL BERRIES   (4) COARSE TEXTURE   (5) FLAT TOP

A lot can go wrong with blueberry muffins. Some problematic muffins we encountered in our testing, from left to right: (1) Muffins made with mashed berries taste fine but look all wrong. (2) Cottony grocery-store muffins often have sticky, clammy tops. (3) A quick packaged mix with artificial berries baked up into hockey pucks. (4) This deli muffin is dry and coarse, with mushy, marble-sized blueberries. (5) If the muffin cups are overfilled with batter, the baked muffins will have flat tops.

Apple Cake

Some apple cakes turn out shellacked and inedible while others are eggy and sodden. Fifty apple cakes later, we discovered a better way.

⋟ BY RAQUEL PELZEL ⋞

Easier to bake than a home-made apple pie but more refined than a quick-cooking apple crisp, an apple cake serves up sweet-tart apples married to a gracious, buttery cake. It can be baked in many forms—loaf pan, cake pan, glass baking dish, even cast-iron skillet. Another part of the apple cake's changing wardrobe is the placement of the apples. They can be found inside, on top of, or underneath the cake. In fact, the only constant in the apple cake recipes I explored was the apples themselves.

I began my tests by gathering a small mountain of apple cake recipes and baked off five that were representative of the group. Most were disappointing. One cake tasted like an overly spiced apple muffin, with flavorless apple chunks suspended in a grainy, gingerbread-colored interior. A loaf-pan cake made by layering McIntosh apples in the batter came out heavy and eggy, with wet pockets of cake and steamed, supersoft apples. I tried an apple upside-down cake consisting of partially cooked apples arranged in a round cake pan with the cake batter poured on top. This one turned out like one of my third-grade craft projects, shellacked, inedible, and ready to hang on the wall. The fourth recipe sounded easy—toss sliced apples in a baking dish and pour batter on top—but it resulted in a loose apple crisp–like dessert.

The fifth cake showed some promise. Baked in a springform pan, it consisted of a stiff layer of batter topped with raw chopped apples. Although my tasters found the cake too tightly bound and the apples too heavily spiced, I took a shine to its stand-up presentation. The cake was clean-edged and pretty, with a ring of apples jutting up above its crown.

From these initial tests, I gathered my wish list: I wanted the apples to retain their sweet character and to refrain from exuding so much juice as to affect the cake. The cake should contribute a subtle backdrop in flavor, not a barrage of overwhelming spices, and its texture should be sturdy enough to support the apples without being firm and dense, in the way a quick bread is.

With its crown of golden, tender apples, this cake requires no frosting or glaze, but a dusting of confectioners' sugar can be added just before serving.

A Sinking Feeling

To find a suitable cake to serve as the foundation for the apples, I turned to the yellow cake recipe in the March/April 1999 issue of *Cook's*. While it was buttery, tender, and rich, this cake was also too delicate to stand up to the weight and released juices from the sliced apples, which I had shingled across the top.

To give the cake base more muscle, I increased the ratio of flour to liquids and added a bit more baking powder for greater lift. I then topped the cake with raw sliced apples coated in sugar. Although improved, this cake was too spongy. It was also a touch sodden from the exuded apple liquid, and it dipped slightly in the center from the apples' weight and juices.

I found a partial solution in my choice of apples: Granny Smith. While Grannies don't have superior flavor, they hold their shape nicely during baking and don't give off much juice. Even better choices, if you can find them, are Pink Lady, Cameo, and Gala. Even with the Grannies, however, the cake was still unable to fully support the fruit. After a host of additional tests, including

broiling the apple slices ahead of time, fiddling with ingredient ratios, and baking the cake at different temperatures and on different rack levels in the oven, the center still sank. How could I produce a stand-up cake with a thick top layer of richly flavored apples?

Panned Out

The solution dawned on me when I noticed a Bundt pan sitting inconspicuously on a corner shelf. With this pan, I wouldn't have a sinking problem—there would be no center to sink. What's more, the hollow center of the pan might knock down the baking time (which until this point had been 1½ hours). And if I placed the apples in the bottom of the pan and then inverted it after baking, the fruit could still be perched on top. I happily dusted off the Bundt pan and increased my working recipe by one-half to fill its larger size.

To prevent sticking, I greased the pan with 2 tablespoons of softened butter, then tossed raw, cubed apples in brown sugar and laid them in the pan. (Cubes fit better than slices in the Bundt's fluted shape.) I topped the apples with batter and popped the pan in the oven. Forty-five minutes later, I pulled out the cake and inverted it onto a cake stand. Although perfectly baked, the cake was no showstopper, with some apples hugging the cake and others glued to the pan.

To solve this problem, I tried sprinkling 6 tablespoons of sugar over the bottom of the pan before adding the brown sugar–tossed apples, hoping that the sugar would melt and trap the apple's juices before they hit and then stuck to the pan. This apple cake fell from the pan without any coaxing, and the chopped apples clung to the swells of the cake—not the valleys of the pan.

But this Bundt cake wasn't without fault. It was pale and gummy at its apex. When I tested dark brown sugar in the pan instead of white, the apples looked bruised, a result I attributed to uneven melting of the brown sugar. But the cake wasn't gummy anymore, as the brown sugar had created a semicrisp shell around the apples. Next, I gave a combination of white and brown sugars a try. I sprinkled 6 tablespoons of white sugar in the pan. Then, as evenly as possible, I added 2 tablespoons of dark brown sugar on top of the white. I added the sugared apples and, finally, the batter. This version was still mottled in color—light patch, dark patch, light patch—a problem that was easily solved by substituting light brown sugar for dark. When unmolded, the cake practically glowed with a haloed ring of apples of a lovely, flaxen gold. This apple cake was the one—tall, bountiful, and proud not to be an apple pie.

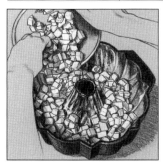  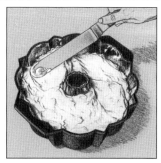

1. Distribute the cubed apples evenly on the bottom of the buttered and sugared pan.

2. Dip a rubber spatula into the mixing bowl, scooping out a large dollop of batter. Drop the batter off the end of the spatula in quadrants.

3. Smooth the batter with an offset spatula or the back of a soup spoon.

APPLE CAKE

MAKES ONE 10-INCH CAKE, SERVING 10 TO 12

Cake flour does this cake the most justice (see "Do You Really Need Cake Flour for Cakes?" below), but if there's none available, use a lower-protein, unbleached all-purpose flour instead. Pillsbury and Gold Medal are good options. The cake must be unmolded right after baking. If bits of apple or caramelized sugar stick to the pan, use a toothpick to remove them and return them to their rightful spots on the cake while still warm. Try Pink Lady, Cameo, or Gala apples rather than Grannies if you can find them. This cake is best served the day it is made, with a dusting of powdered sugar, if you like.

Cake

16	tablespoons (2 sticks) unsalted butter, cut into 16 pieces, softened but still cool, plus 2 tablespoons softened butter for pan
1 1/4	cups granulated sugar, plus 6 tablespoons for pan
2	tablespoons light brown sugar for pan
3	large eggs plus 2 large egg yolks
1/2	cup (4 ounces) heavy cream
2	teaspoons vanilla extract
2 1/4	cups (9 ounces) cake flour
1	tablespoon baking powder
3/4	teaspoon salt

Apples

2	Granny Smith apples (about 1 pound), peeled, and cut into 1/2-inch cubes
2	tablespoons light brown sugar

1. Adjust oven rack to lower-middle position and heat oven to 350 degrees. Grease standard nonstick 12-cup Bundt pan with 2 tablespoons softened butter; dust sides with 2 tablespoons granulated sugar, then evenly distribute remaining 4 tablespoons granulated sugar in bottom of pan. Evenly sprinkle brown sugar on top of granulated sugar, breaking up large lumps with fingers.

2. Whisk eggs and yolks in 2-cup measuring cup to combine. Add cream and vanilla and beat until thoroughly combined.

3. In bowl of standing mixer fitted with paddle attachment, combine flour, 1 1/4 cups sugar, baking powder, and salt. Mix on lowest speed until combined, about 30 seconds. With mixer still running on lowest speed, add butter 1 piece at a time in 1-second intervals, beating until mixture resembles coarse meal, with butter bits no larger than small peas, 1 to 1 1/2 minutes.

4. With mixer still running, add 1/2 cup liquid; mix at lowest speed until incorporated, 5 to 10 seconds. Increase speed to medium-high and beat until light and fluffy, about 1 minute. With mixer still running, add remaining liquid in steady stream (this should take about 30 seconds). Stop mixer and scrape down bowl with rubber spatula, then beat at medium-high speed to combine, about 30 seconds.

5. Toss cubed apples with 2 tablespoons light brown sugar and distribute in an even layer over sugar in pan. Add batter in 4 portions, and gently level with offset spatula. (See illustrations above.) Bake until cake begins to pull away from sides of pan, springs back when pressed with finger, and toothpick or skewer inserted into center of cake comes out clean, 35 to 45 minutes. Meanwhile, line wire rack with 12-inch square of foil. Immediately invert cake onto foil-lined rack. Cool at least 1 hour, then slide onto serving plate; cut into slices and serve.

Do You Really Need Cake Flour for Cakes?

Although most home cooks use all-purpose flour for everything, even cakes, the *Cook's* test kitchen is inclined to use lower-protein flours when a delicate texture and fine crumb is called for. In an effort to resolve this issue once and for all, we used our apple cake recipe to perform head-to-head tests.

First, a bit about the theory of low- and high-protein flours. All-purpose flour has a relatively high protein content (10 to 11.7 percent, depending on the brand: King Arthur is in the 11.7 percent range, Pillsbury and Gold Medal around 10 percent), whereas cake flour runs in the 8 to 9 percent range. When water and flour are mixed, gluten is formed. The higher the protein content, the higher the gluten production. For cakes, biscuits, and other chemically leavened baked goods, lower gluten levels usually translate into a softer, more tender crumb.

There is one additional complication. Cake flour is bleached, whereas one can easily find unbleached all-purpose flour such that it can absorb greater amounts of liquid and fat. While this results in a finer crumb, many people can taste an "off" flavor when bleached flour is used owing to the residual hydrochloric acid left behind from bleaching.

This science was confirmed when we baked two apple cakes, one with unbleached all-purpose and one with bleached cake flour. The former was a bit tough, the latter much more delicate, albeit with a slightly off flavor.

ALL-PURPOSE FLOUR   CAKE FLOUR

Good height and a fine crumb are characteristic of a cake made with cake flour. A cake made with all-purpose flour has a compact, heavier structure.

Clearly, the cake flour was the winner, even when taking flavor into account. We also tested Pillsbury's lower-protein all-purpose flour against the higher-protein King Arthur (both unbleached). Of these two, Pillsbury was preferable, but, all-in-all, the cake flour still produced a more delicate, fine-textured cake. The conclusion? Use cake flour if you have it. If not, choose the lowest protein, unbleached all-purpose flour you can find, Pillsbury and Gold Medal being two widely available brands. —R.P.

Bittersweet Chocolate Sauce

A simple, foolproof technique and the right chocolate make the richest, most flavorful chocolate dessert sauce.

⇒ BY JULIA COLLIN ⇐

Chocolate sauce drapes gracefully over ice cream, pound cake, profiteroles, angel food cake, or a wayward finger. More refined than slow, sticky hot fudge, chocolate sauce has a pure, complex, potent chocolate flavor tempered by a gentle sweetness. It pours with ease and clings with a glossy sheen.

The problem is that chocolate sauce is often waxy or overly sweet, tasting like syrup from a squeeze bottle. If it is too thin, it runs off and away from the dessert it's meant to accompany, and if too thick, it moves slowly and solidifies into hard clumps. Most disappointingly, chocolate sauce is often guilty of having a muted rather than intense chocolate flavor.

Almost all chocolate sauce recipes contain the same few ingredients—chocolate, cream, butter, corn syrup or sugar, and vanilla—and are made according to the same simple technique, but, as I discovered, the resulting sauces can be surprisingly different. I sought to uncover the makings of a rich chocolate sauce that would be as much at home over a bowl of ice cream as beneath a serving of soufflé.

Most recipes I examined used the classic ganache technique, in which hot cream is poured over finely chopped chocolate, gently melting it while the mixture is whisked until smooth. I tested other methods, such as melting the chocolate before adding the warm cream, and heating up all the ingredients together, but they were not as foolproof.

In testing the ganache technique, I made a couple of minor simplifications. Instead of pouring the cream over the chocolate, I added the chocolate to the cream and eliminated another dirty bowl. To ensure that the chocolate melted fully and to minimize whisking (which traps bubbles that mar the appearance of the sauce), I let the hot cream and chocolate stand covered for a few minutes. With a small amount of patience and a bit of restraint with the whisk, I produced a smooth sauce that poured in dark ribbons.

Until now, my working recipe consisted only of heavy cream, sugar, and chocolate. I tried substituting half-and-half and whole milk for the cream,

but neither added the richness or body introduced by the cream. I then made a batch with corn syrup, a common ingredient in chocolate sauce, and compared it with the sauce made with sugar. While the flavor difference was barely perceptible, the corn syrup gave the sauce a shiny, lacquer-like finish and helped it to remain fluid when poured over cold ice cream. Butter contributed a luscious mouthfeel and a luxurious sheen, and a pinch of salt boosted the flavors. Vanilla extract drew attention away from the deep chocolate flavor, so it was out.

Finally, I focused my attention on the chief ingredient: chocolate. In sauces adjusted with appropriate amounts of sweetener, I tested cocoa powder and unsweetened, milk, semisweet, and bittersweet chocolates. Those made with cocoa and unsweetened chocolate were gritty and dull, with harsh, acidic finishes. The milk chocolate produced a smooth sauce, but its flavor was muted and one-dimensional owing to its higher percentage of dairy. Bittersweet and semisweet both made smooth, richly colored sauces, but tasters greatly preferred the less sweet, more complex flavors of the sauce made with bittersweet. They liked the way it stood up to rich ice cream and crisp, buttery profiteroles.

Bittersweet and semisweet chocolates are often believed to be interchangeable in recipes, and the reason may be that the U.S. Food and Drug Administration does not differentiate the two. Most chocolate manufacturers, however, treat them differently, following the European tradition of using a higher percentage of cocoa solids (and therefore a lower percentage of sugar) in bittersweet than in semisweet. Therefore, bittersweet chocolate has a more intense flavor and a more savory edge than the sweeter, mellower semisweet chocolate, making bittersweet a better choice for chocolate sauce.

As I worked with various brands of bittersweet chocolate, I was perplexed to find that they yielded sauces of varying viscosities. I called Thalia Hohenthal, a food scientist with Guittard Chocolate, who explained that cocoa solids are like sponges that soak up

The Right Consistency

Chocolate sauce should be a little thicker than heavy cream. Unlike hot fudge sauce, which will fall off a spoon in globs, chocolate sauce should run off a spoon in a smooth, steady stream.

TASTING: **Choosing a Chocolate**
Making sauces with 10 widely available brands of bittersweet chocolate, I found dramatic differences in flavor. A sauce made with Callebaut received the highest marks and compliments such as "silky," "nutty," and "luxurious." Sauces made with Hershey's Special Dark, Merckens, Lindt Excellence, and Ghirardelli were favored in that order. Bottoming out were Baker's bittersweet squares, which tasters described as "sour," "scorched," and "astringent." —J.C.

moisture. The amount of cocoa solids in bittersweet chocolate differs from brand to brand, making it difficult to standardize the quantity of cream to use in a chocolate sauce. To achieve the perfect consistency, I found it easier to start with the minimum amount of cream and then thin the sauce as necessary.

BITTERSWEET CHOCOLATE SAUCE
MAKES 2 CUPS

When whisking sauce to combine, do so gently so as not to create air bubbles, which will mar its appearance. This sauce can be placed in a container, cooled to room temperature, covered, and refrigerated for up to 3 weeks. To reheat, transfer sauce to heatproof bowl and set over saucepan containing 2 inches simmering water; stir occasionally until melted and warm. Alternatively, transfer sauce to microwave-safe bowl and heat at 50 percent power until melted and warm, stirring once or twice, 2 to 3 minutes.

1–1¼ cups heavy cream
¼ cup light corn syrup
4 tablespoons unsalted butter
   Pinch salt
8 ounces bittersweet chocolate (see "Choosing a Chocolate," above), chopped fine

Bring 1 cup heavy cream, corn syrup, butter, and salt to boil in small nonreactive saucepan over medium-high heat. Off heat, add chocolate while gently swirling saucepan. Cover pan and let stand until chocolate is melted, about 5 minutes. Uncover and whisk gently until combined. If necessary, adjust consistency by heating and stirring in remaining cream.

Big-Name Vanilla Ice Creams Fail to Sweep Tasting

Our panel favors "fresh," "clean" taste over "overwhelmingly vanilla" flavors.

⇒ BY RAQUEL PELZEL ⇐

Vanilla ice cream may be plain, but in the ice cream world, it remains the force to be reckoned with, hoarding 29 percent of the industry's $20 billion annual sales. Its closest rival, chocolate, lays claim to a paltry 8.9 percent. But when it comes to buying vanilla, there are two sides to the bean: Philadelphia-style, made from a milk or cream base, and French-style (often sold under the name "custard-style" or "French vanilla" and sometimes just "vanilla"), made from a precooked custard base that includes egg yolks in the mix. This tasting focused exclusively on the more decadent French-style vanilla ice creams, the style preferred in a *Cook's* taste test conducted for the July/August 1994 issue.

We first tackled the question of what defines an ice cream as "all natural" and whether this would have any impact on the results of the tasting. The surprising answer is that the U.S. Food and Drug Administration (FDA) has no regulations concerning "all natural" labeling of ice cream. Given the lack of guidance by the FDA, we decided to investigate two areas—the use of stabilizers and the type of flavoring—to see if they would affect our results.

Adding Stability, Trapping Flavor

Many ice cream manufacturers add stabilizers—most often carrageenan gum or guar gum—to prevent "heat shock," an industry term for the degradation in texture caused by partial melting and refreezing. This happens when ice cream is subjected to extreme temperature changes during transit to the supermarket or when an ice cream case goes through its self-defrosting cycle. Gum additives stabilize ice cream by trapping water in the frozen mass and slowing down the growth of ice crystals during melting and refreezing.

We thought that the presence of stabilizers might affect our test results. To our surprise, this was not the case. Our top two brands, Edy's Dreamery and Double

Rainbow, use stabilizers. Next we tackled the issue of vanilla flavoring.

Three types of vanilla are used to make vanilla ice cream: vanilla bean specks made from ground vanilla pods, natural vanilla extract, and artificial vanilla flavor. Using vanilla specks in ice cream is a popular technique manufacturers often use to convey to consumers the idea of naturalness or a home-style approach. However, while vanilla beans, which come from the inside of the vanilla pod, carry plenty of flavor, the little black flecks that come from grinding up vanilla pods contribute more to the ice cream's appearance than its flavor. So the presence of flecks of "vanilla" in a commercial ice cream is no indication of quality or taste. Vanilla extract and artificial vanilla flavor are what determine the flavor. (In fact, the top two brands in our tasting do not use ground vanilla pods.)

Natural vanilla extract is made by steeping chopped vanilla beans in an alcohol and water solution. According to FDA guidelines, only ice creams made with natural vanilla extract or naturally derived vanilla flavor can be labeled "vanilla ice cream." The label "vanilla-flavored ice cream" indicates that the ice cream in question was made with a combination of natural vanilla extract or flavor and artificial vanilla flavor. Artificial vanilla flavor is made from vanillin, a product extracted from conifer wood pulp that has been chemically rinsed. Blue

Bell was the only brand in the tasting that contained artificial vanilla flavor, and it rated smack-dab in the middle, thus negating any link between natural flavoring agents and superior flavor. While tasters described Blue Bell ice cream as "cloyingly sweet" and "fleeting on the tongue," its use of artificial vanilla did not automatically relegate it to the bottom of the heap.

In fact, tasters took greater issue with several "naturally flavored" brands—including Häagen-Dazs, Ben & Jerry's, and Edy's Grand—for tasting "artificial" and "boozy." To help explain this odd result we contacted Bruce Tharp, an independent ice cream consultant based in Wayne, Pa. He explained that perceived artificial and alcohol flavors are often caused by the quantity of vanilla extract added to the ice cream. That is, the more extract, the more likely one is to taste the alcohol. Although it's impossible to confirm this theory (manufacturers won't release their recipes to the public), it was clear that the absence of stabilizers and use of natural flavorings were not reliable indicators of a great-tasting ice cream.

Butterfat and Overrun

Next up was the issue of butterfat. A natural byproduct of milk, butterfat, sometimes also called milk fat, is a coveted addition to an ice cream's list of ingredients, contributing to smooth texture, rich flavor, and structure. By law, an ice cream can't be called an ice cream unless its prefrozen mix contains a minimum of 10 percent butterfat. Of the ice creams we tasted, butterfat content ranged from 10 to 16 percent and, in general, the higher the butterfat content, the higher the ice cream rated. Our two top-rated ice creams had butterfat contents of 14.5 percent (Edy's Dreamery) and 15 percent (Double Rainbow). The two lowest rated brands had butterfat contents between 10 and 13 percent.

All commercial ice cream makers also add air to the mix. Oddly enough, this helps to provide

Why Some Ice Creams Melt Faster than Others

Ice cream with a high overrun, such as Edy's Grand (left), contains more air than ice cream with a low overrun, such as Häagen-Dazs (right). The high-overrun ice cream melts more quickly.

structure, as the air cells are distributed evenly throughout the frozen mass. The air that is thus incorporated into ice cream is called overrun—without it, the ice cream would look more like an ice cube. But if used to excess, added air can compromise the ice cream's texture, making it pillowy and light. In addition, an ice cream with a high overrun will melt faster than one with a low overrun (see photos on page 25). This is because there is less frozen mass to melt, and when there is less frozen mass, warm air can penetrate the ice cream more quickly.

Realizing that ice cream with more air has more volume and can be sold in a larger package for more money, the FDA has set a minimum weight of 4½ pounds to the gallon for churned ice cream. This indirectly sets a limit on the amount of air that can be incorporated, since an ice cream that incorporates too much air during the churning process will weigh less than 4½ pounds. Essentially, what all this means is that an ice cream's volume cannot be increased by more than 100 percent through the addition of air. To find out the estimated overrun in the ice creams we sampled, we used a simple calculation (see note in "Tasting Vanilla Ice Cream" on page 27) that takes into consideration the weight of the ice cream and the weight of the liquid ice cream mix before it is frozen. While the top two ice creams had low overruns of 21 and 26 percent, our third favorite had a whopping 93.5 percent overrun. Furthermore, the two last-place ice creams had very different overruns—26 percent and 100 percent (we tested many samples of Edy's Grand and the overrun always came in at 100 percent). Our conclusion? In general, low overrun is preferable, although butterfat content is a better measure of quality. (We also noted that some tasters like high-overrun ice creams—it is, to some degree, a matter of personal preference.)

The last component we researched was emulsifiers, such as mono- and diglycerides, used to control the behavior of fat in ice cream by preventing it from separating out from the ice cream mass. These emulsifiers give an ice cream rigidity and strength, so even if it doesn't have much butterfat or added gums, the ice cream will maintain its round, scooped shape for a prolonged period of time. The only ice cream in our tasting with emulsifiers was also the least favored sample: Edy's Grand. So, according to our taste test, it seems that emulsifiers are not desirable.

What to Buy?

The winner of our tasting, Edy's Dreamery, was described as "rich and velvety," with a "fresh" and "clean" finish. It uses natural flavors as well as stabilizers, has a butterfat content of 14.5 percent, and an estimated overrun of 21 percent. Tasters remarked that its texture was particularly smooth and that it was lighter and softer than other samples. Tasters also responded well to the "clean," "fresh" flavor of our second-place finisher, Double Rainbow. The statistics on this brand are almost identical to those on our winner—natural flavors, stabilizers, 15 percent butterfat, and 26 percent estimated overrun.

Tasters on our 1994 panel crowned Breyer's a winner among supermarket brands sold in half-gallons, so we were not surprised that it placed third in this tasting. Our panelists particularly liked the home-style, "eggy" taste of this product. It even outranked Häagen-Dazs and Ben & Jerry's! (Not bad for an ice cream that's almost 50 percent air—it has a 93.5 percent estimated overrun.)

The real news here is the fourth-place showing of Häagen-Dazs and the seventh-place showing of Ben & Jerry's, out of eight brands sampled. Both of these well-known brands advertise their quality ingredients, have low overruns, and have moderate to high butterfat contents. (Häagen-Dazs is a particularly perplexing case, with a high-end 16 percent butterfat content, natural flavors, a low overrun of 20 percent, and no stabilizers. Judging from the printing on the package, it looks like a winner.) Tasters found the flavor of the Häagen-Dazs and the Ben & Jerry's to be "artificial" and "chemical," with "alcohol" undertones. Is this a function of too much vanilla? Perhaps, but since this information is confidential, we can only hazard a guess.

What we were able to learn after gorging on so much ice cream is that, at least for our tasters, balance is more important than bravado. Clean vanilla flavor and a high butterfat content made more of a difference to us than the presence of stabilizers.

TESTING EQUIPMENT: **In Pursuit of the Right Scoop**

We've all struggled with an intractable pint of rock-hard ice cream—that's where a good ice cream scoop comes in. We gathered 10 readily available scoops in three basic styles—classic, mechanical-release (or spring-loaded), and spade-shaped—and dipped our way through 20 pints of vanilla to find the best. Prices ranged from $3.99 to $21.99.

Classic scoops sport a comfortable thick handle and curved bowl, and they can be used by lefties and righties with equal aplomb. Of the four classic scoops tried, testers were unanimous in assigning first place to the most expensive, the only scoop of all 10 with a self-defrosting feature: the Zeroll Classic Ice Cream Scoop. (This scoop came in first place overall, too.) The defrosting fluid (which responds to heat from the user's hand) and the elegantly curved bowl allowed the scoop to take purchase immediately, curling a perfect scoop with minimal effort. The self-defrosting liquid and nonstick coating also allowed for the perfect release. Only one caveat: Don't run this scoop through the dishwasher, as it will lose its defrosting properties.

Coming in second among the other classic scoops tested was the Oxo Beak Scoop ($11.99). The beak point dug into the ice cream with ease, and the ice cream curled up nicely. Our only minor quibble was the short handle, which forced testers with larger hands to choke up close to the head.

Classic Ice Cream Scoop

Mechanical Scoop

Spade

Mechanical-release scoops come in various sizes and operate by means of a spring-loaded, squeezable handle (or thumb trigger) that connects to a curved steel lever inside the scoop. When the handle or lever is released, the ice cream pops out. Although we frequently use mechanical-release scoops to measure out even portions of cookie and muffin batters, we found them less than ideal for ice cream. They are designed for right-handed users only, and their thin, straight-edged handles were distinctly uncomfortable when considerable pressure was applied—which was often, as their bowl-shaped heads required a high degree of scooping effort. Of the four models we tested, none was worthy of recommendation.

Spades, with their flat, paddle-type heads, are useful when you need to scoop a lot of ice cream quickly, but they are too big to fit into the small bottoms of pint containers. If you make frozen desserts frequently or need to slice through multiple gallon-sized containers of ice cream, a spade might be for you. Our preferred model is the Zeroll Nonstick Ice Cream Spade ($19.60). –Shona Simkin

TASTING VANILLA ICE CREAM

To gather the contestants for our French-style vanilla ice cream tasting, we consulted recent supermarket sales data and included the most widely available top-selling national brands as well as a few brands available through natural food stores. The ice cream had to include egg yolks in its list of ingredients to qualify for the tasting. Twenty *Cook's* staff members tasted the ice creams plain, rating them for overall flavor, texture, and density.

Note: The overrun amounts listed in this chart were estimated by dividing the weight of each brand of ice cream by the weight of the liquid ice cream mix before churning and freezing. According to Bruce Tharp, an independent ice cream consultant, all commercial ice cream mixes weigh approximately 9 pounds per gallon. The weight of the finished product per gallon will vary depending on the amount of air introduced during the churning process. The FDA specifies that 1 gallon of ice cream must weigh at least 4½ pounds, effectively limiting the amount of "overrun" (air) to no more than 100 percent.

HIGHLY RECOMMENDED

EDY'S DREAMERY Vanilla Ice Cream
➤ **One pint, $3.19**

- NATURAL FLAVORS WITH STABILIZERS
- **Estimated overrun:** 21%; **Butterfat:** 14.5%

Our only highly recommended ice cream was described as "rich and velvety," with a "fresh" and "clean" finish. Its texture was called "creamy" and "smooth," decidedly "lighter" and "softer" in body than the other samples.

RECOMMENDED

DOUBLE RAINBOW French Vanilla Ice Cream
➤ **One quart, $2.99**

- NATURAL FLAVORS WITH STABILIZERS
- **Estimated overrun:** 26%; **Butterfat:** 15%

Tasters defined this ice cream as "balanced" and "perfect." Like the Dreamery brand, Double Rainbow was described as "fresh" and "clean" flavored, although some felt it was just a little too sweet. Its texture was deemed "creamy" and "smooth."

BREYER'S All Natural French Vanilla Ice Cream
➤ **Half-gallon, $3.99**

- NATURAL FLAVORS, NO STABILIZERS
- **Estimated overrun:** 93.5%; **Butterfat:** 12 to 14%

Breyer's was liked for its "eggy" and "milky" qualities, which some called "caramel-like." Others found it "too sweet." Its slightly grainy texture "suggests homemade," said one taster, while another said this gave it the appearance of having "separated."

BLUE BELL Homemade Vanilla Flavored Ice Cream *TIED WITH HÄAGEN-DAZS*
➤ **Half-gallon, $5.29**

- NATURAL AND ARTIFICIAL FLAVORS WITH STABILIZERS
- **Estimated overrun:** 47.5%; **Butterfat:** 12%

While some tasters loved Blue Bell's eggy, toffee-like flavor, others found it "cloyingly sweet" and "too eggy." Its texture was described as light and smooth, although a bit "chewy;" other tasters thought it was "too light" and "watery."

HÄAGEN-DAZS Vanilla Ice Cream *TIED WITH BLUE BELL*
➤ **One pint, $3.29**

- NATURAL FLAVORS, NO STABILIZERS
- **Estimated overrun:** 20%; **Butterfat:** 16%

"Eggy" and "artificial" was how Häagen-Dazs was characterized. One taster said it "reeked of extract," while others called it reminiscent of "alcohol." The texture was "fantastic"—dense, creamy, and smooth.

365 EVERY DAY VALUE French Vanilla Bean Ice Cream
➤ **Half-gallon, $4.49**

- NATURAL FLAVORS WITH STABILIZERS
- **Estimated overrun:** 93.5%; **Butterfat:** 14%

"Very average and middle-of-the-road," is how one taster summed up the Whole Foods grocery store home label, while others called it "eggy," "milky," and "just too sweet." Its texture was perceived as somewhat "gluey" and "sticky."

RECOMMENDED WITH RESERVATIONS

BEN & JERRY'S World's Best Vanilla Ice Cream
➤ **One pint, $3.29**

- NATURAL FLAVORS WITH STABILIZERS
- **Estimated overrun:** 26%; **Butterfat:** 13%

Tasters agreed that Ben & Jerry's ice cream had an unmistakably "artificial" quality that was "stale" with a "bad aftertaste" that reminded some of "rubbing alcohol" and others of "cooked milk." Its texture, however, was creamy and smooth.

EDY'S GRAND French Vanilla Ice Cream
➤ **Half-gallon, $3.99**

- NATURAL FLAVORS WITH STABILIZERS AND EMULSIFIERS
- **Estimated overrun:** 100% (we tested five half-gallons of Edy's Grand and found each to have an overrun of 100%); **Butterfat:** 10 to 12%

Edy's Grand was a far cry from its Dreamery brand; some tasters were taken aback by its "shocking fake taste." Many also marked the sample down for "artificial" flavors that were just too "strong" and "boozy." While the texture was "creamy," some complained that it was also "greasy."

Are Expensive Colanders Worth the Dough?

In a word, no. A $25 colander performs as well as a $115 model.

⋻ BY ADAM RIED ⋽

Last year, Americans consumed more than a billion pounds of pasta, and every strand, tube, bow, shell, and twist of it was likely drained in a colander before it hit the sauce. A colander is essentially a perforated bowl designed to allow liquid to drain through the holes. In our initial survey of models, we were not surprised to find colanders made from a range of materials: plastic, enameled steel, stainless steel, anodized aluminum, and wire mesh (which is like a screen). What did surprise us—and how—was the range of prices. Who would have thought that you could drop almost $115 on a simple colander, especially in light of the price tag on the least expensive contestant, just $3.99? This made the idea of a test too tantalizing to resist.

As is our fashion at *Cook's*, we tested the colanders objectively by draining pounds and pounds of cooked spaghetti, orzo, and frozen baby peas in each one. Early in the testing, we splashed scalding water and hot pasta out of a tiny 3-quart model by pouring it too fast from the cooking pot, so we eliminated that size from the running. The 4- to 7-quart models performed on par, so we included them all in the lineup.

Most colanders on the market come with one of two types of base, either a circular metal ring

attached to the bottom, on which the bowl sits pedestal-style, or individual feet soldered to the bottom of the bowl. No matter which type it is, the base should be unfailingly stable to prevent spills. Our research and reading on colanders consistently noted the superiority of the ring over the feet, claiming that a colander on feet is less stable because it touches the ground in only three or four spots.

That sounded like a reasonable theory to us until we tested the two models in the group with feet. These colanders, the Endurance Stainless Steel Footed Colander and the Norpro Expanding Over-the-Sink Colander with Stand, were perfectly stable. During none of the tests did either one tip and spill its contents. (The Norpro can also be suspended between the sides of a sink by extending two metal arms. On our test kitchen sinks, this feature worked just fine, but on some sink designs this colander may be less stable.) In fact, the Endurance remained upright even when we accidentally bumped it with a heavy stockpot. Similarly, and as we expected, the eight colanders with ring bases also enjoyed total stability. In our experience, then, though most colanders on the market have ring bases, you needn't shy away from a model with feet if that's what you happen to find.

We also expected that the size, placement, and

pattern of the drainage holes would be key for quick, efficient draining. Seven of our 10 colanders had the look we expected, that of a metal or plastic bowl with perforations arranged in either straight lines, starbursts, or circles; the remaining three had more unusual designs. True to its name, the Endurance Colander/Strainer was a hybrid with a metal bowl that was so thoroughly perforated it almost looked like wire mesh. Two other colanders, the Harold Imports and the Norpro expandable colander, were made from wire mesh, just like strainers. The three latter colanders had more holes than their more traditional counterparts, and each one performed very well, draining quickly and completely, with no pooling of water and no food—even the wily orzo—slipping through the holes. In truth, though, all of the other colanders also met, or came darn close to meeting, these standards. The traditional colanders with larger holes did allow some orzo to slip through (anywhere from just a few pieces for the Rösle to almost ¾ cup for the Silverstone), but only the Silverstone allowed so much orzo through that it merited a downgrade in the ratings.

Having a keen eye for cookware as we do, we were able to observe subtle quirks and differences in our 10 colanders. Sure, the superperforated

The Colanders We Tested

RECOMMENDED

FAVORITE

Endurance Colander/Strainer
Handsome design and flawless performance.

Hoan 7 Quart
Commodious, cheap, and light.

Harold Imports Steel Wire Mesh
The only colander in our group without handles.

Endurance Footed Colander
Footed design proved stable enough for us.

Norpro Expanding Over-the-Sink
Versatile design does well by those whose sink is always full of dishes.

Farberware Classic Series
Solid phenolic handles are comfortable but will keep cooks who like to hang up their colanders from doing so.

Silverstone Nonstick
Nonstick coating is neither a help nor a hindrance.

All-Clad Stainless Steel
Drains as thoroughly as the mesh colanders.

Calphalon Anodized Aluminum
For $90, we'd prefer that it not dribble water on us.

Rösle Stainless Steel
Performed without a hitch, as it should for a whopping $115.

RATING COLANDERS

RATINGS
★★★
GOOD
★★
FAIR
★
POOR

We rated 10 colanders, with capacities ranging from 4 to 7 quarts, and evaluated them according to the following criteria. Our favorite colander is identified as such and listed first. The remaining colanders are listed in ascending order by price. All of the colanders performed perfectly well, although the 5-quart Silverstone did allow ³/₄ cup of orzo to slip through its holes.

PRICE: Prices paid in Boston-area stores, national mail-order catalogs, and Web sites.

MATERIAL: Material from which the colander is made.

CAPACITY: Colander volume as rated by manufacturer. (In the cases of the Harold Imports, Norpro, and Rösle colanders, manufacturers use inches rather than capacity to indicate size, so we determined the capacity in the test kitchen.)

PERFORMANCE: Our most important test. In each colander, we drained 1 pound of spaghetti cooked in 1 gallon of water, 1 pound of orzo cooked in 1 gallon of water, and one 10-ounce package of frozen baby peas cooked on the stovetop in ¹/₄ cup of water. In each instance, we evaluated the colander based on whether food slipped through the holes, whether water splashed out when poured into the colander at a moderate rate, whether food was fully drained after 30 seconds, and whether water pooled at the base of the colander after 30 seconds. The overall performance score is based on a composite of these factors. Preference was given to colanders in which just 1 tablespoon of food or less was able to slip through the holes, in which the water did not splash, in which food drained fully after 30 seconds, and in which water did not collect in a pool at the base.

DESIGN: Design was assessed based on the colander's stability in the sink and the comfort and heating characteristics of the handles. Preference was given to colanders that remained perfectly stable, with no tipping, while food and water were poured into them, and to colanders with handles that were cool enough to grasp firmly after 30 seconds of draining hot food and boiling water.

Additional observations are noted in the Testers' Comments.

Brand	Price	Material	Capacity	Performance	Design	Testers' Comments
FAVORITE **Endurance** Stainless Steel Colander/Strainer	$24.99	Mega-perforated stainless steel	5 quarts	★★★	★★★	Meshlike perforated bowl is very effective; didn't let a single piece of orzo slip through.
RECOMMENDED **Hoan** 7 Quart Colander	$3.99	Plastic	7 quarts	★★★	★★★	Particularly light and easy to handle. A bit of water pooled at the base after 30 seconds of draining, and a few pieces of orzo slipped through the holes, but neither gave us cause to downgrade the rating.
Harold Imports Steel Wire Mesh Colander	$12.95	Wire mesh with steel support wires	4 quarts	★★★	★★	The absence of handles was not as much of a problem as we anticipated, but still, why not include them?
Endurance Stainless Steel Footed Colander	$19.99	Perforated stainless steel	5 quarts	★★★	★★★	A little water tends to pool at the base, but not enough to be annoying.
Norpro Expanding Over-the-Sink Colander with Stand	$24.99	Stainless steel mesh	5 quarts	★★★	★★★	No-skid, rubber-tipped feet on the bowl and extending arms keep the colander stable whether it's in the sink or suspended over it. (Ability to suspend over a sink depends in part on sink design.)
Farberware Classic Series 7-Quart Colander	$24.99	Stainless steel/phenolic handles	7 quarts	★★★	★★★	Only performance slip was in allowing 2 tablespoons orzo to escape.
Silverstone 5-Quart Nonstick Colander (Model DSCL-50)	$32.99	Nonstick-coated stainless steel with santoprene grip	5 quarts	★★	★★★	Extralarge perforations make for quick draining, but they also allowed noodles and a large quantity of orzo to slip through.
All-Clad Stainless Steel Colander, Model 5605C	$69.99	Perforated stainless steel	5 quarts	★★★	★★★	Larger perforations on the sidewalls make for superquick, splashfree draining, but they also allowed some orzo to escape.
Calphalon Large Anodized Aluminum Colander	$90.95	Hard-anodized with riveted stainless steel handles	5 quarts	★★★	★★★	The ring-type base has an upturned lip that caught and then regularly spilled on the user a tiny amount of water.
Rösle Stainless Steel Colander	$114.95	Stainless steel	5 quarts	★★★	★★★	Handles are solid and easy to grip. Design includes an eye that allows colander to hang from a hook.

Endurance Colander/Strainer drained so thoroughly that not a drop of water pooled at the base, but so did the All-Clad. And sure, the Endurance Footed and Hoan colanders collected a tiny bit of water at the base, but not enough for us to advise against buying them. Every colander in the group got the job done, be it the $4 Hoan plastic model or the gleaming $115 Rösle stainless steel model. To make a recommendation, then, we have to be more subjective than usual. So here it is: Based on this testing and our gut feeling, the colander we'd most like to bring home is the Endurance Colander/Strainer. Reasonably priced at $25, it's solid and comfortable to wield, it drains like a pro and keeps all its contents in check, and many editors here consider it an unusually handsome specimen of a colander.

Comparing Colanders and Strainers

The colander and its cousin, the strainer, accomplish the same work in the kitchen—separating solids from liquids. Beyond that general principle, however, each is designed for different tasks. Colanders have a base that lets them stand up on their own, usually in the sink. The fact that a colander need not be held in place frees both of the cook's hands to lift a hot, heavy pot of water and pasta, for instance. More often than not, foods are drained through a colander when the solid is to be saved and the liquid discarded down the drain. Think pasta, boiled new potatoes, and blanched vegetables.

Strainers are made from wire mesh that can range from very fine (so much so that the strainer's contents must be forced through it by pressing with a wooden spoon, producing a refined puree) to quite coarse. In the case of the conical-shaped, fine-meshed chinois, the strainer's mesh bowl, or cone, is anchored in a solid frame, which is in turn attached to a handle on one side and small hooks on the other. Without a base, a strainer must be held up on the rim of a bowl or pot or by hand, so it is not as well suited as a colander to draining cooked pasta or vegetables. Instead, strainers are often used when you want to save the liquid and discard the separated solids, as is the case when making stock. The wire mesh of a strainer is almost always finer than the holes of a colander, so a strainer catches smaller bits of solids, thereby creating clearer liquid. A reasonably fine-meshed strainer, by the way, also makes a good sifter for dry ingredients such as flour or powdered sugar. —A.R.

⋟ BY KAY RENTSCHLER ⋞

Gathering Laurels

Though most of us appreciate the fact that specialty or mail-order spices are crucial for bringing the flavor of ethnic dishes home, we might question why a recipe, say for a simple chicken stock or white sauce, would demand *Turkish* bay leaves. What are Turkish bay leaves? And what's the alternative? The alternative, as it happens, is the California bay leaf, which is larger and more aromatic than the Turkish. It comes from a shrubby evergreen tree, a different species altogether from the bay, or laurel, tree that produces Turkish bay leaves and grows throughout the Mediterranean. California bay leaves have a potent, eucalyptus-like flavor, whereas Turkish bay leaves have a tea-like, mildly menthol flavor profile.

CALIFORNIAN

TURKISH

To get a closer read on the two, we made side-by-side béchamel (white) sauces. Tasters described the sauce made with the California bay leaf as "medicinal" and "potent," "like something you'd put in a cough drop." The sauce made with the Turkish bay leaf, on the other hand, was described as "mild, green, and slightly clove-like" and "far superior in nuance and flavor." Luckily, Turkish bay leaves are quite easy to find, California bay leaves far less so. McCormick, Spice Islands, and Penzeys spice companies all package Turkish bay leaves. Though recipes occasionally specify one or the other, even giving formulas for substitution (the California bays are stronger tasting), we would advise readers against substituting California bay leaves for Turkish and suggest they think hard before mail-ordering California bay leaves for any recipe.

What Is a Fluid Ounce?

In cooking, foods are usually measured by one of two means: weight (expressed in ounces or grams) or volume (calculated by how much space an ingredient occupies). The term *ounce* is familiar to most as a measurement of weight, but when used in the phrase "fluid ounce" it is a volume measurement of liquid, such as water or milk. If you inspect the side of a liquid measuring cup, you will notice that 8 ounces is exactly 1 cup. This means that 1 cup of milk or water—or a liquid of similar density—weighs 8 ounces. You quickly get into trouble, however, if you use this method with heavier, viscous liquids such as honey or corn syrup or if you use a liquid measuring device to measure dry ingredients by weight. Eight ounces of honey will not fully occupy 1 cup.

Eight ounces of shredded cheese will occupy more than 1 cup. To measure ingredients by weight, use a scale; a liquid measuring cup is good only for measuring by volume.

Cameo Appearance

The Cameo apple, a chance seedling believed to be a cross between the Red and Golden Delicious, is without question This Year's Girl. Developed about 10 years ago in Washington State, the Cameo took honors in all departments when we tested it recently. Not only an outstanding eating apple (similar in taste to the Fuji, with a shimmer of tartness), the Cameo resisted discoloration when sliced and held its contours when baked. We ate Cameos out of hand, used them to make applesauce (against our favored Jonagold) and apple cake (against our favored Granny Smith, page 23), and found them more than equal to every task. Best news of all: Cameo apples are in season from October to August.

Roasted Peppers

Grilling peppers to remove their skins for salads, pizzas, and the like is easy during the summer season. But with no indoor grill, it can be challenging the rest of the year, particularly since broilers sometimes perform this task poorly and unevenly. When just one or two roasted peppers are needed, we prefer the ease of the stovetop. For those cooks with electric stoves, a whole pepper can be grilled directly on a medium-high burner. For our gas stoves here in the test kitchen, we set a whole pepper on an old cooling rack placed directly over a high flame to replicate a grilltop.

A couple of reminders about charring peppers. The point is to char the skin enough to remove it easily, barely cooking the pepper itself. High heat and frequent turning accomplish that. When removing the skin, it's best to avoid running the pepper under water. Though water gets the job done quickly, flavorful oils and juices are washed off.

O Simmer, Where Art Thou?

Boiling and *simmering* are both descriptions of the rate at which a liquid bubbles and vaporizes—what cooks call reduce. Boiling and simmering liquids are often used to cook and poach foods, respectively. A boil refers to a rapidly bubbling and reducing liquid. Water, for example, boils at 212 degrees (at sea level). A simmer is a restrained version of a boil, in which the bubble clusters are small and the steam, by comparison, minimal. We wanted to get a better look at a simmer when one of our interns made the bouillabaisse stock featured in this issue (page 15). At the point when the fish bones are strained out of the stock, the liquid is to have reduced down to 9 cups. She had 11! The discrepancy was, we realized, a direct result of different interpretations of the term *simmer*. Her simmer had been a subtle shimmering movement on the surface of the stock, occasioning a bubble here and there and steam equivalent to what would waft from a hot cup of coffee. Our understanding of simmer was a bit racier: We had constant bursting and reforming bubble clusters along the inner circumference of the pot and a good deal of steam. To be sure, there are slow and brisk simmers, but any true simmer must demonstrate some degree of bubbling—otherwise no real reduction occurs.

BELOW SIMMER

SIMMER

BOIL

First-Class to New York and Seattle

Two chef cookbooks travel from Italy to New York and from Chesapeake Bay (via Asia) to Seattle. Can they make the trip to the home kitchen? BY CHRISTOPHER KIMBALL

My gripe with restaurant cookbooks is that chefs usually make lousy home cooks; they have lost an appreciation for what it is like to be an "army of one." When a chef recipe instructs the reader to stuff 24 kalamata olives "using your fingers," to shell, blanch, and peel a bowl of fava beans, or to use a platoon of saucepans and utensils, I get the urge to call the chef and ask when was the last time he or she made the masterpiece at home unassisted—which means no help washing the dishes, taking out the garbage, or wiping the placemats. That would be justice!

Yet I admit a fascination with restaurant cooking because the better chefs are on the front lines of American cooking. Tired of making asparagus risotto? Try Risotto with Eggplant, Anchovy, and Mint. Sick of slathering desserts with run-of-the-mill whipped cream? Try Country Cream, a whipped mixture of sour cream, mascarpone, yogurt, sugar, and vanilla. Until recently, these gems would be buried in a sea of impossible recipes, a French Laundry list of chef masterpieces that only the culinary insane would make at home.

SECOND HELPINGS FROM UNION SQUARE CAFE
Danny Meyer and Michael Romano
HarperCollins, 352 pages, $35

The Union Square Cafe is a great restaurant (New York's top-rated destination, according to Zagat's guide), but many great chefs have authored real stinkers, the sort of books one buys for the autograph on the title page, not the recipes. So I approached the Cafe's second cookbook, *Second Helpings,* with both enthusiasm and trepidation.

PROS: The Union Square Cafe offers big, hearty, Italian-inspired food. It is neither predictable nor outlandish; it is confident cooking, the sort of cuisine one expects from pros who have a well-centered sense of culinary history. It's also intriguing, like a movie star who is naturally glamorous, without the clothes, the cars, and the makeup crew. Simple but inventive dishes include Olive Mashed Potatoes, Fettuccine with Sweet Corn and Gorgonzola, and Eggplant "Meatballs."

CONS: Generally speaking, *Second Helpings* does not offer quick and easy home cooking. Fava beans have to be shelled, blanched, and peeled. Lamb has to be stuffed. Many recipes have a considerable number of ingredients. This is a book for folks who like to cook and are willing to invest some time doing it.

RECIPE TESTING: All of the recipes we tested were winners, and many were truly inspiring. Eggplant "Meatballs," made from roasted eggplant, Pecorino Romano, egg, bread crumbs, and parsley, are formed into balls and each stuffed with a small chunk of mozzarella. They are then coated with bread crumbs and fried. Scaffata, an Italian vegetable "stew," was extremely time-consuming but worth the effort. The Country Cream was simple and vastly better than ordinary whipped cream. Risotto with Eggplant, Anchovy, and Mint was outstanding, a Strawberry-Rhubarb Pandowdy

was delicious but not pretty (an unavoidable result given the nature of pandowdies), and Portobello Crostini called for too much cheese but was otherwise wonderful. Other winners were Chili and Sage–Rubbed Salmon and Olive-Stuffed Lamb. Although not quick and easy cooking, this food is honest, delicious, and worth every minute of preparation. In short, this cookbook is a rare gem indeed—a chef cookbook that deserves a place in your home kitchen.

TOM DOUGLAS' SEATTLE KITCHEN
Tom Douglas
HarperCollins, 272 pages, $30

Although one can fly from Manhattan to Seattle in a matter of hours, one bite of the food in any one of the three establishments owned by Tom Douglas will convince you that you are a world away. Douglas, a native of the Chesapeake Bay region, came to Seattle in the 1970s with both culinary feet planted firmly in Southern home cooking—pot roast, country ham, grits, and peach cobbler. The

produce, the seafood, and the Asian influence of Seattle have all contributed to his current style of cooking, which is more freewheeling than the Italian-inspired fare offered by the Union Square Cafe.

PROS: The food sounds great. Potato Gnocchi with Roasted Tomatoes and Gorgonzola Cream is irresistible, as are Hot Pepper Wings with Cilantro Sour Cream. There are plenty of good ideas in this book, and Douglas is not shy about combining whatever he finds in the market that day or following whatever culinary whim happens to cross his mind. The food is exciting but never silly.

CONS: If you like your cookbooks to be all of a piece, Tom Douglas is not your cup of tea. Sage Tagliarini lives in the same house with Kasu Zuke Black Cod and Triple Coconut Cream Pie. Sunday dinners at the Douglas household must be wild! Are you going to be served Crusted Smelts, Riesling Rabbit, or barbecued ribs? (For many cooks, however, great diversity within a cookbook may be a blessing, not a limitation.)

RECIPE TESTING: Our test kitchen liked this food a whole lot. Basic Barbecued Baby Back Ribs were very good (although the barbecue sauce, not the ribs, was the star of the show). Potato Gnocchi did not make the easiest recipe for the home cook (a few more visual clues would have been helpful), but they were rich and flavorful. Poppy Seed Coleslaw, Marinated and Seared Tofu, Charred Ahi Tuna with Pasta Puttanesca, as well as Spinach, Pear, and Frisée Salad were winners. Loretta's Buttermilk Pancakes were fine but not outstanding (we like our pancakes fluffier), a Peak-of-Summer Berry Crisp was good but too saccharine (more than 1 cup of sugar for 4 cups of fruit plus the topping), and Chilled Miso Spinach did not roll up or slice properly. Grilled Chicken Skewers needed better directions for incorporating the cornstarch slurry into the glaze (the chicken was nonetheless delicious), and Palace Olive Poppers, while good, were a chore. (This is where the olive stuffing comes in—two dozen in all. One might prefer to order this dish in the restaurant.) Still, if you like both Pink Floyd and Puccini, Tom Douglas delivers.

Most of the ingredients and materials necessary for the recipes in this issue are available at your local supermarket, gourmet store, or kitchen supply shop. The following are mail-order sources for particular items. Prices listed below were current at press time and do not include shipping or handling unless otherwise indicated. We suggest that you contact companies directly to confirm up-to-date prices and availability.

Vanilla Ice Cream and Scoops

Rich, velvety, and fresh-tasting Edy's Dreamery Vanilla Ice Cream topped our list of ice cream contenders (see page 27). The ice cream is widely available in supermarkets, but if you run into trouble in your search, log on to **www.edys.com** and use the Flavor Finder to locate a store near you that carries it. Double Rainbow, which took second place in the tasting, may be harder to come by. It is sold at **Trader Joe's** and **Price Club** stores and can also be located by calling the company directly at **800-489-3580** (West Coast) or **800-844-4258** (East Coast).

After testing 10 ice cream scoops (see page 26), we came up with a favorite and a best buy. The durable, self-defrosting Zeroll Classic Ice Cream Scoop, with its retro ice-cream-parlor design, scoops like a champ. **Professional Cutlery Direct (242 Branford Road, North Branford, CT 06471; 800-859-6994; www.cutlery.com)** carries the scoop, item #WGT109, for $21.99. The Oxo Beak Scoop, priced at a reasonable $11.99, was the only unusually shaped model that we found effective. You can mail-order the scoop from **Kitchen Etc. (32 Industrial Drive, Exeter, NH 03833; 800-232-4070; www.kitchenetc.com)**, item #532837. Zeroll also makes our favorite ice cream spade, available from **Sur La Table (1765 Sixth Avenue South, Seattle, WA 98134-1608; 800-243-0852; www.surlatable.com)**, item #2056, for $15.95.

Colanders

The Endurance Stainless Steel Colander/Strainer emerged as our favorite from the colander testing on page 28. Its mega-perforated, stainless steel, 5-quart hopper is perfect for any straining task, big or small. **Cook's Corner (836 S. 8th Street, Manitowoc, WI 54220; 800-236-2433; www.cookscorner.com)** carries the colander, item #0656, for $24.99.

Apple Cake

While developing the recipe for apple cake on page 22, we found that using a Bundt pan made all the difference. A Bundt pan is a mold (often adorned with decoration) with a center tube for conducting heat to the middle of the cake. **Williams-Sonoma (P.O. Box 7456, San Francisco, CA, 94120-7456; 800-541-2233; www.williams-sonoma.com)** sells a 12-cup, commercial-quality Bundt pan made of heat-responsive cast aluminum with a nonstick surface. The pan's design promotes even rising, uniform baking, and ample browning. And the nonstick interior allows the cake to release with ease. The Bundt pan, item #51-1110527, can be mail-ordered for $26.

Measuring Gear

Long-handled, heavy-duty, and durable is the way to go when deciding what measuring cups and spoons to buy. We like Williams-Sonoma's stainless-steel measuring cups and spoons for their long-lasting dependability and accuracy. A set of both, item #51-2083509, costs $25 at **Williams-Sonoma (P.O. Box 7456, San Francisco, CA, 94120-7456; 800-541-2233; www.williams-sonoma.com)**. The set of cups includes measures with capacities of ¼, ⅓, ½, and 1 cup. The spoons include the hard-to-find ⅛ teaspoon, plus ¼ teaspoon, ½ teaspoon, 1 teaspoon, and 1 tablespoon. The Wonder cup is a great tool for hard-to-measure, semisoft ingredients. Just slide the bottom to the desired measurement, fill, and slide the ingredients out. Measurements are marked in the usual cup increments (one-quarter, one-third, etc.) and in tablespoons, ounces, and milliliters. A 2-cup Wonder cup is available from **The Baker's Catalogue (P.O. Box 876, Norwich, VT 05055; 800-827-6836; www.kingarthurflour.com)**, item #6223, for $7.95.

Steak au Poivre

After testing green, pink, white, and black peppercorns in the steak au poivre recipe on page 9, it was quite clear that only black pepper, the spice that outsells all others, had the rich, bold flavor that is requisite for this dish. But not all black pepper is created equal. As is the case with all other spices, freshness and quality are extremely important. We used Malabar Indian Black Peppercorns, regarded as having the finest flavor of the mass-produced varieties, from **Penzeys Spices (W19362 Apollo Drive, Muskego, WI 53150; 800-741-7787; www.penzeys.com)**. A 2.5-ounce glass jar, item #56157, costs $2.99.

After testing the merits of a variety of steak knives, we found that the cleanest, most effortless cut came from the two priciest contenders. The razor-sharp blades and comfortable-grip handles of the Henckels Four Star Steak Knives and Wüsthof-Trident Classic Steak Knives won us over. The Henckels Steak Knives are available from **Cutlery Express (4551 Falkirk Bay, Oxnard, CA 93035; 888-258-0244; www.cutleryexpress.com)**, item #39190-000, for $139.99, and the Wüsthof-Trident from **Kitchen Etc. (32 Industrial Drive, Exeter, NH 03833; 800-232-4070; www.kitchenetc.com)**, item #485692, for $149.99. Both come in sets of four. Kitchen Etc. also sells the best buy Chicago Cutlery Steak Knives, Walnut Tradition, item #90172, for $39.99.

Grater for Carbonara and Mustard Vinaigrette

We like a Microplane grater to finely grate the cheeses for the carbonara recipe (page 7) and the shallots for the mustard vinaigrettes (page 12). It has extremely sharp teeth that will cut through the cheese and shallots in seconds. Microplane refers to this grater as "coarse." It can be ordered from **Williams-Sonoma (P.O. Box 7456, San Francisco, CA, 94120-7456; 800-541-2233; www.williams-sonoma.com)** for $16.50, item #3720679.

Ratatouille

Roasting the eggplant and zucchini for 30 to 40 minutes on foil-lined, rimmed baking sheets turned out perfectly toothsome and flavorful vegetables for the ratatouille on page 18. A half-sheet pan, which measures about 12 by 18 inches, is perfect for the task. If you don't have the right pans (the recipe requires two), you can mail-order them from **Bridge Kitchenware (214 East 52nd Street, New York, NY 10022; 800-274-3435; www.bridgekitchenware.com)**, item code ABSK-H, for $12.90 each. The store lists them as aluminum half-sheet cake pans.

Bouillabaisse

Saffron, the dried stigmas of the flower of the saffron crocus, is a fundamental ingredient in bouillabaisse (page 13). The crocuses are grown in most Mediterranean countries, in China, and even in Pennsylvania, and the saffron is harvested by hand. Each flower produces only three stigmas, or threads, which means that about one-quarter of a million flowers are needed to produce one full pound of saffron. Needless to say, saffron is exceedingly expensive. Luckily, a little goes a long way. Good saffron should not be more than a year old, and the threads should be a bright orange/red color—not yellow, bleached, or with white streaks. Saffron should have an intense perfume and taste of honey. Your local supermarket is unlikely to carry good-quality, well-kept saffron threads; the best come from specialty shops. And remember, cheap saffron does not exist, so beware any bargains. A gram can run you $5 to $10, depending on quality. You can mail-order saffron from a host of spice merchants, including **Kalustyans (123 Lexington Avenue, New York, NY 10016; 212-685-3451; www.kalustyans.com)**.

RECIPES
September & October 2001

Main Dishes
Bouillabaisse-Style Fish Stew 15
Chicken Cutlets, Breaded
    Crisp 11
    Deviled 11
    with Garlic and Oregano 11
    with Parmesan (Chicken
        Milanese) 11
Spaghetti alla Carbonara 7
Steak au Poivre with Brandied
    Cream Sauce 9

Sauces and Side Dishes
FOR BOUILLABAISSE:
    Garlic-Rubbed Croutons 15
    Rouille 15
Vinaigrette, Mustard
    and Balsamic 12
    and Roasted Garlic 12
    with Lemon and Fines
        Herbes 12
Ratatouille 19

Muffins and Desserts
Apple Cake 23
Blueberry Muffins,
    Best 21
    Cinnamon-Sugar-Dipped 21
    Ginger-Glazed 21
    Lemon-Glazed 21
Chocolate Sauce, Bittersweet 24

PHOTOGRAPHY: CARL TREMBLAY

Crisp Breaded Chicken Cutlet

Best Blueberry Muffins

Spaghetti alla Carbonara

Bouillabaisse-Style Fish Stew

Steak au Poivre with Brandied Cream Sauce

Mustard Vinaigrette

Ratatouille

Apple Cake

Bittersweet Chocolate Sauce

www.cooksillustrated.com

If you enjoy *Cook's Illustrated* magazine, you should visit our Web site. Simply log on to www.cooksillustrated.com. Although much of the information is free, database searches are for site subscribers only. *Cook's Illustrated* subscribers get a 20 percent discount.

Here are some of the things you can do on our site:

Search Our Recipes: We have a searchable database of all the recipes from *Cook's Illustrated* magazine.

Search Tastings and Cookware Ratings: You will find all of our reviews (cookware, food, wine, and cookbooks) plus new material created exclusively for the Web site.

Find Your Favorite Quick Tips.

Get All Your Cooking Questions Answered: Post questions for *Cook's Illustrated* editors and fellow Web site subscribers.

Check Your Subscription: Check the status of your magazine or Web site subscription, pay a bill, or give gift subscriptions online.

Visit Our Bookstore: You can purchase any of our cookbooks, hardbound annual editions of the magazine, or posters online.

Subscribe to *e-Notes:* Our free e-mail companion to the magazine offers cooking advice, test results, buying tips, and recipes on a single topic each month.

Find Out about Our Public Television Show: Watch *America's Test Kitchen* to see the *Cook's* staff at work in our test kitchen. For program times in your area, check www.americastestkitchen.com.

Get All the Extras: The outtakes from each issue of *Cook's Illustrated* are available at Cook's Extra, including step-by-step illustrations.

Need Help with Your Turkey or Ham Dinner? Visit www.turkeyhelp.com and www.hamhelp.com today where you will find recipes for your entire turkey or ham meal, buying guides, carving instructions, and much more.

Rotelle

Farfalle

Cavatappi

Gigli

Orecchiette

Pennoni

Gomitoni

Castellane

Gemelli

Mostaccioli

Radiatore

DRIED PASTA

NUMBER FIFTY-THREE

NOVEMBER & DECEMBER 2001

COOK'S
ILLUSTRATED

High-Roast
Turkey Perfected
90 Minutes, 450 Degrees

Butternut
Squash Soup

Shrimp Fra Diavolo
Tender Shrimp, Mellow Garlic

Brining 101

Testing Coffee
Grinders
Inexpensive Models Win

Best Crème Brûlée

Red Wines
for Cooking
Blends Beat Varietals

Make-Ahead Crescent Rolls
Holiday Green Beans
Breakfast Casserole
Beef Wellington
Perfect Shortbread

www.cooksillustrated.com
$4.95 U.S./$6.95 CANADA

CONTENTS

November & December 2001

2 Notes from Readers
Readers ask questions and suggest solutions.

4 Quick Tips
Quick and easy ways to perform everyday kitchen tasks, from defatting pan drippings to peeling shrimp.

6 Shrimp Fra Diavolo at Home
We get the best of the devil by flambéing the shrimp hot and fast and sautéing the garlic long and slow.
BY ADAM RIED AND MATTHEW CARD

8 Butternut Squash Soup
The secret to great butternut squash soup is steaming the flesh and then using the seeds to add flavor. BY RAQUEL PELZEL

9 High-Roast Turkey
Could we high-roast a turkey without having to call the fire department or drying out the breast meat? We set out to discover the secret of two-hour roast turkey without the smoke. BY BRIDGET LANCASTER

12 Homemade Crescent Rolls
These rich, buttery rolls can be prebaked, frozen, and then heated just before serving. BY RAQUEL PELZEL

14 Introducing Breakfast Strata
The right blend of four staple ingredients—bread, eggs, cheese, and cream—produces a savory breakfast casserole that's simple and satisfying. BY ADAM RIED

16 The Basics of Brining
How salt, sugar, and water can improve texture and flavor in lean meats, poultry, and seafood. BY JULIA COLLIN

18 Make-Ahead Holiday Green Beans
Cooking the beans ahead saves time when you need it most—in the final moments before dinner.

19 Beef Wellington without Fear
Is this dinosaur of a recipe worth making at home? If you like flaky—not soggy—pastry wrapped around perfectly pink, flavorful beef, the answer is an enthusiastic yes.
BY KAY RENTSCHLER

22 Perfecting Crème Brûlée
Lots of yolks, turbinado sugar, an instant-read thermometer, and a final chill are the keys to perfect crème brûlée.
BY DAWN YANAGIHARA

24 Rediscovering Shortbread
A quick, foolproof technique produces shortbread that is miles ahead of the packaged stuff. BY KAY RENTSCHLER

26 Cooking with Red Wine
With the right wine and the right technique, you can make rich, complex-tasting sauces worthy of the finest restaurant at home.
BY JULIA COLLIN

28 Easing the Daily Grind
We tested 10 countertop coffee grinders and found that more money doesn't always buy a better model. BY ADAM RIED

30 Kitchen Notes
Test results, buying tips, and advice related to stories past and present, directly from the test kitchen. BY KAY RENTSCHLER

31 Book Reviews
Top 10 cookbooks for the holidays. BY CHRISTOPHER KIMBALL

32 Resources
Products from this issue, plus coffee grinders, ramekins, and puff pastry.

COOK'S
ILLUSTRATED

Home of America's Test Kitchen
www.cooksillustrated.com

PUBLISHER AND EDITOR
Christopher Kimball

SENIOR EDITOR
Jack Bishop

FOOD EDITOR
Kay Rentschler

MANAGING EDITOR
Dawn Yanagihara

SENIOR WRITER
Adam Ried

EDITORIAL MANAGER
Barbara Bourassa

ART DIRECTOR
Amy Klee

TEST KITCHEN DIRECTOR
Bridget Lancaster

ASSOCIATE EDITORS
Raquel Pelzel
Julia Collin

COPY EDITOR
India Koopman

MANAGING EDITOR,
BOOKS AND WEB SITE
Rebecca Hays

ASSISTANT EDITOR, WEB SITE
Shona Simkin

TEST COOKS
Shannon Blaisdell
Matthew Card
Meg Suzuki

PROOFREADER
Jana Branch

VICE PRESIDENT MARKETING
David Mack

SALES REPRESENTATIVES
Jason Geller
Karen Shiffman

MARKETING ASSISTANT
Connie Forbes

CIRCULATION MANAGER
Larisa Greiner

PRODUCTS MANAGER
Steven Browall

DIRECT MAIL MANAGER
Robert Lee

CUSTOMER SERVICE MANAGER
Jacqueline Valerio

INBOUND MARKETING REPRESENTATIVE
Adam Dardeck

VICE PRESIDENT OPERATIONS
AND TECHNOLOGY
James McCormack

PRODUCTION MANAGER
Jessica Quirk

PRODUCTION ARTIST
Daniel Frey

PRODUCTION COORDINATOR
Mary Connelly

PRODUCTION ASSISTANTS
Ron Bilodeau
Jennifer McCreary

SYSTEMS ADMINISTRATOR
Richard Cassidy

WEBMASTER
Nicole Morris

CHIEF FINANCIAL OFFICER
Sharyn Chabot

CONTROLLER
Mandy Shito

OFFICE MANAGER
Juliet Nusbaum

RECEPTIONIST
Henrietta Murray

PUBLICITY
Deborah Broide

For list rental information, contact The SpecialLISTS, 1200 Harbor Blvd. 9th Floor, Weehawken, NJ 07087; 201-865-5800; fax 201-867-2450. Editorial office: 17 Station Street, Brookline, MA 02445; 617-232-1000; fax 617-232-1572. Editorial contributions should be sent to: Editor, *Cook's Illustrated*. We cannot assume responsibility for manuscripts submitted to us. Submissions will be returned only if accompanied by a large self-addressed envelope. Postmaster: Send all new orders, subscription inquiries, and change of address notices to: *Cook's Illustrated*, P.O. Box 7446, Red Oak, IA 51591-0446. PRINTED IN CHINA.

PEARS Most pears are harvested when still green and placed in cold storage for up to two months to improve their flavor, texture, and fragrance. The pears are then set to ripen in a fairly cool, dark place for up to two weeks. The popular Bartlett turns bright yellow when ripe, and its flesh is sweet and juicy; Red Bartletts are a natural red mutation of their namesake. The Beurré Bosc is very juicy when ripe; look for yellow undertones in its skin. The Beurré d'Anjou has a sharp-edged flavor, while the Doyenné du Comice, a trademark Christmastime pear, is delicate and only slightly sweet, as is the russet-colored Taylor's Gold, also a Comice. *Forelle* is the German word for "trout," and the red speckled skin on the Forelle pear is reminiscent of the fish. Seckels are tiny pears with a sweet, spicy flavor that turn yellow as they ripen. Packhams, which are sweet and juicy, are light green and change little in color as they ripen. Hosui is a variety of Asian pear that is widely available in this country. COVER *(Grapefruit)*: ELIZABETH BRANDON, BACK COVER *(Pears)*: JOHN BURGOYNE

INDIAN SUMMER

There is a time in late October when, in the half-light before dawn, you expect that a few dim-witted bees will be lazing about the frost-stroked goldenrod, the upper pond will be glazed with a skim-coat of ice, and the October skies will look more like November, a northwest wind pushing a heavy gray sky. On such a morning, however, one wakes to find Indian summer, a day when the bees swarm around the hive, you dive buck-naked into the pond, hot from splitting wood, and the heat shimmers up from the hay fields, the skies overhead washed with the powder blue of bachelor's buttons. It is a day too ripe in the nose for August, the sun too strong for November, and one's step too lively for the coming of winter. It is a morning full of promises, like a first date, the warm air ripe with pumpkin, dry hay, wildflower, and the sweet smell of honeysuckle.

There is a man in our part of town whom I respectfully refer to as Mr. President. He is President of the Old Rabbit Hunter's Association, a group whose membership extends only to the President himself, his son, and me, as the devoted disciple. (My apologies and thanks to Gordon MacQuarrie, the best outdoor writer who ever lived.) Mr. President wears green wool pants with suspenders, an orange hunting hat, a gray beard, and an honest, weathered face. The pockets of his hunting vest have long ago given up hope, the stained and tattered bottoms hanging below his waist. He doesn't say much except to start every hunt with the words "I guess we'll eat good tonight"—like a man who, having done the same thing all his life, digs deep and finds a burst of enthusiasm to do it one more time. Now Mr.

President has been at this hunting business awhile, and you notice right off that although he isn't quick to shoot, he usually bags what he's aiming at. I've been known to empty all five shells from my gun in less than two seconds, hitting nothing more than gray birch and red maple. On that occasion, Mr. President simply waited a few seconds, sighted in, and delivered dinner with one shot. His only remark was, "Need shells?"

On this particular late October afternoon, Mr. President and I headed out with his overstuffed rabbit dog, Bucket, and my then 12-year-old daughter, Whitney, on a long amble through some marshy scrub, a Christmas tree farm, and then down through a thicket so dense with milkweed that the only thing I could make sense of was Mr. President's orange hat. Later in the afternoon, after raising a grouse, a woodcock, and two rabbits that were smarter than we were, I flushed a third one but didn't have a clean shot, and Bucket took after it, through the swamp and up a side hill. Mr. President told us to sit and wait—rabbits always run in a circle—so I got comfortable, my back up against one of the few hickories still standing.

The clouds came in, the wind freshened, and it started to feel like late November. I picked up the scent of wood smoke from Mr. President's house as I watched the day being swallowed by shadows. While the snowbirds head south to smile smugly on beach chairs, the pulse of a die-hard Northerner quickens at the first killing frost. Nothing freshens

Christopher Kimball

the blood like the howl of wind, a cold nose ripe with the scent of wet leaves, and the pop of creosote in a stovepipe.

In the middle of my reverie, the rabbit had come full circle, stood up in front of an oak not 20 yards away, looked me in the eye, and headed straight for its hole. I had time for just one badly aimed shot and managed to make short work of a clump of skunk cabbage. Then there were three shots from Mr. President's gun, and all was quiet.

Mr. President came up quickly from behind, looking peevish. He growled, "Next time, I expect, that rabbit will walk right up and plant a kiss on your smacker. Can't eat skunk cabbage." A cold gust blew right through my vest and shirt. The woods were silent, and I was tired.

Then Mr. President looked up with a warm glimmer in his eye, "Yup, why don't the two of you come up to the house for dinner?"

"A rabbit dinner, Mr. President?" I asked.

"Nope, tonight I'm in the mood for pot roast." I looked down and noticed that his left hand was empty. He had fired three times and missed.

"Well, I guess I wasn't in the mood for rabbit anyway," I said, as we headed home. I considered the cold, dark winter that was settling into our narrow mountain valley, the sunset fading into a bitter twilight. Then I thought about Mr. President and smiled. If you know where to look, in the twinkle of an eye or deep in the shadows, you'll find Indian summer when you least expect it.

THE COOK'S ILLUSTRATED PRODUCT LINE

HTTP://WWW.COOKSILLUSTRATED.COM The *Cook's Illustrated* Web site offers a range of products and services related to our magazine, cookbooks, and television show. With just one click, you can order a book, give a gift subscription to *Cook's Illustrated* magazine, sign up for our free e-newsletter, subscribe to the magazine, or check the status of your subscription. Join the Web site and you'll have access to our searchable databases of recipes, cookware ratings, ingredient tastings, quick tips, cookbook reviews, and more.

The Web site also features free recipes, techniques, and answers to cooking questions; original editorial material not found in the magazine; an online bookstore; a question-and-answer message board; and a list of upcoming appearances by editor and publisher Chris Kimball.

Have questions about your subscription? Visit our customer service page, where you can manage your subscription, including changing your address, renewing your subscription, paying your bill, or viewing answers to frequently asked questions.

AMERICA'S TEST KITCHEN TELEVISION SHOW Look for our new television series currently airing on public television. For program times in your area, recipes, details about the shows, or to order *The America's Test Kitchen Cookbook*, visit http://www.americastestkitchen.com.

COOK'S ILLUSTRATED MAGAZINE *Cook's Illustrated* (ISSN 1068-2821) magazine is published bimonthly (6 issues per year) by Boston Common Press Limited Partnership,

17 Station Street, Brookline, MA 02445. Copyright 2001 Boston Common Press Limited Partnership. Periodical postage paid at Boston, Mass., and additional mailing offices, USPS #012487.

A one-year subscription is $29.70, two years is $55, and three years is $75. Add $6 postage per year for Canadian subscriptions and $12 per year for all other foreign countries. To order subscriptions in the U.S. call 800-526-8442; from outside the U.S. call 515-247-7571. Gift subscriptions are available for $24.95 each. Postmaster: Send all new orders, subscription inquiries, and change of address notices to Cook's Illustrated, P.O. Box 7446, Red Oak, IA 51591-0446, or call 800-526-8442 inside the U.S.; from outside the U.S. call 515-247-7571.

COOKBOOKS AND INDEXES *Cook's* also publishes a variety of cookbooks and indexes, including: annual hardbound editions of the magazine; a nine-year (1993–2001) reference index for the magazine; single-subject cookbooks from our *How to Cook* Master Series; our bestseller *The Best Recipe*; and our two newest books, *The Best Recipe: Soups & Stews* and *The America's Test Kitchen Cookbook*. For prices and ordering information, call 800-611-0759 inside the U.S. or 515-246-6911 from outside the U.S. You can also use those same phone numbers to order back issues of the magazine or check the status of your book order.

Romano or Pecorino Romano?

When shopping for the ingredients for your spaghetti alla carbonara (September/October 2001), I realized that I have long been confused about the differences between Pecorino and Romano cheeses. I have seen (and used) Pecorino, Romano, and Pecorino Romano, and I haven't detected extreme differences in flavor. Are they all the same?

CONNOR MCCARTHY
WESTPORT, MASS.

➤ The confusion you have encountered is a matter of nomenclature. Pecorino (derived from *pecora,* the Italian word for ewe or sheep) is the all-encompassing name for pure Italian sheep's milk cheese, of which there are countless varieties. The word is usually used in conjunction with the region of Italy where a cheese was produced. Pecorino Romano, for example, is a sheep's milk cheese traditionally made in Rome. It is undoubtedly the Pecorino best known to Americans.

Though the name implies that this cheese is made in Rome, 60 percent of today's Pecorino Romano is actually made on the island of Sardinia, where production costs are cheaper and sheep are abundant. According to Steve Jenkins, author of *Cheese Primer* (Workman Publishing, 1996), only four Roman companies still produce genuine Pecorino Romano—Locatelli, Fulvi, Brunelli, and Lopez—and their cheeses are considered superior to those made on Sardinia. The rind on genuine Pecorino Romano is often embossed with the image of a sheep's head and the words "Pecorino Romano." But some genuine Pecorino Romanos have painted black rinds that are not embossed, so you may have to rely on the integrity of the cheese monger to find a real Pecorino Romano.

When whole, a Pecorino Romano wheel is an impressively large cylinder weighing up to 40 pounds. Except for cases in which the rind is painted black or is coated with plastic, the rind is generally thin, dry, and bone-white. The cheese is allowed to ripen for at least eight months or up to one year to develop its characteristically piquant, salty, sharp, almost lemony flavor and acrid aroma. The straw-colored cheese is firm-to-hard and can have a slightly grainy, oily texture. Pecorino Romano is perfect for grating over pasta and even for nibbling on its own.

Back to the nomenclature. In many culinary circles and in Italy, Pecorino Romano is often referred to simply as Romano. And sometimes grocers and cheese purveyors label their Pecorino Romano as such. But take caution.

There is a good chance that the Romano in your shopping cart is not the real thing (that is, made exclusively with Roman sheep's milk). If you shop in supermarkets, there's also a good chance that the cheese doesn't even come from Italy. So-called Romanos made in the United States, Canada, and Australia are also used as grating cheeses. These cheeses can be produced from cow's, goat's, or sheep's milk or a mixture thereof. We found that non-Italian Romanos have a texture similar to real Pecorino Romano. When it comes to flavor, only those cheeses made with sheep's milk bear a resemblance to Italian Romanos. Cheeses made with cow's or goat's milk have little or none of the lemony tang contributed by sheep's milk. If you make the carbonara again and want to purchase an authentic Pecorino Romano, check the rind or ask your cheese monger for a Pecorino Romano imported from Rome.

Kitchen Bouquet

In going through a number of my mother's holiday cookbooks I noticed an ingredient called Kitchen Bouquet in a few gravy recipes. I have never heard of it. Can you tell me what it is and if I should seek it out?

STACY HOFFMAN
BANGOR, MAINE

➤ Kitchen Bouquet, a "browning and seasoning" agent for meats, gravies, and stews, is made from caramelized sugars, vegetable extracts, salt, and preservatives. It is slightly thick and has a deep, dark chocolate color. From the bottle, Kitchen Bouquet tastes of burnt and bitter sugar, but we wanted to find out how it influences a recipe. We made two chicken gravies according to the recipe on the bottle, one with Kitchen Bouquet and one without. When presented with them, our panel of tasters immediately commented on the color. Adding a mere ½ teaspoon Kitchen Bouquet transformed a drab "diner-looking" gravy into a deep, dark, meaty-looking one that tasters were certain would taste better. But it didn't. Tasters found the gravy made with Kitchen Bouquet to be "fake-tasting" and to carry a bitter aftertaste ("the kind that burns the back of your throat"). They also found the Kitchen Bouquet–laced gravy to be dominated by a dull, vegetal flavor. The gravy without the Kitchen Bouquet was "fresh" and "clean" and tasted liked chicken.

Basically, Kitchen Bouquet is an impersonator of *fond*—the little brown bits left in a skillet or roasting pan after food has been browned. When dissolved in a liquid added to the pan (in a process called *deglazing),* the fond lends flavor and color to gravies, sauces, and stews. We suggest concentrating on developing a good fond when sautéing or roasting and leaving out the Kitchen Bouquet.

Tapioca Basics

I was surprised to learn that tapioca is a natural substance. From its perfectly round shape, I assumed it was not. Can you please tell me a little about it and its different forms?

HOLLY ROSENBERG
ANNAPOLIS, MD.

➤ Though the small, round pellets referred to as pearl tapioca have a distinctively manufactured look (after all, they are processed into pellets), their content, as you learned, is 100 percent natural. Tapioca is made from starch extracted from the root of the cassava plant, also called manioc or yuca. Cassava is the main source of starch in the diet of people living in many African and South American regions, where it is eaten much like potatoes are in the United States and Europe. Tapioca comes in various forms, with pearl, flour, and instant (or Minute, a trademark) being the most common.

After the cassava starch grains are removed from the root's cells, they are heated and ruptured, which converts the starches into small, irregular masses. These masses are baked into flakes that are finely ground to form tapioca flour or forced through sieves and then baked to form pearl tapioca. Pearl tapioca, which comes in various sizes, requires hydration before cooking. It is used almost exclusively to make the aptly named tapioca pudding. When hydrated, the white pearls become translucent, slightly swollen, and jelly-like; they lend their grain and body to whatever dish they are added. Pearl tapioca's unusual texture elicits passionate responses: It is either loved or hated.

Tapioca flour—though it has considerably less thickening power than pearl tapioca—is used mostly at the commercial level as a thickening agent for soups, fruit fillings, and glazes. In Asian cuisine it is referred to as tapioca starch and is almost as popular as cornstarch for use as a thickener in both sweet and savory dishes.

A third type of tapioca, called instant, Minute, or quick, is made by mixing tapioca flour and water to form a dough, which is slowly cooked and stirred. The dough is then dried, pulverized, and cooled, forming more uniformly sized and shaped granules. Instant, or Minute, tapioca, as the names imply, does not require soaking before cooking, making it a great timesaver in the kitchen, especially when compared with pearl tapioca. Because of its small size, this type of tapioca is often used as a thickener in pie fillings.

The Right Consistency for Pastry Cream

I had some trouble getting the pastry cream to set up when making your fresh fruit tart (July/August 2001). I am quite sure I followed the directions to a T. Any thoughts on what may have happened?

JANET RINGO
HOOD RIVER, ORE.

➤ We have had a handful of questions similar to yours, and it seems that our readers may have a different idea about the consistency of perfect pastry cream. As discussed in the article, our panel of tasters (as well as the author herself) unanimously rejected pastry creams with firm, Jell-O-like qualities. Firm pastry cream slices beautifully, but its texture can be rubbery and gummy. We were after something rich, soft, light, creamy, and smooth. When cold, the consistency of our pastry cream should lie somewhere between homemade mayonnaise and softened butter. But beware. As the pastry cream comes up to room temperature it may slacken a bit, so use it straight from the fridge and then serve the tart swiftly. Although our pastry cream is firm enough to support the fruit in the tart shell, do not expect it to slice neatly. Fresh fruit tarts look best whole. Once sliced, the pastry cream sags slightly and the presentation is not quite as stunning.

If your pastry cream did not achieve the proper consistency (as described above), the sometimes fickle nature of cornstarch was probably the culprit. Mixtures thickened with cornstarch must come to a lively simmer in order to thicken up but will begin to thin if cooked too long. For this reason it is crucial to watch the timing carefully. Once the cornstarch and yolk mixture is added to the simmering half-and-half, the pastry cream is brought to a simmer and then promptly removed from the heat. If the pastry cream is boiled or simmered excessively, the thickening power of the cornstarch may be compromised.

One final warning: As with leavening agents such as baking powder and baking soda, the cornstarch sitting in your pantry will lose its thickening power over time. Make sure you have a fresh box of cornstarch—no more than a year old—on hand.

The Spirit of Bouillabaisse

While going through the ingredient list for your bouillabaisse recipe (September/October 2001), I wondered about possible substitutes for Pernod. I have a bottle of ouzo in my cabinet, and it, too,

I noticed this tool while digging around in a friend's kitchen drawer. Though it is obviously a peeler of some kind, neither of us knows exactly what it is used for. It has odd curves and a small sharp blade at the end of the peeling arm. Can you shed some light on the subject?

PETER NORTH
PENSACOLA, FLA.

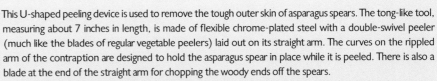

This U-shaped peeling device is used to remove the tough outer skin of asparagus spears. The tong-like tool, measuring about 7 inches in length, is made of flexible chrome-plated steel with a double-swivel peeler (much like the blades of regular vegetable peelers) laid out on its straight arm. The curves on the rippled arm of the contraption are designed to hold the asparagus spear in place while it is peeled. There is also a blade at the end of the straight arm for chopping the woody ends off the spears.

To use this gadget, hold an asparagus spear at an angle with its butt end up, gently place it between the curved nook and the blade of the peeler, and, lightly pressing the contraption closed, slide it up the asparagus spear to remove the outer skin, exposing the tender, moist flesh. Turn the spear to make the next slice; continue until fully peeled. Be sure to squeeze the tong-like tool with a soft hand when peeling the asparagus. Too much pressure may produce too deep a slice. After the spears are peeled, rinse them under cold running water to clean. It is best to peel asparagus just before cooking—certainly not longer than two hours in advance; any more and the asparagus can turn yellow and develop a stringy outer skin.

Why bother peeling asparagus? As no one here at *Cook's* takes the trouble to do so, we were skeptical as to the advantages of this tool. After some research and a host of tests, we came to a firm conclusion. While the tool is easy to use and peels like a champ, when preparing green asparagus, there is simply no good reason to use it. Thin green asparagus need no peeling to begin with, and the tough, woody butt ends of thicker spears can simply be snapped off at their natural breaking point. When we put white asparagus to the test, however, we found that removing the outer skin (which is much tougher than the skin of green asparagus) improved the texture and flavor of the final cooked product immensely. Unpeeled, the skin is stringy, hard to chew, and just plain unpleasant.

And did we need this specific tool to peel the white asparagus? It turns out that we did. Paring knives and regular peelers failed at the task. Lacking the tong-like brace support of the asparagus peeler, it was entirely too easy to break the white spears in half or into other undesirable lengths. If white asparagus frequents your dinner table, this asparagus peeler is a must.

is anise-flavored. Can I use it in place of Pernod? Also, I've found "anise" in the produce section of a local grocery store. Is it the same vegetable as the fennel called for in the recipe?

BARBIE KIPPER
CHAPPAQUA, N.Y.

➤ Both Pernod (pronounced pehr-NOH) and ouzo are anise-flavored spirits made with the essential oil of anise seeds. Pernod is a clear, yellow-green French liqueur with an assertive licorice or anise flavor. As legend has it, dry anise-flavored liqueur made its way into the fisherman's stew, bouillabaisse, in honor of the fish themselves, which are supposedly fond of the strong flavor of anise. Fishermen are said to have lured them with bait of bread soaked in pastis, which is the catchall term for France's many brands of anise-flavored spirits. In our bouillabaisse, Pernod is a component of the marinade that gives flavor and aroma to the fish and shellfish. We call specifically for Pernod because it is the most readily available unsweetened anise liqueur sold in the United States.

Greek ouzo is a favorite spirit of the eastern Mediterranean. Along with a potent anise flavor,

it can have minty herbal notes. Ouzo is sweetened and is therefore inappropriate in bouillabaisse.

Anise (*Pimpinella anisum*), a member of the parsley family, is an annual herb that resembles Queen Anne's Lace, a common wildflower in many parts of the United States. True anise is cultivated only for its seeds, which have a strong licorice flavor and are used to flavor many dishes, from baked goods to fish and meat. Fennel (*Foeniculum vulgare*) bears a resemblance to celery but has a bulbous base and fern-like fronds. Every part of the fennel plant, from its roots to its bulb to its seeds, can be used to infuse a dish, like our bouillabaisse, with the delicate flavor and aroma of licorice. Fennel is sometimes incorrectly labeled "anise" or "sweet anise" in grocery stores. That anise seeds and fennel seeds are similar in appearance and flavor (though anise is more potent) is the likely cause of the confusion about nomenclature.

Errata

In Kitchen Notes of our September/October 2001 issue, we inadvertently transposed the labels identifying the Californian and Turkish Bay leaves. We apologize for the confusion.

Quick Tips

Iceless Ice Bath

Part of the routine for blanching vegetables is to stop the cooking process by transferring the vegetables from boiling water into a bath of ice water, which is called "shocking." When she was blanching vegetables recently, Alice Gordenker of Tokyo, Japan, discovered that she had no ice in the freezer, so she improvised by using frozen ice packs—the type used to chill foods in a cooler—in place of the ice cubes.

Adhering Parchment to Pan

Some cooks, and even a previous *Cook's Illustrated* quick tip, recommend using small bits of the dough or batter you're baking to anchor sheets of parchment paper to their pans. If you'll be using the pans for multiple batches, though, the small bits of dough or batter may well burn and be a nuisance to clean. Karen Greco-Buta of Newton, N.J., avoids this problem by spraying the pan with a light coating of cooking spray. She then lays the parchment sheet down on the sticky surface.

Easy Defatting for Pan Drippings

No one looks forward to spooning that thin layer of liquid fat off the drippings from a roast before making a pan sauce or gravy. Yet if the fat remains, the sauce will be greasy. Both Catherine Hunt of Lancaster, Pa., and Tom Everson of Portland, Ore., suggested a method that makes the process much faster and easier.

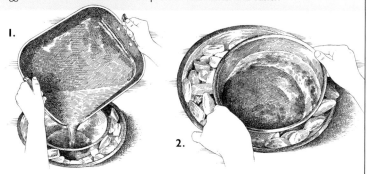

1. Deglaze the roasting pan, fat and all, and scrape up and dissolve the brown bits from the bottom of the pan, but stop short of reducing the liquid. Pour the brown, fatty liquid into a small mixing bowl (metal works best because it reacts quickly to changes in temperature), and set the bowl in an ice water bath.
2. After a few minutes, as the liquid cools, small bits of fat will solidify and rise to the surface. If you rock the inner bowl very gently to create a small wave of liquid moving around its perimeter, the fat will collect around the upper inside edge of the bowl, where it will be easy to remove.

Drying Frosted Cookies

A box or tin of colorful frosted cookies makes a nice gift to friends and neighbors around the holidays. But before the cookies can be wrapped, the frosting has to dry thoroughly, and it can be a real challenge to find enough space to spread out a few dozen cookies in a cramped apartment kitchen. Kip Turnquist of San Francisco, Calif., creates extra space by pressing some paper plates and cups into service.

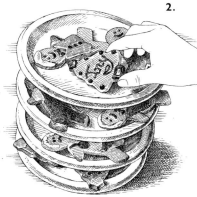

1. Coat the rim of a small paper cup with frosting and invert it onto the middle of a paper plate. Arrange as many drying cookies around the cup as will fit comfortably on the plate. Dab the exposed rim with frosting, then make another plate in the same manner and stack it on top of the first.
2. Repeat until you have a stack of four or five cookie-laden plates.

Fishing Cork Crumbs Out of Wine Bottles

Few things are more frustrating than fishing out bits of cork that have fallen into a freshly opened bottle of wine. Tired of this task, two readers, Ellen Malmon of New Canaan, Conn., and Barbara Satterfield of Fairfax, Va., offered the following remedy. Insert a plastic drinking straw into the neck of the opened bottle and over the cork crumb, then place a finger over the end of the straw and lift it out. A vacuum is created in the straw that traps the cork crumb along with a little wine.

Keeping Cookies Fresh— and Out of Sight

When it comes to storing homemade cookies, decorative cookie jars may be convenient and attractive, but they are not airtight. As Thomas Ferguson of Westlake Village, Calif., discovered, however, there is a way to store cookies in an attractive jar and preserve their freshness at the same time. Simply line the inside of the jar with a large zipper-lock bag, place the cookies in the bag, and seal tightly.

Send Us Your Tip We will provide a complimentary one-year subscription for each tip we print. Send your tip, name, address, and daytime telephone number to Quick Tips, Cook's Illustrated, P.O. Box 470589, Brookline, MA 02447.

Chilling Beverages for a Party

Especially around the holidays, refrigerator space available for chilling beverages before a party is often at a premium. When Melissa Lennon of Phoenixville, Pa., is faced with this problem, she turns her washing machine into something of an icebox. Fill the washer's basket with ice cubes, then nestle in the cans and bottles. When it is time for more cold drinks, they are at the ready. When the party is over and the ice melted, simply run the washer's spin cycle to drain the water.

Rescuing Burnt Cookies

The holidays are prime cookie-baking time, and, inevitably, some of those cookies will end up overbrowned or even burnt. This fate befell Lyn Babcock of New York, N.Y., but she managed to rescue the cookies by gently grating the burnt layer off the bottoms with a Microplane grater/zester. (Of course, if the cookies are too far gone, the Microplane method probably won't work.)

Making Sure Cookies Are Rolled Out Evenly

Making rolled cookies is a holiday tradition for many cooks. So, too, is the problem of rolling the dough to an even thickness. Our food editor, Kay Rentschler, runs a bench scraper lightly over the surface of the dough to feel for high and low points. This way, she knows which area to correct with the rolling pin.

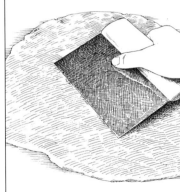

First In, First Out for Onions

It's always best to use up foods that have been sitting in the pantry for a while before breaking into a fresh supply. When it comes to onions, Greta Lieberman of Bala Cynwyd, Pa., has a system to keep track of older specimens so she can use them first. Using a permanent marker, lightly mark a small X on the skin of each onion now in your storage bin. Leave any new onions you add to the bin unmarked. This way, you'll know to reach for the marked onions first. When all of the marked onions have been used, mark the remaining onions.

Rotating Baking Sheets in the Oven

Often when you have two sheets of cookies in the oven at once, the recipe will direct you to reverse them from front to back and top to bottom. In the bustle of a holiday kitchen, however, it can be a challenge to keep track of the direction the pans should be facing in the oven. Pamela Vanderway of Canyon Country, Calif., keeps track by lining her cookie sheets with parchment paper and marking the front edge of the paper, even indicating which pan starts on top and which on the bottom. The notation will help you keep track of which edge goes where when you reverse the pans' positions.

Mess-Free Baker's Pan Coating

Accomplished and novice bakers alike know that the traditional method of greasing and flouring cake pans can be a bit of a nuisance. Jeanne Muller of Ann Arbor, Mich., says that she saves herself some work by combining the greasing and flouring steps. Mix 2 parts shortening with 1 part flour and brush this paste lightly onto the cake pans. This eliminates the messy step of dusting the pans with flour.

Easiest Shrimp Peeling

Between pulling off all the little legs and prying off the shells, peeling shrimp can be a tiresome chore. Over the years, though, Terrence Janericco of Boston, Mass., has perfected an easy, two-step method.

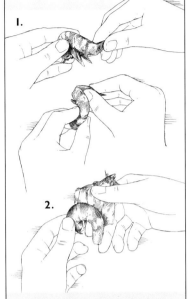

1. Holding the tail end of the shrimp with one hand and the opposite end of the shrimp with the other, bend the shrimp back and forth and side to side to split the shell.
2. Lift off the tail portion of the shell, then slide your thumb under the legs of the remaining portion and lift it off as well.

Turkey Turning

Although *Cook's Illustrated* usually recommends holding large wads of paper towels to turn a hot turkey during cooking, some cooks, including Rebecca Kingswood of Beachville, Ontario, feel more secure using oven mitts. Because she would rather not let the mitts get dirty and greasy, she slips clean plastic produce bags over the mitts to protect them.

Shrimp Fra Diavolo at Home

We get the best of the devil by flambéing the shrimp hot and fast
and sautéing the garlic long and slow.

∋ BY ADAM RIED AND MATTHEW CARD ∈

Fra diavolo, with its abundance of hot red pepper and attendant fiery nature, may be named for the devil—its literal translation from the Italian is "brother devil"—but it can do an angel's work for home cooks. How so? Shrimp fra diavolo, a seriously garlicky, spicy, winey tomato sauce studded with shrimp and served over pasta, takes less than 30 minutes from start to finish. It's a standard restaurant dish that easily makes the transition to home cooking.

That's not to say that this dish doesn't have its challenges, as we discovered after dining on shrimp fra diavolo in restaurants all over Boston's Italian neighborhood, the North End, and then trying published recipes back in the test kitchen. Overall, the sauces we sampled lacked depth and unity of flavor—backbone, if you will. The shrimp contributed little to the overall flavor of the sauce, serving merely as a bulky, lifeless garnish. Ditto the garlic, the flavor of which was often unpleasantly sharp, even acrid. In our ideal fra diavolo, not only would the shrimp themselves be firm, sweet, and well seasoned, but they would commit their flavor to the sauce as well.

The Shrimp

Determined as we were to maximize the flavor of the shrimp, they seemed like the natural starting point for our investigation. We made sauces with several species of shrimp (all medium-large, or 31 to 35 shrimp to the pound) and, as we had found in earlier tests with other shrimp dishes, we preferred Mexican Whites and Gulf Whites equally, followed by Black Tiger shrimp, which are the most widely available.

We learned during testing that the way the shrimp are cooked does have a tremendous effect not just on their texture and flavor but also on the overall flavor of the sauce. Most fra diavolo recipes we encountered add plain raw shrimp to the almost finished sauce; in effect, this means the shrimp are braised in the sauce. While these shrimp do remain tender, our tasters agreed that their flavor was barely developed. We tried seasoning the shrimp with olive oil, salt, and red pepper flakes and then searing them quickly in a very hot pan, adding them back to the sauce just before serving. Every taster noted that the shrimp themselves—and therefore the sauce—had a stronger, more unified flavor. The sear also benefited the red pepper flakes, as they

Flambéing the shrimp in cognac brings out its natural sweetness.

now contributed an earthy, toasty note to the sauce in addition to heat.

Though the searing helped, we wanted to coax still more flavor from the shrimp. Several of the fra diavolo recipes we consulted included cognac. Borrowing an idea from *Cook's* November/ December 2000 recipe for shrimp bisque, we added the cognac to the pan with the seared shrimp and flambéed it for a minute until the flame petered out. The combined forces of cognac and flame made a difference in the flavor. Not only could many tasters detect the spirit's own complexity, but they felt that the shrimp tasted a little stronger, too. This sauce had backbone, which we'd missed in the restaurant versions. All this and drama, too, in an easy, one-minute step.

Curious about why the shrimp flambéed in cognac tasted better, we contacted Dr. Susan Brewer in the department of food science and human nutrition at the University of Illinois in Urbana. She noted that brandy contains hundreds of compounds that undergo profound changes at the roughly 400-degree temperatures of a flambé. One possibility was isomerization, a process in

which heat changes the structure of sugar molecules. A session with the infrared thermometer in our test kitchen confirmed that the flame does burn at more than 400 degrees. We went on to test Brewer's suggestion by tasting side-by-side sauces in which the shrimp and cognac had been flambéed and not. Indeed, tasters noted a slightly fuller, sweeter flavor in the sauce in which the shrimp and cognac had been flambéed.

Sign of the Devil: Garlic and Chile

Fra diavolo's satanic associations arise from its liberal doses of garlic and spicy chile heat. We wanted enough garlic to make the devil proud, and we were frankly surprised to find that tasters agreed, preferring sauces that packed the wallop of almost an entire head, or about eight large cloves, over those with lesser amounts. But there was a caveat: Though we wanted the flavor of browned garlic, we had to mitigate the bitterness that often comes with it. We experimented with cutting the garlic in slices and slivers, grating it, pureeing it, and adding it to the sauce at various times, none of which eliminated the bitterness completely. Then we borrowed the stellar technique from the *Cook's* March/April 2001 recipe for pasta with garlic and oil (*aglio e olio*), wherein a similar quantity of garlic is sautéed slowly, over low heat, until it becomes golden, sticky, mellow, and nutty. What was good enough for aglio e olio proved good enough for fra diavolo; the bitterness was gone, and the sauce had acquired an even sweeter, deeper dimension. Taking another cue from the aglio e olio recipe, we reserved a tablespoon of raw garlic to add to the sauce at the end of cooking, along with a splash of raw olive oil. The tasters appreciated the bright, fruity, high flavor notes of these raw ingredients, which complemented the bass notes now grounding the sauce.

Chile adds fiery heat to fra diavolo. Traditionally, red pepper flakes get the job done (see "Red Pepper Flakes," right), but we also tested cayenne and hot pepper sauce, alone and in various combinations. Though tasters did not detect significant flavor differences, neither cayenne nor pepper sauce bested the traditional pepper flakes, so we stuck with the tried and true.

Our last tests focused on fra diavolo's two remaining major components: tomatoes and wine. We tested canned diced tomatoes (drained of excess liquid), canned crushed tomatoes, canned whole tomatoes (which we chopped by hand), and fresh tomatoes. The winner was drained canned diced tomatoes. The tasters were likewise united behind white wine over its rivals, red wine and white vermouth. The red wine was judged "muddy" and "sour" and the vermouth too herbal. We had been bothered by the compounded acidity of the tomatoes and wine, so we tried adding a little bit of sugar, which balanced the acidity perfectly. We finally had a top-notch shrimp fra diavolo—and the devil by the nose.

SHRIMP FRA DIAVOLO WITH LINGUINE
SERVES 4 TO 6

One teaspoon of red pepper flakes will give the sauce a little kick, but add more to suit your taste.

- 1 pound medium-large shrimp (preferably 31 to 35 count), peeled (and deveined, if desired), preferably Gulf or Mexican Whites
- 1 teaspoon crushed red pepper flakes (or more, to taste)
- 6 tablespoons extra-virgin olive oil
- 1½ tablespoons salt
- ¼ cup cognac or brandy
- 4 tablespoons minced or pressed (through garlic press) garlic (about 12 medium, 8 large, or 5 extralarge cloves)
- ½ teaspoon sugar
- 1 (28-ounce) can diced tomatoes, drained
- 1 cup medium-dry white wine, such as Sauvignon Blanc
- ¼ cup minced fresh parsley leaves
- 1 pound linguine or spaghetti

1. Bring 4 quarts water to rolling boil, covered, in large Dutch oven or stockpot.

2. While water is heating, heat 12-inch heavy-bottomed skillet over high heat for 4 minutes. Meanwhile, toss shrimp, half of red pepper flakes, 2 tablespoons olive oil, and ¾ teaspoon salt in medium bowl. Add shrimp to skillet and quickly spread in single layer; cook, without stirring, until bottoms of shrimp turn spotty brown, about 30 seconds. Off heat, stir to turn shrimp, and add cognac; let stand off heat until cognac warms slightly, about 5 seconds, and return pan to high heat. Wave lit match over skillet until cognac ignites; shake skillet until flames subside, transfer shrimp to medium bowl, and set aside.

3. Off heat, cool now-empty skillet 2 minutes; return to burner and reduce heat to low. Add 3 tablespoons olive oil and 3 tablespoons garlic; cook, stirring constantly, until garlic foams and is sticky and straw-colored, 7 to 10 minutes. Add remaining red pepper flakes, ¾ teaspoon salt, sugar, tomatoes, and wine; increase heat to medium-high, and simmer until thickened and fragrant, about 8 minutes. Stir in reserved shrimp and accumulated juices, remaining 1 tablespoon garlic, and parsley and simmer until shrimp have heated through, about 1 minute longer. Off heat, stir in remaining 1 tablespoon olive oil.

4. While sauce simmers, add linguine or spaghetti and remaining 1 tablespoon salt to boiling water, stir to separate pasta, cover, and cook until al dente; reserve ⅓ cup pasta cooking water and drain pasta. Transfer drained pasta back to now-empty Dutch oven or stockpot; add about ½ cup sauce (without shrimp) and 2 to 3 tablespoons reserved pasta cooking water; toss to coat. Divide pasta among warm serving bowls, top with a portion of sauce and shrimp, and serve immediately.

SCALLOPS FRA DIAVOLO WITH LINGUINE

The scallops, as well as the monkfish in the following recipe, leave more flavorful drippings in the skillet than the shrimp, and these drippings can make the garlic appear straw-colored before it is done cooking. Make sure that it is fragrant, looks sticky, and has cooked for the full 7 to 10 minutes.

Follow recipe for Shrimp Fra Diavolo with Linguine, replacing shrimp with 1 pound sea scallops, with small, crescent-shaped muscles removed.

MONKFISH FRA DIAVOLO WITH LINGUINE

Don't be alarmed if the monkfish sticks to the pan initially; it will loosen after the cognac has been added and flamed.

Follow recipe for Shrimp Fra Diavolo with Linguine, replacing shrimp with 1-pound monkfish fillet cut into 1-inch pieces.

TASTING: **Red Pepper Flakes**

Lending both name and fire to shrimp fra diavolo, dried, crushed red chile pepper (nicknamed *diavolochino* in Italian and referred to as crushed red pepper flakes in *Cook's* parlance) is fundamental to this dish. As we finished one bottle and opened the next during testing, we began to wonder just what, exactly, was in those bottles and whether brand mattered. We purchased four samples of crushed pepper and blind-tasted our way to a surprise answer.

Nearly identical in color and consistency, our line-up included three national brands—McCormick, Durkee, and Spice Islands—and a mail-ordered sample from Penzeys Spices. We infused each sample in vegetable oil, which we tasted plain and sprinkled on rice. Even the most astute tasters on our staff failed to detect appreciable differences, although several participants had a slight preference for the Penzeys brand, in which they detected a fresher flavor. Each sample tasted bright, with a clear, direct heat.

The manufacturing process is straightforward. Before the dried chiles are crushed, they are roasted to attain their characteristic ruddy tone and mildly smoky flavor. Research revealed that the varieties used most often for crushed red pepper are the California or New Mexico. Both are relatively mild, rating from 16,000 to 20,000 units on the Scoville heat scale, which is used to measure chiles' heat. (By comparison, jalapeños rate between 3,000 and 5,000 Scoville units, while superhot habaneros and Scotch Bonnets score above 200,000.) Penzeys was the only product in our lineup to note the variety on its label—which was California.

According to our tests, then, brand makes little or no difference when it comes to crushed red pepper flakes. What does make a difference, as we've discovered in the past, is freshness. Stale pepper flakes that have been sitting in your pantry for a year or more just won't provide the same bite as those from a newly opened bottle. —M.C.

Butternut Squash Soup

The secret to great butternut squash soup is steaming the flesh and then using the seeds to add flavor.

≥ BY RAQUEL PELZEL ≤

With its brash orange color, luxurious texture, and unapologetic squash flavor, butternut squash soup should be anything but meek. Unfortunately, many recipes bury the bold flavor of the butternut squash beneath chicken stock, an excess of cream or milk, or an overabundance of spices. The consistency of the soup is another problem, with some being too thin and others too thick, like a porridge. I set out to preserve the natural flavor of the squash while transforming it into a silky smooth soup.

The first step is to cook the squash. In the recipes I reviewed for this article, three methods prevailed: simmering, sautéing, and roasting. When simmering or sautéing the squash, the first step is to remove its tough, outer skin. Then the flesh must be cut into manageable pieces. After pureeing, the sautéed squash tasted gritty, and although the simmered squash had a smooth, satiny mouthfeel, I concluded that all of the peeling and chopping was too much work.

Infinitely simpler than simmering or sautéing is oven-roasting, for which the skin can be left intact. I rubbed the squash with oil and placed it in a hot oven. The roasting moved at a snail's pace, but it was easy to slip the squash meat away from the shell.

Happy with the simplicity of roasting, I pureed the squash with water. To my surprise, the puree was mealy and caramel-flavored. I gave roasting another chance, this time pureeing the squash with chicken broth in one batch and milk in a second batch. The chicken broth interfered with the flavor of the squash, while the milk made the puree taste like melted squash ice cream.

My testing had reached a dead end. Simmering the squash did it more justice than sautéing or roasting, but that meant peeling and cutting. Thinking that moist heat might be the key, I decided to try steaming. I placed cut, seeded, unpeeled squash in a steamer basket, lowered the basket into a 6-quart Dutch oven, covered the pot, and let the squash steam until tender. Not only did the squash cook in a mere half-hour, but the cooking liquid was perfumed with the squash's essence. After pureeing the squash with some of the cooking liquid, I found it neither mealy nor sugary. What's more, I had avoided peeling the squash by steaming the cut pieces and then scooping the softened flesh from the skin with a spoon, a process just as easy as roasting.

Now I needed to bolster the flavor of the puree, which consisted only of water and steamed squash. I tried three separate tests in which I sautéed garlic, onion, and shallots in butter and then left each in the pot during steaming. Before pureeing, I strained the sautéed bits from the squash-infused broth. The garlic and onion were overpowering, but the shallots complemented the squash nicely. I added salt, and while the soup now tasted good, it still lacked depth of flavor.

As I pored over my notes, it occurred to me that perhaps I was throwing away the answer to more squash flavor—the seeds and fibers. In my next test, instead of ditching the scooped-out remnants, I added them to the sautéing shallots and butter. In a matter of minutes, the room became fragrant with an earthy, sweet squash aroma, and the butter turned a brilliant shade of saffron. I finished the recipe by straining out the shallots, seeds, and pulp. The resulting soup was bold, intensely orange, and, for want of a better word, delightfully "squashy."

Finishing touches included sugar (white sugar added only sweetness, brown sugar added sweetness plus nuttiness) and heavy cream (some recipes call for as much as 2 cups, but I found that ½ cup was sufficient). Velvety and permeated with a heady squash flavor, the soup was thick but not custardy, sweet but not pie-like. Finally, a butternut squash soup worthy of its title.

SILKY BUTTERNUT SQUASH SOUP
MAKES 1½ QUARTS, SERVING 4 TO 6

If you don't own a folding steamer basket, a pasta pot with a removable pasta insert works well. Some nice garnishes for the soup are freshly grated nutmeg, a drizzle of balsamic vinegar, a sprinkle of paprika, or Buttered Cinnamon-Sugar Croutons (recipe follows).

- 4 tablespoons unsalted butter
- 2 medium shallots, minced (about 4 tablespoons)
- 3 pounds butternut squash (about 1 large), unpeeled, squash halved lengthwise, seeds and stringy fibers scraped with spoon and reserved (about ¼ cup), and each half cut into quarters
  Salt
- ½ cup heavy cream
- 1 teaspoon dark brown sugar

1. Heat butter in large Dutch oven over medium-low heat until foaming; add shallots and cook, stirring frequently, until softened and translucent, about 3 minutes. Add squash scrapings and seeds and cook, stirring occasionally, until fragrant and butter turns saffron color, about 4 minutes. Add 6 cups water and 1½ teaspoons salt to Dutch oven and bring to boil over high heat; reduce heat to medium-low, place squash cut-side down in steamer basket, and lower basket into pot. Cover and steam until squash is completely tender, about 30 minutes. Off heat, use tongs to transfer squash to rimmed baking sheet; reserve steaming liquid. When cool enough to handle, use large spoon to scrape flesh from skin into medium bowl; discard skin.

2. Pour reserved steaming liquid through mesh strainer into second bowl; discard solids in strainer. Rinse and dry Dutch oven.

3. In blender, puree squash and reserved liquid in batches, pulsing on low until smooth. Transfer puree to Dutch oven; stir in cream and brown sugar and heat over medium-low heat until hot. Add salt to taste; serve immediately.

BUTTERED CINNAMON-SUGAR CROUTONS

Adjust oven rack to middle position and heat oven to 350 degrees. Remove crusts from 2 slices thick-cut white sandwich bread and cut into ½-inch cubes (you should have about 1¼ cups). Toss cubes with 1 tablespoon melted butter. Combine 2 teaspoons sugar with ½ teaspoon cinnamon, and toss bread cubes with mixture. Spread cubes in even layer on parchment-lined baking sheet; bake until crisp, 8 to 10 minutes.

CURRIED BUTTERNUT SQUASH SOUP WITH CILANTRO YOGURT

Sprinkle lightly toasted pumpkin seeds over each bowl of soup for a nice textural contrast.

Follow recipe for Silky Butternut Squash Soup. While squash is steaming, stir together ¼ cup plain yogurt, 2 tablespoons minced fresh cilantro leaves, 1 teaspoon lime juice, and ⅛ teaspoon salt in small bowl. Add 1½ teaspoons curry powder to squash while pureeing in blender. Continue with recipe, garnishing each bowl of soup with a dollop of cilantro yogurt.

High-Roast Turkey

Could we high-roast a turkey without having to call the fire department or drying out the breast meat? We set out to discover the secret of two-hour roast turkey without the smoke.

⋟ BY BRIDGET LANCASTER ⋞

High-roast turkey is the holy grail of holiday cookery. Not even two hours goes by before the bird is roasted, and with picture-perfect skin. Yet the potential for the piercing shriek of a smoke alarm and torched breast meat are sufficient reason to approach this recipe with more than a pinch of trepidation.

It all started with Barbara Kafka, who introduced America to the high-roast turkey in her book *Roasting* (Morrow, 1995) with a recipe for turkey roasted in a 500-degree oven. In the past five years, we have performed many tests using the high-roast method with chicken, paying particular attention to the problems that high temperatures present for the home cook. We wondered if this technique could be applied to turkey. For this endeavor, we started by placing a 12-pound bird breast-side up on a V-rack, placing the rack in a roasting pan, and then roasting the turkey undisturbed until the thigh meat registered the optimum temperature of 175 degrees—in this case, just under two hours. As promised, there was crisp skin, but only over the breast meat, probably because the turkey was never rotated in the oven. In addition, the breast meat overcooked by the time the thighs were cooked. Even worse, the kitchen filled with black smoke caused by burnt pan drippings. Still, despite the seeming failure of my initial attempt, I was encouraged by the terrific-looking skin and the short amount of time needed to roast the turkey.

Whack 'n Roast

Tackling the problem of the unevenly cooked meat first, I started the turkey breast-side down, then flipped the turkey from side to side, finally finishing breast-side up. This method yielded evenly cooked meat, but since each side of the turkey spent less time face up, the skin was less than crisp.

In their natural form, turkeys are not designed to roast evenly. The vaulted bone structure of the breast promotes faster cooking, while the legs lag behind. I decided a turkey redesign was in order. I butterflied the turkey—a technique in which the

An unusual butchering technique gets a 12-pound turkey out of the oven in less than two hours and delivers supercrisp skin and evenly cooked meat.

backbone is removed and the bird is opened up and then flattened. Logic dictated that with the turkey basically in two dimensions, not three, and all of the meat facing up, the turkey would cook more evenly, and the skin would have equal time to crisp. As it turned out, however, butterflying a turkey is a whole lot harder than butterflying a chicken, a feat I'd accomplished many times with only a little help from a good pair of scissors to cut out the backbone. Because scissors are no match for the sturdier bone structure of a turkey, I found a good-quality chef's knife was necessary to cut along either side of the backbone. Even with a sharp blade, I still needed to apply some serious

pressure to cut through the thicker bones, sometimes literally hacking my way through. Once the backbone was removed, I found that the sturdy rib cage would not flatten under the heel of my hand, as a chicken's would. I reached for my heavy-duty rolling pin, placed the turkey breast-side up, and whacked the breastbone until it flattened—aggressive culinary therapy, if you will. All of this means getting quite physical, but there's no way around it if you want to turn out a perfect high-roast turkey.

I roasted the butterflied bird, and the results were outstanding. As the legs were now in contact with part of the breast, they helped prevent the white meat from overcooking. The thighs, which had been cooking more slowly than the breast meat, zoomed ahead, and by the time the breast meat was up to optimum temperature, 165 degrees, the thighs had reached their target temperature of 175 degrees. If it weren't for the billowing smoke, I would have shouted eureka!

"No Smoking"

The meat was evenly cooked and the skin was crisp, but what to do about the smoke? Filling the roasting pan with water to keep the fat from hitting the bottom of the hot pan solved the smoke problem but delivered soggy skin. (Much of the water evaporates, creating a humid environment, which is anathema to crisp skin.) After many tests, I finally hit on stuffing as the answer. Placed in the bottom of the roasting pan, where it could soak up the drippings, the stuffing could not only eliminate the smoking problem but also pick up outstanding flavor.

The question now was how best to construct this arrangement. A broiler pan was my first thought, since the slotted top would allow the drippings to reach the stuffing. But while the broiler pan top was the perfect size to hold the turkey, the bottom held only enough stuffing for four—not enough for seconds, not to mention leftovers. After going through the kitchen's battalion of roasting pans to use with the broiler pan top, I finally resorted to a disposable rectangular aluminum roasting pan. It was big enough to hold plenty of stuffing, sturdy enough to support the broiler pan top, and, best of all, it was easy to clean up—I just threw it away.

The recipe I had been using, the Cornbread and Sausage Stuffing from *Cook's* November/December 2000 issue, now needed some fine-tuning. After soaking up the fat and liquid from the drippings, our previously well-balanced recipe had become greasy. I lowered the fat in the recipe by reducing the amount of butter from 8 tablespoons to 2 and by cutting the amount of half-and-half and sausage in half. I also reduced the amount of chicken broth; the stuffing got plenty of moisture from the juices of the turkey.

Crisp Skin, Seasoned Meat, Good Gravy

With the mechanics of high-roast turkey in place, I was able to move on to flavor—or lack thereof. As we often do at *Cook's*, I turned to brining—a process in which the turkey is soaked in a solution of salt, sugar, and water. The salt in the solution makes its way into the meat and seasons it. The brine also adds moisture to the meat, which protects it from the effects of overcooking. But with this moisture comes soggy skin. Air-drying the brined turkey in the refrigerator the night before it was roasted (a technique perfected in our November/December 2000 issue) allowed the moisture in the skin to evaporate, and once again the roasted skin was crackling crisp.

So I had great turkey and stuffing, but what about the gravy? I had always made gravy using pan drippings, but now my stuffing soaked up those precious juices. Gravy made only from giblet stock was weak. The solution was the backbone, which I chopped into small pieces and threw into a roasting pan along with the neck and giblets, celery, carrot, onion, and garlic. I roasted the bones and vegetables at 450 degrees until well-browned, then placed them in a saucepan along with chicken broth, white wine, and water, and made a stock. After the stock cooled down, I skimmed off the fat and reserved it to make a roux—a mixture of flour

and fat used to thicken sauces or gravies. This gravy was big on flavor, and, by making it ahead, while the turkey was brining, I was able to cut down the amount of work necessary on Thanksgiving Day. Finally, I had delivered great skin, moist, flavorful meat, and superior dressing—roasted in less than two hours.

CRISP-SKIN HIGH-ROAST BUTTERFLIED TURKEY WITH SAUSAGE DRESSING
SERVES 10 TO 12

If you prefer not to brine your turkey, we recommend a kosher bird. The dressing can be made with cornbread, challah, or Italian bread, but note that they are not used in equal amounts. If you don't own a broiler pan top or if yours does not span the roasting pan, try a sturdy wire rack that rests comfortably on top of a 12 by 16-inch disposable roasting pan. Cover the rack with a large sheet of heavy-duty foil, fold excess foil under, spray it with nonstick cooking spray, and, with a paring knife, cut slits in the foil for fat drainage.

Turkey

2	cups kosher salt or 1 cup table salt
1	cup sugar
1	turkey (12 to 14 pounds gross weight), rinsed thoroughly; giblets, neck, and tailpiece removed and reserved for gravy (recipe follows), and turkey butterflied following illustrations 1 through 5, "Butterflying the Turkey," page 11
1	tablespoon unsalted butter, melted

Sausage Dressing

12	cups cornbread broken into 1-inch pieces (include crumbs), or 18 cups 1-inch challah or Italian bread cubes (from about 1½ loaves)
1¾	cups chicken stock or canned low-sodium chicken broth
1	cup half-and-half
2	large eggs, beaten lightly
12	ounces bulk pork sausage, broken into 1-inch pieces
3	medium onions, chopped fine (about 3 cups)
3	celery ribs, chopped fine (about 1½ cups)
2	tablespoons unsalted butter
2	tablespoons minced fresh thyme leaves
2	tablespoons minced fresh sage leaves
3	medium garlic cloves, minced or pressed through garlic press
1½	teaspoons salt
2	teaspoons ground black pepper

1. **TO BRINE THE TURKEY:** Dissolve salt and sugar in 2 gallons cold water in large stockpot or clean bucket. Add turkey and refrigerate or set in very cool spot (not more than 40 degrees) for 8 hours. (See page 17 for tips on brining outside of refrigerator.)

2. **FOR THE DRESSING:** While turkey brines, adjust one oven rack to upper-middle position

and second rack to lower-middle position and heat oven to 250 degrees. Spread bread in even layers on 2 rimmed baking sheets and dry in oven 40 to 50 minutes for challah or Italian bread or 50 to 60 minutes for cornbread.

3. Place bread in large bowl. Whisk together stock, half-and-half, and eggs in medium bowl; pour over bread and toss gently to coat so bread does not break into smaller pieces. Set aside.

4. Heat heavy-bottomed, 12-inch skillet over medium-high heat until hot, about 1½ minutes. Add sausage and cook, stirring occasionally, until sausage loses its raw color, 5 to 7 minutes. With slotted spoon, transfer sausage to medium bowl. Add about half of onions and celery to fat in skillet; sauté, stirring occasionally, until softened, about 5 minutes. Transfer onion mixture to bowl with sausage. Return skillet to heat and add 2 tablespoons butter; when foam subsides, add remaining celery and onions and sauté, stirring occasionally, until softened, about 5 minutes. Stir in thyme, sage, and garlic; cook until fragrant, about 30 seconds; add salt and pepper. Add this mixture along with sausage and onion mixture to bread and stir gently to combine, trying not to break bread into smaller pieces.

5. Spray disposable aluminum 12 by 16-inch roasting pan with nonstick cooking spray. Transfer dressing to roasting pan and spread in even layer. Cover pan with foil and refrigerate until needed.

6. **TO PREPARE TURKEY FOR ROASTING:** Set slotted broiler pan top on top of roasting pan with foil-covered dressing and spray with nonstick cooking spray; set roasting pan on baking sheet to support bottom. Remove turkey from brine and rinse well under cool running water. Following illustration 6 in "Butterflying the Turkey," page 11, position turkey on broiler pan top; thoroughly pat surface of turkey dry with paper towels. Refrigerate turkey and dressing, uncovered, 8 to 24 hours.

7. **TO ROAST TURKEY WITH DRESSING:** Adjust oven rack to lower-middle position and heat oven to 450 degrees. Remove broiler pan top with turkey and foil cover over roasting pan; replace broiler pan top with turkey. Brush turkey with melted butter. Place entire assembly with turkey in oven and roast until turkey skin is crisp and deep brown and instant-read thermometer reads 165 degrees when inserted in thickest part of breast and 175 degrees in thickest part of thigh, 80 to 100 minutes, rotating pan from front to back after 40 minutes.

8. Transfer broiler pan top with turkey to cutting board, tent loosely with foil, and let rest 20 minutes. Meanwhile, adjust oven rack to upper-middle position, place roasting pan with dressing back in oven, and bake until golden brown, about 10 minutes. Cool dressing 5 minutes, then spoon into bowl or onto turkey serving platter. Carve turkey (see page 11) and serve.

Turkey Timeline

1 TO 2 DAYS BEFORE SERVING:
- Butterfly and brine the turkey.
- Prepare the dressing.

8 TO 24 HOURS BEFORE SERVING:
- Air-dry the turkey.
- Prepare the gravy. (This can also be done earlier, while the turkey brines.)

2 HOURS BEFORE SERVING:
- Roast the turkey with dressing.

WHILE ROASTED TURKEY RESTS:
- Reheat the gravy.

1. Holding turkey upright with backbone facing front, use hacking motion to cut directly to left of backbone with chef's knife.

2. Continue cutting to left of backbone until cut is complete.

3. Holding backbone with one hand, hack directly to right of backbone until backbone is cut free.

4. Using scissors, cut between ribs and skin. Then cut out rib plates and remove any small pieces of bone.

5. Place turkey breast-side up on cutting board and cover with plastic wrap. With large rolling pin, whack breastbone until it cracks and turkey flattens.

6. After brining and rinsing, place turkey breast-side up on broiler pan top. Tuck wings under turkey. Push legs up to rest on lower portion of breast. Tie legs together.

1. With sharp carving knife, cut both leg quarters off turkey.

2. Cut both wing pieces off breast section.

3. Slice straight down along breastbone. Continue to slice down, with knife hugging rib bones, to remove breast meat from bones.

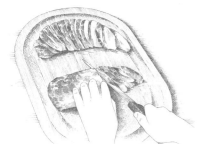

4. Beginning at narrow end of breast, slice meat across grain, about 1/4 inch thick.

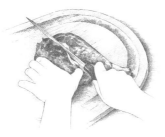

5. Pull thigh and drumstick apart and locate joint. Cut through joint, separating it into two pieces.

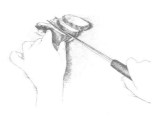

6. Remove largest pieces of meat from thigh and slice meat across grain, about 1/4 inch thick.

TURKEY GRAVY
MAKES ABOUT 1 QUART

To roast the trimmings and vegetables, it's best to use a roasting pan that can sit on the stovetop. If you don't own one, a broiler pan bottom will work; when setting it on the stovetop, however, use medium heat instead of high heat and add only half the amount of chicken broth before scraping up the drippings; add the other half of the chicken broth to the saucepan along with the wine.

Reserved turkey giblets, neck, and backbone, hacked into 2-inch pieces
1   medium carrot, cut into 1-inch pieces
1   celery rib, cut into 1-inch pieces
2   small onions, chopped coarse
6   garlic cloves, unpeeled
3½ cups chicken stock or canned low-sodium chicken broth (two 14½-ounce cans)
2   cups dry white wine
6   sprigs fresh thyme
¼   cup all-purpose flour
    Salt and ground black pepper

1. Heat oven to 450 degrees. Place turkey trimmings, carrot, celery, onions, and garlic in large flameproof roasting pan. Spray lightly with cooking spray and toss to combine. Roast, stirring every 10 minutes, until well-browned, 40 to 50 minutes.

2. Remove roasting pan from oven, and place over burner(s) set at high heat; add chicken stock and bring to boil, scraping up browned bits on bottom of pan with wooden spoon.

3. Transfer contents of roasting pan to large saucepan. Add wine, 3 cups water, and thyme; bring to boil over high heat. Reduce heat to low and simmer until reduced by half, about 1½ hours. Strain stock into large measuring cup or container. Cool to room temperature; cover with plastic wrap and refrigerate until fat congeals, at least 1 hour.

4. To finish gravy, skim fat from stock using soup spoon; reserve fat. Pour stock through fine-mesh strainer to remove remaining bits of fat; discard bits in strainer. Bring stock to simmer in medium saucepan over medium-high heat. In second medium saucepan, heat 4 tablespoons reserved turkey fat over medium-high heat until bubbling; whisk in flour and cook, whisking constantly, until combined and honey-colored, about 2 minutes. Continuing to whisk constantly, gradually add hot stock; bring to boil, then reduce heat to medium-low and simmer, stirring occasionally, until slightly thickened, about 5 minutes. Season to taste with salt and pepper and serve with turkey. (Can be refrigerated up to 3 days; reheat in medium saucepan over medium heat until hot, about 8 minutes.)

Homemade Crescent Rolls

These rich, buttery rolls can be prebaked, frozen, and then heated just before serving.

⇒ BY RAQUEL PELZEL ⇐

Perhaps the most popular dinner roll served at holiday tables is the crescent roll. It's a shame that the crescent rolls most Americans serve come from the supermarket refrigerator case—those diminutive arcs of prefab dough that taste artificial and go stale in minutes. I wanted to make rolls that were tender, rich, and easy enough to accommodate in an already jam-packed holiday schedule.

Restructuring the Roll

My first few attempts turned out rolls that were paunchy, boring, and flat-flavored. They were hard to handle, stuck to the countertop, and had much too much yeast. Many bread recipes try to speed up the rising time of a dough by using an excessive amount of yeast—sometimes as much as 2 tablespoons for 3 or 4 cups of flour. What you get besides speed is a cheesy flavored, lackluster roll that quickly goes stale. So a more modest quantity of yeast was going to be key.

For flour, my options included all-purpose and bread flour. Because crescent rolls should be soft and supple, bread flour, with a high protein content that makes for strong gluten development, would give the rolls more chew and a crustier crust than I wanted. I stuck with our kitchen workhorse, King Arthur unbleached all-purpose flour.

The next variable was the eggs. The working version of my recipe called for one. I compared batches made with one, two, and three eggs, and the latter was the winner. These rolls were soft and pillowy, with a lovely golden crumb.

Although I was using whole milk in my testing, I went on to compare three liquids side by side: water, skim milk, and whole milk. The whole milk rolls tasted the richest but were also the most dense. The rolls made with water lacked flavor and tenderness. The rolls made with skim milk were just right—flavorful and rich.

Up until now, I had been adding 8 tablespoons of softened butter in 1-tablespoon increments while the bread dough was kneaded in a standing mixer. Could these rolls absorb more fat without becoming heavy or greasy? I increased the butter in the next two batches by 4 and 8 tablespoons, respectively. It was clear that these rolls liked their fat; they took to 16 tablespoons

Refrigerating the shaped rolls overnight results in a delicately thin, flaky crust and a tender, flavor-packed interior.

of butter (two whole sticks) with aplomb.

However, adding the softened butter incrementally to the mixing dough was a messy and drawn-out process. To simplify things, I decided to melt the butter and add it to the dough along with the other ingredients. This worked perfectly. So far, I had developed a better-than-average crescent roll recipe, but the crust was not sufficiently flaky, and I was having difficulty rolling out and shaping this sticky dough.

The Big Chill

The easiest way to handle a butter-laden, sticky dough is to let it rest in the refrigerator before rolling it out. This combats two problems. First, the gluten in the dough relaxes, allowing the dough to be rolled without "bucking," or snapping back into shape after rolling. Second, the butter in the dough solidifies, making the dough easier to roll and less sticky to handle.

I had intended to refrigerate the risen and punched-down dough for a couple of hours, but I forgot about it until the next morning. Panic-stricken, I took the dough out of the refrigerator and easily rolled it into a long sheet, cut it, and shaped the pieces into little bundles. After allowing the rolls to rise at room temperature for about an hour, I popped them in the oven. When

they were done, I noticed the difference immediately—blisters! When I bit into a roll, the crust snapped and flaked. This was the kind of crescent roll I had been trying to achieve all along, with flavor and a flaky crust.

To find out why an overnight chill had paid off, I called Maggie Glezer, a baker certified by the American Institute of Baking. She explained that when dough is chilled for a long time—a process bakers call retarding—acetic acid builds up in the dough, giving it a richer flavor as well as a blistered crust. Carl Hoseney, professor emeritus in the department of grain science and industry at Kansas State University, added that blisters are also caused by gases escaping from the dough during retardation.

With these points in mind, I set out to see if a longer refrigerator stay would be even better. I made another batch of dough, let it rise at room temperature, punched it down, and put it in the fridge. The next morning, I formed the dough into crescents, then, instead of letting the rolls rise for an hour and baking them, I put them back in the fridge. The following day, I let the rolls lose their chill at room temperature, then baked them. The crust was even more blistered than before. Next I tried chilling the rolls for three nights; these were better still, with an excellent flavor and a stunning, crackled crust. What I also liked about these rolls is that all you need do on the day they are served is to let them rise one last time and bake them—creating no dirty dishes and taking up no precious workspace.

Now I wondered if the rolls could be frozen and baked off as needed. Because raw dough can't be frozen (the cold temperature kills some of the yeast, affecting both flavor and texture), I prebaked the rolls until they were about three-quarters done, then cooled and froze them. One week later, I defrosted them at room temperature and then finished the baking. Not one taster could tell the difference between these rolls and a batch that had been baked from start to finish without freezing.

All I had to do now was tweak the baking method. Up until this point, I had been baking the rolls at 375 degrees from start to finish. But

STEP-BY-STEP | SHAPING THE ROLLS

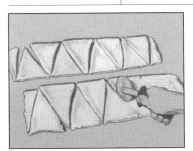

1. Roll dough to a 20 by 13-inch rectangle; use a pizza wheel to trim edges. Cut dough in half lengthwise, then cut 16 triangles, as illustrated.

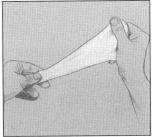

2. Elongate each triangle of dough before rolling crescent, stretching it an additional 2 to 3 inches in length.

3. Starting at wide end, gently roll up dough, ending with pointed tip on bottom.

during my research on retarding dough, I learned that boosting the oven temperature to 425 degrees for the initial bake, then lowering it to 350 degrees when the rolls were just starting to color, would improve the rolls' oven spring. (*Oven spring*, a term used by professional bakers, defines the dramatic increase in size caused when bread gets that initial blast of heat from the oven.) The 425/350 combination worked, making the rolls pleasantly larger and loftier.

Another technique I had read about purported that adding steam to the baking bread would help with oven spring and encourage formation of a thin and delicate crust. After placing the rolls on the lower-middle rack, I poured 1 cup of hot tap water onto a preheated baking sheet on the lowest rack. The burst of steam, combined with the high oven temperature, gave the rolls an even higher rise and turned the crust into a thin and still flakier shell. Now I had a dramatic-looking roll with great flavor, a lovely, tender crumb, and a delicate crust. I bit into a crescent roll with the satisfaction of knowing that making it would be just as easy to fit into a busy holiday schedule as popping open a can.

CRESCENT ROLLS
MAKES 16 ROLLS

When you bake the crescent rolls, make sure the light in the oven is switched off. If the light is on after you shut the oven door, the burst of steam may cause the bulb to crack. You can make the dough up to 4 days ahead of time or even partially bake the rolls and freeze them for longer storage. To do this, begin baking the rolls as instructed, but let them bake at 350 degrees for only 4 minutes, or until the tops and bottoms brown slightly. Remove them from the oven and let cool. Place the partially baked rolls in a single layer inside a zipper-lock bag and freeze. When you're ready to serve them, defrost at room temperature and place them in a preheated 350-degree oven for 12 to 16 minutes. You can freeze the rolls for up to 1 month.

Dough
- ¾ cup skim milk
- 16 tablespoons (2 sticks) unsalted butter, cut into 16 pieces
- ¼ cup sugar
- 3 large eggs
- 3½ cups (17.5 ounces) unbleached high-protein all-purpose flour (such as King Arthur) or 4 cups (20 ounces) unbleached all-purpose flour (such as Pillsbury or Gold Medal), plus extra for work surface
- 1 teaspoon instant or rapid-rise yeast
- 1½ teaspoons salt

Egg Wash
- 1 egg white beaten with 1 teaspoon water

1. Microwave milk, butter, and sugar in 4-cup microwave-safe measuring cup until butter is mostly melted and mixture is warm (about 110 degrees on instant-read thermometer), about 1½ minutes (alternatively, heat milk, butter, and sugar in small saucepan over medium heat until warm; remove from heat). Whisk to dissolve and blend in sugar. Beat eggs lightly in medium bowl; add about one-third of warm milk mixture, whisking to combine. When bottom of bowl feels warm, add remaining milk mixture, whisking to combine.

2. Combine flour and yeast in bowl of standing mixer fitted with paddle attachment; mix on lowest speed to blend, about 15 seconds. With mixer running, add milk and egg mixture in steady stream; mix on low speed until loose, shiny dough forms (you may also see satiny webs as dough moves in bowl), about 1 minute. Increase speed to medium and beat 1 minute; add salt slowly and continue beating until stronger webs form, about 3 minutes longer. (Note: Dough will remain loose rather than forming a neat, cohesive mass.) Transfer dough to large bowl, cover bowl with plastic wrap, and place in warm, draft-free spot until dough doubles in bulk and surface feels tacky, about 3 hours.

3. Line rimmed baking sheet with plastic wrap. Sprinkle dough with flour (no more than 2 tablespoons) to prevent sticking, and punch down. Turn dough onto floured work surface and form into rough rectangle shape. Transfer rectangle to lined baking sheet, cover with plastic wrap, and refrigerate overnight.

4. Turn dough rectangle onto lightly floured work surface and, following illustrations 1 through 3 (above), roll and shape. Arrange crescents in four rows on parchment-lined rimmed baking sheet; wrap baking sheet with plastic wrap, and refrigerate at least 2 hours or up to 3 days.

5. Remove baking sheet with chilled rolls from refrigerator, unwrap, and cover with overturned large disposable roasting pan. (Alternatively, place sheet pan inside large garbage bag.) Let rise until crescents feel slightly tacky and soft and have lost their chill, 45 to 60 minutes. Meanwhile, turn oven light off, place rimmed baking sheet on lowest rack, adjust second rack to lower-middle position, and heat oven to 425 degrees.

6. With pastry brush, lightly dab risen crescent rolls with egg wash. Transfer baking sheet with rolls to lower-middle rack and, working quickly, pour 1 cup hot tap water into hot baking sheet on lowest rack. Close door immediately and bake 10 minutes; reduce oven temperature to 350 degrees and continue baking until tops and bottoms of rolls are deep golden brown, 12 to 16 minutes longer. Transfer rolls to wire rack, cool for 5 minutes, and serve warm.

TASTING: **Supermarket Dinner Rolls**

Is there a supermarket dinner roll worth serving (and eating)? We lined up six readily available brands, plus our homemade roll, and gave them a try. It was no surprise that our crescent roll put the others to shame. Placing a distant second was Pillsbury's crescent roll, defined by tasters as "sweet" and "wheaty," but also "greasy" and "doughy." Almost tying with the Doughboy was our local supermarket's refrigerated crescent roll, judged by tasters

as having an "artificial," "movie popcorn" flavor. The other contenders included Rhode's White Roll Dough (called "gummy" and "squishy"), Bread du Jour Italian rolls ("vapid and offensive"), Sunbeam Brown 'n Serve rolls ("sour"), and J. J. Nissen Brown 'n Serve rolls (likened to "cotton balls" and "gym socks"). —R.P.

A distant second to homemade

Introducing Breakfast Strata

The right blend of four staple ingredients—bread, eggs, cheese, and cream—
produces a savory breakfast casserole that's simple and satisfying.

≥ BY ADAM RIED ≤

What's quicker than quiche, sturdier than soufflé, and combines the best qualities of both? The answer is strata, a layered casserole that in its most basic form comprises bread, eggs, cheese, and milk or cream. Layered among them are flavorful fillings that provide both substance and character, and the result is, in essence, a golden brown, puffed, hearty, savory bread pudding. Strata is easy to prepare, can be made ahead, and feeds a crowd for a holiday—or a garden-variety weekend—breakfast or brunch.

But strata is not without its pitfalls. In our experience, strata often suffers from largesse. Many of the recipes we sampled were too rich for breakfast, with a belly-busting overabundance of custard. And then there were the fillings, where an everything-but-the-kitchen-sink approach led to wet, sagging, overwrought stratas. One we sampled early on included mustard, garlic, nutmeg, marinated artichoke hearts, raw green peppers, cherry tomatoes, ham, Parmesan, fontina, and goat cheese. Such overindulgence not only sends unlucky diners scrambling for Maalox but turns a simple, workhorse dish into a self-parody. Our goal was to scale back strata, keeping it just rich enough while choosing flavorings and fillings that would blend into the chorus, not hog the spotlight.

Strata is a layered, savory bread pudding. Here the filling is spinach and Gruyère.

Lay the Foundation

Bread is the foundation of strata. Although sliced white sandwich bread was the most common choice, recipes also called for Italian, French, sourdough, multigrain, rye, pumpernickel, challah, focaccia, and even hamburger and hot dog buns. We tried them all and preferred supermarket Italian and French breads for their strong crumb and neutral flavor. Since no one objected to the crust, we left it in place. While many recipes specified cubes of bread, we preferred slices because they added to the layered effect of the casserole. Slices ½ inch thick were best; anything thicker was too chewy, and thin slices just melted

away. We also preferred the texture of stale bread (or fresh bread dried in the oven) and found that buttering the slices added richness and flavor.

Our next consideration was the custard that binds the bread. In a battery of tests, tasters were divided between mixtures with equal parts dairy and egg and those with twice as much dairy as egg. The solution was to meet in the middle, adding a little extra dairy to the 50/50 mixture. As for the dairy, we tested low-fat and whole milk, half-and-half, and heavy cream both alone and in combinations. The half-and-half was the clear winner.

Flavor and Fill

As a basic flavoring, sautéed shallots won over onions and garlic. We had a surprise in store when we tested another flavoring common to a few strata recipes—namely, white wine. It showed promise, lightening the flavor of the whole dish. But it also imparted an unwelcome boozy flavor. We corrected this problem by applying a technique used in sauce making—reduction—which cooked off the alcohol and concentrated flavor. The reduced wine brightened the flavor of the whole dish considerably.

One last observation about the most basic seasonings, salt and pepper. Strata required a generous dose of each, and seasoning both custard and filling individually and liberally was the most

effective way to bring all the flavors into focus.

Even with the right basic ingredients in the right proportions, test after test proved that high-moisture fillings such as sausage and raw vegetables ruined the strata's texture. Moisture leached into the casserole, leaving it wet enough to literally slosh and ooze when cut. To correct this problem, we took to sautéing all filling ingredients until they looked dry in the pan, evaporating moisture that would otherwise end up in the strata. Whatever your filling choice, this critical step will make the difference between a moist, tender dish and one that resembles a wet sponge mop.

Assemble and Bake

One of strata's charms, especially during the busy holiday season, is that it can—in fact, most recipes claim it should—be assembled well ahead of time. We rested assembled stratas overnight, for four hours, for one hour, and not at all. Only the fresh-made strata, which was noticeably less cohesive than the rested versions, failed to make the cut. Once assembled, strata can be rested anywhere from one hour to overnight.

A test kitchen colleague suggested weighing down the assembled strata during its rest, and this step had a dramatic effect. Without exception, the weighted stratas had a perfectly even, custardy texture throughout. In stratas rested without the weight, it was not unusual to encounter a bite of bread that had not been fully penetrated with custard.

Once in the oven, the strata cooked much more evenly in a wide, shallow baking dish than in the deep soufflé dish called for in many recipes. Lowering the baking temperature from the widely recommended 350 degrees to 325 was an additional tactic we adopted to even out the cooking. Baking the strata until the top was crisp and golden brown was another common recommendation, but we found that this often signified an overcooked, overly firm, and even rubbery interior. We found it best to remove the strata from the oven when the top was just beginning to brown and the center was barely puffed and still slightly loose when the pan was gently jiggled. With just a five-minute rest, the center finished cooking from residual heat, reaching the perfectly set, supple texture we prized.

BREAKFAST STRATA WITH SPINACH AND GRUYÈRE
MAKES ONE 8 BY 8-INCH STRATA, SERVING 6

To weigh down the assembled strata, we found that two 1-pound boxes of brown or powdered sugar, laid side by side over the plastic-covered surface, make ideal weights. A gallon-sized zipperlock bag filled with about 2 pounds of sugar or rice also works. This recipe and those that follow double easily; use a 9 by 13-inch baking dish greased with only 1½ tablespoons butter and increase the baking times (see recipes for specific timing). Though each strata calls for a certain type of cheese, feel free to substitute any good melting cheese, such as Havarti, sharp cheddar, or colby.

8–10 (½-inch thick) slices supermarket French or Italian bread (6–7 ounces)
5 tablespoons unsalted butter, softened
4 medium shallots, minced (about ½ cup)
1 (10-ounce) package frozen chopped spinach, thawed and squeezed dry
Salt and ground black pepper
½ cup medium-dry white wine, such as Sauvignon Blanc
6 ounces Gruyère cheese, grated (about 1½ cups)
6 large eggs
1¾ cups half-and-half

1. Adjust oven rack to middle position and heat oven to 225 degrees. Arrange bread in single layer on large baking sheet and bake until dry and crisp, about 40 minutes, turning slices over halfway through drying time. (Alternatively, leave slices out overnight to dry.) When cooled, butter slices on one side with 2 tablespoons butter; set aside.
2. Heat 2 tablespoons butter in medium nonstick skillet over medium heat. Sauté shallots until fragrant and translucent, about 3 minutes; add spinach and salt and pepper to taste and cook, stirring occasionally, until spinach and shallots are combined, about 2 minutes. Transfer to medium bowl; set aside. Add wine to skillet, increase heat to medium-high, and simmer until reduced to ¼ cup, 2 to 3 minutes; set aside.
3. Butter 8-inch square baking dish with remaining 1 tablespoon butter; arrange half the buttered bread slices, buttered-side up, in single layer in dish. Sprinkle half of spinach mixture, then ½ cup grated cheese evenly over bread slices. Arrange remaining bread slices in single layer over cheese; sprinkle remaining spinach mixture and another ½ cup cheese evenly over bread. Whisk eggs in medium bowl until combined; whisk in reduced wine, half-and-half, 1 teaspoon salt, and pepper to taste. Pour egg mixture evenly over bread layers; cover surface flush with plastic wrap, weigh down (see note), and refrigerate at least 1 hour or up to overnight.
4. Remove dish from refrigerator and let stand at room temperature 20 minutes. Meanwhile, adjust oven rack to middle position and heat oven to 325 degrees. Uncover strata and sprinkle remaining ½ cup cheese evenly over surface; bake until both edges and center are puffed and edges have pulled away slightly from sides of dish, 50 to 55 minutes (or about 60 minutes for doubled recipe). Cool on wire rack 5 minutes; serve.

BREAKFAST STRATA WITH SAUSAGE, MUSHROOMS, AND MONTEREY JACK

8–10 (½-inch thick) slices supermarket French or Italian bread (6–7 ounces)
3 tablespoons unsalted butter, softened
8 ounces bulk breakfast sausage, crumbled
3 medium shallots, minced (about ⅓ cup)
8 ounces white button mushrooms, cleaned and quartered
Salt and ground black pepper
½ cup medium-dry white wine, such as Sauvignon Blanc
6 ounces Monterey Jack cheese, grated (about 1½ cups)
6 large eggs
1¾ cups half-and-half
2 tablespoons minced fresh parsley leaves

Follow recipe for Breakfast Strata with Spinach and Gruyère through step 1. Fry sausage in medium nonstick skillet over medium heat, breaking sausage apart with wooden spoon, until sausage has lost raw color and begins to brown, about 4 minutes; add shallots and cook, stirring frequently, until softened and translucent, about 1 minute longer. Add mushrooms to skillet, and cook until mushrooms no longer release liquid, about 6 minutes; transfer mixture to medium bowl and season to taste with salt and pepper. Reduce wine as directed in step 2; continue with recipe from step 3, adding parsley to egg mixture along with salt and pepper and substituting sausage mixture for spinach. (For doubled recipe, increase baking time to about 1 hour 20 minutes.)

BREAKFAST STRATA WITH POTATOES, ROSEMARY, AND FONTINA

8–10 (½-inch thick) slices supermarket French or Italian bread (6–7 ounces)
5 tablespoons unsalted butter, softened
Salt and ground black pepper
12 ounces new potatoes (about 2 medium), cut into ½-inch cubes
3 medium shallots, minced (about ⅓ cup)
2 medium garlic cloves, minced or pressed through garlic press
1½ teaspoons minced fresh rosemary leaves
½ cup medium-dry white wine, such as Sauvignon Blanc
6 ounces fontina cheese, grated (about 1½ cups)
6 large eggs
1¾ cups half-and-half
2 tablespoons minced fresh parsley leaves

Follow recipe for Breakfast Strata with Spinach and Gruyère through step 1. Bring 1 quart water to boil in medium saucepan over medium-high heat; add 1 teaspoon salt and boil potatoes until just tender when pierced with tip of paring knife, about 4 minutes; drain potatoes. Heat 2 tablespoons butter in medium nonstick skillet over medium heat and cook potatoes until just beginning to brown, about 10 minutes. Add shallots and cook, stirring frequently, until softened and translucent, about 1 minute longer; add garlic and rosemary and cook until fragrant, about 2 minutes longer. Transfer mixture to medium bowl; season to taste with salt and pepper and set aside. Reduce wine as directed in step 2; continue with recipe from step 3, adding parsley to egg mixture along with salt and pepper and substituting potato mixture for spinach. (For doubled recipe, increase baking time to about 1 hour 10 minutes.)

STEP-BY-STEP | ASSEMBLING THE STRATA

1. Layer the bread and filling in the baking dish.

2. Pour the custard mixture evenly over the assembled layers.

3. Cover the surface flush with plastic wrap and weight the strata.

The Basics of Brining

How salt, sugar, and water can improve texture and flavor in lean meats, poultry, and seafood. BY JULIA COLLIN

Why are some roast turkeys dry as sawdust while others boast meat that's firm, juicy, and well seasoned? The answer is brining. Soaking a turkey in a brine—a solution of salt (and often sugar) and a liquid (usually water)—provides it with a plump cushion of seasoned moisture that will sustain it throughout cooking. The turkey will actually gain a bit of weight—call it, for lack of a better phrase, water retention—that stays with it through the cooking process. This weight gain translates into moist meat; the salt and sugar in the brine translate into seasoned, flavorful meat. And this applies to all likely candidates for brining (see below). For a complete understanding of the process, read on.

HOW IT WORKS

Brining works in accordance with two principles, called diffusion and osmosis, that like things to be kept in equilibrium. When brining a turkey, there is a greater concentration of salt and sugar outside of the turkey (in the brine) than inside the turkey (in the cells that make up its flesh). The law of *diffusion* states that the salt and sugar will naturally flow from the area of greater concentration (the brine) to lesser concentration (the cells). There is also a greater concentration of water, so to speak, outside of the turkey than inside. Here, too, the water will naturally flow from the area of greater concentration (the brine) to lesser concentration (the cells). When water moves in this fashion, the process is called *osmosis*. Once inside the cells, the salt and, to a lesser extent, the sugar cause the cell proteins to unravel, or *denature*. As the individual proteins unravel, they become more likely to interact with one another. This interaction results in the formation of a sticky matrix that captures and holds moisture. Once exposed to heat, the matrix gels and forms a barrier that keeps much of the water from leaking out as the meat cooks. Thus you have a turkey that is both better seasoned and much more moist than when you started.

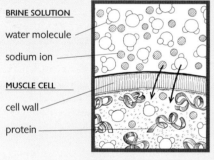 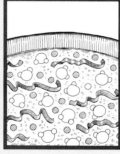 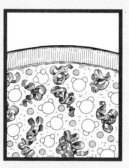

BRINE SOLUTION
water molecule
sodium ion

MUSCLE CELL
cell wall
protein

BEGINNING OF BRINING   **AFTER BRINING**   **AFTER COOKING**

TWO TYPES OF SALT FOR BRINING

Both table salt and kosher salt can be used to make a brine. We prefer kosher salt because it has a cleaner flavor than table salt (which usually contains iodine and anti-caking agents that can affect flavor) and because it has an airier structure, which gives it a higher propensity to dissolve. Essentially, kosher salt is less salty than table salt. A cup of table salt weighs about 10 ounces, while a cup of kosher salt (depending on the precise crystalline structure of the brand purchased) weighs between 5 and 8 ounces. To simplify the math, we use Diamond Crystal Kosher Salt, which weighs 5 ounces per cup, making it exactly half as strong as table salt. If you buy another brand of kosher salt, you may need to adjust the amount called for in the chart on page 17. For instance, Morton Kosher Salt weighs 7.7 ounces per cup. Use 1 1/2 cups of this kosher salt (not 2 cups) to replace 1 cup of table salt.

KOSHER SALT   **TABLE SALT**

THE BEST CANDIDATES FOR BRINING

Lean and often mildly flavored meats with a tendency to overcook—such as chicken, turkey, and pork—are perfect candidates for brining, which leaves them plump and seasoned. Many types of seafood also take well to brining, especially when they are subjected to cooking methods that cause extreme moisture loss. For instance, we don't brine salmon fillets before grilling (the fish has plenty of fat and flavor and won't dry out if pulled from the grill when still translucent in the center). However, when grill-roasting a whole side of salmon, brining allows the fish to spend considerable time on the grill, picking up smoke flavor without becoming dry. Shrimp, which is extremely lean and often mushy, is another good choice for brining (the brine actually firms the shrimp).

CORNISH HEN: whole, butterflied
CHICKEN: whole, parts, butterflied

PORK: loin, tenderloin, chops, fresh ham

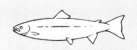

TURKEY: whole, breast, parts, butterflied

SEAFOOD: whole side of salmon (when grill-roasting or smoking), shrimp

In contrast, beef and lamb do not benefit from brining. Unlike poultry and pork, these meats are generally eaten rare or medium-rare and are therefore cooked to a relatively low internal temperature. As a consequence, they do not lose as much of their natural moisture as poultry or pork, which are generally cooked to higher internal temperatures. Beef and lamb also contain more fat, which makes them more flavorful and helps to keep them moist. For many of the same reasons, gamier, fattier birds, such as duck and squab, don't benefit from brining.

Illustration: John Burgoyne

UNIVERSAL FORMULA FOR BRINING

Since we brined our first turkey several years ago, we have been captivated by the benefits of brining. Brines are featured in many of our recipes, which, given the particular time constraints and the nature of the food being brined, recommend a rather wide variety of formulas. We decided to get scientific and come up with a single, all-purpose formula. To start, we reviewed all of our brining recipes and calculated an average ratio of water to salt to sugar as well as an average brining time per pound of meat. Using this new standard formula, we cooked our way through various cuts of poultry and pork and several types of seafood, and it worked in all but a few situations. High roasting (roasting at 450 to 500 degrees), broiling, and high-heat grilling all require a brine with less sugar to ensure the skin or exterior won't burn. (After brining a turkey or fresh ham, rinse well to remove any remaining sugar.) To keep the flavors of the high-heat brine balanced, we also reduced the amount of salt.

HOW TO BRINE

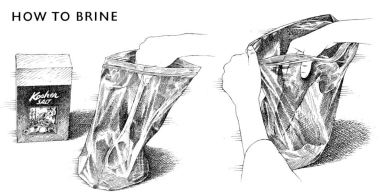

1. Mix cold water, salt, and sugar in brining vessel and stir to dissolve salt and sugar.

2. Immerse food in brine, seal, and refrigerate. (If not refrigerating, add ice packs before covering.)

TYPE OF BRINE	COLD WATER	SALT *	SUGAR	AMOUNT OF BRINE	TIME **
Basic	I quart	• ½ cup Diamond Crystal kosher • ¼ cup + 2 tablespoons Morton kosher • ¼ cup table	½ cup	I quart per pound of food not to exceed 2 gallons brine	I hour per pound, but not less than 30 minutes or more than 8 hours
High-Heat Roasting, Broiling, or High-Heat Grilling	I quart	• ¼ cup Diamond Crystal kosher • 3 tablespoons Morton kosher • 2 tablespoons table	2 tablespoons	I quart per pound of food, not to exceed 2 gallons brine	I hour per pound, but not less than 30 minutes or more than 8 hours

*see page 16 if using kosher salt **when brining multiple items, time based on weight of single item (for example, use weight of 1 of 4 pork chops being brined)

TOOLS OF THE TRADE

From plastic zipper-lock bags that fit on the shelf of the refrigerator to a self-contained cooler chilled with ice packs and stored in a cool garage or cellar, brining vessels come in all shapes and sizes. When brining in coolers or large containers, it may be necessary to weigh the food down with a wide, heavy object such as a dinner plate or soup bowl. This helps keep the food fully immersed in the brine.

PLASTIC ZIPPER-LOCK BAGS (1- or 2-gallon)
USE FOR: Chicken parts, pork tenderloin and chops, shrimp

CAMBRO* OR TUPPERWARE CONTAINERS
USE FOR: Cornish hen (whole or butterflied), chicken (whole or butterflied)
*see Resources on page 32 for information

COOLER/WASHTUB
USE FOR: Turkey, pork loin, fresh ham, whole side of salmon

ICE PACKS
The refrigerator keeps a brine at the ideal temperature of 40 degrees. Ice packs keep the temperature down when refrigerator space is at a premium or the brining vessel is especially large.

HANGING IT OUT TO DRY

Brining does have one negative effect on chicken and turkey: Adding moisture to the skin as well as the flesh can prevent the skin from crisping when cooked. We found that air-drying, a technique used in many Chinese recipes for roast duck, solves this problem. Letting brined chicken and turkey dry uncovered in the refrigerator allows surface moisture to evaporate, making the skin visibly more dry and taut and therefore promoting crispness when cooked. Although this step is optional, if crisp skin is a goal, it's worth the extra time. For best results, air-dry whole brined birds overnight. Brined chicken parts can be air-dried for several hours.

Transfer the brined bird to a heavy-duty cooling rack set over a rimmed baking sheet, pat the bird dry with paper towels, and refrigerate. The rack lifts the bird off the baking sheet, allowing air to circulate freely under the bird.

Make-Ahead Holiday Green Beans

Cooking the beans ahead saves time when you need it most— in the final moments before dinner.

Every cook who has prepared a big holiday meal knows the swell of frenzied activity in the final moments before serving—the last thing you want to deal with is yet another last-minute side dish. To alleviate this problem, we set out to find the best method for cooking green beans ahead of time, putting them in need of only a quick finishing touch before being served.

In the test kitchen, we blanched, steamed, and braised the beans and concluded that blanching—immersing them briefly in boiling water—was the way to go for two reasons. First, blanched beans cook more evenly than steamed ones, and second, they are easier to salt as they cook, which means they become more deeply seasoned.

If the finished, dressed beans are to arrive at the table with a properly crisp-tender texture, it is especially important not to overcook them. Shocking the beans—plunging them in ice water—halts their cooking abruptly and completely. After that the beans can be refrigerated. To find out how long they would hold in the refrigerator, we blanched, shocked, and dried a big batch of beans, stored them in the refrigerator, and sampled them twice a day to test for flavor and texture retention. None of our tasters noted any deterioration until the morning of the fourth day, so we concluded that it is fine to blanch the beans up to three days before serving.

As we developed the butter sauces below, we reheated plenty of chilled beans and learned a thing or two about the process. Most important was to add a little bit of water—1/4 cup will do—to the pan with the beans. This small amount comes to a boil quickly and evaporates almost completely, helping to heat the beans through in just a minute or two.

BLANCHED GREEN BEANS

To blanch, dress, and serve the beans without holding them first in the refrigerator, increase the blanching time to 5 to 6 minutes and don't bother shocking them in ice water. Instead, quickly arrange the warm beans on a serving platter and top with the sauce you've prepared as the beans blanch.

- 1 teaspoon salt
- 1 pound green beans, stem ends snapped off

Bring 2½ quarts water to boil in large saucepan over high heat; add salt and green beans, return to boil, and cook until beans are bright green and crisp-tender, 3 to 4 minutes. Meanwhile, fill large bowl with ice water. Drain beans in colander and transfer beans immediately to ice water. When beans no longer feel warm to touch, drain in colander again and dry thoroughly with paper towels. Transfer beans to gallon-sized zipper-lock bag, seal, and refrigerate until ready to use, up to 3 days.

GREEN BEANS WITH SAUTÉED SHALLOTS AND VERMOUTH
SERVES 4 TO 6

Tongs are the tool best suited to tossing the beans in the pan and arranging them on the platter.

- 4 tablespoons unsalted butter
- 4 large shallots, sliced thin (about 2 cups)
- 1 recipe Blanched Green Beans
   Salt and ground black pepper
- 2 tablespoons dry vermouth

1. Heat 2 tablespoons butter in small skillet over medium heat until foaming; add shallots and cook, stirring frequently, until golden brown, fragrant, and just crisp around the edges, about 10 minutes. Set skillet aside.

2. Heat 1/4 cup water and beans in 12-inch skillet over high heat; cook, tossing frequently, until beans are warmed through, 1 to 2 minutes. Season with salt and pepper to taste and arrange neatly on warm serving platter.

3. Meanwhile, return skillet with shallots to high heat, stir in vermouth, and bring to simmer. Whisk in remaining 2 tablespoons butter, 1 tablespoon at a time; season with salt and pepper to taste. Top beans with shallots and sauce and serve immediately.

GREEN BEANS WITH TOASTED HAZELNUTS AND BROWN BUTTER
SERVES 4 TO 6

- 4 tablespoons unsalted butter
- ½ cup skinned hazelnuts (about 2½ ounces), chopped fine and toasted in small skillet over medium heat until just fragrant, 3 to 4 minutes
   Salt and ground black pepper
- 1 recipe Blanched Green Beans

1. Heat butter in small heavy-bottomed saucepan over medium heat and cook, swirling frequently, until butter turns deep chocolate brown and becomes fragrant, 4 to 5 minutes. Add hazelnuts and cook, stirring constantly, until fragrant and combined, about 1 minute. Season with salt and pepper to taste.

2. Meanwhile, heat 1/4 cup water and beans in 12-inch skillet over high heat; cook, tossing frequently, until beans are warmed through, about 1 to 2 minutes. Season with salt and pepper to taste and arrange neatly on warm serving platter. Top beans with toasted hazelnuts and brown butter and serve immediately.

GREEN BEANS WITH BUTTERED BREAD CRUMBS AND ALMONDS
SERVES 4 TO 6

- 1 slice high-quality white bread, such as Pepperidge Farm, crust removed and torn into rough 1½-inch pieces
- 2 tablespoons sliced almonds (about ½ ounce), crumbled by hand into 1/4-inch pieces
- 2 medium garlic cloves, minced or pressed through garlic press (about 2 teaspoons)
- 2 teaspoons chopped fresh parsley leaves
   Salt and ground black pepper
- 1 recipe Blanched Green Beans
- 4 tablespoons unsalted butter

1. Process bread in food processor until evenly fine-textured, 20 to 30 seconds (you should have about 1/4 cup fresh bread crumbs). Transfer bread crumbs to dry 10-inch nonstick skillet, add almonds, and toast over medium-high heat, stirring constantly, until golden brown, about 5 minutes. Off heat, toss garlic and parsley with hot crumbs; season with salt and pepper to taste, transfer to small bowl, and set aside. (Do not wash skillet.)

2. Heat 1/4 cup water and beans in 12-inch skillet over high heat; cook, tossing frequently, until beans are warmed through, about 1 to 2 minutes. Season with salt and pepper to taste and arrange neatly on warm serving platter.

3. Meanwhile, heat butter in same skillet used for bread crumbs over medium-high heat until foaming; add bread crumb mixture and heat, stirring frequently, until fragrant, about 1 to 2 minutes. Top beans with warm buttered crumbs and nuts and serve immediately.

Beef Wellington without Fear

Is this dinosaur of a recipe worth making at home? If you like flaky—not soggy—pastry wrapped around perfectly pink, flavorful beef, the answer is an enthusiastic yes.

≥ BY KAY RENTSCHLER ≤

Beef Wellington is like the maiden aunt who pays a visit during the holidays: difficult, traditional (and rich), she refuses to be taken lightly. But though you dread dealing with her and pray she'll behave, dinner wouldn't be the same without her.

Even readers on the nod during the early 1960s will recognize beef Wellington, the substantial piece of tenderloin swathed in fine pâté and *duxelles* (a heady mix of mushrooms, shallots, herbs, and butter) and bundled up in a cloak of puff pastry. A pitcher of dark, glossy sauce should be on hand to carry red wine and rich meat juices to the earthy brown of mushrooms and pâté, and onward over buttery, rare beef. The most appealing part of the story is the flaky, golden pastry that holds things in place. Is this a big, aging dinosaur of a dish? Yes. But its interplay of flavors and star presentation make it peerless party fare. Too often, of course, beef Wellington is all dry gray meat, grainy, overcooked pâté, and soggy bottoms or—still worse—served with a metallic tinned jus or packet of thick gravy mix. Even the best claret in the world would bring little comfort.

After examining a couple dozen cookbooks, I found that recipes for beef Wellington showed a consensus as to ingredients—pâté, standard duxelles, preseared beef, and commercial puff pastry—and a uniform lack of detail around the assembly of the beast. Given the potentially irreconcilable differences between a thick log of raw beef and a thin sheet of raw pastry, I had my work cut out for me. My hope was to minimize and secure the efforts needed to deliver the roast to the table in perfect condition: crust golden, meat rare, accompanying flavors rich and compatible, and no leaky pastry. I also wanted a simple, respectable sauce at its side.

The Beef

Beginning with the beef, I discovered that there were multiple issues to work through before even

Wellington features perfectly cooked beef tenderloin swathed with pâté and mushrooms and wrapped in flaky puff pastry.

setting the oven. The first were size and shape. Unquestionably company dinner, to serve eight to 10, beef Wellington requires a piece of tenderloin in the 3- to 4-pound range (untrimmed tenderloins can weigh anywhere between 8 and 10 pounds). Trips to the market turned up surprisingly different shapes and sizes of tenderloin in this weight range. And aesthetics were not the only problem. The shape and diameter of the meat were crucial to recipe consistency as well. To get the proper weight and number of portions, I would need—in the argot of the industry—a center-cut Châteaubriand. (See "Parts of the Tenderloin" at right.)

The tenderloin wanted a brief but high-impact pan-sear before assembly. Wrapping raw meat in dough left the finished Wellington with a spongy texture and unappealing steamed flavor. I found that a sear of one minute per side in a very hot pan afforded depth of flavor and an attractive color contrast in the sliced presentation as well.

Because tenderloin is a watery cut, many recipes suggest dry-aging the meat in the

refrigerator before cooking it. Though I did not expect dry-aging to solve the problem of excessive moisture altogether, I hoped it would, at the very least, evaporate moisture from the meat's surface—creating a more interesting surface texture—and improve the meat's flavor as well. Two days proved ideal: The meat's surface, though leathery, was still malleable enough to accept a pan-sear without needing a trim, and its exterior, once roasted, had a nice chew, tender insides, and meatier flavor.

The Accessories

I moved on to the Wellington's accessories, the pâté and duxelles. It took only a couple of attempts at a quick chicken liver pâté to convince me I could not get close to the smooth richness of an authentic pâté de foie gras. My "homemade" attempts were grainy and disappointing. A smooth, commercial pâté, on the other hand, wafted with cognac and truffles and melted sweetly, playing to the mushrooms and the meat.

Duxelles hearken back to classical times and, in truth, have not changed much since Escoffier. Chopped and sautéed with butter and shallots or onions, the mushrooms cook down into an intense, nubby hash inside of 15 minutes. The food processor brought a pound of them into line very quickly. I chose shallots over onions for their nuanced delicacy. Two tablespoons of heavy cream, directed into the pan once the mushrooms had cooked down, a splash of Madeira, and a toss of fresh thyme gave the duxelles a

Parts of the Tenderloin

BUTT END

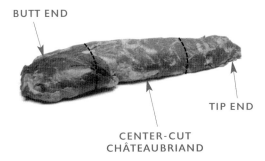

TIP END

CENTER-CUT
CHÂTEAUBRIAND

Ask your butcher for the center-cut Châteaubriand, which has an even thickness from end to end. Ask the butcher to trim excess fat and silver skin and to tie the roast at regular intervals with twine.

1. Turn duxelles onto parchment-lined baking sheet and spread into 8 by 10-inch rectangle.

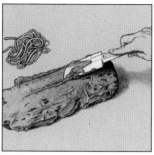

2. Cut off twine from seared roast and discard. Spread pâté evenly on top and sides of tenderloin.

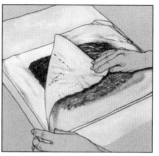

3. Invert duxelles onto dough and peel back the parchment carefully.

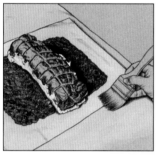

4. Place tenderloin on dough bare-side-up, and brush dough edges with egg wash.

5. Lift dough edges up to encase tenderloin snugly, allowing for 1-inch overlap. Pinch seam to seal.

6. Turn dough corners up, as when wrapping a gift, and press to seal.

moist, supple texture and an earthy perfume.

At first, I wasn't eager to envelope this masterpiece in commercial puff pastry. I resisted, using instead *Cook's* quick puff pastry recipe for Flaky Apple Turnovers (January/February 2001) with great success. The major advantages of homemade puff pastry are flavor and ease of shaping. Nevertheless, I knew most cooks would prefer to get on with the business at hand and duly gave store-bought Dufour all-butter puff pastry a turn. Though problematic to handle when completely thawed—its high water content caused it to pull and stick like chewing gum on hot pavement—Dufour responded well to a leisurely refrigerator thaw that left it still semifrozen, and relatively manageable, after about three hours. The dough's slim dimensions were well-suited to the tenderloin: The 10 by 13-inch rectangle had to be extended only a bit; pressure from a rolling pin repaired cracks along the fold lines.

Assembly

With each component at the ready, it was time to assemble. Potential clashes between texturally and temperamentally different ingredients were mitigated by making everything dead cold. The seared tenderloin, for example, required a minimum of four hours in the refrigerator to become cold enough to stiffen up and get slathered top and sides with pâté. I discovered that flattening the hot duxelles with a spatula into a thin, compatibly sized rectangle on a parchment-lined baking pan, then chilling them, allowed me to invert them onto the center of the rolled out dough, then peel off the parchment. The pâté-slathered tenderloin could then be neatly inverted onto the duxelles, avoiding messy double-layering of pâté and duxelles on the meat. The chilled but malleable dough was simply folded up snugly over the roast and set right-side-up on a parchment-lined baking sheet. The assembled, unbaked Wellington also benefited from advance chilling. Thirty minutes in the fridge helped set and seal the dough.

Though beef Wellington is often shown with leaf and vine decorations made from its own dough scraps, I settled for simple dough ribbons (trimmed in strips from the rolled-out rectangle) draped across the Wellington halfway through baking.

Lift Off

Though I experimented with temperatures between 400 and 450 degrees, as well as lower oven adjustments midway through baking, both meat and dough enjoyed a nice, hot oven. It was 450 all the way. Lesser temperatures produced melting, slippage, and half-baked dough. The bottom oven rack was the place to be. Because juices flow downward, the pastry bottom needed hot, searing heat to fight off sogginess. A low

rack also allowed the top of the Wellington to keep its distance from scarring heat.

When baking the Wellington, 30 minutes will get you rare and 35 minutes will cook the meat medium-rare. At this point, the dough has seen enough of the oven, making higher meat temperatures inadvisable. The finished Wellington needs a full 10 minutes to repose before being sliced—otherwise the red seas will run. (The internal temperature of the meat will also climb as the roast rests.) Its arrival on the counter in the test kitchen always drew a crowd—many of whom were born after Wellington was already out of style. Beef Wellington, meet the new generation.

DRY-AGED BEEF TENDERLOIN FOR BEEF WELLINGTON

1   beef tenderloin center-cut Châteaubriand (see page 19), 3 to 4 pounds trimmed weight, about 12 inches long and 4 inches in diameter, trimmed and tied by butcher

Place roast on wire rack set above rimmed baking sheet and refrigerate, uncovered, for 48 hours.

DUXELLES

1   pound button mushrooms, brushed of dirt and broken in rough pieces by hand
3   tablespoons unsalted butter
2–3   large shallots, minced (about 1/2 cup)
2   tablespoons heavy cream
1   teaspoon Madeira (optional)
1   teaspoon salt
1/2   teaspoon ground black pepper
1   tablespoon minced fresh thyme leaves

1. Process half of mushrooms in food processor until chopped uniformly fine, about ten 1-second pulses, stopping to scrape down bowl after 5 pulses (mushrooms should not be ground so fine as to release liquid). Transfer chopped mushrooms to medium bowl and repeat to chop remaining mushrooms.

2. Heat butter in 12-inch skillet over medium-low heat until foaming; add shallots and cook, stirring frequently, until softened, 3 to 5 minutes. Stir in mushrooms, increase heat to medium-high, and cook, stirring frequently, until most of liquid given off by mushrooms has evaporated, 7 to 10 minutes. Add cream, Madeira, salt, and pepper; cook until mixture is dry, about 3 minutes longer. Off heat, stir in thyme.

3. Line rimmed baking sheet with parchment paper; turn duxelles onto baking sheet and, with rubber spatula, spread into 8 by 10-inch rectangle of even thickness (see illustration 1, above). Cover flush with plastic wrap and refrigerate until completely cold, at least 2 hours or up to 24.

BEEF WELLINGTON
SERVES 8 TO 10

Be sure to use a smooth-textured pâté, not a coarse country pâté. For *Cook's* Quickest Puff Pastry recipe, see the January/February 2001 issue, page 23 or visit www.cooksillustrated.com. If you prefer to use store-bought pastry, look for the Dufour brand in the freezer section of better grocery stores. One 14-ounce package will be enough; defrost it in the refrigerator for 3 hours before using. Pepperidge Farm frozen puff pastry will not work because the size of the sheets is not suited to the recipe, and they cannot be rolled to the correct size.

1	Dry-Aged Beef Tenderloin for Beef Wellington (page 20)
2	tablespoons olive oil
2	teaspoons salt
2	teaspoons ground black pepper
5	ounces fine pâté, mashed until smooth Flour for dusting work surface
1	pound puff pastry, preferably homemade (see note)
1	large egg
1	recipe Duxelles (page 20)

1. Heat 12-inch heavy-bottomed skillet over high heat until very hot, about 4 minutes. Meanwhile, rub tenderloin with oil, then sprinkle with salt and pepper and lightly rub into meat.

2. Set tenderloin in hot skillet, curving it to fit if necessary, and sear on first side without moving, until well-browned, about 1 minute, pressing down on meat so that bottom of roast makes full contact with pan. Using tongs, rotate tenderloin and brown on all sides, about 1 minute per side. Remove from skillet and wrap hot tenderloin tightly in plastic wrap and refrigerate at least 4 hours or up to 24.

3. Unwrap tenderloin and cut off and discard twine. Using small spatula, spread pâté over top and sides of tenderloin (see illustration 2, page 20); set aside.

4. Dust a large sheet of parchment paper with flour. Unwrap puff pastry and place on parchment; dust puff pastry lightly with flour and cover with second large sheet of parchment. Roll into 12 by 15-inch rectangle, mending cracks as you roll. Remove top sheet of parchment and with sharp knife trim two 1-inch bands off long side to form 10 by 15-inch rectangle; refrigerate bands on parchment-lined plate. (If dough is soft and sticky or tears easily, slide parchment with pastry onto baking sheet and freeze until firm, about 10 minutes.)

5. Line rimmed baking sheet with parchment paper and spray lightly with nonstick cooking spray; set aside. Beat egg with 1 tablespoon water; set aside.

6. Remove plastic wrap from duxelles. Following illustration 3, invert duxelles onto puff pastry; peel off parchment. Following illustration 4, place tenderloin pâté-side down onto duxelles-covered dough. Brush edges of dough lightly with beaten egg. Following illustrations 5 and 6, encase tenderloin in dough, wrapping tightly. (There should be about 1-inch overlap forming seam; if overlap is excessive, trim with scissors.) Carefully invert dough-wrapped tenderloin onto prepared baking sheet and brush dough lightly with beaten egg; refrigerate, uncovered, 30 minutes.

7. Adjust oven rack to lowest position and heat oven to 450 degrees. Bake Wellington until light golden brown, about 15 minutes, then arrange decorative ribbons on top. Continue to bake until deep golden brown and instant-read thermometer inserted into center registers between 113 and 115 degrees for rare, about 15 minutes, or around 120 degrees for medium-rare, about 20 minutes. Let stand 10 minutes, transfer to carving platter, and cut crosswise into ½-inch slices. Serve with sauce (see Red Wine Sauce for Beef Wellington, above).

RECIPE: Sauce on the Side

Developing a robust, satiny sauce proved much easier than I had imagined. It took only a package of oxtails, a decent red wine, and some judicious simmering to produce this richly flavorful and full-bodied sauce, which doesn't even require thickening.

RED WINE SAUCE FOR BEEF WELLINGTON
MAKES ABOUT 1¼ CUPS

The stock that is the base of this sauce can—and should—be made in advance. But do not finish the sauce (step 5, below) until the beef Wellington is in the oven.

2½	pounds beef oxtails, trimmed of excess fat
2	medium carrots, chopped into 1-inch pieces (about 1 cup)
2	medium celery ribs, chopped into 1-inch pieces (about 1 cup)
4	small onions, chopped coarse (about 3 cups)
1	large garlic head, broken into cloves, unpeeled
2	teaspoons tomato paste
1	bottle (750 ml) red wine
4–6	large shallots, minced (about 1 cup)
1	bay leaf
10	sprigs fresh thyme
1	(14½-ounce) can low-sodium beef broth
1	(14½-ounce) can low-sodium chicken broth
1	teaspoon whole black peppercorns
6	parsley stems
¼	cup ruby port
4	tablespoons cold unsalted butter, cut into 4 pieces
	Salt and ground black pepper

1. Adjust oven rack to lower-middle position and heat oven to 450 degrees. Combine oxtails, carrots, celery, onions, and garlic in large flameproof roasting pan; spray lightly with cooking spray and toss to combine. Roast, stirring every 10 minutes, until beef and vegetables are well-browned, 40 to 50 minutes, adding tomato paste to roasting pan after 30 minutes.

2. While oxtails and vegetables roast, bring wine, shallots, bay leaf, and thyme to simmer over medium heat in heavy-bottomed 8-quart stockpot or Dutch oven; reduce heat to low, and simmer slowly, uncovered, until reduced to about 1½ cups, about 30 minutes. Set pot aside.

3. Place roasting pan over burner(s) set at high; add beef and chicken broths and bring to boil, scraping up browned bits on bottom of pan with wooden spoon.

4. Transfer contents of roasting pan to stockpot with wine reduction. Add 7 cups water, peppercorns, and parsley stems, and bring to boil over high heat; reduce heat to low and simmer, uncovered, until richly flavored and full-bodied, 3 to 4 hours. Strain broth into large glass measuring cup or container (you should have about 2 cups), discarding solids in strainer. Cool to room temperature; cover with plastic wrap, and refrigerate at least 1 hour or up to 2 days.

5. While beef Wellington bakes, skim hardened fat from surface of stock using soup spoon and discard. Transfer stock to small saucepan and simmer over medium-low heat until reduced to about 1 cup, 10 to 15 minutes. Add port; set aside off heat.

6. While beef Wellington rests, return broth to simmer over medium heat and whisk in butter 1 piece at a time. Season sauce to taste with salt and pepper and serve with beef Wellington. —K.R.

Wellington Timeline

2 TO 3 DAYS BEFORE SERVING:
➤ Dry-age the tenderloin.
(This can be done 2 days before browning or 2 to 3 days before serving, depending on how long you intend to chill the browned tenderloin.)

UP TO 2 DAYS BEFORE SERVING:
➤ Make the stock base for the sauce.

UP TO 1 DAY BEFORE SERVING:
➤ Make the duxelles.
➤ Brown the dry-aged tenderloin.

DAY OF SERVING:
➤ Assemble and bake the Wellington.

WHILE WELLINGTON ROASTS AND RESTS:
➤ Complete the sauce.

Perfecting Crème Brûlée

Lots of yolks, turbinado sugar, an instant-read thermometer, and a final chill
are the keys to perfect crème brûlée.

≥ BY DAWN YANAGIHARA ≤

Beneath either a paltry sugar crust or one that requires a pickax, a majority of crème brûlées suffer from a trio of problems: The custard is tepid, not cold; the custard is leaden, not ethereal; and the flavors are sullen. A proper crème brûlée should have a crackle-crisp bittersweet sugar crust over a chilly custard of balanced egginess, creaminess, and sweetness. Its light, silken, supple texture goes down easily, belying the dessert's richness; it's a masterful work of temperature, taste, and texture.

Crème brûlée is not complicated—it requires only six ingredients—and it can be made well in advance of serving. Despite its charming simplicity, however, there are many opportunities for things to go awry. A search of many recipes revealed standard ingredients, but ratios of eggs and cream varied, as did oven temperatures, so the devil was going to be in the details.

The Crème

First I sought to settle the issue of eggs. Firmer custard, like that in crème caramel, is made with whole eggs, which help the custard to achieve a clean-cutting quality. Crème brûlée is richer and softer—with a pudding-like, spoon-clinging texture—in part because of the exclusive use of yolks. With 4 cups of heavy cream as the dairy for the moment, I went to work. The custard refused to set at all with as few as six yolks; with eight (a common number for the amount of cream) it was better, but still rather slurpy. With 12, however, a surprisingly large number of yolks, I struck gold. The custard had a lovely lilting texture, an elegant mouthfeel, a glossy, luminescent look, and the richest flavor.

I ventured to make crème brûlées with different kinds of cream. Half-and-half (with a fat content of about 10 percent) was far too lean, and the custard was watery and lightweight. With whipping cream (about 30 percent fat), the custard was improved but still a bit loose. Heavy cream (about 36 percent fat) was the ticket. The

To caramelize the sugar crust, sweep the flame from the perimeter of the custard toward the middle, keeping the flame about 2 inches above the ramekin.

custard was thick but not overbearing, luxurious but not death-defying.

I tested various sugar quantities, from ½ cup to ¾ cup. Two-thirds cup was the winner; with more sugar the crème brûlée was too saccharine, and with less the simple egg and cream flavors tasted muted and dull. I also found that a pinch of salt heightened flavors and that vanilla bean was superior to extract.

With proportions in place, I attempted to find the best cooking technique for the custard. Custard made with icebox-cold eggs and cream can go into the oven, but nearly all recipes instruct the cook to scald the cream before gradually whisking it into the yolks beaten with sugar. When compared, a started-cold custard and scalded-cream custard displayed startling differences. The former had a silkier, smoother texture. Past *Cook's* custard-related research explained that eggs respond favorably to cooking

at a slow, gentle pace. If heated quickly, they set only just shortly before they enter the overcooked zone, leaving a very narrow window between just right and overdone. If heated gently, however, they begin to thicken the custard at a lower temperature and continue to do so gradually until it, too, eventually overcooks. In other words, the scalded-cream method is more likely to produce custard with an overcooked—hence inferior—texture.

The downside to starting with cold ingredients is that because the cream is never heated, it is impossible to extract flavor from a vanilla bean. Also, if the cream is heated, the sugar can go into the pot for easy dissolution. Otherwise, the sugar must be vigorously beaten with the yolks to encourage it to dissolve. When I did this, the resulting custard was very frothy and baked up with a dry, soap-foam-like surface. Scalding cream and sugar, steeping with vanilla, then refrigerating until cold seemed an overwrought process, so I tested a hybrid technique. I heated only half the cream with the sugar and the vanilla bean. After a 15-minute off-heat steep to extract flavor from the vanilla bean, I added the remaining still cold cream to bring the temperature down before whisking it into the yolks. This hybrid technique created a custard with a fineness equal to the one started cold—and it baked in less time, too.

Next I investigated oven temperatures. At 325 degrees, the custards puffed and browned on the surface. Too hot. At 300 degrees, they fared beautifully. As for the water bath (or *bain marie*, which prevents the periphery of a custard from overcooking while the center saunters to the finish line), I used a large baking dish that held the ramekins comfortably. (The ramekins must not touch and should be at least ½ inch away from the sides of the dish.) I lined the bottom with a kitchen towel to protect the floors of the ramekins from the heat of the dish.

The golden rule of custards is that they must not be overcooked lest they lose their smooth, silken texture and become grainy and curdled. Judging doneness by gently shaking the custards or by slipping a paring knife into them were not reliable techniques. An instant-read thermometer tells you exactly when the custards must come out of the oven: between 170 and 175 degrees. If you do not have a thermometer, look at the center of the custard. It should be barely set—

shaky but not sloshy. The custard will continue to cook from residual heat once out of the oven. A deep chill then helps to solidify things. If your oven has a history of uneven heating, the custards may finish at different rates, so it is advisable to check each one separately rather than take the whole lot out at once.

The Brûlée

For the crackly caramel crust I tried brown sugar, regular granulated sugar, and turbinado and Demerara sugars (the latter two are coarse light brown sugars). Because brown sugar is moist and lumpy, recipes often recommend drying it in a low oven and crushing it to break up lumps. I found that it just isn't worth the effort. Turbinado and Demerara sugars were superior to granulated only because their coarseness makes them easy to distribute evenly over the custards.

There are a few approaches to caramelizing the sugar. The broiler is almost guaranteed to fail; the heat is uneven and inadequate. A salamander—a long-handled iron plate that is heated and held just above the sugar—is hardly practical since they are hard to come by. A torch accomplishes the task efficiently. A hardware-store propane torch is the tool of choice, but a small butane kitchen torch, available in cookware stores, can do the job, just at a more leisurely pace.

While being "brûléed," the custard is unavoidably warmed a bit. In standard round ramekins, usually only the upper third of the custard is affected. But in shallow dishes (my favorite for their higher ratio of crust to custard), the custard can be completely warmed through. In my opinion, a warm custard can ruin an otherwise perfect crème brûlée. To remedy this problem, I refrigerated the finished crème brûlées, and the crust maintained its crackly texture for up to 45 minutes. Beneath the shattering sugar crust lay an interplay of creamy, cold, sweet, bitter, smooth, and crackly. . . perfect crème brûlée.

Curdled vs. Creamy

A *bain marie*, or hot water bath, makes the difference between overcooked, curdled custard (top) and properly cooked, creamy custard (bottom).

TESTING EQUIPMENT: **Pass the Torch**

Fire up a torch to caramelize the sugar on your crème brûlée—it's the best way to put the crowning glory of a crust on the custard. We tested a hardware-store propane torch (right) against a petite kitchen torch (left) fueled by butane. The propane torch, with its powerful flame, caramelized the sugar quickly and easily, but, admittedly, it's not for the faint-hearted. The butane torch was less intimidating, but its puny flame did the job slowly. If you are looking to buy a propane torch, look for one with a built-in ignition trigger that does not need to be held down for the torch to remain lit. If a kitchen torch is more your speed, purchase a can of butane along with it—otherwise you'll have more luck "brûléeing" with a book of matches. –D.Y.

CLASSIC CRÈME BRÛLÉE
SERVES 8

Separate the eggs and whisk the yolks after the cream has finished steeping; if left to sit, the surface of the yolks will dry and form a film. A vanilla bean gives custard the deepest flavor, but 2 teaspoons of extract, whisked into the yolks in step 4, can be used instead. The best way to judge doneness is with a digital instant-read thermometer. The custards, especially if baked in shallow fluted dishes, will not be deep enough to provide an accurate reading with a dial-face thermometer. For the caramelized sugar crust, we recommend turbinado or Demerara sugar. Regular granulated sugar will work, too, but use only 1 scant teaspoon on each ramekin or 1 teaspoon on each shallow fluted dish.

4	cups chilled heavy cream
2/3	cup granulated sugar
	Pinch salt
1	vanilla bean, halved lengthwise
12	large egg yolks
8–12	teaspoons turbinado or Demerara sugar (see note)

1. Adjust oven rack to lower-middle position and heat oven to 300 degrees.

2. Combine 2 cups cream, sugar, and salt in medium saucepan; with paring knife, scrape seeds from vanilla bean into pan, submerge pod in cream, and bring mixture to boil over medium heat, stirring occasionally to ensure that sugar dissolves. Take pan off heat and let steep 15 minutes to infuse flavors.

3. Meanwhile, place kitchen towel in bottom of large baking dish or roasting pan and arrange eight 4- to 5-ounce ramekins (or shallow fluted dishes) on towel. Bring kettle or large saucepan of water to boil over high heat.

4. After cream has steeped, stir in remaining 2 cups cream to cool down mixture. Whisk yolks in large bowl until broken up and combined. Whisk about 1 cup cream mixture into yolks until loosened and combined; repeat with another 1 cup cream. Add remaining cream and whisk until evenly colored and thoroughly combined. Strain

through fine-mesh strainer into 2-quart measuring cup or pitcher (or clean medium bowl); discard solids in strainer. Pour or ladle mixture into ramekins, dividing it evenly among them.

5. Carefully place baking dish with ramekins on oven rack; pour boiling water into dish, taking care not to splash water into ramekins, until water reaches two-thirds height of ramekins. Bake until centers of custards are just barely set and are no longer sloshy and digital instant-read thermometer inserted in centers registers 170 to 175 degrees, 30 to 35 minutes (25 to 30 minutes for shallow fluted dishes). Begin checking temperature about 5 minutes before recommended time.

6. Transfer ramekins to wire rack; cool to room temperature, about 2 hours. Set ramekins on rimmed baking sheet, cover tightly with plastic wrap, and refrigerate until cold, at least 4 hours or up to 4 days.

7. Uncover ramekins; if condensation has collected on custards, place paper towel on surface to soak up moisture. Sprinkle each with about 1 teaspoon turbinado sugar (1½ teaspoons for shallow fluted dishes); tilt and tap ramekin for even coverage. Ignite torch and caramelize sugar. Refrigerate ramekins, uncovered, to re-chill, 30 to 45 minutes (but no longer); serve.

ESPRESSO CRÈME BRÛLÉE

Place ¼ cup espresso beans in zipper-lock bag and crush lightly with rolling pin or meat pounder until coarsely cracked. Follow recipe for Classic Crème Brûlée, substituting cracked espresso beans for vanilla bean and whisking 1 teaspoon vanilla extract into yolks in step 4 before adding cream.

TEA-INFUSED CRÈME BRÛLÉE

Knot together the strings of 10 bags Irish Breakfast tea. Follow recipe for Classic Crème Brûlée, substituting tea bags for vanilla bean; after steeping, squeeze bags with tongs or press into mesh strainer to extract all liquid. Whisk 1 teaspoon vanilla extract into yolks in step 4 before adding cream.

Rediscovering Shortbread

A quick, foolproof technique produces shortbread that is miles ahead of the packaged stuff.

⇒ BY KAY RENTSCHLER ⇐

Thick, golden shortbread wedges, pierced by the tines of a fork and twinkling with fine sugar, are a tribute to Scottish frugality, as pure as a sacrament, as simple and beautiful as a sand dollar on the beach. Stout for a plain unfilled cookie, shortbread should crumble easily—sandy, sweet, buttery-rich. At the cookie's edge the fine crumb opens slightly and goes tawny and crisp.

If this description sounds unfamiliar, that is because commercial shortbreads are too often stubbornly rigid (when a dough is too lean) or crumbly soft (when vegetable shortening edges out butter). Good homemade shortbread is unfamiliar to most home cooks. It is a transcendent cookie, much more than a simple American butter cookie, and its success depends on a keen eye for proportion and finesse.

Making my way through a host of shortbread recipes, I quickly came to the conclusion that an authentic shortbread should have but four ingredients: butter, sugar, flour, and salt. Shortbreads made with vanilla, cream, or eggs invariably signaled an interloper, one that lured the shortbread down the tawdry path of a sugar cookie or sweet pie dough.

Mixing Methods

Because shortbread contains no proper liquid, the means of transforming the four ingredients into a dough is paramount. The first order of business, therefore, would be to develop a reliable mixing method. The creaming method—in which softened butter and sugar are beaten and the flour folded in—is a standard butter cookie technique. It adapts nicely to shortbread, which contains no real liquids other than the water in the butter. The butter becomes aerated, the sugar partially melts, and the flour folds in comfortably at the end. Shortbreads made this way were fine-pored and fairly delicate.

The biscuit method, in which cold butter and dry ingredients are rubbed together with a pastry cutter or fingertips, is esteemed for delicate biscuits and scones. Even quicker is the food

Once the shortbread has been partially baked, pierce the dough with a skewer to create the design of your choice.

processor (cold butter and a whirring blade). Both the creaming and the biscuit methods, however, resulted in loose, feathery crumbs that required light kneading. Even after this extra step, the resulting shortbread was less than spectacular.

In the end I chose a standing mixer, chilled butter, and low speed, reproducing the biscuit method by "rubbing" the butter into the dry ingredients without softening it unduly. Then, rather than manipulating the crumbs any further, I simply patted them into a disk and baked it. These shortbreads were the best of the lot—fine-pored, tender, and buttery.

Though shortbread cookies want some structure in their crumb, their delicate texture supports a call for a softer, lower-protein flour. I tested flours with protein content in the range of 7 percent to 11 percent, including bleached all-purpose, unbleached all-purpose, and cake flours. Because bleaching alters flavor, shortbread made with cake flour (which is bleached) or bleached all-purpose flour lost every taste test. (Given the lack of additional flavorings, the taste of the flour has a great deal to do with the flavor of shortbread.) Among

unbleached all-purpose flours, I preferred Pillsbury or Gold Medal, which have a moderate protein content of just above 10 percent. (Some all-purpose flours go above 11 percent.)

I was curious to see if a small percentage of rice flour or cornstarch might effect a more tender cookie (many Scottish recipes feature these). Because these starches have virtually no protein and so do not form gluten (the protein that gives structure to baked goods made with wheat flour), I hoped they would work inertly, holding the shape of the dough, keeping the crumb fine, and making the cookies even more tender. Replacing ¼ cup of the flour with either cornstarch or rice flour did the trick; it was just enough to make the shortbread meltingly tender, but not too soft.

Sugar, Salt, and Butter

What would a baking recipe from Great Britain be without castor sugar? In American parlance that is superfine sugar, and it was the clear winner in our tests. Regular granulated sugar produced cookies that were too coarse, and confectioners' sugar had a powdery, drying effect on the crumb. Two-thirds cup superfine sugar was ideal. As insignificant as ¼ teaspoon salt might seem, it is in many ways a crucial ingredient. The shortbread was flavor-deprived and one-dimensional without it.

Butter is definitely the key player here, giving shortbread its rich, nutty flavor and crumbly texture. I wanted to use as much as possible to add flavor and to help hold the dough together. Tests showed that two sticks were just right. Less butter produced doughs that fell apart easily and

Getting the Right Texture

Before pressing, the dough should have the consistency of damp, evenly textured crumbs.

1. Turn half of crumbs into 9-inch parchment-lined cake pan and even lightly with fingers. Press heavily with second cake pan.

2. Add remaining crumbs and press as in step 1. Working quickly, smooth top of dough with back of spoon.

3. Insert paring knife between dough and pan. Leaving knife stationary, rotate pan counterclockwise to free edges of dough.

4. Unmold dough on rimless or inverted baking sheet lined with parchment. Peel parchment round from dough; smooth edges if necessary.

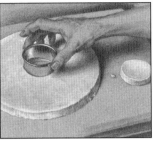

5. Place 2-inch biscuit cutter in center of dough and cut out center. Place extruded round to side, then replace biscuit cutter.

6. After baking 20 minutes, score top surface of shortbread into 16 even wedges with thin knife, then pierce design with skewer.

were slightly dry when baked. More butter made the shortbread lose shape in the oven.

Looks Matter

From the beginning I had been taken with traditionally round, free-form shortbread scored into portions and pierced with a fork. Thus I had ruled out rolling and cutting the cookies. Flouring and rerolling scraps made tough cookies, and the ease and authenticity of a single disk appealed to me. Baking shortbread in a cake pan made sense at first, but the better approach turned out to be using the pan to mold the dough and then unmolding it before baking. This produced a perfectly flat top and crisp, well-defined edges while avoiding the problem of having to turn the delicate baked disk over to expose the fork pattern (which, after unmolding, would be on the underside of the disk). The free-form dough also baked better around the edges than one in a pan.

Thinking shortbread should be a full 3/4 inch thick, I began my baking tests using an 8-inch cake pan and a 300-degree oven. But even after as much as an hour and 15 minutes the shortbread remained soft in the center and precipitously brown in color. Reducing the oven temperature caused the cookies to lose definition; raising it made them too brown. When I traded in my 8-inch cake pan for a 9-inch, the slightly thinner shortbreads baked better in the middle, although the centers were still a bit underdone. To

solve this problem, I tried stamping a small round of dough from the center with a biscuit cutter, replacing the cutter in the center of the cake, and baking the stamped-out round to the side. This accomplished a number of things: the shortbread slices baked evenly without overbrowning, the metal cutter conducted heat to the center of the dough, and there was one wayward cookie to eat right away before the larger disk had cooled.

I also noticed that the shortbread spread a bit in such a low oven, so I tried preheating the oven to 425 degrees to set the dough quickly and turning it down to 300 degrees as soon as the shortbread went in. One hour later the cookies were golden and done, and they had not spread.

In the course of testing one is bound to pick up tips, some of which are simply flukes. Example: Though I had been scoring the shortbread into 16 slender wedges and piercing them through before baking, on one occasion I forgot. When I pulled the shortbread out after 20 minutes to score and pierce it, I noticed the design was easier to execute and prettier than it had been in the raw dough. I also found that a wooden skewer did the piercing more neatly than a fork. (Though tests revealed that this design has no function beyond aesthetics, piercing is both attractive and traditional.) The light spray of superfine sugar is best left until the shortbread comes out of the oven and best kept to a minimum. Early sprinkling mars the design, and too much sugar creates a pasty, suede-like surface.

One tablespoon of sugar reserved from the original 2/3 cup was ideal. Finally, the shortbread cuts nicely right out of the oven.

Perhaps the best news is this: Shortbread improves with age—to a point. Taking far longer to cool than other cookies, shortbread left out on a rack the first night (another oversight) actually improved in texture. A week in a tin or even well-covered on a plate will not dim its greatness.

BUTTERY SHORTBREAD
MAKES 16 WEDGES

If you cannot find rice flour (for mail-order sources, see Resources, page 32), substitute an equal amount of cornstarch; the texture of the shortbread will be slightly affected with a faint chalkiness that dissipates with cooling and over the course of storage. When cutting the butter into cubes, work quickly so that the butter stays cold, and when molding the shortbread, form, press, and unmold it without delay. Be sure to use a plain round biscuit cutter to stamp out the center, not a fluted cutter.

1 3/4 cups (8.75 ounces) unbleached all-purpose flour, preferably Gold Medal or Pillsbury, protein content no higher than 10.5 percent
1/4 cup (1.3 ounces) rice flour
2/3 cup (4.8 ounces) superfine sugar
1/4 teaspoon salt
16 tablespoons (2 sticks) cold, unsalted butter

1. Adjust oven rack to middle position and heat oven to 425 degrees. Line ungreased 9-inch round cake pan with parchment round; set aside.

2. In bowl of standing mixer fitted with paddle attachment, mix flours, all but 1 tablespoon sugar (reserve for sprinkling), and salt at low speed until combined, about 5 seconds. Cut butter into 1/2-inch cubes with 1/4 cup flour mixture on a sheet of parchment paper. Add butter and any remaining flour on parchment to bowl with dry ingredients. Mix on low speed until dough is pale yellow and resembles damp crumbs, about 4 minutes.

3. Remove bowl from mixer and toss mixture lightly with fingers to fluff and loosen; rub any remaining butter bits into flour mixture with fingertips. Follow illustrations 1 through 5 to form and unmold shortbread. Place shortbread in oven; immediately reduce temperature to 300 degrees. Bake 20 minutes; remove baking sheet from oven and follow illustration 6 to score and pierce shortbread. Return shortbread to oven and continue to bake until pale golden, about 40 minutes longer. Slide parchment with shortbread onto cutting board, remove cutter from center, sprinkle shortbread evenly with reserved 1 tablespoon sugar, and cut at scored marks into wedges. Slide parchment with shortbread onto wire rack and cool to room temperature, at least 3 hours. (Can be wrapped well and stored at room temperature up to 7 days.)

Cooking with Red Wine

With the right wine and the right technique, you can make rich, complex-tasting sauces worthy of the finest restaurant at home.

When a recipe calls for red wine, the tendency is to grab whatever is inexpensive or already open on the counter. But as with any ingredient in the kitchen, the choice of wine can make the difference between a sauce worthy of a four-star restaurant and one that's best poured down the drain. In short, the wrong wine can turn an otherwise good sauce bad. The problem is that sifting through the enormous range of wines available is only slightly less confusing than trying to plough through *Ulysses*. Choosing a good bottle for the kitchen can seem like, at best, a shot in the dark.

To find out which red wines are good cookers (as opposed to those which are just good drinkers), I set up three tests—a quick tomato sauce, a pan sauce for steak, and a long-cooked beef stew—through which I could test numerous bottles. With the help of local wine expert Sandy Block (who holds the title Master of Wine, an honor shared by just 18 Americans), I organized those red wines available in even a poorly stocked wine shop into four manageable categories based on flavor, body, and style: light/fruity, smooth/mellow, hearty/robust, and nondescript jug wine. Ironically, the only type of wine not represented in these four categories is the "cooking wine" found on most supermarket shelves. In previous tests, the test kitchen has found that these low-alcohol concoctions have little flavor, a high-pitched acidity, and an enormous amount of salt, all of which combine to produce inedible sauces. Omitting this type of wine from the testing, I began my search for the ultimate red wine for cooking.

Putting Wines to the Test

I began by cooking with a representative from each of the four categories: a light/fruity Beaujolais, a smooth/mellow Merlot, a hearty/robust Cabernet Sauvignon, and a jug of "mountain" (sometimes also labeled "hearty") burgundy. Although none of the groups emerged as the winner from this first round of tests, what did emerge were some important attributes of good and not-so-good cooking wines. While the sauces made with Beaujolais could be described as wimpy, this wine did contribute a refreshing fruitiness that mingled well with the other ingredients and complemented

their flavors. The Merlot-based sauces had a somewhat overcooked, jamlike flavor, but they were also well-structured. The hearty Cabernet Sauvignon gave the sauces an astringent, woody bite that bullied all other flavors out of the way. This wine is aged in oak barrels, and its resulting oak flavors did not soften as they cooked but turned bitter and harsh. The jug wine, meanwhile, made sauces that were overly sweet and simple. Based on these findings, I decided to try to find wines that would combine the most appealing qualities of the light/fruity and smooth/mellow wines, shying away from wines with an oaky influence and inexpensive jug wines.

Focusing on this more narrow category—fruity/smooth/mellow—I selected four new bottles of wine: Sangiovese (a medium-bodied wine from Italy), red Zinfandel (from California), Pinot Noir (from Burgundy, France), and Côtes du Rhône (from southern France). The Sangiovese tasted great in the tomato sauce but made an astringent pan sauce and a cardboard-tasting stew. The Zinfandel tasted overcooked and jammy in the tomato sauce and turned the pan sauce bitter. While both the Côtes du Rhône and Pinot Noir turned in impressive results across the board, the Côtes du Rhône was stellar. When compared with the sauces made from Pinot Noir (a wine made from just one type of grape), the Côtes du Rhône (a blend of several grapes) had a fuller, more even-keeled flavor. The different grape varieties in the blend appeared to compensate for each other's shortcomings to produce a potent, well-rounded flavor.

I then tested several more fruity, medium-bodied blends with little oak, including wines from the greater Rhône Valley (in southern France), Languedoc (also in southern France), Australia, and the United States. These blends were not made from the same grape types, but they all made tasty, well-balanced sauces. My conclusion? Most red wines made from a blend of grapes will produce good sauces—just steer clear of wines aged in oak.

Does Price Matter?

Next came the question of price. Would a $30 blend make a better pan sauce for steak than a $5 blend? To find out, I cooked with fruity, medium-bodied red wines made from a blend of grapes at four price points: $5, $10, $20, and

$30. Tasters found that the results produced by a $5 bottle were much different from those produced by bottles in the other price categories. As wine cooks and reduces, it becomes an intensely flavored version of itself, making the wine's defining characteristics unbearably obvious. The sweet, bland $5 wines cooked down to candy-like sauces, while the $10, $20, and $30 bottles were smoother, making sauces with multiple layers of flavor. Although tasters favored wines in the two more expensive price ranges for their slightly more balanced and refined flavors, none thought the difference justified spending an extra $10 or $20. And I found that limiting the price to around $10 still left me with plenty of options when shopping. I had consistently good results with several widely available wines, including E. Guigal Côtes-du-Rhône ($9.95),

---

RED WINE REDUCTION FOR SAUCES
MAKES ABOUT 2 TABLESPOONS

Two tablespoons of this potent wine reduction can be substituted in a recipe, such as a pan sauce, tomato sauce, or roast beef jus, that calls for one-half to three-quarters cup of wine. Add this reduction near the end of the cooking time—the way you might finish a sauce by swirling in some butter. The reduction can be kept for up to two weeks in an air-tight container in the refrigerator. This recipe can be doubled or tripled.

1	small carrot, chopped fine (about 2 tablespoons)
1	medium shallot, minced (about 2 tablespoons)
2	button mushrooms, chopped fine (about 3 tablespoons)
1	small bay leaf
3	sprigs fresh parsley
1	cup fruity, smooth, medium-bodied red wine blend

Heat all ingredients in 12-inch nonstick skillet over low heat; cook, without simmering (liquid should be steaming but not bubbling), until mixture reduces to 1 cup, 15 to 20 minutes. Pour through strainer and return liquid (about ½ cup) to clean skillet. Continue to cook over low heat, without simmering, until liquid is reduced to 2 tablespoons, 15 to 20 minutes.

COOK'S ILLUSTRATED

26

TASTING RED WINES FOR COOKING

We tested nine types of red wine (more than 30 bottles in total, all priced around $10) in three different applications—a hearty tomato sauce, a quick pan sauce reduction for steaks, and a slow-simmering beef stew. Here are the results by type of red wine, with specific bottles recommended below. Preference was given to types of wine that performed well in all tests.

HIGHLY RECOMMENDED

RED BLENDS Wines made with more than one variety of grape yielded sauces that were especially "full" and "even-keeled." For best results, choose a fruity wine with medium body and little or no oak. See specific recommendations at right.

RECOMMENDED

PINOT NOIR Good results in all tests. Just one notch below the highly recommended wines made from a blend of grapes.

RECOMMENDED WITH RESERVATIONS

AMERICAN JUG WINES "Mountain" and "hearty burgundies" made "sweet, simple" sauces with little character. Not great, but not offensive, either.

MERLOT Overcooked, "jammy" flavor, but sauces had decent structure and proper heft.

BEAUJOLAIS Wimpy and "metallic" sauces with a refreshing acidity and fruitiness. Wine melded well with other sauce ingredients but tasted "underdeveloped."

NOT RECOMMENDED

SANGIOVESE (Chianti) Great in tomato sauce but "scorched" and "astringent" in steak pan sauce. The beef stew was "corky" and "cardboard-tasting."

ZINFANDEL Overcooked, "jammy," and "boozy" in tomato sauce; bitter and "tannic" in pan sauce.

CABERNET SAUVIGNON Wines aged in oak turned bitter and harsh when cooked. Sauces were deemed "astringent," with a "woody bite that bullies other flavors."

SPECIFIC RECOMMENDATIONS

E. GUIGAL, 1998, Côtes-du-Rhône
➤ **$9.95**

This blend of four grapes from southern France was a "good team player," making "gorgeous" garnet-colored sauces with a "well-balanced" flavor.

BONNY DOON, 1999, Ca' del Solo
➤ **$12.25**

Made from at least six grapes, this California blend produced "ultrasmooth" and "complex" sauces with a handsome crimson hue.

FRANCIS COPPOLA, 1999, Rosso
➤ **$10.95**

This California blend of four grapes, including Syrah and Zinfandel, produced "deep," "plummy" sauces with a "slightly sweet" finish.

VIGIL, Non-Vintage, Vigilante Red
➤ **$10.95**

A blend of six grapes, including Syrah and Carignan, this California table wine cooked up "slightly spicy," with a "pronounced berry" flavor.

ROSEMOUNT ESTATE, 2000, Grenache/Shiraz
➤ **$8.95**

This Australian blend of two grapes made "full," "round" sauces with "mild acidity" and bright, ruby color.

Rosemount Estate Grenache/Shiraz ($8.95, from Australia), and Bonny Doon Ca' del Solo ($12.25, from California).

Now We're Cooking

As I cooked my way through multiple bottles of wine, I found that it is not only the type of wine that matters but also the way you cook with it. The right wine can taste all wrong if cooked badly. That's because as wine is heated, delicate flavor compounds known as esters break apart, turning fruity flavors and aromas muddy and sour. The higher the heat, the more rapidly these esters will change from good to horrid.

Transferring this knowledge to cooking, reason suggests that wine would best be treated with low, slow heat. In fact, our testing had demonstrated this point. The beef stew was much more forgiving than the tomato or pan sauce, both of which are typically made by means of a fast and furious reduction over high heat. To further test this proposition, I made two more steak pan sauces, one by rapidly simmering the wine, the other by slowly reducing it, just below a simmer. The results were so radically different that tasters thought the sauces had been made from different wines. The sauce made from the rapidly simmered wine was tart and edgy, while that from the slowly reduced wine was round and smooth. The fast reduction had bruised the wine's esters; the slow reduction allowed their true, fruity flavor to shine through.

As I tested a few more pan sauces and did a little more research, I was introduced to another cooking trick by chef and wine importer Richard Kzirian. He suggested adding small amounts of aromatics to the wine as it reduced to add an extra dimension of flavor and polished texture. Treating the wine almost like a stock, I infused small amounts of shallot, carrot, mushroom, parsley, and bay leaf into the reduction. This made for a pan sauce that was rich and voluptuous, with complex layers of flavor.

Although this reduction is cooked over low, slow heat, I found the process can be speeded up by using a skillet rather than a saucepan. The increased surface area of a wide skillet allows the wine to evaporate more rapidly, even when cooked over low heat. I also found it easiest to remove the syrupy reduction from a nonstick pan, although a regular pan also works. The aromatics are strained out before the reduction is fully complete to keep them from soaking up too much of the increasingly valuable wine as it reduces.

To sum up the test results: A good bottle of cooking wine is likely to be made from a blend of grapes and can be had for about $10. The wine should have good fruit flavor, medium body, and little or no oak flavor. In the kitchen, this wine should be cooked just below a simmer with aromatics and not treated to a hot boil. While this technique is not necessary in recipes that already call for cooking wine slowly with aromatics, as in a stew, it makes all the difference with wine intended for a pan sauce or a quick tomato sauce.

Easing the Daily Grind

We tested 10 countertop coffee grinders and found that more money doesn't always buy a better model.

⇒ BY ADAM RIED ⇐

Just as corn on the cob tastes best if it's boiled within minutes of being picked, coffee tastes best if the beans are ground fresh before they are brewed. With a wide variety of countertop coffee grinders on the market, it is no problem for home cooks to grind beans on demand. The greater challenge is deciding which grinder to buy. Most of the reasonably priced grinders, which generally cost around $20, employ propeller-type blades that work like a blender, literally chopping the beans as they spin. But any coffee enthusiast will quickly allege that blade grinders are rife with problems—namely, that they grind unevenly, they produce too much superfine coffee dust, and the friction from the spinning blades overheats the coffee grounds. We wondered if any of this would really affect the flavor and body of the brewed coffee or if these allegations barely amounted to a hill of beans.

With a self-imposed price cap of $50, a limit that allowed us to include several low-end burr grinders (a fancier type of machine that works like a motorized pepper mill) we bought 10 popular models from seven manufacturers and 30 pounds of coffee beans. Then we let the grounds fly to determine just how good a grinder $50 (or less, in many cases) would buy.

Grinding Tests

We tested each unit by grinding 2 ounces of coffee beans (about 8 tablespoons) and using those grounds to brew full, 40-ounce pots of coffee. Because most everyone we know uses an automatic drip machine, we did, too, choosing a brand new unit from Cuisinart with a thermal carafe.

The first issue we addressed was the evenness of the grind. Michael Kramm, president of Capresso, maker of the Capresso Cool Grind included in our tests, explained that blade grinders actually chop the beans with their furiously spinning blades. In a burr grinder, on the other hand, beans are truly ground a few at a time between two grooved disks, one stationary and the other rotating just above it. The grounds are fed out through a chute into a sealed container. According to Kramm, the disks operate at roughly 7,000 to 9,000 revolutions per minute (RPM), while the motors in most blade grinders spin at 14,000 to 20,000 RPM.

Kramm agreed with other coffee authorities that the blade grinders' rough treatment of the beans often results in unevenly ground coffee,

with particles ranging from dust to large chunks in the same batch. Our observations corroborated this, although we found we could improve the evenness of the blade grind either by grinding in short, quick bursts, with stops in between to shake the grinder to redistribute the grounds, or by shaking the grinder as it ground, much as you would a martini in a cocktail shaker.

The burr grinders produced a more even grind, but tasters did not find that more evenly ground coffee translated into improved flavor. Tasters did prefer the rich body of burr-ground coffee, but they also noticed the tendency of this coffee to taste slightly bitter, owing in part, no doubt, to the more fine and even grind, which made for the coffee's greater exposure to and prolonged contact with the water in the coffee maker. These combined forces

caused what coffee experts call overextraction, which occurs when too much flavor is extracted from the beans. In our tests, we were less likely to encounter this problem if the coffee was ground coarse, moreso than even the coarsest setting on the burr grinders could accomplish.

We were surprised to discover that the coffee brewed with blade-ground beans was less likely to turn out bitter. The tasters did note that coffee from blade-ground beans had less body than coffee from burr-ground beans, but we were happy to sacrifice a little body for the reduced risk of brewing bitter coffee. We also learned that we could improve the body of the coffee somewhat by defying the blade grinders' instructions and grinding the beans for a little longer, 20 to 25 seconds, rather than the recommended 10 to

The Coffee Grinders We Tested

RECOMMENDED

Capresso Cool Grind
Did not grind beans very evenly, but effective nonetheless.

Krups Fast-Touch
Design is sleek and compact, though it has no cord wrap.

Mr. Coffee Grinder
Evenness of grind was not perfect, but brewed coffee was fine.

Braun Aromatic
Ground finely and evenly compared with most of the other blade grinders.

Mr. Coffee Burr Mill
Simplest and best on/off switch of all the burr grinders.

NOT RECOMMENDED

Proctor-Silex
Small capacity is a nuisance. You have to grind twice for one full pot.

Cuisinart Coffee Bar
Shallow lid and loose fit make it easy to spill ground coffee.

Starbucks Barista
Looks good, but the design of the lid is impractical.

Braun Coffee/ Espresso Mill
Grinds evenly and offers internal cord storage.

Capresso Burr Grinder
Beware the power switch when you reach to remove the full hopper.

RATING INEXPENSIVE COFFEE GRINDERS

RATINGS
★★★
GOOD
★★
FAIR
★
POOR

We rated 10 coffee grinders, none priced higher than $50, and evaluated them according to the following criteria. The grinders are listed in order of preference within each category.

PRICE: Prices paid in Boston-area stores, in national mail-order catalogs, and on the Web.

CAPACITY: Number of tablespoons of coffee beans accommodated in the hopper.

DESIGN: Our most important test. Grinders with lids deep enough to accommodate all of the ground coffee without spills were preferred. Lids that were shallow or shaped to allow spills were downgraded. In addition, grinders with on-board cord storage were preferred, but this feature was not essential to earn a rating of good in this category. Design considerations for the burr grinders in the group were different. Since the hoppers on all of them accommodated the ground coffee amply, we judged them on the design of their on/off mechanism. We preferred a manual switch, with no automatic timer.

CLEANING: Grinders that could be cleaned with a few wipes of a damp cloth were preferred. Grinders with hard-to-reach crevices into which a brush had to be maneuvered for cleaning were downgraded.

TEMPERATURE INCREASE: The temperature of the coffee was measured three times immediately after grinding with an infrared thermometer (in degrees Fahrenheit). The results were then averaged to determine the average temperature increase for that mill. According to coffee industry experts, the lower the temperature increase, the better.

Additional observations are noted in the Testers' Comments.

Brand	Price	Capacity	Design	Cleaning	Temperature Increase	Testers' Comments
RECOMMENDED						
Capresso Cool Grind, Model 501	$19.95	★★★ 12 Tbs	★★★	★★	7.3°	Has large capacity and a deep cup, the features we value most in a blade grinder. Some large pieces of bean were left after grinding, however.
Krups Fast-Touch Coffee Mill, Model 203	$19.99	★★★ 12 Tbs	★★★	★★	10.6°	No cord wrap, but excellent fit between lid and base. Grinds fine, yet does not create excessive amount of coffee dust.
Mr. Coffee Coffee Grinder, Model IDS55	$14.99	★★★ 10 Tbs	★★★	★★	9.6°	Nice deep lid prevents the (unevenly) ground coffee from spilling. No cord wrap.
Braun Aromatic Coffee Grinder, Model KSM 2B	$19.99	★★ 9 Tbs	★★★	★★	10°	Tended to grind on the fine side, rarely leaving large chunks of bean. Did create a noticeable quantity of coffee dust, though.
Mr. Coffee Burr Mill, Model BM3	$29.99	★★★ 36 Tbs	★★★	★	12.3°	Grinds thoroughly and pretty evenly, but not completely without dust. No automatic timer, which is fine. We like the control offered by a simple on/off toggle.
NOT RECOMMENDED						
Proctor-Silex Fresh Grind Coffee Grinder, Model E160B	$12.99	★ 5 Tbs	★★★	★★	6.6°	Clever internal cord storage system, but that doesn't make up for a capacity so small that you have to grind twice to get enough coffee for one 8-cup pot.
Cuisinart Coffee Bar Coffee Grinder, Model DCG-20BK	$19.95	★★★ 10 Tbs	★★	★★	8°	Cord stores in an internal chamber, which makes it difficult to use. Shallow lid spills ground coffee, and there was a loose fit between lid and base.
Starbucks Barista Blade Grinder	$19.95	★★ 9 Tbs	★★	★★	5.6°	A study in contrasts: Attractive design, but the lid is so small that coffee spills easily. The coffee is ground evenly, except for the few whole beans usually left behind.
Braun Coffee/Espresso Mill, Model KMM 30	$49.99	★★★ 30 Tbs	★★	★	8.3°	We didn't care for the automatic timer because the machine's notion of the proper grind time often did not jibe with ours.
Capresso Burr Grinder, Model 551	$49.99	★★★ 30 Tbs	★	★	12.6°	Creates more coffee dust than we expected. Also, the power switch is too easy to hit by mistake, an error that sends coffee grounds flying to every corner of the room. Did not care for automatic timer.

15, without overheating the beans or jeopardizing smooth flavor in the coffee.

Overprocessing the beans into superfine coffee dust was another concern. Experts agree that the best grinders produce minimal dust, which can block waterflow through the filter in many coffee-brewing devices. None of the grinders we tested, however, produced enough dust to clog the filter.

The temperature of the coffee grounds was another factor we considered. Ideally, the beans should not heat up too much as they are ground because heat causes the evaporation of flavorful oils and results in a loss of flavor. Most experts claim that cheap blade grinders overheat the coffee beans. According to the infrared thermometer we used to measure the temperature of the grounds, this isn't true. The burr grinders actually caused a greater increase in temperature, albeit a slight one. Our tasters, however, were not able to correlate a greater increase in temperature with poorer coffee flavor. The temperature increases we measured seemed to make very little difference.

User-Friendly Design

Any appliance that you use first thing in the morning, while you are half-asleep, had better be well designed and user-friendly. The two design factors that came to matter to us most were capacity and depth of the cup (on blade grinders). Any grinder should have a capacity large enough to grind in a single batch the beans necessary for a full pot of coffee. Likewise, the cup should be deep enough to contain the grounds without spilling as you remove them from the grinder. All of the burr grinders and the Capresso Cool Grind, Krups Fast Touch, Mr. Coffee Coffee Grinder, and Braun Aromatic blade grinders made the cut here. But the blade grinders offered additional advantages. They were easy to clean, often requiring just a careful wipe of the hopper with a damp paper towel to remove coffee dust, and they were inexpensive, hovering around the $15 to $20 mark. Truth be told, we recommend all of the four blade grinders mentioned above.

That said, we do have one caveat for espresso drinkers. Most manufacturers advise against using a blade grinder—any blade grinder—to grind coffee for use in a pump-driven espresso machine. These grinders simply cannot grind the coffee fine enough. We concur. If this limits your choice to a burr grinder, then we'd go for the Mr. Coffee model because it has a simple on/off switch, which we felt worked better than the timers found on the other two burr models.

=BY KAY RENTSCHLER=

The Magic of Storing Mushrooms

Given their damp, shady habitat, it is no surprise that button mushrooms have little tolerance for careless storage. When stored at home, mushrooms go quickly from proud and plucky to shriveled and dispirited or slimy and discolored. To test the best storage method, we purchased several 12-ounce packages of button mushrooms. We stored one in its original sealed container, one in a paper bag (suggested by the Mushroom Council and thought to promote air circulation), one in a perforated plastic bag (thought to promote air circulation and hold moisture simultaneously), and one in its original cardboard container with the wrap removed and mushrooms then covered with a damp paper towel. (We did not clean the mushrooms, which can cause bruising and would affect our results.)

At the end of five days, the mushrooms in the paper bag were completely dehydrated. The mushrooms in the perforated plastic bag were spongy and discolored. The mushrooms under the (ever-refreshed) damp paper towel were also discolored, but in relatively good condition. The mushrooms in their original sealed container experienced the least deterioration; they were perfectly good after four days. By the fifth day they looked slightly dry and flaky in their container. The moral of this story: Sometimes ready-made packaging has a function beyond simple convenience—sometimes it actually helps to preserve the contents. If you open a sealed package of mushrooms but don't use all the contents, simply rewrap the package (with the remaining mushrooms still inside) with plastic.

Is It a Cure (or a Brine)?

During tests for our illustrated spread on brining in this issue (pages 16–17), we began to wonder what, precisely, constituted the difference between cured and brined meats. To understand this confusing topic better, we consulted Dr. Bob Cassens of the University of Wisconsin and Rytek Kutas, a professional sausage maker. Curing, as most people know, began as a way of preserving meats. The noun *cure*, according to both of our sources, is now commonly used in place of the term *sodium nitrite*, whose by-product, nitric oxide, is what preserves the meat. A cure is introduced into meat by way of a brine—a solution of salt, sugar, spices, and water—by soaking, injection, or both. This technique is known as brine-curing. The goal of brine-curing is to have maximum penetration and distribution of the cure to the center of the meat before it spoils. (Thereafter the meat is cooked.) Nitrites serve not only as a preservative (protecting against botulism, for example) but also produce changes in the flavor, color, and texture of the meat.

Our brines, used to enhance flavor and provide a cushion of moisture, are, properly speaking, flavor brines. Flavor-brining promotes changes in the flavor, color, and texture of meats in a manner similar to curing. The difference is largely one of degree: Flavor-brining is less concentrated, contains no nitrites (and thus has no preservative effects), and, owing to its short duration, penetrates to the center of the meat only in very thin cutlets. Flavor-brined meat, once roasted, grilled, or sautéed, is still fresh meat.

Think Global, Buy Local

While everyone knows that saffron is the most expensive spice in the world, few are aware that it is grown in a variety of locations and that price and quality can vary considerably. Though the bulk of commercially produced saffron comes from Spain and Iran, it is also harvested on a small scale in India, Greece, France, and, closer to home, in Lancaster County, Pa. We decided to toss saffron from different places purchased at different prices into a few pots and set up a test. We prepared three batches of risotto alla Milanese and flavored one with Spanish saffron, one with Indian, and one with American.

The finished risotti were similar in hue, though the Indian "Kashmir" saffron threads were darkest prior to cooking. In a blind tasting, editors overwhelmingly chose the Pennsylvania-grown saffron over both the Spanish and Indian, judging it the "most potent" and "perfumed" of the three. Surprisingly, no one cared much for the Indian saffron, almost twice as costly as the other two and generally regarded as one of the best in the world. Despite its heady aroma, floral tones, and earthy scent, many tasters found it "tinny" and "bland" when cooked in risotto.

EQUIPMENT UPDATE: Reconsidering Copper

In our January/February 2001 issue, we considered the merits and demerits of premium sauté pans—those in the range of $80 to $235. After a variety of tests, we gave the All-Clad Stainless Steel Covered 3 Quart Sauté Pan the highest marks in design and performance. The single copper entrant—and the

Mauviel Cuprinox 2.5 mm 3 Quart Copper Sauté Pan

priciest contestant overall—was the Mauviel Cuprinox 3 Quart Copper Sauté Pan, a pan whose hot-tempered performance landed it in our "Not Recommended" category. But when a reader (and chef) faulted this particular pan for being a poor representative for all copper sauté pans—claiming it was constructed from a copper gauge that was too thin to perform well (better suited, in his words, to table service)—we decided to have another look at copper in general.

Toward that end, we purchased a second 3-quart copper sauté pan, a professional grade (listing just shy of $400), and conducted another series of tests, this time with three pans: the winning All-Clad, our original 2.0 millimeter copper pan, and the new 2.5 mm copper pan. Sure enough, a 0.5-mm advantage in thickness translated into real performance differences. The thicker copper heated up less quickly, maintained its heat better, and was easier to control; its cast-iron handle also lacked the blistering brass grip of the thinner pan. But the most profound difference between the three pans was in temperament overall. The All-Clad, retailing at $165, still garnered high marks for its solid, user-friendly reliability, which demands relatively little from the cook. The two copper pans, on the other hand, were both highly responsive, heating up and cooling down quickly, demanding more active attention from the cook. In the end, it's analogous to the difference between driving with an automatic or a manual transmission. Both will get you where you want to go, it just depends on how you want to get there. For serious cooks who fancy copper pans for more than their good looks, we recommend French professional-grade cookware (about 2.5 mm thick). Mauviel makes such a professional line, as does the French company Bourgeat.

Cookbooks for the Holidays

Here are 10 cookbooks on our shopping list that have
stood the test of time. BY CHRISTOPHER KIMBALL

Cookbooks are deceiving. The one that looks the best or has recipes that sound the most interesting is often the one that is quickly discarded after a few lackluster test runs in the kitchen. Others hold our attention for a time but then fade, the spell broken by lack of character. This holiday season, we offer our top-10 list, those books published in the last five years that really deliver in the long run in terms of both well-tested recipes and their overall contribution to the culinary repertoire. (Reviews are listed in alphabetical order.)

AMERICAN HOME COOKING
Cheryl Alters Jamison and Bill Jamison
Broadway Books, 1999

The Jamisons have created a classic American cookbook that succeeds admirably, being fresh and modern as well as comforting and solid. The excellent, well-tested recipes are a mix of classics such as bread pudding and local specialties such as Honolulu Poke and Iowa Skinny. There are a few missteps in terms of cooking times, but the vast majority of these recipes are winners.

CHEZ PANISSE VEGETABLES
Alice Waters
HarperCollins, 1996

The author's calling card is her devotion to simplicity of preparation, allowing the deep, natural flavors of fresh-picked vegetables to shine through. Waters stands there on a bare stage and, with modest sleight of hand, works wonders with a few garden vegetables. She does include the odd foraged vegetable, and cooking directions can be vague, but there is genius here and, to her great credit, we all can go home after the show and, indeed, pull a rabbit out of our hat.

HOT SOUR SALTY SWEET
Jeffrey Alford and Naomi Duguid
Artisan, 2000

If I could have just one book to awaken my sense of culinary adventure, this would be it. The recipes are fresh, fascinating, well-tested, and nicely adapted to the American kitchen. Based on years of travel through the Mekong Delta region of Southeast Asia, *Hot Sour Salty Sweet* not only delivers Buddhist Sour Soup I can make at home, but it also functions as a travelogue, one written by two individuals with a nicely honed writing style.

IN NONNA'S KITCHEN
Carol Field
HarperCollins, 1997

In Nonna's Kitchen won our hearts as well as our admiration. This collection of recipes from Italian grandmothers ("nonnas") brings us on a journey beyond the high gloss of Italian restaurant food and directly into simple, working-class kitchens. The recipes are not only delicious but straightforward and well-suited to the modern American cook. And then there are the stories. As one goes, in Purgatory, every crumb of bread wasted during a lifetime is counted, and then the penitent must pick up an equivalent number with her eyelashes. This book is heaven.

THE ITALIAN COUNTRY TABLE
Lynne Rossetto Kasper
Scribner, 1999

Kasper has ventured to foreign shores and returned with a voice that rings of authenticity. Her cooking has a sense of place and history, yet the recipes—cantaloupe served with black pepper, olive oil, and vinegar or grilled chicken with mint sauce—are easy to prepare at home. As a bonus, Kasper is a skilled writer, and her anecdotes (on, for example, the sexual benefits of fava beans) make wonderful reading.

JACQUES PÉPIN'S TABLE
Jacques Pépin
Bay Books, 1997

Based on a television series, *Jacques Pépin's Table* delivers French cooking slimmed down and retooled for the American home cook. Here is a culinary pro who knows how to cook, how to write a recipe, and how to deliver fresh, interesting food that is both sure-footed and mature. Although we could do without the nutritional breakdowns and the restraint in the butter department, this book is a must for any even half-serious cook.

MEXICO: ONE PLATE AT A TIME
Rick Bayless
Scribner, 2000

Bayless is the reigning king of Mexican food—at least here in America—and his food is fresh, interesting, and often revelatory. (When was the last time you had tequila-flamed mangoes with vanilla ice cream?) In *Mexico: One Plate at a Time,* he does a top-notch job of bringing this cuisine to the home cook. Although this sort of cooking does require a serious investment of time and effort, the results are more than worth it.

THE NAKED CHEF
Jamie Oliver
Hyperion, 2000

This is a book—based on a TV show that is long on charm and short on serious cooking—that we were determined not to like. But Oliver delivers the goods here: simple food with big flavors. Although his recipes would benefit from less chat and more specifics, the food is modern yet sensible—just what most of us dream of at 5 P.M. on a weeknight.

THE PIE AND PASTRY BIBLE
Rose Levy Beranbaum
Scribner, 1998

The author's first book, *The Cake Bible* (1988), was an original. And so is she. Beranbaum is at heart a quantum physicist whose attention to detail and the inner workings of desserts is beyond question and sometimes beyond reason. This obsessive personality sometimes leads to unnecessary complexity, but it also produces definitive cookbooks, ones that we at the magazine find ourselves referring to time and time again. If you take your baking seriously, buy *The Pie and Pastry Bible*.

SWEET SIMPLICITY: JACQUES PÉPIN'S FRUIT DESSERTS
Jacques Pépin
Bay Books, 1999

Great cooks are reductionists, stripping away what is unnecessary to find classic culinary marriages. This is the essence of *Sweet Simplicity,* a book in which Pépin is at the top of his game. Who thought that frozen raspberries covered with buttered and sugared bread crumbs, baked, and served with sour cream would be transcendent as well as insanely simple? As we noted two years ago, "If we had the time, we would systematically make every recipe." We are almost done.

RESOURCES

Most of the ingredients and materials necessary for the recipes in this issue are available at your local supermarket, gourmet store, or kitchen supply shop. The following are mail-order sources for particular items. Prices listed below were current at press time and do not include shipping or handling unless otherwise indicated. We suggest that you contact companies directly to confirm up-to-date prices and availability.

Coffee Grinders
After grinding more than 30 pounds of coffee beans, we found four grinders we could depend on. Capresso's Cool Grind, model 501, with its large capacity and deep cup, is a workhorse. You can buy it from **Sur La Table (1765 Sixth Avenue South, Seattle, WA 98134-1608; 800-243-0852; www.surlatable.com)**, item #23385, for $19.95. Another first-rate performer is the Krups Fast Touch, model 203, which produces a fine grind with minimal unwanted coffee dust. **Kitchen Etc. (32 Industrial Drive, Exeter, NH 03833; 800-232-4070; www.kitchenetc.com)** carries the grinder, item #97941, for $19.99. We purchased our other recommended grinders, Mr. Coffee, model IDS55, and Braun's Aromatic, model KSM2, for between $15 and $20 each from local kitchen supply stores, but they can be had for even less online. The Mr. Coffee grinder, item #IDS55XU, sells for the low price of $15.34 at **Service Merchandise (www.servicemerchandise.com; 888-764-4387)**. (The grinder is available only through the Web site.) Braun's Aromatic grinder can be ordered online from **Wal-Mart (www.walmart.com; 800-966-6546)** for just $14.96.

For readers who own a pump espresso machine and need a fine grind, we recommend the Mr. Coffee Burr Mill, model BM3-2, available at **Target (200 Rivertown Drive, Woodbury, MN 55188; 888-304-4000; www.target.com)**, item #01414, for $29.99. (Order online or over the phone, or buy the grinder at the store nearest you, which you can find by clicking the Store Locator at the bottom of the company's homepage.)

Crème Brûlée
With a few ingredients and the right tools, it's actually quite easy to make our rich, decadent crème brûlée (page 23). The trademark vessels for the dessert are 5-ounce round ramekins. Those made by Apilco are the perfect size, shape, and weight, are high-fired for maximum resistance to chipping, and are safe for use in the oven, broiler, microwave, and dishwasher. **A Cook's Wares (211 37th Street, Beaver Falls, PA 15010; 800-915-9788; www.cookswares.com)** carries the ramekins, item #5813, in sets of six for $28.50. We also liked the look and

performance of shallow, oval, fluted 5-ounce ramekins. They are sold by **Bridge Kitchenware (214 East 52nd Street, New York, NY 10022; 800-274-3435; www.bridgekitchenware.com)**, item code APAP-TD-O, for $8.95 each.

It can be tricky to determine exactly when the custard is done. We found the most reliable indicator to be a digital instant-read thermometer. We recommend the Thermapen. It has a wide temperature range and is highly accurate (within 0.5 degrees), easy to read, and fast. The Thermapen has a sharp, stainless steel probe that folds back (turning off the thermometer automatically) and locks in place when not in use. What's more, the probe is activated when just ⅛ inch is inserted into the custard (useful if making crème brûlée in shallow oval ramekins). **The Baker's Catalogue (P.O. Box 876, Norwich, VT 05055; 800-827-6836; www.kingarthurflour.com)** sells the Thermapen, item #4325, for $79.95.

If your natural foods store doesn't stock either of the sugars we recommend for the crust, you can order the coarse, crunchy, amber-colored Demerara through **The Baker's Catalogue.** The sugar, which has a light molasses taste, comes in a 1-pound bag, item #1095, for $2.95. To caramelize the sugar, we recommend a professional-caliber torch (BenzOmatic propane torches are available at most hardware stores) or a smaller kitchen torch. Kitchen torches have an adjustable flame and a safe, rubber grip. **Williams-Sonoma (P.O. Box 7456 San Francisco, CA, 94120-7456; 800-541-2233; www.williams-sonoma.com)** sells a butane kitchen torch for $30.00, item #51-1139674. (Butane is available in hardware stores.)

High-Roast Turkey
If brining has become part of your Thanksgiving routine, you might want to invest in a large, sturdy Cambro bucket. A 22-quart, clear, cylindrical bucket will last you a lifetime. You can mail-order the bucket from **Superior Products (P.O. Box 64177, St. Paul, MN 55164-0177; 800-328-9800; www.superprod.com)**, item #800396, for $20. Superior Products also carries smaller Cambro buckets (in 1, 2, 4, 6, 8, 12, and 18 quarts). We like the 6-quart bucket (item #800386, $7.50) for brining smaller items, such as chicken parts or pork chops. (Lids sold separately.)

We roast our butterflied turkey (page 10) on the removable top of a broiler pan set over a disposable roasting pan and use the broiler pan bottom to roast turkey trimmings and vegetables for the gravy. If you don't own a broiler pan, you can purchase a good-sized one (12 by 17 inches), item #28630, for $24.99 from **Cooks Corner (836 South Eighth Street, Manitowoc, WI 54221-0220;**

800-236-2433; www.cookscorner.com). The surface, inside and out, is nonstick for easy cleanup.

Crescent Rolls
Two pieces of equipment crucial to rolling and shaping the dough for our crescent rolls (page 13) are a good rolling pin and a reliable pizza wheel. **Bridge Kitchenware** sells a 20-inch, tapered, hardwood French rolling pin (item code ABRP-FT for $9.95) that allows for more controlled contact with and gentler rolling of the delicate dough than a standard rolling pin. The pizza wheel used to cut the crescent wedges should be sharp and easy to grip and roll. **Cooks Corner** carries such a wheel, item #20781, for $5.99.

Shortbread
Although our shortbread recipe (page 25) calls for just five basic ingredients, a couple of them might be hard to track down. If you can't find rice flour at supermarkets (which are carrying more and more varieties of flour these days) or natural foods stores, you can order a 1-pound bag, item #3035, for $1.95 from **The Baker's Catalogue.** Superfine sugar is also available at some supermarkets, but most of what's out there is beet sugar. We prefer all-natural cane sugar and like to use C&H Baker's Sugar. You can purchase this brand online by the bag (4.4 pounds goes for $3.19) at **www.bakerssugar.com** or over the phone by the case (eight bags for $28) at **925-688-1731.**

Beef Wellington
One surefire way to impress your holiday guests is to serve them beef Wellington. If you don't have a good source for the pork and chicken liver pâté called for in our recipe (page 21), try **Taylor's Market (2900 Freeport Boulevard, Sacramento, CA 95818; 916-443-6881; www.taylorsmarket.com)**, which carries the Trois Petits Cochons (Three Little Pigs) all-natural and handmade Truffle Mousse Pâté we used to develop the recipe. An 8-ounce package, item #TCPM01, costs $8.99 (not including overnight shipping).

We found that homemade puff pastry made a more delectable wrapping for the Wellington than store-bought, but if you don't have time to make your own, try to get your hands on Dufour's all-butter puff pastry. It is a specialty item, so give **Dufour Pastry Kitchens (25 Ninth Avenue, New York, NY 10014; 212-929-2800)** a call before you head out to find it; Dufour will help you locate a retailer near you that carries its product. You can also order a 14-ounce package directly from Dufour for approximately $50 (overnight shipping included).

RECIPES
November & December 2001

Breakfast Dishes
Breakfast Strata
  with Potatoes, Rosemary, and
    Fontina 15
  with Sausage, Mushrooms, and
    Monterey Jack 15
  with Spinach and Gruyère 15

Main Dishes
Beef Wellington 21
  Dry-Aged Beef Tenderloin for 21
Turkey, Crisp-Skin High-Roast
  Butterflied, with Sausage
  Dressing 10
Fra Diavolo
  Monkfish, with Linguine 7
  Scallops, with Linguine 7
  Shrimp, with Linguine 7

**Soups, Sauces, Side Dishes, and
Garnishes**
Butternut Squash Soup
  Curried, with Cilantro Yogurt 8
  Silky 8

Green Beans
  Blanched 18
  with Buttered Bread Crumbs and
    Almonds 18
  with Sautéed Shallots and
    Vermouth 18
  with Toasted Hazelnuts and Brown
    Butter 18
Red Wine Reduction for Sauces 26
FOR BEEF WELLINGTON:
  Duxelles 20
  Red Wine Sauce 21
FOR BUTTERNUT SQUASH SOUP:
  Buttered Cinnamon-Sugar
    Croutons 8
FOR TURKEY:
  Turkey Gravy 11

Breads and Sweets
Buttery Shortbread 25
Crème Brûlée
  Classic 23
  Espresso 23
  Tea-Infused 23
Crescent Rolls 13

PHOTOGRAPHY: CARL TREMBLAY

Breakfast Strata with Spinach and Gruyère

Green Beans with Toasted Hazelnuts

Shrimp Fra Diavolo

Crescent Rolls

Crisp-Skin High Roast Turkey with Sausage Dressing

Silky Butternut Squash Soup

Beef Wellington

Buttery Shortbread

Classic Crème Brûlée

http://www.cooksillustrated.com

If you enjoy *Cook's Illustrated* magazine, you should visit our Web site. Simply log on at http://www.cooksillustrated.com. Although much of the information is free, database searches are for site subscribers only. *Cook's Illustrated* subscribers are offered a 20 percent discount.

Here are some of the things you can do on our site:

Search Our Recipes: We have a searchable database of all the recipes from *Cook's Illustrated*.

Search Tastings and Cookware Ratings: You will find all of our reviews (cookware, food, wine, cookbooks) plus new material created exclusively for the Web site.

Find Your Favorite Quick Tips.

Check Your Subscription: Check the status of your subscription, pay a bill, or give gift subscriptions online.

Visit Our Bookstore: You can purchase any of our cookbooks, hardbound annual editions of the magazine, or posters online.

Subscribe to *e-Notes:* Our free e-mail companion to the magazine offers cooking advice, test results, buying tips, and recipes about a single topic each month.

AMERICA'S TEST KITCHEN

Join the millions of cooks who watch our show, *America's Test Kitchen*, on public television each week. For more information, including recipes from the show and a schedule of program times in your area, visit http://www.americastestkitchen.com.

Seckel

Bartlett

Forelle

Red Bartlett

Beurré Bosc

Packham

Hosui

Doyenné du Comice

Taylor's Gold

Beurré d'Anjou

PEARS